The Handbook of
National Population
Censuses

The Handbook of National Population Censuses

LATIN AMERICA
AND THE
CARIBBEAN,
NORTH AMERICA,
AND
OCEANIA

Doreen S. Goyer and Eliane Domschke

GREENWOOD PRESS

Westport, Connecticut • London, England

Library of Congress Cataloging in Publication Data

Goyer, Doreen S., 1930-
 The handbook of national population censuses.

 Bibliography: p.
 Includes indexes.
 1. Census—Handbooks, manuals, etc. 2. Latin America—
Census—Handbooks, manuals, etc. 3. Caribbean Area—
Census—Handbooks, manuals, etc. 4. North America—
Census—Handbooks, manuals, etc. 5. Oceania—Census—
Handbooks, manuals, etc. I. Domschke, Eliane. II. Title.
HA36.G67   1983   304.6'0723   82-9390
ISBN 0-313-21352-6 (lib. bdg.)   AACR2

The preparation of this volume was made possible
in part by a grant from the Program for Research
Tools and Reference Works of the National Endowment
for the Humanities, an independent federal agency.

Library of Congress Catalog Card Number: 82-9390
ISBN: 0-313-21352-6

First published in 1983

Greenwood Press
A division of Congressional Information Service, Inc.
88 Post Road West
Westport, Connecticut 06881

Printed in the United States of America

10 9 8 7 6 5 4 3 2 1

To the thousands of people in the world who were ever involved in the taking of a census—a thankless task performed with dedication and quite a few miracles.

Contents

Preface

Census publications are difficult to find—and to use—for a multitude of reasons: changes over time in content and format, lack of uniformity in census taking, differing concepts and terminology, and changes in boundaries and place names. One cannot assume anything about any census; it must be consulted directly to verify its content. Researchers have often wasted precious time seeking out a census publication only to find the topic of interest was not included.

The goal of this handbook is to ease that difficulty and others related to the use of census publications.

SOME BASIC INFORMATION ABOUT THE HANDBOOK

Due to the size of the handbook, it was decided to group countries and territories by world regions. This volume contains three: Latin America and the Caribbean, North America, and Oceania. Subsequent volumes will contain Asia, Africa, and Europe.

The criteria for inclusion of sovereign nations in this handbook are obvious. The inclusion of certain territories is not. To be eligible a territory must fulfill some, if not all, of the following:

1. Be geographically separated from the homeland.
2. Have performed its own census.
3. Have published its own results, even if the census was conducted by or in cooperation with the homeland.
4. Have been independent once or have recently become so.

There are some groups that pose problems to the A to Z listing of the entries within continents—the British West Indies, for example. Separate listings are carried for each component with a general entry listing as well, if deemed necessary. In any case all referrals are clearly indicated.

The ground rules of the handbook are as follows:

1. Post-1945 censuses will be discussed in more detail than pre-1945 censuses.
2. The information, unless otherwise stated, comes from the census publications themselves.
3. In some cases where it was not possible to locate copies of the actual census forms and instructions, inferences as to the nature of the questions and definitions used have been made on the basis of the available tabulations.

4. When there were no extant publications for a specific census, information has been gleaned from other, usually subsequent, census publications and so stated.
5. The language of the handbook is condensed in order to conserve space. We have tried to include as much information as possible in this volume and still remain intelligible.

The Introduction to this volume and the complete work contain the "what" of definitions, concepts, trends, and contents. It was never our intention to discuss what should or should not be nor the logic behind the choices involved in the making of a population census. There are many books and documents that present those discussions authoritatively. Some are listed in the bibliography that follows the Introduction. We did not judge it necessary to repeat or to summarize their content in this work.

We wish to acknowledge with gratitude the National Endowment for the Humanities for the core funds that turned an idea into reality; the members of the Population Research Center for supplying other funds, work space, and moral support; our colleagues from APLIC who supplied materials with all speed in response to our urgent requests; and especially Richard Hankinson, editor of the *Population Index*, who granted us permission to use the bibliography of "Governmental and Intergovernmental Serial Publications Containing Vital or Migration Statistics," vol. 46, no. 4, as the basis for the "Other Statistical Publications" section in each country entry. Readers are referred to the *Population Index* if further information is desired.

Abbreviations

APLIC	The Association for Population/Family Planning Libraries and Information Centers—International.
CAME	Concilio de Ayuda Mutual y Económica, Moscow.
CELADE	Centro Latinoaméricano de Demografía, Santiago, Chile.
CICRED	Comité International de Coordinatión des Recherches Nationales de Démographie, Paris.
COTA	Census of the Americas.
ECA	Economic Commission for Africa.
ECAFE	Economic Commission for Asia and the Far East.
ECE	Economic Commission for Europe.
ECLA	Economic Commission for Latin America.
ECWA	Economic Commission for Western Asia.
ESCAP	Economic and Social Commission for Asia and the Pacific.
FOSDIC	Film Optical Sensing Device for Input to Computers.
IASI	Inter-American Statistical Institute.
ILO	International Labour Office.
ISCED	International Standard Classification of Education.
ISCO	International Standard Classification of Occupations.
ISIC	International Standard Industrial Classification (of all Economic Activities).
OAS	Organization of American States.
UNESCO	United Nations Educational, Scientific and Cultural Organization.
UNFPA	United Nations Fund for Population Activities.

The Handbook of
National Population
Censuses

Introduction

THE POPULATION CENSUS IS PROBABLY THE MOST PROLIFIC AND FUNDAMENTAL SOURCE OF INFORMATION ABOUT A NATION.... IT REVEALS NOT ONLY THE BASIC DEMOGRAPHIC TRENDS, SUCH AS POPULATION GROWTH, INTERNAL POPULATION REDISTRIBUTION, URBANIZATION AND ALTERATIONS IN THE AGE AND SEX STRUCTURE, BUT ALSO CONTRIBUTES INDISPENSABLY TO A KNOWLEDGE OF CHANGES IN THE NATION'S OCCUPATIONAL AND INDUSTRIAL COMPOSITION, IN ITS LEVEL OF LIVING, EDUCATION AND EMPLOYMENT.

ABOVE ALL, THE CENSUS MAKES POSSIBLE THE ESTIMATION OF FUTURE TRENDS AND IS THEREFORE ESSENTIAL TO ALL KINDS OF PLANNING: NATIONAL, LOCAL, PUBLIC AND PRIVATE. IT IS ESSENTIAL FOR KNOWING FUTURE ECONOMIC MANPOWER POTENTIALS, FUTURE CONSUMER NEEDS, FORTHCOMING SCHOOL REQUIREMENTS, FUTURE GROWTH IN METROPOLITAN AREAS, POTENTIAL COSTS OF SOCIAL SECURITY MEASURES, FUTURE REQUIREMENTS FOR HIGHWAYS, UTILITIES, PARKS, WATER, ENERGY AND HEALTH SERVICES. —KINGSLEY DAVIS
"CENSUS," *ENCYCLOPAEDIA BRITANNICA*, 1967

It is common to liken a census to a photograph of a population at one moment in time. From it one gains a recognition of who people are and where they are. It is not a collection of dry statistics but a reflection of a society, complete with its problems and preoccupations. This has not always been so in the past. Early countings equated people to things, as units of potential tax revenue and/or the means to fill military ranks. The modern population census has certain features, especially universality and individual enumeration, that illustrate the more humanistic motivation behind these censuses than the purely mercenary motivation typical of the very early censuses.

ESSENTIAL FEATURES THAT DISTINGUISH A CENSUS FROM OTHER FORMS OF POPULATION ACCOUNTING

1. Sponsorship. For a proper census, an extensive administrative machinery has to be mobilized and supported with adequate legislative and legal authority.

The legal basis for the census determines the office responsible for conducting the census, establishes the scope of the census program, ensures cooperation among government agencies at various levels, requires compliance of the population to answer the questions and lastly requires confidentiality on the part of those involved in the taking of a census.

2. Defined territory. Population figures have no meaning unless they refer to a precisely defined territory. The territory covered, along with any changes in its area in successive censuses, should be clearly stated. This applies to any geographical subdivision as well as to national boundaries.

3. Universality. A census should include every person present (*de facto*) and/or residing (*de jure*) within its territory without omission or duplication.

4. Individual enumeration. A census enumerates each individual separately and records his/her characteristics separately. Only by this procedure can the data on various characteristics of an individual be cross-classified. Recording only aggregate or summarized information on the characteristics of a group of persons (that is, group enumeration) inhibits the cross-tabulation of data on several characteristics.

Individual enumeration, however, does not preclude the use of sampling techniques for obtaining data on specified characteristics, providing that the sample design is consistent with the size of the areas for which the data are to be tabulated and with the degree of detail in the cross-tabulations to be made.

5. Simultaneity and specified time. Each person should be enumerated as nearly as possible to the same well-defined point in time, and the collected data should refer to a well-defined reference period. This time-reference period need not, however, be identical for all the data collected. For most of the data, it will be the day of the census; in some instances, it may be a period prior to the census. The census moment serves as a chronological line by which the census official decides to include or exclude newborn and recently deceased members of the population.

6. Periodicity. Census data gain in value if censuses are conducted at regular intervals because a single census provides a static photo of a population, while consecutive censuses can create a motion picture.

7. Compilation and publication. Raw data, whether tucked away in archives or in computers, are of no use to anyone. A census is not complete unless the data collected are compiled and published by geographic areas and by basic demographic variables. Since the value of census results diminishes with the passage of time, they should be published as soon as possible. The publications should also include all definitions, concepts, methodologies, corrections, sampling errors, and so forth.

Various kinds of counting done in the past did not include these features. Estimates, population counts, and parish register counts were not concerned with individual enumeration; these three methods were often tallies of records or registration slips. If individuals were not duly signed up, their existence was ignored. A partial census by itself cannot serve in the place of a full national census; it lacks universality.

The last common method, the group enumeration, appeared to cover the essential features at first glance. The following is an acknowledged oversimplification, but it will serve to illustrate the essential difference between a group and an individual enumeration. In a household enumerated in the group fashion, the number of persons is indicated for each characteristic asked:

Age—Adults: 2
       Children: 2
Sex—Males: 2
       Females: 2

To the question of how many adult males are there in the household (crossing age by sex), the answer would have to be as many as two or as few as none. In an individual enumeration, on the other hand, the characteristics are indicated for each person:

A. 1. Head—male—adult
   2. Spouse—female—adult
   3. Son—male—child
   4. Daughter—female—child

B. 1. Head—female—adult
   2. Son—male—child
   3. Servant—female—adult
   4. Son—male—child

In household A there is only one adult male; in B there are no adult males.

This ability to cross-classify characteristics gives a human dimension to the results because it reflects the infinite variability that exists among people.

THE DEVELOPMENT OF THE MODERN POPULATION CENSUS

There are numerous histories of the census available for detailed study; there is no need to repeat their efforts here. The purpose of the following section is to provide a quick perspective of the development of the modern census.

There are alleged censuses of populations from the past that are now regarded as nothing of the kind. The word is often lightly applied to those rather casual inquiries made on the part of ecclesiastical or civil authorities that did not aim to discover the total size or the detailed composition of the population but merely those who were available for military service, official members of the church, or the taxable part of the community. Who was counted and why constitute the basic differences between ancient and modern censuses, between population counts and true censuses.

Counts were concerned only with how many people there were (as a total or a specific part); there was no interest in determining what the basic socioeconomic characteristics of the population were, where they lived, or how processes of social and biological change may have affected them. The scope and motivation of ancient "censuses" were limited to matters of wealth, military campaigns, or defense. People per se did not matter.

Scientific interest in the application of the numerical method, which was well developed for fiscal and administrative functions among the Romans and Greeks as well as others, was not applied to the study of population groups. As the fall of the Roman Empire approached, private freedom and initiative were sacrificed to the survival of the state. The growth of the Christian church and its subsequent internal disputes found countries moving toward, but not yet achieving, the development of national attitudes, since allegiance to religious authorities became dominant in the feudal society.

The effect of the church on the paucity of even population counts during the Middle Ages may have been due to an event described in the Old Testament of the Bible (2 Sam. 24; 1 Chron. 21, 23, 27). According to the account, King David ordered Joab, the commander of his armies, to determine the total population of Israel. After making the count, Joab reported only the number of men who could bear arms. Some time after the "census" was taken, Israel suffered a great plague. Biblical scholars differ over the reason for the Lord's anger, but in the Judeo-Christian world the enumeration of people came to be regarded as sinful. As late as the eighteen century there was an avoidance of censuses for fear of arousing the Lord's displeasure; Great Britain delayed its first census until 1801 for this reason. Whatever the reason or reality, the result was that throughout the Middle Ages there was very little counting of people. To their feudal lords, they were sources of revenue or cannon fodder; at best their number was indicative of the size of property. To the church, they were a rich mine of souls to be saved. It made little difference to either as to how people survived. The growth of population at that time posed no problem; wars and pestilence kept their numbers in check, and governments either ignored, or were incapable of providing, basic services needed for civilized existence even at that time.

One known accounting of people during this period was the compilation of the Domesday Book in England. It was ordered by William the Conqueror to begin Christmas Day, 1085. Its purpose was to establish a fairer basis for taxation. As before, the motive of taxation was applied, but the word "fairer" implied that some concern for people was being implemented. The commissioners traveled throughout the kingdom and listed all the landholders, their lands, houses, tenants, and classes of servants and serfs. The king, lords and clergy, and the lowliest landholders were included. The detail and precision of the Domesday Book were remarkable for its time.

With the advent of the Renaissance, discovery and trade increased, ports and other cities grew, and the counting of goods and people became commonplace. Scholars began to realize the importance of genuine enumerations and argued for their implementation. A sense of nationalism was taking hold. "Humanism" on the part of government was not the result of concern for its people but rather the need to survive as a nation. People, however, began to be regarded as another form of economic asset; in addition to serving as soldiers and taxpayers, they were becoming the manpower of an expanding labor force.

The "censuses" during this period were still basically population counts, but other information was beginning to be gathered (for example, age and sex), and the coverage was expanding to include more of the total population, although the tendency remained to consider the person enumerated as an impersonal unit. The data were of the number of units in each category; in other words, a group enumeration rather than an individual enumeration.

Toward the end of the seventeenth century a new form of the census began to appear, a prototype of what we now recognize as a modern census. In 1666, the king of France requested that a census of the colony of New France (Quebec) be conducted regularly (Periodicity). In it, the name was recorded for each person (Universality) along with various facts about him or her (Individual enumeration) by means of a house-to-house visitation. The characteristics asked were sex, age, relation to household head, marital status, and occupation. From this were determined total population, locality population, and household composition. There was no implication of the use of this census for taxing or military purposes; it seems the king just wanted to know how the colony was progressing—a decided change in motivation.

The 1703 census in Iceland became the next landmark in census development due to its size. In addition to being an individual enumeration, it covered the whole island by the canvasser method, and for at least one segment of the population, the wandering paupers, it was taken as of a fixed date (Simultaneity). Its motivation was to inquire into the effects of the adverse economic conditions and natural disasters afflicting the island and to search for means of improvement. The results were detailed enough to allow for basic cross-classification and derived figures. Publication, however, was not to be one of this census's features. After being lost in archives for centuries, the results were used for a study published in 1947, and the tables appeared in printed form in 1960.

It is said that the first census of a large populous nation was that of Sweden in 1749. However, it was a tally made from a continuous register of births, deaths and parish membership. It is not known if there was a house-to-house canvass as well. Without the opportunity to examine this census it is difficult to give an opinion about it or to verify such references that it counted only males and not the total population.

The last of the prototypes to be mentioned here is that of the United States in 1790. Like that of Iceland, it was based on a canvass of the whole country as it existed at that time. It was, however, a group enumeration. The name of the household head was written and the number of units in each category was listed. The scope of topics was minimal: the number of free white males sixteen years of age and over, free white males under sixteen, free white females, all other free persons, and slaves (each of which counted for only three-fifths of a person). There were no questionnaires, boundaries were poorly defined, and no tabulation beyond simple addition of entries made by the marshals, who also published on their own the summaries for each state by county. Its motivation, however, was democratic; it served as a legal basis for legislative representation.

Because it was generally believed until the beginning of the nineteenth century that any attempt to enumerate the residents of a large populous country would founder on administrative difficulties, over a century elapsed before the 1666 beginnings of census taking developed into a national census along modern lines. During this interval there were various attempts to enumerate the population of cities, provinces, or cantons, but no successful ones to count the whole population of large countries. The success of the 1790 census of the United States and that of the City of Paris in 1817 instilled enough confidence that a large scale census was deemed possible. Although population size was conquered from 1800 to 1830, the scope and especially the methods to be used still had to be resolved.

The state of the recent modern population censuses vary from the primitive types typical of yesteryear to the highly sophisticated ones of today's industrialized nations. Even so, and even with the benefit of four world population census programs, a perfect census has yet to be taken.

THE DEVELOPMENT OF WORLD POPULATION CENSUS PROGRAMS

The activities of international organizations concerned with population censuses began in the mid-nineteenth century. The First International Statistical Congress, held in Brussels in 1853, adopted perhaps the first formal international recommendations and established some basic requirements, aiming at comparability of population census data and the standardization of techniques. The meeting of the International Statistical Institute in St. Petersburg, Russia, in 1872 adopted certain standards with regard to methods of and topics taken in population censuses. In the 1897 meeting of the same organization, also in St. Petersburg, the idea of a simultaneous census of the "whole world" was formed using the standards agreed upon in 1872. Various international and regional organizations from time to time continued to urge simultaneous censuses or to recommend topics to be investigated along with definitions and methods to be used.

The Population Commission and the Statistical Commission of the United Nations were concerned with international comparability and the need for census statistics from their inception in 1946. Four world population census programs have been sponsored by the United Nations since then.

The Organization of American States (OAS) plans for the 1950 Census of the Americas (COTA) sparked the development by the UN of its own 1950 recommendations at the international level on the basis of information on country experience in the censuses taken from 1925 to 1944. The first recommendations, prepared to guide countries in taking censuses during the period 1945-1954, were relatively simple. They made no pretense of reflecting regional or national differences in conditions. In essence, they were the result of a crash program to promote census taking and, to a lesser degree, comparability between contents and results of such censuses.

The 1960 principles and recommendations were also primarily developed at the international level on the basis of country experience (1945-1954), and only then were they adapted by the regions to their special needs. The recommendations went further than the 1950 set; they were supplemented by suggested programs for analysis and by a set of principles for projecting population values as determined by the census.

The basic recommended content for censuses had not changed a great deal from the proposals that were made in 1853 by the International Statistical Congress. By 1965 international comparability of censuses had not progressed much beyond those traditional basic topics. For this reason, the 1970 World Population Census Program, the most sophisticated set of principles and recommendations so far, aimed to assist countries in producing population statistics of adequate scope and satisfactory quality, properly evaluated and analyzed, to be used for sound decision making on questions of population policy and of planning social and economic action. Development of the 1970 program, unlike the preceding sets, progressed in such a way that regional action and opinion on operations, topics, and tabulations were taken into account at the drafting stage. Decentralization thus ensured that the recommendations were not based only on the experience of a limited number of countries but would give proper weight to the expressed needs of developing countries.

The *Principles and Recommendations for Population and Housing Censuses*, published by the UN in 1980, are not limited to only the 1980 round of censuses: "They are intended as a guide to help countries in planning and carrying out population and housing censuses in the coming years." They have been developed over a period of years by a process of consultation between the UN, the regional commissions, and individual countries with the regional commissions taking the lead, especially with topics to be covered. The Statistical Office of the UN continues to prepare the appropriate guidelines on the organization, timing, staffing, and costs of various census operations. These recommendations differed from the 1970 set in the following fashion:

1. They treat both population and housing censuses as a combined program.

2. They omit any reference to a specific year in the title to reflect the move away from an emphasis on international simultaneity in census-taking.

3. They revise and expand the operational aspects to reflect recent technical and policy developments related to census-taking and orient them toward the needs and circumstances of developing countries.

4. They distinguish among topics recommended as "priority" by a majority of the regions, those that appeared most in both the "priority" and "other useful" lists, and those also mentioned by at least one region as "of interest."

Table 1 is a comparison of the topics that were recommended in the four UN world population census programs.

In short, international comparability has remained as one principle of the World Population Census Program. Emphasis, however, has moved from the simultaneity of census-taking worldwide toward the quality of data collection and compilation that best serve national needs. The underlying belief is that a continuing coordinated program of data collection and compilation can best be served if the relationship between the population census, the housing census, and other statistical investigations is considered when census planning is underway and if consistent concepts and definitions throughout the integrated program of data collection and compilation are used.

GENERAL OUTLINE OF COUNTRY ENTRY WITH EXPLANATION OF VARIATIONS IN TERMS, CONCEPTS, AND DEFINITIONS

I.   Heading.
   A.   Common English version of geographic name of country.
   B.   Official, long-form name.
   C.   Name of the capital city.
   D.   Official statistical agency, especially that in charge of the national census.
   E.   National repository of censuses. Library in the country where most, if not all, of the census publications may be found.
   F.   Main United States repository. Library in the United States where copies of most, if not all, of the census publications may be found.
II.   General entry introduction. General comments on the country's history as may be pertinent to its census history (territorial affiliation to another country, independence, major additions or changes to boundaries, inclusion with other territories in a joint census, and so forth). Traditional practices in conducting a census and characteristics common to most or all censuses of the country.
III.   Specific census entry headed by year of the census, and the date in parentheses in the case of the post-1945 censuses.
   A.   Details on particular censuses, noting relevant information about the country's name, capital, geographical divisions, and political status if different from that during the previous census.
   B.   Type of census. In a population census, information about each person can be collected and entered on the census questionnaire either where he/she is (or was) present on the day of the census (de facto) or at his/her usual residence (de jure). This seems simple enough but strict adherence to either of these types is rarely found. Usually there are modifications demanded, which in essence are contributions of the other. Labeling a count as de jure or de facto is to identify the dominant mode, not its purity of condition.
      1.   De facto: Place where present at the time of the census. In practice, the concept is generally applied to the place where the person slept on the night

Table 1
A Comparison of the Topics Recommended by the UN World
Population Census Programs
(P = priority, O = other useful, — = not cited)

	1950	1960	1970	1980
Place of usual residence	—	P	P	P
Place where present at time of census	P	P	P	P
Place of birth	P	P	P	P
Duration of residence	—	—	O	P
Place of previous residence	O	—	O	P
Place of residence at [year]	—	—	—	P
Place of work	—	—	O	—
Relationship to household head or other reference member	P	P	P	P
Relationship to family head	—	P	O	—
Sex	P	P	P	P
Age	P	P	P	P
Marital status	P	P	P	P
Citizenship	P	P	O	P
Religion	—	—	O	O
Language	P	P	O	O
National/Ethnic origin (race)	O	P	O	O
Children born alive	P	P	P	P
Children living	O	—	P	P
Age at marriage	O	—	O	P
Duration of marriage	O	—	O	P
Marriage order	—	—	O	—
Live births, 12 mos. preceding census	—	—	—	O
Infants born & died last 12 mos.	—	—	—	O
Maternal orphanhood	—	—	—	O
Educational attainment	P	P	P	P
Literacy	P	P	P	P
School attendance	P	P	P	P
Educational qualifications	—	—	O	O
Economic activity status	P	P	P	P
Occupation	P	P	P	P
Secondary occupation	—	O	—	—
Industry	P	P	P	P
Status in employment/occupation	P	P	P	P
Time worked	O	O	—	O
Income	—	—	O	O
Sector of employment	P*	—	—	O
Economic dependency	P	O	O	—
Socioeconomic status	—	O	O	—
Derived topics				
Total population	P	P	P	P
Locality	O	P	P	P
Urban/rural	P	P	P	P
Household composition	P	P	P	P
Family composition	P	P	—	P

*Agriculture only.

preceding the census day (or the night preceding the day of actual enumeration). This question is not asked per se in a *de facto* enumeration. In a *de jure* enumeration it may be asked to determine the *de facto* population for geographic areas, and/or it may serve as a check so that no one is counted twice. Special groups that need specific resolution are:

    a.   persons traveling during the entire night;

    b.   persons who spent the night at work.

Information should be collected in sufficient detail to satisfy the tabulation program.

The 1970 principles and recommendations of the UN indicated that because of the growth of interest in household and families and in internal migration, there is an increasing interest in basing the census on usual residence (*de jure*) rather than on place where present at time of census (*de facto*).

2. *De jure*: Place of usual residence. The basis on which the count of the total population is made should not be confused with the basis of the geographic and household allocation of persons within the country. The place of usual residence is the household and its geographic location where the enumerated person usually resides. Usual residence is not synonymous with legal residence, although in many cases they may be the same place. Usual residence is based generally on a minimum time period spent (or even intended to spend) in one place. The minimum period should be defined in each census. Special groups that need specific resolution are:

    a.   persons who maintain two or more residences;

    b.   students at boarding schools;

    c.   members of armed forces housed on base but still maintaining private living quarters off base;

    d.   persons who sleep away from home during the work week but who return for a couple of days each week;

    e.   persons who have resided more than the minimum time in one place but who do not consider it a residence because they intend to return to the previous residence at some future time;

    f.   persons who have left the country temporarily but are expected to return after some time;

    g.   seamen and fishermen at sea.

Decisions have to be made as to whether to include or exclude any of the above not only from the geographic place but from the household as well.

C.   Method of enumeration. There are two major methods of enumeration. The first has been commonly used in African, American, and Asian censuses; the second, in European and Oceanian.

1. Canvassed. Responses are recorded by the enumerator who interviews one or more responsible members of the family or household. This is the only method that can be used in largely illiterate populations or in other population segments that may be unwilling or find it difficult to complete

the census forms themselves. Well-trained enumerators have greater accuracy in understanding the question, eliciting the correct response, and inscribing uniform and consistent answers. They are also able to code certain responses that cannot fit into the preprinted multiple choices on the form. The number of enumerators needed is greater as is the size of the training program to prepare them. Canvassing also consumes more time to cover the enumeration district. An expanded period of enumeration can very easily lead to an over- or undercount.

2. Self-enumeration. Information is entered by a person in the unit enumerated, usually the head of household. The questionnaire is usually distributed, collected, and checked by a census official. Postal distribution and/or return of the questionnaire is often used with this method. Fewer well-trained enumerators are needed. The householder has more time to ponder questions, and responses may be more accurate. Respondents may feel a greater sense of confidentiality, and greater simultaneity is possible. Postal distribution of questionnaires requires the preparation of a comprehensive and up-to-date list of addresses. The questionnaire must be prepared with adequate instructions so that misinterpretations are minimized. The callback procedure used when questionnaires are not returned or are returned with incomplete data can cause an added expense.

There exist, however, combinations of the two methods that compensate for the differences in segments of the population. The self-enumeration method can be used in urban areas and canvasser in remote areas. There can also be a part of the questionnaire that is to be self-enumerated and the other, canvassed. The choice of method or combination is judgmental, based on the density of the population, the distance to be covered by one enumerator, and the literacy of the respondent.

3. Nonconventional. Such methods are usually used when enumerating nomadic or autochthonous populations. Their situation in society as inhabitants living outside the predominant social and economic structure of a country complicates enumeration, if they are to be included in the national census. Estimates have been used in some censuses. Generally there is a reliable count of the total population, but very few characteristics can be canvassed. A simplified questionnaire can be used for the indigenous population, but because of their remote location, the time reference (census date) used for the more accessible population may be changed to the date of the actual enumeration. Other methods are administrative censuses, group-assembly, tribal or hierarchical approach, enumeration-area approach, among several. Many times, however, the results of such methods are group enumerations (counting so many units per characteristic) rather than individual enumeration.

Systems to maintain simultaneity in enumeration in one country:

a. single-stage enumeration. When the enumerator cannot cover his territory in one day, schedules are delivered to the household in advance for partial or total self-enumeration. The enumerator then makes one trip on the census day to pick up each schedule, look it over for errors or omissions and make corrections on the spot.

b.   two-stage enumeration. The canvasser makes a first round of his territory to fill out schedules as much as possible, then returns on the census day to update information such as births or deaths occurring before the census date or the presence of other people not censused the first time.

c.   mail-out/mail-in. An example of the method in which the household receives the schedule in advance to fill out as of the census date and then returns it by a certain date. The enumerator is used only to seek corrections or fill in omissions not obtainable from the schedule itself; this occurs usually well after the census day.

D.   Enumeration period. The time in which the actual enumeration is performed.

1.   Time of the year. Elements that can affect selection of when the census is to be conducted are seasonal climatic conditions, migrations due to agricultural or other economic activities, holidays, and the availability of potential census personnel.

2.   Length of enumeration. The period should be as short as possible (a few days to two weeks) to avoid double countings and omissions. Large countries or those with vast, sparcely inhabited territories may require more time.

E.   Units of enumeration. The person is the literal basic unit in keeping with the feature of individuality. However, the household is generally the working basic unit in the administration of the census itself. Household lists that carefully identify these units facilitate the collection of data and the control of complete coverage. The household as determined for the population census has often helped determine the concept of the private dwelling especially for certain topics taken in the housing census. In early censuses the household was often the term given to all persons dwelling in the same structure that was intended for habitation. This equation of household to dwelling, however, was too broad; it could not account for persons or groups living in separated quarters within the dwelling, for example, a lodger's room or a hotel guest room. Households may occupy the whole, part of, or more than one housing unit; they may also be found to be living in camps, boarding houses, hotels, or to be homeless.

The family is at times used as a unit of enumeration in place of household. The differences between the household and the family are that a household may consist of only one person but a family must have at least two members and the members of a multiperson household need not be related to each other but members of a family must. Where family is used as the unit of enumeration, households cannot be identified. However, where the household is the unit, families within the household can be identified.

The nonhousehold or institution population is the unit of enumeration that covers persons who do not reside as members of households (persons living in military installations, correctional and penal institutions, dormitories of schools and universities, religious institutions, hospitals, and so forth).

F.   Forms of schedules/questionnaires (these terms are synonymous when used in the context of the census).

1.   Individual. A separate questionnaire is used for each individual enumerated. It is usually grouped with others into a family folder. These folders in turn are grouped into a household folder. The form could also be an individual slip filled out by the canvasser after the interview, containing the information previously taken and entered in the household or general schedule.

2.   Household. A questionnaire on which there is room for separate entries, one for each of several individuals who constitute one household. The household schedule may appear as a short form that contains only the questions to be asked of 100 percent of the population. This is used along with a long form that includes the same questions plus a number of questions on topics that are only to be taken on a sample enumeration basis and are distributed to a pre-selected sample of households.

3.   General. A long questionnaire sheet with room for many individual entries, which is to be used until filled up. Households are indicated by a line drawn between one set of entries and the next.

4.   Special population. A questionnaire prepared for any one of several specific population groups for some special reason, for example, for confidentiality, for the temporarily absent resident in a *de jure* enumeration, for infants, for the disabled or persons with infirmities, or for an ethnic group. The questions asked on this form generally are not those included in the regular form.

G.   Methods of tabulation. The choice of the following is determined by the circumstances of each country, the funds available, and the technical expertise present on the staff.

1.   Manual. Obviously this method was used before mechanical and electronic data processing were available. However, it may still be a preferred method today for a few tabulations that do not warrant the expense of a computer run especially if the questionnaire used was not machine readable. Various means are used: hand tallies in the field by enumerators, transcription of household data to individual slips and vice versa for rearrangements of variables into different combinations. This method is very slow for final results, especially for cross-tabulations, and prone to error in the re-sorting phase. Content errors are difficult to detect, if at all.

2.   Mechanical. Usually performed by use of punched cards and mechanical sorters. Cards are run and rerun for each set of variables or cross-tabulations. It is not effective in multiple cross-classifications, for example, three or four or more variables in one table. Speed is improved over manual tabulation, but the time spent in preparing punched cards limits that. Another moment when error is possible comes in transcription.

3. Computer. With properly edited and coded machine readable questionnaires, this is the speediest and most versatile method of tabulation. However, much time must be spent in developing the software. Nevertheless, the computer is capable of spotting errors, evaluating results, and analyzing data.

H. Total population. This is determined by the segments of the population included or excluded from the census. For census purposes, the total population of the country consists of all the persons falling within the scope of the census. What is to be considered the total population depends first on whether the country chooses a *de facto* or *de jure* type of enumeration. In either type there are population groups that may be included or excluded from the total, depending on national circumstances. Each country needs to describe in detail what constitutes the figure accepted as the total. Special groups to be considered are:

1. Nomads.
2. Persons living in areas to which access is difficult.
3. Military, naval, and diplomatic personnel and their families located outside the country.
4. Merchant seamen and fishermen resident in the country but at sea at the time of the census (including those who have no place of residence other than their quarters aboard ship).
5. Civilian residents temporarily in another country as seasonal workers.
6. Civilian residents who cross a frontier daily to work in another country.
7. Civilian residents other than those in groups 3, 5, and 6 who are working in another country.
8. Civilian residents other than those in groups 3 through 7 who are temporarily absent from the country.
9. Foreign military, naval and diplomatic personnel and their families located in the country.
10. Civilian aliens temporarily in the country as seasonal workers.
11. Civilian aliens who cross a frontier daily to work in the country.
12. Civilian aliens other than those in groups 9, 10, and 11 who are working in the country.
13. Civilian aliens other than those in groups 9 through 12 who are temporarily in the country.
14. Transients on ships in harbor at the time of the census (shipping population).

I. Territorial divisions. These are the geographic designations generally used in censuses.

1. Administrative entities/political divisions. There are greater or lesser variations depending on the country. The only general feature is that the next smaller division is a subdivision of the larger:

a. National and territories. Changes in boundaries may have occurred since the last census. External territories may have been included or excluded in the calculation of total population. Both of these occurrences should be clearly stated in the census report.

b. Major subdivision. This is the primary unit that subdivides the national area (state, province, "département," "entidad federativa," and so forth).

c. Secondary subdivision. The subdivider of the major subdivision (county, "municipio," parish, "arrondissement," and so forth).

d. Places. The cities, towns, and villages that are incorporated under one administrative government with well-defined boundaries. It may have to fulfill a minimum population size in accordance with its urban character.

e. Urban subdivisions. Wards, barrios, sectors of urban places with a distinct administrative character may, for example, be an electoral unit or have a specific name and/or socioeconomic character.

f. Localities. Other population clusters often without urban character and no administrative identity.

2. Statistical and other entities. These are artificially derived for statistical purposes and may be based on economic and/or social affinities. The administrative/political boundaries may be utilized, but the statistical entity has no administrative government of its own.

a. Regions (natural or traditional). Often titled by compass point names such as north, east, south central, and so forth. They can also be litoral as opposed to interior, mountain as opposed to plains, or may be designations of health or electoral districts.

b. Metropolitan areas. Starting with a large central city, the urban fringe or suburbia are combined to indicate a large urban area that may or may not follow administrative boundary lines of one or more secondary subdivisions and may even cross major subdivision boundaries (for example, Standard Metropolitan Statistical Area, Ciudad Metropolitana, and so forth).

c. Subdivisions of regions or metropolitan areas. Census tracts, enumeration districts, zip code districts, and church parish districts.

J. Census reference periods. To establish uniformity in responses, specific reference periods should be decided upon in advance.

1. Census moment (usually midnight before the census date). It is the moment by which determination can be made as to whom to include or exclude in the count due to births or deaths that occur just before or after the moment.

2. Census day/Census night. Either may also be used to determine inclusions or exclusions (temporarily absent resident, temporarily present visitors). This is the reference period used for most of the characteristics of the population (age, marital status, and so forth).

3. Week before the census day. Used in a census that employs the labor force concept to determine the type of activity of the population and the hours worked.

4. Up to twelve months preceding the census date. Used in a census that employs the gainfully employed concept to determine the type of activity. This period is also common in determining the number of live births,

number of deaths, or the number of months worked as a measurement of unemployment or underemployment.

5.   One year or five years. Used in reference as of a specified date in the past to determine internal migration and immigration.

6.   No time reference. One can interpret a question asked without what seems to be a needed reference period as having occurred or being the state at the moment the census was taken. However, some topics need a "no specified time" reference, for example, usual occupation, number of children ever born alive.

K.   Definitions and Concepts.

URBAN/RURAL—Only when an area is totally urban or totally rural is it clearly perceived. Most areas, depending on the designation, occupy a relative position that falls on a graduated distribution along a continuum from the least urban to the most urban. There is no international recommendation or standard that can satisfy each country's desire to label an area as urban. There are six concepts that have been applied singly or in combinations to determine urban in various countries.

1.   Administrative area. The whole division or a specific part, for example, governorates, *chefs-lieux*, capital cities or primary subdivisions with historical or political boundaries.

2.   Population size. Places having either a specified minimum number of inhabitants or a minimum number of inhabitants per unit or area (density). There is usually a political boundary involved but it may extend past the boundary to include surrounding zones.

3.   Local government area. Areas within fixed city limits, or historical or political boundaries.

4.   Urban characteristics. Presence of amenities such as stores, hospitals, water and utility services, and post offices, for example.

5.   Nonagricultural. An area in which the predominant economic activity is other than agricultural.

6.   An area designated by authorities without specified reference to any of the above.

Once urban is defined according to national preference, all the remaining area is considered rural. There are countries, however, that include a third category, semiurban.

HOUSEHOLD—one or more persons living in a private dwelling. The concept is based on the arrangements made by persons individually or in groups for providing food and other essentials for living. The group may or may not be related by blood or marriage as a whole or even in part.

1.   One-person household. An individual living alone in his/her own private dwelling (house, apartment, hotel room, and so forth).

2.   Multiperson household. A group sharing a private dwelling. The multiperson household may consist of many combinations of family and nonfamily sets with or without the presence of live-in servants, boarders,

relatives, and visitors. Some types are: one family, two or more families, unrelated individuals, all of which may have live-in servants or not.

Whatever the type of schedule used, the household can be identified. The individual questionnaires of one household can be grouped together in a special folder. The schedule itself will indicate the head of the household and the relationship of the other members are noted on theirs. The household folder may list the head and the other members separately. The household questionnaire only needs to indicate by statement of relationship and/or order of placement of names what constitutes one household. The general schedule must indicate the head and the standard order of placement with the statement of relationship for each member. A line must be drawn to separate one household from the next.

FAMILY—Two or more persons related by blood or marriage, living together and sharing a common budget. Because the one family household is quite common, people tend to consider the two terms as synonymous. Some censuses have used the word "family," although the definition given is that of a household. Confusion arises when no definition is given. Occasionally a table giving "family" composition or relationships will clarify the term as one or the other.

When individual schedules are used they can be grouped by family before being grouped into the household folder. Both household and general schedules must indicate both household and family relationships or there must be an order of placement of names designed to indicate family units within the household.

INSTITUTIONAL POPULATION—This is the category under which persons are grouped who do not reside as members of a private household nor do they maintain private residences outside of their institution. They are those who have little or no choice in where they reside. Those with no choice are persons committed to correctional and penal institutions, mental hospitals, tuberculosis and Hansen's disease treatment facilities, and similar institutions. Those with little choice are persons who are members of armed forces living on base, students in dormitories, members of religious orders in convents and monasteries, and the like.

HOMELESS—People without domicile who sleep in the streets, doorways, or any other spaces on a random basis and those who find shelter that does not fall into the scope of living quarters (intended for habitation). A special form and a precise census moment is most important for this category.

SEX—The question should appear on the schedule; however, other methods have been used such as color-coded schedules, or sex may be taken from the current population registers. One would think there could be no problem concerning data on sex in the census, but if there is a strong enough motive, for example, military draft, a young male may be listed as female by his family. Occasionally there is a census that lists "indeterminate" along with "male" and "female."

AGE—The majority of censuses ask for completed years as of the last birthday. Occasionally it may be as of the next birthday or as of the nearest birthday. Date of birth is asked by other countries instead. When the date is not known then age in completed years is asked; if that is not known, then an estimate of the age is made by the trained canvasser following determined guidelines, for example, that based on a calendar of local historical events, or a chart relating animal year to numerical year. Those who are not estimated and do not state age may be allocated to an age group according to statistical patterns. When none of these substitutes can be used, it is better to use a column entitled "not stated." Infants under one year may be tabulated by the number of completed months and those under one month, by completed days. Sources of misstatements of age are ignorance of correct age, carelessness, preference for certain digits, or conscious misrepresentation due to social, political, and economic reasons or customs.

1. Real and generational age. The age in completed years at the time of the census is real age. Some tables may be tabulated according to the year of birth, or generational age, because they treat age as of December 31 or January 1, although the census was taken at a different time of the year.

2. Age groups and single years. Where feasible, single year tables for the country as a whole and perhaps for the major civil divisions are useful for recombinations into special groups. Most tables appear in five-year age groups; the standard groups are: 0-4, 5-9, to 85 and over. The group 0-4 may be in single years as well. Other age groupings may be used that are most suitable to the topic of other tables.

MARITAL STATUS—This can be asked of the total population (all ages) or only of the segment whose age is the country's legal marriage age and older. If most of the possible categories of marital status were consistently used, there would be little confusion. Even in today's world, very few individuals could not be assigned to one of the following:

1. Unmarried, single, never married.
2. Legally married.
3. *De facto* or consensually married.
4. Widowed and not remarried nor in some form of union.
5. Legally divorced and not remarried nor in some form of union.
6. Legally separated.
7. *De facto* separation.
8. Annulled.

However, not all are used because a few of the categories above may not be of significant numbers to matter in an individual country. The problem lies in where the persons are assigned who are not of the categories chosen. Some censuses assign the legally separated to divorced, others to married; others divide the separated and list the legally separated as a category and assign the *de facto* separated to married. Where should annulled be put—in divorced, in unmarried, or in married?

As with every topic, the country selects the categories that are significant to its circumstance and therefore should clearly state where the others are to be included.

RELATIONSHIP TO HOUSEHOLD HEAD OR OTHER REFERENCE MEMBER—It is traditional to identify first on the schedule the household head as designated by the other members. This is followed by the remaining members, according to their relationship to the head. In the past, and still in many countries today, the head has customarily been the one who has primary authority and responsibility for household affairs and in the majority of cases is its chief economic support. This concept was and is convenient for the determination of dependency statistics. Even in the time and place where such traditional households predominate, other kinds of households exist that cannot comply with this definition, for example, siblings without parents, unrelated individuals. Where nontraditional households have developed, that is, where spouses are considered equal in household authority and responsibility and share economic support of the household, a variation in the traditional concept is needed. The 1980 United States census, for example, asked that the person in column 1 be the adult in whose name the home is owned or rented.

The standard order of placement on the schedule according to relationship to head may be expanded or reduced to accommodate a nation's need. The usual order is head, spouse, unmarried child, married child, spouse of child, grandchild/great-grandchild, parent of head, parent of spouse, other relative, domestic employee (then spouse, child), and other person not related.

HOUSEHOLD COMPOSITION—There are four main ways to indicate the composition of a household. They are not mutually exclusive; one or all four or any combination have been used in censuses.

1. By size. The simplest and most common classification of households is to group them by the number of household members. Since the definition of a household may vary from country to country the average size also may vary. A household of twenty-four members may indicate a family with many children or a commune of unrelated individuals.

2. By relationship. Occasionally there will be a table indicating the constituent members of a household by their relationship, for example, spouse of head, child of head. Every census contains this information, but not every report gives these relationships in a tabulation.

3. By characteristics of the head. This method of depicting a household is almost as common as classifying by size. The status of the head, especially when he/she is considered the dominant member of the household, is used to indicate the social, cultural and economic situation of the household.

4. By type. Classifying by type is usually based on the number of conjugal family nuclei and/or by the presence or absence of spouse, children, and

unrelated individuals. Some examples are: one-family household, spouse present and "x" number of unmarried children; one person household; two or more family household with "x" number of children and live-in servants, and others. There are other simpler classifications by type: family/nonfamily households, private/institutional households; one person/multiperson households.

PLACE OF BIRTH—This can be used for determining three different topics.

1. Nativity. The place of birth (not necessarily related to citizenship or to nationality) determines whether or not a person is a native of the country.

    a. for natives, it also includes the geographical subdivision where the birth took place or that was the residence of the mother at the time of birth. The choice should be stated.

    b. for foreign born, the name of the country is sufficient, or, if that is not known, the continent should be determined. It is recommended that information taken on the country of birth should be according to the national boundaries existing at the time of the census.

2. Internal migration. Place of birth for natives and usual residence at the time of the census indicates a very simple form of internal migration. This may be improved on if the questions distinguish those born in the city, born elsewhere in the same major civil division, and those born in a different major civil division. It is best, however, if place of birth and usual residence are supplemented with data on duration of residence and place of previous residence or of residence at a specified date in the past.

3. Ethnic composition. For the foreign born only, but if they do not constitute a significant part of the population, it is of little use.

USUAL RESIDENCE—This is basic in determining the *de jure* population. Please note that the usual residence of an individual is not necessarily his/her legal residence. Usual residence is based on residence in a territorial unit (not one house) for a specified minimum period, generally six months. There are, however, exceptional cases that need to be dealt with, for example, students boarding at schools away from their parents' home territory. (See page 10, *de jure*, for remaining cases.) Usual residence is also used in conjunction with place of previous residence, duration of residence, or residence at a specific date in the past to determine the migration patterns of the population.

A very basic form of migration can be seen by crossing the place of birth with usual residence. It can reveal only one move in the period between birth and the time of the enumeration. At first this seemed sufficient and so was commonly used in early censuses when the population was less mobile. Since 1945, however, circumstances of war and industrialization have affected almost every country, and this simple migration measurement no longer serves. Place of previous residence has been added to place of birth and usual residence to indicate population mobility. It has become necessary to cite more than the major subdivision of each residence, and more detail has been added. Smaller divisions, such as counties and places, are asked, and in some cases, whether previous residence was in a rural or urban area. Duration of residence in the form of the number of completed years or the year of first arrival or of the latest return from overseas residence has added another dimension. A variant of duration, residence at a specified date in the past, checks current internal migration, if the specified date is no more than one year previous, and both international migration as well as internal migration, if the date was five years before. The main problem is in the treatment of infants and young children not yet born at the specified date in the past.

CITIZENSHIP—Citizenship as defined by each country may be simple or complex. It relates to the legal nationality of the individual based on political allegiance. The basic terms used to describe this status in a census are: Citizen/Alien or National/Nonnational. Citizens or nationals are often subdivided by birth, by marriage, and by naturalization. Aliens or nonnationals can be subdivided by resident or nonresident status. These terms should not be confused with Native/Foreign-born. Citizenship focuses more on nationals while nationality (derived from country of birth) focuses more on nonnationals. Segments of the population whose position needs to be clarified are stateless persons, those with dual citizenship, and persons in process of naturalization.

RACE, ETHNIC ORIGIN, NATIONALITY—The definitions and criteria applied by each country investigating racial/ethnic characteristics of the population must be determined by the groups that it desires to identify. In early censuses, it seemed simple enough to distinguish, for example, the colonizers from the indigenous population. Pairs such as free/slave, white/nonwhite, European/aborigines, for example, were no longer useful when the population began to mix. This resulted in white/black/colored (mixed) and other variations even to the extreme of the percentage of white or black blood. This, too, became insufficient as a means of characterizing segments of a population. As the complexity of variants of racial/ethnic origin grew, three major trends developed among the countries that conducted censuses:

1. All reference to race or ethnic origin was dropped.
2. Certain racial and ethnic terms were combined in one list, depending on the groups to be identified.
3. Other criteria such as self- or community identification were used instead of race or ethnic origin.

EDUCATION—Educational systems vary from country to country. The development of an International Standard Classification of Education has been a recent project of UNESCO (1976). Countries may use the ISCED, their own national classification system, or merely the number of years of school attendance or level of education completed.

The situation of population groups, however, does not easily lend itself to classification; it depends on what the country wants to identify.

1. Literacy. The ability to read and write a simple paragraph about his/her own life is considered the minimum. The problem arises in whether the determination was made through a test administered by the canvasser, by

completion of a specified number of years of formal education, or by claim of the respondent. The definition and method of determination should be specified. The minimum age limit should exclude those still in process of learning (no higher than age fifteen).

2. School enrollment. Asked of the age group most likely to be attending school, for example those from the age of five to twenty-nine. The grouping depends on the minimum age limit (usually age five) and the maximum, which is not so easily defined. Some countries have significant numbers of students in advanced academic studies, adult education, and other programs, while other countries may have few students past the elementary or secondary level. The upper age level should be dependent on the country's circumstances and should be clearly stated. It should also be stated whether the schooling is formal, tutorial, vocational, special education for the handicapped, and so forth, or not.

3. Educational attainment. This is usually intended to determine the education of the population that has completed formal schooling; therefore, the group is often age twenty-four and over. Again, depending on national circumstance, the minimum age can vary. In any case, it should be clearly stated. Persons with no schooling should also be identified. The level is determined by several methods: age at termination of schooling; number of years completed; level completed; or level and years combined. Degree earned may also be used.

4. Educational qualification. This is determined by the degrees, diplomas, or certificates that an individual has acquired whether by full-time, part-time, or private study and whether earned in the home country or abroad. It implies the successful completion of a course of study. The title of the highest degree, diploma or certificate received should be included along with an indication of the field of study if the title is not clear.

LANGUAGE—When asked, it is usually to indicate the language or languages that are numerically important not just the dominant one.

1. Mother tongue. The language usually spoken in the individual's home in early childhood. It has ethnic significance.

2. Usual language. That which is currently spoken or most spoken in the present home. Indicates assimilation of the foreign born.

3. Ability to speak one or more designated languages.

RELIGION—This is generally asked in two different although similar fashions.

1. Religion. The religious or spiritual belief or preference, whether in an organized group or not.

2. Specific denomination. Affiliation with an organized group with religious or spiritual tenets.

The question on religion is generally optional. Most countries that ask religion do not restrict themselves to (1) or (2) but rather use a combination of the two. They list specific denominations for the most popular religions and only the religion for others. Occasionally the response depends on active membership and not just preference.

ECONOMIC CHARACTERISTICS—With the possible exception of income, the time reference period for census data on economic characteristics should be the same.

1. One week before the census date yields information on *current* activity, employment and unemployment, and other *labor force* information. It may not be appropriate where the predominant employment is seasonal (for example, agricultural, fishing).

2. Up to twelve months before the census date provides information on the *usual* economic activity, the one of most importance to the *individual*, intensity of activity over the period (underemployment), and household income. Determining activity status, occupation, and industry over a long time period has difficulties.

3. Combination of both short and long periods can avoid the difficulties inherent in either but needs detailed instructions and carefully worded questionnaires to be effective.

Persons employed full time in one job in the same industry pose no problem to either period; difficulties arise when dealing with (1) those who are economically active for only a part of the year and (2) those who engage in more than one occupation or who work in different industries during the longer period. The minimum age limit should be set according to the country's need (the United States uses sixteen). It is recommended, however, that it should not be over age fifteen. Tabulations that separate the under fifteen from the fifteen and over permit international comparison.

TYPE OF ACTIVITY—The active are those who supply labor for the production of economic goods and services during the chosen time-reference period. It includes civilian labor force and those serving in armed forces, those who work for pay (wage and salary workers) or profit (self-employed, owners) and unpaid family workers in a family enterprise. They are classified as:

1. Employed: With a job whether working, on vacation, or ill.
2. Unemployed: Those seeking work for pay or profit, including first-time job seekers as well as experienced workers.

The inactive are generally:

1. Homemakers: Performing household duties in own home without pay.
2. Students.
3. Income recipients: Income from property, investment, pensions from former activities.
4. Others: Beneficiaries of public or private support, children not attending school, invalids, and other dependents not listed above.

OCCUPATION—The kind of work done. The main or principal occupation asked is usually determined by the amount of time spent in that occupation or the one most remunerative. Secondary occupation of persons with a main occupation is sometimes asked.

OCCUPATIONAL CLASSIFICATION—It took longer to establish a standard classification of occupations than of industries especially at the three- and four-digit levels. Not all countries use the International Standard Classification of Occupations (ISCO) but most other systems are similar enough to it at the 1-and 2-digit levels that comparability is not too difficult. An explanation of the differences should be given in the census publications. Older forms of occupational classification were (1) an alphabetical listing, (2) a hierarchical listing of occupations by descending order based on status in the community, and (3) a listing based on industry or products made.

INDUSTRY—The activity of the establishment in which the economically active person worked during the time-reference period, or last worked if unemployed. The main industry is asked as in occupation as may a secondary industry.

INDUSTRIAL CLASSIFICATION—The standard classification of industries seems to have developed with more ease than the occupation system, probably because industries are more tangible. Most systems other than the International Standard Industrial Classification of All Economic Activities (ISIC) are similar enough to it that there is some comparability if sufficient explanation of the differences is given. Early forms of industrial classifications were (1) two or three broad economic sectors, usually only the predominant ones, and (2) some subdivisions of these, again only in the predominant sectors.

OCCUPATIONAL STATUS/STATUS IN EMPLOYMENT—More or less a hierarchical ranking of positions within economic activity.

1. Employer. Owner of the enterprise who has one or more salaried personnel working for him/her.

2. Own-account worker/self-employed. Generally the owner of an enterprise who does not have salaried personnel. Occasionally a census may have a subcategory of own-account worker with fewer than three employees.

3. Employee. Person who is remunerated in wages, salary, commission, tips, piece-rates, or pay in kind for his/her time at work.

4. Unpaid family worker. A person who usually works one-third the normal working hours or more per week without pay in an economic enterprise operated by a relative living in the same household. "Same household" is optional to the definition if the circumstances demand.

5. Member of a producer's cooperative. Used only if it is numerically significant, otherwise the worker is assigned to one of the other categories.

6. Persons not classifiable. Experienced workers whose status is not known or is inadequately described; first-time job seekers are put in this category.

7. Unpaid apprentices. Excludes those who receive pay in kind, for example, meals and sleeping quarters, who are placed in "employee."

INCOME—It may be taken for individuals and/or households. It should be stated whether only wages or salaries are counted or whether total income from all sources is included.

Other topics asked in economic characteristics are:

1. Time worked and/or unemployed—usually in hours per week or in months per year.

2. Reasons for unemployment.

3. Sector of employment.

    a. public—subdivided into general government, publically owned enterprises, or

    b. private—privately owned and/or controlled enterprises, household and unincorporated enterprises.

    c. cooperative enterprises and semipublic enterprises may be separately identified.

4. Economic dependency—may indicate the number of dependents per provider or the number of persons dependent on a specific industry.

FERTILITY—This topic indicates the frequency of births in a population and may be determined by a variety of questions or combinations thereof. Sources of fertility data are:

1. General census information (age and sex, analysis of household composition) can establish a child-woman ratio.

2. Fertility of marriage. A combination of marriage frequency and/or duration of married life (date of marriage, age at marriage, number of marriages) and the number of children born alive during that marriage. Back-up questions are age of mother at first birth and number of children living.

3. Maternal fertility. Number of children ever born alive asked of all women ever married or of all women regardless of marital status, with or without age limits.

4. Paternal fertility (rarely used). Number of children ever born alive asked of all men ever married or of all men regardless of marital status.

5. Current fertility. Number of children born alive in the twelve months before the census date and sometimes the number of children surviving.

The main problem to be dealt with is that memory may not serve accurately, especially in countries where both fertility and infant mortality are high. It should be clearly stated the population from whom the data was collected: married women (within "at risk" age limits); all women; women ever married; married men and women; all women who had borne children; married women and widows; married men and widowers; and so forth. Some countries may include adopted children within the number of children ever born alive.

INFIRMITIES—The early censuses were more interested in determining the number of the blind, deaf-dumb, insane, mentally incompetent, or lepers than later censuses. Nowadays, the concentration is primarily to determine those who are too incapacitated to work.

L.   Special elements and features. Included in this section are new or reinstated topics and topics that have been dropped. Mention is made of the
presence of maps, copy of the questionnaire, enumerator's instructions, and
sample tabulations. If there are comparative tables, a section on the analysis of
the country's data, or any special studies or history, they are also noted in this
section. In short, anything present that would not usually appear in a census
publication but is of interest to a researcher is cited here.

M.   Quality of the census. This refers primarily to how the census was
organized and conducted and its resulting publications. Determining the accuracy of the data contained therein is not within the intent of this work. Any
comments about data are as stated in the census itself or by other authoritative
sources, for example, Whipple's Index published in the UN Demographic
Yearbooks of 1955, 1963, 1973, and 1979.

Some of the elements to look for are: a permanent census office as opposed
to one reinstated for each census, a long history of census taking, and prompt
publication of main results. The most important is that all definitions and
concepts are published within the resultant volumes along with any information about test censuses conducted, postenumeration surveys used, development and training of field organization, problems encountered and steps taken
to overcome them, specimens of the questionnaires used, instructions for
enumerators, methods used for the evaluation of the data, and a stated quality
of information on each topic (determination of coverage error, amount and
type of data editing done, internal consistency of data, examination of the
reasonableness of results, comparison of results with those of data collected
elsewhere, and other official statistical agency sources).

Not having all of the above does not mean that the census or its data are
poor, but it is reassuring to a user to see all the effort expended as the above
indicates.

N.   Publication plan. The dissemination of results comes in various stages.

1.   Preliminary. Raw data summaries prepared quickly, usually based on
field tallies, that give the number of inhabitants by geographic areas. The
figures have not had the benefit of evaluation and analysis of results.

2.   Provisional. Preliminary results of other demographic, social and economic characteristics, usually by sample tabulation, to give results for national and sometimes major subdivision levels. The size of the sample
tabulation dictates the degree of geographic detail.

3.   Advance. Cleaned results of the number of inhabitants (on a detailed
geographic level) plus one or two other characteristics such as race/ethnic
origin, and/or age by sex. There could also be cleaned national totals for
other selected characteristics. Advance figures may also result from a sample tabulation.

4.   Final. Cleaned results of all variables, in all predetermined cross-
classifications, derived from complete tabulation of 100 percent as well as
sample enumeration.

5.　Sample. Some topics, not needed for small areas, are taken only on a sample basis during enumeration. The results of these have to have proper weights applied in the tabulation stage to produce valid national estimates. Sample error must accompany tables.

The forms of census publication in the broad sense of the word are:

1.　Computer tapes. With accompanying guides to their use, this form is the most versatile for the researcher who works especially in small-area studies.

2.　Microforms. For the convenience of storing large multivolume sets of census publications.

3.　Printed publications. The most efficient forms from the standpoint of time and money when the data sought are general and not complicated by special geographic areas. Most publication plans of printed results include preliminary and/or advanced tabulations; the final results, however, have a variety of formats:

　　a.　single volume. Results of all planned tabulations for all geographic areas are collected in one volume. Generally used by smaller countries.

　　b.　total country and major subdivision volumes. All results for each subdivision collected in one volume to the smallest geographic division; all results for the whole country usually without repeating the small geographic division results contained in the state volumes. A locality publication may also be used.

　　c.　subject volumes. The results of tabulations by subject for all the geographic areas in one volume. May be used with b.

　　d.　general report. The information usually contained in this report may be included within the volumes listed above or may appear as a separate publication.

Included in the section of the entry labeled Publication Plan are the main entry bibliographic descriptions as well as the answer to whether unpublished data are available on request or whether computer tapes with accompanying guides are available, and the language or languages of the printed publications.

O.　Topic chart. A national topic chart is included for quick reference to the general content of the censuses conducted from 1945 to the latest available.

P.　Other statistical publications. With the kind permission of Richard Hankinson, editor of *Population Index*, the list of other statistical publications was taken from the latest issue containing the "Governmental and Intergovernmental Serial Publications Containing Vital or Migration Statistics" (volume 46, no. 4). There are a few (very few) other publications not listed in the *Population Index* which have been added.

OTHER COMPONENTS OF THIS VOLUME

Maps. We have found referring to maps very helpful and therefore have included one with most entries. Major subdivision boundaries are marked on the majority of the maps.

International Population Charts. The first chart in this section contains international population figures for total country, capital, and large cities, as found in the official published results of each census for the period 1945-present. The second chart contains international population figures for metropolitan areas, as found in the official published results of the latest census. There is no standard among countries for the designation of metropolitan areas. In the event that a city of one million or more was not designated a metropolitan area, it was included rather than leave a gap. The other problem involved in this table was the lack of 1975 to 1980 results for all countries.

International Topic Charts. This section contains compilations of the individual national topic charts found in the main entries to this volume. It covers sixteen general subjects and may serve as an aid to users who wish to make cross-national studies. Once the countries have been tentatively identified from these charts the specific country entries should be consulted for more detail.

Variant Country Names and Capital Cities Cross-Reference. The purpose of this index is to direct the user to the current name of a country or capital city. Entries in this volume are arranged alphabetically under the current country name.

BIBLIOGRAPHY

All the official census publications, census result volumes, methodologies, guides, and enumerator instructions that were available were consulted in the preparation of this work. At first an individual country bibliography of all such works as well as nonofficial publications was intended, but these lists became too long to be included in this book. We would like to mention briefly, however, some comprehensive sets that will not be listed below. The CICRED World Population Year series proved helpful in many cases, as did the many CELADE publications, *The Asian and Pacific Forum* (a periodical), and the UN Demographic Yearbooks, especially the 1955, 1962 through 1964, 1971 through 1973, and 1979 volumes with the special topic on population censuses.

Alterman, Hyman. *Counting People; The Census in History.* New York, 1969.

Consejo Latinoaméricano de Ciencias Sociales. *Los censos de población y vivienda in la década de 1980 en América latina.* Buenos Aires, 1981. (Investigación e información sociodemográficas, No. 2)

Davis, Kingsley. "Census." In *Encyclopaedia Britannica,* Volume 5. Chicago, 1966.

Goyer, Doreen S. *The International Population Census Bibliography: Revision and Update, 1945-1977.* New York, 1980.

Kuczynski, R. R. *Demographic Survey of the British Colonial Empire.* London, 1948-1953. Volumes 1-3.

McArthur, Norma. *Island Populations of the Pacific.* Canberra, Australia, 1967.

Office of Population Research. *Population Index,* 1935-   . Quarterly. Princeton, NJ, 1935-

Shryock, Henry S. Jr. and Conrad Taeuber. *The Conventional Population Census. Systems of Demographic Measurement. Data Collection Systems.* Chapel Hill, NC, 1976. (Laboratories for Population Statistics, scientific report series, No. 25)

Shryock, Henry S. Jr., Jacob S. Siegel, and Associates. *The Methods and Materials of Demography.* 2d printing, revised. Washington, D.C., 1973. 2 volumes.

Texas, University of. Population Research Center. *International Population Census Bibliography.* Austin, TX, 1965-1968. Volumes 1-6 and supplement.

United Nations Fund for Population Activities. *National Censuses and the United Nations.* New York, 1977. (Population profiles, 3)

1950 Censuses

U.N. Statistical Office [and] Population Division. *Studies of Census Methods.* Lake Success, NY, 1947-1949. Reports Nos. 1-15.

U.N. Statistical Office [and] Population Division. *Population Census Methods.* Lake Success, NY, 1949. (Population studies, No. 4)

U.N. Statistical Office. *Handbook of Population Census Methods.* New York, 1954. (Studies in methods, Series F, No. 5)

1960 Censuses

U.N. Statistical Office. *Principles and Recommendations for National Population Censuses.* New York, 1958. (Statistical papers, Series M, No. 27)

U.N. Statistical Office. *Handbook of Population Census Methods.* New York, 1958-1959. Volumes 1-3. (Studies in methods, Series F, No. 5, Rev. 1)

U.N. Statistical Office. *Handbook of Population and Housing Census Methods.* New York, 1972-1974. Volume 4. (Studies in methods, Series F, No. 16 and Add. 4)

U.N. Statistical Office. *Handbook of Population and Housing Census Methods.* New York, 1971. Part 6. (Studies in methods, Series F, No. 16)

Inter-American Statistical Institute. *Censo de población. Estudios sobre métodos y procedimientos.* Washington, D.C., 1960. (IASI document, 4065 Esp.)

Conference of European Statisticians. *European Population Censuses: The 1960 Series. International Recommendations and National Practices.* New York, 1964. (Statistical standards and studies, No. 3)

1970 Censuses

U.N. Statistical Office. Department of Economic and Social Affairs. *Principles and Recommendations for the 1970 Population Censuses.* New York, 1967. (Statistical papers, Series M, No. 44)

U.N. Economic Commission for Africa. *African Recommendations for the 1970 Population Censuses.* New York, n.d. (E/CN.14/CAS.6/1)

U.N. Economic Commission for Asia and the Far East. *Asian Recommendations for the 1970 Population Censuses.* (Sales No. 67.II.F.3)

U.N. Economic Commission for Europe. *European Recommendations for the 1970 Population Censuses.* 1968. (Sales No. E.69.II.E/Mim.17)

Inter-American Statistical Institute. *Programa del censo de América de 1970 (COTA 1970). Censos de población: temas, definiciones, clasificaciones y cuestionarios utilizados por los países de la región americana.* Washington, D.C., 1977. (IASI document 7094 Esp.)

1980 Censuses

U.N. Statistical Office. Department of International Economic and Social Affairs. *Principles and Recommendations for Population and Housing Censuses*. New York, 1980. (Statistical papers, Series M, No. 67)

U.N. Economic and Social Commission for Asia and the Pacific. *Asian and Pacific Recommendations for the 1980 Population and Housing Censuses*. (ST/ESCAP/52)

U.N. Economic Commission for Europe. *Recommendations for the 1980 Censuses of Population and Housing in the ECE Region*. New York, 1978. (CES, Statistical standards and studies, No. 31)

Inter-American Statistical Institute. *Program of the 1980 Census of America (COTA 1980): Standards for the Population and Housing Census*. (IASI document 7357a-3/16/78-25)

U.N. Economic Commission for Africa. *Report of the Working Group on Recommendations for the 1980 Population and Housing Censuses in Africa*. (E/CN.14/CPH/47)

U.N. Economic Commission for Western Asia. Expert Group Meeting on Census Techniques, 12-16 December 1977. *Final Report*. (E/ECWA/POP/WG.9/2)

INDEX TO TERMS DEFINED IN THE INTRODUCTION

LATIN AMERICA AND THE CARIBBEAN

The Caribbean

Antigua

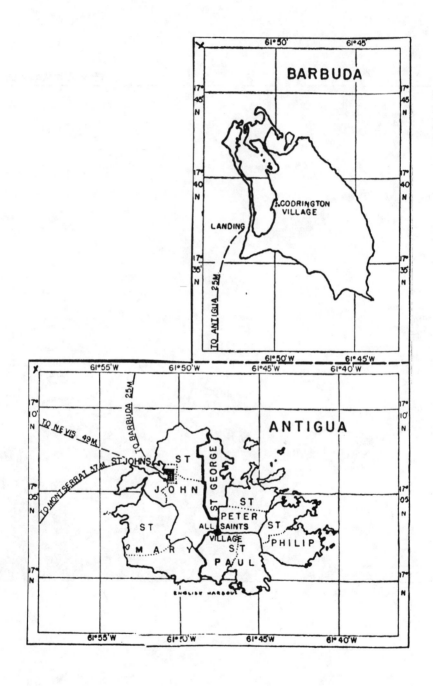

Antigua

Antigua and Barbuda (1981)

CAPITAL: St. John's.
STATISTICAL AGENCY: Statistics Division, Ministry of Planning, Development, and External Affairs.
NATIONAL REPOSITORY: Antigua Public Library, St. John's.
MAIN U.S. REPOSITORY: Population Research Center (Univ. of Texas).

Antigua, including its dependencies of Barbuda and Redonda, was first colonized in 1632. Once one of the Presidencies of the Leeward Islands of the British West Indies, in 1967 it became an Associated State with full internal self-government. Independence was achieved in 1981.

Censuses were said to have been taken in 1844, 1851, 1856. The only information extant from these are total numbers of inhabitants. Information from the census of 1861 was found in the census of England and Wales of that year, volume 3, *General Report*.

1861

Taken presumably by the government authorities. It was *de facto* and self-enumerated on household schedules, but because of the weakness of literacy most of the schedules were filled out by the canvasser. It was manually tabulated. The scope included sex, age, marital status, birthplace, occupation, infirmities, and race.

1871

Like the previous censuses, no publications have been located with results of the census of 1871.

1881

Some data from this census were found in comparative tables in the report for the census of 1891. No census date was cited but it was *de facto*, supposedly self-enumerated (see 1861), and manually tabulated. The scope was sex, age, race, occupation, and number of dwellings.

1891

Taken as part of the Leeward Islands, the census was *de facto*, supposedly self-enumerated, and manually tabulated. It included the shipping population in the harbor. The scope was sex, age, relation to household head, birthplace, marital status, race, occupation (from which the economically active and inactive and the industry can be determined to some degree), and occupational status.

1901

The only data available is the total number of inhabitants by sex, found in the 1901 Census of the British Empire volume. "For financial or other reasons, unable to take a complete census."

1911

Taken by the Registrar General who was appointed census officer for this enumeration. It was *de facto* and self-enumerated with manual tabulation. The scope was sex, age, birthplace, marital status (not cross-classified by age), education (literacy and school attendance), race, religion, occupation, industry (determined through occupation list), number of dwellings, and infirmities.

1921

Taken by the census officer (Registrar General), the census was *de facto* and self-enumerated with manual tabulation. It included shipping population in the harbor. Redonda was uninhabited at this time. The scope was sex, age, relation to household head, number of separate families, birthplace, marital status, education, race, religion, household composition (new), occupation, industry (same as 1911), infirmities, and housing.

1946 (April 9)

The Registrar General of Antigua served as census officer for the Presidency. There were six parishes in Antigua plus Barbuda, the seventh. Included were the shipping population in the harbor and the institutional population.

Definitions and Concepts. [See British West Indies 1946 for the full entry; the following are differences only.] AGE—No infants under one year were coded in completed months. Tables have single years of age to 100 and over, standard five-year age groups to eighty-five and over. MARITAL STATUS—the categories divorced and common-law marriage were new to Antigua. RACE—white, black, Asian, and mixed were the only categories in the tables. HOUSEHOLD COMPOSITION—by size only. OCCUPATIONAL STATUS—employer, own-account worker, unpaid helper, and wage earner (at work, learner, unemployed). INFIRMITIES—blind and deaf-mute only.

Special Elements and Features. Same, plus infirmities and duration of union.

Quality of the Census. Whipple's Index rating was category III—Approximate age data.

Publication Plan. Part F of the West Indian set is devoted to the Leeward Islands. Language of publication is English.

1960 (April 7)

Taken by the territorial census office (not permanent). [See British West Indies 1960, West Indies section, for full entry; the following are the differences only.] Individual schedules were used instead of household. Antigua's territorial divisions are the same as 1946. Because its volume 1 was never published, there are no enumeration district tables.

Definitions and Concepts. RACE—did not include Amerindians, only European, Chinese and East Indian, Syrian, mixed, black, and other. EDUCATION—no literacy taken. FERTILITY (all females age fifteen and over, not fourteen and over)—number of children ever born alive was the only item taken. OCCUPATION—tables list only major groups, no detailed list.

Special Elements and Features. No duration of union or number of children surviving. Literacy, infirmities, and agriculture were dropped.

Quality of the Census. Same as for the British West Indies, but volume 1 was not published. No Whipple's Index rating was available.

Publication Plan. Jamaica. Department of Statistics. *West Indies Population Census. Census of Antigua, 7th April 1960*, Volume 2. Language of publication is English.

1970 (April 7)

Antigua chose not to take part in the Commonwealth Caribbean census. Conducted by the Statistics Division of the Ministry of Planning, Development, and External Affairs, it was both *de jure* and *de facto*, perhaps self-enumerated, and mechanically tabulated. Not much is known of the conduct of this census; all information is taken from the sparse introduction and tables. Results are given for the six parishes of Antigua, for Barbuda (the seventh parish) and for the Port of St. John's, which was divided into three parts. It is not known if an individual, general, or household schedule was used.

Definitions and Concepts. SEX, BIRTHPLACE, RACE, RELIGIONS, EDUCATION—same as 1960. AGE—completed years last birthday, tables give under one, one, two, three, four, then standard five-year age groups with one column entitled "not stated." MARITAL STATUS—married, common-law union, divorced/legally separated, widowed, single/never married, and "not stated." MIGRATION—derived from place of birth and former residence of nationals who returned and years since migration. ECONOMIC ACTIVITY—(last twelve months and last week) all persons age fourteen and over: working, looking for work, incapacitated, other/not stated. The labor force tables indicate both the employed and unemployed. There are no figures for the inactive population. The number of months worked in the last year was also taken. OCCUPATION—eight major groups. INDUSTRY—ten major groups that are similar to ISIC. OCCUPATIONAL STATUS—government employee, private employee, unpaid worker, own-account worker, employer, and not working/not stated.

Special Elements and Features. No complete tabulation of results was made. Housing and social and demographic characteristics were based on 20 percent sample of returns; the economic characteristics on 15 percent. Fertility was not taken.

Quality of the Census. There was a paucity of staff resources. That and the large number of "not stated" responses made tabulation difficult. There is very little description about the conduct of the census, and with no copy of the schedule it makes it awkward to work with this census. The census office is not permanent.

Publication Plan. Antigua. Ministry of Planning, Development, and External Affairs. *Census of Population, 1970.* St. John's, 1974-1975. One volume each on housing, social and demographic characteristics, and economic characteristics. Unpublished data is available. Language of publication is English.

OTHER STATISTICAL PUBLICATIONS: Issued by Statistics Division, *Report for the Years . . .* (biennially), *Statistical Yearbook.*

National Topic Chart

	1946	1960	1970
De facto	X	X	X
Usual residence	X	X	X
Place of birth	X	X	X
Duration of residence	X	X	
Place of prev. residence			
Urban/rural			
Sex	X	X	X
Age	X	X	X
Relation to household head	X	X	
Marital status	X	X	X
Children born alive	X	X	
Children living	X		
Citizenship			
Literacy	X		
School enrollment	X	X	
Ed. attainment		X	X
Ed. qualification			
National/Ethnic origin	X	X	X
Language			
Religion	X	X	X
Household composition	X	X	
Econ. active/inactive	X	X	X
Occupation	X	X	X
Industry	X	X	X
Occupational status	X	X	X
Income			
Housing	X	X	X

Argentina

Argentine Republic

CAPITAL: Buenos Aires Federal Capital.
STATISTICAL AGENCY: Instituto Nacional de Estadística y Censos (INEC).
NATIONAL REPOSITORY: Library of INEC.
MAIN U.S. REPOSITORY: Population Research Center (Univ. of Texas).

Several attempts at a census were made at the beginning of the nineteenth century, but the results lacked uniformity and did not cover all the provinces of the country. The first national census of population was taken in 1869. It was conducted by the superintendent of the census (Diego de la Fuente) on a *de facto* basis, and canvasser was the method used to record information on general schedules. The "terrestrial" population was enumerated separately from the "fluvial" population. At the time of the first census, the country was divided into fourteen states or provinces, four territories, and subdivided into "departamentos." The territorial division of the country changed throughout the years. The scope of the census included: age, sex, marital status, nationality, place of birth, literacy, occupation or profession, and the number of families per house. Under the category of "special condition" were recorded: number of persons living in a house who suffered from certain infirmities (blindness, mental illness, and so forth), number of those considered illegitimate, and school enrollment.

In spite of the effort, the notation of the schedules was deficient, thus making it impossible to differentiate some age groups; age composition did not separate natives from immigrants, except for those living in the city of Buenos Aires. In addition, it was impossible to differentiate persons who did not have an occupation from persons who did not give the information or did not know their occupation. Total population for some cities and subdivisions, a table with approximate figures of the population since 1809, and projections of population for the following decades (1879 to 1919) were provided.

1895

The second general census of population was conducted by the Comisión Directiva del Censo. The census was *de facto*, canvassed, and general schedules were utilized. The territory covered by the census was divided into fourteen states or provinces, one federal district (capital of the country), and nine national

Argentina

— International boundary
–·– Provincia boundary
★ National capital
◉ Provincia capital
┼┼┼ Railroad
── Road

0   300 Kilometers
0   300 Miles

Boundary representation is
not necessarily authoritative.

territories, subdivided into "departamentos." The scope was expanded to include
the following topics: religion, fertility, duration of marriage, and type of construction and ownership of properties. Although more complete than the previous
census, notations on schedules still presented problems. There was no separate
place in the schedules to record the number of houses as opposed to the number
of families living therein. Fertility data was inaccurate; there was no way of
separating the number of women without children from those who did not answer
the question. Data on religion also presented problems. Because it was assumed
that the majority of the people were Catholics, only the persons whom the
enumerator thought were not Catholic were asked their religious preference.

Between 1869 and 1900 several estimates and separate censuses for provinces
were made. In 1904 and 1909 special censuses for the city of Buenos Aires were
carried out.

1914

The third general census was taken by the Comisión Nacional del Censo. It
was *de facto*, canvassed, and for the first time, individual schedules were utilized. Also for the first time, the population living outside the country was
enumerated. In these cases, the consulate was responsible for their enumeration.
In addition to the census of population, industrial, agricultural, commercial and
property ("imobiliario") censuses were taken in the same year.

The territory covered by the census was divided into fourteen provinces, one
federal district, and ten national territories, all of which were subdivided into
"departamentos." Total population, nationality, rural and urban populations,
age, sex, marital status, literacy, school enrollment, educational attainment,
fertility of married women, years of marriage, infirmities, place of birth, occupation or profession, and property ownership were recorded.

Questions about economic activities were not well defined, especially those
concerning women's occupations. Comparability among censuses is difficult due
to the change of concepts throughout the years. Analysis of results, comparative
tables with previous censuses and those of other countries, and density of population were also provided.

1920

This was a general census of the national territories (La Pampa, Misiones, Los
Andes, Formosa, Chaco, Neuquén, Río Negro, Chubut, Santa Cruz and Tierra
del Fuego). It was conducted under the direction of the Asesoría Letrada de
Territorios Nacionales in cooperation with local governments. The censuses of
commerce, agriculture, and industry were taken simultaneously. The census was
de facto, and canvasser was the method used. The scope included residents of
urban and rural areas, nationality, localities, sex, race, age, literacy, school
enrollment (six to fourteen years of age), marital status, vaccination, and place of
birth. Density was also reported.

1947 (June 1)

The fourth general census of population was conducted by the Dirección Nacional del Servicio Estadístico. The census was *de facto*, but resident population was also indicated. Canvasser was the method utilized to record information on three kinds of schedules—household, "convivencia" (used in group quarters), and individual schedules (mainly used in group quarters by an individual who did not wish his personal data to be known by others). Simultaneity was observed, and mechanical tabulation was used. Persons living in the Antarctic sector and Argentinian islands in the Atlantic were not included in the census. The territory was divided into provinces and territories. Buenos Aires Province was subdivided into "partidos" and the other provinces and territories into "departamentos." For the purpose of the census "partidos" and "departamentos" were also subdivided into "fracciones," "circunscripciones," and "radios censales." Furthermore, the Federal District and the "partidos" of the province of Buenos Aires constituted a separate unit called Greater Buenos Aires.

Definitions and Concepts. AGE—date of birth, results were tabulated in single years and standard five-year age groups. URBAN—persons living in cities and villages with more than 2,000 inhabitants. Those living in places with fewer inhabitants were classified as rural. MARITAL STATUS—the question was asked of all persons fourteen years of age and over. Categories were: single, married (legally only), widowed, divorced, and unknown. Common-law marriages were not recorded. PLACE OF BIRTH—for native born, the name of the province; for foreign born, the continent of birth. The place of birth of parents was also recorded. EDUCATION—literacy was asked only of persons fourteen years of age and over because they were above the age for compulsory elementary education. RELIGION—divided into two major groups: Christians and non-Christians, and subdivided into Catholics, Orthodox, Protestants; Jewish and Muslims. Persons without religion or "unknown" were also recorded. INFIRMITIES—physical and mental disability. FAMILY (that is, household) —person or group of persons, related or not by blood, living in the same house and in some way economically dependent on the head of the household. Lodgers, guests, and servants were also included. Married sons and daughters, however, were excluded, although they lived in the same house. ECONOMIC ACTIVITY— lower age limit was fourteen years; reference period was at the time of the census (not specified). The concept of an economically active population was not utilized. Instead, the population was divided into three categories: employed with or without pay, unemployed ("no ocupado") with or without income, and not working ("desocupado") with or without job. A later publication (*Cuadros inéditos...*) showed that the economically active population was equivalent in 1947 to: paid employed, persons not working but with job or profession, and persons not working without a job or profession. The inactive population consisted of: persons working without pay (students, homemakers, and so forth), unemployed with income (persons of independent income, retired, pensioners), and unemployed without income (invalids without income). INDUSTRY—classification presented ten divisions and major groups (two-digits). OCCUPA-TION—was asked but not tabulated (main occupation). OCCUPATIONAL STATUS—categories were: employer, self-employed, employee or laborer, apprentice, "cadete" (less than eighteen years of age), domestic servants, and unpaid family workers.

Special Elements and Features. Publication of results, previously planned to be forty tables, was reduced to fourteen tables. Some tables relating to economic activity were published in 1977, and the remaining tables are available in the form of unpublished documents. Since the schedules were not available (not published) and the number of tables reduced, the complete scope is not known. Tables of the population of localities of 100 inhabitants and more in alphabetical and ranked orders, an index for quick location of tables, comparative tables of population growth for several countries, mortality and life expectancy tables, and an alphabetical list of places for which it was not possible to obtain information were also provided.

Quality of the Census. Whipple's Index classified age accuracy into category I—highly accurate data. Completeness of enumeration was not possible in some areas because of the lack of detailed maps of all regions. The most common source of error was found in the categories of place of birth, place of residence, occupation, family composition, and educational attainment, but careful revision reduced the inaccuracies. Results were only partially published, but a supplementary publication related to economic activities became available in 1977.

Publication Plan. Argentina. Dirección Nacional de Estadística y Censos. *IV censo general de la nación, 1947.* Buenos Aires, 1951. Nos. 1-2. And *IV censo general de la nación.* Buenos Aires, 1948-1952. Tomos 1-3. Argentina. Instituto Nacional de Estadística y Censos. *Cuadros inéditos, IV censo general de la nación, año 1947: características económicas de la población.* Buenos Aires, 1977. Language of publication is Spanish.

1960 (September 30)

The fifth general census of population was conducted by the Dirección Nacional de Estadística y Censos. The census was *de facto*, but usual resident population was also recorded. Canvasser was the method used to record information on household schedules. The censuses of agriculture and housing were taken simultaneously with the population census. The territory covered by the census was divided into provinces, subdivided into departments, except for the province of Buenos Aires, which was subdivided into "partidos." "Fracciones," "radios," and "circuitos censales" were further subdivisions. Tabulation was mechanical.

Definitions and Concepts. AGE, RELIGION, URBAN/RURAL, and INFIRMITIES—same as 1947. MARITAL STATUS—categories were: single, married (legally and common law), widowed, separated, and divorced. The date of the last marriage was also recorded. PLACE OF BIRTH—for native born, province and detailed minor subdivisions were recorded. Aliens recorded the country of birth. CITIZENSHIP—if naturalized, year and place of arrival (province, city, or locality) were recorded. PLACE OF RESIDENCE—usual place (provided information on *de jure* population), duration, and previous residence (indicated migration). EDUCATION—literacy (ability to read and write in any language), school enrollment (if not enrolled, the year of last attendance was recorded as well as reasons for leaving school), and educational attainment (highest degree completed) were recorded. Professional and vocational education were distinguished. HOUSEHOLD—one or more persons living in the same housing unit. The concept of "familia" is identical to household, including related or not by blood, servants, and persons living in the same house, sharing social and economic dependency. ECONOMIC ACTIVITY—lower age limit was fourteen years. Period of reference was the time of the census. Economically active population included: persons employed either in gainful occupation or in nongainful occupation (working in the production of goods and services with commercial value in an enterprise owned by a member of the family); persons with a job but temporarily out of work because of infirmity, accident, vacation, and so forth, and unemployed persons looking for a job or not looking for a job because of temporary suspension or because a new job would begin after the census date. The economically inactive included: homemakers, students, inmates of institutions, the retired, pensioners, or income recipients. In addition, if the person fell into both categories, the criterion used was that the retired or pensioners with or without work were considered inactive; homemakers and students who had an occupation were considered active. OCCUPATION—classification based on COTA 1960. Only major groups (twelve) were tabulated. INDUSTRY—classification based on COTA 1960. Only the nine major divisions were tabulated. OCCUPATIONAL STATUS—categories were: employers, self-employed, employees, and unpaid family workers. Note: the tabulation of occupational and industrial subgroups can be consulted at the Dirección Nacional de Estadística y Censos. FERTILITY—for married, widowed, or divorced women: number of children ever born alive.

Special Elements and Features. Facsimile of the schedules, maps, graphs, and comparative tables for 1947 and 1960 (literacy, occupation, age, and sex), a separate volume for Greater Buenos Aires (city of Buenos Aires and suburban areas surrounding it) were all provided. A list of localities with total population by sex was presented in ranked order.

Quality of the Census. For the first time, a complete map of census zones was realized, providing better coverage of the territory. The provinces of Río Negro, Neuquén, Chubut, Santa Cruz, National Territory of Tierra del Fuego, Antártica, and Islands of South Atlantic were enumerated separately from the rest of the country (November 4). Sample tabulation was utilized for faster availability of results. Census tests were taken to check the questionnaires and the organization for the final enumeration. Whipple's Index category was not available.

Publication Plan. Argentina. Dirección Nacional de Estadística y Censos.

Censo Nacional de Población, 1960. Buenos Aires, 1965. Tomos 1-9 in 11 volumes. Language of publication is Spanish.

1970 (September 25)

The sixth general census of population and housing was conducted by the Instituto Nacional de Estadística y Censos on a *de facto* basis, but resident population was also determined. Canvasser was the method used to record information on household schedules. Tabulation was totally computerized. The final results have not appeared as yet and may never appear. The information gathered here was taken from provisional results published in 1972; sampling results were based on a 2 percent sample tabulation of households, published in 1974; and some comments contained in the *Cuadros inéditos*, published in 1977.

Definitions and Concepts. AGE—date of birth results were tabulated in single years and standard five-year age groups. PLACE OF BIRTH—same as 1960. PLACE OF RESIDENCE—usual place, residence in 1965, and for foreign-born persons, the year of arrival in the country. EDUCATION—literacy, school enrollment (attends now, has attended, never attended), and educational attainment (last level attended and last degree completed). In addition, specialization or professional degree was recorded. Questions on education were asked of all persons five years of age and over. FERTILITY—for all women twelve years and over, number of children ever born. The number of children still living and number of children dead were asked, but tables are still not available. ECONOMIC ACTIVITY—economically active included: employed and unemployed looking for a job (new and experienced workers). Inactive population included: retired, pensioners, persons of independent income, students, and homemakers. OCCUPATION—classification based on ISCO, revised 1968. Only major groups were tabulated. INDUSTRY—classification based on ISIC, second revision. Only major divisions were tabulated. OCCUPATIONAL STATUS—categories were the same as 1960. MARITAL STATUS—same as 1960. HOUSEHOLD—person or group of persons, related or not by blood, living in the same house and sharing arrangements to provide food and other essential things for survival. Private and collective households were distinguished. The private household could be of three kinds: nuclear (parents with unmarried children), extended (nuclear plus other relatives), and compound (nuclear or extended plus other nonrelatives).

Special Elements and Features. Population growth for 1950, 1960, and 1970 in relation to other countries; rates of annual growth of population in Latin America for 1970; estimates of population, fertility and mortality rates; migration and annual growth for the years 1943 to 1970; total population by provinces for 1914, 1947, 1960, and 1970; and a map of population density, 1970, for each province are included in publications.

Quality of the Census. Whipple's Index category was not available. Reliability of sampling data was estimated at 95 percent. Final results have not been published as yet.

Publication Plan. Argentina. Instituto Nacional de Estadística y Censos. *Censo nacional de población, familias y viviendas, 1970. Resultados obtenidos por muestra*. Buenos Aires, 1974. 25v. One for the whole country, one each for provinces. Preliminary results were published. Language of publication is Spanish.

1980 (October 22)

The seventh general census of population and housing was conducted by the Instituto Nacional de Estadística y Censos on a *de facto* basis. A publication with provisional results is the only one available so far, thus no information on organization and methods was given. The following tables were provided: total population by jurisdiction (provinces), by sex, and by the number of housing units; total population by school districts (federal capital only), by sex, and by number of housing units; total population by "partidos" or departments in each province, sex, and number of housing units. Results on population were compared to 1970 with a notation of the percentage of growth between 1970 and 1980.

OTHER STATISTICAL PUBLICATIONS: Issued by Instituto Nacional de Estadística y Censos, *Anuario Estadístico, Boletín Estadístico Trimestral, Serie Investigaciones Demográficas*.

National Topic Chart

	1947	1960	1970
De facto	X	X	X
Usual residence		X	X
Place of birth	X	X	X
Duration of residence		X	X
Place of prev. residence		X	X
Urban/rural	X	X	X
Sex	X	X	X
Age	X	X	X
Relation to household head	X	X	X
Marital status	X	X	X
Children born alive		X	X
Children living			X
Citizenship	X	X	X
Literacy	X	X	X
School enrollment		X	X
Ed. attainment		X	X
Ed. qualification		X	X
National/Ethnic origin			
Language			
Religion	X	X	X
Household composition		X	X
Econ. active/inactive	X	X	X
Occupation	X	X	X
Industry	X	X	X
Occupational status	X	X	X
Income			
Housing			X

Bahamas

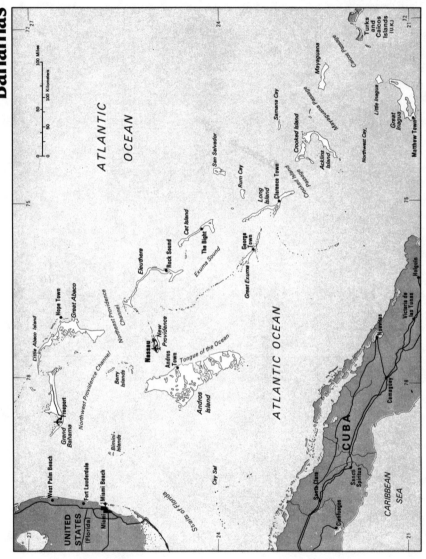

Bahamas

Commonwealth of the Bahamas

CAPITAL: Nassau.
STATISTICAL AGENCY: Department of Statistics, Cabinet Office.
NATIONAL REPOSITORY: Library of the Department of Statistics.
MAIN U.S. REPOSITORY: Population Research Center (Univ. of Texas),
New York Public Library.

The British settlement began in 1647, and it became a colony in 1783. Full independence within the commonwealth was attained in 1973. The Bahamas consist of almost 700 islands only 30 of which are inhabited. Presently there are eighteen administrative districts.

The only extant copies of census reports date from 1891, and these are usually abstracts of the results only. However, censuses were taken in 1838, 1845, 1851, 1861, 1871, 1881, 1891, 1901, 1911, 1921, 1931, 1943 (delayed by World War II rather than cancelled), 1953, 1963, and 1970 (switched in order to participate in the UN World Census Program).

1891

The seventh census, taken by the Office of the Superintendent of Census (Colonial Secretary) was *de facto*, canvasser, and manually tabulated. Tables give results for twenty islands. The scope was sex, age, marriage (only), rank or occupation (prestige ranking), birthplace, infirmities, literacy, vaccinations, and land holdings.

1901

The eighth census, conducted by the Office of the Superintendent of Census (Colonial Secretary), was *de facto*, self-enumerated, and manually tabulated. A household schedule was used. The colony had eighteen administrative districts, that is, islands. The scope was the same as that of 1891.

1911

The ninth census, conducted by the Office of the Supervisor of Census (Colonial Secretary), was *de facto*, self-enumerated, and manually tabulated. Household schedules were used. The tables gave results for the eighteen administrative districts (islands) and chief towns. The scope was place of birth, sex, age, marital status, literacy, nationality, occupation (alphabetical listing), infirmities, vaccinations, and number of inhabited houses.

1921

The tenth census, conducted by the same office as 1911, was *de facto*, self-enumerated, and manually tabulated. Household schedules were used. Tables gave results for twenty-one islands and districts and chief towns, which were considered urban. The scope was birthplace, sex, age, relation to household head (new), marital status, literacy, nationality, occupation (same order, but expanded), infirmities, vaccinations, and the number of inhabited houses.

1931

The eleventh census, conducted by the same office, was *de facto*, self-enumerated, and manually tabulated. Household schedules were used. Results were given for twenty-one islands, districts, and chief towns. The scope was the same as 1921.

1943

The twelfth census, conducted by the Office of the Supervisor of Census (Colonial Secretary), was *de facto* with *de jure* number of inhabitants determined (new), self-enumerated, and manually tabulated. Household schedules were used. The scope was place of birth, sex, age, relation to household head, marital status, citizenship (new), literacy, race (new), religion (new), economic activity (gainfully employed concept), occupation (alphabetical listing), infirmities, vaccinations, and number of inhabited houses. It was recommended that an inquiry be made to revise the census in view of changed conditions.

It was stated that the 1943 census of Bahamas was in no way comparable to the much more extensive censuses that were taken uniformly in the other West Indian colonies in 1946. In the Bahamas census report, much useful information was lost through inadequate tabulation of results.

1953 (December 6)

The thirteenth census, conducted by the same office, was *de facto*, self-enumerated, and manually tabulated. Household schedules were used. The results were given for twenty-two islands, districts and chief towns, and towns and settlements. The population enumerated also included persons on board ship in or enroute to Nassau.

Definitions and Concepts. PLACE OF BIRTH—district for natives and island or territory for foreigners. AGE—completed years last birthday. Tables have single years from one to sixteen, and age groups (under one, one to five, five to ten, and so forth to eighty-five and over). MARITAL STATUS—married, never married, widowed. EDUCATION—literacy. RACE—European (white), African (black), mixed, Mongolian (Asiatic), and other. RELIGION—denominations. ECONOMIC ACTIVITY—gainfully employed concept. OCCUPATIONS—listed according to economic sector. INFIRMITIES—blind, deaf, deaf and dumb, incapacitated. VACCINATIONS—number of people receiving them. HOUSING— type, ownership, number of rooms, and sanitary and water facilities available.

Special Elements and Features. Housing questions expanded from just the number of inhabited, uninhabited, and under construction houses.

Quality of the Census. Long history of census taking but no permanent office. No Whipple's Index listing was given.

Publication Plan. Bahamas. Supervisor of the Census. *Report on the Census of the Bahama Islands, Taken on the 6th December, 1953.* Nassau, New Providence, the Nassau Guardian, 1954. 1 volume. Language of the publication is English.

1963 (November 15)

There was a radical departure in the conduct of this census from the traditional practice in the Bahamas. The Census Act of 1910 had to be discarded in order to make the necessary changes. "One of the results of using the householder method in the past had been the need for a grossly over-simplified census schedule capable of being readily understood and completed by all." As a result there had been no attempt in previous censuses to gather data about fertility, immigration, occupation as separate from industry, employment status, or educational attainment. Also very little information had been taken with regard to dwelling units.

The fourteenth census, conducted by the Department of the Registrar General, was *de jure* (new), with a determination of the *de facto* population, was canvassed (see above), and mechanical tabulation was performed in England. The colony had twenty-one islands divided into enumeration districts and settlements. Household schedules remained with appropriate changes, and special forms were prepared for the transient population. New groups included were tourists, Haitian "transients" with "floating" addresses, and short-term institutional inmates. The census was taken in two stages.

Definitions and Concepts. HOUSEHOLD—a group of persons living together in one dwelling, including boarders and live-in servants. BIRTHPLACE—name of island for natives, name of country for nonnatives. AGE—completed years last birthday, single years zero to twenty-one, then standard five-year groups. MARITAL STATUS—never married, married, legally separated, divorced, widowed. DURATION OF MARRIAGE—of present union. FERTILITY—asked of all women fourteen years and over: number of children ever born live, number of births last year, age at first birth. EDUCATION—all persons age ten and over: educational attainment. For all persons aged five to nineteen years: school enrollment. RELIGION—specific denominations. MIGRATION—immigrant population and internal migrants. ECONOMIC ACTIVITY—all persons fourteen years and over, reference period last twelve months. The gainfully employed concept was used to determine the classifiable labor force (not to be confused with labor force). Active were all employed and unemployed. Inactive were students, homemakers, the retired, those not seeking work, first-time job seekers, institutional inmates, and those unable to work due to illness or incapacity. LABOR FORCE—reference week was not stated but may have been that preceding the census date. The category included all the economically active plus the first-time job seekers. OCCUPATION—listed in thirteen major groups, not the standard classification. INDUSTRY—listed in thirteen major groups, similar to ISIC. OCCUPATIONAL STATUS—government employee, private employee, unpaid family worker, employer, own-account worker, unable to or did not work.

Special Elements and Features. This was a first attempt at international comparability. For the first time results were available for enumeration districts. Fertility, educational attainment, industry, and occupational status were new topics in this census. No race information was gathered. Tables of *de facto* population by settlements and of British residents by enumeration districts are included.

Quality of the Census. A break from tradition was made to coincide with changes in society and to attain international comparability. Increased preparation, especially mapping, helped its accuracy and coverage. No Whipple's Index ranking was given.

Publication Plan. Bahamas. Registrar General's Department. *Report on the Census of the Bahama Islands taken 15th November, 1963.* Nassau, 1965. 1 volume. Language of publication is English.

1970 (April 7)

The fifteenth census, conducted by the Department of Statistics, was *de jure* with a *de facto* total, canvassed, and computer tabulated. Household schedule for control was used along with individual schedules. Population included all Bahamian residents (for at least six months per year), students studying abroad, and ship and aircraft crews abroad. The legal population excluded foreign consular personnel and U.S. military personnel on bases. Results were given for eighteen islands or island groups.

Definitions and Concepts. HOUSEHOLD—private: one or a group of persons sharing meals and living arrangements whether in a dwelling, small hotel, or boarding house. Nonprivate: persons in large hotels and institutions (schools, hospitals, prisons). DWELLING—a unit with its own bathroom, toilet, and kitchen facilities. Bahamian residents who were passengers on board ship in the harbor were censused on board with the ship labeled as a household. AGE—date of birth, coded as completed years as of last birthday, tables of single years for the whole country and each island. MARITAL STATUS—single, married (legally), married (common law), widowed, separated (legally), divorced. EDUCATION—educational attainment (completed years of schooling). MIGRATION—recent immigration from abroad (last twenty years); internal migration within last ten years (place of previous residence). RELIGION—specific denominations, as stated by respondent. NATIONALITY—nationality status defined as legal citizenship. ECONOMIC ACTIVITY—asked of all persons fourteen years and over: main employment situation during the previous six months. Active: all but students, homemakers, unemployed for health or other reasons, the retired, and persons of independent means. OCCUPATION—major and minor groups (two-digits) equal to ISCO, the three-digit level varies in small degree. INDUSTRY—classified to three-digits according to ISIC. OCCUPATIONAL STATUS—private employee, government employee, employer, own-account worker, unpaid family worker. INCOME—both household and individual incomes. HOUSEHOLD COMPOSITION—by size only.

Special Elements and Features. Income data were new. The department participated in the UN World Census Program, 1970. It was the first time that the entire operation from organization through publication was done within the country. Tables by enumeration districts are available. Fertility was not taken.

Quality of the Census. Standard classifications were used in economic activity. However, editing might be questioned as one table had a potentially economic active person age fourteen with no schooling in a professional, technical, and related occupation. Whipple's Index rating was category III—approximate data. Ages were not smoothed.

Publication Plan. Bahamas. Department of Statistics, Cabinet Office. *Commonwealth of the Bahama Islands, Report of the 1970 Census of Population.* Nassau, n.d. 1 volume. Census monographs Nos. 1 and 2. Computer tapes are available. Language of publication is English.

OTHER STATISTICAL PUBLICATIONS: Issued by Department of Statistics, *Quarterly Statistical Summary, Statistical Abstract* (annually).

National Topic Chart

	1953	1963	1970
De facto	X		
Usual residence		X	X
Place of birth	X	X	X
Duration of residence		X	X
Place of prev. residence			X
Urban/rural	X		
Sex	X	X	X
Age	X	X	X
Relation to household head		X	X
Marital status	X	X	X
Children born alive		X	
Children living			
Citizenship			X
Literacy	X	X	
School enrollment		X	
Ed. attainment		X	X
Ed. qualification			
National/Ethnic origin	X		
Language			
Religion	X	X	X
Household compostion			X
Econ. active/inactive	X	X	X
Occupation	X	X	X
Industry		X	X
Occupational status		X	X
Income			X
Housing	X	X	X

Barbados

Barbados

CAPITAL: Bridgetown.
STATISTICAL AGENCY: Barbados Statistical Service.
NATIONAL REPOSITORY: The Department of Archives, St. Michael.
MAIN U.S. REPOSITORY: New York Public Library.

From the arrival of the first British settlers in 1627 until independence in 1966, Barbados was under uninterrupted British control. There were numerous "censuses" in Barbados' history. Although some of the early estimates are known to have been based on individual enumerations, the first modern census of population was that of June 3, 1844. The results of the censuses from 1844 through 1921 were published in abstracts with no explanation of definitions and concepts or organization of the census. There was no uniform treatment of shipping population in the early censuses; in some this group was excluded, in others it was an integral part of the tabulated population.

1844

There was concern on the part of the British government and the planter class over the strength of plantation labor force after slavery was abolished in 1834. This prompted the first all British Caribbean set of censuses. The census was *de facto* and taken as of June 3. Its scope was, at least, the parish population, sex, and age (over and under eighteen). Data from this census have only been found in comparative tables in later censuses.

1851

Taken by the Colonial Secretary's Office, the census was *de facto*, and its scope was age, sex, complexion (white, black, colored), and birthplace. Results were in abstract form only, and a few figures can be found in the *West Indies Census 1946*, Part C, Barbados. The compiler of the census of 1871 stated that it was a defective enumeration.

1861

The census was taken by the Colonial Secretary's Office as part of the census of the British Empire. Some data from this census may be found in the *General*

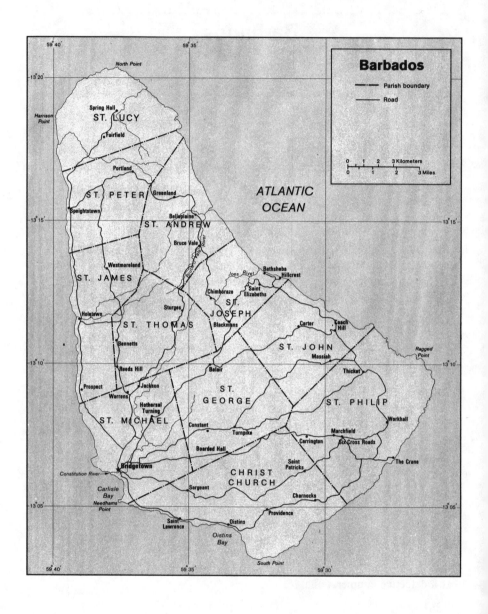

Report of the Census of England and Wales, 1861, volume 3. The scope was sex, age, complexion, legal marital status, occupations, birthplace, infirmities, the instruction and employment of children, and the number of inhabited houses.

1871

The report of this census written by the governor was considered a landmark not only for Barbados but for the entire British Caribbean. It was a revealing demographic analysis of the island. The scope was age (more data for children under six), sex, number of persons in the family, birthplace, complexion, marital status, occupations, religion (new), the instruction and employment of children, number and size of sugar estates, and housing.

1881

Most of the results from this census are found in comparative tables in the *West Indies Census 1946*, Part C, Barbados. The scope was age, sex, complexion, marital status, birthplace, occupations, religion, infirmities, instruction and employment of children, military, and habitation. The inclusion of the shipping population in the total indicated that this was a *de facto* enumeration.

1891

Taken by the Colonial Secretary's Office, it was *de facto*, self-enumerated on household schedules, and manually tabulated. The island was divided into eleven parishes plus the city of Bridgetown. The scope was sex, age, race, marital status, religion, infirmities, school attendance, birthplace, occupations, and housing.
No census was taken in 1901.

1911

Taken by the Colonial Secretary's Office, which was charged with taking the census, it was *de facto*, self-enumerated on household schedules, and manually tabulated. The colony was divided into eleven parishes plus the city of Bridgetown. The scope was sex, age, race, marital status, religion, infirmities, school attendance, birthplace, occupations, and housing. Included was a separate table of occupations of visitors to the island.

1921

Taken by the Colonial Secretary's Office, it was *de facto*, self-enumerated on household schedules, and manually tabulated. The island's eleven parishes and Bridgetown were divided into fourteen census divisions, which were further divided into 149 districts. The results, however, are for the parishes and city only. The scope was birthplace, urban/rural, sex, age, marital status, school attendance, race, religion, occupation, infirmities, and housing. Orphanhood was added, but the results were considered unreliable. There were separate tables for visitors and for the shipping population.
There were twenty-five years between censuses. No census was taken in 1931

due to financial stringency, and the census of 1941 was abandoned due to World War II.

1946 (April 9)

Conducted through the Colonial Secretary's Office, this was the first census that Barbados conducted in close collaboration with the other British colonies in the Caribbean area. The island was subdivided into enumeration districts within administrative boundaries, but the results were given for its eleven parishes and the city of Bridgetown.

Definitions and Concepts. [See British West Indies 1946 for full entry; the following are the differences only.] URBAN—specified areas: Bridgetown and its suburbs (including shipping), most of St. Michael parish, and Speightstown. AGE—tables for single years and standard five-year age groups. FERTILITY— for women of completed fertility (age forty-five and over): legitimacy of children, birth order, and children living. RACE—white, black, East Indian, Syrian, Chinese, other Asiatic, mixed or colored (African with white or with Asiatic).

Special Elements and Features. An appendix has the population of localities of fifty or more inhabitants. For the first time data were taken for literacy, duration of unemployment, and duration of union.

Quality of the Census. Whipple's Index category was II—fairly accurate data.

Publication Plan. Part C of the West Indian census is devoted to Barbados.

1960 (April 7)

Taken by the census office of the territory. [See British West Indies 1960, East Caribbean section, for full entry; the following are differences only.] The colony's eleven parishes and Bridgetown were divided into enumeration districts. Results are given down to that level.

Definitions and Concepts. URBAN—no figures given.

Quality of the Census. No Whipple's Index rating was given.

Publication Plan. Trinidad and Tobago. Central Statistical Office. *East Caribbean Population Census of 1960.* Volume 1, part A, Administrative report; part C, Boundaries of enumeration districts (Barbados): Volume 2, Summary tables 1-19, Barbados; Volume 3 (Barbados), Cross-classifications, part A in one volume, parts B, D, F, and G in one volume, and part E in one volume. Language of publication is English.

1970 (April 7)

Barbados published on its own five bulletins with preliminary results. [See British West Indies 1970 for final results entry.] There are no noticeable differences between the scope of the following set and that of the British West Indies 1970 set. Barbados has eleven parishes and the city of Bridgetown. Results are published for the parishes. The census office is not permanent. Whipple's Index category II—fairly accurate data.

Publication Plan. Volumes 3; 4.4; 4.16; 5; 6.2; 7; 8 abc; 9.2; 10.1; and 10.4 of the British West Indies 1970 set contain the results for Barbados. The following is the citation for the preliminary publications.

Barbados. Statistical Service. *Commonwealth Caribbean Population Census, 1970. Barbados. Preliminary bulletins.* Garrison, St. Michael, 1972-1974. Volume 1. Housing; 2. Working population, part I; 3. Working population, part II; 4. Population; 5. Education. Computer tapes are at the Census Research Programme, University of the West Indies. Language of publication is English.

1980

The preliminary count by parish and sex has been released. Provisional results are said to be available on request.

OTHER STATISTICAL PUBLICATIONS: Issued by Barbados Statistical Service, *Monthly Digest of Statistics.* Issued by Registration Office, *Report on Vital Statistics and Registrations for the Year . . .*, (annually).

National Topic Chart

	1946	1960	1970
De facto	X	X	X
Usual residence		X	X
Place of birth	X	X	X
Duration of residence	X	X	X
Place of prev. residence		X	X
Urban/rural	X	X	X
Sex	X	X	X
Age	X	X	X
Relation to household head		X	X
Marital status	X	X	X
Children born alive			
Children living	X	X	X
Citizenship	X		
Literacy	X	X	
School enrollment	X	X	X
Ed. attainment		X	X
Ed. qualification			
National/Ethnic origin	X	X	X
Language			
Religion	X	X	X
Household composition	X	X	
Econ. active/inactive	X	X	X
Occupation	X	X	X
Industry	X	X	X
Occupational status	X	X	X
Income	X	X	X
Housing	X	X	X

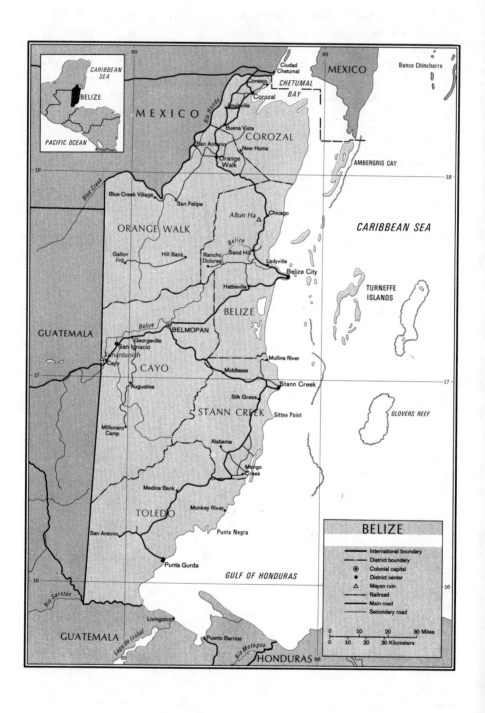

Map of Belize showing districts, cities, roads, and geographic features.

BELIZE

Legend:
- International boundary
- District boundary
- ⊛ Colonial capital
- ● District center
- △ Mayan ruin
- Railroad
- Main road
- Secondary road

Scale: 0 10 20 30 Miles / 0 10 20 30 Kilometers

Belize

Belize

CAPITAL: Belmopan (moved from Belize City in 1970).
STATISTICAL AGENCY: Central Planning Unit, Ministry of Finance and
Economic Development.
NATIONAL REPOSITORY: n.a.
MAIN U.S. REPOSITORY: Population Research Center (Univ. of Texas).

The British dependency, formerly known as British Honduras, was first settled in 1638. The settlement was completely self-governing until 1786 when it received its first British superintendent; however, it was not an official British colony until 1862. Granted internal self-government in 1964, it changed its name to Belize in 1973. Belize became an independent country in 1981.

The first census of record of the Belize settlement was taken in 1816. The scope was sex, age (adult/child), race, free or slave. A census of the slave population only was taken in December 1820. In 1823 a census appears to have been taken but did not prove satisfactory. Its scope was sex, age (adult/child), free or slave. The censuses of 1826, 1829, 1832, and 1835, still only of the British settlement in Belize, repeated the same scope. There is no trace of a further census until 1861.

1861

The first duly organized census was conducted by the Census Superintendent's Office. It was cited as the first census taken with any precision in spite of having an undercount of 4,000 to 5,000. "The inhabitants embrace a peculiarly great variety of nationalities; 37 countries and 42 races (including mixtures, of course) are represented in this settlement." Its scope was sex, age, race, marital status, occupations, birthplace, religion, and infirmities.

The records of the censuses of 1871 and 1881 were destroyed by fire in 1918. However, partial scope was determinable through comparative tables in later censuses.

1891

Taken by the Census Commissioner's Office, it was *de facto* and self-enumerated on household schedules. However, due to lack of literacy much was taken by the canvasser. It was manually tabulated. Schedules were printed in English, but some were available in Spanish. The colony was divided into five districts. The scope was place of birth, sex, age, relation to household head, marital status, citizenship, literacy, occupation, economic dependency, infirmities, inhabited houses, and land ownership. The Acting Colonial Secretary and Registrar, who also served as census commissioner, complained that the census did not contain some items needed but deferred to the desire for colonial uniformity. He also felt that the woodcutters and their families temporarily absent in the Yucatan and Honduras should have been included, that the returns as to marital status should not be trusted as the institution of marriage was in a rudimentary stage, and finally that the column on infirmities was insufficient. The results were published in an abstract form.

1901

Taken by the Registrar General who served as census commissioner, it was *de facto*, self-enumerated and canvassed, and manually tabulated. Household schedules were in English with some available in Spanish. The colony was divided into six districts, towns, and settlements. The scope was place of birth, urban/rural, sex, age, relation to household head, marital status, citizenship, literacy, occupation, economic dependency, infirmities, inhabited houses, and land ownership. The report includes an historical sketch of the census in British Honduras and abstract table comparing 1881 and 1901 by district.

1911

Taken by the Registrar General (census commissioner), it was *de facto*, self-enumerated and canvassed, and manually tabulated. Household schedules were in English with some in Spanish. The colony was divided into six administrative districts, towns, and enumeration districts. Scope included that of the 1901 census plus fertility (married couples only), language, religion, employment status, and description of housing.

1921

Taken by the Registrar General (census commissioner), it was *de facto*, self-enumerated and canvassed, and manually tabulated. Household schedules were in English; the Spanish language ones did not arrive in time to be used. It used the same geographic divisions as 1911. The scope was that of 1901 and 1911 plus place of work, duration of marriage, school attendance, nationality, and some industry. It also featured parental conditions of children (orphanhood), remarriages after widowhood and divorce, and a summary of East Indians. Unlike the previous censuses and some following ones, the results of which were abstracts, the 1921 report had quite detailed tables.

1931

Taken by the Registrar General (census commissioner), it was *de facto*, self-enumerated and canvassed, and manually tabulated. Household schedules were in English and some in Spanish. The scope included all that was included in the 1921 census. The report was limited in scope because of the financial restrictions, resulting from a hurricane. Unpublished data are available "at cost."

1946 (April 9)

Conducted by the census office, which was formed from the General Registry Office, this was the first census closely coordinated with the West Indies program. Household and institution schedules were printed in English only. The colony was again divided into five administrative districts (Northern District was formerly Corozal and Orange Walk Districts); these in turn were subdivided into census districts and subdistricts. As in all previous censuses, persons on board ship in the harbor were included.

Definitions and Concepts. [See British West Indies 1946 for the full entry; the following are the differences only.] AGE—tables in single years and in standard five-year age groups. FERTILITY—also asked were legitimacy and birth order. RACE—tables also included data for Amerindians (Mayans), Carib (Indian and African mix), and mixed included Spanish and Indian mix. LANGUAGE—the one "generally spoken" (Mayan, English, Spanish, Carib, others). HOUSEHOLD COMPOSITION—by size only, from one person to ten plus. OCCUPATIONAL STATUS—employer, own-account worker, unpaid helper, wage and salary worker. INFIRMITIES—totally blind, deaf, deaf and dumb, and mentally defective. AGRICULTURE—instead of the regular census of agriculture, only number of operators of land holdings was asked.

Special Elements and Features. In addition to language and infirmities, which were not included in some of the other 1946 sets, unemployment by cause was also asked. It was the first time fertility was canvassed in Belize.

Quality of the Census. Whipple's Index category was III—approximate age data. Census office is not permanent.

Publication Plan. Part E of the *West Indian Census 1946* is devoted to the census of British Honduras. Language of the publication is English.

1960 (April 7)

Taken by the British Honduras Census Office (General Registry Office). [See British West Indies 1960, West Indies section, for full entry; the following are the differences.] The colony returned to six administrative divisions (Northern District was split again into Corozal and Orange Walk), then divided into census districts and enumeration districts. Included were the shipping population, but foreign, non-West Indian armed forces were excluded.

Definitions and Concepts. RACE—no "mixed" category appears. LANGUAGE—primary language spoken (same as 1946) plus any other in descending order of ability.

Special Elements and Features. The topic infirmities was dropped. For the first time results for enumeration districts were published (see volume 1 under Publication Plan).

Quality of the Census. Whipple's Index rating was not given.

Publication Plan. Jamaica. Department of Statistics. *West Indies Population Census. Census of British Honduras, 7th April 1960.* Volumes 1-2. Language of publication is English.

1970 (April 7)

Conducted by the Central Planning Unit, Belize did not issue any separate reports. [See British West Indies 1970 for full entry]. Six administrative districts plus Belize City and the new capital (Belmopan) were divided into census districts and subdistricts (enumeration districts). Some institutional population and tourists were excluded from tabulation. Volumes 3; 4.5; 4.16; 5; 6.2; 7; 8 abc; 9.2; 10.1; and 10.4 of the British West Indies 1970 set contain the results for Belize. Whipple's Index classified age data into category III—approximate data. Language of publication is English.

OTHER STATISTICAL PUBLICATIONS: Issued by Central Planning Unit, *Abstract of Statistics* (annually). Issued by General Registry, *Report of the Registrar General's Department* (irregularly).

National Topic Chart

	1946	1960	1970
De facto	X	X	X
Usual residence		X	X
Place of birth	X	X	X
Duration of residence		X	X
Place of prev. residence			
Urban/rural	X	X	
Sex	X	X	X
Age	X	X	X
Relation to household head	X	X	X
Marital status	X	X	X
Children born alive	X	X	X
Children living	X		
Citizenship			
Literacy	X		
School enrollment	X	X	X
Ed. attainment		X	X
Ed. qualification			
National/Ethnic origin	X	X	X
Language	X	X	
Religion	X	X	X
Household composition	X	X	
Econ. active/inactive	X	X	X
Occupation	X	X	X
Industry	X	X	X
Occupational status	X	X	
Income			X
Housing	X	X	X

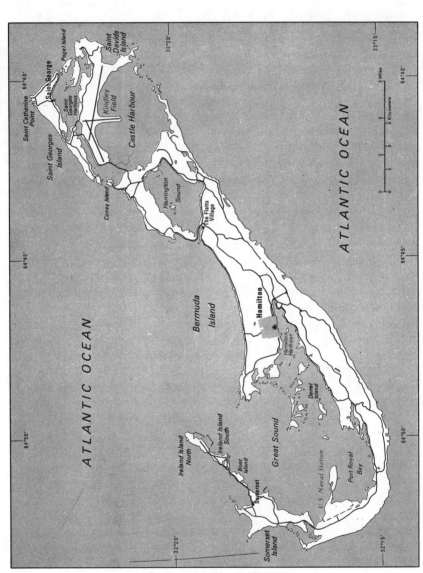

Bermuda

Bermuda

British Colony of Bermuda

CAPITAL: Hamilton.
STATISTICAL AGENCY: Statistical Office, Finance Department.
NATIONAL REPOSITORY: Bermuda Library; Bermuda Archives, Hamilton.
MAIN U.S. REPOSITORY: Population Research Center (Univ. of Texas).

Not actually located in the Caribbean area, Bermuda is one of the British West Indies associated states and colonies. First settled in the early seventeenth century as the Somers Islands, it became a British colony in 1684. Like the other British West Indian possessions it had numerous "censuses" during its early years. The more modern group began in 1841 and continued decennially until 1931; the pattern was broken by a census taken in 1939. The censuses began again in 1950 and have continued decennially through 1970. Most census results for the early years were published in abstracts only, separately or in other publications. It was stated that quite apart from the inadequate presentation of the results, the returns differed so much from census to census as to arouse serious doubts as to their accuracy.

No data have been found from the 1841 or 1851 censuses.

1861

The *General Report* (Vol. III) from the 1861 Census of England and Wales contains a table giving sex and race for Bermuda. Other data were found in comparative tables in later Bermudian census reports. The scope was age, sex, birthplace, civil status (free/slave), military status, race, and religion.

1871

A *de facto* census with the scope of sex, age, birthplace, literacy (new), race, religion, housing, and agriculture was taken.

1881

Same as 1871 with the addition of occupation to the scope.

1891

Also a *de facto* census, which this time included temporarily absent residents. The scope was sex, age, race, marital status, literacy, school attendance, religion, occupation, birthplace, citizenship, infirmities, number of inhabited houses, institutional population, and agriculture. There were also summary results from the military and naval installation schedules.

1901

The *de facto* results of this census were given for the colony's nine parishes and two cities. The scope was usual residence, sex, age, race, marital status, birthplace, literacy, religion, occupation, infirmities, agriculture (land under tillage and products), houses, and military manpower.

1911

Taken by the Census Commissioner's Office (Colonial Secretariat), it was *de facto*, canvassed, and manually tabulated. The colony had nine parishes and two cities. It also included temporarily absent residents, foreign visitors not included in the general population residing in private houses, and residents of hotels and boarding houses not in the general population. The scope was sex, age, race, marital status, usual residence, birthplace, literacy, school attendance or private instruction, religion, occupation, infirmities, agriculture, houses, and a summary of separate naval and military schedules.

1921

It was *de facto*, self-enumerated, and manually tabulated. The scope was sex, age, race, occupation, marital status, relation to head of family (that is, household), religion, birthplace, nationality, citizenship, literacy, infirmities, fertility (new), agriculture, vehicles and boats, and houses and buildings.

1931

Conducted the same as 1921. The scope was same as 1921 except fertility was not taken. "Tables for 1921 and 1931, while claiming to show for all persons 'where born' did so only for those born in the British Empire and showed for all others the nationality and not the birthplace."

1939

A special census, self-enumerated and *de facto* but with *de jure* tables. The scope was sex, age, race, birthplace (see 1931), marital status, citizenship, employment, occupation, religion, literacy in English, economic activity, and infirmities.

It excluded tourists and their servants and personnel on board British ships in port. Included in total but not in other tables were British forces on base and in dockyard establishments, temporary absentees, bona fide guests and nonresident workers.

A medical section of the survey determined legitimacy, fertile women (ages fifteen to forty-six), mental and physical disabilities, and persons living in institutions (medical, penal, and charitable). A recruiting section determined number of males ages eighteen to thirty-six prepared to enlist, those in military units or fire brigades, those on reserve, those with previous experience in service or the merchant marine, and females under age fifty-five with nursing experience. Portuguese and other white were tabulated separately (new).

1950 (October 9)

Taken by the Census Committee, it was *de facto* and *de jure*, self-enumerated, and mechanically tabulated. Two schedules, one for resident households and one for visitors and transients, were used. The colony had nine parishes and two cities (Hamilton and St. George), each of which constituted a census district. These were divided into enumeration districts. Published tables, however, are only for the eleven districts. The civilian population was separated from the visitors and transients.

Definitions and Concepts. HOUSEHOLD—one or a group of persons sharing living quarters and meals, including live-in servants and boarders. DWELLING—the housing unit of a household. The number of dwellings equals the number of households. USUAL RESIDENCE—name of parish. BIRTHPLACE—parish for natives, country (nationality) for nonnatives. DURATION OF RESIDENCE—asked of foreign born only. AGE—completed years as of last birthday. Tables in single years and standard five-year age groups. MARITAL STATUS—single, married (spouse present or absent or in army), widowed, divorced, or cohabiting. FERTILITY—asked of all females age fourteen and over: number of children born live and number of children surviving. LITERACY—at least the ability to read in any language, according to respondent. RACE—Portuguese, other white, colored, others. (Prior to 1939, Portuguese and other whites were tabulated together.) RELIGION—specified denomination. ECONOMIC ACTIVITY—gainfully employed concept. Active were employed, unemployed, apprentices and learners, those seeking first job, and unpaid family workers. Inactive were the retired, homemakers, those of independent and private means, dependents (over school age but under twenty, those over twenty, students, those under school age). OCCUPATION—long list of professions with no classified order. OCCUPATIONAL STATUS—employer, own-account worker, salaried, and wage-earner. INFIRMITIES—totally blind, totally deaf, deaf and dumb, mentally defective.

Special Elements and Features. For the first time since 1921 fertility of any kind was asked; children surviving was new. Occupation was reinstated after being skipped in 1939. For the first time occupational status, unemployment, illegitimacy, and ages of married couples were asked.

Quality of the Census. Long census history but no permanent census office. "One of the main difficulties experienced on this occasion [taking the 1950 census] was the almost complete lack of information with regard to the procedure followed when a census has been taken in previous years," so by comparison to previous censuses, this is a better one. It also has extensive detailed tables. There is an indication of unreliability of data about common-law marriages and illegitimacy in the report.

Publication Plan. Bermuda. Census Committee. *Census of Bermuda, 9th October, 1950. Report of Census and Statistical Tables Compiled in Accordance with the Census Act 1950.* 1 volume. Unpublished data is available for enumeration districts. Language of publication is English.

1960 (October 23)

Taken by Census Office (Medical and Health Department), it was *de facto* with some *de jure* tables, self-enumerated, and computer tabulated in London. Two household schedules were used (same as 1950). Total population included Bermuda population (residents), armed forces and dependents (both off and on base), and overseas visitors and transients. Tables give results by parish (nine), Hamilton City, and St. George's Town. Two extra districts were added for the armed forces (K.A.F.B. and N.O.B. equal "on and off base," respectively).

Definitions and Concepts. HOUSEHOLD, DWELLINGS, RELIGION—same as 1950. AGE—month and year of birth, coded in completed years. Tables in single years and standard five-year age groups. RACE—returned to terms used in 1931 and previous censuses: colored, white, others. BIRTHPLACE—Bermudan status for natives and foreigners ("by birth, acquired status, no status"). Country or island of birth and length of residence for foreign born. MARITAL STATUS—asked of all persons sixteen and over; same as 1950 except no common-law marriage. EDUCATION—literacy (same as 1950) and educational attainment for all age thirteen and over: formal education completed by age when left school. LANGUAGE (new)—principal language other than English for those over and under thirteen. FERTILITY—motherhood (all females age thirteen and over): mother or nonmother. For mothers: number of children ever born alive and number surviving, and number of children under thirteen years of age (new). For married men (new): duration of existing marriage and number of children ever born. ECONOMIC ACTIVITY—gainfully employed concept. Active and inactive determined through occupation table. OCCUPATION—gainfully employed occupations classified in major and minor groups that reflect industry. Table of subsidiary occupations. Separate table of occupations of those unemployed at the time of the census. INDUSTRY—minimal list indicating employer's business or service. OCCUPATIONAL STATUS—self-employed, employed, unemployed, no employment, not stated. INFIRMITIES—same as 1950 plus blind and deaf and physically handicapped. HOUSEHOLD COMPOSITION—by size and race (in dwelling tables). HOUSING—type, tenure, rent, number of rooms, water and waste facilities, and household equipment.

Special Elements and Features. New topics—language other than English, educational attainment, "sort of" industry, male fertility.

Quality of the Census. There seems no pattern to the census; economic activity especially seems to be a mixture of different concepts.

Publication Plan. Bermuda. Census Committee. *Census of Bermuda, 23rd October, 1960. Report of Census and Statistical Tables Compiled in Accordance with Census Act 1950.* Hamilton, Bermuda Government, 1961. 1 volume. Language of publication is English.

1970 (October 25)

This is the first time that Bermuda was included in the Caribbean West Indies census program. As a participant, it received a prepared questionnaire, technical advice for conducting the census, access to training materials, and programming and tabulating facilities. Taken by the census office (Government Statistical Office), it was a slightly modified *de facto* (including residents on short-term vacations outside Bermuda), canvassed, and tabulation by computer using mark-sensed questionnaires. The island was divided into regions, supervisory units, and enumeration districts. (Each hotels and the naval bases were designated as ED's). Population in institutions, visitors, armed forces on base, and persons on shipping answered only the first ten questions on the individual schedule. There was a separate questionnaire for hotels and guest houses, which included name, hotel, sex, age, marital status, place of usual residence, and length of stay (nights). The noninstitutional civil population was the basis of most of the tables (see Table 2). Information about this census has come from the Bermuda publication, not the British West Indies 1970 set. (See that entry.)

Definitions and Concepts. BIRTHPLACE—country of foreign born; country of mother's usual residence for children; parish for native born. This should not be confused with Bermuda status, which was legal status of citizenship. "Local

Table 2
Segments of the Population of Bermuda that Constitute the Four Categories Used, 1970

	Total population	Resident	Civil	Civil non-institutional
Bermudians	X	X	X	X
Imported workers	X	X	X	X
Institutional population	X	X	X	
Foreign armed forces, off base	X			
Bermudians on short vacations	X	X	X	X
Visitors	X			
Foreign armed forces, on base	X			
Persons on shipping	X			

movers and Non-movers" were determined by whether parish of residence was the same or different from that of birth. HOUSEHOLD—a person or group living together and sharing at least one daily meal, plus boarders, live-in servants and their family, and visitors spending the census night. Subtenants and lodgers (no meals) constituted a separate household as did someone who slept most nights away from family for the purpose of work. DWELLING—a room or group of rooms intended for living purposes that had separate access. Private, that in which a private household resided. Nonprivate, group dwellings: living quarters for educational, religious, military, and work reasons, including hotels and boarding houses with six or more guests. Institutional, living quarters for mental and physical health and disciplinary reasons. AGE—completed years last birthday, single years and under two, two to four, then standard five-year age groups. RACE AND ETHNIC ORIGIN—Negro/black, East Indian, Chinese, Amerindian, Portuguese, Syrian/Lebanese, white, mixed, other races, not stated. However, tables cite only Negro/black, white, other, and not stated. Children with one black parent were coded mixed; children of nonblack mixed unions were coded as others. MARITAL STATUS—all persons age fourteen and over: never married, married, widowed, divorced, and legally separated. See relation to household head for "common-law partner" and union status (females). RELIGION—affiliation with a specific denomination, voluntary response. USUAL RESIDENCE—parish for natives, imported workers, and foreigners who are seasonal residents. MIGRATION—internal: usual residence, duration of residence, birthplace (parish), number of parishes ever lived in. Immigration: country of birth and period of entry. EDUCATION—educational attainment of all persons age fifteen and over: highest public examination passed. For all ages, highest level attained. School enrollment, by type of nonvocational educational institution. Vocational education, occupation, method, and period of training. FERTILITY—for all females age sixteen and over (other countries in West Indies used different minimum ages): number of children born live and stillborn in the last twelve months; number of children ever born live; age at first birth; union status at present or at age forty-five; duration of union in completed years. ECONOMIC ACTIVITY—asked of all persons age fourteen and over, not attending school full-time (different minimum age): main activity, both active and inactive, and months worked. Working population, plus first-time job seekers and the unemployed were considered active. Homemakers, students, the retired or disabled, others, and not stated were considered inactive. Labor force—economic situation during past week and total number of hours worked. OCCUPATION— main occupation, including former job of the unemployed. Classified to the three-digit level of the 1968 ISCO. Subsidiary occupation asked. INDUSTRY— classified to the three-digit level of the 1958 ISIC. OCCUPATIONAL STATUS— government employee, nongovernment employee, own-account worker with or without paid help, unpaid family worker, unpaid learner/apprentice. HOUSE-HOLD COMPOSITION—by size and relationship. HOUSING—by tenure, type of building, number of rooms, outer wall material, water supply, toilet facilities, year built, and rent paid.

Special Elements and Features. Use of different minimum age for fertility and economic activity than other West Indies countries. For the first time migration and educational attainment for all persons were asked. Bermuda status, subsidiary occupations, rent, and housing categories were also different from the rest of the countries in the Commonwealth Caribbean census. Income did not appear on the copy of the schedule included in the Bermudan census publication. The miscellaneous section of the Bermuda publication presented extra fertility related tables.

Quality of the Census. A more coordinated pattern for the census than that of 1960. The Bermuda publication gives results, definitions and concepts, organization, and so forth, whereas the British West Indies 1970 administrative report has not been issued as yet. "Professional undermanning at the University Computation Center and at the Bermuda Census Office caused delay in publication." Income not on schedule used in Bermuda but income figures appear in British West Indies 1970 publications.

Publication Plan. Bermuda. Census Office. *Report of the Population Census 1970*. Hamilton, 1973. 1 volume. Also, West Indies University. Census Research Programme. *1970 Population Census of the Commonwealth Caribbean*. Kingston, Herald Ltd., 1973-. Volumes 1-10. Unpublished data are available. Language of publication is English.

1980 (May 12)

Census Office is now permanent. Unpublished data are available.

OTHER STATISTICAL PUBLICATIONS: Issued by Office of the Registrar General, *Report of the Registrar General for the Year*...(annually). Issued by the statistician's office, *Digest of Statistics* (annually).

National Topic Chart

	1950	1960	1970
De facto	X	X	X
Usual residence	X	X	X
Place of birth	X	X	X
Duration of residence	X	X	X
Place of prev. residence			X
Urban/rural			
Sex	X	X	X
Age	X	X	X
Relation to household head			X
Marital status	X	X	X
Children born alive	X	X	X
Children living	X	X	X
Citizenship	X	X	X
Literacy	X	X	
School enrollment			X
Ed. attainment		X	X
Ed. qualification			
National/Ethnic origin	X	X	X
Language		X	
Religion	X	X	X
Household composition			
Econ. active/inactive	X	X	X
Occupation	X	X	X
Industry		X	X
Occupational status	X	X	X
Income			
Housing	X	X	X

Bolivia

Republic of Bolivia

CAPITAL: La Paz.
STATISTICAL AGENCY: Instituto Nacional de Estadística (INE).
NATIONAL REPOSITORY: Centro de Informaciones y Documentación of the INE.
MAIN U.S. REPOSITORY: Population Research Center (Univ. of Texas) and Benson Collection (Univ. of Texas).

Six national enumerations were taken before 1950. In reality, the censuses of 1831, 1835, 1845, 1854 and 1882 were estimates arbitrarily made by geographers and publicists and thus lack the techniques and rigor demanded by statistical operations of this sort. The effects of these deficiencies are especially noticeable in the lack of uniformity of schedules and in the oversimplification of tables. When the 1950 census staff tried to make a comparative table of the earlier censuses, it was found that the totals listed were unrealistic, indicating either an over- or an underestimation. In addition, in the nineteenth century the territorial boundaries of the country were greatly modified, thus imposing obstacles to comparability of results.

The sixth national census in 1900 was conducted by the Comisión Nacional del Censo. It was *de facto*, but place of legal residence was also recorded, and canvasser was the method of enumeration used. Due to local conditions and economic difficulties, it was not possible to follow the models adopted by other countries, and the census schedules presented only those questions in greatest demand: total population, age, sex, place of legal residence, marital status, literacy, race, religion, place of birth, physical handicap, and occupation (nineteen professions cited). The territorial division presented eight "departamentos," subdivided into "provincias," "cantones," "vicecantones" and "misiones." Distinction between urban (200 inhabitants and more) and rural (less than 200 inhabitants) was also recorded.

Although more complete than the previous censuses, it still cannot be taken as a base for comparison. Final results indicated that 14.3 percent of the population was not enumerated.

The realization of a new census was postponed mainly because of economic problems and political instabilities in the country. Vital statistics of the years 1941 to 1948 were kept, but a general census was only taken in 1950.

Bolivia

1950 (September 5)

The seventh general census of population was conducted by the Dirección General de Estadística y Censos on a *de facto* basis, and canvasser was the method used to record information. Apparently individual schedules were utilized. The census of agriculture was taken simultaneously, and some housing questions were recorded (number of persons per housing unit, type of tenure, housing units with running water). Reports carried very little on organization and methods and less of definitions. The information that follows was taken directly from table headings and some introductory notes. The tabulation was manual, and the territory covered by the census was divided into departments, provinces, and cantons.

Definitions and Concepts. AGE—in completed years, tabulated in single years and standard five-year age groups. MARITAL STATUS—categories were: single, married, common-law marriage, widowed, divorced, and not declared. PLACE OF BIRTH—native born and foreign born were distinguished. Country of birth of foreigners was recorded. NATIONALITY—apparently country of citizenship. Tables presented the population divided into three groups: native born, foreign born and naturalized. RACE—distinction made between Indian population and non-Indian population only. LANGUAGE—languages spoken. Three Indian dialects and eight foreign languages were recorded. EDUCATION—literacy, school enrollment, and educational attainment (highest degree completed). ECONOMIC ACTIVITY—economically active population included all employed persons, ten years of age and over. Inactive population was divided into the following groups: homemakers, students, unemployed, retired, independent income recipients, and invalids. INDUSTRY—classification presented major divisions and subgroups (two-digits). OCCUPATION—classification presented 336 groups. OCCUPATIONAL STATUS—categories were: employer, employee, self-employed, unpaid family worker, laborer ("obrero" and "jornalero"), "colono," and "comunario."

Special Elements and Features. Comparative table of total population for the six previous censuses with corrections of inaccurate results was provided. For all features, an additional table expressing percentages was presented. The results for the Indian population were presented separately. Graphs and maps were included but not a copy of the schedule. The results for total population by departments, provinces, and cantons presented enumerated population compared to estimated population and the calculated error.

Quality of the Census. The final results indicated a total population of 3,019,031, but only 2,704,165 were actually enumerated; the remainder was determined by estimates or correction of errors. It was stated that although the results of the census provided a more realistic measurement of the demographic situation of the country still a large number of persons were not enumerated (10.5 percent). Whipple's Index classified age accuracy into category V—very rough data. Household data was considered incomplete and inaccurate.

Publication Plan. Bolivia. Dirección General de Estadística y Censo. *Resultados generales del censo de población de la República de Bolivia levantado el día 5 de septiembre de 1950.* La Paz, 1955. Language of publication is Spanish.

1976 (September 29)

The Instituto Nacional de Estadística conducted the eighth national census. It was *de facto*, but place of usual residence was also recorded. Canvassing was the method used to record information on household schedules, and tabulation was computerized. A housing census was taken simultaneously with the census of population. Territorial divisions were departments, provinces, cantons, and cities.

Definitions and Concepts. AGE—number of years completed at the date of the census. Tables in single years and standard five-year age groups. PLACE OF BIRTH—for natives, detailed information of department, province, and city where born; for aliens, the name of the country. RESIDENCE—divided into two questions, usual residence at the time of the census, including country if alien, and usual residence five years before the census. LANGUAGE—the number of Bolivian (that is, Indian) dialects understood and spoken by all persons, and the language most frequently spoken within the family or in everyday life. EDUCATION—literacy (ability to read and write), school enrollment (ages five and over), educational attainment (last grade completed and last one attended). Traditional and new levels were asked to prevent misunderstanding. MARITAL STATUS—all persons age twelve and over; categories were single (never married or in stable union), married (legally and common law), widowed, divorced and/or separated. HOUSEHOLD—one person or a group of persons living in the same housing unit, related or unrelated by blood or marriage, and sharing arrangements for food. HOUSEHOLD COMPOSITION—by type (private—nuclear, extended, compound—and collective) and relationship. ECONOMIC ACTIVITY—all persons age seven and over. Active were employed (in gainful occupation or unpaid family worker), employed but temporarily not at work, and unemployed, looking for a job. Inactive were homemakers, students, the retired, and independent income recipients. OCCUPATION—asked of all economically active except those looking for their first job. Ten major groups of the COTA 1970 classification were used (one-digit). INDUSTRY—major, minor and subgroups (three-digits) of the ISIC. OCCUPATIONAL STATUS—salaried (manual or intellectual labor), and nonsalaried (family workers, self-employed, and employers). FERTILITY—all women age twelve and over: number of children ever born alive, number of children still living and birth date of last child.

Special Elements and Features. Map of the country divided into the nine departments; age and sex pyramids, plus graphs representing literacy by age and sex, school enrollment by age and sex, school attainment by age, economic activity, and number of children born were presented. Copy of schedules in report. Nationality was dropped, and fertility was recorded for the first time.

Quality of the Census. Census office is permanent. The sample tabulation results indicated 95 percent reliability of data. Final results were published in 1978. Whipple's Index category was IV—rough age data.

Publication Plan. Bolivia. Instituto Nacional de Estadística. *Censo nacional de población y vivienda, 1976.* La Paz, 1977-1978. Advance sample results (1 volume); provisional results for each state (9 volumes); final results for each state (9 volumes); and general resume (1 volume). Computer tapes and accompanying guides are available, and the language of publication is Spanish.

OTHER STATISTICAL PUBLICATIONS: Issued by Instituto Nacional de Estadística, *Boletín Estadístico* (monthly).

National Topic Chart

	1950	1976
De facto	X	X
Usual residence		X
Place of birth	X	X
Duration of residence		
Place of prev. residence		X
Urban/rural	X	X
Sex	X	X
Age	X	X
Relation to household head	X	X
Marital status	X	X
Children born alive		X
Children living		X
Citizenship	X	
Literacy	X	X
School enrollment	X	X
Ed. attainment	X	X
Ed. qualification		
National/Ethnic origin	X	
Language	X	X
Religion		
Household composition	X	X
Econ. active/inactive	X	X
Occupation	X	X
Industry	X	X
Occupational status	X	X
Income		
Housing	X	X

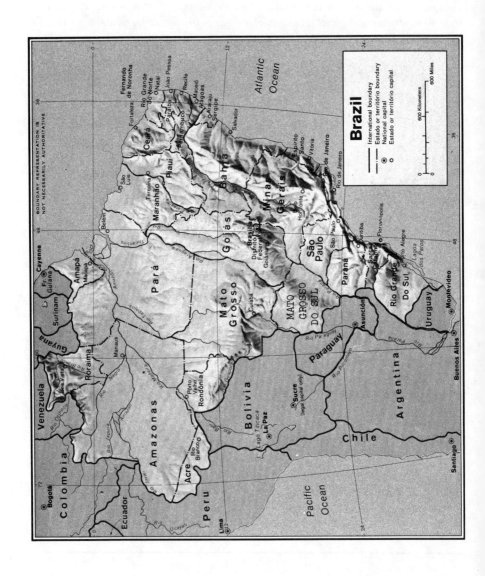

Brazil

Brazil

Federal Republic of Brazil

CAPITAL: Brasilia.
STATISTICAL AGENCY: Fundação Instituto Brasileiro de Geografia e
Estatística (IBGE), Instituto Brasileiro de Estatística.
NATIONAL REPOSITORY: Biblioteca Central—IBGE, Rio de Janeiro.
MAIN U.S. REPOSITORY: Population Research Center (Univ. of Texas).

Estimates of population were made in separate provinces of the country during
the colonial period, but most of the documents containing these results were lost.
A few of these estimates were collected and published in *La population du
Brésil*, CICRED series, 1974.

1872

The first national census was conducted by the Directoria Geral de Estatística.
It was both *de facto* and *de jure* with a distinction made between the temporarily
absent and the transient population.

Very little is known about the organization and methods adopted and even less
of the definitions. Canvassing was the method used for enumeration, and the
results were manually tabulated. The country was divided into provinces, parishes, and "curatos," and separate tables for free and slave populations were
presented. The scope included age, sex, race, marital status, religion, nationality, literacy, school enrollment, physical handicap, and professions. The figure
for total population did not include 181,583 persons, the estimated population for
thirty-two parishes not enumerated during the census period. This census, although the first one, was considered more accurate and the return of results more
complete than the two following censuses.

1890

The second national census was the first after the country was proclaimed a
republic. It was taken on a *de facto* and a *de jure* basis; however, the results were
incomplete and the *de jure* population was not obtained. The census was conducted by the Directoria Geral de Estatística, but its organization was damaged
by administrative and political changes that included the first elections in the

country and general economic difficulties. The distribution of schedules was deficient, and the return of results was incomplete and lacked accuracy. The territory covered by the census was divided into twenty states and one federal district, subdivided into "municípios," districts, and parishes.

The number and complexity of questions posed enormous obstacles for the tabulation of results. The scope included: age, sex, race, marital status, nominal list of individuals with ninety years of age and over, nationality, nationality of parents, date of arrival in the country, number of legitimate and illegitimate children, physical handicaps, date of marriage, times married, age at time of marriage, age of spouse at the time of the census, fertility in marriage, intrafamilial marriages, duration of marriage, number of children living and dead, number of children with physical handicap, race and nationality of spouse, religion, education, and profession. In addition, housing occupancy and total population on ships were also recorded.

All tables presented subtitles in French. Information on parishes that were not enumerated or with incomplete results was supplemented by estimates based on 1872 census results. Because of the costs, publication of results was extremely slow, and only the Federal District, the state of Alagoas, and a synopsis of the country with reduced format for the other states were published. In the volume for the Federal District, vital statistics and comparative tables with comments on previous partial enumerations were also presented.

1900

The third general census of population was conducted by the Directoria Geral de Estatística on a *de facto* and a *de jure* basis. Canvasser was the method used to record information on individual schedules. Credibility and completeness of information varied from state to state; that is, some states presented complete results, others compensated for the loss of schedules by mathematical calculations, and a third group of states in which the nonenumerated population was quite large presented estimates based on comparison with the previous census. Manual tabulation was utilized. The scope included: age, sex, marital status, nationality, literacy, religion, physical handicap, number of legitimate and illegitimate children, and professions. The results for the Federal District were so inaccurate and incomplete that another census was taken in 1906. In this census, household schedules were used, and the question about religion was dropped. Comparative tables with previous censuses and some vital statistics based on national registration were also furnished.

1920

The fourth general census of population was conducted by the same agency, on a *de facto* and a *de jure* basis; canvassers recorded information on household schedules. Private and collective households received different schedules. Agricultural and industrial censuses were taken simultaneously. Mechanical tabulation was used. The scope was basically the same as the 1900 census with the addition of source of livelihood. Religion was dropped again as it was in the 1906 census. This census was much better organized than the previous ones, and the results were fairly accurate. The problem of inaccessibility of certain areas and the extension of the country, however, posed difficulties for completeness of enumeration. In more remote areas, where the results could not be obtained, estimates supplemented data information.

1940

The fifth general census of population and housing was conducted by the Instituto Brasileiro de Geografia e Estatística on a *de facto* and a *de jure* basis. Canvasser was the method used to record information on individual and household schedules and on the list of collective domiciles. Industrial, agricultural, commercial, transportation and communication, and services censuses were taken simultaneously. The scope included: age, sex, race, marital status, place of birth, citizenship, religion, literacy, school enrollment, educational attainment, place of school, physical handicap, language, occupation, occupational status and industry, property ownership, insurance, and fertility. The territory covered by the census was divided into twenty states, one territory and one federal district, subdivided into "municipios" and districts. The results referring to total population excluded 17,913 persons whose data could not be obtained because of loss of schedules. The region of Serra dos Aimorés, because of litigation between the states of Espirito Santo and Minas Gerais, was enumerated separately.

1950 (July 1)

The sixth general census of population and housing was conducted by the Serviço Nacional de Recenseamento, IBGE. Censuses of agriculture, industry, commercial and services were taken simultaneously. The census was *de facto* and *de jure*, but the majority of tables refers to present population (*de facto*). Canvasser was the method used for collection of data, and the forms of enumeration were the same used in 1940 (household, individual, and list of collective domiciles). The results of total population excluded 31,960 persons enumerated in the states of Minas Gerais (10,461), São Paulo (7,588) and Paraná (13,911) whose schedules were lost. As in the previous census, the region of Serra dos Aimorés was enumerated separately. Mechanical tabulation was utilized. Territorial divisions were twenty states, five territories, and the Federal District (seat of the government). The states and territories, except the Federal District and Fernando de Noronha territory, were divided into "municípios," districts and cities, and villages and sectors (smallest unit). The Federal District was divided into districts and "circunscrições", and the Fernando de Noronha territory was classified as an urban area.

Definitions and Concepts. AGE—date of birth. If age was not known, presumed age was recorded. Tabulated in single years and standard five-year groups and ten-year groups. URBAN—areas within cities and villages. RACE—four groups were recorded: white, black, yellow and "pardos" (Indians, mulattos,

"Caboclos" and "Cafusos"). Classification was based on the color of the skin. MARITAL STATUS—categories were: single, married (civil and religious ceremonies had equal value, but common-law marriages were excluded), "desquitados" (legally separated), divorced (aliens married and divorced in foreign countries), and widowed. RELIGION—seven religious groups were recorded, based on the number of followers. Children less than twelve years of age took the religion of their parents, if both belonged to the same group. NATIONALITY—three groups were distinguished: native born, aliens with Brazilian citizenship, and foreign born. For the foreign born, the name of the country of citizenship was not provided because of the changes of sovereignty resulting from World War II. PLACE OF BIRTH—state or territory of birth for native born and country of birth for aliens. PLACE OF RESIDENCE—usual place. If the person was resident but absent at the time of the enumeration, the state or country where the person was living was recorded; if the person was present but was not a permanent resident, the usual place of residence was asked. LANGUAGE—question asked of persons five years of age and older: language spoken at home other than Portuguese. EDUCATION—literacy (ability to read and write in any language), educational attainment (highest degree completed), and educational qualification. ECONOMIC ACTIVITY—defined in terms of main occupation at the date of the census. Lower age limit was ten years. The secondary activity was also recorded. Economically active were all persons with an occupation at the date of the census, excluding unpaid domestic activity, students without any other occupation, unemployed, pensioners, inmates of institutions, and persons of independent income. The industrial and occupational classifications included all of the inactive groups. Persons dependent on agriculture were separately identified. INDUSTRY—classification based on COTA 1950, divisions and major groups (two-digits). OCCUPATION—classification based on COTA 1950, major groups and subgroups (two-digits). OCCUPATIONAL STATUS—categories were: employer, employee, self-employed, and unpaid family worker. Federal, state and municipal employees were classified separately. FERTILITY—total number of children born (stillbirths included) and number of children still living. Questions were asked of women fifteen years of age and over and of men from twenty to seventy-nine years of age. FAMILY—term used to identify households, that is, person or group of persons, related by blood or domestic dependency, living in the same housing unit (lodgers and servants included). The concept took into account not only residents present or absent, but also the nonresidents present. The results referred exclusively to families enumerated in private houses.

Special Elements and Features. The demographic characteristics were analyzed in comparison to 1940 census. New features such as economically active population, dependence on agriculture, and number of employees according to their administrative position were added. Marital status excluded the category of separated. Industrial classification was expanded. The table with total population by age, sex, color, marital status, religion, nationality and literacy for all previous censuses (1872, 1890, 1900, 1920 and 1940) in comparison with 1950 results is of interest. A copy of the schedule is included.

Quality of the Census. Final results were published in 1956. Municipal maps were reviewed for census purposes. Indigenous population was not totally enumerated, and only partial information on color and language was indirectly obtained. Whipple's Index classified age information in category IV—rough data.

Publication Plan. Brazil. IBGE. Serviço Nacional de Recenseamento. *VI recenseamento do Brasil, 1950.* Rio de Janeiro, 1954-1958. Volumes 1-30 in 51 volumes. Volume 1, Brasil: censo demográfico. Volumes 6-30 state and territory volumes (2-5 for other censuses). An equivalent series of publications with selected principal data was also published. Language of publication is Portuguese.

1960 (September 1)

The seventh national census of population and housing was conducted by the Departamento de Estatística de População, IBGE, on a *de facto* and a *de jure* basis, but most of the tables refer to present population (*de facto*). The method of enumeration was canvasser, and two forms were utilized—general household schedules and sampling schedules. The sampling schedules were distributed to 25 percent of households. A list of collective domiciles and the notebooks of the census agents were used for control and the selection of housing units to be included for sampling. Industrial, agricultural, commercial, and services censuses were taken simultaneously, and special inquiries about construction, production, distribution of energy, and administration of real estate were added. Tabulation was computerized for the first time. The territory was divided into twenty-one states, five territories, and the federal district. The federal district was transferred to Brasilia and the city of Rio de Janeiro became the state of Guanabara.

Definitions and Concepts. AGE—in completed years. If less than one year, the number of months was recorded. Tabulated in single years and standard five-year age groups. Unlike 1950, persons who did not know their age were classified under the category "age unknown." RELIGION, RACE, FERTILITY and NATIONALITY—the same as 1950. PLACE OF BIRTH—for native born, the state of birth; for aliens and naturalized Brazilian citizens, country of birth. URBAN—same as 1950, but this time, tables clearly cited urban or rural. PLACE OF RESIDENCE—residents, present or not, and nonresidents were recorded. Usual place, duration of residence (new), previous residence (new), and whether previously living in rural area were asked. FAMILY—same as 1950. If two families shared the same housing unit they were considered "famílias conviventes." DWELLINGS—were divided into private (maximum of three families) and collective (group quarters). EDUCATION—literacy, school enrollment, educational attainment (highest degree completed), number of years of schooling, and educational qualification. MARITAL STATUS—living with the spouse or not was the main concern. Categories were single (never married nor in consensual union), married (civil, religious, and common-law marriages), separated (married but not living with spouse), "desquitados" (legally separated), divorced (only for those married and divorced in foreign countries), and widowed (not remarried or in union). The duration of marriage was also recorded. ECONOMIC ACTIVITY— defined in terms of usual occupation performed during the last twelve months before the census. Lower age limit was ten years. The concept of "gainfully occupied" was adopted. Occupation the week before the census was also asked of all economically active persons. Economically inactive groups included home-makers, students, retired, persons of independent income, invalids, inmates of institutions, and persons without occupation during the year before the census. If a person had a different occupation at the date of the census, it was asked if the new occupation was adopted as definite. INDUSTRY—classification based on COTA 1960, divisions and major groups (two-digits). OCCUPATION— classi-fication based on COTA 1960, major groups, groups, and subgroups (three-digits). Although occupation the week before the census was asked, classification was based on the usual occupation (one performed during most of the year before the census). OCCUPATIONAL STATUS—categories were: employer, employee (public and private), self-employed, unpaid family worker, unpaid worker for other institutions, and share cropper. INCOME—(recorded for the first time) included salaries, pensions, tips, commissions, donations regularly received, or any other source, such as insurance, and rents, correspondent to the last month before the enumeration date. If income was varied, the average of twelve months was recorded. Income levels were determined by taking into consideration the differences of minimal salaries in different regions of the country. ECONOMIC DEPENDENCY—persons economically active were considered dependents of their sector of activity or usual occupation. Economically inactives, but members of a family group, were classified as dependent on the kind of activity or occupa-tion of the head of the family. Economically inactive, living in group quarters, were simply classified as inactives.

Special Elements and Features. For the first time sampling schedules were used. Urban and rural population were, for the first time, clearly distinguished. Industrial and occupational classification was provided. School enrollment, dura-tion of and previous residence, and income were new features. Language was dropped. A special volume was dedicated to socioeconomic conditions of slums in the city of Rio de Janeiro. Although most of the tables referred to *de facto* population, questions related to household composition referred to *de jure* popu-lation. A list of the fifty most populated cities in 1940, 1950, and 1960 was provided.

Quality of the Census. Changes of organization, elaboration of schedules, and definitions of terms pose difficulties for comparisons with previous censuses. Complete tabulation of data was concluded much later; a synopsis of results, however, was available from 1961. Whipple's Index ranking was not available.

Publication Plan. Brazil. IBGE. Departamento de Estatística de População. *VII reconseamento geral do Brasil. Série regional.* Volume 1, Censo demográfico. Rio de Janeiro 1967-1977(?). Volumes 1-19 in 25 volumes. *Série nacional.*

Censo demográfico. Brasil. Rio de Janeiro, 1976. Other volumes dedicated to other censuses. Unpublished data is available and language of publication is Portuguese.

1970 (September 1)

The eighth national census operation, conducted by the Departamento de Censos, IBGE, included simultaneously population, housing, agricultural, industrial, commercial and services censuses with special inquiries about institutions of credit and insurance, and production and distribution of energy. The census was *de facto* and *de jure* but did not include family members of diplomatic representations, military residents in embassies outside of the country, crews and passengers of foreign ships in national ports, and aborigines living in tribes without contact with civilization.

For the first time, the region of Serra dos Aimorés was enumerated in conjunction with the rest of the country. Canvasser was the method utilized to record information on household schedules (a short form and a longer sampling form, used for 25 percent of the population). All results presented referred to the resident population, *de jure*, with exception of Table 1 (urban and rural population by sex and age) where *de facto* and *de jure* population were recorded. Tabulation was computerized. The territorial divisions were twenty-two states, four territories, and the federal district, subdivided into "municípios" and districts. The former territory of Acre was elevated to state category, and the territory of Rio Branco changed its name to Roraima.

Definitions and Concepts. AGE—date of birth or completed years if date is not known. If less than a year, the number of months was recorded. Tabulated in single years and standard five-year age groups. PLACE OF BIRTH, NATIONALITY, PLACE OF RESIDENCE, MARITAL STATUS, LITERACY, EDUCATION and URBAN—same as 1960. RELIGION—three groups were distinguished for having large representations (Catholic, "Evangélica" and "Espírita"), persons belonging to other religious affiliations were classified as "others." In the case of children, the religion of the mother was recorded. ECONOMIC ACTIVITY—lower age limit was ten years of age. Economic activity was defined in terms of usual occupation performed during the last twelve months before the census. The economically active population included persons who had worked during the period of reference and those unemployed looking for a job at the date of the census. The economically inactive included: unemployed (persons who although capable of work, live on donations, alms, and so forth), students, retired, homemakers, pensioners, invalids, inmates of institutions, and persons of independent income. Duration of unemployment, place of work, months worked and weeks worked were also recorded. OCCUPATION—usual occupation was the basis of classification. Also asked was the occupation one week before the census. Major groups, groups, and subgroups were recorded (three-digits). INDUSTRY—classification based on COTA 1970, divisions and major groups (two-digits). List of industries was provided with comments for comparability with 1960. OCCUPATIONAL STATUS—categories were the same as 1960 with the inclusion of persons looking for a job for the first time, who were classified as unpaid workers. ECONOMIC DEPENDENCY—the same as 1960. INCOME—source, last monthly income, and average of monthly income were recorded. FERTILITY—questions asked of all women fifteen years of age and over: number of children born alive, number of stillbirths, number of children born within twelve months before the census, and number of children still living. FAMILY—family group may constitute a person or persons, related by blood or domestic dependency, who lived in the same housing unit. Also included in this group were guests and lodgers. If two families shared the same housing unit they were considered "famílias conviventes." This concept was also applied in 1960, but in 1970 the "famílias conviventes" were divided into main and secondary family, related or not by blood.

Special Elements and Features. Fertility questions were worded differently. Place of work, number of hours worked during the week before the census, number of weeks worked during the twelve months before the census, and duration of unemployment were new features. Duration of marriage was dropped. Results of the census presented comparative tables for the years 1940 through 1970, a table with the most populated cities in 1960 and 1970 (cities of 50,000 and more), another table with the most populated "municípios" for 1970 and one with population density for all "municípios." The occupational and industrial classifications were given with an indication of the numerically important ones. List of microregions was also included.

Quality of the Census. Both date of birth and completed years were asked to improve accuracy of age data, but Whipple's Index classified age accuracy into category IV—rough data. Preliminary results, obtained by sampling 1.3 percent of the population, were published ten months after enumeration date; final results began to be published soon after that.

Publication Plan. Brazil. IBGE. Departamento de Censos. *VIII recenseamento geral—1970. Série regional.* Volume 1, Censo demográfico. Rio de Janeiro, 1972-1973. Volumes 1-24 in 28 volumes. *Série nacional. Brasil.* Rio de Janeiro, 1973. Other volumes dedicated to other censuses. Unpublished data are available, computer tapes are available, and language of publication is Portuguese.

1980 (September 1)

The ninth general census of population and housing was conducted by the Fundação Instituto Brasileiro de Geografia e Estatística (IBGE) in conjunction with censuses of agriculture, industry, commerce, and services, and other special inquiries. The census was *de jure* and *de facto*. Indigenous populations living in reservations were included, but those tribes living in remote areas were excluded. A combination of self-enumeration and canvasser was the method utilized to record information on household schedules (short and long forms; the latter a sampling questionnaire distributed to 25 percent of the population) and a special questionnaire for group quarters. A two-stage enumeration system was used. Tabulation was computerized.

Information supplied here was obtained from the enumerator's handbook and a copy of schedules available before the census date. Preliminary results have just been published. The territorial divisions are twenty-two states, four territories, and the federal district. The state of Guanabara was annexed to the state of Rio de Janeiro, and the state of Mato Grosso was divided into two states—Mato Grosso do Norte and Mato Grosso do Sul.

Definitions and Concepts. FAMILY—concept is identical to household. If two or more families live in the same housing unit they are called "famílias conviventes." AGE—date of birth and presumed age in completed years, if date of birth is not known. If less than one year, the number of months was recorded. RELIGION—religious affiliation. For minors, the religion of the mother was recorded. RACE—color was the basis for classification. Categories: white, black, yellow and "parda" (mesticos, Indian, "Cabocla," "Cafuza," or "Mameluca"). ORPHANHOOD—derived from the question: Is your mother alive? NATIONALITY—three groups were distinguished: Brazilian born, naturalized Brazilian, and foreigner. PLACE OF BIRTH—for Brazilian born, the state or territory of birth; for foreign-born or naturalized Brazilians, the country of birth was recorded. PLACE OF RESIDENCE—questions asked of residents present or absent at the time of the census: Were they living in the same place of birth; had the persons moved from rural to urban area, always lived in urban or always lived in rural area; place of previous residence, indicating whether it was rural or urban zone; and duration of residence, whether in the same state or territory or in the same "município." If the person had been living in the same "município" for less than ten years, the name of the state or the country where living previously was recorded. EDUCATION—literacy (ability to read and write), educational attainment, and school enrollment recorded for persons five years and older. Educational qualification recorded for persons ten years and older. MARITAL STATUS—questions asked of persons ten years and older. Categories were based on the presence or absence of spouse: Single, married (divided into four groups, civil and religious marriage, civil only, religious only, and other), separated, "desquitado" (legally separated), divorced, and widowed. ECONOMIC ACTIVITY—period of reference was twelve months before the census date. Lower age limit was ten years of age. The questions were intended to identify the persons who worked in the last twelve months before the census, including seasonal workers, those temporarily absent for sickness and other reasons, those supported by scholarships, those retired in the last twelve months, and unpaid workers who regularly work fifteen hours or more per week for a family member or any other institution. Those who were not included in this group were: unemployed (experienced or new workers), retired or pensioners, persons of independent income, inmates of institutions, students, invalids, and homemakers. Unemployed persons were also asked whether or not they were looking for a job. The following additional information was also recorded: "município" where working or studying, whether paying into social security or any kind of retirement plan, and the number of hours worked per week (usual and other occupations). Occupation, industry, and occupational status during the week before the census were also recorded. OCCUPATION—usual occupation or principal occupation in case of being engaged simultaneously in more than one. Classification based on ISCO, major groups, groups, and subgroups (three-digits). INDUSTRY—classification based on ISIC, divisions, major groups, and subgroups (three-digits). OCCUPATIONAL STATUS—categories were migrant worker, share cropper, employee, employer, self-employed, and unpaid worker (family or other institution). INCOME—average monthly gross income (salary, wages, and so forth), number of salaries per year. FERTILITY—questions asked of all women fifteen years and over: number of children born alive, number of stillbirths, number of children still living and date of birth of the last child born alive.

Special Elements and Features. A new state was created when Mato Grosso was divided into two states. Guanabara was annexed to Rio de Janeiro state. The question on orphanhood was new. Questions on place of residence and education were worded differently. Income questions were expanded, and an inquiry about insurance was added.

Quality of the Census. Final results are not published yet. No evaluation is available at this time.

Publication Plan. Unpublished data and computer tapes are available. Language of publication is Portuguese.

OTHER STATISTICAL PUBLICATIONS: Issued by Fundação IBGE, *Anuário Estatístico, Boletim Estatístico* (quarterly), *Pesquisa Nacional por Amostra de Domicílios* (annually), *Sinopse Estatística* (annually).

National Topic Chart

	1950	1960	1970	1980*
De facto	X	X	X	X
Usual residence	X	X	X	X
Place of birth	X	X	X	X
Duration of residence		X	X	X
Place of prev. residence		X	X	X
Urban/rural	X	X	X	X
Sex	X	X	X	X
Age	X	X	X	X
Relation to household head	X	X	X	X
Marital status	X	X	X	X
Children born alive	X	X	X	X
Children living	X	X	X	X
Citizenship	X	X	X	X
Literacy	X	X	X	X
School enrollment		X	X	X
Ed. attainment	X	X	X	X
Ed. qualification		X	X	X
National/Ethnic origin	X	X	X	X
Language	X			
Religion	X	X	X	X
Household composition	X	X	X	X
Econ. active/inactive	X	X	X	X
Occupation	X	X	X	X
Industry	X	X	X	X
Occupational status	X	X	X	X
Income		X	X	X
Housing	X	X	X	X

*Note: The 1980 census final results are not yet available.

British Virgin Islands

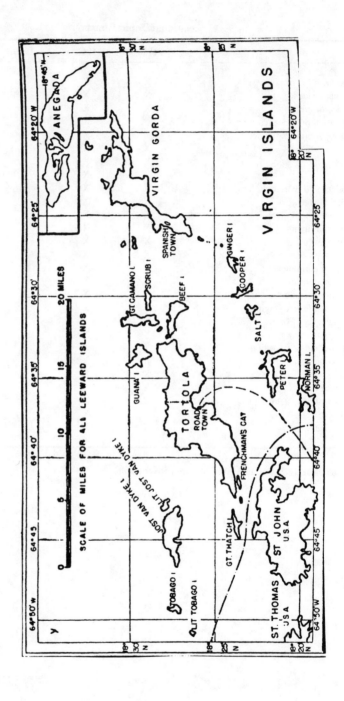

British Virgin Islands

British Crown Colony

CAPITAL: Road Town on Tortola.
STATISTICAL AGENCY: Office of the Financial Secretary.
NATIONAL REPOSITORY: Public Library, Road Town, and Colonial Office
                     Group, London, for early censuses.
MAIN U.S. REPOSITORY: Library of Congress, New York Public Library.

The constituent parts of the Leeward Islands colony, termed the Presidencies, were federated in the last quarter of the nineteenth century. After dissolution of the short-lived West Indies Federation (1958-1963), the British Virgin Islands returned to its status as a colony.

There is mention of censuses in 1678, 1720, and 1756, but it is generally conceded that the first modern census was that of 1844. However, no extant copies of that census seem to have been found. There were decade censuses beginning in 1861 that extended through 1921. These were followed by 1946, 1960, and 1970. The censuses in the British West Indies up to 1946 have traditionally been *de facto* and self-enumerated. The latter is qualified since in practice most were canvassed in major part due to lack of literacy, especially during the early years.

1861

Supposedly there was no census taken in the Virgin Islands in this year but a few tables were found in the *Census of the British Empire 1861*, volume 3, *General Report*. The scope was age, sex, birthplace, marital status, race, occupation, and infirmities.

1871

No information could be found on this census in the Virgin Islands.

1881

Comparative tables found in the censuses of 1891 and 1946 indicate some of the scope of this census: age, sex, race, size of household, occupation, number of houses, and acreage held.

1891

Scope: birthplace, age, sex, marital status, race, size of household, occupation, occupational status, infirmities, acreage held, and fishing.

1901

One table is available in the *Census of the British Empire, 1901*. The scope was sex and number of inhabitants.

1911

A few tables were found in the *Census of England and Wales, 1911, General Report with Appendices*. The scope was number of inhabitants, sex, literacy, race, religion, and number of houses.

1921

Through comparative tables in the 1946 census, the only known scope is number of inhabitants, sex, literacy, race, and religion.

1946 (April 9)

Conducted through the Office of the Commissioner, this was the first census closely coordinated with the West Indies program. The results were given only for six of the thirty-two islands that make up the Virgin Islands: Tortola, Anegada, Virgin Gorda, Peter, Salt, and Cooper Islands. There was no separate census publication for the Virgin Islands; there was one volume for the Leeward Islands colony.

Definitions and Concepts. [See British West Indies 1946 for the full entry; the following are the differences.] No URBAN distinction since Road Town was under 1,000. RACE—tables indicate only white, black, Asiatic, and mixed. AGE—tables for single years and standard five-year age groups. INFIRMITIES—totally blind, and deaf and dumb (collected on a special schedule). FERTILITY—number of children surviving not taken in the British Virgin Islands. HOUSEHOLD COMPOSITION—by size only. OCCUPATIONAL STATUS—employer, own-account worker, unpaid helper, and wage and salary earner (at work, learners, unemployed).

Special Elements or Features. Infirmities and duration of union were included in British Virgin Islands part of the census.

Quality of the Census. Whipple's Index category was III—approximate age data.

Publication Plan. Part F of the *West Indian Census, 1946* is devoted to the colony of the Leeward Islands. Language of publication is English.

1960 (April 7)

Taken by the territorial census office. [See British West Indies 1960, West Indies section, for full entry; the following are the differences.] The British

Virgin Islands number thirty-two in all but only six were censused. The islands were subdivided into enumeration districts for the census, but because volume 1 was not published, there are no printed results at that level.

Definitions and Concepts. FERTILITY—If the child born during the last twelve months was the first? was a new question.

Special Elements and Features. Same.

Quality of the Census. Same. No Whipple's Index rating given. Volume 1 was not published.

Publication Plan. Jamaica. Department of Statistics. *West Indies Population Census. Census of British Virgin Islands, 7th April 1960.* Volume 2. Language of publication is English.

1970 (April 7)

British Virgin Islands did not publish separate reports from this census. [See British West Indies 1970 for full entry.] The only known difference is that BVI was one of the countries not included in the migration volume. Volumes 3; 4.14; 4.16; 6.3; 7; 8 abc; 9.4; 10.3; and 10.4 of the BWI 1970 set contain the data for this colony. Language of publication is English.

1980

The 1980 census has been conducted, but neither data nor methods are available as yet.

National Topic Chart

	1946	1960	1970
De facto	X	X	X
Usual residence	X	X	X
Place of birth	X	X	X
Duration of residence	X	X	X
Place of prev. residence			X
Urban/rural			
Sex	X	X	X
Age	X	X	X
Relation to household head		X	X
Marital status	X	X	X
Children born alive		X	X
Children living	X		
Citizenship			
Literacy	X	X	
School enrollment	X	X	X
Ed. attainment			X
Ed. qualification			
National/Ethnic origin	X	X	X
Language			
Religion	X	X	X
Household composition	X	X	
Econ. active/inactive	X	X	X
Occupation	X	X	X
Industry	X	X	X
Occupational status	X	X	X
Income			
Housing	X	X	X

British West Indies

The British West Indies were made up of the Caribbean set, which included mainland areas of Guyana and Belize, and the islands of Jamaica, Trinidad and Tobago, Barbados, the Leeward Islands (Antigua and its dependencies Barbuda and Redonda, St. Kitts-Nevis-Anguilla, Montserrat, Virgin Islands), the Windward Islands (Dominica, Grenada, St. Lucia, St. Vincent), Cayman Islands, and Turks and Caicos. Although the Turks and Caicos are geographically an extension of the Bahamas, these islands had been a dependency of Jamaica since 1871 and so have been associated traditionally with the Caribbean group. The British West Indies also include islands in the Atlantic, namely the Bahamas and Bermuda.

Keeping track of these islands and their censuses is just as embroiled in confusion as their history and changes in political status through the years. Each entity has its own entry in this book up to the 1946 census. The 1946 through 1970 censuses will be described here in full with only the differences cited in the respective entry, or if a separate publication of results exists, that, too, will be described in the respective entry.

There are three periods of censuses for the BWI: those taken from 1678 up to 1840; those that date from 1841 through 1943; and those from 1946 to the present.

1678-1840

There were colonial censuses before 1776, but these materials are not readily available in the United States. Some of the older censuses contain a few comparative tables, giving mainly population totals or estimates from this period.

1841-1943

After emancipation of the slaves in the West Indies, the British government decreed that a regular census should be taken in the area with an eye toward uniformity in time and content. Although there were times in which individual territories or the whole group could not comply with the decree due to financial or political circumstances, the censuses of this period were fairly coordinated. The year 1844 was to have been the first, but because a few had taken censuses just before that year, they did not repeat. There were censuses in 1851, 1855, 1856, and then they seemed to settle into a decade pattern from 1861 through 1921. The 1901 and 1931 censuses were two that were not taken by all territo-

West Indies

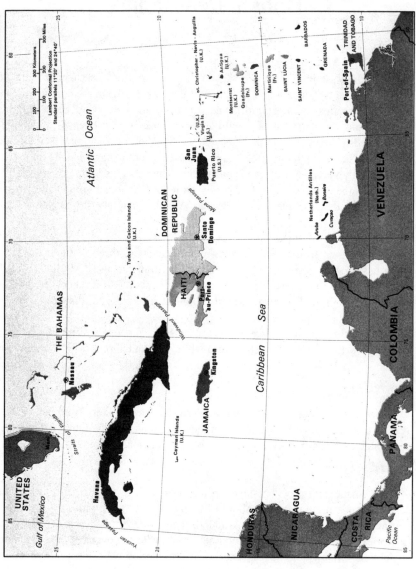

UNITED STATES

Gulf of Mexico

Straits of Florida

Havana

Yucatan Passage

Nassau

THE BAHAMAS

Atlantic Ocean

0   100   200   300 Miles
0   100   200   300 Kilometers
Lambert Conformal Projection
Standard parallels 11°20' and 24°40'

Turks and Caicos Islands (U.K.)

L. Cayman Islands (U.K.)

JAMAICA

Kingston

Caribbean Sea

Windward Passage

HAITI

Port-au-Prince

DOMINICAN REPUBLIC

Santo Domingo

Mona Passage

San Juan

Puerto Rico (U.S.)

Virgin Is. (U.K.) (U.S.)

St. Christopher - Nevis - Anguilla (U.K.)

Antigua (U.K.)

Montserrat (U.K.)

Guadeloupe (Fr.)

DOMINICA

Martinique (Fr.)

SAINT LUCIA

SAINT VINCENT

BARBADOS

GRENADA

TRINIDAD AND TOBAGO

Port-of-Spain

Netherlands Antilles (Neth.)

Aruba   Curaçao   Bonaire

HONDURAS

NICARAGUA

COSTA RICA

PANAMA

COLOMBIA

VENEZUELA

Pacific Ocean

ries. Of the publications available for consultation, very few have even a minimal description of the organization and methods of the census nor are there copies of schedules and rarely a direct statement referring to them. Most of the information here was gleaned from tables and references made in other censuses as well as other sources.

1946-Present

This is a period of as close coordination and uniformity of census content and methodology as is possible within the differences of interest and tradition that these countries have, considering the changes of political status that have occurred during these years.

Table 3 tracks the dates of the censuses taken from 1900 to the present.

1946 (April 9)

The taking of a census had hitherto been a matter for each colony separately, and each had its own census tradition. But this census represented a return to a closer uniformity throughout the Caribbean island colonies than had existed before. Bermuda and the Bahamas, which were to conduct their own censuses in 1950 and 1953, respectively, and Jamaica and its dependencies, Turks and Caicos and Cayman, which had conducted a census in 1943, were excluded.

There was central planning, uniform schedules and instructions were used, and the results were centrally tabulated in Jamaica. Although the enumerations were made within the framework of the laws of each separate colony, a high degree of coordination in detail was possible. The experience of the Jamaican census was referred to at every stage of the planning and also during tabulation. Nevertheless, the 1946 census differed from the Jamaican 1943 census in a number of ways. The scope was simpler. There were less data collected in housing, agriculture, earnings, employment, and school attendance. The addition of a census of agriculture to the original census of population occurred in seven of the nine colonies; Guyana and Belize deferred.

The conduct of the census was performed through the respective statistical office of each colony and presidency. The census was *de facto*, canvassed in two stages, and mechanically tabulated. Household schedules were used, and there was a separate schedule for the census of agriculture, where it was taken. It was agreed, however, that the taking of the latter should not interfere in the taking of the former. The population on board ships registered in the West Indies was included. Each territory established geographic divisions for census purposes but the results generally were published for natural and administrative units.

Definitions and Concepts. URBAN—towns of 1,000 or more. In territories where a town was smaller than 1,000, an urban/rural distinction was not made. HOUSEHOLD—one person living alone or a group of persons living in a single dwelling house, including live-in servants and boarders and visitors who shared one meal per day. Instead of an inhabited house, a dwelling equalled the quarters of a private house (new). Boardinghouses and small hotels serving meals were

Table 3
British West Indies Censuses

	1901	1911	1921	1931	1939	1943	1946	1950	1953	1960	1963	1970	1979	1980	1981
MAINLAND															
Guyana (Brit. Guyana)		X	X	X			X			X		X		X	
Belize (Brit. Honduras)	X	X	X	X			X			X		X		X	
ISLANDS—CARIBBEAN															
Jamaica		X	X	X		X				X		X			
Cayman		X	X			X				X		X	X		
Turks-Caicos		X	X			X				X		X		X	
Barbados		X	X				X			X		X		X	
Trinidad-Tobago	X	X	X	X			X			X		X		X	
Leeward															
Antigua-Dep.	X	X	X				X			X		X			X
St. K-N-A	X	X	X				X			X		X		X	
Montserrat	X	X	X				X			X		X		X	
Virgin Isls.(Brit)	X	X	X				X			X		X		X	
Windward															
Dominica	X	X	X				X			X		X			X
Grenada	X	X	X	X			X			X		X			X
St. Lucia	X	X	X				X			X		X		X	
St. Vincent		X	X	X	X		X			X		X		X	
ISLANDS—ATLANTIC															
Bahamas	X	X	X	X		X			X	X		X		X	
Bermuda	X	X	X	X	X			X		X	X	X		X	

included in private households rather than listed with institutions (group quarters). AGE—month and year of birth was taken and coded as completed years as of last birthday. Tables included single years (up to as high as the oldest respondent in each territory) and standard five-year age groups. In some territories, infants under one year were coded in completed months. MARITAL STATUS—all persons age ten and over: single (never married), married, common-law marriage (new), widowed, divorced, and not stated. DURATION OF UNION—taken of all with common-law marital status only. HOUSEHOLD COMPOSITION—some specified categories in tables, for example, spouse, son; some only listed groupings, for example one family or two family; some cited only size, such as number of persons. FERTILITY (and MOTHERHOOD)—all females fourteen years of age and over: number of children born alive, age at birth of first child, and number of children surviving. BIRTHPLACE—name of locality for native born, name of island or country for nonnatives. The latter and any return migrants were also asked their duration of residence in the colony. RELIGION—specific denomination, based on preference rather than membership. Response was not compulsory. LITERACY—at least the ability to read considered literate, according to respondent's declaration (no test given). RACE—white (including Portuguese), black, East Indian, Syrian, Chinese, other Asiatic, mixed or colored (African with white or with Asiatic). Tables reflected only the categories pertaining to each territory. ECONOMIC ACTIVITY—all persons age ten and over were asked main activity during the last twelve months. The active were all who worked for pay or profit, the temporarily unemployed, unpaid family workers, and those engaged in subsistence farming. The inactive were first-time job seekers, homemakers, the retired and those of private means, students and all other dependents (children, invalids, inmates, and so forth). The labor force (no reference time period) was made up of the active plus first-time job seekers. OCCUPATION—main and, at times, subsidiary occupations asked. The classification used was according to the list used in the Jamaican 1943 census. Although it was a system independent of industry (new), still its fifteen major groups followed the same order as the industry groups plus special categories for clerical workers and laborers. Within each group the occupations were listed in descending order with owners, supervisors, and managers first. INDUSTRY—the nature of enterprise or service classified in twelve major groups as used in the Jamaican 1943 census. Subdivisions gave more detail to lists. OCCUPATIONAL STATUS—employer, own-account worker, unpaid helper, wage or salary earner in employment, apprentice or learner, and unemployed wage earner. Tables for individual territories listed only their individual preference of terms.

Special Elements or Features. Some territories included additional items in their scope. The reports carried comparative tables for some topics as far back as 1844 wherever figures were available. Fertility and industry were gathered for the first time, although industry could be traced in earlier censuses through the occupation lists. Some other "firsts" also existed for individual territories. Separate tables for adolescents—in school or in the labor force—are included.

Quality of the Census. Although there was a long history of census taking, in each colony or territory the various census offices were not always a permanent fixture. Cooperation with the West Indies census program helped by supplying expertise, as well as technical and financial aid. This census was fuller and more comprehensive than any other taken. The reports usually indicated where data appeared unreliable. The variance in the Whipple's Index rating (II-IV) may be due more to the educational level of the populations than to the census methodology.

Publication Plan. Jamaica. Central Bureau of Statistics. *West Indian Census, 1946.* Parts A-H. Kingston, 1948-1950. Part A, General report; Part B, Census of agriculture; Parts C-H, reports for individual colonies. Language of publication is English.

1960 (April 7)

The second closely coordinated census was divided into two geographic sections. The Eastern Caribbean section included the countries of Guyana, Barbados, Windward Islands (Grenada, Dominica, St. Lucia, St. Vincent), and Trinidad and Tobago which served as the location for the tabulation and the publication of the census results. The West Indies section included Belize, Leeward Islands (Antigua, Montserrat, Virgin Islands, and St. Kitts-Nevis-Anguilla), Turks and Caicos, Cayman Islands, and Jamaica which tabulated and published the results. The adoption of a minimum schedule acceptable to all territories was proposed, although the right of individual territories to include specific questions to cater to special local conditions was acknowledged. There was a great deal more variation among the West Indies group than among the Eastern Caribbean group. There were also some differences between the two groups as to content and methodology.

EASTERN CARIBBEAN

The census was *de facto* only, relaxed for assessing internal migration. It was canvassed in two stages in urban areas and in one stage in remote areas and computer tabulated in Trinidad. There were separate household schedules for population and for housing, income cards (for a 10 percent sample), and infant cards for children born between January 1, 1960 and the census date. All the countries were divided into enumeration districts, and for the first time the results were published for ED's (in Volume 2).

Definitions and Concepts. URBAN—places of 2,000 or more inhabitants plus the presence of basic social amenities. HOUSEHOLD—private, one person living alone or a group of persons residing together and sharing at least one daily meal, including live-in servants, boarders, and visitors. Hotels and guest houses with fewer than twenty guests were included in private. Institutional group quarters included large hotels and guest houses. FAMILIES—the relation to household head was taken in such a manner as to also indicate the family. The family is related by marriage and kinship; parents and siblings of the family head or spouse were included along with the spouse and children. AGE—completed years last birthday, infants under two years by completed months. Tabulated in single years and standard five-year age groups. RACE—Negro, white, East Indian, Chinese, mixed (born of parents of different racial groups, not just African), Portuguese, Amerindian, Carib, Syrian and Lebanese, and other. RELIGION—specific denomination according to respondent's reply. (Trinidad and Tobago requested particular sect if Hindu and particular association if Muslim.) BIRTHPLACE and USUAL RESIDENCE—for the native born, the specific territory, parish, town, ward was requested. If the same as residence, the individual was classed as a nonmover; if different, a mover (internal migration). Those born outside the territory gave island or country of birth plus year of residence (immigration). EDUCATION—educational attainment, name of school attending, and type. Tables also indicated teachers and school populations. MARITAL STATUS (age fifteen and over, legal status only): married, registered and not registered (for East Indians only), divorced, widowed, separated, never married. UNION STATUS (all women) if under age forty-five, present status; if over forty-five, status at age forty-five: married (with legal spouse), common law (with partner), single (no longer with spouse or partner), none (never lived with spouse or partner), visiting (child born during last twelve months while not living with spouse or partner). FERTILITY (all women)—number of children ever born alive, age at birth of first live born child, number of children born during last twelve months. ECONOMIC ACTIVITY—main activity, occupation, industry, and occupational status all based on "last 12 months." Active were those who worked or had been looking for work during most of the reference period. Inactive were homemakers, students, the retired or incapacitated, voluntarily idle and first-time job seekers. The number of months worked during the period and whether it was the first job were also asked. Labor force status was determined by economic situation during the last week before the census: worked and number of days; temporarily absent; wanted work; not wanting work. OCCUPATION—type of job (main). Classification system had twenty major groups and subdivisions to three-digit level, similar to ISCO but mainly followed the order of the industry groups. INDUSTRY—name of employer and type of business. Classification was in nine major groups of the ISIC, detailed to the three-digit level. OCCUPATIONAL STATUS—paid employee, own-account worker, employer, unpaid apprentice, unpaid family worker. SOCIOECONOMIC CLASS—classification developed during processing of results: agricultural, nonmanual, manual, and residual. INCOME (10 percent sample)—the exact figure was not asked, only an indication of the range. Gross salary and gross receipts of the last pay period. Unfortunately, tables with income results were not published.

Special Elements and Features. Fertility, migration, and educational characteristics taken in greater depth than in earlier censuses. Union status taken as separate from marital status. Income and months worked were asked for the first time. The socioeconomic class was also determined for the first time. Specimen forms, classification schemes, and codes are found in Volume 1, *Administrative Report*. Volume 2, *Summary Tables*, gives general characteristics for parishes and enumeration districts. Volume 3, *Detailed Cross-Classification*, gives cross-classified and detailed characteristics for parishes, places, and special areas. The parts of Volume 3 that were to give detailed results on fertility, income distribution, and miscellaneous were never published, but summary data on fertility are available in Volume 2. No income data appear in published volumes.

Quality of the Census. This was the first use of a test census to check training, schedules, and field work. There is a full explanation of definitions and concepts, procedures, organization, and so forth. The lack of a complete publication is regretted, although the quality of printing is superior to the West Indies set. There is no Whipple's Index rating for any of the Eastern Caribbean set.

WEST INDIES

The census was *de facto* and *de jure*; the tables were primarily of the *de jure* population. It was canvassed in two stages in urban areas and in one stage in rural areas. Population and housing questions were on a single household schedule, except for Jamaica, Turks and Caicos and Cayman, which used individual mark-sensing schedules for the resident population. Income and infant cards were not used. It was computer tabulated in Jamaica. All countries were divided into enumeration districts, and for the first time the results were published for ED's. Unfortunately, only Jamaica and Belize for which a Volume 1 was issued have results for ED's.

Definitions and Concepts. URBAN—places of 2,000 and more, and places of 1,000 and over with social amenities. HOUSEHOLD—private, one person living alone or a group of persons residing together and sharing at least one daily meal, including live-in servants and boarders. Hotels and guest houses with five or less guests were included in private. Institutional were group quarters, hotels and guest houses of six or more guests. FAMILY—relation to household head did not indicate family relationships within households. AGE—completed years last birthday, infants under one year grouped under zero. Tabulated in single years and standard five-year age groups. RELIGION—specific denominations according to the respondent's reply. RACE—African/Negro, European/white, East Indian, Chinese/Japanese, Maya/Keckchi, Carib, Syrian, mixed (African and European), mixed (Indian and European), other mixed, other race. BIRTHPLACE and USUAL RESIDENCE—native born cited parish, town. If the residence differed from birthplace, the individual was classed as a mover, if the same, as a nonmover. Those born outside of the territory gave the name of the island or country, plus the year of residence. Some of the countries in the West Indies section also took the total number of places lived in. EDUCATION—literacy, educational attainment, and school enrollment. Some also took vocational training. MARITAL STATUS (age fourteen and over, legal status): married, divorced, widowed, separated, never married. UNION STATUS and DURATION OF UNION—married (legal spouse present), common law (with partner present), single (no longer with spouse or partner), none (never lived with spouse or partner), visiting (child born during last twelve months while not living with spouse or partner). FERTILITY—(all women age fourteen and over): number of children ever born alive, age at birth of first live-born child, number of children born in the last twelve months. ECONOMIC ACTIVITY (age fourteen and over)—main activity, occupation, industry, and occupational status were based on the last twelve months reference period. Active population (classifiable labor force) were those who worked. Inactive (not in CLF) were homemakers, students, retired/disabled, first-time job seekers, and unemployed through last twelve months. Labor force status determined by economic situation during the last week before the census: worked, number of days; temporarily absent; wants work; not wanting work. OCCUPATION—main, and subsidiary, if latter in agriculture or fishing. Classification system was that used in Jamaica, which had some similarities to ISCO, nine major divisions and subdivisions to the three-digit level. INDUSTRY—nature of business or service. Classification in nine major divisions (ISIC type) and subdivisions to the three-digit level. OCCUPATIONAL STATUS—private employee, government employee, unpaid family worker, own-account worker with employees, own-account without employees.

Special Elements and Features. Compared with the Eastern Caribbean, this census did not take income (except for Jamaica), family characteristics, or develop socioeconomic classes; it did take literacy, duration of union, subsidiary occupation, and acreage of land held; it varied in *de jure* tables, urban definition, infant age, racial-ethnic designations, and employment status categories. Also the West Indian countries had more variations among themselves than the Eastern Caribbean group. [See respective entries for differences]. Items not seen in earlier censuses included urban definition, union status used for fertility, educational attainment, occupational classification not tied to industry, and tables published for enumeration districts.

Quality of the Census. Recommendations from the University of the West Indies Census Research Organization and of the United States Bureau of the Census were considered in the preparation of this census. A pilot census was also conducted to test the recording and analysis of data. The term "classifiable labor force" is too similar to "labor force" and thus confusing. The quality of the printing in the reports issued was inferior to that of the Eastern Caribbean set (incorrect table titles, wrong pages indexed). The results were to be issued in two volumes for each of the countries participating. Only Jamaica and Belize had Volume 1 printed, the remaining printed only Volume 2. The former is the main source of enumeration district data. Whipple's Index ranked only Jamaica.

Publication Plan. Jamaica. Department of Statistics. Jamaica Tabulation Centre. *West Indies Population Census.* Kingston, 1963-1964. Eight censuses in twenty-five parts: *Census of Jamaica, 7th April, 1960.* (Vols. I-II in 17 v.); *Census of British Honduras, 7th April 1960* (Vols. I-II); *Census of Cayman Islands, 7th April 1960* (Vol. II only); *Census of Turks and Caicos, 7th April 1960* (Vol. II only); *Census of Antigua, 7th April 1960* (Vol. II only); *Census of*

British Virgin Islands, 7th April 1960 (Vol. II only); *Census of Montserrat, 7th April 1960* (Vol. II only); *Census of St. Kitts-Nevis-Anguilla, 7th April 1960* (Vol. II only). Language of publication is English.

1970 (April 7 and October 25)

This census was coordinated, computer tabulated, and printed through the direction of the University of the West Indies, Census Research Programme, Jamaica. Fifteen countries participated in the program, two of which, Bermuda and Turks and Caicos, took the census on October 25. As in 1960 each country was allowed to add or amend topics that were of specific interest if they would not drastically change the basic unity. The conduct of the census was performed through the respective statistical office of each country.

The Commonwealth Caribbean set of publications covers the basic topics. However, the administrative report and the enumeration district tabulation volumes have not been published as yet, so description of this census must come from the abbreviated introductions of the volumes published. These volumes do not explain the country differences; rather, they refer the user to the nonexistent administrative report. A few of the countries published their own preliminary reports, and one, Bermuda, published a final report from which a few differences have been noted. This entry is of the Commonwealth Caribbean set. The individual country publications appear under the country's entry.

The census was essentially a *de facto* one for all except Jamaica, which continued its *de jure* pattern started in 1943. Special mark-sensing individual schedules were used by the canvasser. All the countries were divided into ED's but Volume 2, parts 1-15, which were to contain the summary (general) tabulations for this level, have not been published yet.

Definitions and Concepts. URBAN—no definition available except in some individual country entries. No urban/rural tables in the volumes published to date. HOUSEHOLD—a person living alone or a group living together and sharing at least one daily meal, including live-in servants (plus their relatives) and boarders (plus their relatives). In the volume published one household equals one dwelling, following the pattern used by Jamaica. FAMILY—there is no indication if this was taken in the manner used in the Eastern Caribbean 1960 or in that used in the West Indies section. AGE—completed years as of last birthday. Tables are available in single years and age groups (less than two, two to four, then standard five-year age groups). RACE—Negro/black, East Indian, Chinese, Amerindian, Portuguese, Syrian/Lebanese, white, mixed, other races—classification supplied by respondent. RELIGION—specificied religious denomination according to respondent's preference not official membership. MIGRATION—birthplace for native born, parish; for foreign born, country and year of immigration. Usual residence: same as birthplace. Duration of residence, place of previous residence, number of parishes ever lived in (including birthplace). EDUCATION (all ages)—type of school now attending (except vocational), full- or part-time attendance, educational attainment (type of school, years of primary schooling, exam passed). Vocational training, occupation for which trained or being trained and method and period of training. MARITAL STATUS—never married, married, widowed, divorced, legally separated. Tables only for ages fifteen to sixty-four not attending school. UNION STATUS—same as 1960. For females age fourteen and over: status at present if under forty-five, or if older, status at age forty-five. Tables for females fifteen to forty-four and forty-five to sixty-four not attending school. One table for each country with those age forty-five and over. FERTILITY—for females age fourteen and over: number of live-born children ever had, age at first live-born birth, age at last live-born birth, number of live/stillbirths in last twelve months, union status, duration of union. Tables only for females not attending school ages fourteen to sixty-four. ECONOMIC ACTIVITY—all persons ages ten and over, not attending school full-time: main activity, employment status, months worked, occupation and industry during last twelve months. Active are those who worked, that is, provided a supply of labor for the production of goods and services. Inactive are assumed to be homemakers, students, persons of independent income, retirees, disabled, or dependent children. Since the distinction between active and inactive is not clearly spelled out, it is difficult to determine to which category belongs the first-time job seeker. Labor force is determined by the economic situation as of the week before the census: worked; with job but not working; looked for work; home duties; at school, and so forth. Jamaica and Bermuda kept "wanted work and available" in this question. OCCUPATION—main, during last twelve months. Classification is according to the 1968 ISCO. Tables do not have detailed occupation, only groups. INDUSTRY—type of business last year. Classification according to 1958 ISIC. Tables do not have detailed industry, only groups. OCCUPATIONAL STATUS—employer, government employee, non-government employee, own-account worker with paid help, own-account worker without paid help, unpaid family worker or apprentice. INCOME—total gross income and/or receipts for the last specified pay period. Tables give annual equivalents.

Special Elements and Features. New items were vocational training, private study, and other forms added to type of schooling, and full- or part-time attendance. The tables for internal migration are only for the five most populous countries: Jamaica, Trinidad and Tobago, Guyana, Barbados, and Belize.

Quality of the Census. All the preparation, organization, and other procedures recommended to achieve a good census seemed to have been followed. However, during the processing of the results of this census, the data in the volumes published appear to have been patterned after Jamaica's preference, for example, household equaling dwelling. The lack of Volume 1, the administrative report, and Volume 2, the enumeration district tabulations, has a greater effect than just their content. Without the guide to the geographic codes used in many of the volumes, small areas so designated cannot be researched. There are no comparative tables, no institutional population figures, and no migration figures for ten of the fifteen countries. There is no Whipple's Index rating for this census.

Publication Plan. Jamaica. University of the West Indies, Census Research Programme. *1970 Population Census of the Commonwealth Caribbean.* Kingston, Herald Limited, 1973-. Volumes 1-10 in 48 volumes. Administrative report (not published); Enumeration district tabulations (not published); Age tabulations; Economic activity; Internal migration; Education; Race and religion; Fertility-Union status-Marital status; Housing and household; Miscellaneous—income. Language of publications is English.

1980 (May 12)

In the few preliminary publications received from the Caribbean countries that participated in the 1980 census program there has been no mention of this census being as closely coordinated as the 1970 one. It seems only the date is being observed and that not even by all of the fifteen countries.

National Topic Chart

	1946	1960(E)	1960(W)	1970
De facto	X	X	X	X
Usual residence		X	X	X
Place of birth	X	X	X	X
Duration of residence	X	X	X	X
Place of prev. residence				X
Urban/rural	X	X	X	X
Sex	X	X	X	X
Age	X	X	X	X
Relation to household head	X	X	X	X
Marital status	X	X	X	X
Children born alive	X	X	X	X
Children living	X			
Citizenship				
Literacy	X		X	
School enrollment		X	X	X
Ed. attainment		X	X	X
Ed. qualification				
National/Ethnic origin	X	X	X	X
Language				
Religion	X	X	X	X
Household composition	X	X	X	X
Econ. active/inactive	X	X	X	X
Occupation	X	X	X	X
Industry	X	X	X	X
Occupational status	X	X	X	X
Income		X		X
Housing	X	X	X	X

Cayman Islands

British Crown Colony

CAPITAL: Georgetown on Grand Cayman.
STATISTICAL AGENCY: Department of Finance and Development.
NATIONAL REPOSITORY: Cayman Public Library, Georgetown.
MAIN U.S. REPOSITORY: New York Public Library.

A group of three islands (Grand Cayman, Little Cayman, Cayman Brac), there is not much known of its early history. It was a dependency of Jamaica until 1959 when it returned to being a colony. However, it was administered through the governor of Jamaica until 1962 when it received its own administrator. The censuses up to 1943 were *de facto* and self-enumerated; from 1943 on, they were *de jure* with *de facto* totals and canvassed.

1881

The earliest census from which there are results published was appended to the census of Jamaica in 1881. It contained data for the Grand Cayman only. There were schedules for households, plantations, and ships. The scope was age, sex, race, marital status, birthplace, religion, occupations, and infirmities.

1891

Again appended to the census of Jamaica, its scope was similar to the previous census. Religion was dropped, but education was added.

No census was taken in 1901.

1911

In addition to the items covered in 1881 and 1891, the scope of this census included religion (reinstated) and citizenship.

1921

This census had the same scope as that of 1911.

There was an enumeration of the Cayman Islands in 1934 (August 7), which was of limited scope. It was *de facto* and only sex and race data were found in comparison tables in later censuses.

Cayman Islands

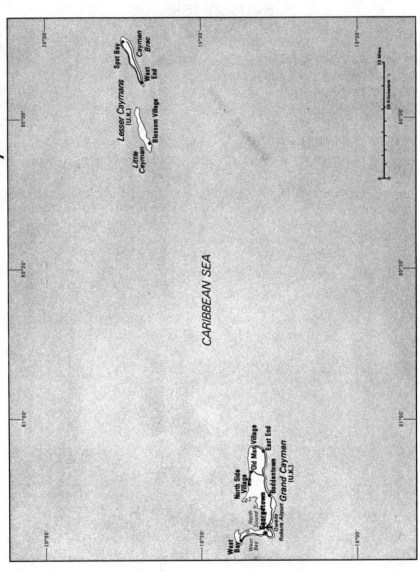

1943

Reflecting the basic changes occurring in the Jamaican census, this was *de jure* with *de facto* totals, canvassed, and mechanically tabulated. There was no separate administrative report for the Cayman Islands, and there were some slight variations. [See Jamaica 1943 for full entry.] The items not present in the Cayman tables are: usual residence, age (no completed months for infants), relation to household head (only numbers of persons per household), nationality (for immigrants only), economic activity (gainfully employed only), industry (only as basis of the occupational classification), income, and migration.

1960 (April 7)

Although no longer a dependency of Jamaica, the Cayman Islands' census was very similar to that of Jamaica. [See British West Indies 1960, West Indies section, for the full entry.] The following are the differences: Additions: acreage of land held, duration of union, and if child born alive in last twelve months was the first child.

Not in tables: year of immigration, total number of places lived, first-time job seekers, number of days worked per week, and characteristics of the household head.

Quality of the Census. Volume 1 was never published. There were more and better occupation and industry tables in the Cayman report than in the Turks and Caicos, but they still were not as detailed as those referring to Jamaica. Used the same classification systems for occupation and industry as Jamaica.

1970 (April 7)

Cayman Islands did not issue any separate results for this census. [See British West Indies 1970 for entry.] It was also not included in the migration volume. Volumes 3; 4.13; 4.16; 6.3; 7; 8 abc; 9.4; 10.3; 10.4 of the BWI 1970 set contain results for the Cayman Islands.

OTHER STATISTICAL PUBLICATIONS: Issued by Department of Finance and Development, *Statistical Abstract* (semiannually).

National Topic Chart

	1960	1970
De facto	X	X
Usual residence	X	X
Place of birth	X	X
Duration of residence	X	X
Place of prev. residence		
Urban/rural		
Sex	X	X
Age	X	X
Relation to household head	X	X
Marital status	X	X
Children born alive	X	X
Children living		
Citizenship		
Literacy	X	
School enrollment	X	X
Ed. attainment	X	X
Ed. qualification		
National/Ethnic origin	X	X
Language		
Religion	X	X
Household composition	X	X
Econ. active/inactive	X	X
Occupation	X	X
Industry	X	X
Occupational status		X
Income		
Housing	X	

Chile

Republic of Chile

CAPITAL: Santiago.
STATISTICAL AGENCY: Instituto Nacional de Estadística.
NATIONAL REPOSITORY: Library of the Instituto Nacional de Estadística, Santiago.
MAIN U.S. REPOSITORY: Population Research Center (Univ. of Texas).

Chile was part of the Spanish Empire until 1810, but only in 1833 was it constituted a republic. It is assumed that at the time of the discovery and colonization of the country the conquistadors had taken censuses within the territory, but no documents are available, and even the articles published at that time only vaguely mentioned the population of the land; therefore, not even an approximate number of inhabitants is known. During the independence days, the several attempts made for the realization of a general census were unsuccessful.

1831

A census was taken in the provinces of Chiloé, Valdivia, Concepción, Maule, and some "departamentos" of Santiago. In 1835, another census was taken in the provinces of Talca, Colchagua, Aconcagua, Coquimbo, and the rest of the "departamentos" in Santiago not included in 1831. The results of these two censuses were put together, and it was called the first general census of the republic. The scope of the census included age, sex, literacy, and number of naturalized citizens. Two other questionnaires were developed containing questions about fertility and mortality; however, the records were incomplete and inaccurate. Later, the number of undercount was estimated at 10 percent.

1843

Second general census of population was taken. Before the census, the Servicio Nacional de Estadística and several statistical committees were created with the intention of gathering all the information related to each province and assuring the success of the census operations. However, despite the preparations, the results were incomplete, and only the province of Maule published detailed results. For the rest of the country, records were limited to total population. A minimal 10 percent undercount was estimated.

Chile

Railroad
Road

BOUNDARY REPRESENTATION IS
NOT NECESSARILY AUTHORITATIVE

Isla Sala
y Gómez

Easter Island
(Isla de Pascua)

1854

The third general census of population was the first conducted by a central office, Oficina Central de Estadística, which established the system of decennial censuses. The country was divided into thirteen provinces and subdivided into "departamentos," "paroquias," "subdelegaciones," and districts (the smallest units). Urban population was obtained for the first time but not for all provinces. The scope of the census included type of dwelling, name, age, sex, marital status, usual profession or occupation, literacy, nationality, and presence of physical or mental disability that limited work activity.

The questions were printed on a general schedule, a form that prevailed until 1930 when the first household schedule was adopted. Coverage and accuracy of results varied in each province. The questions about nationality and occupation were not well understood, thus data had to be edited. Despite these problems 1854 was the most complete of the first three censuses.

All censuses were *de facto*, and canvasser was the method used for enumeration. Tabulation was manual. Indians and persons living in isolated areas were excluded.

1865

The fourth general census followed the same organization as the previous one. Isolated areas of difficult access and the Indian population were not enumerated making a total of 10 percent of undercount. The territory covered by the census included fourteen provinces and the territory of Magallanes, subdivided into "departamentos," "subdelegaciones," and districts. The scope was the same as 1854, but the distinction between urban and rural population was more accurate. In addition, the introductory part of the census presented comments on the history of the census and the total populations of some European, African, Asian, and American countries.

1875

The fifth general census of population was conducted by the Oficina Central de Estadística. It was *de facto* and canvassed on general schedules. Manual tabulation was used until 1920. The territory covered by the census included seventeen provinces (Bío-Bío, Linares, and Curicó added) and two territories (Magallanes and Angol). The scope of the census was the same as in 1854 and 1865, but the words urban/rural were added to the type of dwellings in the schedule. Indians were counted in some provinces but still were usually not part of the census. The amount of undercount was estimated at 10 percent. The introductory part included population density and some comparative tables for the years 1865 and 1875. The territory of Magallanes included Patagonia, Tierra del Fuego, and all the islands located in the southwest and northwest of the Strait of Magellan.

1885

The sixth general census of population, conducted by the same agency, followed the same organization as 1875. The territory covered by the census included twenty provinces (O'Higgins, Tarapacá, and Tacna added) and three territories (Antofagasta added). The scope included type of dwellings, name, sex, age, relationship to head of the family, marital status, occupation, language, literacy, school attendance, place of birth, place of residence (usual or temporary), vaccination, and nationality.

1895

The seventh general census of population varied very little from the 1885 census. As far as the scope, two topics were added—religion (if not Catholic) and parent's nationality. Twenty-three provinces and one territory were divided into "departamentos," "subdelegaciones," and districts. Indians were not enumerated.

1907

Eighth general census conducted by the Oficina Central de Estadística was *de facto*, canvassed, and the general schedule was presented in two colors; one was used for the enumeration of Indians (Araucanos). The term Indian applied only to aborigines living in villages and native compounds. Therefore, some pure Indians living among whites were counted in the general census, whereas some mestizos following the old habits and speaking the Indian language were counted as Indians.

Although in the previous censuses the population was separated into urban and rural, no criterion was adopted for classification. The 1907 census was the first one to set a technical definition for urban population, that is, places of 1,000 or more inhabitants, except for those places where the saltpeter farms were located. A list of houses was made in preparation for the census, which specified types of dwellings and whether inhabited or not.

The scope of the census included name, sex, age, marital status, occupation, religion (if not Catholic), nationality (if not Chilean), literacy, and infirmities (deaf-dumb or blind). Maps, graphs, a copy of schedule, a list of cities in alphabetical order with number of inhabitants, and the number of foreigners by sex were component parts of the introductory notes.

1920

Ninth general census of population was conducted by the Oficina Central de Estadística; the organization was very similar to the 1907 census. The scope included the topics of 1907 except that infirmities was dropped, and the following topics were added: industry, occupational status, property ownership, and physical and mental disability. The area covered by the census included twenty-three provinces and one territory.

1930

The tenth general census was conducted by the Dirección General de Estadística. It was *de facto* and canvassed on household schedules, which were used for the first time. The Indian reservations received schedules of a different color. The area covered by the census was the same as 1920, still divided into provinces, "departamentos," "subdelegaciones," and districts. The "departamentos" were also subdivided into communes and localities. The scope of the census included: name, locality (complete address), type of dwelling, property ownership, type of construction, number of rooms, running water, electricity, sex, age, marital status, physical disability, nationality, religion, literacy, education, occupation, industry, occupational status, date of first marriage, number of children living, and number of children dead. Race was not included because the population was almost all of European descent and the few Indians were incorporated in the rest of the population except for the Araucanos who lived separately and preserved primitive customs. Persons living in the cities and towns were classified as urban population, the remaining, rural. Mechanical tabulation was used for the first time.

1940

The eleventh census of population was conducted by the Dirección General de Estadística. The results were published in monthly issues from 1941 to 1946 of the *Revista Estadística Chilena*. Only a few libraries have the total number of issues. In order to remedy the lack of information, the Instituto Nacional de Estadística and the Centro Latinoaméricano de Demografía (CELADE) decided to reprint about 90 percent of the data in one volume. The information given in this handbook was taken from the reprint edition.

The tables presented the following topics: total population (provinces, "departamentos" and communes), age, sex, literacy, marital status, economic activity, occupation, industry, occupational status, and nationalities. Urban and rural population were distinguished, and additional tables with population of cities of 5,000 and more inhabitants as well as population of pueblos (population centers—1,000 to 5,000 inhabitants) were furnished.

Mechanical tabulation was used, and underenumeration was calculated at 4 percent. The results were not of the enumerated population but rather the results already adjusted by the Dirección Estadística, and no official documentation exists revealing the percentage of adjustment used.

The province of Tacna was not part of this census, since in 1930 it had been given back to Peru. The census covered twenty-five provinces divided into "departamentos," communes and districts.

1952 (April 24)

The twelfth general census of population, conducted by the Dirección General de Estadística, was *de facto* and canvassed. The household schedule was divided into three parts: geographical location, population, and housing. For the first time the census of housing was taken simultaneously with population. Mechanical tabulation and punched cards were used. Precensuses were taken with the objective of listing location and number of inhabitants per house as well as setting the boundaries of districts and other areas of enumeration.

For the first time sampling was used. A 2 percent sample tabulation was used for demographic analysis of population and housing characteristics. Two types of schedules were selected—those containing information for twelve persons or less and those with data about dwellings with thirteen persons or more. An additional schedule was used to verify the accuracy of the birth registration.

The area covered by the census included twenty-five provinces divided into "departamentos," communes, and districts. In the Antarctic territory eighty-seven persons were enumerated but they were included only in the introductory pages and the table of total population.

Definitions and Concepts. URBAN—population centers that had definite urban characteristics that were contributed by certain public and municipal services. AGE—in completed years and if less than one year the number of months was recorded. Tables presented age in single years and five-year groups. MARITAL STATUS—single, married (legally or common law), separated, widowed, and annulled. NATIONALITY—native born and foreigner (Chilean citizens and noncitizens). PLACE OF BIRTH—if native born, place or province of birth was recorded; if foreigner, country of birth. RELIGION—religious affiliation recorded. EDUCATION—literacy (ability to read and write in any language), school enrollment, and educational attainment (last degree completed and grade or course attending). In addition, if received military training and name of the armed force where military instruction was received. INFIRMITIES—blind or deaf-mute. ECONOMIC ACTIVITY—questions asked of all persons twelve years of age or more. Those considered economically active were: persons at work receiving wage or salary, unpaid family worker, presently unemployed, homemaker with a secondary paid occupation helping family income, and student with a secondary occupation. The following groups were considered economically inactive: homemaker without a secondary occupation, persons looking for a job for the first time, students, persons of independent income, the retired and pensioners, invalids, inmates or members of a religion living in seclusion, and other inactive persons. Only economically active persons answered questions about occupation, industry, and occupational status. OCCUPATION—usual occupation or last occupation in the case of unemployed. Classification based on COTA 1950—eleven groups and subgroups (two-digits). INDUSTRY—classification based on COTA 1950—nine major divisions. OCCUPATIONAL STATUS— categories were employer, own-account worker, employee (predominantly intellectual work, or white collar), worker (manual labor, or blue collar), housekeeper, and unpaid family worker. FAMILY ("familia censal")—group of people living in the same house, including servants and boarders.

Special Elements and Features. History of censuses with comparative tables since 1779 for several provinces, tables of population density from 1835 to 1952 by provinces, analysis of internal migration, urban and rural population of provinces since 1865 to 1952, population of most important cities from 1854-1952, copy of the schedules, maps, and graphs are included. First sample tabulation methods and results are described.

Quality of the Census. Whipple's Index made no reference to age accuracy. The country has a long history of censuses but regularity has not always been observed. Precensus of housing in urban areas improved location of houses and delimitation of zones per district. A pretest census was taken in Santiago where 125,000 persons were enumerated with the intention of improving the census questionnaire.

Publication Plan. Chile. Servicio Nacional de Estadística y Censos. *XII censo general de población y I de vivienda.* Santiago, n.d. Tomos 1-6, Regional volumes. Language of publication is Spanish.

1960 (November 29)

The thirteenth general census of population and second of housing were taken simultaneously. Conducted by the Dirección de Estadística y Censos, the census was *de facto*, and canvasser the method used to complete the household questionnaire. The schedule, like the previous census, was divided into three parts—geographical location, housing, and population questions. Two precensuses were taken for checking methods and procedures and served as basis for the general census. Electronic equipment and punched cards were used for tabulation. A 2 percent sample tabulation was used to speed up the availability of information of the basic characteristics of the population. The area covered by the census included twenty-five provinces and the Antarctic territory. The provinces were divided into "departamentos," communes, and districts. In the Antarctic territory 202 persons were enumerated but few tables were presented.

Definitions and Concepts. AGE, MARITAL STATUS, PLACE OF BIRTH, LITERACY, RELIGION and URBAN—the same as 1952. PHYSICAL DISABILITY and NATIONALITY were dropped from the schedules. PLACE OF RESIDENCE—duration of residence (year moved into the present residence), whether permanent or temporary resident, name of country or province of previous residence, causes of moving, and whether moved from urban or rural area. EDUCATION—school enrollment and educational attainment (last degree completed). FERTILITY—question asked of all women twelve years of age or older: number of children born alive. ECONOMIC ACTIVITY—reference period was the census day. Those considered economically active were the following: employed, unemployed, and persons looking for a job for the first time. The economically inactive were: homemakers, students, retired or pensioners, persons of independent income, invalids or inmates, and others not included in the economically active population. Questions were asked of all persons twelve years of age and older. OCCUPATION—Classification based on COTA 1960, twelve major groups and subgroups (two-digits). If more than one occupation, the main occupation was recorded; the unemployed recorded the last occupation, and the category "looking for job for the first time" recorded training, if any. INDUSTRY—classification based on ISIC, eleven divisions and major groups. However, tables presented only the eleven divisions. OCCUPATIONAL STATUS—categories included: employer, own-account worker, employee (white collar), laborer (blue collar), domestic worker (housekeeper, cook, babysitter, butler), paid family worker and unpaid family worker. HOUSEHOLD—constituted the occupants of a dwelling, whether or not related by blood, also guests and servants.

Special Elements and Features. Nationality and physical disability were dropped, whereas fertility and place of residence were added. List of occupations and industries, total population of Greater Santiago and major cities, total population of 1940, 1952, and 1960 by age and sex, and tables of internal migration are included in the introductory notes.

Quality of the Census. Whipple's Index classified age data in category I—highly accurate data. Methods and procedures as well as modification of the schedule were tested by two precensuses. Sample tabulation increased rapid availability of basic data. Census office is permanent.

Publication Plan. Chile. Dirección de Estadística y Censos. *XIII censo de población, 29 de noviembre de 1960*. Santiago, 1963-1965. Series A and B in 26 volumes, whole country and province volumes. Unpublished data are available. Language of publication is Spanish.

1970 (April 22)

The fourteenth general census of population and third of housing were conducted by the Instituto Nacional de Estadística, formerly the Dirección de Estadística y Censos. The census was *de facto* and canvasser the method used on household schedules. The questionnaire was divided in the same fashion as the previous census. Tabulation was computerized. A 5 percent sample tabulation was used to provide faster availability of results. The results of the sample were tabulated on the level of communes and localities of 150,000 inhabitants or more rather than only on the national and state levels as in the previous census. The area covered by the census was the same as 1960. In 1961 the Antarctic territory became part of the province of Magallanes.

Definitions and Concepts. HOUSEHOLD—one or more persons, whether or not related by blood, who occupied part or a whole dwelling. The household might be private, including members of the family, boarders (no more than five), guests, and servants; or nonprivate (group quarters), including persons living in the same dwelling for reasons of health, religion, discipline, studies, and so forth. AGE—same as 1960, but for persons less than one year old, "00" was recorded. Tables presented in single years and standard five-year age groups. MARITAL STATUS—same as the previous censuses. RELIGION—whether Catholic or other religious denomination. PLACE OF BIRTH—for native born, province, commune, or locality of birth. Foreigners recorded their country of origin. PLACE OF RESIDENCE—usual place of residence and previous place of residence (five years before the census—1965). Usual residents were persons living in a place for six or more months whether or not intending to remain in the same residence and persons that although not living in the same residence for a period of six months had the intention of staying. EDUCATION—the same as 1960 with slightly different wording. The questions were asked of all persons five years of age and older. ECONOMIC ACTIVITY—questions asked of all persons twelve years of age and older; the reference week was April 13 to 18. Those considered economically active were: employed, working or temporarily absent from the job, unemployed looking for a job, and looking for a job for the first time. The economically inactive were: retired, pensioners, persons of independent income, students, homemakers, invalids and inmates. OCCUPATION—main occupation. Classification based on COTA 1970, eleven major groups and subgroups (two-digit). INDUSTRY—classification based on ISIC 1968; only the ten divisions were presented in the tables. OCCUPATIONAL STATUS—employer, own-account worker, employee, manual laborer, domestic servant, and unpaid family worker. FERTILITY—asked of all women fifteen and over: number of children born alive, number of children born dead, number of children still living, and number of children who were born alive but since died.

Special Elements and Features. A larger sample tabulation (5 percent) was taken and the results were tabulated for smaller areas than in the previous censuses. The results of the Antarctic territory were included in the province of Magallanes. A larger number of cross-classifications were presented than in previous censuses.

Quality of the Census. The census office is permanent, but due to no report giving the methods, procedures, and the like, it is not known whether precensuses or a postenumeration survey were taken. Whipple's Index category was III—approximate age data.

Publication Plan. Four sets of results were published. Chile. Instituto Nacional de Estadística. *XIV censo nacional de población y III de vivienda, abril 1970.* (1) Muestra de adelanto de cifras censales (Vols. 1-14); (2) Caracteristicas básicas de la población (26v.); (3) Viviendas, hogares y familias (26v.); and (4) Población. Resultados definitivos del XIV censo de población, 1970 (Vols. 1-26). Unpublished results and computer tapes are available. Language of publication is Spanish.

OTHER STATISTICAL PUBLICATIONS: Issued by Instituto Nacional de Estadística, *Anuario Estadístico, Compendio Estadístico* (annually), *Demografía* (annually), *Informativo Estadístico* (quarterly).

National Topic Chart

	1952	1960	1970
De facto	X	X	X
Usual residence		X	X
Place of birth	X	X	X
Duration of residence		X	X
Place of prev. residence		X	X
Urban/rural	X	X	X
Sex	X	X	X
Age	X	X	X
Relation to household head	X	X	X
Marital status	X	X	X
Children born alive		X	X
Children living			X
Citizenship	X		
Literacy	X	X	X
School enrollment	X	X	X
Ed. attainment	X	X	X
Ed. qualification	X	X	X
National/Ethnic origin			
Language			
Religion	X	X	X
Household composition	X	X	X
Econ. active/inactive	X	X	X
Occupation	X	X	X
Industry	X	X	X
Occupational status	X	X	X
Income			
Housing	X	X	X

Colombia

Republic of Colombia

CAPITAL: Bogotá.
STATISTICAL AGENCY: Departamento Administrativo Nacional de Estadística (DANE).
NATIONAL REPOSITORY: Banco Nacional de Datos—Biblioteca (DANE).
MAIN U.S. REPOSITORY: Library of Congress (early censuses) and Benson Collection (Univ. of Texas).

During the colonial period (1538-1810) the Kingdom of New Granada covered an area that corresponds today to Colombia, Ecuador, and Venezuela. Toward the end of the eighteenth century, movements for independence from Spain had developed, and a ruling junta deposed the viceroy of New Granada in 1810. However, it was in 1819 that independence was securely achieved. Since then, constant changes in territorial expansion have occurred, and Colombia has existed under five different names: Gran Colombia in the early days of independence while still united with Venezuela and Ecuador; Republic of New Granada, in 1830 when separated from the other two republics; Grenadine confederation, in 1858, when the various provinces became federal states; United States of Colombia in 1863; and Republic of Colombia, its present name, adopted in 1886. In 1903 present-day Panama separated from Colombia and formed an independent nation.

The organization and methods that were applied to the censuses taken up to the twentieth century are not known. In addition, there were no official publications, and the results vary among sources. Population counts and estimates have been made since 1770 and may be found in the *Anuario Estadístico de 1940*. Other official records provided the information that follows.

1825

The results of the census included total population (divided into broad age groups), marital status, sex, and civil condition (free or slave population). A table with total population of indigenous tribes was also published. These results, however, were not considered accurate because of the large under-enumeration.

Colombia

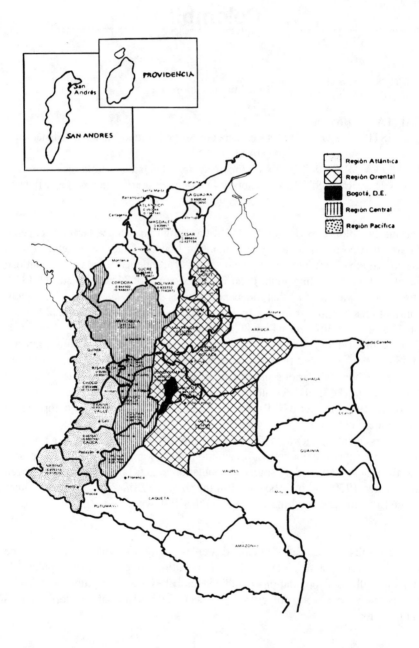

1835

Census of the Republic of New Granada covered twenty provinces divided into cantons. Total population by sex, marital status, age, and religious groups was published in the *Gaceta de la Nueva Granada*, No. 211.

1843

The results of this census were considered only an approximation of reality. A large underenumeration was estimated. The scope was similar to that of 1835, but in addition, the number of foreign born, number of births and deaths, number of buildings and inmates of institutions, and number of schools and students per province were recorded.

In 1851 and 1864 records are limited to total population. In 1858 it was established that a census should be taken every eight years. However, regularity has not been observed in the past or in the present. From 1871 to 1912 some partial censuses were taken, and an attempt was made of a general census in 1905, but the results were considerate inaccurate.

1912

General census of population had the first separate official publication devoted entirely to census results. It was conducted by the Junta Central del Censo Nacional on a *de jure* and a *de facto* basis. A combination of self-enumeration and canvasser was utilized to record information on individual and household schedules. A list of houses was made before the census to improve coverage. The scope included name, sex, age, marital status, nationality, place of birth, place of residence, relationship to head of household, religion, literacy, school enrollment, race, occupation, occupational status, infirmities, and vaccination. Although the best census yet taken in the country, it was not approved by the Colombian congress.

1918

General census of population conducted by the Dirección General de Estadística. It was established that a census should be taken every ten years. The organization and method were the same as 1912, and the scope was virtually the same except that ownership and urban or rural location of property were recorded.

1928

Although an extensive census, the results were not approved by the congress because of the large overenumeration of the inhabitants.

1938

General census of population conducted by the Contraloría General de la República on a *de facto* basis. Canvasser was the method used to gather information on household schedules. The census of housing was taken simultaneously, and for the first time, mechanical tabulation was utilized. The territory covered by the census included fourteen "departamentos," four "intendencias," and six "comisarías," subdivided into "municipios" and "localidades." The scope was age, sex, marital status, education, nationality, religion, occupation, and industry.

1951 (May 9)

The general census of population was conducted simultaneously with census of housing by DANE. Its organization and methods followed the recommendations of COTA 1950. The census was *de facto*, and canvasser was the method used to record information on household schedules. Tabulation was mechanical. Information was tabulated for "departamentos," "intendencias," and "comisarías," subdivided into "municipios" and capital cities.

Definitions and Concepts. URBAN—cities with 1,500 or more inhabitants. HOUSEHOLD—persons living in the same house, related or not by blood, and sharing food arrangements. AGE—in completed years. Recorded in standard five-year age groups and number of months if less than one year of age. MARITAL STATUS—categories were: single, married, widowed, common-law marriage, and separated. PLACE OF BIRTH—for native born, municipality, and for foreign born, the continent of origin were recorded. NATIONALITY—country of citizenship. EDUCATION—literacy (ability to read and write) and educational attainment (highest degree completed). ECONOMIC ACTIVITY—economically active were all persons twelve years of age and older who were employers, employees, self-employed, family workers, or laborers. There is no indication whether or not unemployed persons were included. Inactive were homemakers, students, pensioners, persons of independent income, invalids, inmates of institutions, and beggars. OCCUPATION—main occupation. Classification based on COTA 1950, major groups and groups (two-digits). INDUSTRY—classification based on ISIC, nine divisions and major groups (two-digits). OCCUPATIONAL STATUS—Categories were employer, self-employed, unpaid family worker, employee, and laborer.

Special Elements and Features: Fertility, language, and religion were not part of the census. Data about unemployment and income, although part of the schedule, were not published. Maps and graphs were included but a copy of the schedule was not published.

Quality of the Census. Not cited in Whipple's Index. Some "municipios" and sections of the country were not enumerated, but it was estimated that they represented 1.7 percent of the total population of the country. Tabulation and publication of results started two years after the census. The population of those "municipios" not enumerated was estimated, based on the method of geometric growth of population.

Publication Plan. Colombia. DANE. *Censo de población de 1951.* Bogotá, 1954-1959. One summary and sixteen department volumes. Language of publication is Spanish.

1964 (July 15)

The thirteenth census of population was conducted by DANE. The number of general censuses of population taken up until now vary according to the source consulted. This work followed the number printed in the 1964 title page. The census was *de facto*, and canvasser was the method used to gather information on household schedules. The census of housing was taken simultaneously. Tabulation was computerized. For the first time, remote areas of the country were directly enumerated instead of estimated. The territory covered by the census was divided into eighteen "departamentos," four "intendencias," and five "comisarías." Bogotá was declared a special district in 1954.

Definitions and Concepts. AGE—recorded in completed years as of last birthday and tabulated in single years and standard five-year age groups. PLACE OF BIRTH—same as 1951. MARITAL STATUS—same as 1951 but it was pointed out that divorced persons were not recorded because divorce was not legally recognized in the country. HOUSEHOLD—same as 1951, however, the term "familia censal" was replaced by "hogar censal." PLACE OF RESIDENCE—previous place of residence, duration, and whether located in rural or urban areas were recorded. EDUCATION—literacy of those fifteen years of age and older, literacy of those seven years and older (for comparison with previous census), and educational attainment (highest degree completed). ECONOMIC ACTIVITY—economically active were all persons twelve years and older who were engaged in a paid occupation on the day of the census; persons without an occupation who had worked at least nine months during the year before the census; unpaid family workers who had worked for at least four months; and unemployed persons looking for a job either for the first time or with previous experience. Inactive were homemakers, students, pensioners, persons of independent income, invalids, inmates of institutions, religious persons living in isolation, and other persons without salary. Persons dependent on agriculture (those working in this activity and their dependents) were recorded, but only if they were present at the date of the census. OCCUPATION—classification based on COTA 1960, major groups and subgroups (two-digits). INDUSTRY—classification based on ISIC, divisions and subgroups (two-digits). OCCUPATIONAL STATUS—categories were employer, self-employed, unpaid family worker, employee, and laborer.

Special Elements and Features. Place of previous residence and time of permanence (internal migration) were introduced in this census. A cross-classification of internal migration by age, education, and economic activities was provided. Nationality was dropped. Information on the unemployed was available. Comparative tables for 1951 and 1964 were included in the reports.

Quality of the Census. The coverage of the census was considered satisfactory with an estimated error of 1.8 percent. A census test was taken in preparation for the final enumeration, with the intention of checking adequacy of questionnaires as well as revision of maps. A precensus was taken in February 1964 in all cities of 10,000 and more inhabitants. In this census the number of buildings and their inhabitants were recorded. A postenumeration survey was conducted in thirteen cities in the country. One percent of households was selected in the six most populated cities and ten percent selected for the remaining seven cities. Whipple's Index classified age data into category IV—rough data.

Publication Plan. Colombia. DANE. *XIII censo nacional de población y II censo nacional de edificios y viviendas (julio 15 de 1964).* Bogotá, D.E., 1967-1971. One population and one housing volume for the whole country and four departments; a single volume combined population and housing for each of the remaining departments. Unpublished data are available and language of publication is Spanish.

1973 (October 24)

The fourteenth general census of population and third of housing were conducted simultaneously by the Departamento Administrativo Nacional de Estadística. The census was *de facto*, and canvassers recorded information on household schedules. A 4 percent sampling tabulation was made to provide quick access to topics investigated in the census. The territory covered by the census included twenty-three "departamentos," five "intendencias," and four "comisarías." Some of the "departamentos" were subdivided thus creating some difficulties for comparisons with 1964. Tabulation was computerized. The information was taken from works already published. All final results volumes have not been published as yet.

Definitions and Concepts. URBAN—same as 1951 and 1964. AGE—same as 1964 but the number of months for persons less than one year of age was not recorded. Presented in standard five-year age groups and single years. MARITAL STATUS—the category "divorced" was added. The number of persons who did not answer the question was recorded, and the concept of separated considered as disrupted marriage (legal or common law) was added. PLACE OF BIRTH—same as 1951 and 1964. PLACE OF RESIDENCE—same as 1964. EDUCATION—questions asked of all persons five years of age and older. Literacy, school enrollment (new), and educational attainment. ECONOMIC ACTIVITY—for all persons ten years and older. The reference period (the week before the census) was introduced. In 1964, the age limit was twelve years of age instead of ten. Labor force concept was utilized. The economically active were all persons working (employed) for salary and wage, unpaid family workers who worked fifteen hours or more during the reference week, unemployed persons looking for job (for the first time or not). Inactive population included the retired, pensioners, students, persons of independent income, homemakers, inmates of institutions, and invalids. The number of months worked in 1973 was also recorded. OCCUPATION—a national classification of occupations was utilized (CNO, 1970), ten major groups and the category "without occupation" were presented in the sampling results; the final results are not yet available. These groups were rearranged in a few tables to provide comparisons with 1964.

INDUSTRY—classification based on ISIC, 1968, ten divisions (sampling results). OCCUPATIONAL STATUS—categories: employee, laborer, employer, self-employed, unpaid family worker, domestic worker. INCOME—for the first time recorded. Income of any kind recorded in twelve groups. FERTILITY—for the first time included. Questions asked of all females fifteen years of age and older: number of children ever born alive, and number of children still living.

Special Elements and Features. Sample tabulation employed for the first time. Income and fertility included for the first time. Education questions were expanded to include school enrollment. Labor force concept substituted gainfully occupied. Age limit for inclusion into the labor force changed to ten years of age. Changes in the classification of occupation requires regrouping for comparisons with 1964. Maps and a copy of the schedule were included.

Quality of the Census. Final results are becoming available. Some preliminary results have been published in separate issues of monthly bulletins in addition to final results obtained by sampling (4 percent of households). A postenumeration survey was conducted. Whipple's Index category was not available; it was stated, however, that in comparison to the 1964 census the results for 1973 related to age were more accurate.

Publication Plan. Colombia. DANE. *XIV censo nacional de población y III de vivienda, octobre 24 de 1973*. Bogotá, D.E., 1980-. One general resume (whole country) and one or two volumes for each department. There were also one preliminary, four advanced samples, and one coverage adjustment volumes. Printed final result volumes have only selected tables. The rest are available on computer tapes; a guide is printed in each volume. Unpublished data and computer tapes are available. Language of publication is Spanish.

OTHER STATISTICAL PUBLICATIONS: Issued by DANE, *Anuario Demográfico, Anuario General de Estadística, Boletín Mensual de Estadística*.

National Topic Chart

	1951	1964	1973
De facto	X	X	X
Usual residence			
Place of birth	X	X	X
Duration of residence		X	X
Place of prev. residence		X	X
Urban/rural	X	X	X
Sex	X	X	X
Age	X	X	X
Relation to household head	X	X	X
Marital status	X	X	X
Children born alive			X
Children living			X
Citizenship	X		
Literacy	X	X	X
School enrollment			X
Ed. attainment	X	X	X
Ed. qualification			
National/Ethnic origin			
Language			
Religion			
Household composition	X	X	X
Econ. active/inactive	X	X	X
Occupation	X	X	X
Industry	X	X	X
Occupational status	X	X	X
Income			
Housing	X	X	X

Costa Rica

Republic of Costa Rica

CAPITAL: San José.
STATISTICAL AGENCY: Dirección General de Estadística y Censos.
NATIONAL REPOSITORY: ?
MAIN U.S. REPOSITORY: New York Public Library (early censuses), Population Research Center (Univ. of Texas).

Although Costa Rica was colonized by Spain in 1564, records on its population started only after independence in 1821. A population count made in 1824 to provide basic numbers for the election of representatives was not accurate since the population was not totally enumerated. In 1844 another population count took place; however, the methods used are not known, and the records are limited to total population by provinces, main cities, and villages. The first recognized general census was taken in 1864, when it was established that a census should be taken every ten years. Regularity, however, was not observed except for the last two censuses (1963 and 1973).

1864

The first general census was conducted by the Oficina Central de Estadística on a *de facto* basis. Canvasser mainly and some self-enumeration were the methods used to record information on "house" schedules (the household was equated with the house). The indigenous population was not enumerated, only estimated. The territory was divided into six provinces, subdivided into cantons and districts. Tabulation was manual. The scope included name, sex, age, infirmities, religion, marital status, occupation or profession, place of residence, place of birth of foreign born, and literacy.

1883

Second census of population was conducted by the Dirección General de Estadística, which was created in the same year. The organization was virtually the same as the previous one, but the territory covered by the census included seven provinces divided into cantons, cities, villages, and pueblos. The province of Limon was established in 1882. The indigenous population was still not enumerated, and for the remainder of the population the undercount was esti-

COSTA RICA

International boundary
Provincia boundary
⊛ National capital
○ Provincia capital
Railroad
Road

0   20   40 Miles
0   20   40 Kilometers

ISLA DE COCO
0 1 2 Miles

mated at 10 percent. The scope was the same as 1864. Comparative tables of total population for the years of 1844, 1864, 1875, and 1883 were also presented.

1892

The third census of population was conducted by the Dirección General de Estadística, and organization was basically the same as the previous censuses. Territorial division was not altered. The scope included total population, age, sex, marital status, nationality, religion, occupation or profession, and literacy. Underenumeration was estimated at between 6 and 10 percent.

1904

Census of the city of San José (capital of the country). The scope included age, sex, marital status, religion, and literacy for the city and its districts.

1927

Thirty-five years had passed before the fourth general census of population was taken. The census was conducted by the Oficina Nacional del Censo, which was created in the same year. It was *de jure*, and canvasser was the method used to gather information on household schedules. The territorial divisions remained the same. The scope included total population, age, sex, race, marital status, place of birth, nationality, education, industry, occupation, infirmities, relationship to head of the family, and property ownership. The results, however, were only published in 1960, and by this time many tables were missing. In addition, the large underenumeration generated controversies about accuracy of results.

1950 (May 22)

After twenty-three years, the fifth general census of population was taken in conjunction with the census of agriculture. It was conducted by the Dirección General de Estadística y Censos on a *de jure* basis, and canvasser was the method utilized to record information on household schedules. Tabulation was mechanical. The territory covered by the census included the seven provinces divided into cantons and districts. Methods and concepts were based on the recommendations of COTA 1950.

Definitions and Concepts. URBAN—the main districts of the cantons selected by the existence of social services and amenities. HOUSEHOLD ("familia censal") —group of persons, related or not by blood, living in the same place and sharing food arrangements. AGE—completed years as of last birthday. Presented in single years and standard five-year age groups. For persons less than one year the number of months was recorded; if less than one month, the number of days. RACE—simple observation criterion. In case of doubt, the geographic location, place of birth, nationality, and mother tongue were taken into consideration. Categories were whites and mestizos, blacks, yellows, Indians, and others. MARITAL STATUS—single, married, separated, common-law marriage, widowed, and divorced. EDUCATION—literacy, school enrollment (new), and educational attainment (first time results were available). PLACE OF BIRTH—province and canton for native born and country of birth for foreigners. NATIONALITY—country of citizenship. LANGUAGE—mother tongue. ECONOMIC ACTIVITIES—economically active included persons twelve years and older who were employed during the month before the census and all those who were unemployed and capable of working, new or experienced, looking or not looking for a job. Inactive were: minors, students, homemakers, pensioners, the retired, persons of independent income. OCCUPATION—main occupation or last occupation in case of unemployed. Classification based on COTA 1950, major groups, groups, and subgroups (three-digits). INDUSTRY—classification based on ISIC, ten divisions and subgroups (two-digits). OCCUPATIONAL STATUS—employee, self-employed, unpaid family worker, and employer.

Special Elements and Features. Historical notes of earlier censuses; comparative tables of earlier censuses; maps, graphs, and a copy of schedules were in the report. Fertility was not asked, but tables based on the number of children less than five years of age per 1,000 women between the ages of fifteen and forty-four were presented. Place of birth was recorded on the level of provinces and cantons instead of just provinces as in 1927. Migration data was obtained by comparing data on place of birth and place of residence. Race categories were different from those in 1927. Educational attainment and school enrollment data for the first time were available. Economic activities questions were expanded.

Quality of the Census. A precensus was taken to improve quality and coverage of final enumeration. Training programs were provided for enumerators and technical personnel involved in the census. Underenumeration was considered low, not reaching 5 percent. Whipple's Index classified age data into category IV—rough data.

Publication Plan. Costa Rica. Dirección General de Estadística y Censos. *Censo de población de Costa Rica (22 de mayo de 1950).* San José, 1953. 1 volume. Language of publication is Spanish.

1963 (April 1)

The sixth general census of population was conducted by the Dirección General de Estadística y Censos on a *de jure* basis. Canvasser was the method used to record information on household schedules. The censuses of housing and agriculture were taken simultaneously. Tabulation was mechanical. For the first time, sample tabulation was used to speed up availability of census results (5 percent of households randomly selected). The territory was divided into seven provinces, subdivided into cantons and districts. For census purposes districts were subdivided into zones and segments (new).

Definitions and Concepts. AGE, MARITAL STATUS and EDUCATION—same as 1950. URBAN—same as 1950, except that in the province of San José several districts were considered urban and not just the main district. In the province of Cartago, two districts forming the city of Cartago were urban while the cantons of San Pablo, Nandayure, and Buenos Ayres were all rural. MET-

ROPOLITAN AREA—for the first time included in the census, it corresponded to the central canton (main) and the eight surrounding cantons in the province of San José. PLACE OF RESIDENCE—previous residence (new) and duration of residence (new). PLACE OF BIRTH—place of residence of mother at the time of birth of the enumerated persons (canton or foreign country, if the case). NATIONALITY—citizens and noncitizens were distinguished and in case of double nationality, the country of birth. SOCIAL SECURITY—for the first time the number of social security receivers was recorded. ECONOMIC ACTIVITIES— questions asked of all persons twelve years of age and older. Economically active were: employed persons during the reference period (a month before the census) and persons unemployed but able to work. A minimum of six working days during the reference month was required for the person to be considered employed. Inactives were students, homemakers, pensioners, persons of independent income, inmates of institutions, and invalids. OCCUPATION—classification based on ISCO, major groups and groups (two-digits). Duration of occupation was also recorded (months worked one year before the census). INDUSTRY— classification based on ISIC, divisions, major groups and subgroups (three-digits). Not all tables presented complete occupational and industrial classifications. OCCUPATIONAL STATUS—categories were employer, unpaid family worker, employee, and self-employed. INCOME—for the first time recorded, gross income during the reference month.

Special Elements and Features. A housing census was taken simultaneously with population census. Place of residence, social security recipients, income, and months worked in past year were new questions introduced in this census. Census data stressed economic activities. There was also a separate volume with data about the metropolitan area of San José, including not only results of population and housing census of 1963 but results from the economic census taken in 1964 as well. Language and race were dropped.

Quality of the Census. A test census was taken to improve accuracy and coverage as well as to provide training for enumerators and to check questions to be included in the schedules. The use of sample tabulation provided faster availability of results. Evaluation of results was done through revision of 5 percent of segments (that is, the smallest division) including twenty-five units in urban areas and sixty units in rural areas of the country. Whipple's Index classified age data within the category III—approximate data.

Publication Plan. Costa Rica. Dirección General de Estadística y Censos. *1963 censo de población.* San José, 1966. There is also a volume on the San José metropolitan area and one on evaluation. Language of publication is Spanish.

1973 (May 14)

The seventh general census of population was conducted by the Dirección General de Estadística y Censos on a *de jure* basis. It was the first census taken at a ten year interval. Canvasser was the method utilized to gather information on household schedules. The censuses of housing and agriculture were taken simultaneously with that of population. Tabulation was computerized for the first time. The territory was divided into seven provinces, subdivided into cantons and districts. In addition, data were also available for metropolitan areas, capital cities, and total population for inhabited centers ("centros poblados") and neighborhoods.

Definitions and Concepts. AGE, MARITAL STATUS, PLACE OF BIRTH, and EDUCATION—the same as 1963. FERTILITY—for the first time recorded: number of children born alive, and number of children still living. PLACE OF RESIDENCE—usual place (five years or more). If residing in the place where enumerated for less than five years, the name of canton or country of previous residence was recorded. NATIONALITY—same as 1963, except that persons with double nationality recorded the nationality of their preference. SOCIAL SECURITY—number of social security receivers and type. ECONOMIC ACTIVITY—lower age limit for questions was twelve years; reference period, the week before the census. Economically active were persons working or with a job (for an hour or more during the reference week); unemployed able to work and looking for a job; and unemployed looking for a job for the first time. Inactives were students, homemakers, persons of independent income, the retired, invalids, pensioners, and inmates of institutions. The number of hours worked during the reference week was recorded for the first time. OCCUPATION— main occupation. Classification based on ISCO, major groups, groups, and subgroups (three-digits). INDUSTRY—classification based on ISIC, divisions, major groups, groups, and units (four-digits). OCCUPATIONAL STATUS— categories were paid worker, own-account worker, employer, and unpaid family worker. INCOME—gross income received per month, week, or daily according to the case.

Special Elements and Features. Fertility and number of hours worked were recorded for the first time. Previous place of residence and time worked were not recorded. The question on social security was expanded. The economic activity period of reference was changed from one month to one week before the census. A list of occupations and industries was furnished. In addition to the metropolitan area of San José, a separate volume was published with data on the capital cities of all provinces.

Quality of the Census. Remapping of regions, particularly within the metropolitan area of San José, facilitated completeness of coverage. A test census was taken in six districts in the provinces of San José and Alajuela to improve organization and methods as well as to check questions to be included in the schedules. An evaluation of the results of the 1973 census, based on comparison of birth and death certificates and the results of the previous censuses (1950, 1963), was published separately in conjunction with the population projections by sex and ages, 1950-2000. Whipple's Index category was III—approximate age data.

Publication Plan. Costa Rica. Dirección General de Estadística y Censos. *Censos nacionales de 1973.* San José, 1973-1977? Nos. 1-12. Three volumes on agriculture, three on housing, and six on population. There is also an evaluation volume. Language of publication is Spanish.

OTHER STATISTICAL PUBLICATIONS: Issued by Dirección General de Estadística y Censos, *Anuario Estadístico, Estadística Vital* (annually), *Población de la República de Costa Rica por Provincias, Cantones y Distritos* (semi-annually).

National Topic Chart

	1950	1963	1973
De facto			
Usual residence	X	X	X
Place of birth	X	X	X
Duration of residence		X	X
Place of prev. residence		X	
Urban/rural	X	X	X
Sex	X	X	X
Age	X	X	X
Relation to household head	X	X	X
Marital status	X	X	X
Children born alive			X
Children living			X
Citizenship	X	X	X
Literacy	X˙	X	X
School enrollment	X	X	X
Ed. attainment	X	X	X
Ed. qualification			
National/Ethnic origin	X		
Language	X		
Religion			
Household composition	X	X	X
Econ. active/inactive	X	X	X
Occupation	X	X	X
Industry	X	X	X
Occupational status	X	X	X
Income		X	X
Housing		X	X

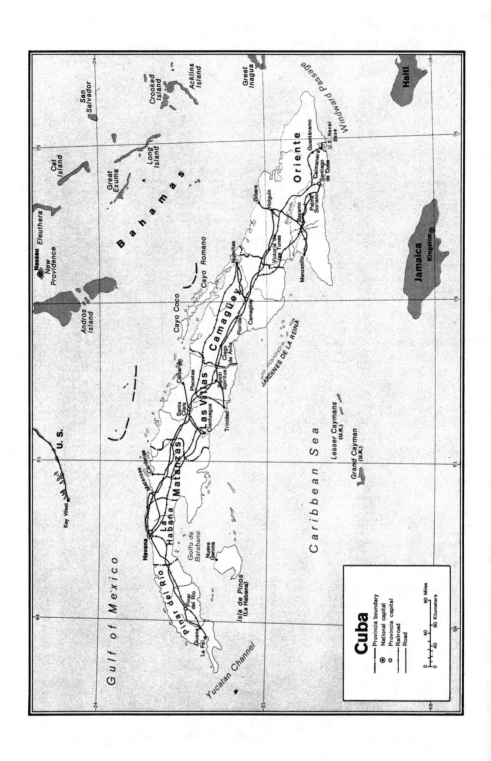

Cuba

Cuba

Republic of Cuba

CAPITAL: Havana.
STATISTICAL AGENCY: Dirección Central de Estadística.
NATIONAL REPOSITORY: Centro de Información Científico-Técnica, Comité
Estatal de Estadísticas, Havana.
MAIN U.S. REPOSITORY: Population Research Center (Univ. of Texas).

Cuba was discovered by Columbus in 1492 and remained under Spanish rule until 1898 when it became an independent republic under U.S. protection. In 1934 the United States gave up the right to intervene in Cuban affairs.

Official publications with the results of earlier enumerations in Cuba are scarce. A lengthy list of secondary sources is available (1907 census) starting from the year 1768 up until 1899, the end of the Spanish colonial period. The exact nature of the data of the earlier enumeration is a matter of discussion, but 1774 seems to be the first "census" of the island. After this date a series of counts and estimates were made in 1787, 1804, 1810, 1819, 1825, 1849, 1850, 1852, 1855, 1859, 1860, 1867, 1869, 1874, and 1879. However, these records were generally rejected for their lack of completeness and accuracy. The only alleged census information gathered from secondary sources that may have some credibility are those following.

1774

Total population by sex and race was recorded. In addition, the "colored" race was divided into two categories, free or slave. A list of buildings and occupied dwellings was also available.

1792 and 1817

Recorded the same type of information as 1774.

1827

The island was divided into three "departamentos" (states)—Occidental, Oriental, and Central. In addition to a simple summary of population like the earlier censuses, description of public wealth classified by products was furnished. The census was considered a good one; however, there is no official publication of its results. Some data from this census can be found in the introductory part of the 1841 census.

1841

This is the first official census taken on the island for which primary source material is available. The census was taken on a *de facto* basis, and canvasser was the method used to record information on general schedules. The scope included number of inhabitants, sex, age, marital status, and race. Results were presented by "departamentos," towns and urban districts grouped as "poblaciones," and rural districts (sugar plantations, coffee plantations and farms).

1846

Nonofficial census that contained the same number of questions as asked in 1841. The results were considered inaccurate with a large estimated undercount among the slave population.

1861

Taken in conjunction with the census of Spain by the Centro General de Estadística. No details of organization were furnished. The scope included number of inhabitants, race or color, age, marital status, sex, civil status (slave or free), occupation, literacy, nationality, residence, and infirmities.

1877

Third official census of the colonial period. It was also taken in conjunction with Spain, on a *de facto* and a *de jure* basis. The scope included number of inhabitants, nationality, race, and sex.

1887

The fourth official census was also taken on a *de facto* and a *de jure* basis, and canvasser was the method used. The scope consisted of the number of inhabitants, sex, nationality, and race.

The accuracy of these censuses (1861, 1877, and 1887) was considered questionable for numerous reasons, including the continuous state of revolution occurring in this period and until the Spanish American War.

1899

The first national census was conducted by the War Department of the United States. Results were published in English and Spanish. This census was *de facto*, and canvasser was the method used for gathering information on general schedules. Although following the general design used in the eleventh census of the United States, a reduced number of questions was asked. Tabulation was mechanical. The scope included name, relationship to head of the family, color, sex, age, marital status, place of birth, citizenship, illegitimacy, occupation, literacy, school attendance, and some housing questions. The country was divided into six provinces, subdivided into municipal districts and "barrios" (wards).

1907

Second national census was conducted by the Oficina del Censo under the direction of the United States provisional governor. The census followed the same organization as the previous one, but the report was published in Spanish. Later an extract was published in English. The scope was very similar to the 1899 census, but the number of persons per family, number of families, number of public schools, and number of teachers were added.

1919

The third national census was conducted by the Dirección General del Censo. The report was printed in English and Spanish. The census was *de jure*, and canvasser was the method used to gather information on individual schedules. Mechanical tabulation and punched cards were utilized. The electoral census was taken simultaneously, but the industrial and agricultural features usually present in the population census were abolished. The scope included: number of inhabitants, age, sex, illegitimate children, place of residence, race, school attendance, literacy, academic or professional title, marital status, occupation, industry, economic activity, citizenship, place of birth, relationship to head of the family, number of families, and number of persons per family.

1931

The fourth national census of population was conducted by the Dirección General del Censo. The original publication of results was very incomplete and consisted only of number of inhabitants and voters per province, municipal districts ("municipios"), and wards ("barrios"). In 1935 attempts were made to have the complete results published; however, they were not successful. Forty years later (1978), parts of the original publication were collected and published under the title *Memorias Inéditas del censo de 1931*. The information gathered here was taken from the latter work. No details about organization were furnished, and some parts of the original results were suppressed and others summarized. The tables published included the following topics: number of inhabitants, age, sex, race, nationality, marital status, literacy, school atttendance, occupation, number of families, number of persons per family, and number of families per dwelling. Vital statistics, density of population, and migration were also recorded.

1943

The fifth national census of population was conducted by the Dirección General del Censo simultaneously with the electoral census. The census was *de jure*, and canvasser was the method utilized to record information on household schedules. The enlarged scope included: place of residence, name, relationship to head of the family, ownership or tenure of the dwelling, sex, place of birth and parents' birth place, race or color, age, marital status, illegitimate children, nationality, year of arrival in the country, literacy, economic activity, occupation, industry, occupational status, infirmities, number of families, and number of persons per family. Urban and rural populations were distinguished.

1953 (January 28)

The sixth national census of population was conducted simultaneously with housing and electoral censuses by the Oficina Nacional de los Censos Demográficos y Electoral. The census was *de jure* and canvasser the method used to record information on household and individual schedules. Tabulation was mechanical with the use of punched cards. Because of lack of time for preparation, the schedules were copied from the 1950 census of Puerto Rico. The territory covered by the census included the six provinces, subdivided into "municipios" and "barrios."

Definitions and Concepts. URBAN—places of 150 inhabitants or more with social services and amenities. AGE—as of last birthday in completed years. Presented in single years and standard five-year age groups. RACE—the categories were white; black; yellow; mixed of white and black, white and yellow, and yellow and black. MARITAL STATUS—the question was asked of men fourteen years of age and older and women twelve years of age and older. The categories were: single, married (legally), common-law marriage, widowed, and divorced. Before this census, in 1931 and 1943, the category "common-law marriage" was included in the singles. NATIONALITY—legal citizenship was recorded. PLACE OF BIRTH—the native born recorded the "municipio" of birth and foreigners, the country of origin. FAMILIA CENSAL—identical to the household concept; that is, included all persons, related or not by blood, living in the same house and sharing food arrangements. FERTILITY—for the first time asked in the census. Only women twelve years and older answered this question: number of children born alive, regardless of marital status. EDUCATION—literacy, educational attainment (last degree completed), and school attendance (during the year before the census). PLACE OF RESIDENCE—usual residence. Foreigners and naturalized Cubans recorded date of first and last arrival in the country. ECONOMIC ACTIVITY—The period of reference was a week before the census. The questions were asked of all persons fourteen years and older. Economically active included the following groups: own-account workers, unpaid family workers, employed, and unemployed looking for a job. Members of the armed forces were also included. Inactive population consisted of homemakers, persons of independent income, students, pensioners, the retired, and invalids. Reasons for unemployment, number of hours worked during the reference period, and number of weeks worked in 1952 were also asked. OCCUPATION—classification based on COTA 1950, major groups and subgroups (two-digits). INDUSTRY—classification based on ISIC, divisions and major groups (two-digits). OCCUPATIONAL STATUS—the categories were: employee (divided into private and government), unpaid family worker, and own-account worker including employer.

Special Elements and Features. The general organization of the census was in accordance with the program of the 1950 Census of the Americas (COTA 1950). This was the first complete census of housing. There are comparative studies and tables for the 1931 and 1943 censuses. A different concept of urban was adopted. For the first time a question on fertility was included, and more detailed information on education was taken. Alphabetical list of "municipios" and "barrios" in each province, mortality data, maps, graphs, and a copy of the schedule are present in the report.

Quality of the Census. No reference was made in the Whipple's Index as far as accuracy of age data. Although with a long history of censuses (since 1899, considering only the period after independence from Spain), regularity has not been observed. The interval between censuses varied from eight to seventeen years.

Publication Plan. Cuba. Oficina Nacional de los Censos Demográfico y Electoral. *Censo de población, viviendas y electoral, enero 28 de 1953. Informe general.* Havana, 1955. 1 volume. Language of publication is Spanish.

1970 (September 6)

The seventh national census of population was conducted by the Dirección Central de Estadística simultaneously with the housing census. The census was taken on a *de jure* basis, but the territory occupied by the U.S. Naval Base of Guantanamo was not included. Canvasser was the method used to record information on household schedules. The enumeration was done in one day in the urban areas due to the immobilization of the population. In the rural areas, however, enumeration was done in three days. Tabulation was computerized.

Precensuses were taken in two different areas to test public attitudes toward the questionnaires, to train enumerators, to test methodology on all aspects of sampling, and to improve coverage. In addition, a listing of dwellings was made to obtain complete address and number of inhabitants per dwelling.

Sample tabulation was utilized for the first time to provide advance results of selected characteristics and to measure quality and coverage of the census. Quality and coverage also were checked through a postenumeration survey of 2 percent of the population (10 percent urban and 5 percent rural areas). No details were given relating to sampling size used for preparation of advanced results.

Definitions and Concepts. URBAN—places of 2,000 or more inhabitants and places of 500 to 2,000 inhabitants with social services and amenities. Some "pueblos" built by the revolution were also included in the list of urban places although not fitting into the definition adopted. NUCLEO CENSAL—the same as household. FAMILY—a group of two or more persons who are members of the same household and related by blood to the fourth degree of consanguinity. Orphanhood was also recorded. AGE—complete date of birth. Presented in single years and standard five-year age groups. RACE—color of skin. Four categories were presented: white, black, mulatto and yellow. MARITAL STATUS —questions were asked of all persons twelve years of age and older. Categories were: single, married (legally), common-law marriage, divorce, and widowed. NATIONALITY—present legal citizenship. PLACE OF BIRTH—the native born recorded state and "municipio" of birth; the foreign born, the country of origin. FERTILITY—questions asked of women twelve years of age and older: Number of children born alive and number of children living. EDUCATION— literacy, school enrollment, educational attainment (last course attended), and type of academic or professional degree. PLACE OF RESIDENCE—whether resident was present or absent, time and cause of absence, and duration of residence. ECONOMIC ACTIVITY—question asked of all persons ten years or older. Period of reference was the week before the census. Economically active population consisted of employed, own-account workers, unpaid family workers, unemployed looking for a job, and persons looking for a job for the first time. Inactive population included the homemakers, students, maids and servants, pensioners, the retired, invalids, inmates of institutions, and others. OCCUPA-TION—no tables were presented in the final results, nor was the classification presented. A separate volume for the province of Matanzas, however, presented the following occupational groups (not based on ISCO): professional and techni-cians, managers, administrative workers, agricultural workers, nonagricultural workers, and service workers. INDUSTRY—no indication of basis for classifi-cation, seven divisions and subgroups (two-digits). OCCUPATIONAL STATUS— categories were state employee, private employee, employer, own-account worker, small agriculture worker, and unpaid family worker.

Special Elements and Features. Sample tabulation, electronic tabulation, and a postenumeration survey were used for the first time. Guantanamo area was not included in the census. At least two sets of publications by province were implied with the appearance of a Matanzas volume from each; however, no further volumes were seen.

Quality of the Census. The PES revealed a 1.77 percent overcount and a 2.53 percent undercount; the percentage of errors was higher in rural areas than in urban. Whipple's Index ranking was category I—highly accurate data. An in-complete publication of sets of reports by province is unfortunate.

Publication Plan. Cuba. Dirección Central de Estadística. *Censo de población y vivienda de 1970.* Havana, 1973-1975. Three advanced sample tabulation results, two separate volumes for Matanzas, and one main volume. Language of publication is Spanish.

1981

Cuba has divided its six former provinces into fourteen. The new administra-tive divisions were adopted in the census. It included basic topics recommended by the UN and CAME (Council of Economic and Mutual Help, based in Mos-cow). Main aspects of the 1981 census are that it was *de jure* and canvassed.

Sampling was used, tabulation computerized, and a housing and population census was carried out simultaneously.

OTHER STATISTICAL PUBLICATIONS. Issued by Comité Estatal de Estadísticas, Dirección de Demografía, *Anuario Estadístico, Resumen de Estadísticas de Población*, annually, *Statistical Yearbook Compendium*.

National Topic Chart

	1953	1970
De facto		
Usual residence	X	X
Place of birth	X	X
Duration of residence	X	X
Place of prev. residence		
Urban/rural	X	X
Sex	X	X
Age	X	X
Relation to household head	X	X
Marital status	X	X
Children born alive	X	X
Children living		X
Citizenship	X	X
Literacy	X	X
School enrollment	X	X
Ed. attainment	X	X
Ed. qualification		
National/Ethnic origin	X	X
Language		
Religion		
Household composition	X	X
Econ. active/inactive	X	X
Occupation	X	X
Industry	X	X
Occupational status	X	X
Income		
Housing	X	X

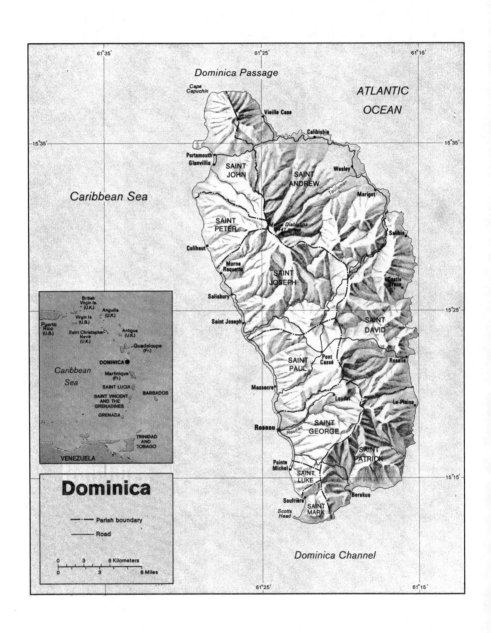

Dominica

Dominica

Commonwealth of Dominica

CAPITAL: Roseau.
STATISTICAL AGENCY: Statistical Office, Ministry of Finance.
NATIONAL REPOSITORY: ?
MAIN U.S. REPOSITORY: Library of Congress, Population Research Center
(Univ. of Texas).

Discovered first by Columbus and claimed by the Spanish, the French established settlements along the coast in the mid-eighteenth century. In 1783 it was ceded to the British. Dominica became a Presidency of the Leeward Islands colony in 1832 and then transferred in 1940 to the Windward Islands group as a colony on its own. As all the British West Indies territories, it was part of the West Indies Federation from 1958 to 1962. It became a West Indies Associated State in 1967 and then received independence in 1978.

All census offices from 1860 through 1946 were formed from the Registrar General's staff. All censuses were *de facto*, and although some reports implied self-enumeration, in all practicality they were canvassed due to the rate of illiteracy. Extant copies of census reports begin with the census of 1871; information about the census of 1860 comes from the comparative tables in the 1871 report.

1860

Scope: total, parish, and town populations, sex, age, occupation, and economic activity (in occupation table).

1871

Scope: birthplace, total and local populations, sex, age, marital status, religion, occupation and economic activity, and infirmities.

1881

Scope is the same as 1871 plus race.

1891

Scope is the same as 1881 plus employment status, number of dwellings, and acreage. Religion was not taken this census.

1901

Only total and local populations by sex was taken.

1911

Cited as the first attempt at approaching a complete census, the scope was place of birth, total and local populations, sex, age, relation to household head, marital status, citizenship, literacy, school attendance, race, religion, economic active/inactive, occupation, infirmities, and number and material of construction of dwellings.

1921

Scope and conduct exactly the same as the census of 1911.
No census taken in 1931.

1946 (April 9)

Dominica was transferred to the Windward Islands in 1940 and participated in the first closely coordinated census of the Caribbean. Results were given for ten parishes and the town of Roseau. [See British West Indies 1946 for full entry; the following are differences.] FERTILITY—no separate tables for Dominica only Windward Island totals. OCCUPATIONAL STATUS—included unemployed and those in institutions. LANGUAGE—one most commonly spoken. MIGRA-TION—only residential status tables. OCCUPATION—main and subsidiary, detailed tables. INDUSTRY—detailed tables. RACE—added Carib to Dominica's categories because previous censuses carried tables for the Carib population. Census of agriculture and of fishing conducted at the same time. Whipple's Index category was IV—rough age data.

Publication Plan. Part H—Windward Islands, contains data for Dominica in the British West Indies 1946 set. Language of publication is English.

1960 (April 7)

The second closely coordinated census; territorial division is same as 1946 but this time data for enumeration districts was published. [See BWI 1960, Eastern Caribbean section, for full entry.] Only difference is there is no table for duration of marriage.

Publication Plan. Volume 1, parts A and D; Volume 2, Windward Islands; and Volume 3, Windward Islands, contain data for Dominica in the BWI 1960 set, in the Eastern Caribbean section. Language of publication is English.

1970 (April 7)

The third closely coordinated census of population. [See British West Indies 1970 for full entry.] No differences. Dominica was not included in the migration volume and issued no separate publications.

Publication Plan. Volumes 3; 4.9; 4.16; 6.3; 7; 8 abc; 9.3; 10.2; and 10.4 of the BWI 1970 set contain data for Dominica. Language of publication is English.

OTHER STATISTICAL PUBLICATIONS: Issued by Statistical Office, *Annual Statistical Digest.*

National Topic Chart

	1946	1960	1970
De facto	X	X	X
Usual residence	X	X	X
Place of birth	X	X	X
Duration of residence	X	X	X
Place of prev. residence			X
Urban/rural		X	X
Sex	X	X	X
Age	X	X	X
Relation to household head	X	X	X
Marital status	X	X	X
Children born alive	X*	X	X
Children living	X*		
Citizenship			
Literacy	X		
School enrollment		X	X
Ed. attainment		X	X
Ed. qualification			
National/Ethnic origin	X	X	X
Language	X		
Religion	X	X	X
Household composition		X	X
Econ. active/inactive	X	X	X
Occupation	X	X	X
Industry	X	X	X
Occupational status	X	X	X
Income			
Housing	X	X	X

*Note: No separate table was presented for Dominica, only for Windward Islands total.

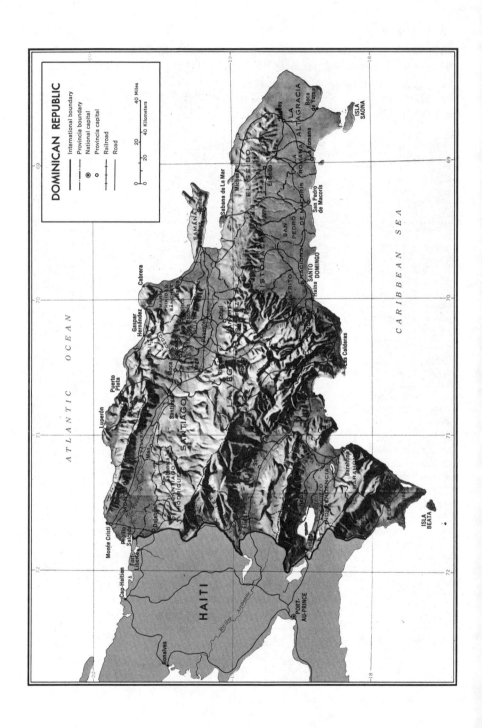

Dominican Republic

Dominican Republic

CAPITAL: Santo Domingo.
STATISTICAL AGENCY: Oficina Nacional de Estadística.
NATIONAL REPOSITORY: ?
MAIN U.S. REPOSITORY: Population Research Center (Univ. of Texas).

At the time of its discovery, the island of Santo Domingo was called "La Española." Although not a census per se, the first document mentioning the population of the island was dated 1606. A treaty between Spain and France was signed in 1697 dividing the island in two parts: the eastern part was granted to Spain and the western to France. In 1795, Spain ceded its part to France, but because the island remained divided in two different cultures, the beginning of the nineteenth century was marked by constant struggles for unification and independence.

In preparation for the election of the House of Representatives, a population count was taken in the five provinces that constituted the Spanish part of the island in 1812. After 1844, when independence was proclaimed, several population estimates and parochial censuses were taken but results are not known.

1920

The first national census of the country was taken in this year; however, because of economic and political instability, lack of experience on the part of enumerators, and an epidemic in several provinces, the results were unsatisfactory. The census was conducted by the Oficina Central del Censo on a *de facto* basis, and canvasser was the method utilized to record information. Further details about organization of the enumeration are not known. The territory covered by the census included twelve provinces, divided into communes; the adjacent islands were not included. The scope was total population by provinces and communes, urban/rural, age, sex, race, nationality, marital status, occupation or profession, literacy, religion, property ownership, and number of voters per commune. The percentage of land utilization was also recorded.

1935

Second national census was conducted by the Dirección General de Estadística. Details of organization are not available. The electoral, housing, and agricultural censuses were taken at the same time. It was established that a census should be taken every fifteen years. The scope was total population, age, sex, nationality, marital status, race, literacy, religion, occupation, and infirmities. The results, however, were not totally published. A separate volume was published with total population according to the 1935 census and in the territorial divisions adopted between 1939 and 1946.

1950 (August 6)

The third national census of population was conducted by the Dirección General de Estadística. It was not stated whether the census was taken on a *de jure* or *de facto* basis. A question on usual place of residence was included, but tables gave no indication of whether they referred to resident or present population. Previous and following censuses, however, were *de facto*. An Inter-American Statistical Institute (IASI) publication classified the census as *de facto*. Housing questions were included in the questionnaire, although a separate census of housing was planned to be taken in 1955. Canvasser was the method used to record information on household questionnaires. The territory was divided into nineteen provinces, the district of Santo Domingo, communes, and municipal districts. Tabulation was mechanical.

Definitions and Concepts. PLACE OF RESIDENCE—usual place. HOUSEHOLD—("Familia censal"), group of persons living in the same house, related or not by blood, and sharing food arrangements. RACE—based on color. Categories were: white, black, mestizo and yellow. The question was not directly asked; the enumerator was the one to decide. AGE—in completed years, presented in single years and standard five-year age groups. The number of completed months was given for infants under one year. MARITAL STATUS—categories were: never married, married, widowed, common-law marriage, separated, and divorced. RELIGION— religious affiliation. PLACE OF BIRTH—province of birth for native born and country of birth for foreign born persons. NATIONALITY—legal citizenship. If a foreign born but naturalized Dominican, the country of origin was also recorded. LANGUAGE—mother tongue. EDUCATION—literacy, school enrollment (new), educational attainment (new), and educational qualification (new). INFIRMITIES—blind, deaf-mute, paraplegic, and so forth. FERTILITY—question asked of women between the ages fifteen and seventy-four: number of children born alive (new). ECONOMIC ACTIVITY—lower age limit was seven years of age. Main and secondary occupations, industry or place of work, and occupational status were asked; persons not working on the day of the census were asked whether they were looking for a job. Criteria followed for inclusion in the economically active population was not clear. As for the economically inactive, the following groups were cited: children, students, homemakers, and others. OCCUPATION—classification based on COTA 1950, major groups and subgroups (two-digits). INDUSTRY—classification based on COTA 1950, divisions and major groups (two-digits). OCCUPATIONAL STATUS—categories were employee (with salary), employer, unpaid family worker, self-employed, and not declared. INCOME—of salaries and other sources was asked but results were not published.

Special Elements and Features. The results for the commune of San Cristobal were published separately. Geographical divisions differed from previous census (1935), seven new provinces were created. Comparative tables with censuses of 1920 and 1935; alphabetical list of communes, municipal districts, and sections of population all were furnished. New features: usual place of residence, place of birth, relationship to head of household, language, fertility, school enrollment, educational attainment and qualification, and detailed economic activity. Income was asked but no tables were published.

Quality of the Census. A housing list was made to obtain the number of enumerators needed in each locality and improve coverage of census. A precensus and a census test were conducted to improve organization and methods to be applied in the final enumeration. Preliminary and final results were published. It was considered the most complete and detailed census as yet taken. However, Whipple's Index classified age data into category V—very rough data. A permanent census office was established in 1948.

Publication Plan. Dominican Republic. Dirección General de Estadística. *Tercer censo nacional de población, 1950.* Ciudad Trujillo, 1952-1958. One general summary, one territorial division, one for Común de San Cristóbal, and one main volume. Language of publication is Spanish.

1960 (August 7)

The fourth national census of population was conducted by the Dirección General de Estadística y Censos. For the first time, sample tabulation (10 percent of households) was applied to accelerate availability of results. Organization was based on COTA 1960 program. The census was *de facto*, including residents of the country, military personnel, and diplomatic missions living abroad as well as foreign persons living temporarily in the country. Canvasser was the method used to record information on household questionnaires. The territory was divided into twenty-five provinces, and the national district, all of which were subdivided into "municipios," municipal districts (urban), and sections (rural).

Definitions and Concepts. URBAN—chief cities or capitals ("cabeceras") of the "municipios" and municipal districts. Rural population were those living in the sections. Results were also given for localities (agglomerations, inhabited places or centros poblados of any size) with a name and functioning as a socially integrated entity. HOUSEHOLD ("hogar censal")—same as 1950. AGE—in completed years, presented in single years and standard five-year groups. The number of months for infants under one year of age was not included. MARITAL STATUS—categories were: never married, married, common-law marriage, widowed, and divorced/legally separated. RELIGION—the following religious groups were recorded: Catholic, Evangelic, Adventist, other religions, and none. RACE—white, black, mulatto and yellow. PLACE OF BIRTH—"municipio" and city for native born and country of birth for foreigners. In addition, nationality was asked of all foreign born. EDUCATION—questions asked of all persons five years of age and older: literacy, school enrollment, and educational attainment (last degree completed). ECONOMIC ACTIVITY—questions asked of persons ten years and older. Economically active were all persons who provide the labor for the production of goods and services, including employed, and those unemployed looking for a job (for the first time or not) at the time of the census. Inactives were: homemakers, students, inmates of institutions, persons of independent income, pensioners, the retired, and others not included in the active population. OCCUPATION—classification based on COTA 1960, twelve major groups were presented (one-digit). INDUSTRY—classification based on COTA 1960, ten divisions (one-digit). OCCUPATIONAL STATUS—employee, employer, self-employed, and unpaid family worker. INCOME—monthly income or salary; no specification whether gross or net income.

Special Elements and Features. The scope of the census was reduced: place of residence, fertility, educational qualification, and language were dropped. Nationality was not a separate question, but rather part of the question on place of birth. Sampling used for the first time. The publication of results was significantly reduced as compared to 1950. Most of the tables refer to the country as a whole, divided into urban and rural areas. Data on provinces was limited to total number of inhabitants. Results of income were published this time. The number of occupied houses with total population was provided for provinces, "municipios," municipal districts, and sectors.

Quality of the Census. Editing, tabulation, and analysis of data started in 1963. Publication of results was limited to preliminary results and general summary; detailed results were not published. There was no Whipple's Index category given.

Publication Plan. Dominican Republic. Oficina Nacional de Estadística. *Cuarto censo nacional de población, 7 de agosto. Resumen general.* Santo Domingo, 1966. 1 volume. One territorial division volume was also published. Language of publication is Spanish.

1970 (January 9 and 10)

The fifth national census of population was conducted by the Oficina Nacional de Estadística simultaneously with the census of housing. The census was *de facto* and canvassed on household schedules. The short form (general characteristics) was distributed to 100 percent of the population; the long form (general, plus economic, fertility, and migration characteristics) was distributed to 50 percent of urban population and 25 percent of the rural population. The territory was divided into twenty-six provinces and the national district, subdivided into "municipios," municipal districts, and zones. Tabulation was computerized.

Definitions and Concepts. URBAN—chief cities/capitals of "municipios" and municipal districts. HOUSEHOLD—same as 1960. AGE—in completed years, or number of months if less than one year of age. Presented in single and standard five-year age groups. MARITAL STATUS—categories were: never married, married, widowed, divorced, separated, common-law marriage, and annulled. EDUCATION—literacy, school enrollment, and educational attainment (last degree completed). FERTILITY—questions asked of women age fifteen and over: number of children born alive, number of children still living, and number of children born in the year before the census (new). PLACE OF BIRTH—for native born, municipal district of birth was recorded and for foreign born, the country of birth. ECONOMIC ACTIVITY—for persons ten years of age and over. Reference period was the week before the census. Economically active population included: employed and unemployed looking for a job (for the first time or not) during the reference period. Inactive population included: homemakers, students, persons of independent income, pensioners, the retired, invalids, and inmates of institutions. OCCUPATION—classification based on COTA 1960, revised. Since the volume corresponding to economic characteristics has not been published yet, the number of groups and subgroups is not known. INDUSTRY—classification based on ISIC, divisions and major groups not known. OCCUPATIONAL STATUS—categories were: employer, employee, self-employed, and unpaid family worker. The usual occupation during the year before the census was also recorded.

Special Elements and Features. Publication format changed, and because of the use of computerized tabulation and sampling method, more information became available. The volumes corresponding to economic characteristics and fertility and migration are not yet available. Fertility questions were revived from 1950 and expanded. Race, religion, and nationality were dropped. A copy of schedules was presented. A separate volume with documents and analysis of the 1970 census data was published in 1972.

Quality of the Census. A census test was taken in 1968 to improve organization and personnel training and to check questionnaires for the final enumeration. A precensus of housing was carried out to improve coverage and to provide data on the personnel and material needed for the census. Preliminary results were published one year after the census; the availability of results was speeded up with the use of sample tabulation (20 percent of schedules). Whipple's Index classified age data into category V—very rough data.

Publication Plan. Dominican Republic. Oficina Nacional de Estadística. *V censo nacional de población, 1970, 9 y 10 de enero de 1970.* Santo Domingo, 1976-. Volumes 1-4 (3 and 4 not published yet). Four subject volumes. Language of publication is Spanish.

OTHER STATISTICAL PUBLICATIONS: Issued by Oficina Nacional de Estadística, *Estadística Demográfica* (irregularly), *República Dominicana en Cifras* (irregularly). Issued by Secretaría de Sanidad y Asistencia Pública, *Cuadros Estadísticos* (annually).

National Topic Chart

	1950	1960	1970
De facto	X	X	X
Usual residence	X		
Place of birth	X	X	X
Duration of residence			
Place of prev. residence			
Urban/rural	X	X	X
Sex	X	X	X
Age	X	X	X
Relation to household head	X	X	X
Marital status	X	X	X
Children born alive	X		X
Children living			X
Citizenship	X	X	
Literacy	X	X	X
School enrollment	X	X	X
Ed. attainment	X	X	X
Ed. qualification			
National/Ethnic origin	X	X	
Language	X		
Religion	X	X	
Household composition	X	X	X
Econ. active/inactive	X	X	X
Occupation	X	X	X
Industry	X	X	X
Occupational status	X	X	X
Income	X	X	
Housing	X	X	X

Ecuador

Republic of Ecuador

CAPITAL: Quito.
STATISTICAL AGENCY: Instituto Nacional de Estadística y Censos (INEC).
NATIONAL REPOSITORY: Biblioteca, INEC.
MAIN U.S. REPOSITORY: Population Research Center (Univ. of Texas).

During the colonial period, Ecuador was alternately part of the viceroyalties of
Peru and New Granada (Columbia). Under the Colombian administration, a
census was taken in 1825 and the results included total population divided into
broad age groups, marital status, sex, and civil condition (free or slave). A table
with the total population of indigenous tribes was also published. Organization
and methods applied are not known, and the results were considered inaccurate
due to a large underenumeration.

Although attempts to establish its independence started at the beginning of the
nineteenth century, only in 1830 did Ecuador withdraw from the Federation of
Gran Colombia and become independent. Disputes over frontiers, however,
remained between Ecuador and its two neighbors Colombia and Peru, and in
1942 a great part of its territory was ceded to Peru.

In 1906 a census of Quito was taken, but it was not until 1950 that the first
general census of population was carried out.

1950 (November 29)

The first general census of population was conducted by the Dirección General
de Estadística y Censos on a *de jure* basis. Canvasser was the method used to
record information on household schedules. The census followed the recommendation of COTA 1950, and tabulation was mechanical. The territory covered by
the census was divided into seventeen provinces and the archipelago of Colon
(Galápagos) and subdivided into cantons and parishes. Housing questions were
included such as type of construction, tenure, and water facilities.

Definitions and Concepts. URBAN—corresponded to the capitals of provinces and cantons. AGE—in completed years, presented in single years up until
twenty-four years of age and then standard five-year age groups. MARITAL
STATUS—categories were: single, married, widowed, divorced and common-

law marriage. Questions were asked of all males age fourteen and over and females age twelve and over. EDUCATION—lower age limit was ten years. Literacy (ability to read and write), educational attainment (last degree completed), and educational qualification. LANGUAGE—lower age limit was six years. Population was divided into monolingual (Spanish, Quechua, other languages, and dialects) and bilingual (speaking two different languages or one language and one indigenous dialect). HOUSEHOLD COMPOSITION—family groups and nonfamily groups, number of heads, number of persons per household. INFIRMITIES—physical or mental illness was recorded. ECONOMIC ACTIVITY—asked of all persons age twelve and over. Economically active were persons gainfully occupied including employers, employees, members of the armed forces, self-employed, unpaid family workers, and students and homemakers who had a gainful occupation. Inactives were students and homemakers without another occupation, persons of independent income, invalids, inmates of institutions, and members of religious congregations living in isolation. OCCUPATION—based on COTA 1950, twelve major groups (one-digit). INDUSTRY—based on ISIC, nine divisions (one-digit). OCCUPATIONAL STATUS—categories were employer and self-employed, employee and laborer, unpaid family worker. NATIONALITY—country of citizenship. PLACE OF BIRTH—province for native born and country of birth for foreign born.

Special Elements and Features. Housing questions were included. Migration data, although recorded, were not published. There are maps and graphs but no copy of the schedules. A separate publication, *La Población del Ecuador—un análisis del censo de 1950*, was released in 1959, providing additional analysis of census results.

Quality of the Census. The original publication scheme was never completed, but in 1960 a general summary of the final results was published. Information was presented for the country as a whole and by provinces. The main deficiency of the census was the lack of information on indigenous population in some regions of the country. Census tests were taken in preparation for the final enumeration to check applicability of schedules, to provide training of personnel, and to improve the organization and methods to be utilized. Whipple's Index was category V—very rough data. No attempt was made to determine the scale of census omissions or to verify accuracy.

Publication Plan. Ecuador. Dirección General de Estadística y Censos. *Primer censo nacional de población del Ecuador, 1950.* Quito, 1953-. Only five of twelve subject volumes in this set were published. *Primer censo nacional de población, 29 de noviembre de 1950. Resultados definitivos.* Quito, 1953-. Only two of the province volumes were published. Unpublished data are available, and language of publication is Spanish.

1962 (November 25)

The second general census of population and first census of housing were conducted simultaneously by the Dirección General de Estadística y Censos.

They were taken on a *de facto* basis, and canvasser was the method used to gather information on household questionnaires. The organization followed the recommendations of COTA 1960. Tabulation was mechanical. Sample tabulation was used (3 percent of questionnaires) for rapid publication of preliminary results. The territory covered by the census included nineteen provinces (two provinces split into four between 1950 and 1962 censuses) and the archipelago of Colon (Galápagos), all subdivided into cantons and parishes.

Definitions and Concepts. URBAN, PLACE OF BIRTH, AGE—same as 1950. Ages were presented in single years and standard five-year groups. HOUSEHOLD—a person or group of persons occupying a dwelling. Households were divided into private and nonprivate (group quarters). PLACE OF RESIDENCE—previous place and duration of residence were recorded (new). EDUCATION—literacy, school attendance (new), and educational attainment were recorded for persons six years of age and older; school attendance, for persons between the ages six and twenty-nine years. ECONOMIC ACTIVITY—asked of all persons age twelve and over. Economically active population included employed as well as unemployed persons looking for a job. Inactives were: homemakers, students, persons of independent income, inmates of institutions, invalids, and others not classified in previous groups. OCCUPATION—last occupation or occupation of larger income in case of more than one. Classification based on COTA 1960, twelve major groups (one-digit). INDUSTRY—classification based on ISIC, nine divisions (one-digit). OCCUPATIONAL STATUS—employer, self-employed, paid employee, unpaid family worker or any other unpaid worker (apprentice), and other (members of religious congregations, looking for a job for the first time and persons whose occupational status was not well defined).

Special Elements and Features. First census of housing taken in the country. New features: duration and previous place of residence and school attendance. The following features were dropped: citizenship, educational qualification (professions and trade), and language. A larger number of cross-classifications, mainly related to economic activity, were published. Analysis of data is not available.

Quality of the Census. Whipple's Index category was V—very rough data. Census tests of buildings, housing, and population were taken in several cities in preparation for the final enumeration.

Publication Plan. Ecuador. División de Estadística y Censos. *Segundo censo de población y primer censo de vivienda, 25 de noviembre 1962.* Quito, 1964. 3 volumes, population; 1, housing; 16, state volumes; and one summary. Unpublished data are available and language of publication is Spanish.

1974 (June 8)

The third general census of population and second of housing were conducted by the Instituto Nacional de Estadística y Censos on a *de facto* basis. Canvasser was the method used to record information on household schedules. Preliminary results were published based on 10 percent sample tabulation. Tabulation was computerized for the first time. The territory covered by the census included nineteen provinces and the Galápagos subdivided into cantons and parishes. Results were also found for "zonas en discusión", areas under dispute.

Definitions and Concepts. HOUSEHOLD, URBAN, AGE, PLACE OF BIRTH— same as 1962. PLACE OF RESIDENCE—usual residence (new), duration of residence, and place of previous residence. EDUCATION—literacy (ability to read and write), educational attainment, and school enrollment (six years was the lower age limit). MARITAL STATUS—for persons twelve years of age and older. Categories were single (never married), married, common-law marriage, divorced, widowed, and separated. FERTILITY—recorded for the first time for women fifteen years of age and older: number of children born alive and number of children still living. ECONOMIC ACTIVITY—for all persons age twelve years and older. Reference period was the week before the census. Economically active population included employed and unemployed looking for a job. Inactive population: students, homemakers, the retired, pensioners, and others not included in previous categories. OCCUPATION—classification based on ISCO and revised by IASI, major groups and subgroups (two-digits). INDUSTRY— classification based on ISIC, divisions and major groups (two-digits). OCCU- PATIONAL STATUS—categories were: employer or active partner, self-employed, employee, unpaid family worker, and others (members of religious groups and cooperatives).

Special Elements and Features. Computerized tabulation was new. Although a *de facto* census, tables with total *de jure* population of provinces by usual place of residence were provided. Fertility was recorded for the first time. The category "separated" was introduced in marital status. Economically active population was recorded according to period of reference (the week before the census) for the first time. Copy of schedule was available. Occupational and industrial classifications were published with the final results.

Quality of the Census. Census office is permanent. Preliminary results were available two months after enumeration and provisional results, based on sample tabulation, were published a year after the census. Analysis of data was not available. Coverage and accuracy of results are not known. Whipple's Index category was IV—rough age data.

Publication Plan. Ecuador. Instituto Nacional de Estadística y Censos. *III censo de población, 1974. Resultados definitivos.* Quito, 1976-1978. 22 volumes in 37 volumes (one national summary, twenty-one provincial volumes). Preliminary and sample results also published. Unpublished data are available. Language of publication is Spanish.

OTHER STATISTICAL PUBLICATIONS: Issued by Instituto Nacional de Estadística y Censos, *Serie Estadística* (irregularly).

National Topic Chart

	1950	1962	1974
De facto		X	X
Usual residence	X		X
Place of birth	X	X	X
Duration of residence		X	X
Place of prev. residence		X	X
Urban/rural	X	X	X
Sex	X	X	X
Age	X	X	X
Relation to household head	X	X	X
Marital status	X	X	X
Children born alive			X
Children living			X
Citizenship	X		
Literacy	X	X	X
School enrollment		X	X
Ed. attainment	X	X	X
Ed. qualification	X		
National/Ethnic origin			
Language	X		
Religion			
Household composition	X	X	X
Econ. active/inactive	X	X	X
Occupation	X	X	X
Industry	X	X	X
Occupational status	X	X	X
Income			
Housing	X	X	X

El Salvador

Republic of El Salvador

CAPITAL: San Salvador.
STATISTICAL AGENCY: Dirección General de Estadística y Censos (DGEC).
NATIONAL REPOSITORY: Punto Focal Nacional, DGEC.
MAIN U.S. REPOSITORY: Population Research Center (Univ. of Texas).

During the colonial period, El Salvador was part of the Capitanía General de Guatemala. Repeated attempts for independence were made from 1811 on. In 1821 it became independent from Spain and was annexed to Mexico. In 1824, El Salvador separated from Mexico and became part of the short-lived Central America Federation. Finally, in 1841, El Salvador was constituted an independent state; the republic was proclaimed in 1856.

El Salvador does not have a long history of censuses. In the colonial period the records are limited to parish registrations of births, marriages, and deaths. After independence, population counts and estimates were made, but results were inaccurate and cannot be used for comparison with later censuses. Methodology and organization are not known. The Oficina Central de Estadística was created in 1881, and in 1892 population was counted in eight departments. Based on these results, an estimate of the total population of the country was made. The first statistical yearbook was published in 1911 containing the number of administrative divisions (fourteen "departamentos") with respective estimated population, density, and school enrollment. The lack of qualified personnel, however, makes these results of doubtful accuracy.

In 1929, a test census was taken in the "municipio" of San Salvador in preparation for the first general census. Simultaneity was not achieved and overenumeration was attributed to the inexperience of enumerators.

1930

First general census of population, conducted by the Dirección General de Estadística, was the first attempt to use statistical methods for census purposes. Canvasser was the method utilized to record information, but details of organization were not provided. The statistical agency established that a census should be taken decennially. The territory covered by the census included the fourteen departments subdivided into "municipios." The scope was age, sex, marital

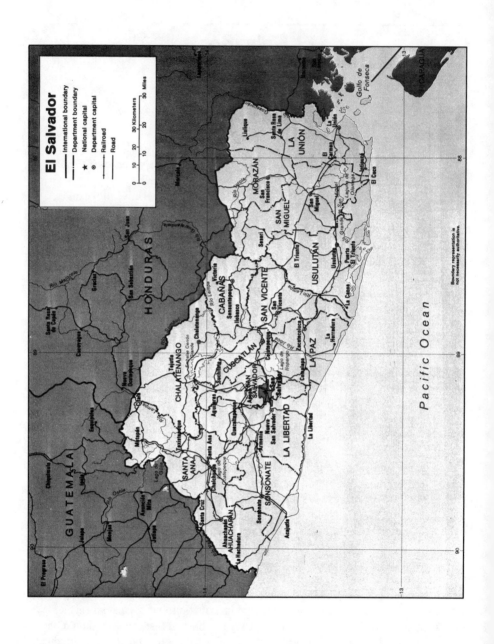

status, nationality, literacy, profession or occupation, race, housing tenure and place of domicile (whether urban or rural).

1950 (June 13)

The second general census of population was conducted by the Dirección General de Estadística and followed the recommendations of COTA 1950. Censuses of housing, agriculture, industry, and commerce were taken in the same year. The census was *de facto*, and canvasser was the method used to record information on general schedules. Tabulation was mechanical. The territory covered by the census was divided into departments, districts, "municipios," and cantons. Data was also available for the most important cities.

The results were published by the Dirección General de Estadística y Censos. A permanent census office was established in 1952.

Definitions and Concepts. URBAN—population in capitals of "municipios" regardless of size. HOUSEHOLD ("familia censal")—persons or groups of persons, related or not by blood, living in the same house and sharing food arrangements. Servants and other persons who ate with the family but did not sleep in the same house were not considered members of the household. AGE—in completed years, or completed months if less than one year of age. Presented in single years and standard five-year age groups. MARITAL STATUS—categories were: never married, married, common-law marriage, widowed, and divorced. Question was asked of persons fourteen years of age and older. PLACE OF BIRTH—recorded for the first time: native born gave department (state) of birth, foreign born, country of birth. NATIONALITY—question asked of foreign born only: country of citizenship. EDUCATION—literacy and educational attainment (last degree completed—new) for ages ten and over, school enrollment for ages six to fourteen (also new). The causes for not attending school were also recorded. PLACE OF RESIDENCE—department, city, and zone (urban/rural) of usual residence. ECONOMIC ACTIVITY—all persons ten years of age and over. Gainful worker approach was used. The usual occupation was recorded, and the economically active population included employed as well as unemployed persons. Inactive population: students, homemakers, pensioners, invalids, and others not included in the previous categories. OCCUPATION—classification based on COTA 1950, major group, groups, and subgroups (three-digits). INDUSTRY—classification based on ISIC, divisions and major groups (two-digits). OCCUPATIONAL STATUS—categories were: employer, employee, self-employed, and unpaid family worker.

Special Elements and Features. First census to provide a detailed study of the economic structure of the population. The following features were presented for the first time: place of birth, school attendance, educational attainment, and relationship to head of household. Within the categories of marital status, common-law marriage was recorded for the first time. Race was dropped. Although the census was *de facto*, place and type of usual residence were recorded. A table with the population of diplomatic personnel by age and marital status was supplied. Complete data were given for important cities. No comparative tables were provided. Maps, graphs, and schedules are available.

Quality of the Census. The lack of a census history contributed to the limited experience of the personnel engaged in census operations. This was the first census that applied international recommendations. Whipple's Index was category V—very rough age data.

Publication Plan. El Salvador. Dirección General de Estadística y Censos. *Segundo censo de población, julio 13 de 1950.* San Salvador, 1954. 1 volume. A census atlas was also published. Language of publication is Spanish.

1961 (May 2)

The third general census of population was conducted simultaneously with a census of housing by the Dirección General de Estadística y Censos. The census was taken on a *de facto* basis, and canvasser was the method used to record information on individual and household schedules. Tabulation was mechanical (punched cards and sorters). The territory covered by the census was divided into states, "municipios," and cantons; however, most results were released on state level.

Definitions and Concepts. HOUSEHOLD AND MARITAL STATUS—same as 1950. URBAN—place where municipal authorities live, not taking into consideration the number of inhabitants nor the presence of social services and amenities. AGE—in completed years or number of months if less than one year of age. Presented in single years. PLACE OF BIRTH—same as 1950. NATIONALITY—citizenship. EDUCATION—literacy (age ten years and older); school enrollment (between six and twenty-nine years of age); and educational attainment (age six years and older), last degree completed. ECONOMIC ACTIVITY—lower limit was ten years of age. Period of reference was the month before the census. Economically active population included the employed and unemployed persons looking for a job. Inactives were: homemakers, students, inmates of institutions, pensioners, persons of independent income, and others not classified in previous groups. OCCUPATION—classification system is their own for this census, major groups, groups, and subgroups (three-digits). INDUSTRY—classification based on ISIC, only nine divisions (one-digit). OCCUPATIONAL STATUS—categories were: employer, self-employed, unpaid family worker, employee, and others (looking for a job for the first time, and other persons without clearly identified occupations).

Special Elements and Features. Comparative tables for the 1950 and 1961 censuses, density of population, and analysis of results were presented. Most of the results were given on state level; results on the city level were not published. Place of usual residence was dropped. Different criteria were used for classification of economically active population—period of reference was a month before the census instead of a year before as in 1950.

Quality of the Census. The census office is permanent. Census coverage was verified through comparisons with results obtained in the 1950 census and through a direct method of revisiting certain areas. In addition, a special questionnaire was distributed by public services and in elementary schools asking whether any family member or employee had not been enumerated.

Special training was given to those engaged in postcensus operations. Sample tabulation was utilized for the elaboration of preliminary results. Housing data were many times omitted due to the use of separate questionnaires for housing and population. Maps of rural areas were not as complete as those for urban areas. This census was not given a Whipple's Index rating.

Publication Plan. El Salvador. Dirección General de Estadística y Censos. *Tercer censo nacional de población, 1961.* San Salvador. 1 volume. A sample volume and one for localities were also published. Language of publication is Spanish.

1971 (June 28)

The fourth general census of population was realized simultaneously with a census of housing and conducted by the Dirección General de Estadística y Censos. The enumeration was taken on a *de facto* basis; both self-enumeration and canvasser were used to record information on household schedules. Organization and methods applied followed the recommendations of COTA 1970. Tabulation was computerized. The territory covered by the census was the fourteen states and their "municipios."

Definitions and Concepts. HOUSEHOLD, MARITAL STATUS, PLACE OF BIRTH—same as 1950. AGE—in completed years; number of months not recorded. Presented in single years and standard five-year age groups. NATIONALITY—country of citizenship. PLACE OF RESIDENCE—usual place of residence two years and five years before the census (new). EDUCATION—questions asked of all persons age six years and older: literacy, school enrollment, and educational attainment. FERTILITY—for the first time recorded. Questions asked of all women fourteen years of age and older: number of children born alive, and number of children still living; for women between fourteen and forty-nine years of age: number of children born in 1970 and among those how many were still alive. ECONOMIC ACTIVITY—questions asked of all persons age ten years and older. Period of reference was the week before the census. Classification of economic activity was based on main occupation. Economically active population included employed and unemployed persons. The unemployed included those looking for a job and those not looking for a job because of temporary infirmity or because of unavailability of employment. Inactives were: students, homemakers, pensioners, retired, persons of independent income, inmates of institutions. OCCUPATION—classification based on ISCO, major groups, groups, and subgroups (three-digits). INDUSTRY— classification based on ISIC, ten divisions (one-digit). OCCUPATIONAL STATUS—categories were employer, self-employed, employee, unpaid family worker, and others (looking for job for the first time and apprentices).

Special Elements and Features. New questions: place of residence (usual and previous) and fertility. Occupational and industrial classifications were modified since the last census. Analysis and comparisons were provided. Tabulation was computerized for the first time. Self-enumeration was also utilized for the first time but only for public employees.

Quality of the Census. A precensus was taken for personnel training, applicability of questionnaires, evaluation of maps, and testing the methods of propaganda used. Census personnel were specially trained and selected by competitive examination. A postenumeration survey was conducted to determine coverage (50,000 urban families and the total rural population). Preliminary results were published five months after enumeration. Sample tabulation was utilized (5 percent of private households and 100 percent of group quarters). The results by sample were published a year after the census. Whipple's Index category was IV—rough age data.

Publication Plan. El Salvador. Dirección General de Estadística y Censos. *Cuarto censo nacional de población, 1971.* San Salvador, 1974-1977. Volumes 1-2, Subject volumes. Language of publication is Spanish.

OTHER STATISTICAL PUBLICATIONS: Issued by Dirección General de Estadística y Censos, *Anuario Estadístico, Avance Estadístico* (monthly), *Boletín Estadístico* (quarterly), *El Salvador en Cifras* (biennially). Issued by Ministerio de Planificación y Coordinación del Desarrollo Económico y Social, *Indicadores Económicos y Sociales* (semiannually).

National Topic Chart

	1950	1961	1971
De facto	X	X	X
Usual residence	X		X
Place of birth	X	X	X
Duration of residence			
Place of prev. residence			X
Urban/rural	X	X	X
Sex	X	X	X
Age	X	X	X
Relation to household head	X	X	X
Marital status	X	X	X
Children born alive			X
Children living			X
Citizenship	X	X	X
Literacy	X	X	X
School enrollment	X	X	X
Ed. attainment	X	X	X
Ed. qualification			
National/Ethnic origin			
Language			
Religion			
Household composition	X	X	X
Econ. active/inactive	X	X	X
Occupation	X	X	X
Industry	X	X	X
Occupational status	X	X	X
Income			
Housing	X	X	X

Falkland Islands

British Crown Colony

CAPITAL: Stanley.
STATISTICAL AGENCY: Registrar General's Office or Colonial Secretary's
Office.
NATIONAL REPOSITORY: ?
MAIN U.S. REPOSITORY: Population Research Center (Univ. of Texas).

Discovered in 1592 by the British, it has been occupied at various times by
France, Spain, and Argentina as well. Britain repossessed the islands in 1833.
Argentina claims sovereignty over what is also called the Islas Malvinas.

East and West Falklands are the two main islands; South Georgia Island has
had periods of greater and lesser populations, especially during whaling seasons.
The South Sandwich Islands are uninhabited.

Population figures for 1851, 1861, and 1871 are estimated; 1881 began the
long series of censuses, decennially from 1881 through 1931, then 1946, 1953,
1962, and 1972. All the censuses are similar. They are *de facto* (including the
shipping population) and self-enumerated (at least since 1901). Reports carry
very little about organization and methodology and less about definitions.

The scope, shared by all ten censuses, is birthplace, total population, urban/rural
(Stanley isolated from the remainder), sex, age (in groups only: under one, one
and under five...twenty to under thirty...to eighty and over), marital status,
citizenship (born or naturalized British subjects), school attendance (noted in
occupation table), religion (except in 1921), occupation, economically active/inactive
(in occupation table), and some form of housing inquiry. They have generally
excluded British armed forces and imported temporary foreign labor, while
including population on ships in the harbors. The following are differences noted
in each census.

1881

Territorial divisions: Stanley and suburban area, Darwin and Falkland Island
Company territory, remainder of East Falkland Island, West Falkland and adja-

The Falkland Islands appear on the map of Argentina, p. 42.

cent islands, colonial shipping, casual British shipping, and foreign shipping. The occupations list is not alphabetized nor is it classified in the standard manner; however, there are some natural groupings.

1891

No report could be located for this census, but comparative tables from the 1901 report indicate the same scope with the possible exception of occupation. The lack of a comparative table does not mean it was not taken; only that the data are not available. Age groups were not cross-classified by sex.

1901

Size of household appears in addition to the general scope. Age groups by sex table reappears.

1911

The island of South Georgia was added to the territorial divisions, and there was one brief statement in the text referring to infirmities.

1921

Same as 1911 except religion was not taken.

1931

Same as 1911 (not 1921) plus a reference in the text to the number of illiterates. There was a crude form of industry division because there are only sheepherding, whaling, and government cited as industries. Nationality was added. There were separate tables for the dependencies.

1946 (March 31)

Conducted by the Registrar General's Office, this census was *de facto* and self-enumerated. The territorial divisions were Stanley, remainder of East Falkland, West Falkland, and Shipping. There are no definitions in the report. A household schedule was used, and tabulation was manual. The dependencies were not included. The scope was birthplace, total and Stanley populations, sex, age (same age grouping as used since 1881), marital status (unmarried, married, divorced included with widowed), citizenship and nationality, school attendance (still in occupation table), religion (specific denomination), economically active/inactive (in occupation table), occupation (alphabetized and partially grouped by the three industries), and number of dwellings and rooms.

Special Elements and Features. Tables on births and deaths, and immigration and emigration from other sources were included. Social and economic report not based on the census was also included.

Quality of the Census. Very comparable to all the preceding censuses because very little had changed over the decades. No permanent census office nor extensive preparation for the census. Since it seems that life in the Falkland Islands has changed little, the repetitiveness of the censuses seems suitable for their purposes.

Publication Plan. Falkland Islands. Registrar General. *Report of the 1946 Census: Report of Census Taken on the Night of the 31st March, 1946.* Stanley, 1946. 1 volume. Language of publication is English.

1953 (March 28)

Conduct, scope, and features of this census were the same as that of 1946.

Publication Plan. Falkland Islands. Registrar General. *Report of the Census Taken on the Night of the 28th March, 1953.* Stanley, 1954. 1 volume. Language of publication is English.

1962 (March 18)

Conduct and scope was the same as 1946 and 1953.

Special Elements and Features. Birth and deaths by sex for single years from 1853-1961 included in report.

Publication Plan. Falkland Islands. Census Supervisor's Office. *Report of Census 1962 [Taken on the Night of 18th March, 1962].* Stanley, 1962. 1 volume. Language of publication is English.

1972 (December 3)

Conduct, scope, features, and so forth were the same as 1946, 1953, and 1962.

Publication Plan. Falkland Islands. Census Office. *Report of Census 1972.* Stanley, 1973. 1 volume. Language of publication is English.

National Topic Chart

	1946	1953	1962	1972
De facto	X	X	X	X
Usual residence				
Place of birth	X	X	X	X
Duration of residence				
Place of prev. residence				
Urban/rural	X	X	X	X
Sex	X	X	X	X
Age	X	X	X	X
Relation to household head				
Marital status	X	X	X	X
Children born alive				
Children living				
Citizenship	X	X	X	X
Literacy				
School enrollment*	X	X	X	X
Ed. attainment				
Ed. qualification				
National/Ethnic origin	X	X	X	X
Language				
Religion	X	X	X	X
Household composition				
Econ. active/inactive	X	X	X	X
Occupation	X	X	X	X
Industry				
Occupational status				
Income				
Housing				

*Note: School enrollment was included in the occupation tables.

French Guiana

French Overseas Department (DOM), called Guyane

CAPITAL: Cayenne.
STATISTICAL AGENCY: Institut National de la Statistique et des Études Économiques (INSEE), Service Départemental de la Guyane.
NATIONAL REPOSITORY: Observatoire Economique de Paris.
MAIN U.S. REPOSITORY: University of California at Los Angeles and Population Research Center (Univ. of Texas).

The smallest and least populated of the three former Guianas located on the northern coast of South America, French Guiana was settled in the early seventeenth century. It changed hands many times until 1816 when it came firmly under French control. In 1947 it became a French Overseas Department.

Censuses taken previous to 1946 were considered of poor quality due to the primitiveness of part of the population and its extreme mobility, and difficult terrain. These also caused difficulties in later censuses.

The complexity of the legal population definition used in French possessions was not present in French Guiana censuses until 1961. Age, however, was presented in both real and generational modes, again later than in the other French overseas departments. The urban definition, of such concern elsewhere, was simpler here because of the way the population was naturally distributed, about 90 percent resided along the coast, especially in Cayenne.

1946 (March 25)

France decreed that a census of the nonindigenous population (foreigners, metropole French, and all persons whose mother or father was born outside the territory) should be taken in all overseas possessions. A census of the total population was optional. French Guiana tried to census its total population, but the items taken were minimal and the results poor. The form for the "non-originaire" census was supplied by the Service Colonial des Statistiques (Paris). The schedules were individual, canvassed, and were to be mechanically tabulated in France by INSEE. The census here was *de facto*. The territorial divisions were: arrondissement de Cayenne (Guyane) and the arrondissement de Inini.

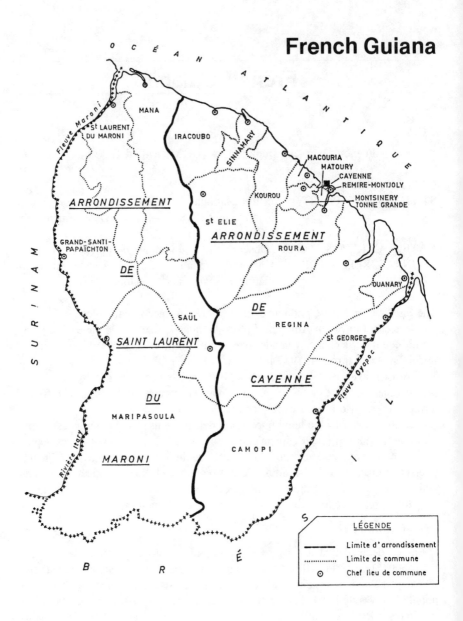

French Guiana

These in turn were subdivided into communes. The following refers only to the "non-originaire" census.

Definitions and Concepts. AGE—month and year of birth. Tables gave real age in standard five-year groups and generational age in single years. BIRTHPLACE—department in France, name of other French possession, or country for foreign born, non-French citizens. Birthplace of mother was also asked. NATIONALITY—citizenship: born or naturalized French, or name of country of political affiliation. MARITAL STATUS—single, married, widowed, divorced, and common-law union. FERTILITY—asked of males and females: number of children born alive and the number surviving. ECONOMIC ACTIVITY—no reference period stated, assumed to be as of the moment of the census. Active were those citing an occupation and inactive were those citing no occupation. OCCUPATION—classed in twenty groups resembling the French list. INDUSTRY—classed in twenty-one groups (French code). OCCUPATIONAL STATUS—employer, employee, own-account worker, not stated, without occupation.

The following refers only to the total population census: AGE—broad age groups only (under fifteen, fifteen to sixty, sixty and over). NATIONALITY—French or foreigner. A footnote cited numbers for the army, penal population, and freed convicts.

Special Elements and Features. Very little data taken for the total population.

Quality of the Census. The 1954 census cited that the numbers of 1946 were manifestly inexact. The lack of qualified, trained enumerators, the mobility of the rural population, and the difficulty of terrain in the interior certainly contributed to that inexactitude.

Publication Plan. France. INSEE [and] Service Colonial des Statistiques. *Résultats du recensement de 1946, territoires d'outre-mer (Français d'origine métropolitaine et étrangers): Guyane et Inini.* Paris, 1948. In *Bulletin Mensual de Statistique d'Outre-Mer*, série "statistique", no. 7. Tables with results for the total population are in appendix. Language of publication is French.

1954 (July 1)

Taken in conjunction with a census of industry, crafts, and business, this census was *de facto* and *de jure* (tables mainly for *de jure* population) and canvassed on household schedules as were the censuses of the other overseas departments. However, it was stated that individual schedules were used for the nonprimitive population of Cayenne district. The primitive population (Indian and African tribes) were excluded in the Guyane enumeration, whereas, both primitive and nonprimitive peoples in Inini were counted, but only global figures are given in the tables. Results published are for nontribal population only, whether primitive or not.

Definitions and Concepts. AGE, BIRTHPLACE, NATIONALITY, EDUCATION, ECONOMIC ACTIVITY—same as 1946. MARITAL STATUS—same as 1946 but common-law union was moved to household composition tables.

OCCUPATION and OCCUPATIONAL STATUS were taken, but tables contain only the socioeconomic status designations determined by crossing the two. French code was used. HOUSEHOLD COMPOSITION—by size, by characteristics of head, and by four main categories of type based on spouse and/or children present and presence of other relatives and nonrelatives in the household.

Special Elements and Features. No separate occupation or occupational status tables. Some tables divided by primitive and nonprimitive population. Tables available for Cayenne City and St. Laurent du Marone. Fertility was dropped.

Quality of the Census. Census operations were still plagued by the adverse conditions of nature. There was not as much detail as in the other overseas department result publications.

Publication Plan. France. INSEE. *Résultats statistiques du recensement général de la population des departements d'outre-mer effectué le 1er juillet 1954: Guyane.* Paris, 1957. Language of publication is French.

1961 (October 9)

Conducted in the same fashion as the censuses of the other overseas departments, this census was *de jure*, canvassed on household schedules, and under the responsibility of the local authorities. The schedules were edited and underwent mechanical tabulation in Cayenne before being forwarded to INSEE in Paris, where only the legal population results were checked again before being mechanically tabulated there. The published results for all but the legal population numbers were based on the Cayenne tabulations. In this census, there was an attempt to enumerate more precisely the tribal population in various regions of the interior. A second slip was used to get their tribal group, summary of civil state, family relationship, marital status, place of residence at the moment of the census, and some elements of their economic status.

The designation of the legal population in French possessions is different from the usual. The totaling of two, or all three, of the following segments constitutes the legal population for the specific area:

1. "Population municipale"—private households and collective households inhabited by those who freely choose to reside there, for example, live-in hospital staff, hotel residents.

2. "Population comptée à part"—populations in institutions, inhabitants who have little or no choice to reside there, for example, military on base, boarding students, prisoners, patients (not staff) in hospitals of all kinds of relatively long term duration, and public works labor in barracks.

3. "Double compte"—inhabitants of "comptée à part" institutions in one commune who maintain a personal residence in another are counted sometimes in both communes, sometimes in only one or the other (in the colonies). Generally, the legal population of the commune is a combination of all three, whereas the legal population of larger administrative units or of the whole territory is the total of numbers one and two only.

Definitions and Concepts. AGE—same as 1954 but only the table of single years by generational age gives age for those under fifteen. MARITAL STATUS, BIRTHPLACE, EDUCATION, HOUSEHOLD COMPOSITION—same as 1954. NATIONALITY (reinstated)—French citizenship (born or naturalized), tribal membership (Indian and African in the interior), and affiliation of foreigners. USUAL RESIDENCE—crossed with birthplace to give minimal data on internal migration and immigration. ECONOMIC ACTIVITY—all persons age fifteen and over; reference period was the preceding twelve months. Active were those who declared an occupation; inactive, those "without." OCCUPATION— forty-five groups. All occupations were classed in detail as was done in the other departments according to the list used in France in 1954, but in the publication occupations were "regrouped" according to relative importance in Guyane. INDUSTRY—forty groups following the order of the nine major groups of the ISIC. OCCUPATIONAL STATUS—taken but there are no tables of this category alone; it was used to create the socioeconomic status, which followed the French code. ECONOMIC DEPENDENCY (new)—number of children under fifteen in household and number of economically active in household.

Special Elements and Features. Nationality was reinstated, and economic dependence was added. Table on tribes by sex and broad age groups was given. Emphasis was on housing. Both tribal and nontribal populations were included for the first time.

Quality of the Census. The results lack details of lower ages, occupations, and industries; however, fewer of the population were left out of the enumeration than before, which indicates that they are overcoming the conditions of nature and society that are adverse to a good census.

Publication Plan. France. INSEE. *Résultats statistiques du recensement général de la population des départments d'outre-mer effectué le 9 octobre 1961. Guyane*. Paris, 1964. Language of publication is French.

1967 (October 16)

It is supposed that the conduct of this census was similar to that of 1961. There is no description of organization, methodology, or definitions. The following information is taken from tables and notes. Tables are for the *de jure* population. The conduct was in the hands of local governments. The "comptée à part" population was divided into two groups: (1) prisoners, minors in institutions, inmates of psychiatric facilities and (2) military housed on base, patients of TB and Hansen's Disease treatment facilities, boarding students, and public works laborers in barracks. Housing data was also taken. Previous censuses had almost the same content, but the tables lacked the detail given for Martinique and Guadeloupe. Many commune boundaries and names were changed in 1969, and one table in the publication gives the legal population of the new communes while the remaining tables are of the communes as they were at the census.

Definitions and Concepts. AGE, USUAL RESIDENCE, BIRTHPLACE, MAR-

ITAL STATUS, EDUCATION, HOUSEHOLD COMPOSITION and ECONOMIC DEPENDENCY—appear to have been the same as 1961. NATIONALITY—same as 1961 but no table for tribes. OCCUPATION and INDUSTRY—same as 1961 but tables contain more detailed entries to two- or three-digits as needed. Classed according to the French lists. OCCUPATIONAL STATUS—same as 1961 except "colon" (tenant farmer?) was omitted from the list. A table was presented with this breakdown as well as socioeconomic status derived from crossing this with occupation.

Special Elements and Features. Fertility was not taken. There was greater detail in occupation, industry, and socioeconomic status. Emphasis was on household composition, economic dependency (children under age fifteen), and housing.

Quality of the Census. Greater involvement of INSEE seemed to have upgraded the results of the censuses. At least, the tables contained more detailed information. The absence of definitions and so forth, which are evidently to be included in an analysis volume (not yet published) is a lack. No Whipple's Index category is given.

Publication Plan. France. INSEE. *Résultats statistiques du recensement général de la population des départements d'outre-mer effectué le 16 octobre 1967. 1ʳᵉ partie: tableaux statistiques. Guyane.* Paris, n.d. Language of publication is French.

1974 (October 16)

Only a number of inhabitants volume has been issued formally; however, some tables with 1974 results have been distributed. The information for this entry is taken from whatever was available. It was computer tabulated by INSEE. Although the departmental census office is reestablished for each census, the regional office of INSEE is permanent.

Definitions and Concepts. AGE—real and generational age by five-year age groups and single years for ages fifteen to twenty-four only. ECONOMIC ACTIVITY—(PAEA) reference period twelve months preceding census and (PAES) reference period seven days preceding census. Footnotes indicating active are poorly printed and cannot be read. The inactive are students, homemakers, the disabled, the retired, and others (those doing compulsory military service). An employment survey was conducted in 1969-1970. Results of both census and survey were compared. INDUSTRY—primary, secondary and tertiary sectors divided by the nine major groups based on ISIC. Also indicated were the number of unemployed (both experienced and first-time job seekers). The final results were due to be published in 1982, but no copy has appeared in the United States as yet.

Publication Plan. France. INSEE. *Recensement général de la population en 1974. Population de la France, départements d'outre-mer: arrondissements, communes.* Paris, 1976. Unpublished data and computer tapes are available from INSEE—Département de la Coopération et des Services Statistiques des DOM-TOM (Paris). Language of publication is French.

OTHER STATISTICAL PUBLICATIONS: Issued by INSEE (Paris): *Annuaire Statistique, Bulletin de Statistique* (monthly), *Bulletin Trimestriel de Statistique, Bulletin de Statistique des Départements et Territoires d'Outre-Mer* (quarterly), *Statistique du Mouvement de la Population dans les Départements d'Outre-Mer,* (irregularly).

National Topic Chart

	1946	1954	1961	1967	1974*
De facto	X	X			
Usual residence		X	X	X	
Place of birth	X	X	X	X	
Duration of residence					
Place of prev. residence					
Urban/rural					
Sex	X	X	X	X	X
Age	X	X	X	X	X
Relation to household head		X	X	X	
Marital status	X	X	X	X	
Children born alive	X				
Children living	X				
Citizenship			X	X	
Literacy		X	X	X	
School enrollment					
Ed. attainment		X	X	X	
Ed. qualification					
National/Ethnic origin	X	X	X	X	
Language					
Religion					
Household composition		X	X	X	
Econ. active/inactive		X	X	X	X
Occupation	X		X	X	
Industry	X		X	X	
Occupational status	X		X	X	
Income					
Housing		X		X	

*Note: Census taken but very little information is available.

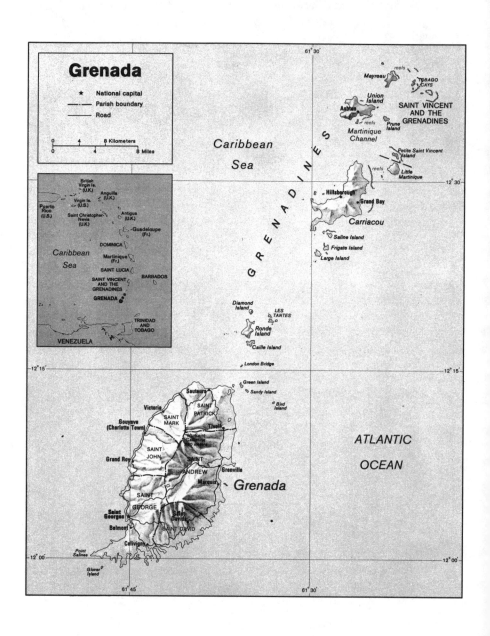

Grenada

★ National capital
–·–·– Parish boundary
—— Road

0   4   8 Kilometers
0   4   8 Miles

Caribbean
Sea

Caribbean
Sea

British
Virgin Is.
(U.K.)
Anguilla
(U.K.)
Virgin Is.
(U.S.)
Puerto
Rico
(U.S.)
Saint Christopher-
Nevis
(U.K.)
Antigua
(U.K.)
Guadeloupe
(Fr.)
DOMINICA
Martinique
(Fr.)
SAINT LUCIA
SAINT VINCENT
AND THE
GRENADINES
BARBADOS
GRENADA
TRINIDAD
AND
TOBAGO
VENEZUELA

61° 30′

Mayreau
TOBAGO
CAYS
Union
Island
Ashton
SAINT VINCENT
AND THE
GRENADINES
reels
Prune
Island
Martinique
Channel
Petite Saint Vincent
Island
Little
Martinique
12° 30′

Hillsborough
Grand Bay
Carriacou
Saline Island
Frigate Island
Large Island

G R E N A D I N E S

Diamond
Island
LES
TANTES
Ronde
Island
Caille Island
London Bridge

12° 15′

Green Island
Sandy Island
Bird
Island

Sauteurs
Victoria
SAINT
MARK
SAINT
PATRICK
Tivoli
Gouyave
(Charlotte Town)
SAINT
JOHN
Saint
Andrews
SAINT
ANDREW
Grenville
Grand Roy
Marquis
Grenada
SAINT
GEORGE
Saint
Georges
Saint
David's
Belmont
SAINT DAVID
Calivigny
Point
Salines
12° 00′
Glover
Island

ATLANTIC

OCEAN

61° 45′   61° 30′

12° 15′

12° 00′

Grenada

Independent British Commonwealth State

CAPITAL: St. George's.
STATISTICAL AGENCY: Statistical Officer; Ministry of Finance, Trade, Industry, and Planning.
NATIONAL REPOSITORY: Colonial Office Group, London and ?
MAIN U.S. REPOSITORY: Population Research Center (Univ. of Texas).

First settled briefly by the British in 1609, it was taken over by the French, who controlled it from 1650 to 1762. Britain then regained control, which lasted until 1974 except for a brief period during the American Revolution. It was included in the Windward Island group until their independence. Like the other British West Indies countries, Grenada supposedly had a long series of "censuses" or estimates. Publications, however, have been found only for those censuses beginning with 1891. This one does contain comparative tables that give a few figures back to 1861. Instead of the usual (for the British West Indies) abstract tables for these early censuses, there are narrative reports included from which more information is available about the country. There is still, however, a lack of definitions and concepts.

1861

Scope included sex, age, marital status, birthplace, occupations, religion, and the number and material of inhabited houses.

1871

Scope was the same as 1861 but no trace of occupations was indicated.

1881

Scope included birthplace, sex, age, relation to household head, marital status, race (new), religion, infirmities (new), and number and material of inhabited houses.

1891

The first report seen with essential tabulations plus discussions of the data. This census contained adequate geographical breakdowns. It was *de facto* and self-enumerated. Scope included sex, age, marital status, occupations plus separate tables of trades and handicrafts, birthplace, religion, infirmities, East Indians (instead of all races), number of children attending different types of schools, housing, and agricultural information. The enumeration district table has number of inhabitants by sex.

1901

It appears to have been *de jure* ("all people resident"); however, it may be that the tables published referred only to this group. Scope was the same as 1891 plus illegitimacy. The report cited the probable inaccuracy of some results especially in illegitimacy, land holdings, and number of livestock.

1911

Scope was the same as 1891.

1921

De facto, self-enumerated. The population also included those in public institutions, shipping, and the houseless. The scope was birthplace, urban/rural, sex, age, relation to household head, marital status, literacy, school attendance, race (last taken in 1881), nationality (new), language spoken (new), religion, occupation, infirmities, and housing.

There was a span of twenty-five years before the next census.

1946 (April 9)

Conducted through the Government Office, this census was coordinated with the 1946 West Indies program. The colony's six parishes plus the island of Carriacou were divided into census and enumeration districts, but the tables give results for the natural and administrative divisions only.

Definitions and Concepts. [See British West Indies 1946 for full entry; the following are the differences.] URBAN— the population within towns and the suburbs of the capital. AGE—infants coded in completed months under one year. Tables have single years of age and standard five-years age groups. EDUCATION—school attendance is listed in "occupation." RACE—tables indicate white (including Portuguese), black, East Indian, Syrian, Chinese, other Asiatic, aboriginal Indian (Carib), mixed or colored. OCCUPATIONAL STATUS —employer, own-account worker, unpaid helper, wage or salary earner in employment, apprentice or learner, and unemployed wage earner and duration of unemployment.

Special Elements and Features. The report for Grenada gives the history and comparison of censuses up to 1946. Occupational status was asked for the first time.

Quality of the Census. Whipple's Index is category IV— rough age data.

Publication Plan. Part H of the West Indies Census is devoted to the census of the Windward Islands.

1960 (April 7)

The census was taken by the census office of the territory. [See British West Indies 1960, Eastern Caribbean section, for full entry; the following are the differences.] Grenada is made up of six parishes and Carriacou makes the seventh. All were divided into enumeration districts and tables give results for that level.

Quality of the Census. Grenada lacks one of the publications issued in all other countries, Part G—detailed characteristics of economic activity. Whipple's Index category is not available.

Publication Plan. Trinidad and Tobago. Central Statistical Office. *Population Census 1960. Eastern Caribbean Region. Windward Islands.* Port-of-Spain, 1963-1969. Volume 1, Part A—*Administrative Report*, Part D—*Boundaries of Enumeration Districts* (Windward Islands); Volume 2, *Summary Tables 1-19*, Windward Islands; Volume 3, *Detailed Cross-Classifications*, Part A (1 volume), Parts B, D, E, and F (1 volume). Language of publications is English.

1970 (April 7)

Conducted by the Census Office, territorial division was same as 1960. [See British West Indies 1970 for full entry.] Grenada issued no separate publications. It was not included in the migration volume.

Publication Plan. Volumes 3; 4.7; 4.16; 6.2; 7; 8 abc; 9.2; 10.2; and 10.4 contain data for Grenada. Language of publication is English.

OTHER STATISTICAL PUBLICATIONS: Issued by Statistical Office: *Abstract of Statistics* (annually).

National Topic Chart

	1946	1960	1970
De facto	X	X	X
Usual residence		X	X
Place of birth	X	X	X
Duration of residence	X	X	
Place of prev. residence			
Urban/rural	X		
Sex	X	X	X
Age	X	X	X
Relation to household head	X	X	X
Marital status	X	X	X
Children born alive	X	X	X
Children living	X		
Citizenship			
Literacy	X		
School enrollment	X	X	X
Ed. attainment		X	X
Ed. qualification			
National/Ethnic origin	X	X	X
Language			
Religion	X	X	X
Household composition	X		
Econ. active/inactive	X	X	X
Occupation	X	X	X
Industry	X	X	X
Occupational status	X	X	X
Income		X	X
Housing	X	X	X

Guadeloupe and Dependencies

French Overseas Department (DOM)

CAPITAL: Basse-Terre.
STATISTICAL AGENCY: Institut National de la Statistique et des Études Économiques (INSEE), Service Départemental de la Guadeloupe.
NATIONAL REPOSITORY: Observatoire Economique de Paris.
MAIN U.S. REPOSITORY: Population Research Center (Univ. of Texas).

One of the four French overseas departments established in 1946, Guadeloupe was one of the "Old Colonies," first settled by the French in 1635. The censuses taken previous to 1946 were considered of poor quality due to circumstances of time and place and to the tendency of local administrators to inflate population numbers for fiscal reasons. Even the censuses of this century, using modern methods, were not of reliable quality because tabulation was performed in the local area. The first modern census was that of 1867, and there were ten censuses up until 1946. The censuses of 1954, 1961, 1967, and 1974 have been conducted with more care due to the involvement of the French statistical agency (INSEE) in their preparation, conduct, and tabulation.

The designation of the legal population in French possessions is different from the usual. The totaling of two, or all three, of the following segments constitutes the legal population for the specific area:

1. "Population municipale"—private households and collective households inhabited by those who freely choose to reside there, for example, live-in hospital staff, hotel residents.

2. "Population comptée à part"—populations in institutions, inhabitants who have little or no choice in residing there, for example, military on base, boarding students, prisoners, patients (not staff) in hospitals of all kinds of relatively long term duration, and public works labor in barracks.

3. "Double compte"—inhabitants of "comptée à part" institutions in one commune who maintain a personal residence in another are counted sometimes in both communes, sometimes in only one or the other (in the colonies). Generally, the legal population of the commune is a combination of all three, whereas the legal population of larger administrative units or of the whole territory is the total of numbers one and two only.

Guadeloupe and Dependencies

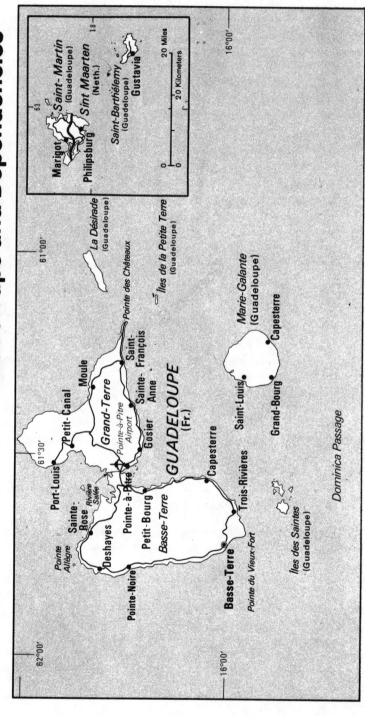

The legal population in Guadeloupe in the 1946 and 1954 censuses was the total of the "municipale" plus those residents temporarily absent. In 1961, the legal total was determined in the same fashion as was used in France. That is, that described above.

A second difference in French censuses is how age is presented. Both real and generational age are represented in the tables. The real age, usually in five-year age groups, is similar to what is used in most censuses. The generational, however, is different. The specific year of birth determines the age rather than the amount of time passed. In other words, anyone born in 1950 is thirty- one years old whether he has passed his thirty-first birthday or not by the date of the 1981 census.

The urban distinction is also complex; however, it is not necessary to explain this here as there are rarely any tables presented with urban figures.

1946 (May 16)

France decreed that a census of the nonindigenous population (foreigners, metropole French, and all persons whose mother or father was born outside the territory) should be taken in all overseas territories and departments in this year. It was optional as to whether a full census (including the indigenous) would be conducted at the same time. Guadeloupe chose to take only the "non-originaire." There are no results because "the census of Guadeloupe was tabulated there and was kept confidential because it gave total results so much smaller than the previous countings. This seemed to indicate that the census methods were some- what effective in counteracting the traditional inflation of results due to electoral and financial interests."

1954 (July 1)

Taken in conjunction with a census of industry, crafts, and business, it was *de facto* and *de jure* (tables mainly for *de jure* population), canvassed on household schedules, and mechanically tabulated in Paris. A second schedule was used for the "population comptée à part," which contained fewer questions. The house- hold schedule had a special section for visitors' and the temporarily absents' information and also collected housing data. Territorial divisions in tables: com- munes grouped by island. Basse-Terre (ten), Grande-Terre (sixteen), Marie-Galante (three), Les Saintes (two), and La Désirade, Saint-Martin, Saint-Barthelémy (one each). This is the first time census methods were adapted to local condi- tions, such as hierarchy of socioeconomic status.

Definitions and Concepts. URBAN—Basse-Terre, Pointe-au-Pitre, and com- munes of aggregated populations of 2,000 and over. HOUSEHOLD—one per- son or a group living in one dwelling. Specification of a dwelling became more precise in later censuses. AGE—year of birth and completed years. Tables of real and generational age in standard five-year age groups. MARITAL STATUS (legal)—single, married, widowed, divorced. Common-law union appears only in type of household tables. BIRTHPLACE—department in France, name of other French possession, or name of country, if foreign. The birthplaces of mother and of father were also asked. NATIONALITY—only of the foreign born. FERTILITY—asked of females age fourteen years and over: number of children born alive. EDUCATION—asked of all age fourteen and over: literacy and educational attainment (diploma received). ECONOMIC ACTIVITY—age fourteen and over: reference period was the moment of the census. Active included employed, unemployed looking for work, unpaid family helpers, and the military. Inactive were homemakers, those of independent income, students, inmates of institutions, beggars, and so forth. OCCUPATION—age fourteen and over: main and secondary occupation. Classified according to the 1954 edition of the list used in France (to four-digits where necessary). OCCUPATIONAL STATUS (new)—employer, own-account worker, "colon" (tenant farmer?), salaried worker, family helper, and apprentice. SOCIOECONOMIC STATUS—cross-classification of occupation with occupational status. ECONOMIC DEPENDENCY—number of children under sixteen in the household.

Special Elements and Features. Occupational status and socioeconomic status are new. Marital status, nationality, and fertility were not taken for the "population comptée à part." No industry as a separate census of industry was taken (results in *Bulletin Mensuel de Statistique d'Outre-Mer*, serie "statistique," No. 19). The appendix has a copy of the schedules used and there is a history of censuses in the introduction.

Quality of the Census. "The 1954 census taken in the French Antilles is considered very accurate because taken by the 'prefet' [chief administrative office of the department] instead of by local governments as was done previous to this census. The reason was to avoid over-estimating of results which had become traditional throughout a number of Antilles cities." INSEE (Paris) supplied schedules and tabulated results. Whipple's Index category is not available.

Publication Plan. France. INSEE. *Résultats statistiques du recensement général de la population des départements d'outre-mer effectué le 1ᵉʳ juillet 1954: Antilles Françaises: Martinique et Guadeloupe.* Paris, 1956. Language of publication is French.

1961 (October 9)

Conducted by the local governments under guidance of INSEE, this census was *de facto* and *de jure* with mainly *de jure* tables. It is not known if it was self-enumerated or canvassed on the household schedules that also collected housing information. Institutional schedules were also used, and both were mechanically tabulated by INSEE. Territorial divisions were the same as 1954. The legal population for communes was the "municipale" and the "comptée à part" without double count.

Definitions and Concepts. URBAN—only the aggregated population of 2,000 and more, not the total population of the commune. AGE—year of birth only. Tables in real age and generational age in standard five-year age groups, generational age in single years. MARITAL STATUS—same as 1954. NATIONALITY—

citizenship, of the French nationals and the foreign born. BIRTHPLACE—department in France, commune for native born, name of TOM or DOM, name of country for foreign born. This plus usual residence gave basic internal migration and immigration. EDUCATION—age fifteen and over: literacy and highest degree attained. ECONOMIC ACTIVITY—age fifteen and over: reference period one year before the census. Active were employed, underemployed, and certain unemployed; inactive were others (not listed under separate categories). OCCUPATION—main or latest occupation. Classified by the French list of 1954, major, minor and subgroups (three-digits). INDUSTRY—divided by primary, secondary, and tertiary sectors with major, minor and subgroups. Nine major groups based on ISIC. OCCUPATIONAL STATUS—same as 1954. SOCIOECONOMIC STATUS—cross-classification of occupation and status further classed by public or private sector and adapted to local conditions. HOUSEHOLD COMPOSITION—by type, which was based on the basic core (spouse, and/or children present and so forth) and presence of others in the household; also by size and by characteristics of the head. ECONOMIC DEPENDENCY—number of children under age fifteen in the household, and the number of economically active in household.

Special Elements and Features. No fertility, but household composition and industry were added. Copy of schedule and codes used are in appendix. Emphasis was on household composition and economic activity.

Quality of the Census. The closer involvement in the control of the census by INSEE should have improved accuracy even though the responsibility for the conduct was returned to local governments. However, it was conceded that this census had an overcount in spite of INSEE's action. Whipple's Index category ranking is not available.

Publication Plan. France. INSEE. *Résultats statistiques du recensement général de la population des départements d'outre-mer effectué le 9 octobre 1961: Guadeloupe.* Paris, 1965. Language of publication is French.

1967 (October 16)

It is supposed that the conduct of this census was similar to that of 1961. There is no description of organization, methodology, or definitions. The following information is taken from tables and notes. Tables are for *de jure* population. "Care for the operations of each commune is in the hands of the local government." There is a slight change in the organization of the "comptée à part" designation; it is divided into group I (prisoners, minors in institutions, inmates of psychiatric facilities) and group II (militáry living on base, patients of TB and Hansen's Disease treatment facilities, boarding students, and public works laborers in barracks). Housing data was also taken.

Definitions and Concepts. AGE, USUAL RESIDENCE, BIRTHPLACE, MARITAL STATUS, EDUCATION, NATIONALITY, OCCUPATION, INDUSTRY, SOCIOECONOMIC STATUS, HOUSEHOLD COMPOSITION and ECONOMIC DEPENDENCY—appear to be the same as 1961. FERTILITY (reinstated)—females born in the territory or other overseas department only, age fifteen and over: number of children ever born alive. OCCUPATIONAL STATUS—same as 1961 and 1954 except "colon" (tenant farmer?) dropped from the list. However, one table gives results using the 1961 set of terms.

Special Elements and Features. There was a reinstatement of fertility and emphasis on household composition. No copy of schedule nor descriptive text was published.

Quality of the Census. Lack of definitions in final result volume may make it awkward to use. Whipple's Index category is not available.

Publication Plan. France. INSEE. *Résultats statistiques du recensement général de la population des départements d'outre-mer effectué le 16 octobre 1967. 1er partie, tableaux statistiques. Guadeloupe.* Paris, n.d. Language of publication is French.

1974 (October 16)

Only a number of inhabitants volume has been issued formally; however, some tables with 1974 results have been distributed. The information for this entry is taken from whatever was available. The results were computer tabulated by INSEE. Although the departmental census office is reestablished for each census, the regional office of INSEE is permanent. The final results are due to be published in 1982.

Definitions and Concepts. AGE—real and generational age in standard five-year age groups, and both in single years to age twenty-four. ECONOMIC ACTIVITY—two reference periods: preceding twelve months, active are "those having had a job during the last twelve months (PAEA) all of whom declared having exercised an activity remunerated or on own account during that period"; the same for the preceding seven days (PAES) was also taken. Inactive are students, homemakers, invalids, the retired, others (including those doing compulsory military service). INDUSTRY—primary, secondary, and tertiary sectors subdivided by major industry groups plus unemployed (subdivided by "having had work but not that week" and "seeking first job").

Publication Plan. France. INSEE. *Recensement général de la population en 1974. Population de la France, départements d'outre-mer: arrondissements, communes.* Paris, 1976. Unpublished data and computer tapes are available from INSEE, Département de la Coopération et des Services Statistiques des DOM-TOM (Paris). Language of publication is French.

OTHER STATISTICAL PUBLICATIONS: Issued by INSEE (Paris): *Annuaire Statistique, Bulletin de Statistique* (monthly), *Bulletin de Statistique des Départements et Territoires d'Outre-Mer* (quarterly), *Statistique du Mouvement de la Population dans les Départements d'Outre-Mer* (irregularly).

National Topic Chart

	1946	1954	1961	1967	1974
De facto	X	X	X		
Usual residence	X	X	X	X	X
Place of birth		X	X	X	
Duration of residence					
Place of prev. residence					
Urban/rural		X	X		
Sex		X	X	X	X
Age		X	X	X	X
Relation to household head		X	X	X	
Marital status		X	X	X	
Children born alive		X		X	
Children living					
Citizenship			X	X	
Literacy		X	X	X	
School enrollment					
Ed. attainment		X	X	X	
Ed. qualification					
National/Ethnic origin		X	X	X	
Language					
Religion					
Household composition			X	X	
Econ. active/inactive		X	X		X
Occupation		X	X	X	X
Industry			X	X	X
Occupational status		X	X	X	
Income					
Housing		X	X	X	

Guatemala

Guatemala

Republic of Guatemala

CAPITAL: Guatemala, C.A.
STATISTICAL AGENCY: Dirección General de Estadística (DGE).
NATIONAL REPOSITORY: Biblioteca—DGE.
MAIN U.S. REPOSITORY: Library of Congress, Population Research Center
(Univ. of Texas).

Guatemala was a colony of Spain from 1524 to 1821. The first population count was taken in 1778; however, it cannot be considered a census per se but rather a compilation of tax and parish reports. Of these records, only the total number of inhabitants is known. After independence from Spain in 1821, Guatemala was annexed briefly to Mexico. With the other Central American nations Guatemala became part of a federation called the United Provinces of Central America. The federation was disbanded in 1839 and Guatemala became a republic. A case study done by the United Nations summarized "although the census of 18 April 1950 is referred to as the sixth, it is hardly comparable with earlier censuses. It may in fact be regarded as the first to provide reliable data, since the others contain serious errors" (UN Economic Commission for Latin America. *Case Studies of Arrangements for Evaluation and Utilization of Population Census Results*. Report 2, the Republic of Guatemala. 1960).

1880

Second census of population was conducted by the Secretaría de Fomento, Sección de Estadística, on a *de facto* basis. Canvasser was the method used to record information on general schedules. Simultaneity was not observed, and the results were considered only an approximation in preparation for the census to be taken in 1885. The scope included age, sex, race, nationality, religion, marital status, literacy, usual place of residence, profession, infirmities, and type of dwelling. Only nineteen "departamentos" (states), subdivided into "municipios," were covered by the census. Three states were not enumerated, and the total population of the country was estimated.
The 1885 census was not taken.

1893

The third general census of population was conducted by the Dirección General de Estadística on a *de facto* basis. The organization was practically the same as the 1880 census, but this time all twenty-two states were enumerated. In addition, the population was divided into urban, rural, and special population (those in group quarters). The scope was the same except that vaccination and school enrollment were added. The results were considered inaccurate, and an estimated 10 percent of the population was omitted.

1921

The fourth census of population was taken by the Dirección General de Estadística on a *de facto* basis, and canvasser was the method used to record information on household schedules. The scope included age, race, literacy, marital status, sex, nationality, and occupation. The results were not totally tabulated, and 15 percent was added to make up for the underenumeration. Comparative tables with 1880 and 1893 census results are included in the report.

1940

The fifth census of population was conducted by the same agency following basically the same organization as 1921 census except that individual schedules were utilized, and tabulation was mechanical. Territory covered by the census was divided into five zones, subdivided into "departamentos" (states) and "municipios." Urban and rural population were distinguished. Scope included age, sex, race, religion, language (new), literacy, persons of school age (seven to fourteen), marital status, infirmities, nationality, industry, and occupation. Tables comparing results with 1880, 1893, and 1921 censuses were also presented. There was a questionnaire with housing topics, but results were not tabulated. The figures emerging from this census were greatly inflated. Results were published nineteen months after enumeration.

The permanent census office was established in 1948, and it was decided that a census should be taken decennially.

1950

The sixth census of population was conducted simultaneously with an agricultural census by the Dirección General de Estadística. The census organization followed the recommendations suggested by COTA 1950. Enumeration was carried out on a *de facto* basis, including foreign diplomatic personnel living in the country while excluding its own diplomatic personnel living in other countries. Canvasser was the method utilized to gather information on household schedules. Tabulation was mechanical with punched cards. The territory was divided into twenty-two "departamentos" (states) and subdivided into "municipios." Urban and rural areas were distinguished as well.

Definitions and Concepts. URBAN—all places with 2,000 or more inhabitants and places with a population between 1,500 and 2,000 with water services. Preliminary results, however, followed the traditional definition of urban; that is, all cities, villages, and pueblos. HOUSEHOLD ("familia censal")—person or groups of persons, related or not by blood, living in the same house and sharing food arrangements. Servants who eat with the family but sleep in different dwellings were counted separately. AGE—in completed years. If less than a year of age the number of months or the number of days was recorded. Presented in single years and standard five-year age groups. Tabulation for months or days of persons less than one year was not presented. MARITAL STATUS—categories were: never married, married, common-law marriage, widowed, and divorced. ETHNIC GROUP—only two groups were recorded: Ladino (nonindigenous) and indigenous. Social and cultural criteria were used for classification. As a result, persons belonging to the yellow and black races were classified as Ladino. PLACE OF BIRTH—state and "municipio" for native born and country of birth for foreigners. NATIONALITY—used to indicate citizenship rather than ethnicity. PLACE OF RESIDENCE—usual place and previous place of residence ("municipio" or country of residence on January 1, 1945). RELIGION—the following religions were recorded: Catholic, Protestant, Israelites, and others. In case of omission, the religion of the family or the dominant religion of the area was allocated. LANGUAGE—language spoken at home. Categories were: Spanish, "lengua indigena" (indigenous language) and other languages (English, German, French, Italian, Chinese, and other). The indigenous language was subdivided into sixteen languages, following the classification of the Linguistic Institute of Guatemala. The questions were asked of all persons three years of age and older. EDUCATION—literacy, school enrollment, and educational attainment (new). Questions asked of all persons seven years and older. CULTURAL CHARAC-TERISTICS—type of food and clothing, and whether the person was living in a "rancho" (ranch). The definition of ranch was not given. ECONOMIC ACTIVITY—lower age limit was seven years of age. Period of reference was the month before the census. Economically active included: employed and unemployed persons looking for a job. Labor force criteria was followed. Inactive population: students, homemakers, invalids, inmates of institutions, pensioners, persons of independent income, the retired, and others not included in previous categories. OCCUPATION—classification based on COTA 1950, major groups, groups, and sub-groups (three-digits). INDUSTRY—classification based on ISIC, divisions, major groups, and groups (three-digits). OCCUPATIONAL STATUS—categories were: employer, employee, self-employed, and unpaid family worker. Reasons for inactivity were also recorded.

Special Elements and Features. Practically all tabulations were prepared taking into consideration ethnic groups as a criterion for classification. Cultural characteristics, previous place of residence, place of birth, educational attainment, occupational status, reasons for unemployment or inactivity were recorded for the first time. Graphs, maps, and a copy of the schedules were included. Labor force criteria were utilized for the first time.

Quality of the Census. Preliminary results were published four months after enumeration. Permanent census office was established. Test censuses were taken to improve quality of enumeration, coverage, and to check applicability of the questionnaire. A special program was set for personnel training. Whipple's Index classified age data into category V—very rough data. Despite a long history of censuses, regularity has not been observed; the interval between censuses varied from three to twenty-eight years. Publication of final results began three years after the census.

Publication Plan. Guatemala. Dirección General de Estadística. *Sexto censo de población, abril 18 de 1950* [Guatemala 1953]. *Sexto censo de población* [Guatemala, 1957]. Other volumes were promised but none have been seen. Language of publication is Spanish.

1964 (April 18)

For various reasons this census, planned to be taken in 1960, had to be postponed. The seventh census of population was conducted by the Dirección General de Estadística, simultaneously with censuses of housing and agriculture. The census was *de facto*: canvasser was the method used to gather information on household schedules. Tabulation was mechanical with punched cards. Manual tabulation was also utilized to obtain preliminary results. Census organization followed recommendations suggested by COTA 1960. The territory covered by the census was divided into five zones, subdivided into "departamentos" (states) and "municipios."

Definitions and Concepts. URBAN—population in officially recognized cities, towns, and villages. HOUSEHOLD—persons or groups of persons, related or not by blood, living like a family, or together for disciplinary, health, or religious reasons. Households are divided into private and group quarters. AGE, MARITAL STATUS, LANGUAGE—same as 1950. ETHNIC GROUP—based on social consensus and divided into two major groups, indigenous and non-indigenous. PLACE OF BIRTH, LANGUAGE and CULTURAL CHARAC-TERISTICS—same as 1950. NATIONALITY—citizenship by birth or natural-ization. If foreign born the name of the country was also recorded. PLACE OF RESIDENCE—duration and previous residence. RELIGION—same categories used in 1950. EDUCATION—literacy, school enrollment, and educational at-tainment (last degree completed) same as 1950. FERTILITY—for the first time recorded in the census. Questions asked only of all women who have had chil-dren: number of children ever born alive, and age of mother at birth of the first child. ECONOMIC ACTIVITY—lower age limit was seven years of age. Pe-riod of reference was the same as 1950 (the month before the census) but in 1950 those who were classified as working (employed) were all persons who worked at least one day during the reference period; whereas in 1964 the criterion was at least six continuous days. Economically active were all employed persons and unemployed looking for a job. Inactive included homemakers, students, inmates of institutions, the retired, pensioners, persons of independent income, and invalids. The number of months worked was also recorded. OCCUPATION—main occupation or occupation at the day of the census. Unemployed persons recorded the last occupation. Classification based on ISCO, major groups, groups, and subgroups (three-digits). INDUSTRY—classification based on ISIC, divisions, major groups, and units (three-digits). OCCUPATIONAL STATUS—employers, employees, self-employed, paid family workers, unpaid family workers. Affiliation to IGSS (Social Security Institute of Guatemala) was recorded for the first time.

Special Elements and Features. Number of months worked, fertility, and IGSS membership were recorded for the first time. The definition of urban was changed. The population of the main cities of the American countries (North, Central, and South America) was presented. Occupational and industrial classifications were furnished.

Quality of the Census. Test censuses were taken to check effectiveness of schedules as well as to estimate the time needed for the final enumeration. Preliminary results and sampling results were published by 1964, but final results were only available in 1971. A postenumeration survey was, for the first time, carried out. The results indicated a 3.7 percent underenumeration with practically no difference between omissions in rural and urban areas. Discrepancies of answers to the questionnaires amounted to 9.2 percent, and the question that presented the largest percentage of error was age (20.3 percent). Results of the PES were published in June 1965. Evaluation of census results was also based on comparisons with birth registration records. Whipple's Index was category IV—rough age data.

Publication Plan. Guatemala. Dirección General de Estadística. *VII censo de población, 1964.* Guatemala, 1971-1972. Volumes 1-3, plus four sample tabulation volumes. Language of publication is Spanish.

1973 (March 26)

The eighth census of population was taken by the Dirección General de Estadística in conjunction with a census of housing. The organization of the census was based on previous census operations, U.N. recommendations, and COTA 1970. The census was taken on a *de jure* basis for the first time; canvasser was the method used to record information on household schedules. Tabulation was computerized. Territory covered by the census was divided into areas (urban/rural), "departamentos" (states) and "municipios."

Definitions and Concepts. URBAN, AGE—same as 1964. HOUSEHOLD—person or group of persons, related or not by blood, living in the same dwelling and sharing food arrangements. MARITAL STATUS—categories were the same in 1950 and 1964, but at this time persons less than thirteen years of age were considered never married. ETHNIC GROUP—based on social consensus and direct question. In previous censuses cultural characteristics and language were asked to complement the answers about ethnic groups; in this census however, these characteristics were not included in the schedules. PLACE OF BIRTH—

same as 1950. PLACE OF RESIDENCE—usual place of residence, residence five years before the census; year of arrival in the country was also asked of foreign-born, permanent residents. EDUCATION—literacy, school enrollment, and educational attainment (last degree completed). There is a slight difference in the way the questions were asked in 1964 and 1973. ECONOMIC ACTIVITY— lower age limit was ten years of age. Period of reference was the week before the census (new). Economically active population included persons who worked, persons who did not work but had a job, unemployed (experienced) looking for a job, and unemployed looking for a job for the first time. Inactive population included homemakers, students, the retired, pensioners, persons of independent income, and others (inmates of institutions). OCCUPATION—main or last occupation. Classification based on ISCO, major groups, groups, and subgroups (three-digits). INDUSTRY—classification based on ISIC, divisions, major groups and units (three-digits). OCCUPATIONAL STATUS—categories were employer, employee, self-employed, unpaid family worker (fifteen hours per week minimum). FERTILITY—questions asked of all women age fifteen and older: number of children born alive and number of children still living. Affiliation to IGSS (Social Security Institute of Guatemala) was also recorded.

Special Elements and Features. De jure census conducted for the first time. Cultural characteristics, language, religion, nationality, and age at first birth were dropped. Place of residence similar to 1950. Fertility was asked of all women age fifteen and older instead of only women with children as in 1964. Economic activity presented different age limit and period of reference. Computerized tabulation provided larger number of cross-classifications; not all were published but results are available on request. The tables for Guatemala City were also tabulated by zones (twenty-five neighborhoods). Orphanhood was introduced in this census.

Quality of the Census. The organization and methodology employed were based on international recommendations. Three test censuses were carried out in preparation for the final enumeration. Preliminary results were manually tabulated and available in 1973, sampling results (5 percent of households) were available in 1974, and final results were published 1974-1977. Maps were made for all cities and urban places of thirty and more dwellings. Whipple's Index was category IV—rough age data.

Publication Plan. Guatemala. Dirección General de Estadística. *Censos, VII de población y III de habitation, 26 de marzo-1 de abril 1973.* Guatemala, 1973-1977. Series 1-3 in five volumes (published so far). Unpublished data and computer tapes are available. Language of publication is Spanish.

OTHER STATISTICAL PUBLICATIONS: Issued by Dirección General de Estadística, *Anuario Estadístico, Boletín Estadístico* (semiannually), *Informador Estadístico* (weekly), *Trimestre Estadístico.*

National Topic Chart

	1950	1964	1973
De facto	X	X	
Usual residence	X		X
Place of birth	X	X	X
Duration of residence		X	
Place of prev. residence	X	X	X
Urban/rural	X	X	X
Sex	X	X	X
Age	X	X	X
Relation to household head	X	X	X
Marital status	X	X	X
Children born alive		X	X
Children living			X
Citizenship	X	X	
Literacy	X	X	X
School enrollment	X	X	X
Ed. attainment	X	X	X
Ed. qualification			
National/Ethnic origin	X	X	X
Language	X	X	
Religion	X	X	
Household composition	X	X	X
Econ. active/inactive	X	X	X
Occupation	X	X	X
Industry	X	X	X
Occupational status	X	X	X
Income			
Housing		X	X

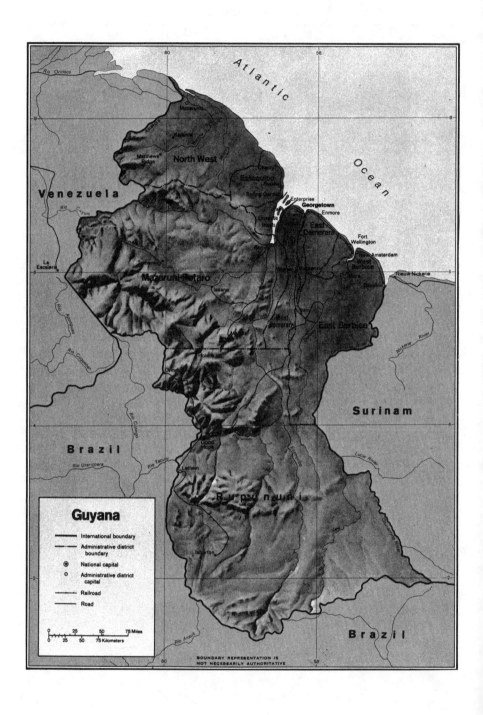

Guyana

— International boundary

—·— Administrative district boundary

⊛ National capital

○ Administrative district capital

——— Railroad

——— Road

0 · · · 25 · · · 50 · · · 75 Miles

0 25 50 75 Kilometers

BOUNDARY REPRESENTATION IS
NOT NECESSARILY AUTHORITATIVE

Guyana

Cooperative Republic of Guyana

CAPITAL: Georgetown.
STATISTICAL AGENCY: Statistical Bureau, Ministry of Economic Development.
NATIONAL REPOSITORY: Libraries of the Statistical Bureau and the University of Guyana at Turkeyen.
MAIN U.S. REPOSITORY: New York Public Library (early censuses), Population Research Center (Univ. of Texas).

Although geographically South American, Guyana is identified as Caribbean. Guyana (former British Guiana) was first settled in the late seventeenth century by the Dutch who built seawalls and drainage systems to make the below sea-level land along the Atlantic Coast habitable. The British firmly established rule in 1815 in the three colonies of Berbice, Essequibo, and Demerara. In 1831 the three were united as one colony, known as British Guiana. Guyana became an independent state within the British Commonwealth in 1966 and proclaimed itself a republic in 1970. Ninety percent of the population lives in 5 percent of the land area, the narrow coastal strip. The Amerindians, 4 percent of the population, mainly live in the interior and have not been integrated into Guyana society. The 1851 to 1946 censuses enumerated only those who lived in settled areas; the rest of the population was estimated. The censuses since 1841 have been *de facto*, canvassed, and conducted by the Registrar General's Office. Guyana has traditionally used a realistic treatment of areal breakdown; the cities of Georgetown and New Amsterdam were separated from the remainder of their counties in the tables. There were also tables with numbers of inhabitants by race for every sugar estate, village, farm, and institution. They have also traditionally distinguished between the local and foreign born by race.

There was a rough count of people in 1831. The 1841 census gave total population, urban/rural (Georgetown and New Amsterdam/remainder), and sex. Results can be seen in comparative tables, censuses of 1931 or 1946. Comparative tables in the 1861 census gave the scope of the census of 1851 as country of birth, urban/rural (same as 1841), sex, and age (over and under twenty).

1861

Conducted by the Registrar General's Office, it was *de facto* and probably canvassed. Details as to its organization and methodology are missing. Scope included country of birth, total and detailed local populations, urban/rural, sex, age, marital status (new), race (origin rather than complexion), occupation, and number of dwellings. Tables included numbers of indentured immigrants.

1871

Same as 1861 plus infirmities.

1881

Same as 1871 plus economically active/inactive in the occupation table.

1891

Same as 1881 plus school attendance in the occupation table. Race was changed from origin to complexion.
No census was taken in 1901.

1911

The same conduct and scope as 1891 plus religion. There are an index to the tables (geographic area by subject), a separate section on East Indians, and comparative tables. Figures of immigration and emigration from other sources were incorporated in the report.

1921

Same as 1911 plus size of household, orphanhood, registered voters, and place of work. Table of immigration (arriving and leaving) from 1835 to 1921 was included in the report.

1931

Same as 1921 but dropped place of work, orphanhood, and registered voters. First report to have a copy of the schedule used (household) and first to state that the census was self-enumerated. Marital status expanded to include divorce, occupation included both main and subsidiary. Age groups are nonstandard (one, two, three, four, five, six to ten, eleven to fifteen...).

1946 (April 9)

First of the closely coordinated Caribbean censuses conducted by the Registrar General's Office. [See British West Indies 1946 for full entry.] As a result of this coordination, this is the first time that other Asiatics were included as well as Chinese and East Indians. Race is more complexion than origin, continuing a trend started in the 1891 census. For the first time industry was taken with detailed tables for both occupation and industry. Fertility included legitimacy and birth order. Farm holdings were also asked. Household composition asked size only.

Geographic divisions: Three counties were divided into eight administrative districts, two cities divided into wards. All divided into enumeration districts.

Whipple's Index category was III—approximate age data.

Publication Plan. Volume D of the British West Indies 1946 set is devoted to Guyana (British Guiana). Language of publication is English.

1960 (April 7)

This was the second coordinated Caribbean census. [See British West Indies 1960, Eastern Caribbean section, for full entry.] No differences from that entry in Guyana. This was, however, the first attempt made to enumerate the Amerindians in remote areas. This was done in January 1960 because April was the rainy season in that area. No adjustments were made in the data for the difference.

No Whipple's Index rating was available.

Publication Plan. Volume 1, parts A and E; Volume 2, parts 1 and 2; and Volume 3, parts A and G (1 volume), B and D (1 volume), and E and F (1 volume) contain the data for Guyana in the British West Indies 1960, Eastern Caribbean, set. Language of publication is English.

1970 (April 7)

Third coordinated Caribbean census is described in the British West Indies 1970 entry. Geographic divisions were the same as 1960. Whipple's Index category is III—approximate age data.

Publication Plan. Volumes, 3; 4.3; 4.16; 5; 6.1; 7; 8 abc; 9.1; 10.1 and 10.4 of the British West Indies 1970 set contain the results for Guyana. The following is a separate publication: Guyana. Statistical Bureau. *Population Census, 1970; Summary Tables.* [Georgetown], 197? Computer tapes are available at the Census Research Programme, University of the West Indies. Language of publication is English.

OTHER STATISTICAL PUBLICATIONS: Issued by Statistical Bureau, *International Migration Report* (annually), *Quarterly Statistical Digest, Statistical Abstract* (annually).

National Topic Chart

	1946	1960	1970
De facto	X	X	X
Usual residence		X	X
Place of birth	X	X	X
Duration of residence		X	X
Place of prev. residence			X
Urban/rural			X
Sex	X	X	X
Age	X	X	X
Relation to household head	X	X	X
Marital status	X	X	X
Children born alive	X	X	X
Children living	X		
Citizenship			
Literacy	X		
School enrollment	X	X	X
Ed. attainment		X	X
Ed. qualification			
National/Ethnic origin	X	X	X
Language			
Religion	X	X	X
Household composition	X	X	X
Econ. active/inactive	X	X	X
Occupation	X	X	X
Industry	X	X	X
Occupational status	X	X	X
Income		X	X
Housing	X	X	X

Haiti

Republic of Haiti

CAPITAL: Port-au-Prince.
STATISTICAL AGENCY: Institut Haitien de Statistique.
NATIONAL REPOSITORY: Institut Haitien de Statistique et d'Informatique.
MAIN U.S. REPOSITORY: Population Research Center (Univ. of Texas).

Discovered by Columbus in 1492, it became a haven of French buccaneers who later turned planters. In 1804 Haiti became the world's first Negro republic and the second oldest republic in the Western Hemisphere (after the United States). In 1822 it captured the present-day Dominican Republic but lost it again in 1844. Due to political and economic disorder it was occupied by the United States from 1915 to 1934. The territory includes the islands of Tortuga and Gonâve. The first national census was taken in 1950 and the second in 1971.

1950 (August 8)

The first census of Haiti was conducted by the Institut Haïtien de Statistique. It was *de jure*, canvassed, and probably mechanically tabulated. There were household, group quarter, and institution schedules used. The territorial divisions were five departments subdivided into "arrondissements" and "communes." Information is available to the commune level.

Definitions and Concepts. URBAN—designated cities (no minimum population size stated). HOUSEHOLD—one person living alone or a group of persons sharing common household arrangements, including live-in servants and boarders. USUAL RESIDENCE and BIRTHPLACE—commune for the native born, and country for the foreign. Combined, these give basic data on internal migration and immigration. AGE—in completed years. Tables in standard five-year age groups only. MARITAL STATUS—single (never married nor cohabiting), legally married (totals included married who live with other than legal spouse), common law (cohabiting but not legally married persons only), widowed, legally divorced, legally separated. EDUCATION—literacy (ability to read and write more than just name) and educational attainment (highest grade completed). NATIONALITY—taken to distinguish those of Haitian citizenship from foreigners. ECONOMIC ACTIVITY—(age fourteen and over). Reference period was the week before the census date. The active were those working for pay or

Haiti

profit and the unemployed who were looking for work. This group also included the unpaid family worker, part-time and religious workers, and apprentices. The inactive were homemakers, students, those of independent income, the retired, invalids and all others not elsewhere classified. OCCUPATION—main occupation. Classified in ten major divisions according to COTA 1950. INDUSTRY—Classed in nine major groups according to ISIC, 1948. OCCUPATIONAL STATUS—government employee and private enterprise employee (salaried), unpaid family worker, own-account worker with employees, own-account worker without employees. HOUSEHOLD COMPOSITION—size, type (with or without live-in servants or boarders), and characteristics of head.

Special Elements and Features. Census taken in conjunction with censuses of housing and agriculture.

Quality of the Census. Special questions on urban population afflicted and cured of Yaws asked, but no results appear in publications. Age had to be smoothed and unknown ages grouped proportionally. Even so the Whipple's Index category was V—very rough data. The census office is permanent.

Publication Plan. Haiti. Institut Haïtien de Statistique. *Recensement général de la République d'Haiti, août 1950.* Department volumes 1-5 in 8 volumes plus a preliminary and a revised final population numbers volume. Language of publication is French.

1971 (August 31)

The conduct and organization was very much like the census of 1950. The main difference was that the rural population was enumerated by a ten percent sample. The territorial division was the same as 1950, but the tables were for metropolitan areas and cities as well as for communes.

Definitions and Concepts. URBAN—specified metropolitan areas and cities (no minimum population size cited). HOUSEHOLD, BIRTHPLACE, NATIONALITY, and INDUSTRY—same as 1950. AGE—same as 1950 plus number of completed months for children under one year. Table of single years was also included. MARITAL STATUS—the married but cohabiting with other than legal spouse included in common law category, instead of married. Separated included with divorced. RELIGION (new)—major denominations (Catholic, Protestant, other). FERTILITY (new)—asked of women fifteen to forty-nine years of age: number of children born alive in last twelve months. EDUCATION—same as 1950 plus school enrollment. ECONOMIC ACTIVITY—reference period changed from one week to six months preceding the census. Amount of time worked in last six months and days worked in preceding week were also asked. OCCUPATION and INDUSTRY—same as 1950 but classification expanded to two-digit level. OCCUPATIONAL STATUS—employer, own-account worker, salaried, paid or unpaid family helper, other.

Special Elements and Features. There is emphasis on internal migration with the addition of questions on duration of residence and place of previous residence. Questions on fertility, on religion, and on school enrollment were added.

Also new to this census was the number of deaths during the last twelve months (name, age, sex).

Quality of the Census. The census office was aided by the United Nations with finances and technical advice. Census maps were prepared; however, some rural ones were lacking in detail; schedules and instructions were tested by a pilot census. ISIC and ISCO were adapted to local conditions. The report claims this census to be "of reasonably good reliability." Selection of "cities" (that is, urban) based on purely administrative notions so some areas of urban character were not included. Other quotes of interest: "Intended as a *de jure* census it turned out to be more a *de facto* one" and "Data on housing and economic activity are a bit weak." Whipple's Index was category IV—rough age data.

Publication Plan. Haiti. Institut Haïtien de Statistique. *Recensement général de la population et du logement, août 1971.* Port-au-Prince, 1978-79. Volume 1, whole country; volumes 2-6, departments; volume 7, agriculture. The preliminary results publication gives number of houses, households, and persons for the nine new departments, which were expanded from the traditional five in 1971. The final result publications, however, give results for the original five departments. Language of publication is French.

OTHER STATISTICAL PUBLICATIONS: Issued by Institut Haïtien de Statistique, *Bulletin de Statistique—Supplément Annuel, Bulletin Trimestriel de Statistique, Fiche Statistique, Guide Economique.*

National Topic Chart

	1950	1971
De facto		
Usual residence	X	X
Place of birth	X	X
Duration of residence		X
Place of prev. residence		X
Urban/rural	X	X
Sex	X	X
Age	X	X
Relation to household head	X	X
Marital status	X	X
Children born alive		X
Children living		
Citizenship	X	X
Literacy	X	X
School enrollment		X
Ed. attainment	X	X
Ed. qualification		
National/Ethnic origin	X	X
Language		
Religion		X
Household composition	X	X
Econ. active/inactive	X	X
Occupation	X	X
Industry	X	X
Occupational status	X	X
Income		
Housing	X	X

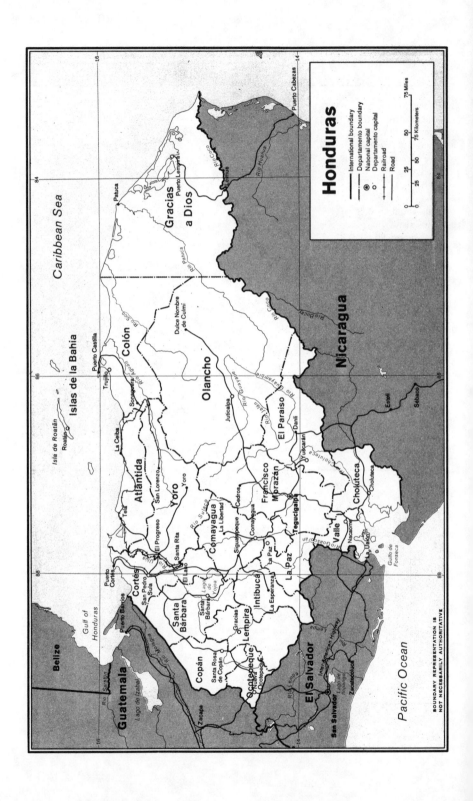

Honduras

Republic of Honduras

CAPITAL: Tegucigalpa.
STATISTICAL AGENCY: Dirección General de Estadística y Censos (DGEC).
NATIONAL REPOSITORY: Biblioteca of DGEC.
MAIN U.S. REPOSITORY: New York Public Library, Population Research Center (Univ. of Texas).

The colonial period lasted from 1524 to 1821 when Honduras along with other Central American countries declared its independence from Spain. In 1823, it became part of a Central American federation and finally in 1838 an independent republic. Tegucigalpa was established as capital of the country in 1880.

The number of enumerations and estimates taken in the early days vary according to the source consulted, mainly because of the lack of a central office responsible for census operations. The later censuses (1961, 1974), however, seem to agree that four censuses were taken in the nineteenth century and were followed by ten to date.

1791

The first census was actually a resumé of church records from 1789 to 1791.

1801

Record of total population collected from 1791 to 1801.

1881 and 1887

Censuses taken by statistics officers. Simultaneity seemed to have been achieved in the 1887 enumeration, which, although better conducted than the previous one, still greatly underenumerated the population. In some places omissions reached 50 percent because of the refusal of the indigenous to be counted.

1901

An enumeration was carried out and compared with the records of military personnel and civilians that were organized by the government. Total population of "departamentos" (states) and "municipios" by sex was recorded. Tribes were not included and results were considered incomplete (10 percent omitted).

1910

Census taken by the Dirección General de Estadística, but no details of organization and methods were furnished. Many tribes were not enumerated, and the questionnaire used included the following features: total population, age, sex, marital status, citizenship, literacy, race, language, number of children with elementary education, number of professionals, property ownership, and vaccination. Available results, however, are limited to total number of inhabitants in comparison with 1905, number of houses, and number of inhabitants per house.

1916

Census taken by the Dirección General de Estadística but there were no details as far as organization and methods. Results included: total population by sex and number of private houses and buildings. A comparison with records of 1910 and 1916 numbers of inhabitants indicated it was largely underenumerated. The territory was divided into seventeen "departamentos" and "municipios."

1926

Census of population was taken by the Dirección General de Estadística on *de jure* and *de facto* bases. Canvasser was the method implied ("empadronamiento directo"), but no details were given. Scope included total population of "departamentos" and "municipios" by sex, nationality, and literacy. Population was divided into residents and transients.

1930

The Dirección General de Estadística was established as a central office. The country was divided into seventeen "departamentos" (states) and "municipios." No details of the census operation were given. Comparative tables for 1910, 1916, and 1926 were presented. The scope was the most extensive so far: total population, age, sex, urban/rural, race, infirmities, citizenship, marital status, property ownership, occupation, religion, literacy, school enrollment, number of private houses, and number of families.

1935

Census was taken by the Dirección General de Estadística. Again there were no details of organization, and the scope was the same as 1930.

1940

Census was taken by the same office. Conduct, scope, and territorial division were the same as 1930 and 1935.

1945 (June 24)

Census of population was taken by the Dirección General de Estadística. No details were furnished as far as organization and methods utilized, and only a reduced number of tables were published. The territory covered by the census was divided into seventeen "departamentos," subdivided into "municipios." The "departamentos" of Tegucigalpa and Gracias changed their names to Francisco Morazán and Lempira, respectively. It is not known whether there were territorial size changes involved. Information gathered here was taken from introductory notes and table headings.

Definitions and Concepts. AGE—presented in ten-day groups (zero to nine, ten to nineteen, twenty to twenty-nine days), five-month groups (one to five and six to eleven), single years (one to four), and standard five-year age groups. MARITAL STATUS—categories were: single, married, widowed, and divorced. RACE—the following groups were recorded: indigenous, mestizos, whites, yellow, and blacks. NATIONALITY—country of citizenship, including Honduras. EDUCATION—literacy (ability to read and write), school enrollment (only for ages seven through fifteen), educational attainment (only for the first five grades) recorded for the first time. RELIGION—categories were: Catholics, Protestants, Buddhists, Muslims, and others. OCCUPATION—not divided into groups, but rather 122 professions were alphabetically presented.

Special Elements and Features. Educational attainment was recorded for the first time. Legitimacy of the whole population was recorded. Property ownership was recorded for native and foreign born persons.

Quality of the Census. Whipple's Index made no reference to age accuracy. Based on 1950 census comments, the early censuses (those before 1950) were inaccurate and with a large percentage of underenumeration.

Publication Plan. Honduras. Dirección General de Estadística y Census. *Resumen del censo general de población levantado el 24 de junio de 1945.* Tegucigalpa, 1947. Language of publication is Spanish.

1950 (June 18)

The census of population was conducted by the Dirección General de Censos and Estadística. As was cited in the introduction, the number of censuses taken differs from source to source. The censuses of 1961 and of 1974 indicate that this is the twelfth national census taken even though the report of this census called it the thirteenth.

The census was conducted during a transition time when the Dirección General de Censos and Estadística was being reorganized. Therefore, the census did not differ fundamentally from the previous ones. The methods suggested by the COTA 1950 could not be closely followed. The census was *de facto*, and canvasser was the method utilized to record information on general schedules.

Tabulation was manual, and the data was presented for "departamentos" (states), "municipios," and districts.

Definitions and Concepts. AGE—in completed years, and number of months if the person was less than one year of age. Tables were presented in standard five-year age groups and single months. MARITAL STATUS: asked of all persons over fourteen years of age. Categories were: married, separated, common-law marriage, widowed, divorced, and never married. URBAN—inhabited centers and seats of the municipalities. The number of inhabitants was not taken into consideration. PLACE OF BIRTH—departamento (state) of birth was recorded of persons born in the country. NATIONALITY—derived from the question of whether a citizen or foreign born. The latter also recorded the country of birth. EDUCATION—for all persons age ten years and older: literacy and educational attainment (last degree). College educated persons were tabulated by separate fields. HOUSEHOLD ("familia censal")—included all persons, related or not by blood, living in the same place on the day of the census. SOCIOECONOMIC CHARACTERISTICS—derived from the following questions: whether the person used shoes or not; whether the person ate wheat bread, and the type of bed the person used. ECONOMIC ACTIVITY—gainfully employed concept was adopted. The following groups were considered economically active: employees, employers, self-employed, unpaid family workers, homemakers and students who also had a paid occupation, members of the armed forces, and the unemployed looking for a job. Inactive population indicated only homemakers without further details. The time worked during the census year and causes of unemployment were also recorded but not tabulated. INDUSTRY—classification based on ISIC, nine divisions (one-digit). OCCUPATION—main occupation. Classification based on COTA 1950, major groups and subgroups (two-digits). OCCUPATIONAL STATUS—categories were employee, employer and self-employed, and unpaid family worker.

Special Elements and Features. A separate volume was published in 1954 (two years after the publication of general results) with more detailed information for "municipios" and districts and corrections of errors detected in the previous publication; however, economic activities were omitted. Details of organization, maps, and graphs were available as was a copy of the schedules. It was the most complete census yet taken. Place of birth, economic activity, industry, occupational status, and socioeconomic status were recorded for the first time. School attendance, race, religion, infirmities, and property ownership were dropped.

Quality of the Census. Underenumeration was considered high in some areas. Accuracy was deficient mainly due to lack of preparation of census personnel. Some questions were answered inappropriately, especially the ones related to economic activities. Missing data were supplied based on information from other sources. Not all personal characteristics were cross-classified by age and sex; in most cases tabulation considered sex differentiation only. Ten percent was added to the total population enumerated to compensate for the underenumeration. Whipple's Index category was not available.

Publication Plan. Honduras. Dirección General de Estadística y Censos. *Resultados generales del censo general de la república levantado el 18 de junio de 1950.* Tegucigalpa, 1952. 1 volume. *Detalle del censo de población por departamentos, levantado el 18 de junio de 1950.* Volumes 1-2. Tegucigalpa, 1954. Language of publication is Spanish.

1961 (April 17)

The thirteenth census of population was conducted by the Dirección General de Estadística y Censos simultaneously with a census of housing. The organization was based on the recommendations suggested by COTA 1960. The enumeration was carried out on a *de facto* basis, and canvasser was the method used to record information on household schedules. Tabulation was mechanical. The territory covered by the census was divided into five zones, subdivided into eighteen "departamentos" (states) and "municipios." The departamento of Gracias a Diós was enumerated for the first time, but estimates for 1950 were available.

It was established in 1960 that a census of housing and population should be taken every ten years, but for economic reasons it took place in 1961.

Definitions and Concepts. HOUSEHOLD—one person or group of persons, related or not by blood, living in the same place. Guests and pensioners were included if not more than five. Private and group quarters were distinguished. URBAN—places with 1,000 or more inhabitants with social services and amenities present. AGE—in completed years or months, if the case. Tabulated in single years, single months, and standard five-year age groups. MARITAL STATUS—ten years and over. Categories were the same as 1950. EDUCATION—literacy (for ten years and older), school enrollment (five years and older) during the month of the census, and educational attainment (last degree completed). PLACE OF BIRTH—state of birth for native born and country of birth for foreign born persons. NATIONALITY—country of citizenship. Honduran nationality included native born and naturalized. ECONOMIC ACTIVITY—economically active population included employed, unemployed looking for a job during the month before the census, and others (not defined before, but who had worked for some time during the year before the census date). Inactives: homemakers, students, persons of independent income, the retired, pensioners, invalids, and inmates of institutions. OCCUPATION—classification based on COTA 1960, major and subgroups (two-digits). INDUSTRY—classification based on ISIC, divisions and major groups (two-digits). OCCUPATIONAL STATUS—categories were: employer, government employee, private employee, self-employed, unpaid family worker (working at least two days per week), others (not well defined occupations such as active members of cooperatives), not known, and looking for job. Time worked during the year before the census was also recorded.

Special Elements and Features. Maps were updated; however, some municipal boundaries remained inaccurate because of unresolved controversies. Household schedules were used for the first time. Sample tabulation and postenumeration survey were applied for the first time. Comparative table of population density for the years 1950 and 1961 was included. Housing census, for the first time, was taken simultaneously with the census of population. No comparison of urban/rural areas is possible between 1950 and 1961 because of the differences in the concepts adopted. Socioeconomic status (shoes, clothing and type of bed) was dropped and school enrollment was revived. Most data were published on departamental level (state).

Quality of the Census. Several test censuses were taken to check applicability of questionnaires, to estimate costs of operations, to prepare census personnel, to check possibility of taking simultaneously the three censuses (population, housing, and agriculture), and to test methods to be applied in the enumeration and postenumeration periods.

Postenumeration studies were done in two different ways: comparing the census results with birth registration and reenumeration of some "municipios" by sample survey. The results of postenumeration indicated that omissions amounted to 5.3 percent in the population census and 6.1 percent in the housing census. Sample tabulation permitted faster availability of results. Whipple's Index was not available. Age and educational attainment questions presented the largest percentage of inaccurate answers.

Publication Plan. Honduras. Dirección General de Estadística y Censos. *Población y vivienda, abril 1961. Departamento de . . .* Tegucigalpa, 1962-1964. 18 volumes plus four preliminary and sample volumes, four volumes for places, and two subject volumes for the whole country. Language of publication is Spanish.

1974 (March 5)

The fourteenth national census of population was conducted by the Dirección General de Estadística y Censos on a *de jure* basis. Canvasser was the method utilized to record information on household schedules. The census of population was taken simultaneously with housing. The territory covered by the census was divided into eighteen "departamentos" (states) subdivided into "municipios."

Definitions and Concepts. HOUSEHOLD—one person or group of persons, related or not by blood, living in the same dwelling and sharing food arrangements. AGE—in completed years, presented in single years and standard five-year age groups. For persons less than one year of age, "00" was recorded. MARITAL STATUS—categories were: never married, married, married but separated, common-law marriage, common-law marriage but separated, divorced, and widowed. ORPHANHOOD—derived from the question, Is your mother alive? PLACE OF BIRTH—"departamento" and "municipio" for native born and country of birth for foreign-born persons. NATIONALITY—questions asked of foreign born only: citizenship and year of arrival in the country. PLACE OF RESIDENCE—(five years of age and older) usual, previous (in March 1969), and duration of residence. EDUCATION—literacy, school enrollment, educational attainment (last degree completed), educational qualification. Questions were asked of all persons six years and older. ECONOMIC ACTIVITY—lower age limit was ten years of age. Reference period was the week before the census. Economically active included employed and unemployed persons (looking for a job for the first time or not). The inactive were: students, homemakers, the retired, invalids, persons of independent income, pensioners, inmates of institutions. OCCUPATION—classification based on COTA 1970, major and subgroups (two-digits). INDUSTRY—classification based on ISIC, divisions and major groups (two-digits). OCCUPATIONAL STATUS—categories were: employer, self-employed, employee, unpaid family worker (fifteen hours or more per week). FERTILITY—questions asked of all women fifteen years of age or older: number of children born alive, how many live in the same house, how many live outside, how many are dead, date of birth of last child, and whether still alive. No tables, however, were presented in the census volume; some data are available in the *UN Demographic Yearbook*.

Special Elements and Features. This was the first totally *de jure* census. Usual, previous, and duration of residence were recorded. Fertility, year of arrival in the country, educational qualification, and orphanhood were asked for the first time. Fertility, however, was not published in the census report.

Quality of the Census. Whipple's Index was category IV—rough age data. No comments were made as far as accuracy of results or coverage of the census. Although with a long history of censuses, only after 1950 were international recommendations taken into consideration. Regularity was observed to some degree, but the exact number of national censuses is subject to controversy. The census office is permanent.

Publication Plan. Honduras. Dirección General de Estadística y Censos. *Censo nacional de población*. Tegucigalpa, 1976-1977. Volumes 1-3. There were also preliminary and sample result volumes. Computer tapes are available. Language of publication is Spanish.

OTHER STATISTICAL PUBLICATIONS: Issued by Dirección General de Estadística y Censos, *Anuario Estadístico*.

National Topic Chart

	1941	1950	1961	1974
De facto		X	X	
Usual residence				X
Place of birth		X	X	X
Duration of residence				X
Place of prev. residence				X
Urban/rural	X	X	X	X
Sex	X	X	X	X
Age	X	X	X	X
Relation to household head	X	X	X	X
Marital status	X	X	X	X
Children born alive				X
Children living				X
Citizenship	X	X	X	X
Literacy	X	X	X	X
School enrollment	X		X	X
Ed. attainment	X	X	X	X
Ed. qualification				X
National/Ethnic origin	X			
Language				
Religion	X			
Household composition				
Econ. active/inactive		X	X	X
Occupation	X	X	X	X
Industry		X	X	X
Occupational status		X	X	X
Income				
Housing			X	X

Jamaica

Independent state of the Commonwealth (1962)

CAPITAL: Kingston.
STATISTICAL AGENCY: Department of Statistics.
NATIONAL REPOSITORY: Department of Statistics.
MAIN U.S. REPOSITORY: New York Public Library, Population Research
Center (Univ. of Texas).

The first Europeans to inhabit Jamaica were Spaniards in 1509, who remained until the English captured the island in 1655. It was made a crown colony in 1866; self-government was granted in 1944, and full internal autonomy was received in 1953. It was a member of the West Indies Federation until 1962 when it received full independence and status as a commonwealth state. The first capital was Spanish Town until 1872 when Kingston was so designated. The major administrative subdivisions are called parishes. The first census (1844) had five parishes, the second (1861), twenty. From 1871 to the present there were fourteen parishes, which allows comparability over that period. Censuses previous to the one of 1943 were *de facto* and self-enumerated. From 1943 on, the censuses have been *de jure* and canvassed.

1844

The first census was at the request of Britain and the island's plantation owners who were worried about the status of the labor force after emancipation (1833-1838). This census was apparently carried out in a manner similar to that used in the English census of 1841. The results were presented by enumeration districts, and the three tables were submitted by letter from the Island Secretary. The figures were considered an underenumeration. Scope included age, sex, race, country of birth, trade or avocation, and number of houses on the several types of plantations.

1861

There is an eight page document, giving the results of this census, but the information also appeared in the *Census of England and Wales for the Year 1861* (Volume 3, *General Report*). Scope included age, sex, race, country of birth, occupation, plus marital status, infirmities, literacy, and numbers attending school.

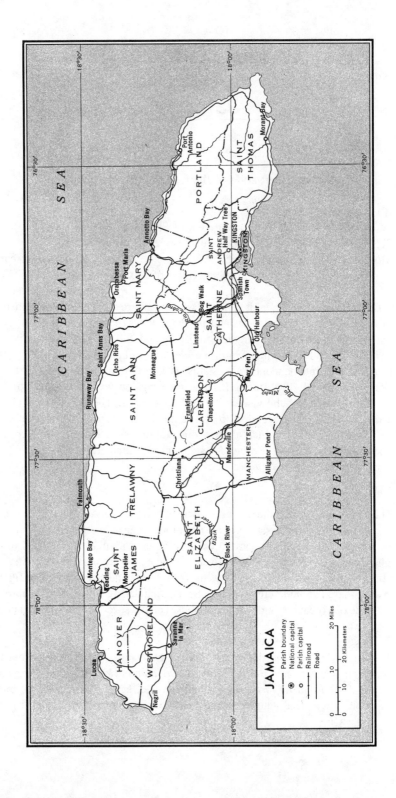

1871

The conduct and scope was the same as that of 1861 plus religion and minus infirmities. One improvement was that instead of the exhaustive list of occupations given in 1861, there was an attempt at recognizing broad categories.

1881

This was the first time that the Registrar General's Office conducted the census. The conduct and scope were more or less the same as that of 1871. There was, however, a description of the main administrative procedures and a further refinement of age groups. Race was expanded to include Indian coolies and Chinese, and occupation was listed in a more orderly fashion following the six major classes used in the England and Wales census of 1861. Houses listed in six categories was last used in 1844. New to this census was the inclusion of the Turks and Caicos Islands in the enumeration.

1891

Conducted in much the same fashion as the census of 1881. There were some improvements in the presentation of data, for example, occupation was given by age groups. Religion was dropped. There were also special returns on the East Indian population. The population numbers given for electoral districts became a regular feature. Infirmities was reinstated.

1911

The conduct and scope was the same as 1891 plus literacy by age and the reinstatement of religion in a new form (preference rather than membership). Cayman Islands was added.

1921

Similar to 1911, the scope was name, relation to family head, age as of last birthday, sex, marital status, race, occupation (not cross-classifed by age, however), literacy and school attendance, religion, country of birth, nationality of foreign born, infirmities, and housing.

A census office was established in June 1942.

1943 (January 4)

The eighth census of Jamaica, conducted by the Central Bureau of Statistics, was *de jure* (new), canvassed (new), and mechanically tabulated. It continued to include Cayman Islands and the Turks and Caicos Islands. Household schedules for population and housing were used with a supplemental schedule for the blind and the deaf-mute. A separate census of agriculture was conducted at the same time.

Definitions and Concepts. USUAL RESIDENCE—specific address. AGE—completed years as of last birthday. Tabulated in single years and standard five-year age groups. Infants under one year were listed by number of completed months. PLACE OF BIRTH—for natives, parish; for nonnatives, country and period of immigration. RELATION TO "FAMILY" HEAD—that is, household head. HOUSEHOLD—a person or group of persons living in one housekeeping community, who may or may not be related but live together with common housekeeping arrangements. Included live-in servants, boarders, and lodgers. MARITAL STATUS—married, single, widowed, divorced, and common law. FERTILITY—asked of all women ever married and all women reporting children: total number of children ever born alive and number of children living. RACE—specific question as to racial origin rather than complexion. NATION-ALITY—British subject by birth, marriage, naturalization (that is, citizenship), and for foreign born, name of country. EDUCATION—literacy, school attendance, and educational attainment. RELIGION—affiliation to specific denominations. HOUSEHOLD COMPOSITION—by size and by number of children. ECONOMIC ACTIVITY—gainfully employed only; inactive were indicated by occupation: retired, homemaker, student, inmate of institution, and so forth. OCCUPATION—subdivisions under industry rather than own classification. INDUSTRY—major divisions similar to ISIC. OCCUPATIONAL STATUS—employer, own-account worker, wage earner, unpaid family worker. INCOME—wages earned only. MIGRATION—length of residence.

Special Elements and Features. First inclusion in the census of common-law marriage; first fertility and migration questions. Table of contents lists cross-analysis tables in addition to tables by single subject. Separate census result tables for the Jamaican dependencies (Turks and Caicos, Cayman) are included in the report.

Quality of the Census. "A landmark, fuller than any other taken in the Colonies of the British Empire to the present time, more comprehensive in detailed analysis, not wanting in accuracy of collection and compilation," according to the census office. A long history of census taking, but no permanent census office until 1942. Canada's Dominion Bureau of Statistics extended advice.

Publication Plan. Jamaica. Central Bureau of Statistics. *Eighth Census of Jamaica and its Dependencies, 1943: Population, Housing and Agriculture.* Kingston, 1945. 1 volume. Language of publication is English.

A sample census was conducted in 1953 in Jamaica and in 1954 in the dependencies.

1960 (April 7)

The ninth census of Jamaica was conducted by the Department of Statistics. [See British West Indies 1960, West Indies section, for full entry; the following are the differences.] Individual mark-sensing schedule cards were used for the resident population. There was also a self-enumeration form for nonresidents. Jamaica has fourteen parishes, which were subdivided into enumeration districts for the census. Tables give data down to the ED level.

Definitions and Concepts. AGE—tables available in single years and standard five-year age groups. FERTILITY—the question "if the child born during the last 12 months was the first" was not asked. EDUCATION—also asked vocational training completed. USUAL RESIDENCE—number of parishes lived in was also requested. INCOME (earnings)—approximate annual income from wages and salaries only.

Special Elements and Features. Census emphasized economic activity.

Quality of the Census. Whipple's Index category was IV—rough age data.

Publication Plan. Jamaica. Department of Statistics. *West Indies Population Census. Census of Jamaica, 7th April 1960.* Volumes 1-2 in 17 volumes. 1, Parts A-D, *Administrative Report*; 2, Parts A-J, *Tables.* Language of publication is English.

1970 (April 7)

The tenth census of Jamaica, conducted by the Department of Statistics, was *de jure* with a *de facto* total, canvassed, and computer tabulated. It included the shipping population in port. [See British West Indies 1970 entry.] The following comes from Jamaica's own set of publications.

Definitions and Concepts. URBAN—same as 1960, except minimum number of inhabitants increased to 2,500. USUAL RESIDENCE—where one spends the greater part of the year (home, boarding school, long-time institutional resident, and so forth; fishermen [home], seamen [vessel]). For native, parish and locality; for foreign born, country. HOUSEHOLD—a person who lives alone or a group who live together and may or may not eat together. DWELLING—all the living quarters of a household (dwelling equals household). Hence, dwellings and households are divided into private and nonprivate (six or more paying boarders or lodgers). AGE, BIRTHPLACE, RACE, RELIGION, MIGRATION—same as 1960. MARITAL STATUS—same as 1960 plus "legally separated." East Indians married by custom are included in married. EDUCATION—school enrollment, educational attainment, and vocational training. ECONOMIC ACTIVITY—all persons age ten and over not attending school: gainfully employed concept, main activity during past year asked. Active and inactive were the same as 1960. OCCUPATION—main occupation. INDUSTRY—type of business. Both classification schemes were developed for this region and based largely on those developed or proposed by the ILO (ISCO, ISIC). OCCUPATIONAL STATUS—same as 1960 plus number of months worked. There is also a labor force type of question: the economic situation and total hours worked, including overtime, in the past week. FERTILITY—all females age fourteen and over: number of children ever born alive, age at first live birth, age at last live birth (new), number of live births and stillbirths during the last twelve months, union status at present or at age forty-five, duration of union (new). INCOME— all age ten and over: total wages and pay period.

Special Elements and Features. In the migration results, the intermediate moves of those still resident in parish of birth were discounted. Literacy was dropped. Census maps were provided. Stillbirths asked for the first time. The method and length of vocational training were asked. Two newly published volumes give geographic codes of all areas.

Quality of the Census: Maps as well as verbal descriptions of boundaries are provided. With a long history of census taking and a permanent census office, Jamaica published its own census result volumes in addition to the Commonwealth Caribbean set. Whipple's Index is not available. There were 34,800 persons for whom incomplete data was obtained.

Publication Plan. Jamaica. Department of Statistics. *Commonwealth Caribbean Population Census, 1970. Jamaica*. Kingston, 1974. Volumes, 1-6 in ? volumes. 1, *Administrative Report*; 2, *Subject Matter at Parish, Constituency or Special Area*; 3, *Subject Matter at Education Level*; 4, *Enumeration District Tables*; 5, *Enumeration District Maps and Descriptions*; 6, *Demographic Atlas of Urban Areas*. Also the Commonwealth Caribbean set. Computer tapes are available. Language of publication is English.

OTHER STATISTICAL PUBLICATIONS: Issued by Department of Statistics, *Demographic Statistics* (annually), *Pocketbook of Statistics* (annually), *Statistical Abstract* (annually), *Statistical Yearbook*. Issued by Registrar General's Department, *Registrar General's Annual Report*.

National Topic Chart

	1943	1960	1970
De facto		X	
Usual residence	X	X	X
Place of birth	X	X	X
Duration of residence	X	X	X
Place of prev. residence			X
Urban/rural		X	X
Sex	X	X	X
Age	X	X	X
Relation to household head	X	X	X
Marital status	X	X	X
Children born alive	X	X	X
Children living	X		
Citizenship	X		
Literacy	X	X	
School enrollment	X	X	X
Ed. attainment	X	X	X
Ed. qualification			
National/Ethnic origin	X	X	X
Language			
Religion	X	X	X
Household composition	X	X	
Econ. active/inactive		X	X
Occupation	X	X	X
Industry	X	X	X
Occupational status	X	X	X
Income	X	X	X
Housing	X	X	X

Martinique

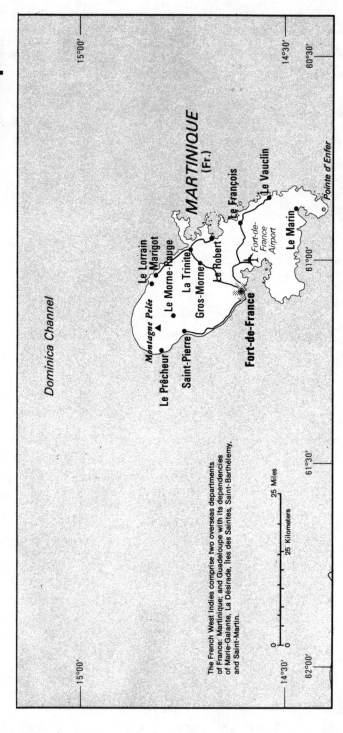

Dominica Channel

MARTINIQUE
(Fr.)

Le Lorrain
Marigot
Le Morne-Rouge
Montagne Pelée ▲
La Trinité
Le Prêcheur
Gros-Morne
Saint-Pierre
Le Robert
Le François
Le Vauclin
Fort-de-France Airport
Fort-de-France
Le Marin
Pointe d'Enfer

The French West Indies comprise two overseas departments
of France: Martinique; and Guadeloupe with its dependencies
of Marie-Galante, La Désirade, Îles des Saintes, Saint-Barthélemy,
and Saint-Martin.

25 Miles
25 Kilometers
0
0

15°00'
14°30'
15°00'
60°30'
61°00'
61°30'
62°00'
14°30'
61°00'

Martinique

French Overseas Department (DOM)

CAPITAL: Fort-de-France.
STATISTICAL AGENCY: Institut National de la Statistique et des Études
                      Économiques (INSEE), Service Départemental de
                      la Martinique.
NATIONAL REPOSITORY: Archives of the Ministry of Overseas Territories
                       (early censuses), Observatoire Economique de
                       Paris (later).
MAIN U.S. REPOSITORY: UCLA (early censuses) and Population Research
                        Center (Univ. of Texas).

One of four French overseas departments established in 1946, Martinique was one of the "Old Colonies" settled in 1635. The censuses taken previous to 1946 were considered of poor quality due to the circumstances of time and place and to the tendency of local administrators to inflate population numbers for fiscal reasons. Even the censuses of this century, using modern methods, were not of reliable quality because tabulation was performed in the local area. The first modern census was that of 1867 and there were ten up until 1946. The censuses of 1954, 1961, 1967, and 1974 have been conducted with more care due to the involvement of the French statistical agency (INSEE) in their preparation, conduct, and tabulation.

The designation of the legal population in French possessions is somewhat different from the usual. The totaling of two, or all three, of the following segments constitutes the legal population for the specific area:

1. "Population municipale"—private households and collective households (inhabited by those who freely choose to reside there, for example, live-in hospital staff, hotel residents).
2. "Population comptée à part"—populations in institutions (inhabited by those who have little or no choice to reside there, for example, military on base, boarding students, prisoners, patients—not staff—in hospitals of all kinds of relatively long term duration, and public works labor in barracks).
3. "Double comptée"—in the colonies inhabitants of "comptée à part" institutions in one commune who maintain a personal residence in another area were counted sometimes in both communes, sometimes in only one or the other.

Generally, the legal population of the commune is a combination of all three; whereas, the legal population of larger administrative units or of the whole territory is the total of numbers one and two only.

The legal population in Martinique in the 1946 and 1954 censuses was the total of the "municipale" plus those residents temporarily absent. In 1961 the legal total was determined in the same fashion as was used in France. That is, that described above.

A second difference in French censuses is how age is presented. Both real and generational age are represented in the tables. The real age, usually in five-year age groups, is similar to what is used in most censuses. The generational, however, is different. The specific year of birth determines the age rather than the amount of time passed. In other words, anyone born in 1950 is thirty-one years old whether he has passed his thirty-first birthday or not by the date of the 1981 census.

The urban distinction is also complex; however, it is not necessary to explain this as there are rarely tables present with urban figures.

1946 (May 16)

France decreed that a census of the nonindigenous population (foreigners, metropole French, and all persons whose mother or father was born outside the territory) should be taken in all overseas territories and departments this year. It was optional to conduct a full census at the same time. Martinique chose to conduct both. The form for the "non-originaire" census was supplied by the Service Colonial des Statistiques (Paris) for the European and assimilated populations. The schedules were individual, self-enumerated, and were to be mechanically tabulated in France by the INSEE. The territorial divisions in this census were: north, containing three cantons; and south, containing five cantons, each of which was subdivided into communes. This subdivision made the results comparable to the total census, which was prepared and tabulated in Martinique. The responsibility for the conduct of the censuses was with the local governments. The total census was also on individual schedules and self-enumerated as much as possible.

Definitions and Concepts. URBAN—communes with population of 2,000 or more aggregated to the seat of commune government. HOUSEHOLD—one person or a group in one dwelling. Specification of a dwelling became more precise in later censuses. USUAL RESIDENCE—asked of only those temporarily absent from their domicile. BIRTHPLACE—department in France, other French possession, or name of country if foreign. The birthplaces of mother and of father were also asked. AGE—month and year of birth. Tables of real age in standard five-year age groups and single years in the generational mode. HOUSEHOLD COMPOSITION—by size and characteristics of the head. MARITAL STATUS—single, married (including separated), widowed, divorced, common-law union. FERTILITY—asked of both males and females: number of children born live and the number surviving. EDUCATION—literacy and educational attainment. School enrollment from noncensus source was found in the publication. NATIONALITY—mixed citizenship and ethnic origin: native-born French (France or possessions), naturalized French, and foreign born. OCCUPATION— usual profession rather than occupation at a specified time. Grouped by employers, employees, seamen-fishermen, civil servants, liberal professions, other professions, and a few subdivisions. INDUSTRY—name and nature of business, grouped broadly in agriculture, industry, other. HOUSING—if house owned or if landholder.

Special Elements and Features. School enrollment, voters, vital statistics, immigration were included but all were from noncensus sources. No special topic was emphasized.

Quality of the Census. There was no established statistical service in Martinique at this time. It was acknowledged that the numbers in ages six and under were questionable; some differences existed in results tabulated mechanically in Paris and those manually tabulated in Martinique. Occupation data were weak because of tendency to cite former occupation rather than declare self as "without occupation." "The census of 1946 seems to have been carried out with more care; the excessively inflated results found in previous censuses have disappeared." However, because the "non-originaire" population had to fill in two similar schedules, there was the likelihood that only one was returned in some cases. No Whipple's Index category is given.

Publication Plan. Non-Originare: France. INSEE [and] Service Colonial des Statistiques. *Résultats de recensement de 1946 dans les territoires d'outre-mer (Français d'origine métropolitaine et étrangers): Martinique.* Paris, 1948. (*Bulletin Mensual Statistique d'Outre-Mer [BMSOM]*, Serie "statistique," no. 5.) Total: France. INSEE [and] Service Colonial des Statistiques. *Recensement de la population de la Martinique en 1946.* Paris, 1947. (*BMSOM*, Serie "etudes," no. 13) Language of publication is French.

NOTE: [*BMSOM*, Serie "etudes," no. 18, contained results for all "non-originaires" in all overseas territories.]

1954 (July 1)

Taken in conjunction with a census of industry, crafts, and business, it was *de facto* and *de jure* (tables mainly for *de jure* population), canvassed on household schedules, and mechanically tabulated in Paris. A second schedule was used for the "population comptée à part," which contained fewer questions. The household schedule had a special section for information about visitors and the temporarily absent and also collected housing data. Territorial divisions in tables are communes only. This is the first time that census methods were adapted to local conditions (for example, hierarchy of socioeconomic status).

Definitions and Concepts. URBAN—Fort-de-France and communes of aggregated populations of 2,000 and over. HOUSEHOLD—same as 1946. AGE— year of birth and completed years. Tables in real and generational age in standard five-year age groups. MARITAL STATUS—same as 1946 except common law appears only in type of household tables. BIRTHPLACE—same as 1946 except year of immigration of foreign born not asked. NATIONALITY—only of foreign born. FERTILITY—asked of all females fourteen years and over: number of children born alive. EDUCATION—asked of all ages fourteen and over: literacy and educational attainment (diploma received). ECONOMIC ACTIVITY—age fourteen and over. No reference period stated; assumed to be moment of the census. Active were employed, unemployed looking for work, unpaid family helpers, and the military. Inactive were homemakers, those of independent income, students, inmates of institutions, beggars, and so forth. OCCUPATION—age fourteen and over: main and secondary occupation. Classified according to the 1954 edition of the list used in France (four-digits). OCCUPATIONAL STATUS (new)—employer, own-account worker, "colon" (tenant farmer?), salaried worker, family helper, and apprentice. SOCIOECONOMIC STATUS—cross-classification of occupation with occupational status. ECONOMIC DEPENDENCY—number of children under sixteen in household.

Special Elements and Features. Occupational status and socioeconomic status are new. Marital status, nationality, and fertility not taken for the "population comptée à part." No industry, as a separate census of industry was taken (results in *BMSOM*, Série "statistique," no. 19). The appendix has a copy of the schedules used, and there is a history of censuses in the introduction.

Quality of the Census. "The 1954 census taken in the French Antilles is considered very accurate because taken by the 'prefet' (chief administrative office of the department) instead of by local governments as was done previous to this census. The reason was to avoid the over-estimating of results which had become traditional throughout a number of Antilles cities." INSEE (Paris) supplied schedules and tabulated the results. No Whipple's Index category is given.

Publication Plan. France. INSEE. *Résultats statistiques du recensement général de la population des départements d'outre-mer effectué le 1er juillet 1954: Antilles Françaises: Martinique et Guadeloupe.* Paris, 1956. Language of publication is French.

1961 (October 9)

Conducted by the local governments under guidance of INSEE, this census was *de facto* and *de jure* with mainly *de jure* tables. It is not known if it was self-enumerated or canvassed on household schedules that also collected housing information. Collective (institutional) schedules were also used, and both were mechanically tabulated by INSEE in Paris. Territorial divisions were communes only. The legal population for communes is the "municipale" and the "comptée à part" without double count.

Definitions and Concepts. URBAN—only the aggregated population of 2,000 and more, not the total population, of the commune. AGE—year of birth only. Tables in real age and generational age in standard five-year age groups, generational age in single years. MARITAL STATUS—same as 1954. NATIONALITY—citizenship of French nationals and the foreign born. BIRTHPLACE—department in France, commune for native born; French overseas department or territory, or country of birth for foreign born. This plus usual residence gave basic internal migration and immigration. EDUCATION—age fifteen and over: literacy and highest degree attained. ECONOMIC ACTIVITY—age fifteen and over: reference period one year before the census. Active were employed, underemployed, and certain unemployed; inactive were others (not listed under separate categories). OCCUPATION—main or latest occupation. Classified by the French 1954 list, major, minor and subgroups (three-digits). INDUSTRY—divided by primary, secondary, and tertiary sector with major, minor, and subgroup subdivisions. Major groups (nine) based on ISIC. OCCUPATONAL STATUS—same as 1954. SOCIOECONOMIC STATUS—cross-classification of occupation and status further classed by public or private sector and adapted to local conditions. HOUSEHOLD COMPOSITION—by type, which was based on the basic core (spouse and/or children present, and so forth) and presence of others in the household; also by size and by characteristics of the head. ECONOMIC DEPENDENCY—number of children under fifteen in the household, and the number of economically active in household.

Special Elements and Features. No fertility, but household composition and industry were added. Economic dependency was included as were a copy of the schedule and the codes used. Emphasis was on household composition and economic activity.

Quality of the Census. The closer involvement in the control of the census by INSEE would improve accuracy even though the responsibility for the conduct was returned to local governments. However, it was conceded that this census had an overcount in spite of INSEE's action. No Whipple's Index category is given.

Publication Plan. France. INSEE. *Résultats statistiques du recensement général de la population des départements d'outre-mer effectué le 9 Octobre 1961. Martinique.* Paris, 1965. Language of publication is French.

1967 (October 16)

It is supposed that the conduct of this census was similar to that of 1961. There is no description of organization, methodology, or definitions. Information below is taken from tables and notes. Tables are for *de jure* population. "Care for the operations of each commune is in the hands of the local government." There is a slight change in the organization of the "comptée à part" designation; it is divided into group I (prisoners, minors in institutions, inmates of psychiatric facilities) and group II (military living on base, patients of TB and Hansen's Disease treatment facilities, boarding students, and public works laborers in barracks). Housing data was also taken.

Definitions and Concepts. AGE, USUAL RESIDENCE, BIRTHPLACE, MARITAL STATUS, EDUCATION, NATIONALITY, OCCUPATION, INDUSTRY, SOCIOECONOMIC STATUS, HOUSEHOLD COMPOSITION and ECONOMIC DEPENDENCY—appear to be the same as 1961. FERTILITY (reinstated)—only females born in the territory or other overseas department, age fifteen and over: number of children ever born alive. OCCUPATIONAL STATUS—same as 1961 and 1954 except "colon" (tenant farmer?) dropped from the list. However, one table gives results using 1961 set of terms.

Special Elements and Features. Fertility was reinstated. Emphasis is on household composition. No copy of schedule nor descriptive text was included.

Quality of the Census. Lack of definitions in result volume may make it awkward to use. No Whipple's Index category is given.

Publication Plan. A brief publication of provisional main results [and] France. INSEE. *Résultats statistiques du recensement général de la population des départements d'outre-mer effectué le 16 Octobre 1964. 1ᵉʳ partie. Tableaux statistiques. Martinique.* Paris, n.d. Language of publication is French.

1974 (October 16)

Only a number of inhabitants volume has been issued formally; however, some tables with 1974 results have been distributed. The information for this entry is taken from whatever was available. It was computer tabulated by INSEE in French Guiana. Although the departmental census office is reestablished for each census, the regional INSEE office is permanent. The final results were due to be published in 1982, but have not appeared in print as yet.

Definitions and Concepts. AGE—real and generational age in standard five-year age groups, and both in single years to twenty-four. ECONOMIC ACTIVITY— two reference periods were used. Preceding twelve months: active were "those having had a job during the last 12 months (PAEA), all of whom declared having exercised an activity remunerated or own account during that period." Other reference period, seven days preceding the census (PAES). Inactive were students, homemakers, invalids, retired, others (including those doing compulsory military service). INDUSTRY—primary, secondary, and tertiary sectors subdivided by major industry groups plus unemployed (subdivided by "having had work but not that week" and "seeking first job").

Publication Plan. France. INSEE. *Recensement général de la Population de la France, Départements d'Outre-Mer: Arrondissements, Communes.* Paris, 1976. Unpublished data and computer tapes are available from INSEE, Departement de la Cooperation et des Services Statistiques des DOM-TOM (Paris). Language of publication is French.

OTHER STATISTICAL PUBLICATIONS: Issued by INSEE (Paris), *Annuaire Statistique, Bulletin de Statistiques* (monthly), *Bulletin de Statistique des Départements et Territoires d'Outre-Mer* (quarterly), *Statistique du Mouvement de la Population dans les Départements d'Outre-Mer* (irregularly).

National Topic Chart

	1946	1954	1961	1967	1974
De facto	X	X	X		
Usual residence	X	X	X	X	
Place of birth	X	X	X	X	
Duration of residence	X				
Place of prev. residence					
Urban/rural	X	X	X		
Sex	X	X	X	X	X
Age	X	X	X	X	X
Relation to household head	X	X	X	X	
Marital status	X	X	X	X	
Children born alive	X	X		X	
Children living	X				
Citizenship	X	X	X	X	
Literacy	X	X	X	X	
School enrollment	X				X
Ed. attainment	X	X	X	X	
Ed. qualification					
National/Ethnic origin	X	X	X	X	
Language					
Religion					
Household composition	X		X	X	
Econ. active/inactive		X	X	X	X
Occupation	X	X	X	X	
Industry	X		X	X	X
Occupational status		X	X	X	
Income					
Housing		X	X	X	

Mexico

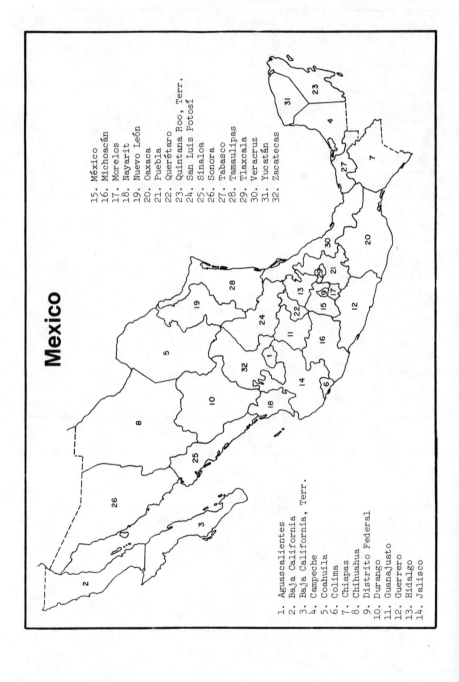

1. Aguascalientes
2. Baja California
3. Baja California, Terr.
4. Campeche
5. Coahuila
6. Colima
7. Chiapas
8. Chihuahua
9. Distrito Federal
10. Durango
11. Guanajuato
12. Guerrero
13. Hidalgo
14. Jalisco

15. México
16. Michoacán
17. Morelos
18. Nayarit
19. Nuevo León
20. Oaxaca
21. Puebla
22. Querétaro
23. Quintana Roo, Terr.
24. San Luis Potosí
25. Sinaloa
26. Sonora
27. Tabasco
28. Tamaulipas
29. Tlaxcala
30. Veracruz
31. Yucatán
32. Zacatecas

Mexico

United Mexican States

CAPITAL: Mexico City.
STATISTICAL AGENCY: Dirección General de Estadística.
NATIONAL REPOSITORY: "Gilberto Loyo", Balderas no. 71, P.B.
MAIN U.S. REPOSITORY: Population Research Center (Univ. of Texas).

During the pre-Hispanic period, population counts were known among Indian tribes. These early counts were later used by the governors of the colony, and similar counts were taken during the fifteenth, sixteenth, and seventeenth centuries, mainly for the purpose of taxation. Most of the records of this period were lost or are unavailable for public use. From 1793 until 1890 frequent population estimates were made; but only total population is known. The first officially recognized census of population was taken in 1895. The Distrito Federal is geographically located within the State of Mexico but constitutes a separate entity. Inside the "Distrito Federal" is located the city of Mexico, which is divided into "cuarteles."

1895

The first general census was taken by the Dirección General de Estadística, and canvasser was the method used on general schedules. This census, although more carefully taken than the previous ones, presented numerous deficiencies mainly due to the confusion arising from the division of the population into three groups: the present, the absent, and visitors. The scope included age, sex, place of birth, nationality, marital status, religion, literacy, occupation, language, and physical and mental deficiencies. The territory covered by the census included thirty federal entities (states and territories) and the Federal District, subdivided into departments, "partidos," and districts.

1900

The second general census was the first taken during a year ending in zero in conformity with a majority of the countries. The organization and scope were virtually the same as 1895, but at this time, information on naturalized citizens was recorded, and the population was counted on a *de facto* basis. The territorial division was basically the same except Baja California was divided into north and south districts.

1910

The third general census of population was conducted by the Dirección General de Estadística. It was *de facto* and a combination of canvasser and self-enumeration was used on a single household schedule. A housing list with the number of inhabitants per house was made before the census with the purpose of determining the number of questionnaires needed for the enumeration. The scope of the census included age, sex, language, literacy, religion, nationality, occupation, marital status, place of residence, place of birth, and physical and mental illness. Housing information was limited to type of house and the number of houses under construction. The following tables were also presented: total population since 1793; comparative tables for the years 1895, 1900, and 1910; and estimates of population for individual years from 1901 to 1912. Rural and urban populations were distinguished. Territory covered included twenty-eight states, three territories, and the Federal District. The states were subdivided into districts and "partidos" and the Federal District into "municipios" and localities.

1921

The fourth general census of population was conducted by the same agency, following basically the same organization of the 1910 census. The publication of results, however, was not finished until 1928. The country was divided into twenty-eight states, three territories and the Federal District, subdivided into "municipios" and localities. The scope included those items taken in 1910 plus race and fertility. There are comparative tables of 1910 and 1921 data.

1930

The fifth general census of population was taken along with agricultural and industrial censuses. It was conducted by the Departamento de Estadística Nacional on a *de jure* basis for the first time, and canvasser was the method used on general schedules. A pilot census was taken in the state of Morales with the purpose of testing the organization to be adopted in the final census. The territory covered by the census included twenty-eight states, three territories and the Federal District, subdivided into "municipios" and localities. The scope included age, sex, marital status, relationship to head of the family, literacy, occupation, nationality, language, physical and mental illness, place of birth, property ownership, and time of unemployment. Fertility and race were dropped. The military forces were enumerated separately but the results were not made available to the public.

1940

The sixth general census of population was conducted by the Dirección General de Estadística. It was taken on a *de jure* basis, and canvasser was the method used on general schedules. It was the first census to publish information on each "municipio" and localities of 10,000 or more inhabitants. The territorial division was the same as 1930. No general report was available, and information gathered here was taken from introductory notes and table headings. The scope included age, sex, place of birth, marital status, literacy, nationality, language, family, religion, physical and mental disabilities for work, economic activity, industry, occupation, occupational status, educational attainment, school attendance, property ownership, and customs (eating habits, kind of clothes, and whether or not a person used shoes).

1950 (June 6)

The seventh general census of population was conducted by the Dirección General de Estadística on a *de jure* basis, and canvasser was the method used on general schedules. Housing questions were included in the population questionnaire. The agricultural census was taken simultaneously, but a separate schedule was used. Tabulation was mechanical using punched cards. The census covered thirty-two entities (twenty-eight states, three territories and the Federal District).

Definitions and Concepts. URBAN—localities with more than 2,500 inhabitants. LOCALITY—place with buildings or any kind of construction set together, inhabited temporarily or permanently, with a name and political characteristics based on the law or custom. AGE—in completed years or number of months if less than one year of age. Presented in single years and standard five-year age groups. EDUCATION—asked of persons six years or older: literacy, school attendance, and educational attainment (highest grade completed). FERTILITY— asked of all women who ever had children: number of children born alive. FAMILY—broad sense, including the head, spouse, the unmarried children, any relative living in the same house, those economically dependent on the head of the family, and servants. Visitors, guests, boarders, and married children with an occupation were not included. MARITAL STATUS—asked of all men sixteen years and older and women fourteen years and older. Categories were: single, married (civil or religious ceremony), common-law marriage, widowed, and legally divorced. PLACE OF BIRTH—state or territory for native born and country of birth for foreigners were recorded. NATIONALITY—country of citizenship. LANGUAGE—asked of all persons five years of age and older: mother tongue (Indian dialect or foreign language) and ability to speak Spanish. ECONOMIC ACTIVITY—asked of all persons twelve years of age and older. The economically active were all persons with a paid occupation (employed) and those without occupation, divided into two groups (unemployed up to twelve weeks and unemployed for thirteen or more weeks). Those included in the labor force were, however, only the employed and those unemployed for twelve weeks or less at the time of the census, as well as unpaid family workers. The inactive included homemakers, students, invalids, inmates of institutions, and persons of independent income. The following were also recorded: main occupation one week before the census, paid secondary occupation one week before the census, number of days worked, number of weeks unemployed, and looking for a job. OCCUPATION—classification based on COTA 1950, only nine major groups were presented. INDUSTRY—classification based on ISIC 1950, only nine divisions were presented. OCCUPATIONAL STATUS—employer, employee, laborer, own-account worker, and unpaid family worker. INCOME (new)—that earned during one month of 1950 and other kinds of income obtained during the year before the census (1949) was taken. In addition, costs of food and rent were recorded for each head of household. CUSTOMS—eating habits and whether a person usually wears shoes were recorded. RELIGION—religious denomination recorded.

Special Elements and Features. Housing questions were included in the population schedule. For the first time, principal occupation one week before the census, paid secondary occupation, number of days worked, number of weeks unemployed, and income were recorded. Physical and mental illness were dropped from the schedules. An alphabetical list of municipios with population by sex and comparative tables for the 1930, 1940, and 1950 censuses were included. Costs of housing and food were asked.

Quality of the Census. Mapping and revision of territorial divisions improved the coverage of the enumeration. An experimental census was taken in 1948 to test organization and feasibility of the census questionnaire. Selective tests and training were given to the personnel involved in the census operation. Whipple's Index classified age data in category V—very rough data.

Publication Plan. Mexico. Dirección General de Estadística. *Séptimo censo general de población, 6 de junio de 1950.* Mexico, D.F., 1952-1953. 1 volume for each state and territory plus a general summary and a separate report. Unpublished data are available in-house only. Language of publication is Spanish.

1960 (June 8)

The eighth general census of population was conducted by the Dirección General de Estadística at the same time that the agricultural census was being taken (May 2 to June 15). The census of population was taken on a *de jure* basis, and canvassers recorded information on general schedules. The tabulation was computerized. The territory covered by the census included thirty-two federal entities (twenty-nine states, two territories, and the Distrito Federal). The territory of Baja California Norte became a state in 1951.

Pretest censuses were taken in the states of Mexico, Oaxaca, and the Distrito Federal. During the census test in Mexico City, self-enumeration was used in three different zones.

Definitions and Concepts. AGE, URBAN, PLACE OF BIRTH, NATIONALITY, LITERACY, and FAMILY ("familia censal")—same as 1950. PLACE OF RESIDENCE—duration and previous residence were asked (new). LANGUAGE—all persons five years of age and older: mother tongue or dialect of persons of Indian origin as well as foreigners. The ability to speak Spanish was also recorded. RELIGION—religious affiliation was recorded. The categories were:

Catholic, Protestant, Jewish, other, and none. EDUCATION—all persons six years and older: literacy, educational attainment (highest degree completed), and school attendance, including vocational, professional, and sub-professional schools. MARITAL STATUS—for persons twelve years and older. The categories were the same as 1950. FERTILITY—asked of all women regardless of marital status: number of children ever born alive. ECONOMIC ACTIVITY—asked of all persons eight years of age and older. The economically active were all persons who had a job, profession, or paid occupation the week of the census, those unemployed for twelve weeks, and those unemployed for thirteen weeks or more. The tables presented the active age eight to eleven years separately from those age twelve and over. The inactive included students, homemakers, inmates of institutions, pensioners, persons of independent income, and invalids. OCCUPATION—classification was based on COTA 1960 and presented only eight major groups. The results are not directly comparable to 1950. In 1950 the "labor force" concept included only employed and short-term unemployed (twelve weeks or less). The occupation tables, however, did not separate the under twelve years of age from the twelve and over. INDUSTRY—classification based on ISIC presented only the nine divisions. The results were not comparable to 1950 for the same reasons as occupation above. OCCUPATIONAL STATUS— categories were: employee, employer, "obrero" (manual laborer), "jornalero" (agricultural worker receiving salary), own-account "ejidatário" (agricultural worker cultivating his own land), and unpaid family worker. The following were also asked of all employed persons: days worked during the week before the census and income received during the month before the census. Unemployed persons were asked the number of weeks without a job or whether looking for a job for the first time. INCOME—obtained through work or other sources during the month before the census. CUSTOMS—eating habits (wheat bread, fish, milk, and eggs) and whether or not the person wears shoes.

Special Elements and Features. There is a table with total population based on counts and estimates since 1521. Electronic tabulation was introduced in this census. Results for localities were limited to total population by sex. Special attention should be given to the totals for economically active and labor force for comparisons to other censuses. Maps and a copy of the schedule were included. A separate volume was issued with the rectification of Tables 25, 26, and 27 of the general summary. Occupational classification was not presented in the volumes for the individual states.

Quality of the Census. To improve completeness of the census, maps and a list of localities were prepared in 1958. Precensuses were taken in several regions of the country to test the questionnaires and the possibility of using self-enumeration. In addition, the precensus provided training for the personnel employed in the final census operation. Whipple's Index classified age data in category IV—rough data.

Publication Plan. Mexico. Dirección General de Estadística. *VIII censo general de población, 1960.* Mexico, D.F., 1963-1964. One or more volumes for each state and territory, two volumes for localities, a general summary and its "rectification," one volume on income, and the report. Unpublished data are available in-house only. Language of publication is Spanish.

1970 (January 28)

The ninth general census of population, conducted by the Dirección General de Estadística, was taken on a *de jure* basis, and canvassers were used to collect information on household schedules. The questionnaire was divided into three parts: identification data, housing data, and personal data for each member of the household. The census of housing was taken simultaneously and an additional questionnaire was used to gather information about agricultural products and subsistance farming. Four pretest censuses were taken to check applicability of the household questionnaire, the method of enumeration to be adopted in the final census, and to provide updating of maps and lists of localities in each "municipio." The territory covered by the census included thirty-two federal entities (twenty-nine states, two territories and the Distrito Federal). Tabulation was computerized.

Definitions and Concepts. AGE, URBAN, LOCALITY, PLACE OF BIRTH, PLACE OF RESIDENCE, EDUCATION, RELIGION and LANGUAGE—same as 1960. CUSTOMS—question was reduced to the regular use of shoes. FERTILITY—asked of women age twelve and over: number of children ever born alive. Marital status and fertility were cross-classified. MARITAL STATUS— categories were: married (civil and/or religious ceremony), common-law marriage, widowed, divorced, separated, and single. ECONOMIC ACTIVITY—for persons twelve years of age and over. Two reference periods were used: the week before the census and one year before the census (1969). Economically active the week before the census included employed, unpaid family workers, own-account workers, and the unemployed looking for a job, whether for the first time or not. The active during the year before the census consisted of all persons who worked at any time during 1969, either in gainful occupation or as unpaid family worker working at least fifteen hours per week. The economically inactive (week) were students, homemakers, persons of independent income, inmates of institutions, invalids, pensioners, and so forth. Other questions concerning economic activity: number of months worked, main occupation in 1969, number of weeks looking for job for the first time or not. INDUSTRY—classification based on ISIC with eleven divisions and ninety-one major groups (two-digits). The name of the firm was also recorded. OCCUPATION—classification based on COTA 1960 and revision according to ISCO with eight major groups, seventy-five groups, and 292 subgroups (three-digits). OCCUPATIONAL STATUS—categories were: employer, "jornalero" (agricultural worker receiving salary), employee or "obrero," own-account worker, unpaid family worker, and "ejidatários" (agricultural worker fulfilling specific requirements such as legal ownership of government land). Although the categories were the same as 1960, employees and "obreros" were joined in one class, and "ejidatários" were no longer part of the own-account worker class. INCOME—gross income within a year, a month, and a week were recorded.

Special Elements and Features. The two reference periods for economic activity were explicitly stated for the first time. There is more information for localities than was presented in the 1960 census. Occupational and industrial classifications were used, and comparisons with 1960 are included. Nationality was dropped from the schedules. There is extensive information about census operation and data processing. Alphabetical index of subjects gives the number of the tables. A copy of the schedule and instructions for the enumerators are also included.

Quality of the Census. Four census tests were carried out to improve completeness and accuracy of data. Mexico has a long history of censuses, regularly taken every ten years since 1900 (except for 1921 because of social and political reforms). The census office is permanent. Whipple's Index classified age data in category IV—rough data.

Publication Plan. Mexico. Dirección General de Estadística. *IX censo general de población, 1970. (28 de enero de 1970).* Mexico, D.F., 1970-1973. One volume for each state (Oaxaca has two) and territory, an abbreviated summary, one general summary, four locality volumes, and manuals have been published. Unpublished data are available in-house only. Language of publication is Spanish.

1980 (June 4-11)

This is the tenth census of population taken in Mexico. So far only a preliminary report has been issued by the Coordinación General de los Servicios Nacionales de Estadística, Geografía e Informativa.

OTHER STATISTICAL PUBLICATIONS: Issued by Dirección General de Estadística, *Agenda Estadística* (annually), *Anuario Estadístico, Anuario Estadístico Compendiado, Revista de Estadística* (quarterly).

National Topic Chart

	1950	1960	1970
De facto			
Usual residence	X	X	X
Place of birth	X	X	X
Duration of residence		X	X
Place of prev. residence		X	X
Urban/rural	X	X	X
Sex	X	X	X
Age	X	X	X
Relation to household head	X	X	X
Marital status	X	X	X
Children born alive	X	X	X
Children living			
Citizenship	X	X	
Literacy	X	X	X
School enrollment	X	X	X
Ed. attainment	X	X	X
Ed. qualification			
National/Ethnic origin			
Language	X	X	X
Religion	X	X	X
Household composition	X	X	X
Econ. active/inactive	X	X	X
Occupation	X	X	X
Industry	X	X	X
Occupational status	X	X	X
Income	X	X	X
Housing	X	X	X

Montserrat

British Crown Colony

CAPITAL: Plymouth.
STATISTICAL AGENCY: Statistics Office, Chief Minister's Office.
NATIONAL REPOSITORY: Statistics Office.
MAIN U.S. REPOSITORY: Population Research Center (Univ. of Texas).

Montserrat was a Presidency of the Leeward Islands colony until the dissolution of the West Indies Federation in 1962. In 1967 it elected to remain a British colony instead of becoming an Associated State. There were censuses before 1844 but that one was considered the first modern census. Censuses are cited for 1851, 1859, 1871, 1881, etc., through 1921, 1946, 1960, 1970. The pre-1946 censuses have traditionally been *de facto*.

1859

In the *Census of the British Empire, 1861*, volume 3, *General Report*, there is one table of total population, probably coming from the 1859 census.

1881

No publications but comparative tables in the census of 1891 give data for total and parish populations, sex, race, and occupation.

1891

The first report on the Leeward Islands census was prepared by the Colonial Secretary and implied that the census was coordinated and compiled centrally in the colony. Scope included total and parish population with figures for Plymouth, age groups, sex, birthplace, marital status, race, occupation, employment status, infirmities, and number of houses.

1901

Again no publication could be located. The 1911 census of England and Wales gave a total population by sex in one comparative table.

1911

Conducted by the Registrar General's Office of Montserrat, the scope was total and parish populations, age groups, sex, marital status, birthplace, citizenship,

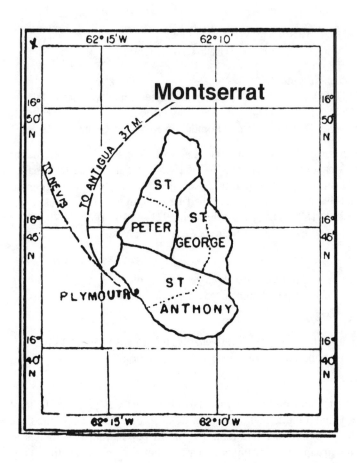

religion, literacy and the number attending school, occupation, infirmities, and number of houses.

1921

The conduct and scope were the same as 1911.

1946

Conducted by the Office of the Registrar, Montserrat participated in the West Indies census program. The presidency has three parishes, one of which, St. Anthony, absorbed that of St. Patrick, which had been listed separately in earlier censuses.

Definitions and Concepts. [See British West Indies 1946 for the full entry; the following are differences.] No URBAN distinction. AGE—tables in single years and standard five-year age groups. Infants were not listed by completed months. RACE—white, black, Asian, and mixed. OCCUPATIONAL STATUS— employer, own-account worker, unpaid helper, and wage and salary earner (at work, learner, unemployed). INFIRMITIES—totally blind, deaf and dumb.

Special Elements and Features. In addition to the variations above, duration of union was also asked.

Quality of the Census. Whipple's Index category was III—approximate age data. The census office is reestablished for each census.

Publication Plan. Part F of the *West Indian Census 1946* was devoted to the Leeward Islands colony. Unpublished data are available. Contact the Jamaica statistics office for computer tapes. Language of publication is English.

1960 (April 7)

This was also a census conducted with the other Caribbean colonies and was taken by the territorial census office. [See British West Indies 1960, West Indies section, for full entry; the following are the differences.] Montserrat had three parishes which were subdivided into enumeration districts for census purposes. Because its Volume 1 was not published, no data are available for that level.

Definitions and Concepts. FERTILITY—also asked was if the child born during the last twelve months was the first.

Special Elements and Features. Occupations and industries are listed by major groups only, no detailed classifications.

Quality of the Census. No Volume 1 published; no Whipple's Index rating given.

Publication Plan. Jamaica. Department of Statistics. *West Indies Population Census. Census of Montserrat, 7th April 1960.* Volume 2.

Unpublished data are available. Contact Jamaica statistics office for computer tapes. Language of publication is English.

1970 (April 7)

No separate publications from this census were issued by Montserrat. [See British West Indies 1970 for full entry.] Results for this island were not contained in the migration volume. Volumes 3; 4.12; 4.16; 6.3; 7; 8 abc; 9.4; 10.3; and 10.4 of the British West Indies 1970 set contain the results for Montserrat. Unpublished data are available. Contact the Census Research Programme (University of West Indies, Jamaica) for computer tapes. Language of publication is English.

1980 (May 12)

Montserrat participated in the 1980 population census program of the Commonwealth Caribbean countries. Final results will be processed by computer in Barbados. The first preliminary result volume was processed by hand and contains data on households and housing. Montserrat intends further publications. Meanwhile, unpublished data are available. Language of publication is English.

OTHER STATISTICAL PUBLICATIONS: Issued by Statistics Office, *Statistical Digest* (annually), *Vital Statistics Report* (annually).

National Topic Chart

	1946	1960	1970	1980
De facto	X	X	X	X
Usual residence	X	X	X	
Place of birth	X	X	X	
Duration of residence		X	X	
Place of prev. residence		X	N.A.	
Urban/rural		X	X	X
Sex	X	X	X	X
Age	X	X	X	X
Relation to household head		X	X	
Marital status	X	X	X	
Children born alive	X	X	X	
Children living	X		X	
Citizenship				
Literacy	X	X		
School enrollment	X	X	X	
Ed. attainment		X	X	
Ed. qualification			X	
National/Ethnic origin	X	X	X	
Language				
Religion	X	X	X	
Household composition		X	X	X
Econ. active/inactive	X	X	X	
Occupation	X	X	X	
Industry	X	X	X	
Occupational status	X	X	X	
Income			X	
Housing	X	X	X	X

Netherlands Antilles

Autonomous part of the Netherlands

CAPITAL: Willemstad on Curaçao.
STATISTICAL AGENCY: Bureau voor de Statistiek. Department Social & Economische Zaken.
NATIONAL REPOSITORY: Central Bureau of Statistics, Fort Amsterdam.
MAIN U.S. REPOSITORY: Population Research Center (Univ. of Texas).

The Netherlands Antilles consists of two sets of three islands each: Curaçao, Aruba, and Bonaire, located off the Venezuelan coast; and Sint Maarten, St. Eustatius, and Saba, located in the Leeward part of the Caribbean island chain stretching from Puerto Rico to Trinidad. In spite of their location, these three are referred to as the "Windward Islands" and constitute one of the four political units, along with Aruba, Bonaire, and Curaçao.

Like most of the Caribbean islands,they were discovered in the time of Columbus, and their possession by the Dutch was contested, especially by the British, until 1816. They remained a Dutch colony until 1954, when together they gained internal self-government. In 1975 under the new Netherlands constitution, they were granted equality with the mother country.

There was reported to have been a census in 1930, but no publications of results have been seen or cited. Age, sex, and marital status appeared in comparative tables in the 1960 census.

1960

The census of 1960 was two separate censuses taken six months apart by different agencies. The first, of Aruba alone, was taken in June and the second, of the remaining islands, in December.

ARUBA (JUNE 27)

The report of this census was written by Amos H. Hawley who served as technical advisor to the Office of Vital Statistics and Census. The tabulation was performed on the electronic data processing equipment housed at the Lago Oil and Transport Co., whose staff also developed the programs. The census was *de jure* and canvassed on household schedules. There were basically no administrative divisions on the island, and so it was divided into fifty enumeration districts,

Netherlands Antilles

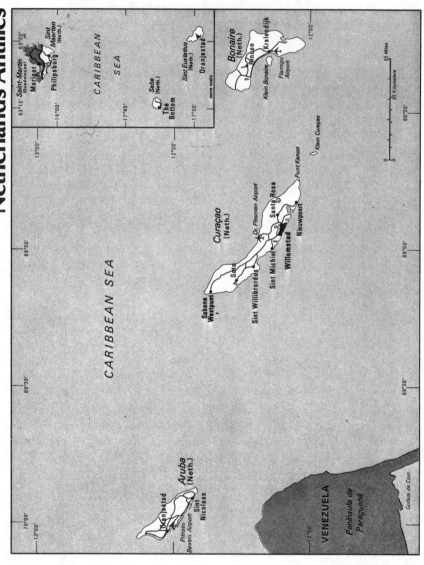

two of which were for the Lago concession. Published tables are for the island as a whole.

Definitions and Concepts. URBAN—"The whole island is essentially an urban area." HOUSEHOLD—One person living alone or a group of persons who normally sleep and eat under the same roof; it includes those residents who are temporarily absent. HOUSEHOLD COMPOSITION—size, characteristics of head, and type based on presence or absence of spouse, children, relatives, lodgers, unrelated persons, and so forth. AGE—in completed years. Age tables are in single years. BIRTHPLACE—island or country of birth for all persons. NATIONALITY—citizenship, political affiliation to what country. EDUCATION— school attendance for those age five and over and educational attainment (last grade of school completed). RELIGION—specific denomination affiliation. MARITAL STATUS—asked of all age thirteen and over: single (never married), married, cohabiting, widowed, divorced. Date of first marriage was also asked. FERTILITY—asked of all women age thirteen and over: number of live births ever had, and number had in the preceding twelve months. ECONOMIC ACTIVITY—asked of all persons age fourteen and over: reference period not stated, assumed to be the week before the census (labor force concept). The active were the employed and the unemployed looking for work. The inactive were housewives, students, the retired/pensioned, those unable to work. Hours worked last week also asked. OCCUPATION—main or principal ocupation (including that of the experienced unemployed). Classified in the nine major groups resembling ISCO. INDUSTRY—nature of establishment. Divided into fifteen groups with no standard order of classification. OCCUPATIONAL STATUS—wage and salary, own-account worker. ECONOMIC DEPENDENCY— number of persons employed per household. INCOME—from all sources.

Special Elements and Features. Number of births and deaths in the preceding twelve months, date of settlement in Aruba, principal sources of news (radio, TV, and so forth), and number of persons with definite plans to emigrate from Aruba were all included.

Quality of the Census. Census results were compared to the demographic profile of the work force of Lago Oil, migration figures that were available at the Office of Vital Statistics and Census, and the population register. Aruba was excluded from the Whipple's Index category I—highly accurate age data—given to the remainder of the Netherlands Antilles for 1960.

Publication Plan. Netherlands Antilles (Aruba). Office of Vital Statistics and Census. *The Population of Aruba: A Report Based on the Census of 1960*, by Amos H. Hawley [Oranjested], Lago Oil and Transport Co., n.d. Language of publication is English.

BONAIRE, CURAÇAO, AND THE WINDWARD ISLANDS (DECEMBER 31)

The census was conducted by the Statistiek en Planbureau Nederlandse Antillen [Netherlands Antilles Statistical and Planning Bureau]. It was *de jure*, canvassed on household schedules, and mechanically tabulated at the Shell Curacao N.V. facilities.

The Netherlands Antilles had a registration system that was quite complete except for Sint Maarten. The registration system was much used in the preparation and checking of the census. Curaçao was divided into four districts, and then into electoral districts; Bonaire had four districts but for the housing census only, and the Windward Islands were a district unto themselves.

Seamen were censused according to resident island. Those included were residents of at least one year as well as those who intended to reside in the territory for more than one year. The temporarily absent were also included. Visitors of less than one year from foreign countries were excluded. Those residents working or studying outside of the territory were not included with the usual residents, but information was collected separately on the schedule: age, sex, birthplace, nationality, usual residence, reason for being abroad, and expected year of return.

Definitions and Concepts. URBAN—the city and suburban district of Curaçao only. HOUSEHOLD—those living and eating together in a dwelling unit in which there was one kitchen; a separate schedule was used for dwellings with no unique kitchen (for example, institutions, group quarters, and so forth). Households include other relatives, boarders and lodgers, and live-in servants. HOUSEHOLD COMPOSITION—size, characteristics of head, language generally spoken in household, and households with domestic servants. AGE—date of birth (day, month, year obtained from the register). Tables in single years and standard five-year age groups. MARITAL STATUS—single, married (legally), common-law marriage, widowed, and divorced. BIRTHPLACE—(information supplied from register), island cited in tables. Country was asked of the foreign born. NATIONALITY/ORIGIN—Dutch citizenship subdivided by origin: Antillian, Suriname, Dutch, elsewhere; the Antillian was further subdivided into the six island parts. Male heads of household were listed according to place of birth whereas wives and children were listed according to head, not according to their actual place of birth. Exception was a male head born elsewhere but married to an Antillian, in which case he was listed as Antillian. RELIGION—as stated by the enumerated: Catholic, Protestant, other, and none. FERTILITY—asked of all women age thirteen and over: number of children born alive ever and in 1960. Age at first legal marriage was also asked of Antillian males age fifteen and over and females age thirteen and over. EDUCATION—literacy not taken but established if three or more years of elementary school were completed. Educational attainment (highest degree received) and qualification (specific field stated) were also taken. School attendance determined through type of activity question. LANGUAGE—that which was most spoken in the household: Papiamento, Dutch, Spanish, English, Portuguese, other. ECONOMIC ACTIVITY—asked of all ages; no reference period. Active were the employed and the unemployed (new and experienced) looking for work. Inactive were homemakers, students, invalids, the retired and those of independent income, the institutionalized and those in religious orders not having an occupation or receiving wages, and all other inactive (established in the question on occupational status). OCCUPATION—all persons age ten and over: usual or normal occupation of employed only. Classified in major and minor groups (two-digits) according to a slightly modified ISCO. INDUSTRY—all persons age ten and over: kind of establishment. Classified in division and major group (two-digits) according to the ISIC. OCCUPATIONAL STATUS—this question also determined type of activity: employer (with at least one half-time salaried employee), own-account worker (at least half-day), contract/casual worker (for set term of specific project), and the unemployed looking for work. The last were also asked the number of weeks unemployed. INCOME—class of income asked but no table of results given. HOUSING—characteristics included.

Special Elements and Features. Year of first settlement in Netherlands Antilles for those born elsewhere and firm emigration plans for 1961 were also recorded. Family members working or studying outside the territory were tabulated separately. Number of deaths of household members in 1960 was also asked. There are a few text tables with comparative figures from 1930.

Quality of the Census. There was a small percent undercount, due primarily to coordination with population register. One week needed for enumeration; however, it was not taken simultaneously with that of Aruba. Because there was little that they could draw on from the 1930 count, enumeration districts had to be drawn from scratch, good land maps were not available, and houses had not yet been numbered systematically. Credit was given for good work performed and for the aid given by others. The report included a list of suggestions for future censuses. Whipple's Index was category I—highly accurate data (excluding Aruba).

Publication Plan. Netherlands Antilles. Bureau voor de Statistiek. *Volkstelling 1960: Curacao, Bonaire, St. Maarten, St. Eustatius en Saba.* Willemstad, 1961. Deel A-D in 1 volume. Language of publication: Dutch with English abstract and table titles and headings.

1966 (February 20)

This was a census taken only of the Windward Islands by the Statistical Bureau. No information was given as to reason, methodology or definitions. Scope was sex, age (standard five-year groups), nationality and origin, marital status, household size, and housing characteristics.

Publication Plan. Netherlands Antilles. Bureau voor de Statistiek. *Volkstelling Bovenwindse Eilanden, 20 Februari 1966.* Fort Amsterdam, Curacao, n.d. Language of publication is Dutch.

1971 (December 31)

The first general population and housing census covering the whole of the Netherlands Antilles was conducted by the Statistical Bureau. It was *du jure*, canvassed, and tabulated by electronic data processing. Individual schedules (in

Dutch, English, Spanish, and Papiamento) were used which were grouped and enclosed in family forms which in turn were grouped and enclosed in the household form. Housing schedules were also used. The individual schedules were preprinted with the basic demographic characteristics contained in the population register. The canvasser verified or changed this data in addition to collecting other information. The forms were sent to the respective island registration offices for checking and control of both the register and the census before being tabulated. The territorial divisions were the six islands subdivided into enumeration districts but the tables were for each island as a whole.

Definitions and Concepts. HOUSEHOLD—one person living alone or a group of persons living together and sharing household arrangements, including live-in servants and boarders. Divided into single person, one family, two or more family, and nonfamily types. FAMILY—legally married couples (and single parents) with or without unmarried children form the nuclear family. BIRTH-PLACE—country or island of birth. NATIONALITY/ORIGIN—same as 1960 but the results on the tables appear only as "Antillian" or "other." AGE—date of birth. Tables in single years and standard five-year age groups. MARITAL STATUS—single, married, widowed, and divorced (legal status only) plus date of marriage; if married before, whether marriage dissolved by death. RELIGION—same as 1960 plus number of specific denominations expanded. FERTILITY—asked of all women age fourteen and over: number of children ever born alive, number who have since died, number of live children under age twenty (plus dates of birth). No tables have been published as yet. EDUCATION—all persons aged six and over: Education given in Dutch? Education taken outside the Netherlands Antilles? Still enrolled? Attending day or evening classes? No tables as yet. School enrollment and transportation to school taken, but there are no tables as yet. Tables are available for educational attainment (highest degree) and educational qualifications (study objective). ECONOMIC ACTIVITY—asked of all persons age fourteen and over; reference period was the week before the census. Active are all who are employed for fifteen hours or more, including family workers; also the unemployed (new and experienced) who were looking for work. Inactive are housewives (home duties), pensioned, and those of independent income, the disabled, patients in health institutions, students, and others. OCCUPATION—main occupation and average hours worked per week; classified in major groups, groups and units (three-digits) of the ISCO. Also asked was unemployment duration, registered as seeking employment, kind of work seeking. INDUSTRY—name, address, and nature of establishment. Classified in division, major group, and subgroup (three-digits) of ISIC. OCCUPATIONAL STATUS—employer (of three or more employees), own-account worker (professional), minor independent (employing less than three), wage or salary worker, family worker, casual laborer, other. INCOME—classes of total income, how is income earned, and source of major part.

Special Elements and Features. Transportation to work includes distance in time units, means, time spent waiting, and average daily expense. Other questions were asked on public health, rental payments, and reason for more than one family in same housing unit. However, no tables have been published so far with the results of these last three topics. A housing census was also taken; results have not been seen as yet.

Quality of the Census. Simultaneity was achieved with this census. The close coordination of the census and the registration system was mutually beneficial. The census was a "relatively dependable mirror of reality." There were test censuses conducted in Aruba and Curaçao the preceding July, and the planners attempted to utilize UN recommendations and international standards. Many topics were sought—fertility, travel to school, national health, available housing, housing condition, community services, and languages—for which no tables have appeared. The set that appeared in 1974, however, was labeled "Deel A," which implies the possible issuance of a "Deel B." Whipple's Index was category I—highly accurate age data.

Publication Plan. Netherlands Antilles. Bureau voor de Statistiek. *Eerste algemene volks—en woningtelling Nederlandse Antillen. Deel A. De uitkomsten van der volkstelling*. Fort Amsterdam, 1974. Volumes A1-A10. Unpublished data are available. Language of publication is Dutch.

OTHER STATISTICAL PUBLICATIONS: Issued by Bureau voor de Statistiek, *Statistisch Jaarbock, Statistische Mededelingen* (monthly).

National Topic Chart

	1960 Aru.	1960 NA	1966 W	1971
De facto				
Usual residence	X	X		X
Place of birth	X	X	X	X
Duration of residence	X	X		X
Place of prev. residence				
Urban/rural				
Sex	X	X	X	X
Age	X	X	X	X
Relation to household head	X	X		X
Marital status	X	X	X	X
Children born alive	X	X		X
Children living				X
Citizenship	X	X		
Literacy		X		
School enrollment	X	X		X
Ed. attainment	X	X		X
Ed. qualification		X		
National/Ethnic origin	X	X	X	X
Language		X		
Religion	X	X		X
Household composition			X	
Econ. active/inactive	X	X		X
Occupation	X	X		X
Industry	X	X		X
Occupational status	X	X		X
Income	X	X		X
Housing	X	X	X	X

Nicaragua

Republic of Nicaragua

CAPITAL: Managua.
STATISTICAL AGENCY: Instituto Nacional de Estadística y Censo (INEC).
NATIONAL REPOSITORY: Biblioteca (INEC) and Biblioteca (Banco Central de Nicaragua).
MAIN U.S. REPOSITORY: Population Research Center (Univ. of Texas).

The colonial period lasted from 1522 to 1821, the year in which the Province of Nicaragua became independent from Spain. After a short period of annexation to Mexico, Nicaragua and other newly independent countries formed what was called the United Provinces of Central America (1823). In 1838, Nicaragua became an independent state.

The earliest population count was done by members of religious groups in 1775. In the following years, several estimates and enumerations were taken (1778, 1779, 1800, 1813, 1820, and 1867), but there is no information regarding organization and methods applied. In 1906, a provisional census was carried out, but again only total population is known. At this time, it was established that a census should be taken every ten years, starting in 1910; however, it was not accomplished. With the destruction of the national archives by an earthquake in 1931 no more details are known besides the previously mentioned.

1920

A general census of population was conducted by the Oficina Central del Censo. The census was *de facto*, and self-enumeration was the method used to record information on household schedules. A canvasser was used only for those who did not know Spanish. Tabulation was manual. The territory covered by the census was divided into thirteen "departamentos" and two "comarcas," subdivided into "municipios," or districts. Nomadic tribes were only estimated, but tribes permanently settled were enumerated. Scope included age, sex, nationality, profession, marital status, race (color), language, religion, and literacy. The results of the census were considered unsatisfactory and 10 percent was the estimated underenumeration.

1940

Very little is known about this census. The tables available refer to total population of "departamentos" and "municipios" divided into urban and rural. Territorial divisions suffered several changes since the last census, but these changes and others that occurred in earlier days did not become available until the publication of the 1950 census results. No details about organization and methods are available.

1950 (May 31)

A general census of population was conducted by the Dirección General de Estadística y Censos. It was considered the best census taken to date in the country and the first one to follow modern techniques and internationally applied methods. The census was *de facto*, and canvasser was the method used to record information on general schedules. Tabulation was mechanical (new). The organization was based on recommendations suggested by COTA 1950. The territory covered by the census was divided into sixteen "departamentos" (states) and the Comarca de Cabo Gracias a Diós. The Departamento de Río San Juan was created in 1949. The territory in dispute with Honduras was not enumerated.

Definitions and Concepts. URBAN—all inhabited centers ("centros poblados") that constitute a county or state capital. A list of these centers with their respective populations was given for international comparability. HOUSEHOLD ("familia censal")—person or group of persons, related or not by blood, living in the same place and sharing food arrangements. Private households and group quarters were distinguished. AGE—in completed years or in months, if less than one year of age. Tabulated in single years and standard five-year age groups. PLACE OF BIRTH—native and foreign born were distinguished. For the first group the state of birth was recorded, and for the second, the country of birth. NATIONALITY—two groups: Nicaraguans (native born and naturalized) and foreigners (declared citizenship). MARITAL STATUS—all persons age fourteen and over. Categories were: single (never married), married (civil and religious ceremony, civil only, and religious ceremony only), widowed, divorced, and common-law marriage. FERTILITY—number of children less than five years of age per 1,000 women between the ages of fifteen and forty-five. LANGUAGE—language or dialect spoken at home. EDUCATION—literacy (ability to read and write), educational attainment (last degree completed), and school enrollment. Lower age limit for the questions was six years of age. RELIGION—three groups were tabulated: Roman Catholics, Protestants, and others (included other religions and persons who did not answer the question). ECONOMIC ACTIVITY—the economically active were all persons fourteen years of age and older engaged in gainful occupations, including unpaid family workers. Inactive population included the following groups: homemakers, students, the retired, persons of independent income, pensioners, and persons less than fourteen years of age. There is no clear indication of the classification of unemployed persons as active or inactive. OCCUPATION—classification based on COTA 1950, major groups and subgroups (two-digits). INDUSTRY— classification based on ISIC, divisions and major groups (two-digits). OCCUPATIONAL STATUS—categories were: salaried worker (seasonal worker, laborer and employee), employer, self-employed, and unpaid family worker.

Special Elements and Features. Almost all the recommended topics other than the basic age, sex, race, marital status, and so forth were recorded for the first time in the Nicaraguan census. Race, however, was dropped. Lists of localities according to size of population and in alphabetical order were presented. For the first time, organization, method, and definitions of concepts were included in the report. Maps, graphs, and a copy of schedule were available.

Quality of the Census. This was the first census in the country to follow modern methods and mechanical tabulation. Nineteen test censuses were carried out in preparation for the final enumeration. Personnel training was provided. Whipple's Index was category V—very rough age data.

Publication Plan. Nicaragua. Dirección General de Estadística y Censos. *Censo general de población de la República de Nicaragua, 1950. Informe general y cifras del departamento de.* . . . Managua, 1952-1954. Only five of sixteen state volumes were published. The general report and an advance report were also issued. Language of publication is Spanish.

1963 (April 25-May 31)

The national censuses of population, housing, and agriculture were simultaneously conducted (new) by the Dirección General de Estadística y Censos. The organization of the census was based on recommendations suggested by COTA 1960. In November 1960 Nicaragua lost the territory that was in dispute with the Republic of Honduras. The census was *de facto*, and canvasser was the method used to record information on household schedules. Tabulation was mechanical. Territory covered by the census was divided into sixteen states and subdivided into "municipios" (similar to counties).

Definitions and Concepts. AGE—the same as 1950. URBAN—state and county capitals, other localities of 1,000 and more inhabitants with social services and amenities. HOUSEHOLD—person or group of persons living in the same place either as member of the same family or as pensioners, guests, servants plus any other occupant. Private households and group quarters were distinguished. MARITAL STATUS—same categories as 1950. FERTILITY—for all women age fifteen and older: number of children ever born alive (new). PLACE OF BIRTH and NATIONALITY—the same as 1950. EDUCATION—asked of all persons ten years of age and older: literacy (ability to read and write), school enrollment, and educational attainment (last degree completed). LANGUAGE—ability to speak Spanish. RELIGION—groups presented were: Catholics, Protestants (Anglicans, Baptists, Moravians, and others), others, and not reported. ECONOMIC ACTIVITY—the economically active population included employed persons as well as the unemployed looking for a job (new and experienced workers). Inactives were homemakers, students, inmates of institutions, the retired, pensioners, and persons of independent income. Questions were asked of all persons ten years of age and older. Period of reference was thirty days before the census. The number of weeks worked in 1962 was also asked. OCCUPATION—main occupation, classification based on COTA 1960, major groups and subgroups (two-digits). INDUSTRY—classification based on ISIC, divisions and major groups (two-digits). OCCUPATIONAL STATUS—Categories were: employer, self-employed, unpaid family worker, employee, manual laborer, and seasonal worker.

Special Elements and Features. The "departamentos" of Jinotega, Nuevo Segovia, and Zelaya had their size changed due to the loss of the territory in dispute with Honduras. Population of localities according to size of population was recorded. Results were also available for the main cities in the country. Fertility (number of children born alive) was recorded for the first time. Economic activity of the head of the household tabulated. Questions on religion and language were modified. For comparison, the results of the censuses of 1906 through 1950 were readjusted to the 1963 administrative boundaries.

Quality of the Census. Sample tabulation of 5 percent of population outside Managua; and 20 percent of population inside Managua was used. Provisional results were published three months after enumeration, sample results one year after the census, and the final results were available from 1964 to 1967. Postenumeration survey was conducted. Whipple's Index was category V—very rough age data.

Publication Plan. Nicaragua. Dirección General de Estadística. *Censos nacionales, 1963, población.* Managua, 1964-1967. Five subject volumes. Language of publication is Spanish.

1971 (April 20)

The national census of population was conducted by the Oficina Ejecutiva de Encuestas y Censos simultaneously with the censuses of housing and agriculture. The enumeration was taken on a *de facto* basis, and canvasser was the method utilized to record information on household questionnaires. The territory covered by the census was divided into three regions, sixteen "departamentos" (states) and subdivided into "municipios." Changes in the divisions of "municipios" have occurred. Tabulation was computerized for the first time.

Definitions and Concepts. URBAN, AGE, EDUCATION—same as 1963. PLACE OF BIRTH—basically the same as 1963 but "municipios" of birth of native born persons were also recorded. MARITAL STATUS—categories were: never married, married, common-law marriage, widowed, and divorced. ORPHANHOOD—recorded for the first time and derived from the question: Is your mother alive? PLACE OF RESIDENCE—Recorded for the first time: usual place and previous place of residence. In addition, the year of arrival in the country was asked of all foreign-born persons. HOUSEHOLD—one person or a groups of persons, related or not by blood, living and eating in the same place. Households were divided into private and group quarters. FERTILITY—number of children born alive, number of children still living (new), number of children born in 1970 (new), and number of children born in 1970 and who also died in 1970 (new). ECONOMIC ACTIVITY—questions asked of all persons ten years and older. Period of reference was the week before the census. Economically active were: employed and unemployed looking for job (new or experienced workers). Inactive population included: homemakers, students, retired, pensioners, persons of independent income, and others not classified elsewhere. OCCUPA-TION—classification based on COTA 1970, major groups only (one-digit). INDUSTRY—classification based on ISIC, divisions (one-digit).

Special Elements and Features. Orphanhood, year of arrival in country, place of usual and previous residence, and expanded number of fertility questions were all recorded for the first time. Age limit for answering questions on economic activity was ten years of age instead of fourteen as in 1963. The period of reference was the week before the census instead of the month as in 1963. The number of weeks worked was not recorded. Language and religion were dropped.

Quality of the Census. Preliminary results were published six months after the census. In the publications available there is no indication of quality of the census (coverage, accuracy, and so forth); however, an enumerator's manual has been published. Whipple's Index is category V—very rough age data. The census office is reestablished for each census.

Publication Plan. Nicaragua. Oficina Ejecutiva de los Censos. *Censos nacionales, 20 de abril de 1971: población.* Managua, 1974-1975. Publication does not appear to be complete at this time. Four subject volumes and four preliminary sample bulletins. Computer tapes are available. Language of publication is Spanish.

OTHER STATISTICAL PUBLICATIONS: Issued by Oficina Ejecutiva de Encuestas y Censos, *Anuario Estadístico, Boletín Demográfico* (irregularly), *Compendio Estadístico* (irregularly).

National Topic Chart

	1950	1963	1971
De facto	X	X	X
Usual residence			X
Place of birth	X	X	X
Duration of residence			
Place of prev. residence			X
Urban/rural	X	X	X
Sex	X	X	X
Age	X	X	X
Relation to household head	X	X	X
Marital status	X	X	X
Children born alive		X	X
Children living			X
Citizenship	X	X	
Literacy	X	X	X
School enrollment	X	X	X
Ed. attainment	X	X	X
Ed. qualification			
National/Ethnic origin			
Language	X	X	
Religion	X	X	
Household composition	X	X	
Econ. active/inactive	X	X	X
Occupation	X	X	X
Industry	X	X	X
Occupational status	X	X	X
Income			
Housing		X	X

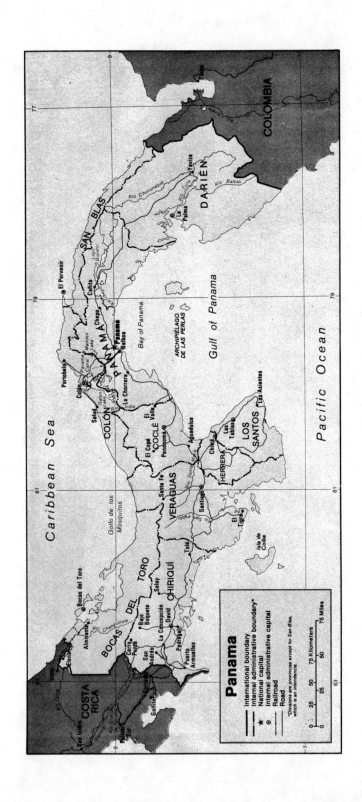

Panama

Panama

Republic of Panama

CAPITAL: Panama.
STATISTICAL AGENCY: Dirección de Estadística y Censo (DEC).
NATIONAL REPOSITORY: Biblioteca de Estadística y Censo.
MAIN U.S. REPOSITORY: Population Research Center (Univ. of Texas).

The colonial period extended from 1513 to 1821, when Panama was freed from Spain and joined Colombia. The struggle for independence was a constant issue until 1903, the year that Panama became a separate republic. Records of the colonial period are not known, except for some doubtful historical data indicating the total population for the year 1793.

During the time Panama was part of Gran Colombia, no official publication of a census was issued; but different sources presented the total population of the country for the years 1827, 1843, 1851, 1870, 1880, and 1896. Details of organization and methods of these "censuses" are not known.

1911

The first general census was conducted by the Dirección General de Estadística on a *de jure* basis, and canvasser was the method used to record information. Reports of these earlier censuses carry very little information on the organization and methods utilized. More detail, however, was revealed in a historical retrospective published in the 1940 census. Simultaneity was not observed. Indigenous population was not directly enumerated but estimated. The Canal Zone was enumerated in 1908, but the results were considered a simple estimate, the accuracy of which could not be assured. The territory covered by the census was divided into seven provinces and subdivided into districts. Scope included age, sex, race, nationality, religion, marital status, literacy, and professions. The number of births and deaths were also recorded for the years 1912 to 1915. Tabulation was manual.

1920

Second general census of population was conducted by the Dirección General del Censo on a *de jure* basis, and the organization was apparently the same as the previous census. Territory was divided into eight provinces (the province of Herrera was created in 1915), and subdivided into districts. Scope was expanded with the following questions: number of legitimate and illegitimate persons (coming from legal marriages or not), urban, school enrollment, country of birth of foreign born, nationality, household, infirmities, residence (whether the person was living in an owned house, rented house, or was a servant or boarder), inmates of institutions (orphans, prisoners, or indigents).

Indian population was irregularly enumerated and mostly over estimated. The population of neighborhoods in each district of the province of Panama was also recorded.

1930

The third general census of population was conducted by the Dirección General del Censo, and the organization adopted, according to the little information available, was very similar to that of 1920. The results were considered more accurate. The numbers for the indigenous population, however, were still considered deficient. Scope was the same as 1920, but educational attainment was added. Questions on legitimacy and inmates of institutions were dropped. Territory was divided into nine provinces (the province of Darién was created in 1922), and subdivided into districts. Tabulation was mechanical. In 1938 it was established that a census should be taken every ten years.

1940

The fourth general census of population was conducted by the Contraloría General, Oficina del Censo. This census is the mark of a new era in the history of demography of the country. Three aspects distinguished it from the previous ones: simultaneity was observed; the enumerated population was *de facto*; and the schedules were expanded, including more details on socioeconomic characteristics. Canvasser was the method utilized to gather information on general schedules. Tabulation was mechanical. The territory covered by the census was divided into nine provinces, subdivided into districts and "corregimientos." The cities of Panama and Colón were separately tabulated which included data of respective neighborhoods. Scope included age, sex, marital status, place of birth, duration of residence, urban/rural, relationship to household head, nationality, literacy, school enrollment, educational attainment, race, religion, economic activity, occupation, industry, employment status, and economic dependency (who supported the household). Comparative tables, a historical view of previous censuses, and an alphabetical list of localities (for the first time published in the country) by province and district were all included in the report. Electoral population by provinces and districts was also recorded. Organization and methods, definitions of concepts, copy of schedules and changes in territorial divisions were available. The indigenous population was not totally enumerated.

1950 (December 10)

The fifth national census of population was, for the first time, simultaneously taken with censuses of housing and agriculture. It was conducted by the Dirección de Estadística y Censo on a *de facto* basis, and canvasser was the method used to record information on five types of questionnaires: household, group quarters, individual, indigenous, and children cards ("tarjeta infantil"). The territory covered by the census was divided into nine provinces and subdivided into districts. Data for localities were also available. The organization of the census followed the recommendations suggested by COTA 1950. Tabulation was mechanical.

Definitions and Concepts. HOUSEHOLD ("familia")—one person or group of persons, related or not by blood, living in the same house. Guests, servants, any person living in the house and persons who spent the night of the census, although not permanently living in the house, were also included. URBAN—localities of 1,500 or more inhabitants with social services and amenities. AGE—in completed years, or number of months if less than a year old. Tabulated in standard five-year age groups. PLACE OF BIRTH—district of birth for native born and country of birth for foreign born. Comparisons with previous censuses are not possible because these questions were only asked in 1940 and then only the province of birth was asked of the native born. NATIONALITY—asked only of foreign born persons: if naturalized citizen or name of the country of citizenship. LANGUAGE—the first time this question was asked: language spoken at home. MARITAL STATUS—categories were: never married, married, common-law marriage, widowed, and divorced. FERTILITY—asked of women twelve years and older: number of children ever born alive. EDUCATION—literacy of all persons age ten and over. The ability to both read and write classified the respondent as literate; the previous censuses asked only the ability to read. School enrollment for all persons seven to fifteen years of age: attendance in elementary school. Educational attainment for all persons age seven and over: highest level or degree completed (new). ECONOMIC ACTIVITY—all persons age ten and over. Reference period was not stated, perhaps the moment of the census. The economically active were the employed, the unemployed, and new workers. The last two groups were included for the first time. The inactive were homemakers, students, minors, the retired, persons of independent income, pensioners, invalids. Duration of unemployment and the educational qualifications of new workers were also asked. OCCUPATION—classification was based on COTA 1950, major groups and subgroups (two-digits). INDUSTRY—classification was based on ISIC, divisions, groups and subgroups (three-digits). OCCUPATIONAL STATUS—categories were: employer, employee, self-employed, and unpaid family worker. Comparisons with 1940 are not possible. INCOME—for the first time recorded in a census. Questions asked only to employees: last salary or wages received. In addition, it was asked whether income was received per month, every fifteen days, per week, or daily. SOCIAL SECURITY (new)—the number of persons paying social security and the respective date of payment were taken.

Special Elements and Features. New topics were language, fertility, income, and social security. Economic activity was expanded, and different concepts for classification were adopted. Place of birth was more detailed. Data on household composition were expanded. Race and religion were dropped. Publication of results followed a different organization. Indigenous population and urban population data were presented separately. Indigenous population was for the first time directly enumerated; however, it included only those living in organized tribes.

Quality of the Census. Maps of districts and localities were prepared, and an estimate of the number of houses and inhabitants, as well as the time needed for their enumeration, were all part of the precensus operations. Test censuses were conducted to check methods and forms to be used in the final enumeration. Simultaneity was achieved for the first time. Preliminary and final results were promptly available. Whipple's Index rated it as category IV—rough age data.

Publication Plan. Panama. Dirección de Estadística y Censo. *Censos nacionales de 1950. Quinto censo de población.* Panama, 1954-1959. There are numerous publications on instructions and preliminary results in addition to the six main subject volumes. Language of publication is Spanish.

1960 (December 11)

The sixth national census of population was conducted by the Dirección de Estadística y Censo on a *de facto* basis; canvasser was the method utilized to gather information on household, indigenous, group quarters and individual schedules. Tabulation was mechanical using punched cards (new). The territory covered by the census was divided into nine provinces and subdivided into districts and "corregimientos" (the political base of the state). The population census was taken simultaneously with the census of housing. The census of agriculture was taken in 1961 except in the indigenous zones where it was taken simultaneously with population and housing censuses.

Definitions and Concepts. AGE—in completed years and, if less than a year of age, the date of birth was recorded. It was tabulated in single years and standard five-year age groups. MARITAL STATUS, URBAN, HOUSEHOLD, PLACE OF BIRTH, NATIONALITY, and SOCIAL SECURITY—the same as 1950. PLACE OF RESIDENCE—Duration of residence was revived and previous place of residence was asked for the first time. EDUCATION—asked of persons seven years of age and older: literacy and educational attainment (the same as that of 1950) and school enrollment (recorded for all levels and not just for elementary school as in 1950). ECONOMIC ACTIVITY—the lower age limit for inclusion in the labor force was ten years of age. Period of reference, as in 1950, was the day of the census. Economically active were: employed persons (including unpaid family workers), unemployed looking for a job, and new workers looking for a job for the first time. Inactive population included: homemakers, students, minors, the retired, pensioners, persons of independent income, and inmates of institutions. Duration of unemployment and educational qualification of new workers were recorded. Whether the person worked during the year of the census (1960) was asked for the first time. OCCUPATION—classification based on COTA 1960, major groups and subgroups (two-digits). INDUSTRY—classification based on ISIC, divisions and major groups (two-digits). As in 1950, a division for the Panama Canal Zone was included to record the sources of work in that zone. However, results provided insufficient data since the answers were limited to the name of the military base. New workers were not classified by industry. OCCUPATIONAL STATUS—same categories as 1950. INCOME—the same as 1950.

Special Elements and Features. Alphabetical list of localities with total population was included. Indigenous schedules excluded questions on housing, marital status, place of residence, and nationality. The questions on education and economic activity were reduced. Language, vaccination, and fertility were dropped altogether.

Quality of the Census. Precensuses were carried out to measure reliability of methods, to test questionnaires, to estimate costs, to check adequacy of maps and to evaluate vehicles of census propaganda. The recommendations of COTA 1960 were followed.

Postenumeration survey was conducted for the first time, and the results indicated 2.1 percent of omissions for nonindigenous population. Underenumeration of indigenous population was not measured. Whipple's Index was category IV—rough age data. Preliminary results were available two months after enumeration and final results became available from 1962 to 1965.

Publication Plan. Panama. Dirección de Estadística y Censo. *Censos nacionales de 1960. Sexto censo de población y segundo de vivienda.* Panama, 1962-1965. Numerous publications on instructions and preliminary results in addition to the nine main subject volumes and the general compendium. Language of publication is Spanish.

1970 (May 10)

The seventh national census of population was taken simultaneously with census of housing and was conducted by the Dirección de Estadística y Censo. The census was *de facto*, and a combination of canvasser and self-enumeration was the method used to record information on household and group-quarters schedules. For the first time, the same questionnaire was utilized by both the indigenous and nonindigenous population. Tabulation was mechanical. The territory covered by the census was divided into nine provinces and subdivided into districts and "corrigimientos." The organization followed the recommendations suggested by COTA 1970.

Definitions and Concepts. URBAN—same as 1950. AGE—in completed years and if less than one year of age "00" was recorded. Tabulation in standard five-year age groups. MARITAL STATUS—categories were: never married, married, common-law marriage, divorced, widowed, separated from legal marriage, and separated from common-law marriage. PLACE OF BIRTH—locality and district of birth were recorded for the native born; and for the foreign born, the country of birth. In addition, persons born in the Canal Zone were so specified. PLACE OF RESIDENCE—usual place of residence was recorded for the first time. Previous place of residence was also taken. FERTILITY (last taken in 1950)—asked of all women age fifteen and over: number of children born alive and the number born in the last twelve months. EDUCATION—asked of all persons age six and over: literacy, school enrollment, educational attainment, and educational qualification (new). Type of diploma, certificate, and the name of the school or college where obtained were asked. ECONOMIC ACTIVITY—lower age limit was ten years of age. Period of reference, the week before the census. Economically active population included employed as well as unemployed persons looking for a job (experienced or new workers). Inactive population: homemakers, students, retired, pensioners, persons of independent income, and inmates of institutions. Number of weeks worked was also recorded. OCCUPATION—classification based on COTA 1970, major and subgroups (two-digits). Main occupation or last occupation was recorded. In the case of a person who had not worked before, it was noted "new worker." INDUSTRY—classification based on ISIC, revision 1968, divisions and major groups (two-digits). OCCUPATIONAL STATUS—categories were: self-employed, employer, employee of the Panama Canal Zone, government employee, private employee, and unpaid family worker. INCOME—questions asked only of employees: gross salary and pay period (by day, week, or month). SOCIAL SECURITY—whether or not the person paid Social Security at any time and whether or not it was paid the month before the census.

Special Elements and Features. For the first time the same questionnaire was used for both indigenous and nonindigenous population. The census of housing was for the first time taken for indigenous population. The census of agriculture was taken simultaneously with population and housing for the indigenous population. Fertility returned to the regular schedule. Duration of residence, duration of unemployment, and nationality were dropped. Usual place of residence and the number of hours worked per week were recorded for the first time. Self-enumeration was used in several cities for the first time. Information on localities was expanded. A special publication was issued with data on Panama City, City of Colón, District of San Miguelito and sectors of metropolitan areas.

Quality of the Census. Enumeration of indigenous still presented several difficulties. Test censuses were taken to check applicability of questionnaires, to test the possibility of using self-enumeration, and to gather sufficient information for the organization of the final enumeration. Sample tabulation was applied (20 percent of population) to provide faster access to results. Analysis of results was not published in the census volumes but was to appear in separate monographs that have not been published as yet. Whipple's Index was not available.

Publication Plan. Panama. Dirección de Estadística y Censo. *Censos nacionales de 1970: VII censo nacional de población y III censo de vivienda, 10 de mayo de 1970.* Panama, 1972-1976. Publications on methodology, preliminary and advance sample results, six main subject volumes, including a general compendium. A plan for provincial volumes was not implemented. Computer tapes are available. Language of publication is Spanish.

1980 (May 11)

The eighth national census of population was taken simultaneously with census of housing and conducted by the Dirección de Estadística y Censo. Only the preliminary results are available; therefore, very little is known of the organization and methods used in the census. The enumeration was *de facto*, and the territory covered by the census was expanded to include two new "corregimientos" —Ancón (district of Panamá) and Cristóbal (district of Colón). The Canal Zone was added to Panama in 1979.

Tables available: total population by provinces from 1911 to 1980; occupied houses and population by provinces for 1970 and 1980; area, population and number of inhabitants per km^2 in 1980; area, population, and density by provinces and districts, 1980; occupied houses and population by localities, 1970 and 1980; occupied houses and population of provinces by districts and corregimientos: 1970-1980; graph of population growth from 1911 to 1980.

OTHER STATISTICAL PUBLICATIONS: Issued by Dirección de Estadística y Censo, *Estadística Panameña: Situación Demográfica, Panamá en Cifras* (annually).

National Topic Chart

	1950	1960	1970	1980
De facto	X	X	X	X
Usual residence			X	
Place of birth	X	X	X	
Duration of residence		X		
Place of prev. residence		X	X	
Urban/rural	X	X	X	
Sex	X	X	X	
Age	X	X	X	
Relation to household head	X	X	X	
Marital status	X	X	X	
Children born alive	X		X	
Children living				
Citizenship	X	X		
Literacy	X	X	X	
School enrollment	X	X	X	
Ed. attainment	X	X	X	
Ed. qualification			X	
National/Ethnic origin				
Language	X			
Religion				
Household composition	X	X	X	
Econ. active/inactive	X	X	X	
Occupation	X	X	X	
Industry	X	X	X	
Occupational status	X	X	X	
Income	X	X	X	
Housing	X	X	X	

Panama Canal Zone

**Former Possession of the United States,
returned to Republic of Panama in 1979**

STATISTICAL AGENCY: Dirección de Estadística y Censo (DEC).
NATIONAL REPOSITORY: Biblioteca de Estadística y Censo.
MAIN U.S. REPOSITORY: Population Research Center (Univ. of Texas).

The control of the Panama Canal Zone was granted to the United States by a treaty with the Republic of Panama signed in 1903. In 1904 a census was taken by the order of the Isthmian Canal Commission. In 1906, a census of towns was taken by the Sanitary Department, and the results showed the number of whites, blacks and yellows. It was stated that 5 to 10 percent should be added to these results to cover the outlying districts connected with the canal work. Another census was carried out in 1908, and to these results were added the populations of rural districts, which were counted in 1907.

1912

The first full census was taken by the Department of Civil Administration of the Isthmian Canal Commission. The territory covered by the census was divided into four districts (Ancón, Empire, Gorgona, and Cristóbal) subdivided into towns and villages; the settlements of Porto Bello, Nombre de Diós, Colón Beach, Taboga Sanitarium and the floating equipment at Chame. Employees of the Isthmian Canal Commission and Panama Railroad residing in the cities of Colón and Panamá, although enumerated, were not included in the Canal Zone results. No more details on organization were published. Scope included age, sex, color, number of persons gainfully employed, occupation, citizenship, place of birth, period of first residence in the Canal Zone, marital status, literacy, migration, and the number of persons born in the United States by state and territories.

Annual police censuses were taken from the 1913-1914 fiscal year until 1920. The censuses were then taken in conjunction with the regular decennial census of the United States. Any differences in organization and conduct will be pointed out in the appropriate census entry. Scope varies among territories and possessions.

The Panama Canal Zone area appears on the map of Panama, p. 266.

1920

First census of population taken under the supervision of the U.S. Bureau of the Census. The territory covered by the census was divided into two districts (Balboa and Cristóbal). The cities of Panamá and Colón were excluded from enumeration. Scope included total population divided into civilian and military, age, sex, color, nativity and parentage, place of birth for foreign born, marital status, literacy, school attendance, and language. Data on industry were recorded for civilian population only.

The large decrease in population since 1912 was due to two major factors: the Executive Order of 1912 for the depopulation of the Canal Zone of native landowners and squatters and the reduction of the labor force employed in the construction of the canal after its completion. Comparative tables were provided.

1930

The census of agriculture, although conducted simultaneously with the census of population in the continental United States and other outlying areas, was not taken in the Canal Zone. The scope of the population census was basically the same as 1920, but year of immigration, number of gainful workers, period of unemployment, and citizenship were added to the schedules. The classification of gainful workers was by industry groups with no attempt to show specific occupation.

1940

Census of population taken in conjunction with the sixteenth decennial census of the United States. Scope included: age, sex, color, nativity, place of birth, school attendance, educational attainment (new), marital status, relationship to head of household, economic activity, occupation (new), occupational status (new), industry, number of hours worked, number of weeks worked in 1939 (new), unemployment and housing (number of rooms and monthly rent). The housing census was taken simultaneously for the first time. Language, literacy, and year of immigration were dropped.

1950 (April 1)

Census of population was taken in conjunction with the seventeenth decennial census of the United States and conducted under the supervision of the Governor of the Canal Zone. For organization and methods, see United States 1950. Differences: territorial division of the Canal Zone has no county organization, instead it was divided into court districts, which were treated, for census purposes, as equivalent to county areas. The territory covered by the census was divided into two districts (Balboa and Cristóbal) and subdivided into towns. Canal Zone adopted general and individual schedules only.

Definitions and Concepts. AGE—in completed years as of the date of enumeration. Tabulated in standard five-year age groups (with median age). For the first time, unknown age was estimated according to other data instead of presented separately as in previous censuses. RACE—(color) two major groups: whites and nonwhites (blacks, black mixed, Indians, Japanese, Chinese, and others). Persons of mixed parentage were classified according to race of the nonwhite parent. NATIVITY—two basic groups: native (born in the United States, its territory or possessions, or born in foreign country but with American citizen parents) and foreign born. Up until 1946 Philippinos were also considered natives, but for the 1950 census they were classified as foreigners. EDUCATION—school enrollment, for all from five to twenty-four years of age; educational attainment (highest degree completed), for the population twenty-five years of age and older. MARITAL STATUS—categories were: never married, married, widowed, divorced, and, for the first time, separated (taken but not in table). Nonreported in marital status was allocated based on the presence of spouse or children. In 1940, nonreported were classified as single only. HOUSEHOLD—all persons, related or not by blood, who occupied a house, an apartment, or other group of rooms, or a room that constituted a dwelling unit. Married couples were, in addition, classified as "with household" or "without household." This classification was based on whether or not the husband was the head of the household. PLACE OF BIRTH—country or territory of birth asked of all persons. ECONOMIC ACTIVITY—period of reference was the week before the census. Lower age limit was fourteen years of age. Since not all persons were enumerated in the same week, the dates of the period of reference varied. In 1940, however, data referred to one fixed week for all persons. Included in the labor force were all persons classified as employed, unemployed looking for a job, and members of the armed forces. Not in the labor force were: homemakers, invalids, inmates of institutions, and others (students, the retired, too old to work, seasonal workers off season, voluntary idle, and not reported). Data not comparable with censuses previous to 1940. OCCUPATION—classification was according to the *Index of Occupations and Industries 1950*, major groups (one-digit). OCCUPATIONAL STATUS—categories were private wage and salary worker, government worker, self-employed, and unpaid family worker.

Special Elements and Features. Citizenship, number of hours worked, number of weeks worked, and period of unemployment were dropped from the schedules. Populations of towns and rural areas were presented in alphabetical order. Comparative tables with the previous census were included.

Quality of the Census. See United States entry for 1950. In addition, it was stated that complete data on employment status and occupation were not always obtained, therefore the size of the labor force was understated. Precise allocation of occupation was not possible due to insufficiently specific occupation designation.

Publication Plan. U.S.Bureau of the Census. *Census of Population: 1950. A Report of the Seventeenth Decennial Census of the United States.* Volume 2, Part 51-54, *Territories and Possessions.* Washington, D.C., 1953. Language of publication is English.

1960 (April 1)

Census of population was taken in conjunction with the eighteenth decennial census of the United States. The field work was the responsibility of the governor of the area. The census was *de jure*, and canvasser the method used to record information on household schedules and individual forms. All questions were asked on a complete-count basis. Manual coding and editing and mechanical tabulation rather than FOSDIC were utilized.

The territory covered by the census was divided into court districts and minor geographic divisions. The amount of information available for the Canal Zone as a whole is greater than for its subdivisions.

Definitions and Concepts. AGE—in completed years and date of birth (new). Assignment of unknown age was the same as 1950. Age was tabulated in single years up until twenty-one and then standard five-year groups. COLOR—two groups, white and nonwhite. The nonwhite group included Negro, American Indian, Japanese, Chinese, Filipino, Korean, Asian Indian, and Malayan races. Mexicans by birth or ancestry, if not belonging to Indian or other nonwhite race, were classified as white. URBAN—towns of 2,500 inhabitants or more. COURT DISTRICTS—equivalent to county areas. PLACE OF BIRTH—asked of population born in the United States, in Canal Zone, in other outlying areas of the United States, and in selected foreign countries. EDUCATION—school enrollment asked of all persons five to thirty-four years of age. Persons seven to sixteen years of age not reporting school enrollment were classified as enrolled. Educational attainment (highest grade attended and highest degree completed), asked of all persons fourteen years of age and older. Median school years completed was also tabulated. MARITAL STATUS—same categories as 1950. HOUSEHOLD—same as 1950, but instead of dwelling unit, housing unit was the basic unit of enumeration. In addition, married couple with their own household could be male or female headed. FAMILY—two or more persons living in the same household who are related to each other by blood, marriage, or adoption. ECONOMIC ACTIVITY—period of reference was the week before the person was enumerated. Lower age limit was fourteen years of age. Included in the labor force were: employed, unemployed looking for job, and members of the armed forces. Inactives were: persons doing only incidental unpaid family work (less than fifteen hours per week), homemakers, students, retired, seasonal workers off season, inmates of institutions, and invalids. Of these groups not in the labor force, only inmates of institutions and students were shown separately. Hours worked per week and the number of weeks worked in 1959 were also asked. OCCUPATION—classification system is basically the same as that used for the United States but condensed into fifty-five occupation groups because of the smaller number of workers. INDUSTRY—classification was basically the same as that of the United States but condensed to seventeen groups. OCCUPATIONAL STATUS—categories were the same as that of 1950. INCOME—for the first time the Canal Zone was included (gross income received during the year before the census). FERTILITY (new)—asked of all women who had ever been married: number of children ever born alive.

Special Elements and Features. A few definitions used in the 1960 census differed from those used in 1950. The following features were included for the first time: fertility and income. The number of weeks worked, the number of hours worked per week, and industry returned to the schedules. The number of rooms and monthly rent, nativity, and veteran status were dropped. For the first time, standard household schedules were utilized.

Quality of the Census. See United States entry, 1960, for general comments about coverage and accuracy of data. Certain requirements for employment of field work staff were established, although the field staff in each area was the responsibility of the governor. Training was administered to enumerators; enumeration maps were prepared; coverage, accuracy, and consistency of data were verified by a crew leader; and callback records were utilized.

Publication Plan. U.S. Bureau of the Census. *Census of Population: 1960. The Eighteenth Decennial Census of the United States.* Volume 1, Part 54-57, *Outlying Areas.* Washington, D.C., 1963. Language of publication is English.

1970 (April 1)

The census of population was taken in conjunction with the nineteenth decennial census of the United States. Like the previous censuses the governor or ranking official of the outlying areas was responsible for the field work under the supervision of the Bureau of the Census. The census of housing was conducted simultaneously with population, but a census of agriculture was not included in the Canal Zone.

The enumerated population was *de jure*, and canvasser was the method used to record information on household questionnaires (FOSDIC readable—new). An individual questionnaire was also used for persons living in hotels and group quarters as in the previous censuses. Tabulation was computerized; the editing, coding, and processing of questionnaires followed the same general procedure used for the United States.

Definitions and Concepts. AGE—same as 1960. URBAN—same as 1960. MARITAL STATUS—categories were: single, married (divided into legally, consensually, and separated), widowed, and divorced. PLACE OF BIRTH—all persons were asked if born in the United States, Puerto Rico, United States territories, or in a foreign country. Foreign-born persons were asked their country of birth. CITIZENSHIP—foreign-born persons were classified as naturalized, permanent alien, temporary alien, and born abroad of American parents. The year of arrival in the area was also asked. PLACE OF RESIDENCE—usual place and previous place of residence in 1965 were recorded. VETERAN STATUS—asked of males, sixteen years and older: whether served in the army, navy, or other armed force and during what war. EDUCATION—school enrollment (tabulated for persons three years old and over), educational attainment (highest grade of school attended and highest degree completed). Vocational training was recorded for the first time. FERTILITY—the same as 1960. Although the schedules referred to all women independently of their marital status, in the Canal Zone only the married women were reported. Single women were counted as having no children in spite of the fact that some of these women have had children. ECONOMIC ACTIVITIES—period of reference was the week before the census. Most of the reports related to economic activities data referred to persons sixteen years of age and older; selected employment status, however, was shown for persons fourteen and fifteen years old. Economically active were: employed and unemployed looking for a job. Not in the labor force included mainly students, homemakers, retired workers, seasonal workers in an off season, inmates of institutions, disabled persons, and persons doing only incidental family work (less than fifteen hours per week). As in 1960, only students and inmates were shown separately in selected tables. Number of hours worked, reasons for not working, number of weeks worked, and whether the person worked for a few days in 1969 were also recorded. OCCUPATION—classification based on the *1970 Census of Population Classified Index of Industries and Occupations*, but only a reduced number of groups were presented, twelve major groups and thirty-two subgroups (two-digits). INDUSTRY—based on the CIIO twelve divisions and major groups (two-digits). OCCUPATIONAL STATUS—same as 1960. INCOME—gross income from wages, salary, and so forth; net income from own nonfarm business, professional practice or partnership; net income from own farm; income other than earnings (Social Security, retirement, public assistance, welfare or any other source).

Special Elements and Features. Race (color) was dropped. Territorial divisions were pointed out on tables. Place of previous residence was recorded for the first time. Citizenship, year of immigration, veteran status, returned to the schedules. Some questions were addressed differently. Vocational training recorded for the first time or expanded. Copies of schedules and maps are present in the report.

Quality of the Census. See United States entry, 1970, for general comments on completeness and accuracy of data. Extensive field pretesting was carried out to determine content and procedures of the census. A number of changes were introduced in this census to improve usefulness of data; however, comparability with 1960 was not affected. Quality control and check measures were utilized throughout the census operation. Missing information was in most cases supplied by allocation.

Publication Plan. U.S. Bureau of the Census. *Census of Population: 1970.* Volume 1, Part 54-58, *Outlying Areas.* Washington, D.C., 1973. Language of publication is English.

1980 (May 11)

In 1979, the Panama Canal Zone was returned to be administered by the Republic of Panama; therefore, more details will be included in the appropriate entry of that country.

National Topic Chart

	1950	1960	1970
De facto			
Usual residence	X	X	X
Place of birth	X	X	X
Duration of residence			X
Place of prev. residence			X
Urban/rural		X	X
Sex	X	X	X
Age	X	X	X
Relation to household head	X	X	X
Marital status	X	X	X
Children born alive		X	X
Children living			
Citizenship			X
Literacy			
School enrollment	X	X	X
Ed. attainment	X	X	X
Ed. qualification			
National/Ethnic origin	X	X	
Language			
Religion			
Household composition			X
Econ. active/inactive	X	X	X
Occupation	X	X	X
Industry		X	X
Occupational status	X	X	X
Income		X	X
Housing		X	X

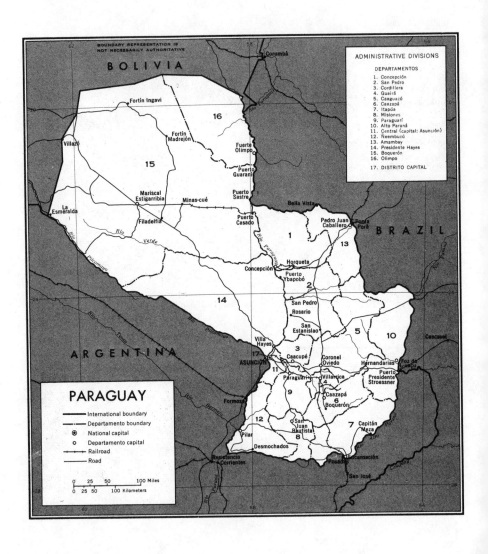

BOUNDARY REPRESENTATION IS
NOT NECESSARILY AUTHORITATIVE

BOLIVIA

Corumbá

ADMINISTRATIVE DIVISIONS

DEPARTAMENTOS

1. Concepción
2. San Pedro
3. Cordillera
4. Guairá
5. Caaguazú
6. Caazapá
7. Itapúa
8. Misiones
9. Paraguarí
10. Alto Paraná
11. Central (capital: Asunción)
12. Ñeembucú
13. Amambay
14. Presidente Hayes
15. Boquerón
16. Olimpo

17. DISTRITO CAPITAL

Fortín Ingavi

16

Fortín
Madrejón

Villazó

Fuerte
Olimpo

15

Puerto
Guarani

Mariscal
Estigarribia

Minas-cué

Puerto
Sastre

Bella Vista

La
Esmeralda

Filadelfia

Río Verde

Puerto
Casado

Pedro Juan
Caballero

Ponta
Porã

BRAZIL

1

13

Río Pilcomayo

Horqueta

Concepción

Puerto
Ybapobó

2

14

San Pedro

Rosario

San
Estanislao

5

10

Cascavel

ARGENTINA

Villa
Hayes

17

ASUNCIÓN

Caacupé

Coronel
Oviedo

Hernandarias

Foz do
Iguaçu

11

Paraguarí

Villarrica

Puerto
Presidente
Stroessner

Formosa

9

4

Caazapá
6
Boquerón

7

Capitán
Meza

12

San
Juan
Bautista

8

Pilar

Desmochados

Resistencia
Corrientes

Posadas

Encarnación

San José

PARAGUAY

———— International boundary
—·—·— Departamento boundary
⊛ National capital
○ Departamento capital
+++++ Railroad
———— Road

0   25   50   100 Miles
0 25 50   100 Kilometers

Paraguay

Republic of Paraguay

CAPITAL: Asunción.
STATISTICAL AGENCY: Direccíon General de Estadística y Censos
NATIONAL REPOSITORY: ?
MAIN U.S. REPOSITORY: New York Public Library (early censuses), Population Research Center (Univ. of Texas).

A Spanish colony since 1535, Paraguay gained its independence in 1811. During the War of Triple Alliance (1865-1870), nearly half of its population and a great part of its territory were lost to Argentina, Brazil, and Uruguay. Apparently, the first census was taken in 1886 by the Oficina General de Estadística. Results of the census were published in the *Anuario Estadístico de la República de Paraguay* of the same year. The territory was divided into "partidos" (states) and the federal capital (Asunción). The scope included age; sex; nationality; nativity; literacy; number of baptisms, marriages, and deaths; infirmities; school enrollment; number of schools, pupils and teachers; and members of diplomatic missions by place of residence. No details of organization and methods were given.

1899

A census was taken but not published except for the total population available in the census report of 1960.

1936

A partial census was carried out and the results were considered only an approximation of reality. Estimated population, with some comments, was published in *Memoria de la dirección general de estadística, 1938*.

These first censuses suffered from serious deficiencies in the enumeration procedure and did not provide reliable or complete data for comparative studies with the 1950 census.

1950 (October 28)

The first national census of population and housing was conducted by the Dirección General de Estadística y Censos on a *de facto* basis, and canvasser was the method utilized to record information on general schedules. The organization and methods adopted followed the recommendations of COTA 1950. Mechanical tabulation was used.

The territory covered by the census was divided into sixteen departments and the Federal Capital. Data were presented by regions, departments, districts, and zones. The federal capital was subdivided into sectors and sections.

Definitions and Concepts. AGE—completed years, presented in standard five-year age groups. URBAN—inhabited places (cities and "pueblos"), and capitals of departments and districts, without considering the number of inhabitants. RURAL—areas outside the limits of respective "municipios." PLACE OF BIRTH—region of birth for native born and country of birth for foreign born. The ethnic group of Mennonites was recorded separately. NATIONALITY—the population was divided into two major groups: Paraguayan citizens (including those born in a foreign country) and foreigners. MARITAL STATUS—categories were: single, married, common-law marriage, widowed, and divorced (included legally and not legally separated). Questions were asked of all persons fifteen years and over. LANGUAGE—that most used at home asked of persons three years old and over. Four groups were recorded: only Spanish, only Guaraní, both Spanish and Guaraní, and other languages. EDUCATION—literacy (of persons ten years and over), and school attendance (from seven to fourteen years of age, compulsory elementary school enrollment). Causes of not attending school were also recorded. Educational attainment (highest degree completed, of all persons seven years and over). ECONOMIC ACTIVITY—lower age limit was twelve years of age. Economically active population included all persons engaged in gainful occupations at the time of the census and unemployed persons able to work and looking for a job. Economically inactive were homemakers, students, the retired, pensioners, invalids, and inmates of institutions. OCCUPATION—classification based on COTA 1950, major groups and subgroups (two-digits). INDUSTRY—classification based on COTA 1950, eight divisions (one-digit). OCCUPATIONAL STATUS—categories were employer, employee, self-employed, unpaid family worker, and member of the armed forces. ECONOMIC DEPENDENCY—the heads of household and members of the family dependent on agriculture and animal husbandry were recorded separately. HOUSEHOLD—group of people, related or not by blood, living in the same house.

Special Elements and Features. Copy of schedules, comparative tables for 1886 and 1950, estimates of population from 1887 to 1950, birth and death rates, number of immigrants registered in the Institute of Agrarian Reform from 1948 to 1954, data on the "colonias Menonitas," and data on internal migration based on comparisons between place of birth and places of present residence are all included in the report.

Quality of the Census. This is the first census that covered the entire population. Maps were prepared, and enumerators were trained to assure completeness and accuracy of results. A permanent census office was established. The publication of results was started in 1953. The totals for the country were published in the *Anuario Estadístico de 1948-53* and for the departments and Federal Capital in separate bulletins. Whipple's Index was not available. According to the *U.N. Demographic Yearbook*, the results for total population excluded 12,881 schedules that were not tabulated, the Indian jungle population estimated at 17,000, and an adjustment of 50,067 for underenumeration.

Publication Plan. Paraguay. Dirección General de Estadística. *Censo nacional de población y viviendas, 28 octubre 1950. Departamento de....* Asunción, 1953-1955. Of the seventeen volumes of this set, those for Concepción, Guaira, and Central are no longer available. A volume on general tables and analytical commentary was published in 1962. Language of publication is Spanish.

1962 (October 14)

National census of population and housing was conducted by the Dirección General de Estadística y Censos. Reports carried very little about organization and methods followed. The enumeration was taken on a *de facto* basis, and canvassers recorded information on household schedules. The territory was divided into sixteen departments and their districts and the Federal Capital, subdivided into sections. Sample tabulation was utilized for elaboration of preliminary results.

Definitions and Concepts. AGE—in completed years, presented in single year and standard five-year age groups. URBAN—cities and towns and administrative centers of departments and districts. PLACE OF BIRTH—two major groups: native born and foreign born, presented by departments. The foreign born were also presented by nationality. MARITAL STATUS—asked of persons twelve years and over. Categories: never married, married (civil and religious ceremonies), married (civil ceremony only), common-law marriage, widowed, and divorced (separated legally or otherwise). LANGUAGE—spoken at home. Categories were: Castellano only, Guaraní only, Castellano and Guaraní, other languages. Questions asked of persons three years and older. EDUCATION—literacy (persons seven years and over): ability to read and write. School enrollment (persons between seven and fourteen years of age): like 1950, the causes for not attending school were also recorded. Educational attainment (persons seven years and over): last degree completed. ECONOMIC ACTIVITY—basically the same concept used in 1950. Economically active population included all persons twelve years of age and older, engaged in gainful occupation or unemployed looking for a job (new worker or experienced). Inactive: homemakers, students, retired, pensioners, persons of independent income, invalids, and inmates of institutions. OCCUPATION—classification based on COTA 1960, major groups only (one-digit). INDUSTRY—classification based on COTA 1960, major divisions only (one-digit). OCCUPATIONAL STATUS—categories were: employer, employee, self-employed, laborer, unpaid family worker, paid family worker, and nonspecified worker. RELIGION—recorded for the first time. Categories were: Catholic, Christian, non-Catholic (including all Protestant denominations), other religions (Buddists, Moslims, Israelites), and no religion. Results for the country as a whole were not present in tables for religion. FERTILITY—asked of women twelve years and over: number of children born alive (new). PLACE OF RESIDENCE—recorded for the first time: number of permanent residents, immigrants, and persons in transit. In addition, duration of residence was asked.

Special Elements and Features. New features included: fertility, religion, and duration of residence. Age was presented in single years for the first time. The total population of the federal capital (Asunción) according to census and official estimates (1793, 1886, 1914, 1928, 1936, 1945, 1950, and 1962) was given in separate table. More detailed information on migrants was provided.

Quality of the Census. Whipple's Index classified age accuracy into category III—approximate data. According to the *U.N. Demographic Yearbook*, the results of total population excluded adjustment for underenumeration and an allowance of 35,000 (estimate) for Indian jungle population. The final results started to be published in 1965.

Publication Plan. Paraguay. Dirección General de Estadística y Censos. *Censo de población y vivienda, 14 de octubre de 1962.* Asunción, 1964-1965. Of the seventeen volumes only the one for Asunción seems to still be available. There were also provisional, preliminary (sample), and whole country volumes issued. Language of publication is Spanish.

1972 (July 2)

The third national census of population and housing was conducted by the Dirección General de Estadística y Censos on a *de facto* basis, but a few tables were presented for the resident population. Canvassers recorded information on household schedules. Sample tabulation (10 percent) was utilized to provide preliminary results. The territory covered by the census was divided into sixteen departments (subdivided into districts or "municipios") and the Federal Capital. New districts and changes of boundaries were indicated in the report.

Definitions and Concepts. URBAN—all capitals of districts without taking into consideration special characteristics. Special attention should be given to some localities classified as urban in 1962 and rural in 1972. HOUSEHOLD—divided into private (person or group of persons living as a family and sharing food arrangements), and collective (group of persons living together for reasons of health, work, religion, military). FERTILITY—asked of all women fifteen years and over: number of children born alive, number of children still living, date of birth of last child and whether still alive. ORPHANHOOD—derived from the question: Is your mother alive? PLACE OF BIRTH—for native born, department of birth and for foreign born, the country of birth. PLACE OF RESIDENCE—the usual place and the previous place of residence (in July 1967) were recorded. The previous place of residence was asked of all persons five years and over. AGE—in completed years and "00" for those less than one year. Recorded in single year and standard five-year age groups. MARITAL STATUS—

asked of persons twelve years of age and older. Categories: single, married, common-law marriage, widowed, separated, or divorced. EDUCATION—questions asked of all persons seven years and over: literacy (ability to read and write), school enrollment, and educational attainment (last degree completed). Causes for not attending school were also recorded for persons between seven and fourteen years of age. ECONOMIC ACTIVITY—period of reference was the week before the census. Lower age limit was twelve years. Population economically active: employed (at work, with a job but not at work) and unemployed (new or experienced looking for a job or not, who were not included within the nonactive population). Inactive population: retired, pensioners, persons of independent income, students, homemakers, and invalids. Employed and unemployed were separately classified by occupation and industry. OCCUPATION—classification based on COTA 1970, major groups and subgroups (two-digits). The more detailed classification is available by request. INDUSTRY—classification based on ISIC, major divisions (one-digit). OCCUPATIONAL STATUS— categories were: employer, employee, laborer, self-employed, and unpaid family worker.

Special Elements and Features. The category "unknown" was eliminated for age, marital status, fertility, school attendance, place of birth, usual and previous place of residence, and housing characteristics. Instead, data were supplied based on data of precedent person with similar characteristics. Fertility questions were expanded; religion, nationality, and language were dropped. Previous place of residence substituted for duration of residence adopted in 1962. Classification of economically active population differed from previous censuses; the period of reference referred to the week before the census instead of the date of the census. Maps, graphs, copy of the schedule, and comparative tables with previous census results were provided, as was a brief history of population growth in the country (1886-1972) and in Asunción (1793-1972). Total population recorded from the censuses taken within the countries participating in the Censo de las Americas de 1970 appeared in comparison with previous estimates. A list was furnished of unpublished tables with detailed cross-classifications that are available.

Quality of the Census. The U.S. Bureau of the Census, CELADE (Centro Latino Américano de Demografía), CEPAL (Comisión Economica para America Latina), and UNFPA (UN Fund for Population Activities) provided technical assistance for the taking of the census. Several national institutions contributed to the updating and preparation of census maps. A precensus was carried out to test the organization and materials to be used during enumeration and to provide training of personnel. Provisional results were available a year after the enumeration; final results available in 1975.

Publication Plan. Paraguay. Dirección General de Estadística y Censos. *Censo nacional de población y viviendas, 1972.* Asunción, 1975-1976. 2 volumes. Provisional and sample tabulation results were also published. Unpublished data are available. Language of publication is Spanish.

OTHER STATISTICAL PUBLICATIONS: Issued by Dirección General de Estadística y Censos, *Anuario Estadístico, Demografía (Hechos Vitales)* (annually).

National Topic Chart

	1950	1962	1972
De facto	X	X	X
Usual residence			X
Place of birth	X	X	X
Duration of residence		X	
Place of prev. residence			X
Urban/rural	X	X	X
Sex	X	X	X
Age	X	X	X
Relation to household head	X	X	X
Marital status	X	X	X
Children born alive		X	X
Children living			X
Citizenship	X	X	
Literacy	X	X	X
School enrollment	X	X	X
Ed. attainment	X	X	X
Ed. qualification			
National/Ethnic origin			
Language	X	X	
Religion		X	
Household composition			
Econ. active/inactive	X	X	X
Occupation	X	X	X
Industry	X	X	X
Occupational status	X	X	X
Income			
Housing	X	X	X

Peru

Republic of Peru

CAPITAL: Lima.
STATISTICAL AGENCY: Oficina Nacional de Estadística y Censos.
NATIONAL REPOSITORY: ?
MAIN U.S. REPOSITORY: Population Research Center (Univ. of Texas).

Vital statistics are known to have existed since the Incan Empire. During the colonial period, however, the estimates and population counts were made only for the purpose of taxation, and the records are neither accurate nor complete.

After independence from Spain (1821-1824), an electoral census was taken in 1828, but the results were not published. General population counts were carried out in 1836, 1850, and 1862, but taxation was still the main purpose and no significant changes of methods and techniques were utilized.

It was not until 1876 that the first national census of population was taken. The census was conducted by the Dirección de Estadística on a *de facto* basis, and canvassers recorded information on general schedules. The population was divided into three categories: urban, special (group quarters), and rural. The scope included name, age, sex, nationality, literacy, religion, occupation, usual place of residence, race, marital status, property ownership, and infirmities. The territory covered by the census was divided into twenty-one departments (states) and subdivided into provinces and districts. The results, although considered not accurate, were the best obtained up to that date.

Partial censuses were taken in several departments and provinces between 1876 and the first quarter of the twentieth century.

1940

Second general census of population was conducted by the Dirección Nacional de Estadística on a *de facto* basis, and canvasser was the method used to record information on four types of schedules: household or family schedule (employed only in a few cities), urban schedules (general questionnaires employed in provincial capitals and departments), rural schedules (general questionnaires used in rural areas), and group quarters schedules. The census office was permanently established, and preliminary tasks were done, including a housing census in 1938 as a preparatory phase for the final population enumeration.

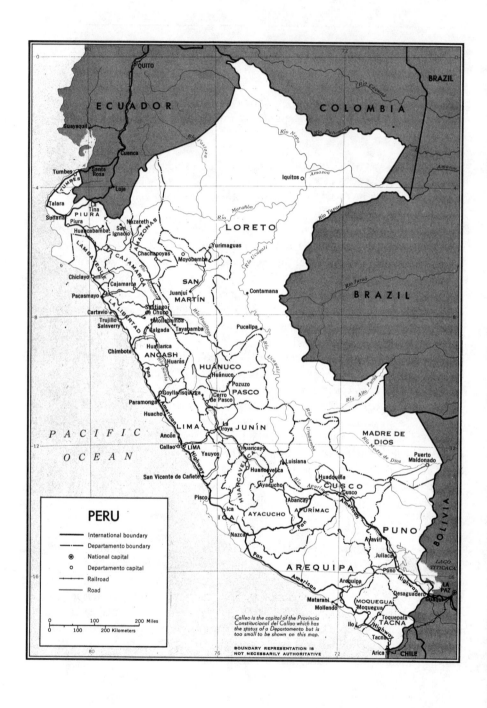

PERU

International boundary
Departamento boundary
⊛ National capital
○ Departamento capital
Railroad
Road

0   100   200 Miles
0   100   200 Kilometers

Callao is the capital of the Provincia
Constitucional del Callao which has
the status of a Departamento but is
too small to be shown on this map.

BOUNDARY REPRESENTATION IS
NOT NECESSARILY AUTHORITATIVE

The territory covered by the census was divided into twenty-three departments (Madre de Diós, San Martín, and Tumbes were added and Tarapacá excluded), subdivided into provinces and districts. The scope included name, age, sex, marital status, race, relationship to head of the family (that is, household), infirmities, language, literacy, educational attainment, religion, nationality, place of birth, place of usual residence, occupation, economic activity, industry, occupational status, and fertility.

The results indicated that remote areas were not directly enumerated, and the indigenous population was estimated at 350,000 persons. In addition, 7.5 percent of the total population was omitted from enumeration (465,144 persons).

1961 (July 2)

Although called "sixth" national census of population, it was actually the third general population census taken in the country. It was conducted by the Dirección Nacional de Estadística y Censos on a *de facto* basis, and canvassers recorded information on household schedules. The organization and methods adopted followed the recommendations of COTA 1960. The territory was divided into twenty-four departments (Department of Pasco was created in 1944) and subdivided into provinces and districts. Tabulation was computerized. The census of housing was taken simultaneously.

Definitions and Concepts. URBAN—all inhabited centers that were classified as capitals of districts, regardless of the number of inhabitants. Also classified as urban were the inhabited centers that, although not the capital of a district, had the same number of inhabitants or more as the capital of the same district and presented social services and amenities. HOUSEHOLD—("familia censal")—included all persons, related or not by blood, living in the same place. The "familia censal" became a nonfamily group ("grupo non familiar") if the number of boarders and lodgers exceeded the number of members of the family (more than five persons in general). AGE—completed years, recorded in standard five-year age groups and also in the following groups: less than a year, one to three, four, five, six, seven to fourteen, fifteen to sixteen, seventeen to nineteen, twenty to thirty-nine, forty to sixty-four, and sixty-five plus. PLACE OF BIRTH —province of birth for native born and country of birth for foreign-born persons. PLACE OF RESIDENCE—province, and duration of residence recorded in number of years. NATIONALITY—the population was divided into three groups: Peruvians, naturalized Peruvians, and foreigners. RELIGION—name of religious affiliation. MARITAL STATUS—categories were: single, married, common-law marriage, divorced, separated, and widowed. LANGUAGE—asked of persons five years and over: ability to speak Spanish and the language or dialect of the person's mother. EDUCATION—for persons six years and over: literacy, school attendance, educational attainment, and educational qualification of persons sixteen years of age and over. FERTILITY—For all women fourteen years and older: number of children born alive and age of mother at the birth of first child. ECONOMIC ACTIVITY—lower age limit was six years of age. Period of reference was date of census. Economically active population included: employed, unpaid family workers, and unemployed looking for a job (new or experienced workers). Inactive population: homemakers, students, persons of independent income, the retired, pensioners, members of religious groups not receiving salary or wages, invalids, minors not working or studying, older persons not receiving pensions, and inmates of institutions. The number of months worked during the year before the census and the time of unemployment were also recorded. OCCUPATION—main occupation or last occupation, if the person was unemployed. Classification was based on COTA 1960, twelve major groups only (one-digit). INDUSTRY—classification based on COTA 1960, nine divisions (one-digit). OCCUPATIONAL STATUS—the categories were: self-employed, employer, employee, manual laborer, and family worker ("trabajador familiar"). INCOME—recorded for the first time. Only monthly income of employees and weekly income of laborers were asked.

Special Elements and Features. It was established that a census should be taken decennially. For the first time the censuses of population, housing, and agriculture were taken simultaneously. Sample tabulation was utilized to provide faster availability of results. For the first time duration of residence, school attendance, educational qualification, income, the number of months worked, and time of unemployment were recorded. Race and the number of children still living were dropped from the schedules. The total population of "centros poblados" (localities of all sizes) and that of the indigenous population by departments and provinces were presented separately.

Quality of the Census. The frequency of censuses (1876, 1940, and 1961) has been irregular. Underenumeration was calculated at 4 percent (412,781 persons), and the indigenous population was only estimated (100,830). Publication of results began to be available in 1963 (preliminary results) and 1964 (final). Whipple's Index ranking is not available.

Publication Plan. Peru. Dirección Nacional de Estadística y Censos. *VI censo nacional de población.* Lima, 1962-1973. Volume 1 (Población) has five subject reports, Volume 2 (Viviendas) has two subject reports, Volume 3 (Agropecuario) one report, Volume 4 has all three census results by department. Four of twenty-three reports were not published, Volumes 5 and 6 were not published. In addition, there were four volumes on localities of all sizes. Language of publication is Spanish.

1970 (October-December)

A national census of population and housing of "pueblos jóvenes" (young cities) was conducted by the former Oficina Nacional de Desarrollo de Pueblos Jóvenes and published by the Oficina Nacional de Estadística y Censos. It covered twenty-five cities where the young cities were located.

"Pueblos Jóvenes" was defined as urban settlements located in the surrounding areas of cities of 10,000 or more inhabitants. They originated through migration and/or population growth in these cities but lack the basic social services and amenities needed for their urban assimilation.

It was a 20 percent sample census, and the canvassers recorded the information on household schedules. The scope included: relationship to head of the household, sex, age, orphanhood, place of birth, years of residence and previous residence, number of children born alive, number of children still living, marital status, literacy, language, school enrollment, educational attainment, economic activity, main and previous occupation, industry, occupational status, and income.

1972 (June 4)

General censuses of population and housing were conducted simultaneously by the Oficina Nacional de Estadística y Censos. The census was *de facto*, and canvasser the method utilized to record information on household schedules. Tabulation was computerized. The territory covered by the census included the twenty-four departments, divided into provinces and districts.

Definitions and Concepts. URBAN—all capitals of districts and inhabited placed with 100 or more contiguous housing units with social services and amenities. CENTRO POBLADO—inhabited centers identified by a name where several families live permanently or, exceptionally, only one family or even one person lives. HOUSEHOLD ("hogar censal")—a person or group of persons, related or not by blood, who live in a housing unit or part of it and share food arrangements. FAMILY—three classes of families were distinguished: nuclear, extended, and compound. Compound family referred to nuclear or extended families living with one or more persons not related by blood to the head. Unrelated persons living together were also considered a compound family. AGE—in completed years. Tabulated in single year and standard five-year age groups. PLACE OF BIRTH—the same as 1961. PLACE OF RESIDENCE— usual place, duration, and place of previous residence were recorded. NATIONALITY—name of country of the foreign born who were not naturalized Peruvians. RELIGION—the same as 1961. MARITAL STATUS—categories were: never married, married, widowed, divorced, separated, and common-law marriage ("conviviente"). FERTILITY—for women twelve years old and older: number of children born alive, number of children dead, and age of the mother at the birth of the first child. ORPHANHOOD—derived from the question: Is your mother alive or not? EDUCATION—literacy, school enrollment, educational attainment, and educational qualification. The questions were asked of all persons five years of age and older. The period of attendance (day, afternoon, or evening) and whether the student had another activity were also recorded. LANGUAGE—mother tongue, regardless of the ability to speak that language at the time of the census. The following groups were recorded: Quechua, Aymara, other autocthonous language, Spanish, and other foreign language. ECONOMIC ACTIVITY—lower age limit was six years. Period of reference was the week before the census. Economically active population included: employed, unpaid family workers, and unemployed looking for a job (new and experienced workers).

Inactive: pensioners, the retired, persons of independent income, students, home-makers, minors (less than seventeen years of age not working or studying), members of religious groups not receiving wages or salaries, older persons not receiving pensions, invalids, and inmates of institutions. The period of unemployment in weeks and period of employment in months were also recorded. OCCUPATION—classification based on ISCO, major groups, groups, and subgroups (three-digits). INDUSTRY—classification based on ISIC, divisions, groups, and subgroups (three-digits). OCCUPATIONAL STATUS and INCOME—the same as 1961.

Special Elements and Features. Previous residence was recorded for the first time. Fertility included a question on the number of children dead. Language question was worded differently. Educational qualification was more detailed. In general, a larger number of cross-classifications was presented.

Quality of the Census. Census tests were taken to improve accuracy of data, to train personnel, and to check the applicability of methods and techniques to be applied in the final enumeration. Sampling enumeration, taken simultaneously with the census, was used to measure completeness of the census. The results indicated 3.86 percent of underenumeration (543,556), and the Indian jungle population was only estimated (39,800). Whipple's Index rating was not available. Provisional results were tabulated manually and were available two months after the census. Final results were published in 1974-1975.

Publication Plan. Peru. Oficina Nacional de Estadística y Censos. *Censos nacionales: VII de población, II de vivienda, 4 de junio de 1972.* Lima, 1974-1975. Two volumes of national results and twenty-four department volumes in 47 volumes. Language of publication is Spanish.

OTHER STATISTICAL PUBLICATIONS: Issued by Oficina Nacional de Estadística, *Anuario Estadístico, Boletín de Análisis Demográfico* (irregularly).

National Topic Chart

	1961	1970	1972
De facto	X		X
Usual residence		X	X
Place of birth	X	X	X
Duration of residence	X	X	X
Place of prev. residence		X	X
Urban/rural	X		X
Sex	X	X	X
Age	X	X	X
Relation to household head	X	X	X
Marital status	X	X	X
Children born alive	X	X	X
Children living		X	X
Citizenship	X		X
Literacy	X	X	X
School enrollment	X	X	X
Ed. attainment	X	X	X
Ed. qualification	X		X
National/Ethnic origin			
Language	X	X	X
Religion	X	X	X
Household composition			
Econ. active/inactive	X	X	X
Occupation	X	X	X
Industry	X	X	X
Occupational status	X	X	X
Income	X	X	X
Housing	X		X

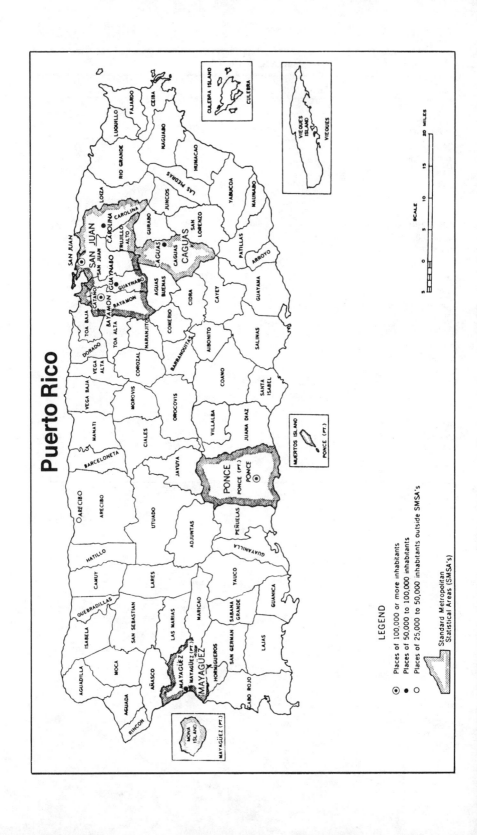

Puerto Rico

LEGEND

⊙ Places of 100,000 or more inhabitants

● Places of 50,000 to 100,000 inhabitants

○ Places of 25,000 to 50,000 inhabitants outside SMSA's

Standard Metropolitan
Statistical Areas (SMSA's)

Puerto Rico

Commonwealth of Puerto Rico

CAPITAL: San Juan.
STATISTICAL AGENCY: Bureau of Economic Planning, Puerto Rico Planning Board.
NATIONAL REPOSITORY: General Library, University of Puerto Rico.
MAIN U.S. REPOSITORY: Population Research Center (Univ. of Texas).

Under Spanish domination since 1509, Puerto Rico together with adjacent islands was ceded to the United States in 1898 after the Spanish-American war. During Spanish administration, censuses were taken in 1765, 1775, 1800, 1815, 1832, 1846, 1860, 1877, 1887, and 1897. Before 1860, enumerations were incomplete, lacked accuracy, and could be considered more an estimate than a census per se. Official records are scarce and mostly limited to total number of inhabitants.

1860

A census of population was conducted under Spanish supervision by the Junta General de Estadística. The census was *de jure*, and the results, although not totally accurate, were considered the closest to the real figure than any other yet taken. The territory covered by the census was divided into eight departments and the city of San Juan, capital of the island. The scope included: age, sex, marital status, nationality, residence, race (color), civil status (free or slave), literacy, and occupation.

1877

Census of population was taken on a *de jure* and a *de facto* basis, and official figures are limited to sex, race, and nationality. No details on organization and methods are available. The results were published in the report of the Civil Secretary of Puerto Rico.

1887

Census taken under the supervision of the Dirección General del Instituto Geográfico y Estadístico of Spain. The enumeration was carried out on a *de jure* and a *de facto* basis, and the results were considered of better quality than the previous one. The following tables were obtained from official census returns: *de jure* and *de facto* population by sex, race, and nationality; total population by sex and marital status; total population by sex and literacy; population by age and sex.

1897

A census was taken, but the results were never published or even tabulated in full.

1899

Census of population was conducted by the War Department of the United States. The first census taken under U.S. administration was *de jure*, and canvassers recorded information on general schedules. The questionnaire, although following the general design of that of the eleventh decennial census of the United States, differed with respect to the number of inquiries. The territory was divided into seven departments and subdivided into municipal districts. The names and boundaries of departments had changed since 1887, but a comparative table was furnished.

The censuses of agriculture and of educational establishments were taken simultaneously with population. The scope included: age, sex, relationship to head of the family, color, marital status, nativity, citizenship, school attendance, literacy, occupation, industry, economic activity, and some housing questions. Mechanical tabulation was used.

1910

Census taken in conjunction with the thirteenth decennial census of the United States. It was *de jure*, and canvassers recorded information on general schedules. The territory was divided into municipalities, cities, towns or villages, and barrios. Urban and rural areas were distinguished. Scope: age, sex, marital status, color, nativity, place of birth, parentage, year of immigration of foreign born, males of voting and militia age, citizenship, school attendance, literacy, language, and number of dwellings and families. Occupation and ownership of homes present in the general schedules of the United States were not asked in Puerto Rico.

1920

Census taken in conjunction with the fourteenth decennial census of the United States. The organization and methods were virtually the same as the previous one. Scope was the same as 1910, but economic activity, occupation, industry, and tenure of home were added. The results were available for municipalities, cities and towns, and places of 2,500 to 5,000 inhabitants. The islands of Culebra and Vieques were included as separate municipalities and the smaller adjacent islands were parts of other municipalities.

1930

Population census taken in conjunction with the fifteenth decennial census of the United States. Organization was basically the same as 1920. Scope: language and economic activities were enlarged (more detailed information). The year of immigration was not asked; the remaining questions were the same as the previous census. Census of agriculture was taken simultaneously. Territorial divisions presented no major changes.

1935

Special census of population taken by the Administración de Reconstrucción de Puerto Rico under the direction of the U.S. Bureau of the Census. The results were printed in English and Spanish, and apparently the organization was similar to the 1930 census. The territory covered by the census was divided into municipalities (including Culebra, Vieques, and adjacent islands), cities, towns, and barrios. Urban and rural areas were distinguished. The scope included: age, sex, race, nativity, place of birth, citizenship, marital status, school attendance, literacy, language, economic activity, occupation, industry, and some housing questions. More extensive information was given for smaller geographical subdivisions. The population of cities and towns in alphabetical order was also provided.

1940

Census taken in conjunction with the sixteenth decennial census of population of the United States. For the first time, the census of housing was taken simultaneously. The enumeration was taken on a *de jure* basis; canvasser was the method utilized to record information on general schedules. The scope included all the features of the previous census, and in addition, place of previous residence (in 1935) and occupational status were recorded for the first time.

1950 (April 1)

The census of population was taken in conjunction with the seventeenth decennial census of population of the United States. A housing census was taken simultaneously. Population was enumerated on a *de jure* basis; canvassers recorded information on general schedules. The territory was divided into municipalities, cities, towns, barrios, and for the first time, in standard metropolitan areas. SMA (standard metropolitan area) was a municipality or group of contiguous municipalities that contained at least one city of 50,000 or more inhabitants. Mechanical tabulation was used.

Definitions and Concepts. URBAN—places with 2,500 inhabitants or more. RACE (color)—the population was divided into two major groups: whites and nonwhites (blacks and persons of mixed blood). AGE—as of last birthday in completed years. For the first time, age not reported was estimated on the basis of related information. Tabulated in single years and standard five-year age groups, with median age indicated. NATIVITY—two major groups: native (persons born in the United States or in any of its territories and possessions, including those who, although born in a foreign country, were of American parentage), and foreign born. PLACE OF BIRTH—country of birth and, if native, whether born in the continental United States or other territory or possession. HOUSE-HOLD—all persons, related or not by blood, who occupy a house or other room that constitutes a dwelling unit. MARITAL STATUS—categories were single, married (legally or common law), widowed, or divorced. Married couples were classified as "with own household" if the husband was the head of the household. FERTILITY (new)—asked of all women: number of children ever born. EDUCATION—school enrollment (at any time after February); for the first time kindergarten enrollment was separately identified. Also taken were educational attainment (year of school in which enrolled for persons between the ages of five and twenty-nine and highest degree completed for all persons five years old and over) and literacy. LANGUAGE—ability to speak English. ECONOMIC ACTIVITY—period of reference was the week before the census. Lower age limit was fourteen years. The labor force included: employed (at work, with a job but not at work, and unpaid family worker) and unemployed looking for a job. Not in the labor force: keeping house, unable to work, inmates of institutions, and others (students, the retired, too old to work, voluntary idle, and seasonal workers in off season not looking for work). The number of weeks worked in 1949 and the number of hours worked were also recorded. OCCUPATION—classification based on the *Classification Index of Occupations and Industries 1950*, major groups, groups, and subgroups (three-digits). INDUSTRY—classification system developed for the 1950 census of Puerto Rico consisted of 156 groups (three-digits). OCCUPATIONAL STATUS—categories were private wage and salary worker, self-employed, unpaid family worker (fifteen hours or more per week), and government worker. INCOME—recorded for the first time. Gross income of wages and salaries, net income from self-employment, and income other than earnings were asked.

Special Elements and Features. Data on standard metropolitan areas were tabulated for the first time, but the usefulness of the data was limited by the lack of comparability with previous censuses. Fertility, educational attainment, and income were recorded for the first time. Citizenship and previous residence were dropped. Comparability of economically active population with that in censuses previous to 1940 was affected by the differences in the "labor force" and "gainful worker" concepts.

Quality of the Census. See United States entry, 1950, for more details on completeness and accuracy of data. The size of the labor force was probably understated because certain groups (students, housewives, and semiretired persons) failed to report the complete information needed. They did not indicate that they were working part time or were looking for a job unless carefully questioned. Whipple's Index was category IV—rough age data.

Publication Plan. U.S. Bureau of the Census. *Census of Population: 1950. A*

Report of the Seventeenth Decennial Census of the United States. Volume 2, Part 51-54. Washington, D.C., 1953. There were also an advance report and a Spanish language index of occupations and industries. Unpublished data are available. Language of publication is English.

1960 (April 1)

In 1952 Puerto Rico acquired the status of a commonwealth, and the census of population and housing was conducted as a joint project of the U.S. Bureau of the Census and the Puerto Rico Planning Board. The census was *de jure*, and a combination of canvasser and self-enumeration was the method used to record information on household schedules. The schedules were of three kinds: a short form, containing questions asked on 100 percent basis, was used in all areas except the three largest cities (San Juan, Ponce, and Mayaguez); a second short form, identical to the first except for three questions (description of property, value, and rent), was used in the three largest cities on 100 percent basis; and a long form, used for 25 percent sample of households and housing units. Supplementary forms were utilized in special situations where direct enumeration was not feasible; and for the first time, the advance census report forms provided for the self-enumeration in the three largest cities.

The territory covered by the census also included Vieques, Culebra, and other small adjacent islands. The area was divided into municipalities and barrios. The urbanized areas were subdivided into cities and towns. The reports were written in English and Spanish, and tabulation was mechanical. Standard metropolitan statistical areas (SMSA) are a county or group of contiguous counties that contain at least one city of 50,000 inhabitants or more, or twin cities with a combined population of at least 50,000 persons. These counties have to be essentially metropolitan in character and socially and economically integrated with the central city. In Puerto Rico, the 1960 SMSA's are identical to the SMA's of 1950.

Definitions and Concepts. URBAN—places of 2,500 inhabitants or more, plus those in the densely settled urban fringe of urbanized areas. AGE—for the first time date of birth (month and year) was recorded. Assignment of unknown ages was as in 1950. Ages were tabulated in single years and standard five-year groups, with median age. PLACE OF BIRTH—two major groups: those born in Puerto Rico recorded mother's place of residence at the time of birth, and those born outside recorded country of birth. NATIVITY—the same as 1950. PLACE OF RESIDENCE—usual place and previous residence (in 1955). CITIZENSHIP— only for foreign born (naturalized and aliens, not reported). EDUCATION—school enrollment at any time since January 1960 (year of school enrolled); educational attainment (highest grade attended and highest degree completed) and literacy. LANGUAGE—ability to speak English. VETERAN STATUS—although asked in 1950, the results were not published. The following was asked of males fourteen years of age and older: whether the person had served in any of the U.S. armed forces and during what war. MARITAL STATUS—categories were: never married, married with subcategories (legally, consensually, and separated), widowed, and divorced. The presence of spouse was recorded; however, persons living in group quarters with their spouse were classified as married, spouse absent. HOUSEHOLD—basically the same as 1950, but housing unit instead of dwelling unit was used as the base for enumeration. FAMILY—like in 1950, consisted of two or more persons living in the same household, related to each other by blood, marriage, or adoption. FERTILITY—asked only of women ever married: number of children ever born alive. ECONOMIC ACTIVITY—period of reference was the week before the census. Lower age limit was fourteen years. In the labor force: employed (at work, not at work but with a job), and unemployed looking for work within the past sixty days. Experienced workers unemployed were distinguished from new workers. Not in the labor force: persons doing only incidental unpaid family work (less than fifteen hours per week), students, housewives, the retired, seasonal workers in off season and not looking for job, inmates of institutions, and the disabled. The number of hours worked and weeks worked in 1959 were recorded; and for the first time, year last worked, place of work, and transportation to work were asked. OCCUPATION—classification based on the *Classified Index of Occupations and Industries*, 1960. A total of 467 occupations were recorded, major groups, groups, and subgroups (three-digits). INDUSTRY—classification based on the *Classified Index of Occupations and Industries*, 1960, a total of 163 categories (three-digits). OCCUPATIONAL STATUS—the same as 1950. INCOME—the same as 1950.

Special Elements and Features. San Juan City annexed the entire city of Rio Piedras in 1951. Census tracts were established in Puerto Rico for the first time. The three largest cities (Mayaguez, Ponce, and San Juan) were included in the block statistics program. For the first time, sampling and partial self-enumeration were utilized. A special report was issued with information on social and economic characteristics of Puerto Ricans (by birth or parentage) living in the United States. Citizenship and place of previous residence were reinstated and veteran status, place of work, and transportation to work were recorded for the first time. Race was dropped.

Quality of the Census. A census pretest was conducted to check the schedule design, and the use of the advance census report form, the method of selecting the sample, and tabulation procedures were new. Enumeration maps, field review, call backs, and an intensive training program were realized to assure completeness and accuracy of results. The final population reports were published a year after the census and the detailed characteristics the following year (1963). Whipple's Index classified age data into category I—highly accurate.

Publication Plan. U.S. Bureau of the Census. *Census of Population: 1960. The Eighteenth Decennial Census of the United States.* Volume 1, Part 53. Washington, D.C., 1964. Also published were census tract volumes for the three major cities. Unpublished data are available. Language of publication is English.

1970 (April 1)

The census of population and housing was conducted as a joint project of the U.S. Bureau of the Census and the Puerto Rico Planning Board. The census was taken simultaneously with the nineteenth decennial census of the United States. Population was enumerated on a *de jure* basis, and a combination of canvasser and self-enumeration was utilized to record information on two FOSDIC (machine readable) household questionnaires. One contained complete-count items, and the other, distributed to 20 percent of the population, had complete-count items and sample questions as well. Both schedules were printed in Spanish. An individual form, printed in Spanish and English, was used for the transitory non-Spanish speaking persons on the island.

The territory covered by the census was divided into "municipios," barrios, SMSA's, urbanized areas, and places. The tabulation was computerized, and table headings were in Spanish and English.

Definitions and Concepts. URBAN, AGE, NATIVITY, PLACE OF BIRTH, LITERACY, LANGUAGE, MARITAL STATUS, HOUSEHOLD, FAMILY and FERTILITY—same as 1960. PLACE OF RESIDENCE—usual place, previous residence (in 1965), year moved into present house, and for the first time, residence in the United States. Data on residence in the United States included: duration of residence in the United States, year of return to Puerto Rico, and the activity the person was engaged in during his stay in the United States. EDUCATION—school enrollment, that is, year of school in which enrolled (nursery school separately identified) and educational attainment (highest grade attended and highest degree completed). In addition, for the first time, data on vocational training of persons fourteen years old and over was recorded. VETERAN STATUS—same as 1960 with the inclusion of the Vietnam conflict. Veterans of both the Korean War and World War II were presented as a separate group. ECONOMIC ACTIVITY—period of reference was the week before the census. Lower age limit was fourteen years; however, most of the data shown in the census reports related to persons sixteen years old and over. In the labor force: employed (at work, with job but not at work) and unemployed looking for work during the four weeks before the census. Reasons for unemployment and date last worked were also recorded. Not in the labor force consisted mainly of students, housewives, retired workers, seasonal workers in off season who were not looking for work, inmates of institutions, disabled persons, and persons doing only incidental family work (less than fifteen hours per week). The number of weeks worked, place of work, means of transportation were also recorded. OCCUPATION—classification based on the *Classified Index of Industries and Occupations*, 1970; 441 categories were presented in major groups, groups, and subgroups (three-digits). INDUSTRY—classification based on the *Classified Index of Industries and Occupations*, 1970; 226 categories classified into twelve major industry groups (three-digits). OCCUPATIONAL STATUS—categories were: private wage and salary worker, government worker, self-employed (own business not incorporated and own business incorporated), and unpaid family worker. INCOME—types presented: wage or salary income, nonfarm net self-employment income, farm net self-employment income, social security income, public assistance income, income from all other sources, income of families and unrelated individuals, median, mean, and per capita, were also shown in the reports. POVERTY STATUS—for the first time data were published. Poverty levels were determined by official agencies.

Special Elements and Features. Census tract reports were furnished for each SMSA. The FOSDIC readable questionnaire was used for the first time in Puerto Rico. Block statistics were not only available for the three largest cities as in 1960, but also for the cities of Arecibo, Caguas, Guayama, and Humacao. Most modifications in the schedules were in the wording and the format. Questions on residence and activity while in the United States and vocational training were new. Information on income was more detailed, and data on poverty status were furnished for the first time. Citizenship was dropped.

Quality of the Census. Pretest census was carried out in order to evaluate the following procedures planned for the final enumeration: feasibility of using machine-readable questionnaires; the possibilities of conducting the population and housing census simultaneously with the agriculture census; and to determine the differences in quality of work of enumerators. Whipple's Index classified age data into category II—fairly accurate data. Certain unacceptable entries were edited, and any missing characteristics were supplied by allocation.

Publication Plan. U.S. Bureau of the Census. *Census of Population: 1970.* Volume 1, Part 53. Washington, D.C., 1974. There were also census tract volumes for each of the three major city areas. Unpublished data and computer tapes are available. Language of publication is bilingual, English and Spanish.

1980

This census was taken in conjunction with the twentieth decennial census of the United States. No data are available as yet.

OTHER STATISTICAL PUBLICATIONS: Issued by Puerto Rico Planning Board, *Statistical Yearbook.* Issued by Department of Health, *Informe Anual de Estadísticas Vitales.*

National Topic Chart

	1950	1960	1970
De facto			
Usual residence	X	X	X
Place of birth	X	X	X
Duration of residence			X
Place of prev. residence		X	X
Urban/rural	X	X	X
Sex	X	X	X
Age	X	X	X
Relation to household head	X	X	X
Marital status	X	X	X
Children born alive	X	X	X
Children living			
Citizenship		X	
Literacy	X	X	X
School enrollment	X	X	X
Ed. attainment	X	X	X
Ed. qualification			
National/Ethnic origin	X		
Language	X	X	X
Religion			
Household composition	X	X	X
Econ. active/inactive	X	X	X
Occupation	X	X	X
Industry	X	X	X
Occupational status	X	X	X
Income	X	X	X
Housing	X	X	X

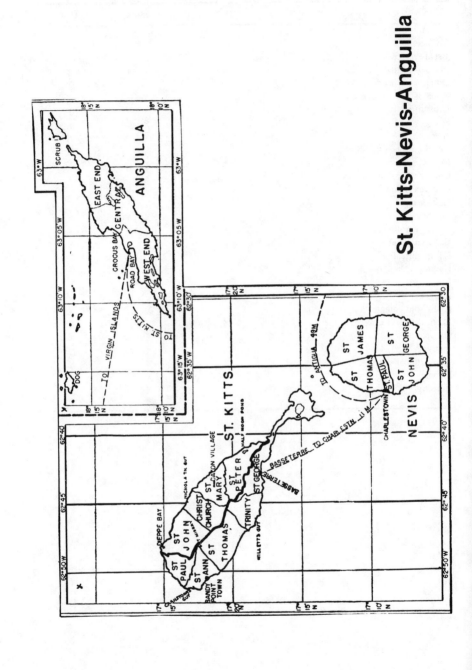

St. Kitts-Nevis-Anguilla

St. Kitts-Nevis-Anguilla

British Associated State and British Dependency, respectively

CAPITAL: Basseterre on St. Christopher Island; The Valley, Anguilla.
STATISTICAL AGENCY: Ministry of Trade, Development, and Tourism.
NATIONAL REPOSITORY: Public Library, Basseterre, St. Kitts.
MAIN U.S. REPOSITORY: Library of Congress.

Along with the other Presidencies of the Leeward Islands, St. Kitts-Nevis-Anguilla was part of the West Indies Federation, 1958-1962; it then attained full internal self-government (1967) as an Associated State.

While legally remaining part of St. Kitts-Nevis-Anguilla, Anguilla became a self-governing British colony in 1976. It did not participate in the 1970 Commonwealth Caribbean census program but conducted its own census in 1974. No publications, however, have been seen from that census.

As with all British West Indies countries St. Kitts-Nevis-Anguilla had censuses during the early colonial period up to 1840. There was supposedly a census in 1841 and 1855, but published results are almost nonexistent. St. Kitts-Nevis-Anguilla followed the same pattern of decade censuses, 1861-1921, 1946, 1960, 1970, as the rest of the British West Indies. The pre-1946 censuses were *de facto* and supposedly self-enumerated.

1861

Results for this census were found in the *Census of the British Empire, 1861*. Volume 3, *General Report*. Scope: St. Kitts—total population, sex, and ages under and over ten years; Nevis—total population, sex, age (under ten and by ten-year age groups to sixty and over), birthplace, race, religion, and occupation; no figures for Anguilla.

1871

The only table found was total population by sex.

1881

Scope was found in comparative tables in the 1891 census: total population, sex, age, occupation, and number of houses.

1891

Part of the Leeward Islands census, the scope included total population, birthplace, sex, age groups, marital status, race, occupation, occupational status, infirmities, number of houses, and acreage held.

1901

The *Census of the British Empire 1901* contained only one table of total population by sex.

1911

The report of the census results for this Presidency contained tables of birthplace, total population for island and chief cities, age groups, sex, marital status, citizenship, literacy, school attendance (in occupation table), race, religion, economic activity (in occupation table), occupation, infirmities, and number of houses. This report has several comparative tables.

1921

The report indicates the exact same conduct and scope as 1911.

1946 (April 9)

Conducted by the Office of the Administrator, St. Kitts-Nevis-Anguilla also participated in the West Indies census program. St. Kitts Island has nine parishes; Nevis, five parishes; and the island of Anguilla, no recognized subdivision. The tables give results for the administrative units, parishes and towns.

Definitions and Concepts. [See British West Indies, 1946, for the full entry; the following are differences.] St. Kitts and Nevis had towns of sufficient size to make an urban distinction; Anguilla did not. AGE—tables of single years and standard five-year age groups. RACE—white, black, Asiatic, mixed. FERTILITY—number of children surviving was not taken. HOUSEHOLD COMPOSITION—size only. OCCUPATIONAL STATUS—employer, own-account worker, unpaid helper, and wage and salary earner (at work, learner, unemployed). INFIRMITIES—totally blind, totally deaf, deaf and dumb, and mentally deranged.

Special Elements and Features. Comparative tables are included. Duration of union was also taken.

Quality of the Census. Whipple's Index category was III—approximate age data.

Publication Plan. Part F of the *West Indian Census 1946* is devoted to the Leeward Islands colony. Language of publication is English.

1960 (April 7)

Conducted by the territorial census office. [See British West Indies, 1960, West Indies section, for full entry; the following are the differences.] Individual schedules were used instead of household. St. Kitts-Nevis-Anguilla have the same parishes as 1946, subdivided into enumeration districts. Unfortunately, because Volume 1 was never published, tables are not available for that level.

Definitions and Concepts. No differences.

Special Elements and Features. Infirmities was dropped. Housing characteristics were expanded over that in 1946. There is a table for temporary heads of household.

Quality of the Census. The census office is reestablished for each census. Volume 1 was never published, and there was no Whipple's Index rating given.

Publication Plan. Jamaica. Department of Statistics. *West Indies Population Census. Census of St. Kitts-Nevis-Anguilla, 7th April 1960.* Volume 2. Language of publication is English.

1970 (April 7)

[See British West Indies, 1970, for full entry.] The only differences were that St. Kitts-Nevis were not included in the migration volume. Volumes 3; 4.11; 4.16; 6.3; 7; 8 abc; 9.4; 10.2; and 10.4 of the BWI 1970 set contain the results for the St. Kitts-Nevis. Anguilla did not participate in this census but conducted its own in 1974. No publications or citations thereof have been seen. Whipple's Index category III—approximate age data was assigned to St. Kitts-Nevis census. Language of publication is English.

1980 (?)

Two tables have been issued so far with the results of the 1970 census compared with the provisional 1980 results entitled "Parochial Comparisons." Content: number of buildings, households, population by sex, and average number of persons per household. The total population includes persons aboard ships in harbor.

OTHER STATISTICAL PUBLICATIONS. Issued by Statistical Office, Planning Unit, *Annual Digest of Statistics.*

National Topic Chart

	1946	1960	1970	1980
De facto	X	X	X	X
Usual residence	X	X	X	
Place of birth	X	X	X	
Duration of residence	X	X	X	
Place of prev. residence			N.A.	
Urban/rural	X	X	X	
Sex	X	X	X	
Age	X	X	X	
Relation to household head		X	X	
Marital status	X	X	X	
Children born alive	X	X	X	
Children living				
Citizenship				
Literacy	X	X		
School enrollment	X	X	X	
Ed. attainment		X	X	
Ed. qualification			X	
National/Ethnic origin	X	X	X	
Language				
Religion	X	X	X	
Household composition	X	X	X	
Econ. active/inactive	X	X	X	
Occupation	X	X	X	
Industry	X	X	X	
Occupational status	X	X	X	
Income			X	
Housing	X	X	X	

St. Lucia

State of St. Lucia (independent 1979)

CAPITAL: Castries.
STATISTICAL AGENCY: Statistical Department.
NATIONAL REPOSITORY: Central Library.
MAIN U.S. REPOSITORY: New York Public Library (early) and Population Research Center (Univ. of Texas) (later).

Initially a Spanish possession, the British attempted to make settlements in St. Lucia in 1605 and 1638. The Carib Indians made colonization difficult for both the British and the French who possessed it until 1803 when it reverted finally to British control. It became an official British colony in 1814 and was combined with the Windward Island group in 1838. St. Lucia was a member of the West Indies Federation, 1958-62, but withdrew from the Windward Island group in 1959. In 1967 it became a West Indies Associated State until it received independence in 1979.

The modern censuses began with that of 1843 (no extant publications) and continued from 1851 by decades through 1921. St. Lucia joined the West Indies census programs of 1946, 1960, and 1970. The censuses have traditionally been *de facto*. The 1911 report implied that self-enumeration was the method used, which was fairly common in this part of the Caribbean. The problem is that very little, if anything at all, is written about the organization and methodology of the pre-1946 censuses. The census office was reestablished for each census.

1851

The census of 1946 indicates that total population and race were taken (in comparative tables). No publication was located.

1861

Tables found in the *Census of the British Empire, 1861*, Volume 3, *General Report* indicate the scope of this census was birthplace, total population, sex, age, race, occupation, economic active/inactive (in occupation table).

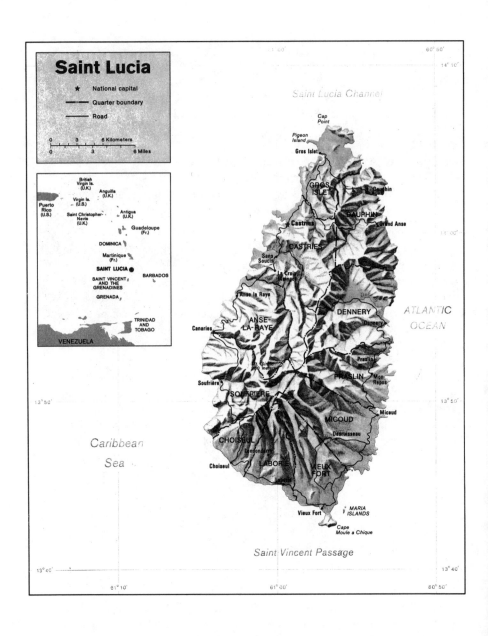

Saint Lucia

★ National capital

╺╍╸ Quarter boundary

━━ Road

0   3   6 Kilometers
0   3   6 Miles

British
Virgin Is.
(U.K.)
Anguilla
(U.K.)
Virgin Is.
(U.S.)
Puerto
Rico
(U.S.)
Saint Christopher-
Nevis
(U.K.)
Antigua
(U.K.)
Guadeloupe
(Fr.)
DOMINICA
Martinique
(Fr.)
SAINT LUCIA ●
SAINT VINCENT
AND THE
GRENADINES
BARBADOS
GRENADA
TRINIDAD
AND
TOBAGO
VENEZUELA

Saint Lucia Channel

Cap
Point

Pigeon
Island

Gros Islet

GROS
ISLET

Dauphin

DAUPHIN

Castries

Grand Anse

CASTRIES

Sens
Soucis

La Croix
Maingot

Anse la Raye

DENNERY

ATLANTIC
OCEAN

Canaries

ANSE-
LA-RAYE

Dennery

Praslin

Mt. Gimie
950 meters

PRASLIN

Mon
Repos

Soufrière

SOUFRIERE

Micoud

13° 50'

MICOUD

Micoud

13° 50'

CHOISEUL

Desruisseau

Londonderry

Choiseul

LABORIE

VIEUX
FORT

Caribbean

Sea

Laborie

Vieux Fort

MARIA
ISLANDS

Cape
Moule a Chique

Saint Vincent Passage

61° 10'

61° 00'

60° 50'

13° 40'

1871

Tables found in the 1946 census indicate the scope as birthplace, total and local populations, and race.

1881

Comparative tables in the censuses of 1891 and 1946 indicate the scope to have been at least birthplace, total and local populations, sex, and marital status.

1891

Very little discussion on organization and methodology of this census appeared in the report; however, the tables cover birthplace, total and local populations, urban/rural distinction, sex, age, marital status, race, religion, occupation, economic active/inactive, infirmities, number and material of dwellings, and agriculture.

1901

Conduct and scope was the same as 1891 minus race.

1911

Conduct and scope was the same as 1901 plus literacy, language, and school attendance (in occupation table). Race consisted only of a separate section of tables for East Indians. Birth, death, and marriage figures for 1901-10 are included in report.

1921

Same as 1911 including birth, death, and marriage data for 1911-20.

1946 (April 9)

This was the first of the closely coordinated censuses in the West Indies. [See British West Indies, 1946, for full entry.] The only difference is that the fertility tables are for the Windward Islands as a whole and not for the individual colonies. Whipple's Index was category IV—rough age data.

Publication Plan. Volume H, Windward Islands, contains the tabulations for St. Lucia. Language of publication is English.

1960 (April 7)

The census was part of the second coordinated census program in the Caribbean. [See British West Indies, 1960, Eastern Caribbean section, for full entry.] No differences occurred in the St. Lucia census. No Whipple's Index rating was given.

Publication Plan. Volume 1, Parts A and D; Volume 2, part for Windward Islands; and Volume 3, Windward, Parts 1 and 2, contain the results of this census for St. Lucia. Language of publication is English.

1970 (April 7)

This is the third Caribbean census program. [See British West Indies, 1970, for full entry.] The only difference is that St. Lucia was not included in the migration volume. No Whipple's Index rating was given.

Publication Plan. Volumes 3; 4.6; 4.16; 6.2; 7; 8 abc; 9.2; 10.2; and 10.4 of the British West Indies 1970 set have the results for St. Lucia. Unpublished data and computer tapes are available. Language of publication is English.

1980

A table of population by sex for administrative areas has been issued so far from the 1980 population census.

OTHER STATISTICAL PUBLICATIONS: Issued by Statistical Department, *Annual Statistical Digest.*

National Topic Chart

	1946	1960	1970	1980
De facto	X	X	X	X
Usual residence		X	X	
Place of birth	X	X	X	
Duration of residence	X	X	X	
Place of prev. residence			X	
Urban/rural	X	X	X	
Sex	X	X	X	
Age	X	X	X	
Relation to household head	X	X	X	
Marital status	X	X	X	
Children born alive	X	X	X	
Children living	X			
Citizenship				
Literacy	X			
School enrollment		X	X	
Ed. attainment		X	X	
Ed. qualification				
National/Ethnic origin	X	X	X	
Language	X		X	
Religion	X	X	X	
Household composition	X	X	X	
Econ. active/inactive	X	X	X	
Occupation	X	X	X	
Industry	X	X	X	
Occupational status	X	X	X	
Income		na	X	
Housing	X	X	X	

St. Vincent

St. Vincent and the Grenadines

CAPITAL: Kingstown.
STATISTICAL AGENCY: Statistical Unit, Government of St. Vincent.
NATIONAL REPOSITORY: The Kingstown Public Library, Kingstown.
MAIN U.S. REPOSITORY: New York Public Library (early) and Population Research Center, (Univ. of Texas) (later)

Discovered by Columbus on his third voyage, St. Vincent was claimed by Britain in 1627, disputed by France, and finally settled by the British in 1783. It became a part of the Windward Island group in 1833, a member of the West Indies Federation from 1958-62, an Associated State in 1969, and independent in 1979.

Its censuses (modern) started in 1844 (no publications located) and then continued by decades 1851 through 1931 (skipped 1901), 1946, 1960, and 1970. They have traditionally been *de facto*, and a few implied that they were self-enumerated.

1851

No publication or comparative tables other than total population has been located.

1861

Tables in the *Census of the British Empire, 1861*, Volume 3, *General Report*, show birthplace, total population, age, sex, race, religion, occupation, and economic active/inactive (in occupation tables).

1871

A few comparative tables in the census of 1946 indicated that partial scope of this census was birthplace, total and local populations, and race.

1881

Comparative tables in the censuses of 1891 and 1946 give data for birthplace, total and local populations, sex, and race.

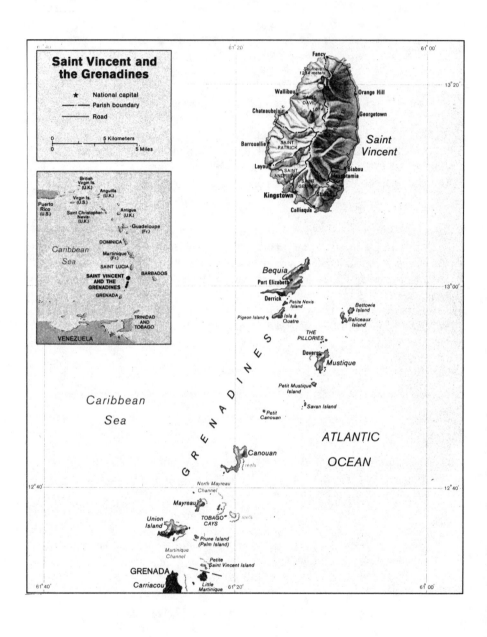

Saint Vincent and the Grenadines

★ National capital
—·— Parish boundary
— Road

0   5 Kilometers
0   5 Miles

British
Virgin Is.
(U.K.)
Anguilla
(U.K.)
Virgin Is.
(U.S.)
Puerto
Rico
(U.S.)
Saint Christopher-
Nevis
(U.K.)
Antigua
(U.K.)
Guadeloupe
(Fr.)
DOMINICA

Caribbean
Sea

Martinique
(Fr.)
SAINT LUCIA
SAINT VINCENT
AND THE
GRENADINES
BARBADOS
GRENADA
TRINIDAD
AND
TOBAGO
VENEZUELA

61° 40'
61° 20'
61° 00'
13° 20'

Fancy
Soufrière
1234 meters
Wallibou
Orange Hill
SAINT
DAVID
Chateaubelair
Georgetown
Barrouallie
SAINT
PATRICK
Saint
Vincent
Layou
SAINT
ANDREW
Biabou
Mesopotamia
SAINT
GEORGE
Kingstown
SAINT
Calliaqua

Bequia
Port Elizabeth
13° 00'
Derrick
Petite Nevis
Island
Bettowia
Island
Pigeon Island
Isla à
Quatre
Baliceaux
Island
THE
PILLORIES
Dovers
Mustique
Petit Mustique
Island
Savan Island
Petit
Canouan

Caribbean
Sea

G R E N A D I N E S

ATLANTIC
OCEAN

Canouan
reefs

12° 40'
North Mayreau
Channel
Mayreau
TOBAGO
CAYS
reefs
Union
Island
Ashton
Prune Island
(Palm Island)
Martinique
Channel
Petite
Saint Vincent Island
GRENADA
Carriacou
Little
Martinique
61° 40'
61° 20'
61° 00'
12° 40'

1891

The report of this census does not give details about the organization and methodology. Scope included birthplace, total and local populations, sex, age, marital status, race, religion, occupation, economic active/inactive (in occupation table), infirmities, number of dwellings, and agriculture.

No census was taken in 1901.

1911

Scope of this census: birthplace, total and local populations, sex, age, marital status, literacy, school attendance (in occupation table), race (limited to distinguishing the East Indians only), religion, occupations, economic active/inactive (in occupation table), infirmities, number and material of dwellings, and agriculture.

1921

Scope and conduct of this census was the same as 1911.

1931

Same as 1921 plus citizenship (British born or naturalized) and all races.

1946 (April 9)

First of the closely coordinated censuses carried out in the West Indies. [See British West Indies, 1946, for full entry.] There were no differences. Whipple's Index is category IV—rough age data.

Publication Plan. Volume H, Windward Islands, of the British West Indies 1946 set contains data for St. Vincent. Language of the publication is English.

1960 (April 7)

This was the second closely coordinated Caribbean census. [See British West Indies, 1960, Eastern Caribbean section, for full entry.] No noticeable differences are present. No Whipple's Index rating was given.

Publication Plan. Volume 1, Parts A and D; Volume 2, part for Windward Islands; and Volume 3, Parts 1 and 2, Windward Islands, of the British West Indies 1960, Eastern Caribbean set give the results of this census. Language of publication is English.

1970 (April 7)

Third census of the British Caribbean in which St. Vincent participated. [See British West Indies, 1970, for full entry.] St. Vincent was not included in the migration volume. No Whipple's Index rating was given.

Publication Plan. Volumes 3; 4.8; 4.16; 6.2; 7; 8 abc; 9.3; 10.2; and 10.4 of the master set contain results for St. Vincent. Language of publication is English.

There is no word as yet as to a 1980 census.

OTHER STATISTICAL PUBLICATIONS: Issued by Statistical Unit, *Digest of Statistics* (annually).

National Topic Chart

	1946	1960	1970
De facto	X	X	X
Usual residence		X	X
Place of birth	X	X	X
Duration of residence	X	X	X
Place of prev. residence			X
Urban/rural	X		X
Sex	X	X	X
Age	X	X	X
Relation to household head	X	X	X
Marital status	X	X	X
Children born alive	X	X	X
Children living	X		
Citizenship			
Literacy	X		
School enrollment		X	X
Ed. attainment		X	X
Ed. qualification			
National/Ethnic origin	X	X	X
Language			
Religion	X	X	X
Household composition		X	X
Econ. active/inactive	X	X	X
Occupation	X	X	X
Industry	X	X	X
Occupational status	X	X	X
Income		na	X
Housing	X	X	X

Suriname

Republic of Suriname

CAPITAL: Paramaribo.
STATISTICAL AGENCY: Algemeen Bureau voor de Statistiek.
NATIONAL REPOSITORY: ?
MAIN U.S. REPOSITORY: Population Research Center (Univ. of Texas).

The former Dutch Guiana attained independence in 1975. The first successful settlement was by the British in 1651. The Dutch acquired Suriname in exchange for their rights to Nieuw Amsterdam (Manhattan Island, N.Y.). The territory was contested by the British until 1815. Slavery was abolished in 1863, and East Indians (mainly from British Caribbean) and Indonesians were imported to provide contract labor for the plantations.

The country is presently divided into nine districts: Paramaribo (city), Nickerie, Coronie, Saramacca, Suriname, Para, Brokopondo, Commewijne, and Marowijne. Brokopondo was added between the 1950 and 1964 censuses and Para between the 1964 and 1971; they were both formerly part of the Suriname district.

1921

This was an administrative census called the first census. It was based on the population register only. No publications giving results were located. Some data were found in comparative tables in the 1971-72 census. The known scope was sex, age, and racial origin.

1950 (October 31)

The second general population census was *de jure* with a *de facto* total. It was canvassed on individual schedules and family/household folders. Separate schedules were used for Indians and Bushnegroes in tribes (sampled), lepers, and foreigners. The results were mechanically processed in the Netherlands, using punched cards.

Those not included (except in the *de facto* total) were foreign nonresidents, tourists, and the Dutch military housed on base. Many items were taken, but many of the publications giving the results have not been seen or cited. Tables for racial origin, sex, age, and lepers and available by geographical distribution and

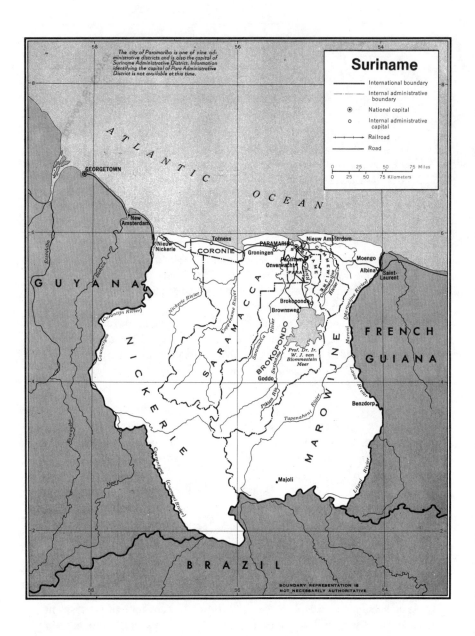

Suriname

International boundary
Internal administrative boundary
⊛ National capital
○ Internal administrative capital
+++ Railroad
— Road

| 0 | 25 | 50 | 75 Miles |
| 0 | 25 | 50 | 75 Kilometers |

ATLANTIC

OCEAN

GEORGETOWN

New Amsterdam

Totness

PARAMARIBO   Nieuw Amsterdam

Nieuw Nickerie

CORONIE   Groningen

Lelydorp   Moengo

Onverwacht

Albina   Saint-Laurent

GUYANA

PARA

Brokopondo

Brownsweg

BROKOPONDO

Prof. Dr. Ir. W. J. van Blommestein Meer

NICKERIE

SARAMACCA

Goddo

MAROWIJNE

FRENCH

GUIANA

Benzdorp

Majoli

BRAZIL

Nickerie Rivier

Coppename Rivier

Saramacca Rivier

Suriname Rivier

Maroni

Marowijne Rivier

Lawa Rivier

Tapanahoni Rivier

Litani Rivier

Pikin Rio

Courantyne (Corantijn River)

Corantijn Rivier

Coesewijne

Berbice

Essequibo

Cuyuni

New R.

BOUNDARY REPRESENTATION IS NOT NECESSARILY AUTHORITATIVE

migration. The territorial divisions are the usual administrative areas (districts, "ressortes" (provinces), cities, and so forth) and the less usual socioeconomic areas (occupation-areas) and "rings" based on distance from Paramaribo.

Definitions and Concepts (in the available volumes only). URBAN—the Paramaribo district. AGE—date of birth asked. Results in real age (as of the census date) in single years and standard five-year age groups; in generational age (as to December 31, 1950) in standard five-year age groups. Infants under one year were tabulated by number of completed months and month of birth. BIRTHPLACE—place for native born, country for foreign born. USUAL RESIDENCE—address (from registration) for residents. MARITAL STATUS—of household head only (the only tables available). HOUSEHOLD COMPOSITION—size, characteristics of head, and type (single person, one family, two or more family, and so forth). RACE/ORIGIN—more race than nationality except for foreigners present: black, colored (mixed), Hindu, Indonesian, Chinese, European, Amerindian, and others.

Special Elements and Features. Emphasis on lepers. Housing characteristics are available.

Quality of the Census. It is strongly tied to the country's registration system. There was a 6.5 percent undercount but this was mainly among the Bushnegroes and Indians in tribes who were extremely isolated and mobile. The greatest lack, however, lies in the incomplete publication of results. Whipple's Index did not cite.

Publication Plan. Suriname. Welvaartsfonds. *Tweede algemeen volkstelling Suriname, 1950.* Paramaribo, 1954-1956. Series A through E (only Volumes 2 through 7, 10, 23 and 24 seem to have been published). Language of publication is Dutch with an English summary, table titles, and headings.

1964 (March 31)

The third general population census was taken in the *de facto* mode, but most tables are for usual residents. It was conducted by the *ad hoc* Census Bureau of the General Statistical Office. Canvassed on household schedules, a simplified schedule was used for enumerating the Bushnegroes (descendants of escaped plantation slaves) and Amerindians (aborigines) who are still living in tribes. Not all tables contain data of the total population. The census was coded on punched cards and mechanically tabulated in Suriname. Territorial divisions were Paramaribo, which was subdivided into electoral districts, and the seven other districts.

Of the fifty-six tables, twenty-five include data for the Bushnegroes and Amerindians in tribes: nationality, age, sex, racial origin, residential district, marital status, religion, size of household, educational level attained, children ever born alive, labor force (only those receiving pay), and housing characteristics. A housing census was taken at the same time.

Definitions and Concepts. URBAN—"regularly occupied areas" as opposed to "scarcely occupied areas" but no table appears. AGE—data of birth (day, month, and year). Tables (as of December 31, 1963) in zero, one, two, three, four then standard five-year age groups. Other tables (in cross-classifications) are in single years and standard five-year age groups. RACIAL ORIGIN—Creole (descendants of original white settlers and slaves and Bushnegroes who have left their tribes), Hindu, Indonesians, Amerindians, Chinese, European, Bushnegroes, others. NATIONALITY—Dutch citizens by origin (Suriname, Antillian, Dutch, elsewhere), Amerindian, Indonesian, Chinese, Americans, others. HOUSEHOLD— one person living alone or a group living together in one dwelling unit plus those spending the night of March 31, 1964, also live-in servants, lodgers, and boarders. HOUSEHOLD COMPOSITION—by size and by characteristics of head. Position in household is not used to characterize composition. BIRTHPLACE—district and place for native born, country for foreign born. MARITAL STATUS—single, married, common-law union, widowed, divorced, plus age at first marriage. FERTILITY—asked of all women ever married: number of children ever born alive and number surviving. RELIGION—compulsory response required, but whatever declared was accepted; specified denominations. LANGUAGE—named all languages spoken and the one spoken best by the individual (Dutch, Surinamese, Hindi, Javanese, other). MIGRATION—established by year of arrival in district of usual residence and district and country of previous residence. EDUCATION— educational attainment (type of school and years completed in last attended day school, final diploma from day school), and educational qualification (most important degree of advanced education). ECONOMIC ACTIVITY—All persons age ten and over; reference period was as of the time of the census. Type of activity was established in the occupational status question. The active are the employed and those looking for work. The inactive are homemakers, students, the pensioned, and others. OCCUPATION—present main occupation (whether in government, private enterprise, or agriculture). Classified in an alphabetical list in one table as well as in major, minor, and subgroups according to the ISCO (1958). Subsidiary occupation also asked (in government, private enterprise, or agriculture). INDUSTRY—whether in government, private enterprise, or agriculture. Specific industry classified in division and major group (two-digits) according to ISIC. OCCUPATIONAL STATUS—expanded to include all types of activity. Employer, own-account worker, family worker (paid and unpaid), wage and salary worker, contract (casual) worker, those seeking work, and the inactives listed above. The number of weeks unemployed was also asked.

Special Elements and Features. Index to tables indicates those tables that include the Amerindians and Bushnegroes in tribes data.

Quality of the Census. Although it is not known if all district volumes were published (Coronie has been cited), at least the whole Suriname volume gives complete results for all the topics taken. It was stated that there was great cooperation on the part of the public. More money was spent on this census than that taken in 1950. A postenumeration check was carried out to determine accuracy. Results of this check were not stated. The census bureau was not permanent but more than a year was spent preparing for this census. No Whipple's Index rating was given.

Publication Plan. Suriname. Algemeen Bureau voor de Statistiek. *Derde Suriname volkstelling, 1964*. Paramaribo, 1964, 1967. (Suriname in Cijfers, No. 33, Parts 1-9). Eight district volumes and one whole Suriname. Language of publication is Dutch, with an English summary and index of tables.

1971 (December 31)

The fourth general population census was *de jure*. The only publication seen at this time is a preliminary result volume that has very little information about content, organization, and methods.

There are comparative tables (1921-1971) rounded to thousands on population by district, racial origin, sex, ratio, and broad age groups. The bulk of the publication has population by sex for each enumeration district of the nine districts comparing 1964 with 1971 (except the table for Paramaribo).

Quality of the Census. "In order to obtain a distribution of the population in the preliminary report by place of usual residence, it was necessary to allocate those who were enumerated elsewhere to the geographic area in which they normally reside. This, however, proved to be too time consuming so that the number of usual residents who were temporarily absent from each district had to be estimated." However, the data was not expected to differ from the final figures.

Publication Plan. Suriname. Algemeen Bureau voor de Statistiek. *Voorlopig resultaat vierde algemene volkstelling*. Paramaribo, 1972. (Suriname in Cijfers, No. 60). Language of publication is Dutch, with a two page English summary.

OTHER STATISTICAL PUBLICATIONS: Issued by Algemeen Bureau de Statistiek, *Suriname in Cijfers, Jaarcijfers*.

National Topic Chart

	1950	1964	1971
De facto		X	
Usual residence	X	X	
Place of birth	X	X	
Duration of residence		X	
Place of prev. residence		X	
Urban/rural	X		
Sex	X	X	X
Age	X	X	X
Relation to household head	X	X	
Marital status	X	X	
Children born alive		X	
Children living		X	
Citizenship		X	
Literacy			
School enrollment			
Ed. attainment		X	
Ed. qualification		X	
National/Ethnic origin	X	X	X
Language		X	
Religion		X	
Household composition	X	X	
Econ. active/inactive		X	
Occupation		X	
Industry		X	
Occupational status		X	
Income			
Housing	X	X	

Trinidad and Tobago

Republic of Trinidad and Tobago

CAPITAL: Port-of-Spain.
STATISTICAL AGENCY: Central Statistical Office.
NATIONAL REPOSITORY: Central Statistical Office.
MAIN U.S. REPOSITORY: Library of Congress and Population Research
Center (Univ. of Texas).

Trinidad was in the possession of (but not settled by) the Spanish until the British took over in 1797 (officially in 1802). Tobago became a British territory in 1814 and was part of the Windward Islands colony until transferred to Trinidad jurisdiction in 1889. Both were part of the West Indies Federation (1958-1962). Trinidad and Tobago gained independence in 1962 and changed to a republic in 1976. It is a member of the British Commonwealth.

Trinidad and Tobago has had censuses since 1844 and is the only former British territory in the Caribbean with an unbroken series. An earlier census for Tobago was taken in 1839. The census of 1891 is the first of the two islands together. All the censuses were *de facto*, canvassed, and conducted by the Registrar General's Office until the 1960 census, which was taken by the Central Statistical Office.

1851 (Trinidad only)

The only known scope of this census was that found in comparative tables in the 1891 census. It appears to have been total population and that of census divisions, race, and religion.

1861

Some tables were found in the *Census of the British Empire, 1861*. Scope for Trinidad: country of birth, total population, census division population, sex, age, marital status, race, occupation, economic activity (in occupation table), and infirmities. Scope for Tobago: country of birth, total population, sex, age, marital status, literacy, race, occupation, economic activity (in occupation table), and infirmities.

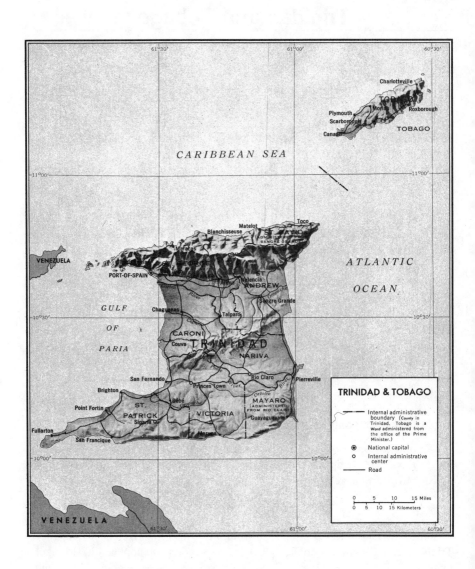

CARIBBEAN SEA

Charlotteville

TOBAGO

Plymouth   Mona   Roxborough
Scarborough
Canaan   TOBAGO

VENEZUELA

ATLANTIC

OCEAN

Matelot   Toco
Blanchisseuse
ST GEORGE
(ADMINISTERED
SANGRE GRANDE)
Maracas

PORT-OF-SPAIN   ST
Arima   Valencia   ANDREW

GULF   Chaguanas   Sangre Grande

OF   Talparo

PARIA   CARONI
Couva   TRINIDAD
NARIVA

San Fernando   Rio Claro   Pierreville
Brighton   Princes Town
Point Fortin   Débé   MAYARO
ST.   Oropuche   (ADMINISTERED
Fullarton   PATRICK Siparia   VICTORIA   FROM RIO CLARO)
San Francique   Guayaguayare

TRINIDAD & TOBAGO

Internal administrative
boundary (County in
Trinidad. Tobago is a
Ward administered from
the office of the Prime
Minister.)

⊛ National capital

○ Internal administrative
   center

— Road

0   5   10   15 Miles
0   5   10   15 Kilometers

VENEZUELA

1871

Scope for Trinidad (only) was found in comparative tables in the 1891 census: country of birth, total and census division population, sex, age, marital status, race, and infirmities.

1881

Scope for Trinidad found in comparative tables in the 1891 census was the same as 1871 plus occupation.

1891

First census taken after Tobago was unified with Trinidad; however, most of the tables in this report are for Trinidad. There is only a summary table for Tobago as a whole. The census of 1901 gives more detailed data for Tobago than the 1891 census. Scope included country of birth, total and census division populations (sixteen plus Tobago), sex, age, marital status (legal or registered only), school attendance (in occupation table), race (based on birthplace rather than complexion), religion (last taken in 1851), occupation, economic activity (in occupation table), and infirmities. There are separate sections for each of the ethnic/racial groups in this report.

1901

The later enumeration date was due to conflict with the Easter holiday. There were nineteen census divisions, including Tobago (included in all pertinent tables). Scope was the same as 1891 plus number of inhabited dwellings and livestock.

1911

Conduct and scope were the same as 1901 plus citizenship (those who were naturalized British subjects) and literacy. Total population was divided into general population and East Indian population in many tables. Maps of the census divisions for Trinidad and Tobago and of the subdivisions of Port-of-Spain were included.

1921

This was the first time that counties appear (eight); other divisions were three towns and Tobago. Scope was the same as 1911, and there were separated sections with tables for institutional population, shipping population, general, and East Indian populations. Maps were included.

1931

Conduct and scope of this census were the same as 1921 plus industries. The report contained an index to tables (geographic division by subject). Tables were available for subdivisions (enumeration districts). The occupation and industry tables were detailed. Maps were included that also included subdivisions for San Fernando Town and Arima Town.

1946 (April 9)

First census closely coordinated with the other colonies in the Caribbean area. [See British West Indies, 1946, for full entry; the following are differences.] There was more information on housing than that taken in the other territories. URBAN—the three main cities only. RACE—added categories East Indian Creole (mixed), and Chinese Creole (mixed), which were combined in some tables. FERTILITY—also asked legitimacy and birth order. OCCUPATIONAL STATUS—added "in institutions." There was also more geographic detail of subjects, more data on the institutional population, and detailed occupation and industry tables than in the other colony reports. Trinidad and Tobago also issued their own census report that contained a summary of the population report prepared by Jamaica, a description of enumeration district boundaries, and a complete report on the agricultural and fishing census. Whipple's Index category was IV—rough age data.

Publication Plan. Part G of the British West Indies 1946 set and the following: Trinidad and Tobago. Registrar General's Office. *Colony of Trinidad and Tobago, Census 1946.* Port-of-Spain, 1948. Language of publication is English.

1960 (April 7)

In this second census closely coordinated with the British West Indies, Trinidad served as tabulation and printing center for the Eastern Caribbean 1960 set. [See British West Indies, 1960, Eastern Caribbean section, for full entry.] The only difference was that Trinidad and Tobago requested the respective sect of those indicating Hindu or Muslim as their religion. They also took no housing census as they had done one in 1958.

Publication Plan. Volume 1, Parts A, B, and S; Volume 2, Parts A and B; and Volume 3, Parts A, B, D, E, F, G of the BWI 1960, Eastern Caribbean section, contain data for Trinidad and Tobago. Language of publication is English.

1970 (April 7)

The third closely coordinated census was conducted by the Central Statistical Office. Trinidad has eight counties, three cities; Tobago, one ward. All were subdivided into enumeration districts (ED's). The tables for ED's have not been published yet. Trinidad and Tobago were included in the migration volume, and they also issued some bulletins on their own. [See British West Indies, 1970, for full entry.] The only difference was that the respective sect of those professing Hindu or Muslim religion was asked again. Whipple's Index was category III— approximate age data.

Publication Plan. Volumes 3; 4.2; 4.16; 5; 6.1; 7; 8 abc; 9.1; 10.1; and 10.4 of the British West Indies 1970 set contain data for Trinidad and Tobago. They also issued the following: Trinidad and Tobago. Central Statistical Office. Population Census Division. *1970 Population Census. Bulletins*. Port-of-Spain 1971-1975. Nos. 1-5 in 6 volumes. Unpublished data may be available. Language of publication is English.

1980 (May 12)

This is a *de facto* census conducted by the Population Census Division of the Central Statistical Office. It is not known if it was canvassed or self-enumerated; the implication is the former. The tabulation is computerized. The total population includes shipping population and foreign military and diplomatic personnel and families in the country. The territorial divisions are twelve major civil divisions (eight counties, three cities, and Tobago), subdivided into wards (Trinidad) and parishes (Tobago). These are further subdivided into enumeration districts. This information was taken from the preliminary result bulletin issued in June 1981.

OTHER STATISTICAL PUBLICATIONS: Issued by Central Statistical Office, *Annual Statistical Digest, Population and Vital Statistics Report* (annually), *Social Indicators* (irregularly), *Statistical Bulletin* (irregularly), *Statistical Pocket Digest* (annually).

National Topic Chart

	1946	1960	1970	1980
De facto	X	X	X	X
Usual residence		X	X	
Place of birth	X	X	X	
Duration of residence	X	X	X	
Place of prev. residence			X	
Urban/rural	X	X	X	
Sex	X	X	X	
Age	X	X	X	
Relation to household head	X	X	X	
Marital status	X	X	X	
Children born alive	X	X	X	
Children living	X			
Citizenship				
Literacy	X			
School enrollment		X	X	
Ed. attainment		X	X	
Ed. qualification				
National/Ethnic origin	X	X	X	
Language				
Religion	X	X	X	
Household composition	X	X	X	
Econ. active/inactive	X	X	X	
Occupation	X	X	X	
Industry	X	X	X	
Occupational status	X	X	X	
Income		na	X	
Housing	X		X	

Turks and Caicos Islands

British colony

CAPITAL: Cockburn Town, Grand Turk Island.
STATISTICAL AGENCY: Chief Secretary's Office.
NATIONAL REPOSITORY: The Victoria Public Library.
MAIN U.S. REPOSITORY: Population Research Center (Univ. of Texas).

From 1799 to 1848 the Turks and Caicos Islands were a part of the Colony of the Bahamas of which they form a physical continuation. They then became a separate colony until 1874 when they were assigned to Jamaica as a dependency. In 1959 they passed to the West Indies Federation. When this organization dissolved in 1962, they again became a direct dependency of Great Britain. Only eight of thirty small islands in the group were inhabited, but both the 1960 and 1970 censuses give results for only six. The censuses up to 1921 have traditionally included the shipping population. The results of the censuses taken while a dependency of Jamaica (1891-1943) are appended to the Jamaican reports. The census office is reestablished for each census.

1861

This is the first census for which results were found. It was *de facto*, canvassed, and manually tabulated. It is not known if an official publication exists. The scope was determined from the results published in the *Census of England and Wales, 1861*, Volume 3, *General Report*. Scope included sex, age, birthplace, race, and occupation (including the inactive and the unemployed).

No publication has been found with 1871 census results.

1881

The first census of Turks and Caicos as a Jamaican dependency was *de facto*, self-enumerated, and manually tabulated. Scope included sex, age, race, marital status, occupation, literacy and numbers attending school, birthplace, religion, infirmities, those vaccinated, houses, and livestock.

Turks and Caicos Islands

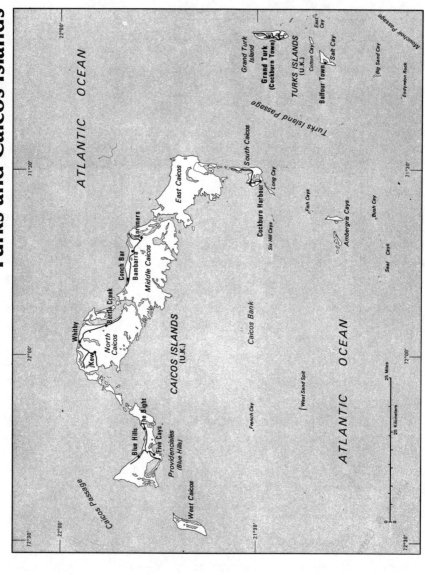

1891

De facto, canvassed, and manually tabulated, the scope of this census was the same as that of 1881 with slight variations. Age listed single years under five then five-year age groups. Religion was not taken.

1901

Again, no official publication was located. The following was included in the *Census of the British Empire, 1901*: sex, age, marital status, birthplace, race, occupation, and literacy and number attending school. (Jamaica did not take a census in this year.)

1911

The scope and conduct of this census was virtually the same as that of the 1891 census, which was referred to in the report of this census as the "last" census. (It was for Jamaica but not for Turks and Caicos.) The only difference in scope was the reinstatement of religion last used in 1881.

1921

Again, the scope and conduct of this census were the same as that of 1881.

1943 (January 4)

The census of the Turks and Caicos was carried out at the same time and with the same type of schedules as the census of Jamaica. [See Jamaica, 1943.] However, there were some differences in the printed results from those of Jamaica due to their size (island results rather than parish) and structure. There were no introductory pages indicating variations. Only the differences are cited here: RACE—did not include separate figures for East Indian coolies or Chinese. AGE—infants under one year were not listed by completed months. No INCOME tables. MIGRATION—referred to the immigrant population only. No INDUSTRY except that used in the classification of occupations.

1960 (April 7)

This census was conducted in conjunction with the Commonwealth Caribbean census program and closely coordinated with Jamaica. It was both *de jure* and *de facto*. [See British West Indies, 1960, West Indies section, for the basic information.] The following are the differences: No URBAN/RURAL distinction due to the size of the territory. RESIDENCE—year of immigration was not asked. ECONOMIC ACTIVITY—first-time job seekers and the number of days worked per week were not determined. OCCUPATION—tables of occupation were for movers only; no table for subsidiary occupation. INDUSTRY—one table only, two divisions (water transportation, all others) only for residents absent abroad. There was no census of agriculture, but acreage of land held was asked.

Quality of the Census. There is a great lack of occupation and industry data in the tables published. A few tables in the publication were inaccurately labeled, and the tables of contents listed many wrong page numbers. Volume 1 was not printed. There is no Whipple's Index rating.

Publication Plan. Jamaica. Department of Statistics. Jamaica Tabulation Centre. *West Indies Population Census. Census of Turks and Caicos Islands, 7th April 1960.* Kingston, n.d. Volume 2 only. Language of publication is English.

1970 (October 25)

Although taken six months later than the others who participated in the Commonwealth Caribbean census program, there are no differences. [See British West Indies, 1970, for full entry.] The census office also issued thirty-one tables as a separate work. This entry contains the information available in the Turks and Caicos publication. Geographical divisions—six islands: Grand Turk, Salt Cay, South Caicos, Middle Caicos, North Caicos, and Providenciales (Blue Hills). The tables have figures for all six islands and the total. The following are tables *not* found in the already published volumes of the Commonwealth Caribbean set: private households by number of persons, relation to household head, religion, marital status, type of school attending, primary schooling (ages five to fourteen and fifteen and over), educational attainment (all persons five and over), vocational and special training (age ten and over, not attending school), number of children ever born (all women fifteen and over, women fifteen to forty-four, women forty-five to sixty-four), live births and stillbirths during last twelve months (women fifteen to forty-four and forty-five to sixty-four), union status (women fourteen and over, at present time or at age forty-five), usual residence (local population and foreign born), duration of residence (local population and foreign born), place of birth (local born population), duration of residence (local born population), previous residence (local born), number of islands ever lived in (local born). Turks and Caicos was not included in the migration volume of the Commonwealth Caribbean set.

Publication Plan. Turks & Caicos. Census Offices. *Turks & Caicos Islands Census, October 1970.* [Cockburn Town]. n.d. Computer tapes are available. Language of publication is English.

1980

It is not known if Turks and Caicos took their census on the same date (May 12) as others of the Commonwealth Caribbean. Only provisional counts of number of inhabitants for the six islands are available.

National Topic Chart

	1960	1970	1980
De facto	X		
Usual residence	X	X	
Place of birth	X	X	
Duration of residence		X	
Place of prev. residence			
Urban/rural			
Sex	X	X	
Age	X	X	
Relation to household head	X	X	
Marital status	X	X	
Children born alive	X	X	
Children living			
Citizenship			
Literacy	X		
School enrollment	X	X	
Ed. attainment	X	X	
Ed. qualification			
National/Ethnic origin	X	X	
Language			
Religion	X	X	
Household composition	X	X	
Econ. active/inactive	X	X	
Occupation	X	X	
Industry	X	X	
Occupational status	X	X	
Income		X	
Housing	X	X	

Uruguay

Uruguay

Oriental Republic of Uruguay

CAPITAL: Montevideo.
STATISTICAL AGENCY: Dirección General de Estadística y Censos (DGEC).
NATIONAL REPOSITORY: Biblioteca of the DGEC.
MAIN U.S. REPOSITORY: Population Research Center (Univ. of Texas).

During the colonial period (1624 to 1828), only estimates and partial censuses were taken, mainly for the province of Montevideo (1803, 1818, 1829, and 1835). The first general census of population was carried out in 1852, but no details on the organization and methods used are available. The results included total population divided into the following groups: males up to fifty-nine years of age, females in the same age group, children up to fourteen years, and old persons of sixty years and over. Marital status, sex, nationality, color, and infirmities were also recorded.

1860

The second general census of population was taken, but only a few tables are available with no indication of organization or methods adopted. The country was divided into thirteen departments and subdivided into sections, cities, and villages. The results presented the total number of inhabitants by sex and nationality. Comparative figures with 1852 were also furnished.

1884 and 1889

Partial censuses were taken on a *de facto* basis, canvassers recorded information on individual schedules. Scope included: total number of inhabitants, age, sex, migration, urban/rural, nationality, usual place of residence, duration of residence, marital status, relationship to head of household, literacy, school enrollment, infirmities, fertility, religion, color, economic activity, occupation, and industry. Results are available for Montevideo only.

In 1896, it was established that a census of population should be taken every eight years. A pilot census was taken in the Department of Flores in preparation for the following general enumeration.

1900

A census of population was conducted by the Comisión Nacional del Censo in the eighteen departments ("departamentos de campana"). Results did not include Montevideo. Only population by sex and nationality was presented; however, there is some indication that age, marital status, race, literacy, and occupation were also recorded.

1908

Third general census of population was conducted by the Dirección General de Estadística simultaneously with the censuses of housing and agriculture, on a *de facto* basis, canvassed on individual schedules. The territory covered by the census included all nineteen departments, subdivided into sections. Scope included: age, sex, nationality, marital status, religion, literacy, place of birth, place and duration of residence, relationship to head of the household, school attendance, occupation, industry, economic activity, infirmities, vaccination, property ownership, number of children ever born, number of children living, and persons of 100 years of age and over. It was the most comprehensive census yet taken in the country; however, there was no evaluation of its results.

For the following half century only estimates of population based on these last results were made for the country.

1963 (October 16)

The fourth general census of population and second of housing were taken simultaneously by the Dirección General de Estadística y Censos on a *de facto* basis. The reports carried very little about organization and methods and less on definitions. Information gathered here was taken from the *UN Handbook of Population and Housing Census Methods (1955-1964)* and from table headings. Tabulation was computerized, and the territory covered by the census included all nineteen departments, divided into sections. Urban and rural population were distinguished.

Definitions and Concepts. URBAN—all cities (no size limit indicated). AGE—In completed years and completed months for infants under one year. Tables available for single years and standard five-year age groups. MARITAL STATUS—categories were: single, married, widowed, divorced, and common-law union. PLACE OF BIRTH—distinction between native and foreign born. Natives recorded department and locality and foreign born, the country of birth. RESIDENCE—duration (year of arrival) and place of previous residence (locality, department, and foreign country). CITIZENSHIP—acquired by birth or naturalization. The country of citizenship was asked of all aliens. EDUCATION—literacy (ability to read and write), school attendance, and educational attainment (highest level attended and highest grade completed). Questions were asked of all persons six years and over. ECONOMIC ACTIVITY—period of reference was as of the census date. Lower age limit was ten years. The economically active population included employed, unemployed looking for a job (new and experienced workers), and unpaid family workers. Persons looking for a job for the first time were asked the profession for which they were prepared and the kind of occupation they were seeking. OCCUPATION—both main and usual occupations were recorded, major groups, groups, and subgroups (three-digits). INDUSTRY—primary and secondary industry were asked, divisions, major groups and subgroups (three-digits). OCCUPATIONAL STATUS—categories were employer, own-account worker, employee, and unpaid family worker.

Special Elements and Features. Complete industrial and occupational classifications were included in the report. Religion, infirmities, vaccination, property ownership, data on persons 100 years and older, and fertility were dropped. Educational attainment, previous residence, and occupational status were recorded for the first time.

Quality of the Census. A post-enumeration survey was carried out to measure coverage and accuracy of the census. Results indicated that 2.05 percent of the population was omitted from enumeration and that accuracy, which was only measured for age, marital status, and literacy, was high. Whipple's Index classified age data in the category II—fairly accurate data. Sample tabulation provided fast availability of preliminary, sample, and advanced results. However, the main final result set did not appear until 1973.

Publication Plan. Uruguay. Dirección General de Estadística y Censos. *IV censo de población y II de vivienda, año 1963.* Montevideo, 1973. Five subject volumes. Unpublished data are available, but computer tapes are for internal use only. Language of publication is Spanish.

1975 (May 21)

The fifth general census of population and third of housing were conducted simultaneously by the Dirección General de Estadística y Censos. The census was *de facto* (with some resident tables) and canvassed on household schedules (with both housing and population). The tabulation was computerized, and a 12 percent sample tabulation was used for early publication of advance results. The territory covered was Montevideo and eighteen departments (interior), subdivided into sections. Tables, however, were for departments only.

Definitions and Concepts. URBAN—in 1963 the law of populated centers was used; although there were modifications to this in 1975, they were not specified. HOUSEHOLD—one person living alone or a group (related or not) living in the same housing unit and sharing meals and other living needs (included domestics). Divided into private and collective types. USUAL RESIDENCE—if other than where found at the time of the census, the department and locality given or name of country (for nonresidents). Place of residence in 1970 was also asked. NATIONALITY—(only for foreign residents) given by continent except for those born in Argentina, Brazil, Spain, and Italy. BIRTHPLACE—(only for residents) department and locality or country. Specifically it was the residence of parents, especially the mother, when birth occurred. AGE—in completed years as of the moment of the census; children under one year were recorded "0." Age was tabulated in single years and standard five-year groups. MARITAL STATUS— single, married (legal), common-law union, widowed, divorced, and separated. Common-law widowhood and separation were also taken, but these categories are not included in tables. FERTILITY—asked of all women fifteen and over who ever had liveborn children: number of children at home, elsewhere, number of liveborn children who died, and number of liveborn children in the last 12 months. EDUCATION—all persons six years of age and over: literacy, school enrollment, and educational attainment. ECONOMIC ACTIVITY—asked of all persons age twelve and over. Reference period was the week before the census. The active were the employed (including unpaid family workers, those with a job but not working, seasonal and temporary workers) and the experienced unemployed looking for a job. Inactive were new job seekers, the retired/pensioned, persons of independent income, students, homemakers, and others. OCCUPATION—main occupation based on the major portion of income and the last occupation of the unemployed. Classification was COTA 1970 (two-digits). INDUSTRY—main industry classified by ISIC (three-digits). OCCUPATIONAL STATUS—employer, own-account worker, wage or salary worker (subdivided into public and private sectors), unpaid family worker (fifteen hours or more per week), member of a production cooperative, and others. HOUSEHOLD COMPOSITION—by size, by type (uniperson, nuclear, extended), and by characteristics of the total household (economically active/inactive, age) and of the head.

Special Elements and Features. The reference period of economic characteristics changed to the week before the census and the age changed to twelve years. Fertility, which was last taken in 1908, was new. Citizenship was dropped. Graphs, maps, comparative tables (1963 and 1975), and industrial and occupational classifications were included. The industry and occupation of the foreign-born, economically active, resident population were given by year of arrival.

Quality of the Census. The early censuses were highly irregular; the 1963 and 1975 are conceded to be the only two that can serve as a basis for statistical programs. The census office is permanent. The census followed the COTA 1970 recommendations. Whipple's Index category was I—highly accurate age data. The preliminary results appeared in 1976, and the advance sample results in 1977. The final results were published in 1979 and 1980.

Publication Plan. Uruguay. Dirección General de Estadística y Censos. *V censo general de población.* Montevideo. 1979-1980. Three subject volumes and support publications (methods, tabulation plans, coverage study). Computer tapes are for internal use only. Language of publication is Spanish.

OTHER STATISTICAL PUBLICATIONS. Issued by Dirección General de Estadística y Censos, *Anuario Estadístico, Boletín Informativo* (quarterly and annually). Issued by Instituto de Estadística, Universidad de la República de Uruguay, *Estadísticas Básicas.*

National Topic Chart

	1963	1975
De facto	X	X
Usual residence		X
Place of birth	X	X
Duration of residence	X	X
Place of prev. residence	X	X
Urban/rural	X	X
Sex	X	X
Age	X	X
Relation to household head	X	X
Marital status	X	X
Children born alive		X
Children living		X
Citizenship	X	
Literacy	X	X
School enrollment	X	X
Ed. attainment	X	X
Ed. qualification		
National/Ethnic origin		
Language		
Religion		
Household composition		X
Econ. active/inactive	X	X
Occupation	X	X
Industry	X	X
Occupational status	X	X
Income		
Housing	X	X

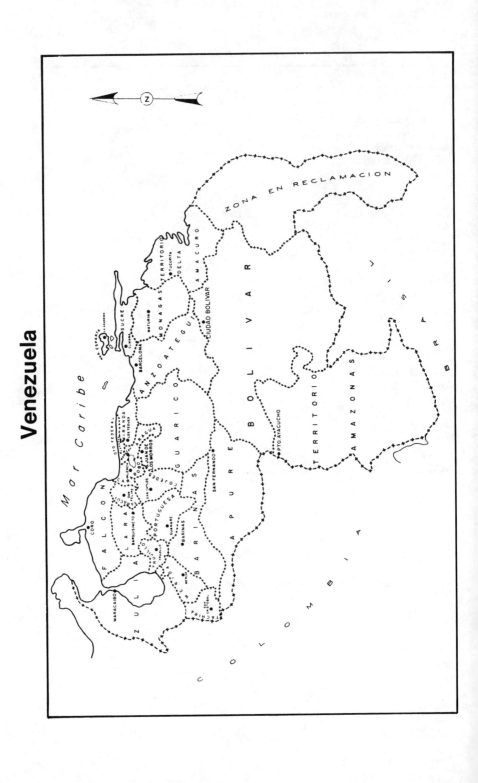

Venezuela

Venezuela

Republic of Venezuela

CAPITAL: Caracas.
STATISTICAL AGENCY: Dirección General de Estadística Y Censos Nacionales.
NATIONAL REPOSITORY: Centro de Documentación e Información de la Oficina Central de Estadística e Informática.
MAIN U.S. REPOSITORY: Population Research Center (Univ. of Texas).

The first estimate of the population of Venezuela was made in 1772; this was followed by several others until the end of the colonial period in 1811. These estimates, however, referred only to about half of the present territory of the country, and most of the results were limited to the total number of inhabitants with some attempts at racial classification.

After independence from Spain, another series of estimates, made either by private or official agencies, covered the period from 1814 to 1857. The results were no better than the previous ones and were generally not considered as representative of the population of the country.

The official censuses started in 1873, but it was not until 1936 that the census operations achieved the amplitude and characteristics of a modern census. The earlier censuses were primarily involved in determining the military and work obligations of the population, taxation, and changes in legal status.

Despite official attempts, regularity of census taking was not always observed; the intervals between vary from five to twenty-nine years. The Dirección General de Estadística was created in 1871, and from then until 1950 it was responsible for the execution of the censuses. In 1950 the name was expanded to Dirección General de Estadística y Censos Nacionales, which implied a permanent census office.

All censuses until 1971 were conducted on a *de facto* basis, and a combination of self-enumeration and canvassing was the method used for enumeration.

1873

This was the first general census of the population that was officially recognized. Detailed results are available only for the Distrito Federal and the state of Carabobo. For all but three of the remaining states, only the total population by sex and the number of houses in each "municipio" were furnished. Mérida, Trujillo, and the Federal Territories had no data available.

1881

The second general census, conducted by the same agency, followed the same organization. The household schedules included the following topics: name, sex, single or multiple birth, legitimate and illegitimate births, age, marital status, relationship to head of the family, occupation, education, literacy, religion, nationality, place of birth of native born, and infirmities. The territory covered by the census included twenty states, the Distrito Federal, four territories and the colony of Guzman Blanco. An alphabetical list of inhabited centers of the federal district, number of foreigners living in Venezuela by country of birth and state of residency, number of persons 100 years old and older, and the number of twins per state were also recorded.

1891

No details of organization were furnished for the third general census of population, but apparently it followed the same method used in the previous enumeration. The tables published included the following topics: sex, age, legitimate birth, marital status, literacy, occupation, military residents, place of residence, infirmities, number of twins, and number of foreign residents (by state, district, and "municipio"). In addition, the number of buildings and type of construction were also recorded.

1920

The fourth general census results were considered extremely inaccurate and the estimated undercount was 400,000 inhabitants. Publication of the results was never issued.

1926

The fifth general census of population was taken on a *de facto* basis; however, persons not present at the time of the census but resident in the "municipios" were also recorded. Self-enumeration combined with canvasser was used to record information on household and personal schedules. The territory covered by the census included twenty states, the Distrito Federal, and two territories. States and territories changed names, probably because of annexations. The scope of the census included: name, sex, age, marital status, legitimate and illegitimate births, literacy, religion, occupation, nationality, physical disabilities, vaccination, single or multiple birth, place of birth, place of residence, and whether parents were living or deceased.

1936

The organization of the sixth general census was the same as the previous census, but the scope was much reduced and included only age, sex, marital status, literacy, education, fertility, place of birth, nationality, and foreign population. The Indian population was estimated and included in the total number of inhabitants. Data on houses and buildings were never published.

1941

The seventh national census of population was conducted simultaneously with a census of housing. It was conducted on a *de facto* basis, and a combination of self-enumeration and canvasser was used to record information on household schedules. Individual schedules were used for enumeration of persons not present at the time of the census. The twenty states, the Distrito Federal, and the territories were divided into districts and "municipios." The tabulation was mechanical with punched cards, and the preliminary results were known less than two months after enumeration. The scope was expanded: age, sex, marital status, school attendance or reasons for not attending, place of birth, nationality, economic activity, industry, occupation, religion, literacy, vaccination, and physical and mental illness. The results presented were divided into rural, urban, suburban, and localities of 500 inhabitants and more. The Indian population again was estimated. Additional tables with density, population change, and comparative results between 1936 and 1941 were furnished. Fertility was dropped.

1950 (November 26)

The eighth general census of population, taken simultaneously with a census of housing, was conducted by the Dirección General de Estadística y Censos Nacionales. The territory covered by the census included the twenty states, the Distrito Federal, two federal territories and the federal dependencies that are formed by several islands in the Caribbean sea. Some districts and "municipios" were redivided; therefore, comparisons with the 1936 and 1941 censuses should be made carefully. The Metropolitan Area of Caracas was created.

The census was carried out on a *de facto* basis and a combination of self-enumeration and canvassing was the method used to record information on household and individual schedules. Mechanical tabulation with punched cards was utilized. A special census was taken of the Indian population (November 22, 1951 to January 15, 1952); however, only the groups living near the inhabited centers were enumerated. The remaining native population was estimated and added to the official total population. It was done in this fashion to separate this group from the total population, which consisted of only those directly enumerated.

Definitions and Concepts. CENTROS POBLADOS (inhabited centers)—a very broad definition that included not only cities and towns but also "caserios," "pueblos," "aldeas" and "vecindarios," petroleum centers, "sitios," and agricultural cooperatives. (These terms do not have English equivalents and were presented in the *UN Demographic Yearbook* without translation). URBAN—places with 1,000 and more inhabitants. HOUSEHOLD ("familia censal")—a person or group of persons, related or not by blood, living in the same place and sharing food arrangements. AGE—in completed years. For children less than one year old, date of birth was recorded. Age was presented in single years and standard five-year groups. Infants under one year were tabulated in single months, and for persons 100 and over in single years. MARITAL STATUS—asked of males age fourteen and older and females age twelve and older. The categories were: single, married, widowed, divorced, and "unido" (common-law marriage). For comparisons with 1941 census the last group ("unidos") should be counted among the singles. PLACE OF BIRTH—state and district for native born, and country of birth for all persons born outside the country whether citizens or not. CITIZENSHIP—three categories were presented: Venezuelan (native born and foreign born with Venezuelan parents), naturalized citizens, and foreigners (country of birth was also recorded). PLACE OF RESIDENCE—state and district, and duration of residence recorded in years and months. EDUCATION—literacy, school attendance (ages seven to fourteen) and for the first time educational attainment (last degree completed and what degree pursuing at the time of the census). ECONOMIC ACTIVITY—economically active population included all persons ten years of age and older employed in gainful occupation, working for a family member without payment, unemployed looking for job, and persons fifteen years and older looking for a job for the first time. Economically inactive population consisted of the following groups: homemakers, students, the retired, persons of independent income, inmates of institutions, and invalids. OCCUPATION—main occupation or last one if unemployed. Classification based on COTA 1950, major groups, groups, and subgroups (three-digits). The armed forces were classified separately. INDUSTRY—classification based on ISIC, divisions and major groups (two-digits). OCCUPATIONAL STATUS—the categories were: laborer (blue-collar worker), employee (white-collar worker), employer, own-account worker, and unpaid family worker. INCOME—gross income per month or per day; number of months worked; number of days worked during the last four weeks and whether in addition to the salary the worker received room, board, or both. However, no tables were presented for income. The number of economically dependent persons was also recorded, but tables were not published. FERTILITY—asked of all females age twelve and over: number of children ever born alive and age of mother at first birth.

Special Elements and Features. New to this census are educational attainment and the Metropolitan Area of Caracas. Income and family dependents were taken, but tables were not published. There is, however, a table by age and sex of the population that is dependent on agriculture for the states. Economic activity, based on different concepts, was emphasized. No reference period was mentioned. There are several comparative tables (1936, 1941, and 1950) on age, marital status, school attendance, place of birth, density, population change, Indian population, and rural/urban populations. For 1941 and 1950 there are comparative tables on economic activity and infirmities. Maps, graphs, a copy of the schedule, and a list of localities of 1,000 and more inhabitants were also included.

Quality of the Census. Whipple's Index classified age data into category IV—rough data. This census was more complete and more accurate than the previous ones because of pilot censuses realized before enumeration. Regularity of decennial censuses mainly started in 1950.

Publication Plan. Venezuela. Dirección General de Estadística y Censos Nacionales. *Octavo censo general de población.* Caracas, 1954-1960. One set of eleven subject volumes and one set of state volumes, plus a two-volume summary for the whole country. Language of publication is Spanish.

1961 (February 26)

The ninth general census of population, taken simultaneously with the census of housing, was conducted by the Dirección General de Estadística y Censos Nacionales. The census was taken on a *de facto* basis, and a combination of self-enumeration and canvassing was the method used to record information on household and individual schedules. No further details were furnished as far as organization and methods used. The information gathered here was taken from introductory notes and table headings.

Definitions and Concepts. CENTRO POBLADO, HOUSEHOLD, MARITAL STATUS, NATIONALITY, LITERACY, PLACE OF BIRTH—same as 1950. URBAN—places with 2,500 or more inhabitants. For the purpose of the census, three areas were established: urban (2,500 or more), intermediate (1,000 to 2,499 inhabitants), and rural (less than 1,000 inhabitants). AGE—in completed years or if less than one year, in completed months. Presented in single years and standard five-year age groups. PLACE OF RESIDENCE—usual residence and duration of residence. FERTILITY—asked of all females age twelve and over: number of children ever born alive was the only question. EDUCATION—asked of all persons four years of age and older: school attendance, educational attainment (last degree completed), and educational qualification. ECONOMIC ACTIVITY—economically active population included all persons ten years or older employed in gainful occupation one week before the census, unpaid family worker, unemployed looking for a job, and persons looking for a job for the first time. The inactive included homemakers, students, retired, persons of independent income, inmates of institutions, and invalids. Causes and length of unemployment were also asked. OCCUPATION—classification based on COTA 1960, groups and subgroups (two-digits). INDUSTRY—classification based on ISIC, divisions and major groups (two-digits). OCCUPATIONALS STATUS—the categories were: employer, employee and worker, own-account worker, unpaid family worker, and other (clergymen, members of cooperatives, and any other not included in the above categories). INCOME—gross income per month, per week, and per day; and whether room, board, or both were provided.

Special Elements and Features. Results of income were published. Educational qualification was asked for the first time. Fertility was cross-classified with present age of the mother, age of first child, and marital status. Distribution of tables for place of birth and nationality differed from 1950.

Quality of the Census. Whipple's Index made no reference to age accuracy in this census. A list of all small places and "centros poblados" with an indication of estimated population was made to improve enumeration in rural areas and to insure completeness. No publication was found containing information on procedures and methods used in the census.

Publication Plan. Venezuela. Dirección General de Estadística y Censos Nacionales. *Noveno Censo General de Población (26 de febrero de 1961).* Caracas, 1964-1969. In addition to the state volumes and whole country summary there were state map volumes and regional lists of populated centers. Language of publication is Spanish.

1971 (November 2)

The tenth general census of population and housing was conducted by the Dirección General de Estadística y Censos Nacionales and was the first taken on a *de jure* basis. Canvassing was the method used to record information on the schedules. Three types of schedules were utilized: household (short form, containing eight questions on population), sampling schedule (long form, containing thirty-six questions on population and sixteen on housing), which was distributed to 25 percent of the households, and the individual schedule (same content as the sampling questionnaire) used to enumerate persons living in group quarters and persons living outside of their usual residence. Tabulation was computerized.

Definitions and Concepts. METROPOLITAN AREAS—inhabited places of 50,000 and more persons. URBANIZED AREAS—the part of the city with a higher density of construction. URBAN ZONES—although not properly defined, urban zones were places with 2,500 and more inhabitants and for the purpose of the census were places that were supposed to be enumerated in fifteen days. AGE—in completed years and date of birth. Presented in single years and standard five-year age groups. MARITAL STATUS—the same categories used in 1950 and 1961. PLACE OF BIRTH—native born recorded state, district, and municipio of birth and foreigners the country of origin. NATIONALITY (citizenship)—two categories were presented: Venezuelan (native born, born in foreign country of Venezuelan parents, and naturalized citizens) and foreigner. PLACE OF RESIDENCE—usual and duration of residence plus place of previous residence. EDUCATION—questions asked of persons five years of age and older but tabulated for different age groups: literacy for ages ten and over, school attendance for those age five through twenty-nine (private or official), educational attainment for ages seven and over (last degree completed), and educational qualification. Reason for not attending school was also recorded. ECONOMIC ACTIVITY—questions asked of all persons fifteen years and older. Labor force concept was used. The reference period was the week before the census. Economically active included employed, own-account workers, unpaid family workers (working at least fifteen hours per week), unemployed looking for a job, and persons looking for a job for the first time. Inactive population included students, homemakers, pensioners, the retired, inmates of institutions, and invalids. Hours worked per week as unpaid family worker, time of unemployment, hours worked during the reference period, number of weeks worked full- or part-time in 1970, and number of jobs in 1970 were also asked. INDUSTRY—classification based on COTA 1970, divisions and major groups (two-digits). OCCUPATION—classification based on COTA 1970, groups and subgroups (two-digits). OCCUPATIONAL STATUS—The categories were: employee or worker (government or private enterprise), employer, own-account worker, unpaid family worker, and others (members of cooperatives, unidentified categories, and unemployed not looking for job). INCOME—gross income the month before the census, and whether room, board or other kind of payment was included in the income. FERTILITY—For women fifteen years and older: number of children born alive. Published results have not appeared.

Special Elements and Features. For the first time the census was *de jure*. More topics were obtained through the use, for the first time, of sampling. The concept for urban areas and the creation of twenty-five metropolitan areas were new. There was a change in the format of publication. Tables with classification of population according to the new concepts of urban, intermediate, and rural areas; table with population change for the years 1936 to 1971; and one with the population of cities of 20,000 or more comparing 1950 and 1971 are included. Distribution of tables related to place of birth and nationality differ from 1961.

Quality of the Census. Whipple's Index category was III—approximate age data. The percent of undercount was estimated at 6 to 7 percent of the population, that is, 650,000 persons. Discrepancies were found between the results obtained by sampling and the ones obtained by total enumeration. The largest amount of omissions and inaccurate answers was found in the area of economic activity, and the number of occupations not specified or not identifiable was calculated at 364,936. The fact that omissions were not uniformly distributed brought another element of limitation for the analysis of data. Pilot censuses were taken to improve mapping of areas, methods and systems of enumeration, questionnaires, and to check sampling, field work, and the application of the *de jure* criterium.

Publication Plan. Venezuela. Dirección General de Estadística y Censos Nacionales. *X censo de población y viviendas*. Caracas, 1974-1977. The final results are subject reports grouped under each of three geographical divisions (national, state, metropolitan area). There are also comparative results for whole country, twenty-five metropolitan areas, twenty-four states, and eight regions. An eight-volume list of populated centers and one national summary complete the set. Unpublished data and computer tapes are available. Language of publication is Spanish.

OTHER STATISTICAL PUBLICATIONS: Issued by Oficina Central de Estadística e Informática, *Anuario Estadístico, Boletín Mensual, Indicadores de Conyuntural* (monthly).

National Topic Chart

	1950	1961	1971
De facto	X	X	
Usual residence		X	X
Place of birth	X	X	X
Duration of residence	X	X	X
Place of prev. residence			X
Urban/rural	X	X	X
Sex	X	X	X
Age	X	X	X
Relation to household head	X	X	X
Marital status	X	X	X
Children born alive	X	X	X
Children living			
Citizenship	X	X	X
Literacy	X	X	X
School enrollment	X	X	X
Ed. attainment	X	X	X
Ed. qualification		X	X
National/Ethnic origin			
Language			
Religion			
Household composition		X	X
Econ. active/inactive	X	X	X
Occupation	X	X	X
Industry	X	X	X
Occupational status	X	X	X
Income	X	X	X
Housing	X	X	X

Virgin Islands (U.S.)

Territory of Virgin Islands (U.S.)

CAPITAL: Charlotte Amalie, St. Thomas.
STATISTICAL AGENCY: U.S. Bureau of the Census and Office of Territorial Affairs, Dept. of the Interior.
NATIONAL REPOSITORY: ?
MAIN U.S. REPOSITORY: New York Public Library (early) and Population Research Center (Univ. of Texas).

The Virgin Islands, formerly the Danish West Indies, consists of three major islands (St. Croix, St. John, and St. Thomas) and about 100 smaller islands and cays, mostly uninhabited. Under Danish administration, the earliest records show the population of St. Thomas since 1688, St. John since 1717, and the number of slaves in St. Croix in 1742. The first census, however, was taken in 1835 followed by a series of quinquennial censuses until 1860. Results from the 1835, 1841, and 1846 censuses were reproduced in the census report of 1855, published in the *Statistiske Meddelelser* of Denmark. From 1860 on, the censuses were taken decennially and were published by the Danish statistical office until 1911, last census taken under Danish administration. Unfortunately, of those early publications the only ones available are the reports of the 1901 and 1911 censuses.

The islands were purchased by the United States in 1917. With the exception of a special census taken in the same year, all the subsequent ones were conducted in conjunction with the regular decennial censuses of the United States.

1901

The census of population was conducted by the Statens Statistiske Bureau (Denmark). The territory covered by the census included the three major islands, which were subdivided into villages and communes. Introductory notes of the report are mostly an analysis of results rather than comments on organization and methods adopted. The report was published in Danish with the table of contents and table headings written in both French and Danish. The following tables were presented: total population by sex, age, and marital status; urban and rural population by sex, age, and marital status; total population by place of birth,

Virgin Islands

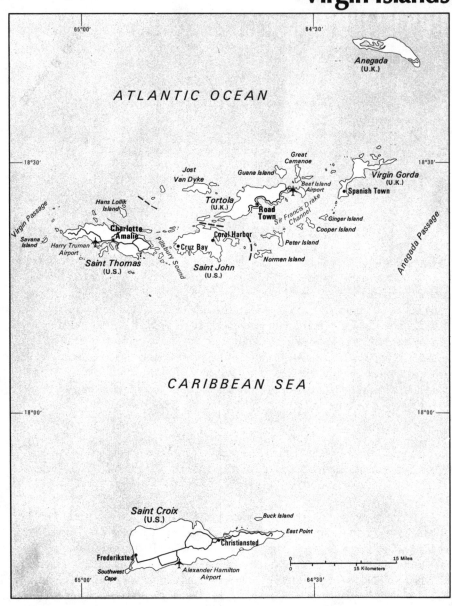

ATLANTIC OCEAN

65°00' 64°30'

Anegada
(U.K.)

18°30' 18°30'

Great
Camanoe

Jost
Van Dyke Guana Island

Virgin Gorda
(U.K.)

Beef Island
Airport Spanish Town

Hans Lollik
Island Tortola
(U.K.) Road
Town Sir Francis Drake
Channel

Ginger Island

Virgin Passage

Cooper Island

Savana
Island Charlotte
Amalie Coral Harbor

Harry Truman
Airport Cruz Bay Peter Island

Pillsbury Sound

Saint Thomas
(U.S.) Saint John
(U.S.) Norman Island

Anegada Passage

CARIBBEAN SEA

18°00' 18°00'

Saint Croix
(U.S.) Buck Island

East Point

Christiansted

Frederiksted

Southwest
Cape Alexander Hamilton
Airport

65°00' 64°30'

0 15 Miles
0 15 Kilometers

religion, infirmities, and occupations. Some occupations were subdivided into broad occupational status (chief and assistants).

1911

Census of population, conducted by the same agency, followed closely the organization and scope of the previous one.

1917

First census conducted under the United States administration. The organization and methods adopted were based on the thirteenth decennial census of the United States, taken in 1910. The censuses of agriculture, manufactures, and fisheries were taken simultaneously. The population was enumerated on a *de jure* basis, and canvasses was the method used to record information on general schedules. Although the census was taken as of November 1, the actual enumeration took place during the months of December 1917 and January 1918. The territory was divided into islands, cities, and rural districts. Scope included: home tenure, relationship to head of the family (household), sex, color, age, marital status, place of birth, citizenship, language, literacy, school attendance, occupation, industry, occupational status, and the number of retired persons and temporarily unemployed. Comparative table with results from 1835 to 1917 was included.

1930

The census of population was conducted in conjunction with the fifteenth decennial census of the United States. It was *de jure*, canvassed, and general schedules were used. The territorial divisions were the same as 1917; urban and rural distinction was present through most of the tables. Scope included: age, sex, color, marital status, relationship to head of household, place of birth, ability to speak English, school attendance, year of immigration, mother tongue, occupation, industry, and items related to dwellings (families and tenure of homes), and unemployment. An agriculture census was taken simultaneously.

1940

This census of population, conducted in conjunction with the sixteenth decennial census of the United States, was the first taken simultaneously with a census of housing. The organization and methods were basically the same as 1930. The scope was virtually the same, except for economic activities, which added number of hours worked, duration of unemployment, and the number of weeks worked in 1939.

1950 (April 1)

The census of population was taken in conjunction with the seventeenth decennial census of the United States. The governor of the islands was responsible for the field work. The population was enumerated on a *de jure* basis, and canvasser was the method utilized to record information on general schedules.

Tabulation was mechanical. The territory covered by the census was divided into islands and municipalities, subdivided into minor civil divisions (city or quarter). Urban and rural populations were distinguished.

Definitions and Concepts. URBAN—places with 2,500 inhabitants or more. RACE (color)—the following groups were recorded: white, Negro and mixed or other races (including Japanese, Filipino, Chinese, and so forth). AGE—as of last birthday in completed years. Presented in standard five-year age groups. The method of assigning unknown ages on the basis of related information was used for the first time. NATIVITY—based on country of birth, the population was classified into two major groups: native and foreign born. CITIZENSHIP—two major categories: citizen (native and naturalized) and alien. Data shown only for persons twenty-one years old and over. PLACE OF BIRTH—classification of foreign born was based on international boundaries recognized by the United States in 1950. MARITAL STATUS—categories were: single, married, consensually married, widowed, and divorced. Questions were asked of persons fourteen years old and over. Married couples were classified as "with own household" (if the husband was the head of the household) and "without own household" (those living in the household as relatives, lodgers, or employees, or those living in group quarters). HOUSEHOLD—included all persons living in the same house, apartment, or group of rooms that constituted a dwelling unit. Members of the household might be relatives or not. EDUCATION—school enrollment (for persons between five and twenty-nine years of age) and educational attainment (recorded for population twenty-five years old and over) referred to the last degree completed. Median number of school years was also tabulated. ECONOMIC ACTIVITY—period of reference was the week before the census. Ages covered were fourteen years old and over. Included in the labor force: employed (at work, with job but not at work, and unemployed looking for a job [experienced and new workers]). Not included in the labor force: persons doing any incidental family work (less than fifteen hours per week), homemakers, unable to work, inmates of institutions, students, the retired, too old to work, seasonal workers in off season, and voluntarily idle. OCCUPATION—classification based on the *U.S. Classified Index of Occupations and Industries, 1950*, reduced form. Only sixty-four occupations were reported (two-digits). INDUSTRY—classification based on *U.S. Standard Industrial Classification (SIC)*, reduced version; only fifty-one industry groups were presented (two-digits). NOTE: The number of employed persons was limited to the civilian labor force, that is, armed forces were excluded. OCCUPATIONAL STATUS—categories were: private wage and salary worker, government worker, self-employed worker, and unpaid family worker. INCOME—amount of money from wages or salary received in 1949, net income from self-employment, and amount of other sources of income.

Special Elements and Features. Period of unemployment, number of hours worked, and number of weeks worked were not recorded. Literacy and language were dropped. Income and educational attainment were recorded for the first time. Data on economic activity are not comparable with that taken in censuses previous to 1940.

Quality of the Census. Omission from the labor force of some workers has probably resulted in some understatement in many of the occupation, industry, and occupational status results. Precise allocation of occupation was not possible due to insufficiently specified occupation and industry designations. See entry for the United States, 1950, for more information on the coverage and accuracy of results.

Publication Plan. U.S. Bureau of the Census. *Census of Population: 1950. A Report of the Seventeeth Decennial Census of the United States.* Washington, D.C., 1953. Volume 2, Part 51-54. Language of publication is English.

1960 (April 1)

This census of population was taken in conjunction with the eighteenth decennial census of the United States. The population was enumerated on a *de jure* basis, and canvasser was the method used to record information on household and individual questionnaires. Manual coding and editing and mechanical tabulation rather than FOSDIC were used. All questions were asked on complete count basis (no sample questions). The census of housing was taken simultaneously. The territorial divisions were the same as 1950.

Definitions and Concepts. URBAN, NATIVITY, and RACE—same as 1950. AGE—same as 1950; however, it was tabulated in single years to twenty-one then standard five-year age groups. EDUCATION—school enrollment (ages five to thirty-four) and educational attainment (ages five and over) measured by highest level attended and degree completed. MARITAL STATUS—categories were: single, legally married, consensually married, separated, widowed, and divorced. Presence of spouse was also recorded. HOUSEHOLD—persons, related or not by blood, living in the same housing unit. FAMILY—two or more persons living in the same household, related to each other by blood, marriage, or adoption. FERTILITY—for the first time, data on number of children ever born alive to women ever married were recorded. ECONOMIC ACTIVITY— reference period was the week before the census. Lower age limit was fourteen years. The labor force included: employed (at work, with a job but not at work, and unpaid family workers) and unemployed (looking for a job in the past sixty days). Not in the labor force: persons doing incidental unpaid family work (less than fifteen hours per week), students, homemakers, the retired, seasonal workers off season and not looking for a job, inmates of institutions, and the disabled. Of these groups, only students and inmates of institutions were shown separately. Number of weeks worked in 1959 and number of hours per week were also recorded. OCCUPATION—classification based on the *U.S. Classified Index of Occupations and Industries, 1960,* reduced form; only forty-eight occupations were recorded (two-digits). INDUSTRY—classification based on *U.S. CIOI,* condensed format; only forty-one groups were presented (two-digits). OCCU-PATIONAL STATUS—the categories were the same as 1950. INCOME—although slightly different wording was used, the concept was basically the same as 1950.

Special Elements and Features. Fertility was recorded for the first time. Citizenship was dropped. The number of weeks worked returned to the schedules. A second question was added to measure educational attainment.

Quality of the Census. See the United States entry, 1960, for general comments on coverage and accuracy of data. Certain requirements for employment of field staff were established by the Bureau of the Census, although the field work was the responsibility of the governor. As in earlier censuses, the general procedure for changing unacceptable entries was to assign an entry for that person that was consistent with entries for other persons with similar characteristics.

Publication Plan. U.S. Bureau of the Census. *Census of Population: 1960. The Eighteenth Decennial Census of the United States.* Volume 1, Part 54-57. Language of publication is English.

1970 (April 1)

The census of population was taken in conjunction with the nineteenth decennial census of the United States. The governor or ranking official of the outlying areas supervised the census. Censuses of housing and agriculture were taken simultaneously. The enumeration was taken on a *de jure* basis, and canvasser was the method used to record information on a single household questionnaire which was FOSDIC readable (new). There were no sample questions. An individual schedule was used for persons who lived in hotels and group quarters. Although the census date was April 1, in most of the outlying areas enumeration was delayed for one to three weeks. Editing, coding, and processing of questionnaires followed the same general procedure as that used for the United States. Tabulation was computerized. The territory covered by the census was divided into islands, cities, and quarters. Urban and rural area distinctions were shown in almost all tables.

Definitions and Concepts. HOUSEHOLD, MARITAL STATUS, EDUCATION, AGE, and FERTILITY—same as 1960. RACE (color)—Negro, white, and other. PLACE OF BIRTH—country of origin according to international boundaries accepted by the United States in 1970. NATIVITY—two major groups: native (born in the U.S. territory, born in the United States, and born in Puerto Rico) and foreign born. CITIZENSHIP—returned to the schedules. Four groups were distinguished: naturalized, permanent alien, temporary alien, and born abroad of American parents. The year of immigration was also recorded. PLACE OF RESIDENCE—for the first time, the place of previous residence (in 1965) was recorded. VETERAN STATUS—for the first time recorded. Questions asked of all persons sixteen years old and over: if they had served in U.S. armed forces and in what war. ECONOMIC ACTIVITY—period of reference was the week before the census. Lower age limit was sixteen years of age. The labor force included all persons classified as employed (at work, and with a job but not at work) and unemployed (looking for a job during the past four weeks, and available to accept a job). Unemployed persons who had worked at any time in the past were classified as experienced unemployed. Those not in the labor force consisted mainly of students, homemakers, the retired, seasonal workers in off season and not looking for a job, inmates of institutions, the disabled, and persons doing only incidental unpaid family work (less than fifteen hours during the reference week). The number of weeks worked was also recorded. OCCUPATION—main occupation or last occupation, if the person was unemployed. Classification based on *CIOI*, condensed form, only thirty-two occupational groups (two-digits). INDUSTRY—classification based on the *CIOI, 1970*, presented in reduced number of groups, only forty industry groups (two-digits). OCCUPATIONAL STATUS—the same categories as 1960. INCOME—from earnings (wage, salary, commissions, from nonfarm business, professional practice or partnership, and from own farm), income from other than earnings (Social Security, retirement, welfare), and income from other sources received in 1969.

Special Elements and Features. Citizenship returned to the schedules. Place of previous residence, veteran status, vocational training were asked for the first time. The economic activity concepts were revised, and questions on income were more detailed. FOSDIC system was utilized for the first time on the schedules of outlying areas.

Quality of the Census. To improve the usefulness of the 1970 census results, a number of changes were introduced based on evaluation of previous censuses, consultation with users of data, and extensive field pretesting. For more details on coverage and accuracy of data see United States entry for 1970.

Publication Plan. U.S. Bureau of the Census. *Census of Population: 1970*. Volume 1, Part 54-58. Language of publication is English.

OTHER STATISTICAL PUBLICATIONS: Issued by Bureau of Vital Records and Statistical Services, *Vital Statistics* (annually). Issued by Office of Territorial Affairs, *Annual Report of the Governor of the Virgin Islands to the Secretary of the Interior*.

National Topic Chart

	1950	1960	1970
De facto			
Usual residence	X	X	X
Place of birth	X	X	X
Duration of residence			
Place of prev. residence			X
Urban/rural	X	X	X
Sex	X	X	X
Age	X	X	X
Relation to household head	X	X	X
Marital status	X	X	X
Children born alive		X	X
Children living			
Citizenship	X		X
Literacy			
School enrollment	X	X	X
Ed. attainment	X	X	X
Ed. qualification			
National/Ethnic origin	X	X	X
Language			
Religion			
Household composition	X	X	X
Econ. active/inactive	X	X	X
Occupation	X	X	X
Industry	X	X	X
Occupational status	X	X	X
Income	X	X	X
Housing	X	X	X

NORTH AMERICA

North America

Canada

Canada

CAPITAL: Ottawa.
STATISTICAL AGENCY: Statistics Canada.
NATIONAL REPOSITORY: 1666-1760 Archives de Paris, copies in Parliamentary Library, Ottawa. 1760 on, Statistics Canada Library.
MAIN U.S. REPOSITORY: Detroit Public Library, Library of Congress, and Population Research Center (Univ. of Texas)

Censuses in Canada date back to 1666 when the first census of the colony of New France was taken. This census lays claim to being the first modern census because it was a *de jure*, nominative census taken by house-to-house canvass that gathered age, sex, conjugal condition, and occupation of the people of the colony. Royal troops stationed in the area were excluded. The clergy, nobility, public functionaries, and farmers were left out of the census of professions and trades. The New France census of 1667 added questions on agriculture: land cleared and number of cattle. Few censuses since then have failed to touch on some aspect of agriculture.

There were over ninety censuses of colonies, territories, and individual provinces from 1666 to 1870. Full national censuses date from 1871, after confederation in 1867. The pre-1871 censuses, with few exceptions, indicated the total population by locality, sex, and marital status. Age breakdowns were generally given in four or more divisions, especially under French domination. The English period of censuses usually distinguished children from adults; or males over and under fifty with females over and under fifteen; or both sexes over and under sixteen. From 1841 on, however, age breakdowns became more detailed again.

Although introduced in one census, the following items were not consistently asked in subsequent censuses. However, it is interesting to note when they first appeared: housing (1685); origins and religion (1767); infirmities (1784); place of birth (1817); rudimentary census of industries (1820); school attendance (1842); literacy and urban-rural division of population (1891); citizenship, language, earnings, weeks worked, and immigration (1901); hours worked per week (1911); internal migration, fertility, educational attainment (literacy dropped), household and family composition, labor force participation, war service, and sample enu-

meration on housing (1940); partial self-enumeration (1961); educational qualification and vocational education (1971).

Canadian censuses began as *de jure* and have never varied from that type. The canvasser method of enumeration was maintained until 1961 when the sample forms on migration, fertility, and income were left with the householder to fill out by himself. In 1971 self-enumeration was used for 98 percent of the population while 2 percent in the remote rural areas were canvassed. Those percentages changed in 1976 to 99 percent and 1 percent respectively.

In 1886 and regularly every ten years until 1956 quinquennial censuses with national coverage began but with a limited number of inquiries.

Indians, at first only those settled near the colonies, were included by enumeration or estimate in the New France censuses of 1685, 1688, 1692, 1698; Acadian census of 1693; Nova Scotian census of 1767; New Brunswick census of 1861; Prince Edward Island census of 1861; and Newfoundland census of 1869. They have been included in all but the 1901 census since confederation. However, they were excluded from the gainfully occupied universe in 1921 and from the labor force in 1951.

With two official languages, English and French, Canada has been interested in the population's knowledge of one or both languages since 1901. Mother tongue has also been asked since then, primarily to help determine national or ethnic origins as, geographically, Canada has three zones with strong cultural division: the eastern section (English and French), the prairie section (English and Central/East European), and the west coast (English and Oriental). The determination of Canadian citizenship versus British subject status also became of interest in the same census even though Canada did not gain national status until 1947.

1851-52

The censuses of 1851 and 1861 are aggregates of censuses of Upper and Lower Canadas conducted separately. The census taken as of January 12, 1852, was *de jure* and canvassed. Scope included origins, religion, trade or occupation, ages, birthplace, births, deaths (by age and cause), school attendance, infirmities (deaf, dumb, blind, lunatics), family composition, marital status, housing, and a "budding" census of industries and agriculture.

1860-61

Same as 1851-52.

1870-71

First census after confederation (Ontario, Quebec, New Brunswick and Nova Scotia) and conducted by the Ministry of Agriculture as of April 2, 1871; it was *de jure* and canvassed. Indian population was estimated in most places. Scope included: place of birth, sex, age, marital status, school attendance, literacy, origins, religion, occupation (listed alphabetically), infirmities, and nominal returns of deaths and births during last twelve months. Also housing, agriculture, industrial establishments, and products were taken. Extensive topographical studies were done before, during, and after census. Feature: Volume 4 contains summaries of censuses taken at different periods in and for territories then part of Canada (1666-1871).

1881

Second census (Ontario, Quebec, New Brunswick, Nova Scotia, Manitoba, British Columbia and territories), conducted by Ministry of Agriculture as of April 4, 1881: it too was *de jure* and canvassed. Indians estimated as in 1871. Scope included place of birth, sex, age, marital status, literacy, school attendance, origins, religion, occupation, infirmities, and nominal returns of deaths, also housing, industries, agriculture, and products. Feature: Volume 20, Appendix A, gives the component parts of several classes of occupations listed in the tables alphabetically—a first move toward an occupational classification.

1884-85

Census of the three provincial districts of the Northwest territories (Assiniboia, Saskatchewan, Alberta).

1885-86

Census of Manitoba. Feature: tables show occupations classified rather than in alphabetical order.

1890-91

Third census (British Columbia, Manitoba, New Brunswick, Nova Scotia, Ontario, Prince Edward Island, Quebec, the Territories [Alberta, Assiniboia East and West, Saskatchewan, and unorganized territories] conducted by Ministry of Agriculture as of April 5, 1891; it was *de jure* and canvassed. Scope included: birthplace of both the individual and parents (new), sex, age, relation to household head (new), marital status, educational status and literacy, origins, religion, occupation, occupational status (new), and nominal returns of deaths, also agriculture, industries and products. Features: first time French Canadians were determined, not just persons of French origin. Those persons away from residence over twelve months were not counted. The first time occupations of females given.

1891

Census of Newfoundland and Labrador.

1901

Fourth census conducted by the Census Office of Ministry of Agriculture as of March 31, 1901; it was *de jure* and canvassed. Scope included: birthplace, sex, age, relation to household head, marital status (divorce added), citizenship (new), literacy, school attendance, origins, mother tongue and knowledge of official language (new), religion, occupation, industry (new), occupational status (own-account worker added), earnings (new), weeks worked (new), immigration, births, and deaths, also housing, agriculture, industries, and products. Feature: the first time the territories of Keewatin, Athabaska, Mackenzie, and Yukon were enumerated.

1901

Census of Newfoundland and Labrador.

1906

Census of population and agriculture of the Northwest provinces: Manitoba, Saskatchewan and Alberta. Indian population numbered but not blacks or Orientals.

1911

Fifth census conducted by the Census and Statistics Office (permanent) as of June 1, 1911; it was *de jure* and canvassed with mechanical tabulation (new). Scope included: birthplace, sex, age, relation to household head, marital status, citizenship, literacy, school attendance, origins, mother tongue and knowledge of official language, religion, occupation, industry, occupational status, earnings, immigration and naturalization, hours worked previous week (new), weeks worked, infirmities, and nominal returns of deaths, also housing, agriculture, manufactures, and products. Features: Volume 2 appendix, census of the Far North of Canada. Index to occupations numbering system consists of three parts: (1) industry, (2) class of workers, and (3) particular trade or occupation.

1911

Census of Newfoundland and Labrador. First record of the sexes in Northern Labrador.

1916

Census of prairie provinces, population and agriculture: Manitoba, Saskatchewan, and Alberta. First mention of difficulties in age gathering among the total population instead of just among Indians.

1921

Sixth census conducted by Dominion Bureau of Statistics as of June 1, 1921; it was *de jure* and canvassed with mechanical tabulation. Scope included: birthplace of individual and parents (reinstated), sex, age, relation to household head, marital status, citizenship, literacy, school attendance, origins, mother tongue and knowledge of official language, religion, occupation, industry, occupational status, weeks worked, earnings, immigration and naturalization, and infirmities. Prior to this census, no distinction was made between the household comprising a group of people in the same housekeeping unit, and the family. In 1921 "census family" was used to indicate household and "private family" to mean the kinship group. Also taken were housing and agriculture. Features: since the Dominion Bureau of Statistics was established the following formerly covered only by the census are now taken annually and thus are dropped: census of industries and vital statistics. Volume 6 contains descriptive analysis of more important results of the census. Variations of population numbers in this census caused by (1) fluctuations in birthrate, (2) cessation of immigration during World War I, and (3) losses occasioned by the war.

1921

Census of Newfoundland and Labrador.

1926

Seventh census ("Depression Census"), conducted by the Dominion Bureau of Statistics as of June 1, 1931, was *de jure* and canvassed with mechanical tabulation. Scope included: birthplace of individual and parents, sex, age, relation to household head, marital status, citizenship, literacy, school attendance, origins, mother tongue and knowledge of official language, religion, occupation, industry, occupational status, earnings, weeks worked, causes of unemployment (new), immigration and naturalization, and infirmities (blind, deaf-mutes only); also housing and agriculture. Features: Volume 1 is a compendium of historical material relating to the Canadian population; comparative tables go back as far as possible. Separate classifications for occupation and industry were new. Previously the Canadian classification scheme was in the main an occupational classification on an industrial framework. Volume 6, *Unemployment*, containing hitherto unpublished data on unemployment in 1921 appears in Appendix II. In volume 7, *Occupation and Industry*, the appendix contains comparative occupation groups by sex, 1891-1931, for Canada and more unpublished data from the 1921 census.

1936

Census of prairie provinces, population and agriculture: Manitoba, Saskatchewan, and Alberta. Indians included.

1931

Census of the prairie provinces. First time asked: years at school, seeking work for those age fourteen to twenty-seven not in school, present and usual occupations.

1941

Eighth census ("War Census"), conducted by the Dominion Bureau of Statistics as of June 2, 1941, was *de jure* and canvassed, with mechanical tabulation. Scope included: birthplace, duration of residence (new), place of previous residence (new), sex, age, relation to household head, marital status, date of first marriage (new), number of children born alive (new), number of children living (new), citizenship, school attendance, education attainment (years of schooling), origins, mother tongue and knowledge of official language, religion, household composition (new), family composition (new), economically active (new), occupation, occupation in 1931 (new), industry, occupational status, earnings, weeks worked, youth not in school seeking work, war service (new), immigration and naturalization, and infirmities. Also housing (a separate one-in-ten sample census), merchandising, and services were taken. Features: first time use of census tracts (two cities). First time use of sample tabulation (1/10) to prepare preliminary results on occupations, earnings, and employment. First time "not stated" ages assigned by making use of all information on the census schedule. Volume 1, Appendix IV, contains intercensal estimates of population for Canada and the provinces, 1867-1941. Volume 7, Appendix A, gainfully employed fourteen years of age and over by selected occupations and sex for "greater" cities of Montreal, Toronto, Vancouver, and Winnipeg, 1931 and 1941.

1945 (October 1)

The last separate census of Newfoundland and Labrador, conducted by the Dominion Bureau of Statistics at the request of the Newfoundland Government, was *de jure* and canvassed, with mechanical tabulation. Separate schedules for population (household), individual (for lodgers and others for whom information not known by household head), displaced persons (temporary nonresidents). Excluded: nomadic Indians and foreign residents (those on official status, diplomats and so forth). Tables for districts and settlements.

Definitions and Concepts. URBAN—those living inside cities, towns, and incorporated villages. HOUSEHOLD—all persons living in a dwelling whether tied by kinship or not. One household per dwelling. DWELLING—structurally separate set of living premises (single house, one part of a semidetached or row house, or each apartment or flat in a building). AGE— completed years at last birthday, completed months for infants. Standard five-year age groups in tables. MARITAL STATUS—single (never married), married, widowed, and divorced (new for Newfoundland this census). FAMILY—spouses with or without unmarried children, or single parent with unmarried children. Single children, twenty-five and over, were counted as persons in families but not as children. BIRTHPLACE— district (or settlement) for natives, name of country for nonnatives. NATIONALITY— citizenship. ORIGINS—English, Irish, Scottish, Welsh, French, Scandinavian, Eskimo, half-breed, Indian, others. EDUCATION—For all persons ten years old and over, literacy. For those five to twenty years old, years of schooling and enrollment, age on leaving school. RELIGION—six denominations plus "others." MIGRATION—for all ten years old and over, residence in 1935 (name of district or settlement, or name of country). GAINFULLY EMPLOYED—all persons receiving remuneration, unpaid family workers and apprentices, and the like who receive no pay. Not gainfully employed—homemakers, retired, students, inmates and those with no occupation. OCCUPATION—classification based on an industry frame. OCCUPATIONAL STATUS—gainfully employed (employers, own-account worker, unpaid worker and apprentice); not gainfully employed (no occupation, student, retired, inmate, or nomadic Indian).

Special Elements and Features. The category of divorced was newly added to marital status designations used by Newfoundland. Question of whether or not an individual had had tuberculosis in the last five years and whether he or she had had chest x-rays. Source and amount of income asked, but tables gave only that of the gainfully employed. Population of Newfoundland, 1836-1945. Volume 1, Appendix C, index of place names with page numbers in which census data can be found in the tables.

Quality of the Census. Benefited from Dominion Bureau of Statistics expertise. Nonstated ages were assigned.

Publication Plan. Canada. Dominion Bureau of Statistics, and Newfoundland Government. *Eleventh Census of Newfoundland and Labrador, 1945. [St. John's], 1949.* Volume 1, *Population.* Volume 2, *Agriculture and Fishing.* Language of publication is English only.

1951 (June 1)

The ninth census, the first since Newfoundland officially became the tenth province of Canada in 1949, was conducted by the Dominion Bureau of Statistics. It was *de jure* and canvassed with electronic mechanical tabulation. Ten schedules, four for population (however, only one main schedule); the remaining were for housing, agriculture, fishing, and the census of distribution. Territorial divisions were provinces, census divisions (paralleled the electoral districts more or less), subdistricts (similar to polling districts), and the census metropolitan area (new), which was an area with close economic, geographic, and social relationships whose main center had a population of 25,000 or more. Excluded were foreign residents (foreign officials, diplomats, and military personnel as well as foreign visitors). Included were Canadians overseas. Special population groups were censused by other appropriate government agencies, for example those living in isolated areas of Northern Canada, by the Royal Canadian Mounted Police.

Definitions and Concepts. URBAN—cities, towns, and villages of 1,000 or more whether incorporated or not, plus urbanized fringes of large cities (new). BIRTHPLACE—district or settlement for natives; name of country for nonnatives. AGE—completed years at last birthday. Tables in single years and standard five-year age groups. MARITAL STATUS—single (never married), married, widowed, and divorced. Those separated whether legally or not were classed as married. HOUSEHOLD—person or group occupying one dwelling. DWELLING—structurally separate set of living premises with private entrance from outside the building or from a common hallway or stairway inside. FAMILY—based on kinship. ORIGINS—National/ethnic/racial classification. Through 1941, origin was traced through the father for all but Indians whose tribe was determined through the mother. This basically remained the same except that this census attempted to use the language spoken as the main indicator. Then if this were not sufficient, origin was that of the paternal ancestor at first arrival in Canada. Mixed Indian and white (termed "half-breeds" in previous census) were classed as native Indians if they resided on a reservation; if not, then origin of father was noted. Other mixed (Negro-white, Chinese-white) were classed according to father's origin. Formerly they had been designated Negro or Oriental whether the father was or not. CITIZENSHIP— national allegiance. EDUCATION—school enrollment and years of schooling. LANGUAGE—mother tongue and knowledge of an official language (English or French). RELIGION—affiliation, official or not, to a specific denomination. ECONOMIC ACTIVITY—labor force concept (new) instead of the gainfully employed definition. That is, any person fourteen years or older who worked some time during the census week ending June 2 for pay or profit was included in the labor force. OCCUPATION—usual or main occupation. Occupational classification was modified from that used in 1941: proprietory and managerial and professional form two new groups, communication split from transportation and increase in number of classes. Most important is that manufacturing was subdivided by kind of product produced (as the Industrial Classification Systems of 1941 and 1951 do). Not ISCO. INDUSTRY—name of establishment (new). Industrial classification was similar to that used in 1941. Forestry and logging split from fishing and trapping, and number of classes increased. Not ISIC. OCCUPATIONAL STATUS—employer, employee, own-account worker, no pay. INCOME—restricted only to earnings over the twelve months prior to the census date in wage-earning employment. IMMIGRATION—period of first arrival to Canada. WAR SERVICE—first asked in 1941; determined if served in Canadian and/or other forces. INFIRMITIES—only totally blind or totally deaf population.

Special Elements and Features. Labor force concept (see above) applied for the first time. Census tracts made for fourteen cities. Urban definition changed. T-night operation was one night just before the census night in which the transient population was sought by enumerators in hotels, camps, and so forth. First census to decentralize processing of results. Comparative tables can be found in respective topic volumes.

Quality of the Census. Long history of census taking by a permanent organization. Pretesting, comparative checks on coverage, and topographical preparation indicate a census of good quality. "Not stated" responses, except in occupation and industry, were statistically assigned.

Publication Plan. Canada. Dominion Bureau of Statistics. *Ninth Census of Canada, 1951. Neuvième recensement du Canada, 1951.* Ottawa, Edmond Cloutier, 1953-1956. Volumes 1-11 in 14 volumes. Subject report volumes, administrative report, general review made up the set. Unpublished data are available. Language of publication is bilingual, English and French.

1956 (June 1)

First nationwide census taken midway between decennial censuses (supplanted the prairie censuses). Conducted by the Dominion Bureau of Statistics it was *de jure* and canvassed with electronic mechanical tabulation. One schedule was used for population because the scope of this census was limited to the basic demographic characteristics of age, sex, relation to household head, and marital status. Excluded and included populations—same as 1951. Census tracts expanded to cover seventeen cities.

Definitions and Concepts. The same as applied in the 1951 census for the subjects enumerated.

Special Elements and Features. Results issued as bulletins rather than completed volumes. Compared only with 1951 figures except for dwellings, which were compared from 1881-1956.

Quality of the Census. Same as 1951. Whipple's Index was category I—highly accurate age data.

Publication Plan. Canada. Dominion Bureau of Statistics. *Census of Canada, 1956. Recensement du Canada, 1956. Population.* Ottawa, 1957-1958. Bulletins Nos. 1-1 through 1-22. Subject volumes. Unpublished data are available. Languages of publication are English and French.

1961 (June 1)

Tenth decennial census, conducted by the Dominion Bureau of Statistics, was *de jure*, canvassed with some self-enumeration, and computer tabulated (new). There were eleven schedules of which five were for population. The remainder were for housing, agriculture, forestry, irrigation, and merchandising. Excluded and included population—same as 1951. Census tracts are available for twenty-three cities.

Definitions and Concepts. All but the following were the same as used in the 1951 census. EDUCATION—school attendance and educational attainment. The latter determined the level or highest grade in school rather than just the number of years of schooling. MIGRATION—(sample) last taken in 1941; asked residence in 1956 (address), and whether it was a farm, a small agricultural holding, or urban. FERTILITY—(sample) last taken in 1941; asked data of first marriage, number of live-born children. INCOME—(sample) gross earning for the last twelve months; earnings from own business or professional practice (new); income from family allowance, old age pensions, government benefits, retirement plans, bonds and bank interest, dividends, other investments, and other money income (new).

Special Elements and Features. There was a one-in-five household sample enumeration on migration, fertility, and income in addition to housing. Self-enumeration was used in sampling. "Not-in-labor-force" groups were not identified in the results of this census. Volume 3, Part 1 (Bulletin 3.1-1) has historical tables, 1911-1961. This was the first use of the computer for tabulation.

Quality of the Census. Same as 1951. Whipple's Index was category I—highly accurate age data.

Publication Plan. Canada. Dominion Bureau of Statistics. *1961 Census of Canada. Recensement du Canda, 1961.* Ottawa, Roger Duhamel, 1962-1971.

Volumes 1-7 in 16 parts (179 bulletins). Advance series, subject volumes, special series, census tracts, and census monographs. Unpublished data and computer tapes are available. Language of publication is both English and French.

1966 (June 1)

Second quinquennial census, conducted by the Dominion Bureau of Statistics, was *de jure*, canvassed, and computer tabulated. Excluded and included population—same as 1951. There were census tracts for twenty-eight cities and census metropolitan areas (CMAs) in addition to the geographic divisions standard in Canadian censuses.

Definitions and Concepts. URBAN, AGE, SEX, MARITAL STATUS, HOUSEHOLD, and FAMILY—were the only topics taken; definitions were the same as 1961.

Special Elements and Features. More housing characteristics were asked in this census. Census of agriculture was also taken.

Quality of the Census. Same as 1951 and 1961. Whipple's Index category I—highly accurate age data. There was a 2.6 percent undercount.

Publication Plan. Canada. Dominion Bureau of Statistics. *1966 Census of Canada. Recensement du Canada, 1966*. Ottawa, 1967-1971. Volumes 1-5. Bulletins, 1 Population—General Characteristics; 2 Population—Household, families, and housing; 3-5—Agriculture. Unpublished data and computer tapes are available. Language of publication is English and French.

1971 (June 1)

Eleventh decennial census ("Hundredth year Census"), conducted by Statistics Canada, formerly the Dominion Bureau of Statistics. It was *de jure* and self-enumerated by 98 percent of the population; remainder in rural areas were canvassed. Computer tabulation used FOSDIC system of data capture. Schedules included: short form with ten questions on population and nine on housing and long form, ten on population, twenty-nine on housing, and thirty socioeconomic questions. The long form (sample) was used in one-in-three self-enumerated households, and exclusively in the canvassed area. The remaining schedules were for agriculture, business, and so on. There were census tracts for thirty-one cities and census metropolitan areas (CMAs).

Definitions and Concepts. BIRTHPLACE, URBAN, SEX, HOUSEHOLD, FAMILY, MARITAL STATUS, CITIZENSHIP, ORIGINS, RELIGION, INDUSTRY, OCCUPATIONAL STATUS and WAR SERVICE—same as 1951. FERTILITY—same as 1961. AGE—month and year of birth. Tables in single years and standard five-year age groups. INFIRMITIES—dropped. IMMIGRATION—same as 1961, plus if parents born in Canada. EDUCATION—in addition to enrollment and educational attainment, the following were asked: where attended highest grade of elementary or secondary school (province or outside Canada); years of schooling since secondary school; university degree, certification or diploma; vocational education. LANGUAGE—in addition to mother tongue and knowledge of official language, language most spoken in the home. ECONOMIC ACTIVITY—same as 1961 (that is, labor force concept), plus when last worked even for a few days. OCCUPATION—same as 1961, plus cite the most important activities or duties and job title; if worked mainly full-time, and place of work (new). INCOME—Same as 1961, plus farm income. MIGRATION—same as 1961, plus number of times moved from one Canadian municipality to another since June 1, 1966. Occupational classification differed from 1961 in the major groups, plus additions to minor and unit groups. Industrial classification—same as 1961.

Special Elements and Features. The basic subjects of the census remained the same as 1961. However, some new questions were inserted to serve as checks because of self-enumeration; others, such as educational qualification and vocational education, language spoken in the home, full- and part-time work and usual place of work, are expansions of the 1961 subject treatment. There was extensive sampling, one-in-three, on birthplace of parents, fertility, citizenship, immigration, income, employment, and education. Geo-coding and generalized tabulation retrieval systems were used. There was computer linkage of population and agriculture documents.

Quality of the Census. Same as 1951 and 1961. Whipple's Index category I—highly accurate age data. There was a 2 percent undercount.

Publication Plan. Canada. Statistics Canada. *1971 Census of Canada. Recensement du Canada, 1971.* Ottawa, 1972-1978. Volumes 1-6 in 21 parts (226 bulletins).Advance series, subject volumes, census tracts, special series, working manuals. Unpublished data and computer tapes are available. Language of publication is English and French.

1976 (June 1)

Third quinquennial census, conducted by Statistics Canada, was *de jure*, self-enumerated (99 and 1 percent), and computer tabulated. Population excluded— same as 1951, 1961, 1971. Schedules: collective dwelling record, population and housing (short form); population and housing (long form—sample); population and housing (outside Canada); individual. Geographic units—same as 1961, 1971. Census tracts are for thirty-one cities and CMAs.

Definitions and Concepts. URBAN—population of 1,000 or more in an area with a density of 1,000 per square mile. AGE, SEX, MARITAL STATUS, LANGUAGE, HOUSEHOLD, EDUCATION, MIGRATION—same as 1971. ECONOMIC ACTIVITY—labor force concept (same as 1971) plus the question "During week before census were there definite arrangements to start new job?" OCCUPATION and INDUSTRY were not asked.

Special Elements and Features. Educational characteristics were asked of all persons fifteen years and over instead of five years and over as in 1971. Household head can be either husband or wife instead of automatically husband as in previous censuses. Sample enumeration of one-in-three households was used for education, labor force activity and migration.

Quality of the Census. Through change of wording from "attendance at university or school" (1971) to "attendance at educational institution" (1976), there was an undercount of fifteen to nineteen year olds who mistook the statement to mean university only. Otherwise quality the same as 1951, 1961, 1971. Whipple's Index, category I—highly accurate age data. Only 2.04 percent undercoverage of the total population.

Publication Plan. Canada. Statistics Canada. *1976 Census of Canada. Recensement du Canada 1976.* Ottawa, 1977-1979. Volumes 1-10 in 107 bulletins. Volumes 1-5, subject volumes; volume 6, census tracts; volume 7, provincial tracts; volumes 8-10, supplementary bulletins. Enumeration area reference lists. Unpublished data and computer tapes are available. Language of publication is English and French.

1981 (July 3)

The census was conducted by Statistics Canada and is *de jure*. Only interim figures have been seen (unpublished), which are said to exclude the populations in temporary addresses (motels, hotels, and hospitals), military personnel living abroad, and those who erroneously listed their usual residence.

OTHER STATISTICAL PUBLICATIONS: Issued by Immigration and Demographic Policy Group, *Immigration Statistics* (annually). Issued by Statistics Canada, *Canada Year Book, Canadian Statistical Review* (monthly), *International and Interprovincial Migration in Canada* (annually), *Principal Vital Statistics by Local Areas* (annually), *Vital Statistics* (annually).

National Topic Chart

	1951	1956	1961	1966	1971	1976
De facto						
Usual residence	X	X	X	X	X	X
Place of birth	X		X		X	X
Duration of residence						
Place of prev. residence			X		X	X
Urban/rural	X	X	X	X	X	X
Sex	X	X	X	X	X	X
Age	X	X	X	X	X	X
Relation to household head	X	X	X	X	X	X
Marital status	X	X	X	X	X	X
Children born alive			X		X	
Children living						
Citizenship	X		X		X	
Literacy						
School enrollment	X		X		X	X
Ed. attainment	X		X		X	X
Ed. qualification					X	X
National/Ethnic origin	X		X		X	
Language	X		X		X	X
Religion	X		X		X	
Household composition	X		X	X	X	X
Econ. active/inactive	X		X		X	X
Occupation	X		X		X	
Industry	X		X		X	
Occupational status	X		X		X	
Income	X		X		X	
Housing	X	X	X	X	X	X

Greenland

Greenland

CAPITAL: Godthaab.
STATISTICAL AGENCY: Danmarks Statistiks, Copenhagen.
NATIONAL REPOSITORY: Danmarks Statistiks Bibliotek.
MAIN U.S. REPOSITORY: New York Public Library (early censuses), Population Research Center (Univ. of Texas).

The largest island in the world was first visited by Norwegian navigators in A.D. 984. During the following centuries, Dutch and English explorers landed on the western and eastern coasts, but no permanent settlement was established. In 1729 Denmark, after constant trading activities, assumed direct control of the island. The inhabitants (native born) are predominantly Eskimos.

The first three censuses were taken in 1834, 1840, and 1845 and published in the *Statistisk Tabelvaerk*. The following censuses, taken in 1850, 1855, 1860, 1870, 1880, and 1890, were published in the *Statistiske Meddelelser*. No details on organization and methods for these and previous censuses were given, and the publication of results was limited to total population published in later census reports.

1901

The tenth census of population was conducted by the Bureau of Statistics of Denmark with cooperation of the Royal Bureau of Commerce of Greenland. No details on organization and methods are available. The territory covered by the census was divided into West Region (divided into north and south) and East Region. The regions were subdivided into districts and villages. The scope of the census included: age, sex, race, marital status, professions and industries, number of houses, and their inhabitants. Results for Europeans and native born were presented separately. Total population for 1805, 1840, 1860, 1880, and 1890; territorial changes from 1890 to 1901; density; size of towns; vital statistics (annually from 1891 to 1901); and causes of death were also published in this report.

The following censuses were taken in 1911 and 1921 and published in the *Statistiske Meddelelser*, but we were not able to get hold of copies to consult.

The CICRED World Population Year volume published about Denmark in

Greenland

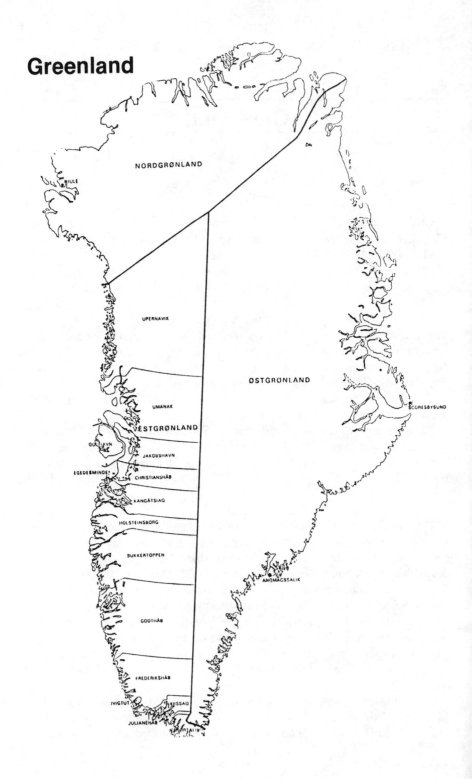

NORDGRØNLAND

THULE

UPERNAVIK

ØSTGRØNLAND

UMANAK

VESTGRØNLAND

SCORESBYSUND

GODHAVN

JAKOBSHAVN

EGEDESMINDE

CHRISTIANSHÅB

KANGÅTSIAQ

HOLSTEINSBORG

SUKKERTOPPEN

ANGMAGSSALIK

GODTHÅB

FREDERIKSHÅB

IVIGTUT

NARSSAQ

JULIANEHÅB

NANORTALIK

1977 indicated that the censuses of Denmark from 1834 to 1860 were taken on a *de jure* basis, from 1870 to 1921 on a *de facto* basis, and returned to *de jure* in 1930. Apparently the same occurred in Greenland since their censuses were taken in cooperation with the government of Denmark. Total population for these years was published in later censuses.

1930

The thirteenth general census of population was taken by the Bureau of Greenland Affairs under the supervision of the Bureau of Statistics of Denmark. No details on organization and methods were provided. The territory was divided into West Region (north and south) and East Region; both were subdivided into communes, or parishes, and places. Like the previous censuses, results for Europeans and native born were presented separately. The scope was basically the same as 1901. The following additional tables were furnished: total population for 1834, 1860, 1880, 1890, 1901, 1911, and 1921 in comparison with 1930; list of communes by size and number of inhabitants; number of parishes and districts; masculinity rates; age distribution per 1,000 inhabitants; birth and death rates from 1922 to 1930 (single years); and comparative tables of professions from 1860 to 1930.

1945 (December 31)

The fourteenth general census of population was conducted by the Greenland government authorities in conjunction with the Bureau of Statistics of Denmark. The census was apparently *de jure*, and a combination of canvasser and self-enumeration was the method used to record information on household schedules. The tables distinguished citizens of Greenland and citizens of Denmark. The territory was divided by regions, West Region including north, south, and Thule (created in 1937), and East Region. The regions were subdivided into districts, communes, and places.

Definitions and Concepts. AGE—in completed years, tabulated in single years and standard five-year age groups. MARITAL STATUS—categories were: single, married, widowed, separated, and divorced. CITIZENSHIP—two major groups were presented: persons under Danish law (persons born outside Greenland; persons born in Greenland with parents under Danish jurisdiction, except if the person has a business in Greenland; persons born in Greenland married to a person under Danish jurisdiction; and persons born in Greenland who have an appointment from the Danish crown); and persons under Greenland law (all persons not previously defined, including Danish women married to Greenlanders not under Danish law). PLACE OF BIRTH—commune of birth for Greenlanders and country of birth for foreign born. OCCUPATION—every person declared whether he had a permanent job, was self-employed, or was a dependent member of the household. Classification presented six major groups and subgroups for Greenlanders and nine major groups for persons under Danish law. OCCUPATIONAL STATUS—categories were: persons with permanent job in the government, persons with temporary or part-time job, the retired or pensioners, and persons of independent income. Apparently homemakers, children, and home assistants were classified under the occupation of the head of the household.

Special Elements and Features. Introduction of the concept of citizens under Danish and Greenland laws and inclusion of the region of Thule were new. Masculinity rates in comparison with the Danish figures and tables with birth and death rates from 1931 to 1945 (single years) were included.

Quality of the Census. There is a long tradition of censuses taken either quinquennially or decennially, although the census office is not permanent. Whipple's Index classified age accuracy into category I—highly accurate data.

Publication Plan. Denmark. Statistiske Department. *Folketaellingen i Grønland den 31 december 1945/Population du Gröenland au 31 décembre 1945.* Copenhagen, 1950. (*Statistiske Meddelelser*, 4th series, volume 134, part 5. Language of publication is Danish. French is used only in the title and in the table of contents.

1951 (December 31)

The fifteenth general census of population was conducted by Greenland government authorities in conjunction with the Bureau of Statistics of Denmark. The census was apparently *de jure*, but no details of organization and methods are available. The results were published in 1956.

The following tables were published: total population by regions; population by age groups by sex, 1951 compared to 1945; population by sex and marital status for 1945 and 1951 in Greenland, compared to 1950 in Denmark; household size, 1951 Greenland and 1950 Denmark; population distributed by major industrial groups and occupational status; and the number of births, deaths, and marriages from 1946 to 1954 (single years).

Quality of the Census. The Whipple's Index classified age accuracy into category II—fairly accurate data.

Publication Plan. Denmark. Statistiske Department. *Befolkningen i Grønland. Fordelt efter kon, alder, civil stand m.v. ved folktaellingen den 31. December 1951.* (*Statistiske Efterretninger*, 1956, no. 69.) Unpublished data are available. Language of publication is Danish.

1955 (December 31)

The sixteenth general census of population was conducted by the Greenland government authorities in cooperation with the Bureau of Statistics of Denmark. Very little was published of this census. A table with total population for 1955 and 1960 for regions and communes was published in 1962.

The United Nations *Handbook of Population and Housing Census Methods* indicated, however, that the usual residents of the household, present at the time of the census, were enumerated, and information on age, sex, place of birth, marital status, economic activity, occupations, and industry were recorded. The following information was taken from this source.

Definitions and Concepts. AGE—date of birth (month, day and year). PLACE OF BIRTH—distinction between natives and foreign born; place and commune for native born and country of birth for foreign-born persons. MARITAL STATUS—categories were: single, married, widowed, divorced, and separated. Type of separation was not specified. ECONOMIC ACTIVITY—period of reference was the census date; lower age limit, fourteen years. Economically active included employed and unemployed looking for job. The following groups were considered inactive: homemakers, students, pensioners, and others (not specified). OCCUPATION—main and secondary occupations were recorded. Classification was not indicated.

There is no indication, however, where and if these tables were published. Unpublished data are available.

1960 (December 30-31)

The seventeenth general census of population was conducted by the Ministry of Greenland in cooperation with the Bureau of Statistics of Denmark. The census was *de facto*, excluding the Danish-American defense control in Thule, the Sdr. Strømfjord, and the naval station in Grønnedal. No details on organization and methods were provided. The territory was divided into regions (West, North-Thule, and East) subdivided into communes and places. Information gathered here was taken from introductory pages and table headings.

Definitions and Concepts. AGE—date of birth, tabulated in single years and standard five-years age groups. PLACE OF BIRTH—four groups were distinguished: born in Greenland, born in Denmark, born in Faroe Islands, and foreign born. Only the total number of persons for each of these groups, without identification of place, was recorded. The place of birth of parents was also recorded. MARITAL STATUS—categories were the same as 1955. ECONOMIC ACTIVITY—period of reference was the census date. Lower age limit, fourteen years. Economically active included employed and unemployed looking for a job. Inactive population: homemakers, pensioners, persons of independent income, others (children, family helpers, and outside helpers working at home). The place of work (state or private enterprise) and form of employment contract (contract workers; month, week, or hourly paid workers, and apprentices) were also recorded. OCCUPATIONAL STATUS—categories were: self-employed, public employee or civil servant, skilled worker, and unskilled worker. OCCUPATION—occupational classification presented as subgroups of occupational status, major, and subgroups (two-digits). INDUSTRY—classification based on ISIC, divisions and major groups (two-digits). HOUSEHOLD—consisted of a group of persons living in one housing unit. The number of households included both private and collective households. The private household included immediate family and other relatives plus servants and lodgers. FAMILY—a single lodger in Greenland is never considered a single family. The family included single parents, a couple legally married or not, with or without children. FERTILITY—for all women fifteen years and over: number of children both stillborn and born alive from 1952 to 1955 and 1956 to 1960 was recorded by age of the mother at birth of the first child. Fertility was considered both inside and outside marriage.

Special Elements and Features. There are tables with total population for court, administrative, police, electoral, medical, school, and commercial districts for the years 1951, 1955 and 1960. Alphabetical list of places in 1951, 1955, and 1960 is included. Questions on economic activities were expanded. Tables of economic activity for 1951, 1955, and 1960 provided details of the changes that occurred. The number of children per private household, size of household, number of families in the household, family size, number of births, deaths, and marriages for 1952 to 1955 and 1956 to 1960 were presented.

Quality of the Census. The census office is not permanent, although there is a long and regular tradition of censuses. Information about organization and methods is lacking. Final results were published in 1965. There is no Whipple's Index category cited.

Publication Plan. Denmark. Statistiske Department. *Grønland. Folketaellingen 1960. Aegteskaber, fødte og døde 1952-1960.* Copenhagen, 1965. (*Statistisk Tabelvaerk*, 1965, II.) Unpublished data are available. Language of publication is Danish.

1965 (December 31)

The eighteenth general census of population was taken for the first time simultaneously with a census of housing. The census was conducted by the Ministry of Greenland in cooperation with the Bureau of Statistics of Denmark on a *de jure* basis. Danish-American defense control in Thule, the Sdr. Strømfjord, and the Naval Station in Grønnedal were not included. Information was recorded on household schedules, printed in Danish and Greenlandic. Details on organization and methods were not provided, and the information here was taken from introductory pages of the census report and table headings. The territory covered by the census was divided into regions (West, Northgreenland-Thule, and East) and subdivided into communes and jurisdictions. As in 1960, total population was also recorded for parishes, court, administrative, electoral, medical, school, and commercial districts.

Definitions and Concepts. AGE, MARITAL STATUS, HOUSEHOLD and FAMILY—same as 1960. PLACE OF BIRTH—commune, city, or weather station was recorded for Greenlanders and country of birth for foreign born. Tables do not show the countries of birth of the foreign born except for Denmark and Faroe Islands. This time, however, detailed information for Greenlanders was given. PLACE OF RESIDENCE—usual place of residence. The usual residents and temporary residents were distinguished. ECONOMIC ACTIVITY— period of reference was the date of the census; lower age limit was fourteen. In Greenland some people have different occupations at different times of the year. The active population included employed and unemployed looking for a job. Inactive population: housewives, children, daughters and house assistants, persons of independent income, students, and inmates of institutions. Housewives, children, and house assistants were assigned the same occupation as the head of the household. Unemployed recorded the most recent occupation. The form of employment contract and the source of income were also recorded (self-employed; part-time fisherman; civil servants; contract workers; temporary workers paid monthly, weekly, daily or hourly; apprentices; and persons of independent income). OCCUPATION—classification based on ISCO, major groups and sub-groups (two-digits). INDUSTRY—classification based on ISIC, divisions and major groups (two-digits). OCCUPATIONAL STATUS—categories were: self-employed, part-time fisherman, civil servant and public employee, skilled worker and unskilled worker, and apprentice and trainee.

Special Elements and Features. The following tables, based on church records, were also included: number of marriages from 1921 to 1965, number of children born per 1,000 women between the ages fifteen and forty-nine for the years 1952 to 1965. For the first time population and housing censuses were taken simultaneously. There was an alphabetical list of places and respective population for 1955, 1960, and 1965. Place of residence was recorded for the first time since 1945. Copy of the schedule was included in the report.

Quality of the Census. Whipple's Index classified age data into category II—fairly accurate data. Final results were published in 1969.

Publication Plan. Denmark. Danmarks Statistisk. *Grønland. Folke- og boligtaellingen 31. December 1965....* Copenhagen, 1969. (*Statistisk Tabelvaerk,* 1969: IX.) Language of publication is Danish.

1970 (December 31)

The nineteenth general census of population and housing was conducted by the Ministry of Greenland Affairs assisted by local city treasurers. The census was *de jure* and again excluded the Danish-American defense territories and the naval station at Grønnedal. Unlike 1965, it included the Danish civilian population in Søndre Strømfjord and the personnel at the airport in Kulusuk. A combination of self-enumeration and canvasser was the method used to record information on household schedules. Tabulation was computerized. The territory covered by the census was divided into regions (Northgreenland-Thule, West, and East), subdivided into communes, towns and villages, stations, and fishing districts.

Definitions and Concepts. AGE—in completed years, plus identification number and date of birth. Tabulated in single years and standard five-year age groups. MARITAL STATUS—same categories as 1965. PLACE OF BIRTH—population was divided into four groups: born in Greenland, born in Denmark, born in Faroe Islands, and foreign born. Detailed information (commune of birth) was given for those born in Greenland only. PLACE OF RESIDENCE—usual place. Temporary residents were recorded separately from permanent residents. HOUSEHOLD—all persons living in the same house, including servants and lodgers. Households were classified as private or collective. The private households were subdivided into families. FAMILY—basic family consisted of a single parent or a couple with unmarried children. EDUCATION (for the first time recorded)—questions asked of all persons from fourteen to thirty-nine years of age: school attendance (regular and technical schools) and educational attainment (highest degree completed). ECONOMIC ACTIVITY—lower age limit was fourteen years; period of reference was the census week. Economically active included the employed and unemployed. Children under fourteen, housewives without job, and house assistants working at home, pensioners, students, and married men working at home duties (classified for census purposes as "housewives") were considered inactive. ECONOMIC DEPENDENCY—the groups classified as inactive were included in the same occupation, industry, and form of employment contract as the head of the household. If the head of the household was not engaged in any industry, the same groups were included into either "persons of independent income" group or "persons receiving government assistance." OCCUPATION—classification based on ISCO, major groups, groups, and subgroups (three-digits). INDUSTRY—classification based on ISIC (two-digits), divisions and major groups. OCCUPATIONAL STATUS—categories were: self-employed, unpaid family worker, part-time fisherman (person who does not own his boat and pays for it by share of catch), civil and public servant, skilled worker including apprentice, and unskilled worker including persons of unspecified activity. Public servants, skilled, and unskilled workers were also classified according to their sector (state or private enterprise) and the form of employment contract.

Special Elements and Features. Education information was recorded for the first time. Vital statistics (marriage, births, and deaths) from 1966 to 1970 were also included. There was an alphabetical list of living places and the changes that occurred between 1965 and 1970. A systematic list of tables, subject index, and map of communes are aids. The region of Ivigtut was tabulated separately. Tables distinguished total population from those born in Greenland.

Quality of the Census. Whipple's Index category II—fairly accurate age data. Final results were published in 1974. Still very little information was given on the methods applied in the census.

Publication Plan. Denmark. Danmarks Statistik. *Grønland. Folke- og boligtaellingen 31. December 1970....* Copenhagen, 1974. (*Statistisk Tabelvaerk*, 1974: VI) [and] *Folke- og boligtaellingen i Grøland, 31. December 1970.* Copenhagen, 1972. (*Meddelelser fra Økonomiststatistisk Kontor*, no. 25.) Unpublished data are available. Language of publication is Danish.

1976 (October 26)

The twentieth general census of population, taken simultaneously with the census of housing, was conducted by local authorities in Greenland. The census was *de jure* and self-enumerated with the assistance of commissioners. Household schedules were utilized. Tabulation was computerized. The territory covered by the census was divided into regions (Northgreenland-Thule, West, and East), subdivided into communes, towns, villages, and stations. If the station was inside a commune, its results were included within that of the commune. The census of housing, however, did not include stations or Ivigtut.

Definitions and Concepts. AGE—same as 1970. PLACE OF BIRTH—same as 1970. MARITAL STATUS—categories were: never married (single), married, and formerly married (widowed, divorced, and separated). PLACE OF RESIDENCE—usual place of residence (registered residents). Information for nonpermanent residents was recorded separately. HOUSEHOLD and FAMILY—same as 1970. EDUCATION—questions asked of all persons between fourteen and thirty-nine years of age: school attendance and educational attainment (highest degree completed in regular and technical school). Industrial training was also recorded. ECONOMIC ACTIVITY—period of reference was the week before the census. Lower age limit was fourteen. The population was divided into three groups: persons with income from their own work; persons who receive income from pensions, independent income, scholarship, retirement, and in general those who receive income from the government; and the third group, persons dependent on another's income (children, housewives, and so forth). Economically active included: those receiving income from work and those temporarily out of work during the week of the census. Unpaid family workers and those seeking education were also classified as active. Inactive population: pensioners, the retired, housewives, and permanently unemployed. Note that students and apprentices (those seeking education) were classified within the same occupation as those who had already finished their education. Source of income during the year before the census and reasons for unemployment were the basis for classification into active and inactive. OCCUPATION—based on ISCO, major groups, groups, and subgroups (three-digits). INDUSTRY—classification based on ISIC, divisions and subgroups (two-digits). Basically the same as 1970. OCCUPATIONAL STATUS—the categories were: self-employed, helping spouse, fisherman (share catch), fisherman in general, civil and public servants (including apprentices and candidates for the position), skilled workers, and unskilled workers. EMPLOYMENT CONDITIONS—civil servants, skilled, and unskilled workers were also classified as: native civil servants and candidates for it, employed by GAS (Greenland workers' contract), natives with some other kind of employment, nonnative civil servants and candidates, nonnatives with other kind of employment, and students and apprentices in industries. In addition these groups were also asked their sector (state or private enterprise).

Special Elements and Features. More detailed information on economic activity; brief summary of censuses; occupational and industrial classifications were provided in the report.

Quality of the Census. Remote areas presented problems for enumeration, and many persons did not report when they moved, especially those who moved within the commune. Information on education and occupation was deficient and, in many cases, made it impossible to determine the results in the tables. Comparisons between census results and national registration showed discrepancies of data for persons with permanent residences in the communes and in districts outside the communes. Whipple's Index category was I—highly accurate age data. Final results were published in 1978.

Publication Plan. Denmark. Danmarks Statistik. *Folke- og boligtaellingen i Grønland, 26. Oktober 1976.* Copenhagen, 1978. (*Statistisk Tabelvaerk*, 1978: 6.) Unpublished data are available. Language of publication is Danish.

OTHER STATISTICAL PUBLICATIONS: Issued by Ministeriet for Grønland, *Grønland i Tal* (annually), *Meddelelser fra Statistisk Kontor, Sundhedstilstanden i Grønland-Landslaegens Årsberetning.* Issued by Danmarks Statistik, *Grønlands befolkning* (annually).

National Topic Chart

	1945	1951	1955	1960	1965	1970	1976
De facto			X	X			
Usual residence	X	X			X	X	X
Place of birth	X		X	X	X	X	X
Duration of residence							
Place of prev. residence							
Urban/rural							
Sex	X	X	X	X	X	X	X
Age	X	X	X	X	X	X	X
Relation to household head	X			X	X	X	X
Marital status	X	X	X	X	X	X	X
Children born alive				X			
Children living							
Citizenship*	X			X	X	X	
Literacy							
School enrollment						X	X
Ed. attainment						X	X
Ed. qualification							
National/Ethnic origin							
Language							
Religion							
Household composition		X		X	X	X	X
Econ. active/inactive	X		X	X	X	X	X
Occupation	X		X	X	X	X	X
Industry		X	X	X	X	X	X
Occupational status	X	X		X	X	X	X
Income							
Housing					X	X	X

*Note: Citizenship refers to the distinction between those persons under Greenland law and those under Danish law.

St. Pierre and Miquelon

French Overseas Territory (T.O.M.)

CAPITAL: Ville de St. Pierre.
STATISTICAL AGENCY: Local administration and INSEE (Statistical Bureau of France).
NATIONAL REPOSITORY: ?
MAIN U.S. REPOSITORY: UCLA (early censuses) and Population Research Center (Univ. of Texas) (later).

St. Pierre and Miquelon are the two main islands of nine in an archipelago in the North Atlantic. A third, Iles aux Marins, was at one time inhabited but has a negligible population today. The original settlers were French Basque with a strong proportion of Normands and Bretons. There was no evidence of any Indian inhabitants when they arrived. As a result, while the other French overseas possessions were concerned with censuses of "indigenous" and "non-indigenous" populations, St. Pierre and Miquelon had only to take "non-originaires" censuses to determine the total population.

Publications of the earliest censuses up to and including that of 1946 have not been located. Only commune totals have appeared in *Bulletins Officiels*. "The previous enumerations consist of a simple compilation of accounts furnished by the village elders." They did not take a census in 1946.

1951 (May 14)

Conducted by the local administration with individual schedules supplied by INSEE, this census was *de facto*, probably self-enumerated, and mechanically tabulated in France. Results are given for St. Pierre and Iles aux Marins, and Miquelon-Langlade (Grand and Petite Miquelon).

Definitions and Concepts. BIRTHPLACE—French citizens indicated department in France or one of the overseas possessions. Foreigners indicated country. Both groups were asked parents' birthplaces as well. AGE—year of birth. Tables appear in single years (generational age) and standard five-year groups. MARITAL STATUS—single, married, widowed, and divorced. EDUCATION—literacy and educational attainment. NATIONALITY—more citizenship than ethnic ori-

St. Pierre and Miquelon appear on the map of Canada, p. 362.

gin and virtually no indication of race. FERTILITY—(all ages, men and women): number of children ever born alive and number surviving. One table has the average number of children surviving for males (eighteen years old and over) and females (fifteen years old and over). Also number of children born alive outside of continental France was asked. MIGRATION—the topic of "tropical sojourn" was not applicable, but it was asked of the civil servants born in France. ECONOMIC ACTIVITY—no specification of reference period or those included in inactive. The active are indicated by occupation and the number of inactive are classed by broad age group only. OCCUPATION and INDUSTRY—given according to INSEE lists. OCCUPATIONAL STATUS—employer (including small fishermen with one or more boats), employee (including sailors hired to work those boats), own-account worker, and person without occupation.

Special Elements and Features. Fertility for males as well as females was taken.

Quality of the Census. Uniform schedules and tabulation done by INSEE and low rate of illiteracy would imply a decent census. Results were compared with vital statistics and other documentation.

Publication Plan. France. INSEE. *Le recensement de la population non originaire des territoires d'outre-mer en 1951. (Analysis).* Paris, n.d. (*Bulletin Mensual de la Statistique d'Outre-Mer [BMSOM]*, supplément série "étude," no. 33) and France. INSEE. *Résultats du recensement de 1951, territoires d'outre-mer: 1re partie, Côte Francais de Somalis, Inde Française, Saint-Pierre-et-Miquelon. (Tables).* Paris, 1952. (*BMSOM*, supplément série "statistique," no. 14.) Language of publication is French.

1957 (October 15)

Conducted by local administration with more involvement of INSEE in the planning and organization of census. It was *de facto* with a *de jure* population total only. It was not stated if it was canvassed or self-enumerated on household schedules (new), but it was mechanically tabulated in France. The results were given for the same territorial divisions as 1951.

Definitions and Concepts. AGE—same as 1951 plus one column with median age for communes. BIRTHPLACE—same as 1951 plus year of arrival for those born outside the territory. MARITAL STATUS, EDUCATION, ECONOMICALLY ACTIVE/INACTIVE, NATIONALITY—same as 1951. FERTILITY—same as 1951 except children surviving was not asked. LANGUAGE—ability to read and write French or another language (primarily a literacy question). OCCUPATION—classification as used by INSEE but this time cross-classed by economic sector (public, semipublic, private, military, other, that is, inactive). Also socioeconomic status determined by cross of occupation with occupational status. INDUSTRY and OCCUPATIONAL STATUS—same as 1951. MIGRATION—immigration of nonnative born only.

Special Elements and Features. Relation to household head and household composition was now possible through use of household schedules. Socioeconomic status and language were new.

Quality of the Census. Greater involvement of INSEE in the census lent expertise to the project.

Publication Plan. France. INSEE. *Recensement de la population de Saint-Pierre-et-Miquelon.* Paris, 1962. Language of publication is French.

1962 (April 20)

Conduct and scope were virtually the same as 1957. Iles aux Marins had separate tables.

Definitions and Concepts. Differences only: MIGRATION—birthplace crossed by usual residence gave internal migration. OCCUPATIONAL STATUS—employer, own-account worker, salaried, apprentice, agricultural farmer. ECONOMIC ACTIVITY—reference period was the year before census. HOUSEHOLD COMPOSITION—in addition to size and number of children under age fifteen (DEPENDENCY), the type of household was given: man alone, man with children, man and other (no children), and the same for women.

Special Elements and Features. Reference period for the economically active/inactive, household type, internal migration were all new. Separate tables for Iles aux Marins.

Quality of the Census. There was further involvement of INSEE in census organization and preparation. Data was evaluated by comparison with vital statistics and other documentation.

Publication Plan. France. INSEE. *Saint Pierre et Miquelon. Recensement de la population, avril 1962.* Paris, 1962. Language of publication is French.

1967 (June 12)

Conduct and scope were almost the same as the census of 1962. There was a definite statement that the census was canvassed. Tables gave results for only St. Pierre and for Miquelon; Illes aux Marins counts were included in St. Pierre.

Definitions and Concepts. All were the same as 1962 with the exception of the following: HOUSEHOLD COMPOSITION—size and characteristics of head were the same but type changed: one person (without spouse or child); married couple alone; married couple with unmarried children; married couple with married, widowed, divorced or common-law children and, perhaps, grandchildren; common-law couple without children at home; single parent of unmarried child; single parent with married, widowed, divorced, or common-law child and, perhaps, grandchildren.

Special Elements and Features. Fertility was not taken.

Quality of the Census. Data were compared with vital statistics and other documentation.

Publication Plan. France. INSEE. *Recensement de la population du territoire de Saint-Pierre-et-Miquelon, 1967.* Paris, 1967. Language of publication is French.

1974 (Feb. 18)

This census had the same basic conduct and scope as 1967. It was taken on a *de facto* basis, but in addition to *de jure* total population there were other tables for the *de jure* population. Literacy was not taken. Whipple's Index is category I—highly accurate age data.

Publication Plan. France. INSEE. *Recensement de la population du territoire de Saint-Pierre-et-Miquelon, 1974.* Paris, 1974. Language of publication is French.

National Topic Chart

	1951	1957	1962	1967	1974
De facto	X	X	X	X	
Usual residence		X			X
Place of birth	X	X	X	X	X
Duration of residence					
Place of prev. residence					
Urban/rural					
Sex	X	X	X	X	X
Age	X	X	X	X	X
Relation to household head		X	X		X
Marital status	X	X	X	X	X
Children born alive	X	X	X		
Children living	X				
Citizenship	X	X	X	X	X
Literacy	X	X	X	X	
School enrollment					
Ed. attainment	X	X	X	X	X
Ed. qualification					
National/Ethnic origin	X	X	X	X	X
Language		X			
Religion					
Household composition		X	X	X	X
Econ. active/inactive	X	X	X	X	X
Occupation	X	X	X	X	X
Industry	X	X	X	X	X
Occupational status	X	X	X	X	X
Income					
Housing			X	X	X

United States

United States of America

CAPITAL: Washington, D.C.
STATISTICAL AGENCY: Bureau of the Census.
NATIONAL REPOSITORY: Library of Congress.
MAIN U.S. REPOSITORY: Bureau of the Census Library.

During the colonial period, at the request of the British Board of Trade, thirty-eight enumerations were taken within the various colonies, but the first federal census of the United States was carried out in 1790, only one year after the inauguration of the first president. The early censuses were administered by the Secretary of State; a permanent census office was not established until 1902.

The primary reason for the establishment of the decennial census of population was to determine electoral representation. From 1790 to 1840 the household rather than the individual was the unit of the enumeration, and only the names of the heads of the household were recorded on the schedules. The census results of 1820 contain two pages describing how the census should be taken. It can be assumed that preceding and succeeding censuses (until the establishment of a federal census office) were conducted in much the same manner.

Prior to 1870 Indians of remote areas (not taxed) were excluded from the enumerations, and the number of slaves were discounted two-fifths. The increase in the territory covered in each census will be indicated in each census entry.

1790

The first general census of population was directed by the Secretary of State, but the actual enumeration was taken under the supervision of the federal marshal of each state. The census was *de jure*, canvassed, and there were no questionnaire forms. Enumerators supplied their own paper. The law required that the totals should be posted in public places "for the inspection of all concerned." The scope included: name of the head of the household, number of persons in each household, number of free white males under sixteen years of age, free white males sixteen years and older, free white females, all other free persons, and slaves.

The enumeration covered the areas occupying the District of Columbia plus the following states: Maine, New Hampshire, Vermont, Massachusetts, Rhode Island, Delaware, Connecticut, New York, New Jersey, Pennsylvania, Mary-

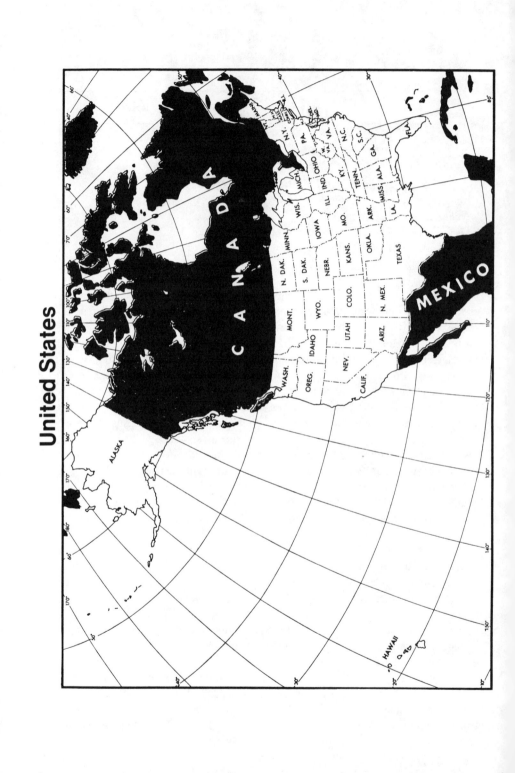

United States

land, Virginia, West Virginia, North Carolina, South Carolina, Kentucky, Tennessee, and part of Georgia. Boundaries of towns and counties were poorly defined.

1800

The second general census followed closely the organization and scope of the first one. Age data were taken in more detail for the free white persons (under ten, ten to under sixteen, sixteen to under twenty-six, twenty-six to under forty-five, forty-five and over). The enumerated territory was extended to include the states of Ohio, Indiana, Illinois, Michigan, Wisconsin, and the south central parts of the states of Alabama and Mississippi.

1810

The third general census of population was identical to 1800 in organization and scope. The territory was further extended to include the areas forming the present state of Arkansas, all but the northwestern corner of Missouri, all but the southwestern part of Louisiana, and the extreme northern parts of Alabama and Mississippi.

1820

The organization of the fourth general census was somewhat described by a letter from the Secretary of State to the marshals giving their instructions for enumerating the population. The census date was that of the start of the enumeration period, the first Monday of August 1820. The enumeration was to be concluded in six calendar months and the results sent to the Secretary of State by April 1, 1821. The marshals were to hire assistants who were residents of the county or city to which they were to be assigned. The marshals were to take care not to appoint more than one assistant to any one portion of the population to be censused and each division must not include more than one county or city. Since there were more inquiries than on the previous census, a sufficient number of assistants should be hired. Their pay was to be one dollar per 100 persons enumerated. The assistants were to direct their inquiries to the head of the family at each dwelling house, follow the order of the columns (copy supplied), each person was counted in the family where he/she resided on census day, the homeless were assigned to the residence where they were found. The actual wording of the questions was also supplied. The assistants were advised to indicate only the main sector of occupation because most persons worked in more than one. Only those who worked were to be tallied in the sector and not entire families. The results sent to the Secretary of State were to be not just aggregate totals for the state but for each subdivision (county, town, parish, ward, and so forth). It is interesting to note that all inquiries on population had to be answered to the best of the individual's knowledge or there was a fine of twenty dollars. However, when it came to situation of property and private concerns asked in the census of manufacturing establishments and products, voluntary responses were acceptable.

The fourth general census was similar in organization, but for the first time the number of persons engaged in agriculture, commerce, and manufacturing was obtained. The schedule was uniform. The scope included: name, sex, color, age, and condition of life, that is, whether head of the family, free or slave, citizen or foreigner (not naturalized). The category "free colored person" was equivalent to "all other free persons" adopted in the previous censuses. For the first time "free colored" and slaves were recorded by age and sex. A census of manufacturing establishments was also taken. An alphabetical list of manufactures was included with the forms supplied the enumerator. The southern parts of Alabama and Mississippi, the northwestern part of Georgia, and the southwestern part of Louisiana were added.

1830

The fifth general census was also *de jure*, canvassed, and uniform schedules were used. The scope was expanded. In addition to age, sex, color, condition of life and citizenship, questions about physical illness (deaf and dumb, blind) were asked. Age was recorded in even more detailed groups. The census of manufactures was dropped. The territory covered by the census now included the state of Florida.

1840

The sixth general census followed a similar organization as the 1830 but a temporary centralized census office was established. The scope was considerably enlarged to include questions about insane and idiotic persons in public and private charge; number of schools, universities, and colleges; number of scholars; number of students; literacy for adult whites; number of pensioners from revolutionary or military services; and industry. The enumerated territory added the state of Iowa, northeastern Minnesota, and the remaining part of Missouri.

1850

In the seventh decennial census the following changes were introduced: six schedules were adopted (free inhabitants, slave inhabitants, mortality, agriculture, manufacture, and social statistics), the marshals were responsible for the subdivision of districts into counties, townships, or wards, the number of population inquiries was expanded, the name of each person was listed (not just that of the household head), and all topics were taken of each individual enumerated. The schedules included: relationship to head of household; number of children living away from parents; years of residence; age; sex; color; occupation; value of estate owned; place of birth; marital status; married within the year; school attendance; literacy; citizenship; whether confined to bed by illness and for how long; whether deaf, dumb, blind, insane, idiotic, pauper, receiving public relief, pensioner, or convict; and whether fugitive or manumitted slave.

The following states were added to the territory previously covered by the census: Texas, Utah, Washington, Oregon, California, and most of New Mexico.

1860

The eighth decennial census followed the same organization as used by the previous one, and the scope was identical except that a question about value of personal property was included. The area covered by the census included almost entirely the present extension of the continental United States, except for Oklahoma, which was first enumerated in 1890.

1870

The ninth census used the same organization and scope adopted in the previous census. However, in keeping with the abolition of slavery, there was no longer a distinction made between free and slave populations. One population schedule was used with supplemental schedules for mortality, agriculture, manufactures, and social statistics. No change occurred in the territory covered by the census. "So much information was collected that some of it could not be published before the next census was due. In addition, hand tallying and lack of any procedure for verification led to many errors."

1880

The tenth general census presented the following innovations: establishment of a census office in the Department of Interior and the appointment of a superintendent of the census for the duration of the census, enumerators and supervisors were used in place of marshals, and confidentiality of census information was imposed by law. The census continued to be *de jure* and the canvasser method was used. In addition to the population schedule and the supplemental schedules, special schedules were used for the enumeration of Indians. In general, the scope was only slightly expanded over that of 1870, but much greater detail was obtained for many of the items. For the first time Alaska was included in the federal decennial census. Citizenship was dropped.

1890

The eleventh census introduced the following innovations: data on farm and home mortgages as well as indebtedness of private corporations and individuals were collected in supplemental surveys, separate schedules were used for each family, punched cards and electric machine tabulation were used for processing information. The number of types of schedules used was the same, but the scope was expanded, and some subjects were covered in greater detail than before. The following items were included: name of the street, house number, name of each person, color, age, sex, relationship to head of family, marital status, occupation, duration of unemployment, health (the disabled, blind, deaf, dumb, idiotic, insane, crippled), school attendance, literacy, place of birth and parents' place of birth, year of immigration, language, number of children living, number of children ever born alive, farm residence, and whether wife or widow of veteran. Citizenship was reinstated.

The Indian territory and Oklahoma territory (later the state) and other Indian reservations were also covered by the census.

1900

The twelfth census was the last to be conducted by the temporary census office. The organization and scope were similar to 1890 with minor changes. Four major areas of inquiries were part of the census: population, mortality, products of agriculture and of manufacturing, and mechanical establishments. Special schedules were used to obtain information on crime, school statistics of the deaf, and persons defective in sight, hearing, or speech. A modified form of the general schedule for population was used in making the enumeration of the Indians.

The area covered by the census included the continental United States, Alaska, and Hawaii (new). The other outlying areas of the United States took their censuses separately; Puerto Rico in 1899, the Philippine Islands in 1903. Guam and American Samoa did not take a census; only an estimate of the total population was available.

1910

The permanent census office (Bureau of the Census) was established in 1902. The thirteenth census was the first to be conducted by the new organization. To improve the quality of temporary employees hired for the census operations, competitive examinations were established as the method of candidate selection. The publication of census results was also improved; data in the greatest demand were released six months to a year before the final reports. Mechanized card punching substituted for the previous hand operated models. The census was *de jure*, and canvassing was the method used on a general population schedule. A slightly modified schedule was used in Hawaii and Puerto Rico and a special schedule was used for Indians. The scope included: name, relationship to head of family, color, sex, age, marital status, place of birth, parents' place of birth, number of years in the country, citizenship, occupation, occupational status, industry, whether employed at the date of enumeration, months of unemployment in the preceding year, school attendance, literacy, ownership of home, whether or not a surviver of the Union or Confederate army or navy, language, name and address of those with infirmities, and fertility. Supplemental schedules were used for paupers, juvenile delinquents, prisoners, the insane in hospitals, and the feebleminded.

The census covered the continental United States, Alaska, Hawaii, and Puerto Rico. The other outlying possessions were not enumerated in the same year.

1920

The organization and scope of the fourteenth decennial census was similar to the previous one; but fertility, veteran status, and time of unemployment were dropped from the schedule. The censuses of agriculture, manufactures, and mines and quarries were still being conducted simultaneously with that of population. Supplemental schedules recorded data on blind and deaf and mutes. More sophisticated equipment was used for mechanized quality control.

The census covered the continental United States, Alaska, Hawaii and Puerto Rico; and for the first time, Guam, American Samoa, and the Panama Canal Zone were canvassed simultaneously with the other outlying areas. The census of the Virgin Islands was a special one conducted by the Bureau of the Census in 1917, and the Philippine Islands carried out their own census in 1918.

1930

The organization and scope of the fifteenth decennial census was similar to the 1920 census, but age at first marriage and veteran status were revived, and more details were recorded on employment. The census of manufactures was taken separately, but the censuses of agriculture and mines and quarries were still being taken simultaneously with population. In addition to the general population schedule, a special schedule on unemployment was introduced to collect data from all persons who usually worked at a gainful occupation but were out of work the day before the enumeration, persons able to work and looking for a job, and persons having a job but on leave without pay (excluding the sick or voluntary idle). Supplemental schedules for the blind and the deaf-mute as well as for the Indian population were supplied.

The census covered the continental United States, Alaska, Hawaii, American Samoa, Guam, Panama Canal Zone, and Puerto Rico. The Virgin Islands were enumerated for the first time with the regular decennial census. The figures for the Philippine Islands were an estimate based on the 1918 census. The statistics of the outlying territories were published separately, and very little was done to adapt topics and issues to their condition.

1940

The sixteenth decennial census of population was, in many ways, the basis for the contemporary U.S. census. Although general schedules were still used, the following changes were introduced: the use of scientific sampling techniques that were previously tried experimentally, and the inclusion of a census of housing. The use of sampling increased the possibility of obtaining more information with reduced cost and burden on the respondents. It also accelerated the publication of preliminary results, increased the number of detailed tables published, and helped in processing the data more efficiently.

The territory covered by the census was the same as in 1930. The enumeration of Alaska was taken in October 1939, and the census of the Philippine Islands was taken by its own government in 1939.

The scope of the census included home ownership, tenure, value of home, and whether or not residing on a farm (household data). Personal data included the following: name, relationship to head of household, sex, color or race, age, marital status, school attendance, educational attainment, place of birth, parents' place of birth, native language, veteran status, citizenship, place of residence in the previous year, urban/rural, economic activity, employment, occupation, industry, occupational status, number of hours worked, duration of unemployment, number of weeks worked, and wages and income. Social Security status, usual occupation, usual industry, and usual occupational status were supplementary questions asked of all persons fourteen years of age and over. For all women ever married, the number of marriages, age at first marriage, and number of children ever born were also recorded.

1950 (April 1)

The seventeenth decennial census of population, conducted by the Bureau of the Census, was *de jure*, and canvassing was the method used on general population and housing schedules and agriculture questionnaires. Individual schedules were available on request. A field test was conducted before the census to measure the applicability of the questionnaires and the public's reaction to them. Agriculture surveys and a survey of residential financing were realized simultaneously with the census. The extensive use of sampling in the 1950 census provided lower costs, less burden on respondents, and the quick release of information. Two sample sizes (20 percent and 3 1/3 percent) were used in the population census. For the first time sampling was used in the housing census. Tabulations were computerized (new) and a postenumeration survey was conducted. The territory covered by the census included: the continental United States, the territories of Alaska and Hawaii, and the outlying possessions of American Samoa, Guam, Puerto Rico, Virgin Islands, Panama Canal Zone, and the Trust Territory of the Pacific Islands. (All the outlying areas have entries of their own; see individual entry for other than decennial censuses.) The Philippine Islands became an independent country in 1946 and were not covered in this census. The smallest areas for which there are published results are census tracts (population) and blocks (housing) for cities of 50,000 and more inhabitants.

Definitions and Concepts. URBAN—places of 2,500 inhabitants that were incorporated as cities, boroughs, towns, and villages; the densely settled urban fringe (including both incorporated and unincorporated areas) around cities of 50,000 or more inhabitants; and unincorporated places of 2,500 or more not in an urban fringe. PLACES—a concentration of population, regardless of the existence of legally prescribed limits, powers, or functions. URBANIZED AREAS—closely settled urban fringe around cities with 50,000 or more. STANDARD METROPOLITAN AREAS—a county or group of contiguous counties (towns and cities in New England) that contain at least one city of 50,000 inhabitants and are socially and economically tied to that city. SMAs and urbanized areas were established to distinguish urban from rural populations in the vicinity of large cities. These areas are subdivided by census tract (population) and block (housing). AGE—as of last birthday in completed years; for children under one year, the month of birth. Tabulated in single years and standard five-year age groups, with median age. RACE—determined by observation. Categories included: white, Negro, American Indian, Japanese, Chinese, and Filipino. Persons with mixed white and nonwhite parents were given the race of the nonwhite parent. If both parents were nonwhite, the race of the father was recorded. White persons with a Spanish surname identified persons of Spanish American and Mexican American origin, but this procedure was limited to the five southwestern states. FAMILY—two or more persons related by blood, marriage, or adoption and living in the same household. HOUSEHOLD—concept based on living arrangements included all persons who occupy a house, apartment, or group of rooms that constitute a dwelling unit. MARITAL STATUS—asked of persons fourteen years of age and older. Categories were related to current marital status: married, widowed, divorced, separated, and never married. Number of times married and duration of marriage were also recorded. PLACE OF BIRTH—name of state, territory, possession, or foreign country was recorded. Canadians were subdivided into Canada-French and Canada-other. Parents' birthplace was also taken. CITIZENSHIP—persons born in a foreign country were classified as naturalized or not. Initials AP were given to persons born abroad of American parents. PLACE OF RESIDENCE—name of county, state, or foreign country were recorded. Place of residence one year before the census (1949), whether living on a farm or living in the same county was also asked. EDUCATION—school attendance (persons aged five to twenty-nine), educational attainment (highest grade and whether finished or not), and educational qualification. ECONOMIC ACTIVITY—reference period was the week before the census. Questions were about current employment status, hours worked during the week, type of job held, duration of unemployment, extent of employment during the preceding year, and income were asked of all persons age fourteen and over. The economically active were those included in the labor force: persons at work, unemployed looking for a job, persons with a job but temporarily absent from it, unpaid family workers (who worked fifteen hours or more per week), and members of the armed forces. Not in the labor force (the economically inactive) were the homemakers, invalids, inmates of institutions, students, the retired, the voluntarily idle, and seasonal workers for whom the census week fell in an off season and so were not reported as unemployed. OCCUPATION—The U.S. classification used is similar to ISCO, organized in twelve major groups and 270 specific occupational categories. Thirteen of these categories were further subdivided to make a total of 469 units (three-digits). A condensed or intermediate classification was used in cross-classification tables. INDUSTRY—The U.S. classification is similar to ISIC, organized into thirteen major groups and a total of 148 categories (three-digits). When industry was cross-classified an intermediate classification of seventy-seven industries was used. NOTE: For counties and small urban places, only major occupation groups and condensed industrial classifications were shown. OCCUPATIONAL STATUS—private wage and salary worker, government worker, self-employed, and unpaid family worker were the categories presented. INCOME—annual income of 1949 earned in wages and salaries; from business, professional practice, or farm; or received from interest, dividends, allowances, pensions, rents, and so forth was recorded. The information was obtained by sample enumeration. If the sample was the head of the household, the income of the family group was also recorded. FERTILITY—number of children ever born alive was asked of all females ever married.

Special Elements and Features. Sampling was used for some housing topics (new). Other features are tables of urban and rural population under new and old definitions, rank of the states under the new and old urban definitions, rank of the states by percent of urban population from 1900 to 1950, a very detailed explanation of territorial divisions, and population of all territorial divisions in alphabetical order by states. Subject reports coordinate data on topics for the United States as a whole, regions and, occasionally, states. Maps, graphs, facsimiles of schedules, and an extensive analysis of census operations were included. Census tracts and block statistics are available.

Quality of the Census. Whipple's Index classified age data into category II—fairly accurate data. The postenumeration survey indicated a total net underenumeration of 1.4 percent. The percent of underenumeration and inaccuracy of age in the group under ten years of age was 4.3. Several devices were used to improve completeness of coverage such as the use of infant cards, missed-person forms published in the newspaper, and a longer training period for enumerators. The postenumeration survey also indicated that the underenumeration was greater in rural than in urban areas and that errors were greater in the enumeration of nonwhite than in the white population.

Publication Plan. U.S. Bureau of the Census. *Census of Population: 1950. A Report of the Seventeenth Decennial Census of the United States.* Washington, D.C., 1952-1957. Volumes for the United States, each state, and territories and possessions; census tract volumes; special reports, and numerous publications on organization, methods, and evaluation. Language of publication is English. One or two items on Puerto Rico are in Spanish.

1960 (April 1)

The eighteenth census of population was also taken with the census of housing. Conducted by the Bureau of the Census, the enumeration was *de jure* with special provision for the counting of persons living overseas. For the first time, self-enumeration was used extensively for the collection of data. "Advance census report" (short form) and household questionnaires were used. The census was taken in two stages; first, the short form was distributed (ten days before the census date), which contained five items to be answered by all persons, then the same household schedule was distributed to 25 percent of the urban population. Most of the questionnaires were to be returned by mail. Tabulation was computerized with the data first being transcribed to special FOSDIC schedules. SMSA data are available in census tracts (population) and blocks (housing).

The territory covered by the census included the fifty states (Alaska and Hawaii attained statehood in 1959), the District of Columbia, the Commonwealth of Puerto Rico, American Samoa, Panama Canal Zone, Guam, and Virgin Islands. The Trust Territory of the Pacific Islands conducted a census in 1958. Guam and the Virgin Islands took a census of agriculture simultaneously with that of population and housing. A standard household schedule was used in these two outlying areas, and all the questions were asked on a 100 percent basis. Tabulation was on punched cards rather than the FOSDIC schedules.

Definitions and Concepts. URBAN, URBANIZED AREAS, FAMILY, HOUSEHOLD, and FERTILITY were the same as 1950. SMSAs—one county or a group of counties containing at least one city (or twin cities) having 50,000 inhabitants or more that were metropolitan in character and economically and socially integrated with the central city. AGE—date of birth asked (first time since 1900). Tabulated in single years and standard five-year age groups. RACE (color)—refers to two groups: white and nonwhite. The nonwhite were further classified as Negro, American Indian, Japanese, Chinese, Filipino, Hawaiian, part Hawaiian, Aleut, Eskimo, and others. Puerto Ricans, Mexicans and other persons of Latin America were classified as white unless they were descendents of Indian or other nonwhite races. MARITAL STATUS—the categories were the same as 1950. The number of times married and date or dates of first and subsequent marriages were also recorded. PLACE OF BIRTH—basically the same as 1950 but no distinction was made about Canadians (French or other) nor the Irish (Northern Ireland or Irish Republic). Parents' birthplace continued to be recorded. CITIZENSHIP—only recorded in New York and Puerto Rico on 100 percent basis. LANGUAGE—mother tongue of the foreign born. DURATION OF RESIDENCE—date the person moved into the present residence, place of residence five years before the census (whether in different city, county, state, foreign country or U.S. possession). EDUCATION—asked of all persons five years and older: school enrollment (private or public school) and educational attainment (highest grade attended and completed). ECONOMIC ACTIVITY—asked of all persons fourteen years of age and older. Occupational status was dependent on the person's activity during the week prior to the census. The following were included in the civilian labor force: persons at work (worked for pay or profit for one or more hours during the reference week or worked for fifteen hours or more as unpaid family worker), persons with a job but not at work, and those who were unemployed and looking for work. Members of the armed forces plus the civilian labor force constituted the total labor force. Not in the labor force were the following: students, homemakers, the retired, seasonal workers in an off season, inmates of institutions, and persons who could not work because of long term physical or mental illness. The number of weeks worked; number of hours worked during the reference week; year last worked; name of the company, business, organization; and journey to work (place and means of transportation) were also recorded. OCCUPATION—The U.S. classification scheme is similar to ISCO, eleven major groups (including not reported) and 297 specific categories. Thirteen of these categories were further subdivided to make a total of 516 items (three-digits). INDUSTRY—U.S. classification used was similar to ISIC, twelve major groups plus a not reported category. The major groups were further subdivided into 149 items (three-digit). Both occupation and industry were given in nondetailed versions when required. OCCUPATIONAL STATUS—categories were: private wage and salary worker, government worker, self-employed, and unpaid family worker. INCOME—basically the same as 1950, but separate data was also obtained for each person of the family who was fourteen years of age or older.

Special Elements and Features. This was the first census to use the mails extensively to collect the population and housing data contained on the sample questionnaire (FOSDIC readable). There were twenty-eight subject reports and five special area reports published. The special report on Spanish surname population contained the only data in printed form for small areas in the five southwestern states. Supplementary reports provided miscellaneous types of data.

Quality of the Census. Whipple's Index classified age data in category I—highly accurate. For the first time in a major U.S. census, a formal program of quality control was established. A postenumeration survey was carried out with the following findings: omissions of persons was 3.0 percent, erroneous inclusions of persons was 1.3 percent, net underenumeration of persons was 1.7 percent. In general, the weakness detected in the 1950 postenumeration survey was avoided in 1960. The more extensive use of sampling cut the quantity of coding work, and the use of the advance census report form reduced the errors of coverage. Pretests and special censuses were carried out in several states in order to test the cost and effectiveness of field operations, the use of machine-readable questionnaires, the methods implemented to improve coverage, applicability of the questionnaire, and the use of the sample (long form) questionnaire.

Publication Plan. U.S. Bureau of the Census. *Census of Population: 1960. The Eighteenth Decennial Census of the United States.* Washington, D.C., 1961-1968. In addition to the main volumes for each state, there were advanced reports, subject reports, selected area reports, census tract volumes, five census monographs, and numerous support volumes (geographic divisions and codes, indexes of occupation and industry, procedural history, and evaluation reports). Unpublished data and computer tapes are available. Language of publication is English.

1970 (April 1)

The nineteenth decennial census was *de jure* and mostly self-enumerated (mail-out/mail-back); some of the rural areas employed canvassers for the additional sample questions. Three kinds of household questionnaires were used: the short form (100 percent) distributed to 80 out of 100 housing units; the second form was distributed to another 15 percent of the population and contained both 100 percent, 20 percent, and 15 percent sample items; the last was distributed to the remaining 5 percent of the population and contained 100 percent, 20 percent, and 5 percent sample items. Sixty percent of the population (in large metropolitan areas) received and returned their questionnaires by mail; the remainder (in smaller towns and rural areas) received their form by mail but enumerators visited each household to collect them. The tabulation was computerized, and the questionnaires themselves were in FOSDIC form; there was no need for transcription.

The territory covered by this census included: the fifty states, the District of Columbia, Puerto Rico, American Samoa, Panama Canal Zone, Guam, Virgin Islands, and the Trust Territory of the Pacific Islands plus other small areas under the jurisdiction of the United States. SMSA data are available in census tracts (population) and blocks (housing).

The Virgin Islands and Guam had population and housing censuses taken simultaneously with agriculture. FOSDIC readable schedules were used here for the first time, but there were no sample questions and the scope differed from that used in the continental United States.

Definitions and Concepts. HOUSEHOLD, FAMILY, URBAN, SMSA, MARITAL STATUS and AGE were the same as in 1960. RACE—the categories were basically the same as 1960; Korean was a new group presented and Negro was changed to Negro or black. The latter included all persons who identified themselves as such as well as those who entered themselves as Jamaican, Trinidadian, West Indian, Haitian, and Ethiopian. American Indians were asked to give the name of the tribe. Mexicans, Puerto Ricans, and Indo-Europeans who did not classify themselves in one of the other categories were included in the group of whites. Persons of mixed parentage, in doubt of their classification, were asked to give the race of their father. PLACE OF BIRTH—name of the state or foreign country was recorded. Ireland and Northern Ireland were distinguished. Persons born in Great Britain were asked to specify whether born in England, Wales, or Scotland. For persons born in the West Indies or the Caribbean, the specification of the island or country was necessary. Parents' place of birth was also recorded. ETHNIC ORIGIN—This question appeared for the first time. It was designed to obtain information primarily from persons of Spanish heritage (Mexican, Puerto Rican, Cuban, Central and South American, and other Spanish). For the five southwestern states questionnaires were coded according to Spanish surname. CITIZENSHIP (reinstated)—categories were: naturalized, alien, and born abroad of American parents. Year of immigration was also recorded. LANGUAGE— the language other than English that was spoken at home. DURATION OF RESIDENCE—year moved into present residence and residence five years before the census (1965); if different, the name of the city, county, state, foreign country, or U.S. possession was recorded. EDUCATION—school enrollment and educational attainment (years completed). Data was collected from all persons three years of age and over. FERTILITY—the question, number of children ever born alive, was the same as 1960; however, it was asked of all women regardless of marital status. VOCATIONAL TRAINING (new)—in the following fields: business, office work, nursing or health fields, trades and crafts, engineering or science technician and draftsman, agriculture or home economics, or other field. WORK DISABILITY (new)—whether disability kept respondent from holding any kind of job, limited the kind or amount of work, and for how long a person had been limited in his ability to work were recorded. ECO-NOMIC ACTIVITY—asked of all persons age fourteen and over; however, most tables are for those sixteen and over. The reference period was the week before the census. Included in the civilian labor force were employed persons (at work, and with job but not at work) and unemployed (looking for a job in the past four weeks and available to accept job). Unemployed who had worked before were classified as experienced. Total labor force includes civilian labor force plus members of the U.S. armed forces. Not in the labor force were students, homemakers, the retired, seasonal workers during off season, inmates of institutions, the disabled, and unpaid family workers who worked less than fifteen hours during the reference week. Number of weeks worked, number of hours worked, reasons for being temporarily absent from job, place of work (complete address), means of transportation, year last worked, and work activity five years before the census were also asked. OCCUPATION—The U.S. classification presented twelve major groups instead of eleven as in 1960. The categories included in the new major group (transport equipment operatives) were split from the original group thus maintaining comparability. The major groups were subdivided into 441 categories and were arranged in four major divisions: white collar, blue collar, farm workers, and service workers. INDUSTRY—the U.S. classification consisted of twelve major groups divided into 227 subgroups. The establishment of smaller (more homogeneous) groups was responsible for the additional seventy-seven categories. The category "not reported" was eliminated. OCCUPATIONAL STATUS—private wage and salary worker, government worker, self-employed (incorporated or unincorporated), and unpaid family worker. Occupation, industry, and occupational status five years before the census were also asked. INCOME—earnings in 1969 from wages, salaries, commissions, bonus or tips, self-employment income (farm and nonfarm), and income other than earnings (Social Security, public welfare, and all other sources) were recorded.

Special Elements and Features. The number of reports presented in 1970 was basically the same as 1960, but there were more cross-tabulations for smaller geographical areas. The following topics were added to the questionnaires: vocational training completed, occupation and industry in 1965, year of immigration, disability, and Spanish origin and descent. The question about place of work was expanded to include street address. This was the first time that poverty status data were included in a decennial census report.

Quality of the Census. Whipple's Index classified age data into category I—highly accurate data. The mail-out/mail-back system, questionnaires and instruction sheets in other languages (Spanish and Chinese), and an information program employing public media and community educators contributed to the accuracy of reponses. A postenumeration post office check (PEPOC), a vacancy recheck, and missing persons campaigns were used to improve coverage. On the basis of demographic analysis, which included comparison of the census counts with estimates of expected population, the net underenumeration in 1970 was

2.5 percent. Mechanical and manual techniques were applied to the editing of unacceptable data, for example, omissions and inconsistencies.

Publication Plan. U.S. Bureau of the Census. *Census of Population: 1970.* Washington, D.C., 1972-1975. Volumes for each state, U.S. summary, subject reports (40), census tract volumes, general demographic trends for metropolitan areas, employment profiles of selected low-income areas, support publications (indexes of occupations and industries, evaluation series, procedural history, data collection forms and procedures, geographic identification code schemes) are the sets published. Unpublished data and computer tapes are available. Language of publication is English.

1980 (April 1)

The twentieth general census of population was conducted by the Bureau of the Census simultaneously with a census of housing.The census was *de jure* and self-enumeration (mail-out/mail-back) was the method used to record information on household questionnaires. Two types of schedules were used: a short form with the 100 percent or complete count items was distributed to 78 percent of the households; and a long form, containing the same questions plus an additional twenty housing and twenty-six population questions, was distributed to the remaining 22 percent of the population. The tabulation was computerized and the questionnaires were FOSDIC readable.

The territory covered by the census was divided into regions and states (including the District of Columbia, Puerto Rico and the outlying areas) and subdivided into counties, metropolitan areas, cities, towns, and other minor civil divisions. All metropolitan areas were subdivided into census tracts (population) and block (housing). Enumeration district data, as in 1970, does not appear in printed publications.

Definitions and Concepts. HOUSEHOLD—the concept was the same as 1970, only the term "head of the household" was dropped in favor of "person in column one" in whose name the home is owned or rented. If none fit that category, any adult member was named. RACE—the word "race" was dropped; the categories are a mix of race and ethnicity. For the first time, all persons were asked a question on Spanish origin. AGE, EDUCATION, VETERAN STATUS, PREVIOUS RESIDENCE, and FERTILITY are the same as 1970. MARITAL STATUS—the same as 1970 plus number of marriages, date of first marriage (and present), and whether married more than once because of spouse's death. PLACE OF BIRTH—name of the state or foreign country of birth. A question on ancestry replaced parents' place of birth (asked in 1970). CITIZENSHIP—same as 1970. LANGUAGE—ability to speak English was added to the inquiry on the language other than English spoken at home. DISABILITY—the scope was expanded to include persons of all ages (not just those under sixty-five) in order to determine those who are limited or prevented from use of public transportation as well as work. ECONOMIC ACTIVITY—asked of all persons sixteen and over; the same questions as used in 1970. Questions related to journey to work were expanded (travel time, carpooling). Questions to measure extent of unemployment and part-time workers were new. INCOME—total income rather than just earnings; sources were classified separately.

Special Elements and Features. The 1980 schedules were only two instead of three. The following were excluded from the questionnaire: parents' place of birth; mother tongue; vocational training; industry, occupation and occupational status in 1975. At this time only the advance final results have been published; there may be more features when publication is complete.

Quality of the Census. Since the beginning of 1975, the Bureau of the Census conducted numerous tests. Several were national tests of the content of the questionnaires; several were tests of enumeration methods to find the best way to distribute and collect questionnaires and to improve coverage. Four small scale censuses were taken. Finally, three dress rehearsals were taken to test and evaluate every detail of the census plans.

Publication Plan. It is uncertain until the sets of reports appear as to what form they will take, printed, microfilm or fiche, and/or computer tapes. Preliminary and advance final reports have been issued for all states and territories.

OTHER STATISTICAL PUBLICATIONS: Issued by the Bureau of the Census, *County and City Data Book* (quinquennially), *Current Population Reports* (irregularly but often), *Pocket Data Book* (biennially), *Statistical Abstract of the U.S.* (annually), *Historical Statistics of the U.S.* (irregularly), and many more issued by other agencies as well as the Bureau of the Census.

National Topic Chart

	1950	1960	1970	1980
De facto				
Usual residence	X	X	X	X
Place of birth	X	X	X	X
Duration of residence	X	X	X	X
Place of prev. residence	X	X	X	X
Urban/rural	X	X	X	X
Sex	X	X	X	X
Age	X	X	X	X
Relation to household head	X	X	X	X
Marital status	X	X	X	X
Children born alive	X	X	X	X
Children living				
Citizenship	X	X	X	X
Literacy				
School enrollment	X	X	X	X
Ed. attainment	X	X	X	X
Ed. qualification				
National/Ethnic origin	X	X	X	X
Language		X	X	X
Religion				
Household composition	X	X	X	X
Econ. active/inactive	X	X	X	X
Occupation	X	X	X	X
Industry	X	X	X	X
Occupational status	X	X	X	X
Income	X	X	X	X
Housing	X	X	X	X

OCEANIA

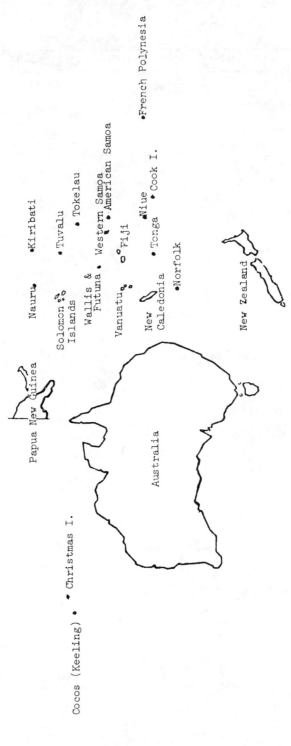

Hawaii

Guam Pacific Islands

Kiribati

Nauru

Tuvalu Tokelau

Western Samoa
American Samoa
Wallis &
Futuna
Fiji
Niue
Vanuatu Tonga Cook I.

Solomon
Islands

New
Caledonia Norfolk

French Polynesia

Papua New Guinea

Australia

New Zealand

Cocos (Keeling) Christmas I.

OCEANIA

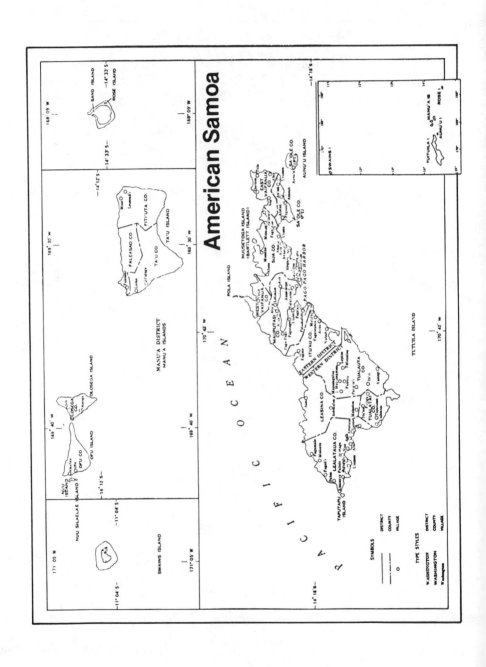

American Samoa

American Samoa

American Samoa (unorganized unincorporated territory, U.S.)

CAPITAL: Pago Pago.
STATISTICAL AGENCY: Development Planning Office and U.S. Bureau of
the Census.
NATIONAL REPOSITORY: U.S. Bureau of the Census Library.
MAIN U.S. REPOSITORY: Same.

Since 1722 the Samoan Islands have been visited by several European expedi-
tions. In 1830, coincident to the arrival of the pioneer missionaries of the London
Mission Society, the natives suffered their first epidemic of influenza. The
epidemic was repeated throughout the nineteenth century, decimating great parts
of the population.

American Samoa was acquired by the U.S. government according to a treaty
with United Kingdom and Germany, signed in 1899. Its territory consisted of six
islands of the Samoan group—Tutuila, Aunuu, Manu'a (Ofu, Olosega and Ta'u),
and Rose. The first two islands and Rose were ceded in 1900, and Manu'a
Islands in 1904. Later in 1925, the Swain Islands were incorporated.

A brief account of the extended family ("Matai") system in Samoa (both
American and former Western) is of fundamental importance for the understanding of its society and its economic activities. A "matai" is the head of the "aiga"
(extended family), which is the basic unit of the social system in Samoa. The
family supports the "matai" in all social and economic matters concerning the
"aiga." In return, the "matai" is responsible for providing leadership and direction to his people as well as the distribution of the "aiga" revenue necessary for
the members' subsistence. The "matai" has the rights to certain land (customary
land). The electoral system of the country is closely tied to the "matai" system.
For census purposes, persons who are under a "matai" are asked the district
where their "maiai's" title is registered, and if the head of the family has more
than one "matai" title, the village of the title he intends to use in the election is
recorded.

Local censuses were taken since 1900, and in 1922 a general report sent by the
governor to the U.S. Secretary of the Navy published the following results: total
population by administrative districts for 1900, 1901, 1903, and 1908; popula-

tion by sex for administrative districts and villages for 1912, and total population of Tutuila and Manu'a Islands by sex.

From 1920 to 1980 the population of American Samoa was enumerated in conjunction with the regular decennial census of population of the United States. In 1956 a census was taken under the New Zealand administration and, in 1974, a special census was taken by the Development Planning Office of the local government. The local census office is not permanent.

1920

First census of population taken under the supervision of the U.S. Bureau of the Census in conjunction with the fourteenth decennial census. The population was enumerated on a *de jure* basis, and canvasser was the method utilized to record information on general schedules. The territory covered by the census included the six islands, divided into districts, counties, and villages. The island of Rose was uninhabited. The scope included age, sex, race, literacy, school attendance, ability to speak English, marital status, and occupations. Comments on living conditions and agriculture were included.

1930

Census of population taken in conjunction with the fifteenth decennial census of the United States simultaneously with a census of agriculture. The organization was basically the same, but at this time the population of the Swain Islands was also part of the census. Scope was the same as 1920 plus a question on nativity.

1940

Census taken along with the sixteenth decennial census of the United States, and organization, methods, and territorial divisions were virtually the same as 1930. The scope was the same as 1930, but family relationship and place of birth were added. In American Samoa, the head of each social group or family is a "matai" literally translated as master. This is particularly relevant for the understanding of the family relationship and their economic and political activities.

1950 (April 1)

The census of population was taken in conjunction with the seventeenth decennial census of the United States. The population was enumerated on a *de jure* basis; however, persons in the armed forces, college students, and inmates of institutions were enumerated as residents of the places where their installations were located. Canvasser was the method used to gather information on general schedules. The territory covered by the census was divided into four districts and subdivided into islands, counties, and villages. The tabulation was mechanical.

Definitions and Concepts. AGE—as of last birthday in completed years. When age was not reported, it was estimated on the basis of related information. Tabulated in standard five-year age groups and median age. RACE—followed the concept accepted by the general public, did not necessarily reflect biological differences, and in many cases referred to nationalities. Groups recorded: Polynesian, part-Polynesian, white, and other (Chinese, Japanese, Korean, and blacks). NATIVITY—two major groups: native (persons born in the United States or any of its territories and possessions, including those who, although born in a foreign country were of American parentage); and foreign born. PLACE OF BIRTH—country of birth and if native whether born in the United States, other territory or possessions, or American Samoa. HOUSEHOLD—all persons, related or not by blood, who occupy a house or other room that constitutes a dwelling unit. Dwelling unit is the basic unit of enumeration. The group quarters were constituted by all persons living in quasi households not classified as dwelling units. MARITAL STATUS—categories were: single, married (legal or common law), widowed, or divorced. Married couples were classified as "with own household," if the husband was the head of the household. LANGUAGE—ability to speak English. EDUCATION—school enrollment (age coverage from five to twenty-four), educational attainment (highest degree completed), recorded for the first time. ECONOMIC ACTIVITY—the population was divided into those who worked as civilians in 1949 (for pay or profit or unpaid family worker, full- or part-time), those who were in the armed forces in 1949, and others (persons not included in the previous categories or persons for whom information was not obtained, primarily homemakers, students, retired, invalids, and inmates of institutions). The age limit was fourteen years or older. OCCUPATION—classification based on the U.S. Classified Index of Occupations and Industries, 1950. Only major groups were presented.

Special Elements and Features. The category "separated" was included in the schedule but not tabulated. Data on economic activity are not comparable with the previous census. College students were enumerated at their college residence rather than at their parental home. Literacy was dropped and educational attainment was introduced.

Quality of the Census. See the United States entry for 1950 for more details on completeness and accuracy of data. Precise allocation of occupation was not possible because of the insufficiency of specific answers.

Publication Plan. U.S. Bureau of the Census. *Census of Population: 1950.* Volume 2, *Characteristics of the Population.* Parts 51-54. *Territories and Possessions.* Washington, D.C., 1953. Language of publication is English.

1956 (September 25)

Unlike 1950, this census of population was conducted by the New Zealand administration in conjunction with Western Samoa and other New Zealand island territories. The census was taken on a *de facto* basis, and canvasser was the method used to record information on household schedules. Tabulation was manual. The entries of the schedules were made in Samoan language for outer districts and optionally in English for urban areas (Western Samoa mainly).

No special details were given for American Samoa and the information that follows was gathered from the Western Samoa census and the tables for American Samoa, which were published separately.

Definitions and Concepts. AGE—date of birth. Tabulated in single years and standard five-year age groups. HOUSEHOLD—group of persons who sleep in the same house. FAMILY—the term "matai" is used to determine the head of the family. PLACE OF BIRTH—country of origin. MARITAL STATUS—the same categories as 1950. RELIGION—the following affiliations were recorded: London Missionary Society, Methodists, Roman Catholic, Latter Day Saints, Seventh Day Adventist and "object" to indicate those who did not wish to answer the question. ECONOMIC ACTIVITY—occupations presented in major groups, occupational status, and relationship to the "matai" (all shown in the same table). No inquiry was made about unemployment. FERTILITY—first time the question was recorded: the number of children living and of children dead plus the age of mother at first birth were asked.

Special Elements and Features. Fertility, mortality, and religion were recorded for the first time. Education and language were dropped.

Quality of the Census. Some difficulties, caused by the previous *de jure* type of enumeration and the large amount of migration among islands, were avoided in this *de facto* census. Although there was no specific mention about American Samoa, the age data collected by the enumerators in Western Samoa were constantly being corrected by comparison with cohorts. Unfortunately, this was not done consistently by all enumerators, thus reducing the value of the results. A two-stage enumeration was used in order to improve completeness and accuracy of the data. The census office was not permanent and the enumerators were not adequately trained in many cases.

Publication Plan. American Samoa. Governor's Office. *Census of American Samoa, September 25, 1956.* [Pago Pago, 1957]. Language of publication is English.

1960 (April 1)

The census of population was conducted in conjunction with the eighteenth decennial census of the United States. The census was *de jure*, and canvasser was the method used to record information on household schedules. The organization and processing of the data followed the same general pattern as in 1950; the differences are to be found in the content and design of the questionnaires and the increased use of machines for editing and tabulation. Territorial divisions are the five districts—Manua, Eastern Tutuila, Western Tutuila, Swains Island, and Rose Island (uninhabited).

Definitions and Concepts. PLACE OF BIRTH—same as 1950. AGE—in completed years and for the first time the date of birth. Tabulated in single years (up to twenty-one only) and standard five-year age groups. Median age was also presented. RACE and NATIVITY—same as 1950. HOUSEHOLD—same as 1950; dwelling unit changed to housing unit for enumeration. MARITAL STATUS— same as 1950 but the category "separated" was added to the tables. The presence of spouse was also recorded. FAMILY—two or more persons living in the same household, related by blood, marriage, or adoption. Family statistics are only for those living in households; therefore, couples living in group quarters were not counted. EDUCATION—School enrollment (age coverage from five to thirty-four) and educational attainment. FERTILITY—for the first time the number of children ever born alive was recorded. ECONOMIC ACTIVITY—reference period was the week before the census. Lower age limit was fourteen years. The labor force included employed and unemployed looking for a job. Not in the labor force are persons not previously classified: students, homemakers, retired workers, seasonal workers off season and not looking for a job, invalids, and inmates of institutions. Only students and inmates of institutions were shown separately. The number of weeks worked in 1959 was also recorded. Data on economic activity are comparable with the previous census except for the number of weeks worked. Although the period of reference was different in 1950, data on the number of persons who worked are generally comparable. OCCUPATION—Questions asked of employed persons only. Classification based on the U.S. Classified Index of Occupations and Industries, 1960. A condensed version was adopted in American Samoa with thirty-three groups. INDUSTRY—Classification based on U.S. CIOI, 1960 condensed version, with twenty-one major groups (new). OCCUPATIONAL STATUS—categories were private wage and salary worker, government worker, self-employed, and unpaid family worker (fifteen hours or more per week). These data were recorded for the first time. INCOME—gross income from wages and salaries; net income from own business, professional practice, partnership or farm and any other kind of income (Social Security, pensions, insurance, rents, and so forth). Questions were asked of all persons fourteen years of age and older (new).

Special Elements and Features. The concept of the housing unit was introduced in substitution for dwelling unit. For the first time the census included the following questions: children ever born, industry, occupational status, occupation for employed persons, weeks worked, and income. Educational attainment referred to last grade attended and last degree completed. Language question was dropped.

Quality of the Census. A more reliable coding and editing system was applied and the use of machines was intensified to correct inconsistencies and unacceptable data. See United States entry for 1960 with general comments about coverage and accuracy of data.

Publication Plan. U.S. Bureau of the Census. *Census of Population: 1960.* Volume 1, *Characteristics of the Population.* Parts 54-57, *Outlying Areas.* Washington, D.C., 1963. Computer tapes are available. Language of publication is English.

1970 (April 1)

The census of population was conducted in conjunction with the nineteenth decennial census of the United States. The censuses of housing and agriculture were conducted simultaneously with the census of population.

The population was enumerated on a *de jure* basis, and canvasser was the method used to record information on a single household questionnaire. FOSDIC (machine readable) questionnaire was used for the first time. Like 1950 and 1960, an individual questionnaire was utilized to enumerate persons living in hotels and group quarters. Sampling was not used in American Samoa.

Although the census date was April 1, in most of the outlying areas enumeration was delayed from one to three weeks. Computerized tabulation. No changes in territorial division have occurred.

Definitions and Concepts. AGE, HOUSEHOLD, FAMILY, FERTILITY and EDUCATION—same as 1960. A question on vocational training was added for the first time. MARITAL STATUS—categories were: never married, now married, consensually married, widowed, divorced, and separated. The category "separated" included legally or otherwise absent from spouse. PLACE OF BIRTH—same as 1950 and 1960. CITIZENSHIP—whether naturalized, permanent alien, temporary alien, and born abroad of American parents. PLACE OF RESIDENCE—usual place and for the first time residence in 1965. In addition, it was asked whether the person had voting, legal, or other residence in the United States. VETERAN STATUS—for the first time recorded: whether served in the armed forces and during what war. ECONOMIC ACTIVITY—reference period was the week before the census. Lower age limit was sixteen years. The labor force included all persons classified as employed (at work, and with job but not at work), and unemployed (looking for job during the past four weeks, and available to accept a job). Unemployed persons who had worked at any time in the past were classified as experienced unemployed. Not in the labor force consisted mainly of students, homemakers, retired workers, seasonal workers in off season and not looking for a job, inmates of institutions, disabled persons, and persons doing only incidental unpaid family work (less than fifteen hours during the reference week). The number of weeks worked was also recorded. OCCUPATION—main occupation or last occupation if unemployed. Classification based on Classified Index of Industries and Occupations but presented in a reduced form—thirty-two occupational groups (two-digits). INDUSTRY—classification based on CIIO, presented in reduced format—forty industry groups (two-digits). OCCUPATIONAL STATUS—categories were private wage and salary worker, government worker, self-employed, and unpaid family worker. INCOME—from earnings (wage, salary, commissions, and so forth, own nonfarm business, professional practice or partnership; and own farm income), income from other than earnings (Social Security, retirement, welfare), income from other sources.

Special Elements and Features. Race was dropped; nativity was replaced by citizenship; place of previous residence for the first time was recorded, and the data were used to determine residential mobility; veteran status, first time recorded. The economic activity concepts were revised; questions on income were more detailed; vocational training was first introduced in the census.

Quality of the Census. To improve the usefulness of the 1970 census results, a number of changes were introduced based on evaluation of previous censuses, consultation with users of data, and extensive field pretesting. For more details on coverage and accuracy of data, see United States entry, 1970.

Publication Plan. U.S. Bureau of Census. *Census of Population: 1970.* Volume 1, *Characteristics of the Population.* Parts 54-58, *Guam, Virgin Islands, American Samoa, Canal Zone, Trust Territory of the Pacific Islands.* Washington, D.C., 1973. Computer tapes are available. Language of publication is English.

1974 (December 25)

Special census of population conducted by the Development Planning Office. The enumerated population was *de facto*, but many tables were presented for the *de jure* population. Canvasser was the method utilized to record information on household and individual schedules. The schedules were written in English only. The tabulation was totally computerized. The island of Tutuila was divided into three districts—Eastern, Central, and Western—and the Swain Islands were incorporated into Manu'a district.

Definitions and Concepts. AGE—date of birth and completed years. Tabulated in single years and standard five-year age groups. RACE—no distinction between American Samoan and Western Samoan, and persons of other Pacific islands were described as Tongan or Nivena (most common). Where ancestry was mixed and contained any Samoan person, it was described as part-Samoan; for mixed ancestry without Samoans, the two parts were listed. Papalagi or European was classified as Caucasian. HOUSEHOLD—group of people who normally sleep in the same house and share their meals. The "matai" was the head of the household. FAMILY—persons related by blood. Legal and customary adoption were not treated differently. To indicate relationship to head, the Samoan system was used—brother's son, wife's mother, and so forth. MARITAL STATUS—Categories were: never married, married, widowed, and divorced. PLACE OF BIRTH—country of birth for foreign born and place or village of birth for native born. The mother's usual place of residence was also recorded. RELIGION—large congregations were listed; but if not listed, the name of the religious affiliation was asked. The word "refuse" replaced "object" that was used in the previous census. EDUCATION—school enrollment (attendance should be understood as full time) and educational attainment (last degree attained and number of years in school). PLACE OF RESIDENCE—usual and recent place of residence. FERTILITY—questions asked of females born in 1960 or before: number of children ever born alive, number of children still living, age of mother at first birth (new), date of birth of the most recent child, whether still alive, and, if dead, the date of death. ECONOMIC ACTIVITY—questions were asked of all persons. All persons should fall into one of these categories: working in communal or commercial agriculture, working in paid employment (except agriculture), receiving other income, dependents and working in household, and not working. Any combination of these five categories was also recorded. Additional questions: whether working full- or part-time, place of work, and name of employer. OCCUPATION—basis for classification was not stated; seventy-three occupational groups were presented.

Special Elements and Features. Changes and additions were made to previous questionnaires in order to obtain information for planning future educational and medical facilities, and to estimate economic development, migration and fertility.

Quality of the Census. Preliminary censuses were taken; editing programs were developed to check and correct various aspects of data. Postenumeration survey was conducted to assure completeness and accuracy of data.

Publication Plan. American Samoa. Development Planning Office. *Report on the 1974 Census of American Samoa.* Part 1, Basic information. Apia, 1974. Unpublished data are available (East-West Population Institute). Computer tapes are available. Language of publication is English.

National Topic Chart

	1950	1956	1960	1970	1974
De facto		X			X
Usual residence	X		X	X	X
Place of birth	X	X	X	X	X
Duration of residence					
Place of prev. residence				X	
Urban/rural					
Sex	X	X	X	X	X
Age	X	X	X	X	X
Relation to household head	X	X	X	X	X
Marital status	X	X	X	X	X
Children born alive			X	X	X
Children living		X			X
Citizenship				X	
Literacy					
School enrollment	X		X	X	X
Ed. attainment	X		X	X	X
Ed. qualification					
National/Ethnic origin	X		X		X
Language	X				
Religion		X			X
Household composition	X		X	X	X
Econ. active/inactive	X	X	X	X	X
Occupation	X	X	X	X	X
Industry			X	X	
Occupational status			X	X	
Income			X	X	
Housing			X	X	

Australia

Commonwealth of Australia

CAPITAL: Canberra.
STATISTICAL AGENCY: Australian Bureau of Statistics.
NATIONAL REPOSITORY: Library, Australian Bureau of Statistics.
MAIN U.S. REPOSITORY: Population Research Center (Univ. of Texas).

To understand the earlier censuses of Australia, a brief historical review is necessary. Australasia consisted of the six states of the Commonwealth of Australia (New South Wales, Victoria, Queensland, South Australia, Western Australia, and Tasmania), and New Zealand, which was separated from New South Wales in 1841. New Zealand will be the subject of a separate entry.

Long before the arrival of the first European to Australia, the country was inhabited by aborigines with various languages and customs. In 1770, James Cook explored the east coast of the continent and claimed it for Britain. As a British dependency, Australia served as a penal colony, and its first immigrants consisted of criminals and their jailers. Only after 1850, attracted by the gold strike in Victoria, were new settlements formed.

During these early days of colonization, enumerations (musters) were frequently carried out by requiring the inhabitants to attend on certain days a specific place in their respective district. However, the actual results of only a few of these enumerations have been preserved.

Before 1911, censuses were carried out in the separate states under the provision of the State Acts and were controlled by local government. Therefore, the date of the census, the subject, and the scope of inquiry varied immensely among them. Following the British tradition, the censuses were *de facto*, and self-enumeration was the method used to record information on household schedules. Another common factor among those censuses was the exclusion of full-blooded aborigines from enumeration. Housing censuses were taken simultaneously. These first censuses included the topic "civil condition," which should not be confused with marital condition. "Civil condition" was a way of distinguishing free men from convicts.

1828

The first regular Australasian census was taken in New South Wales and included the population of Queensland. The subjects of inquiry consisted of

AUSTRALIA

- –··– International boundary
- –·–· Internal administrative boundary
- ⊛ National capital
- ○ Internal administrative capital
- +–+ Railroad
- —— Road

0   200   400   600 Miles
0   200   400   600 Kilometers

name, age, sex, civil condition (born free, came free, free from servitude, holding absolute pardon, holding conditional pardon, holding ticket of leave, convict, colonial sentence, and government servant), duration of residence in the country, housing occupancy, and religion.

1833 and 1836

These following censuses were also taken in New South Wales and included the population of Queensland and Victoria. They had a similar scope to the 1828 census, but the question on housing occupancy was dropped, and the question about civil condition was reduced. In these three first censuses, the military population was enumerated separately.

1841

Another census taken in New South Wales, including the population of Queensland, Victoria, and Norfolk Island. In the same year, Tasmania took its first census. The New South Wales census showed considerable advancement over the previous ones with more complete information, better tabulation of results, and more detailed age groups. Marital status and nature of occupation were added. The housing census was reinstated with inquiries about housing occupancy and type of construction.

The census of Tasmania was taken separately and recorded name, age, sex, civil condition, marital status, religion, and occupation. The housing census included type of construction, number of houses being built, and occupancy.

1844

This is the first census taken in South Australia. Information regarding the historical development of the census is incomplete. Schedules recorded age, name, sex, marital status, religion, occupation, and housing occupancy.

1846

Censuses were taken in New South Wales and South Australia. The South Australian census followed the same pattern as the 1844 census. The New South Wales census included the population of Queensland and Victoria. Scope was name, sex, age, civil condition, marital status, place of birth and occupational status (new), religion, occupation, housing occupancy, and type of construction.

1848

Censuses were taken in Western Australia for the first time and in Tasmania. In Western Australia inquiries included: name, age, sex, religion, and occupation. The census of Tasmania maintained the same scope adopted in 1841.

1851

Censuses were taken in New South Wales (Queensland and Victoria were included), South Australia, and Tasmania. In Tansmania the subjects of inquiry were the same as 1841. In New South Wales the subjects recorded were the same as the ones in 1846. Civil condition was asked for the last time in New South Wales. In South Australia, nationality, duration of residence in the country, and infirmities were added to the subjects recorded in 1844 and 1846; religion, however, was dropped.

1854

Censuses were taken in Western Australia, and for the first time, Victoria took its census separately. In Western Australia, civil condition and marital status were added to the topics taken in 1848. In Victoria, the census schedules included name, age, sex, marital status, religion, occupation, literacy (new), house occupancy, and type of construction.

1855

The South Australian census was the only one taken this year. The scope included name, age, sex, relationship to head of family (new anywhere in Australia), marital status, nationality, duration of residence in the country, infirmities, occupation, and housing occupancy.

1856

The census taken in New South Wales this year was the first to be supplemented by a general report. The scope was practically the same as 1851, but place of birth and occupational classification questions were expanded, while literacy was new. Civil condition was dropped, and the housing census added a question about number of houses being built.

1857

Censuses were taken in Victoria and Tasmania. In addition to name, age, sex, marital status, religion, and literacy asked in 1854, the census of Victoria included relationship to head of family, place of birth, occupational status, higher education (university), number of houses being built, and number of rooms per house.

In Tasmania, the scope of 1841 census was maintained.

1859

This was the third census taken in Western Australia. There was neither a copy nor description of the schedule used. Information was obtained by examination of published tables. In addition to name, sex, age, civil condition, marital status, religion, and occupation, which were part of the 1854 census, place of birth, literacy, and questions related to housing were recorded.

1861

Censuses were taken in New South Wales, Victoria, South Australia, Tasmania, and Queensland (separately for the first time).

For New South Wales, the scope consisted of age, sex, religion, relationship to family head (new), marital status, place of birth, infirmities (new), literacy, and occupation. The housing census dropped the number of unoccupied houses and those being built and added number of rooms.

In Victoria, nationality and infirmities were added to the scope used in 1857.

Queensland was designated a separate colony in 1859. The scope of this first census was: sex, age, relationship to family head, marital status, birthplace, religion, occupation, literacy, and school attendance. Housing data were also taken.

In South Australia, the scope was that of 1855. Birthplace replaced nationality, religion was revived, and literacy added.

In Tasmania, relationship to family head, birthplace, literacy, and higher education were added to 1841 scope, and civil condition was dropped.

1864, 1866, 1868

Queensland (1864 and 1868) and South Australia (1866) both repeated the scopes of their 1861 censuses.

1870

The scope of the Western Australia census was that of 1859 with more details in the results. In Tasmania, the scope of 1861 was used again.

1871

The New South Wales census was the same as 1861, but results of literacy of the Chinese and the aborigines were separate.

Victoria's scope was also that used in 1861, but insanity, occupational status, and past occupation were added.

Queensland added information about persons not going to work due to sickness or accident to the scope used in 1861 and 1868. There was an important change in territorial division, however. Pastoral districts and parishes replaced police districts and municipality boundaries, which had been used in all previous censuses.

South Australia continued with the same scope used in 1861.

1876

Censuses were taken in Queensland and South Australia again. In Queensland, the scope of the census was the same as that of 1871. South Australia remained with the scope used since 1861.

1881

For the first time, a simultaneous enumeration was taken throughout Australia. The following subjects were included in the schedules of all states: name, age, sex, relationship to the head of the family, marital status, place of birth, nationality, house occupancy, type of construction, religion, occupation, literacy, school attendance, and higher education. In addition, Western Australia recorded civil condition, and South and Western Australia recorded duration of residence. Unfortunately, the results of this census were destroyed by fire, but a number of summary tables were preserved.

1886

Census taken in Queensland followed the scope of 1881.

1891

A conference of statisticians was held at Hobart in 1890, and as a result uniformity was achieved in all Australian states as far as date of the census and subjects of inquiry. The following topics were recorded: name, age, sex, relationship to head of the family, marital status, occupation, occupational status, place of birth, nationality, religion, higher education, school attendance, literacy, infirmities, and all the particulars so far recorded in the housing censuses.

1901

Census was taken in all states, and the scope was the same as that of 1891 with the exception of New South Wales and Victoria, which added questions about number of children born to present marriage and duration of marriage. Description of infirmities was quite detailed, including causes of accidents.

1911

The first commonwealth census was conducted by the Commonwealth Bureau of the Census and Statistics. It was established that the census operations would be synchronous with the census of the United Kingdom and other parts of the British Empire. The census was *de facto*, self-enumerated, and information was recorded on household schedules (household cards and personal cards). Scope of the census included: name, sex, age, marital status, date of marriage, number of children ever born from existing and previous marriages, relationships to head of household, infirmity, place of birth, nationality, race, length of residence in the country, date of arrival, religion, education, occupation, and occupational status. To the housing census, questions of nature of the building, tenure, and amount of weekly rent were added.

1921

The second commonwealth census was conducted by the same agency and followed basically the same organization as the previous one. The household schedules, however, presented dwelling slips, personal slips, and shipping slips. Mechanical tabulation was introduced in this census. The territory covered by the census included the six states, two internal territories (Northern and Federal Capital territories) and three external territories (Papua, New Guinea, and Norfolk Island). In addition to the questions asked in 1911, place of birth of parents, causes of unemployment, and number of dependent children were recorded. Age at last birthday was asked to all persons and not just to those whose exact date of birth was unknown. Questions related to housing census were the same as the ones in the previous census.

1933

The third commonwealth census should have been taken in 1931, but for economic reasons was postponed to 1933. The same organization adopted in the 1921 census was followed. One more external territory was included—the mandate territory of Nauru. The additional questions recorded in this census referred to orphanhood, language, war service, industry, and craft, which replaced occupation and income. The question related to number of children in present and previous marriages was dropped.

Aboriginal population was still not included.

1947 (June 30)

The fourth commonwealth census of population and housing was postponed from 1941 to 1947 because of the war. It was conducted by the Commonwealth Bureau of Census and Statistics on a *de facto* basis, and self-enumeration was the method used to record information on household schedules and personal slips.Full-blooded aborigines, members of Allied forces, enemy prisoners of war and internees from overseas were not counted. Refugees, however, were part of the census enumeration. The population of Torres Strait Island, which was previously regarded as full-blooded aboriginal, was included in this census. The territory covered by the census was divided into six states, two internal territories (Northern and Australian Capital territory) and four external territories (Papua, New Guinea, Norfolk Island, and Nauru) and subdivided into local government areas, municipalities, shires, or road districts.

Definitions and Concepts. AGE—as of last birthday in completed years. Tabulated in standard five-year age groups. Children under one year were classified "0." MARITAL STATUS—categories were: never married, married, widowed not remarried, divorced not remarried, and separated (legally or otherwise). Duration of marriage was also recorded. URBAN—metropolitan areas related to capital cities of the states and adjoining municipal areas. Urban provisional division referred to cities of the territories; cities and towns outside metropolitan divisions within the states, except for Tasmania. In Tasmania boundaries of urban provisional divisions were determined only for census purposes because most of the towns were not incorporated. DWELLING—room or collection of rooms occupied by a household group living together as a family unit. RACE—population was divided into two main groups: full-blooded European and non-European and "half-caste." The full-blooded non-Europeans were subdivided into Chinese, Indian, Malay, Syrian, and Polynesian. The "half-caste" persons were subdivided into those with one parent of European origin and those with both parents of non-European origin. For this last group the race of the father was stated. PLACE OF BIRTH—for persons born in Australia, the name of state, territory, and local government area of birth were recorded. For foreign born, the name of the country. PLACE OF RESIDENCE—Only for foreign born and the length of residence in the country. NATIONALITY—Name of the country to which the person owed legal allegiance. In some cases where the nationality changed by reason of annexation, the previous nationality was added; for example, German (Austrian). RELIGION—population was divided into two main groups, Christians and non-Christians, and subdivided into different religious denominations. FERTILITY—the number of children born of existing marriage, number of children living, and number of children dead. ECONOMIC ACTIVITY —defined in terms of participation or not in the work force at the time of the census. Three groups were distinguished: persons not engaged in industry, business, trade, or service (including children, pensioners, inmates of institutions, full-time students or scholars, persons of independent income, persons engaged in unpaid home duties, and others); persons usually engaged in industry, trade, and so forth, but out of work at the time of the census; and persons who were working at the time of the census. Only the first group was not included in the work force. Persons engaged in industry but not at work were also asked the period since last worked, reasons for not working or not looking for job, if able and willing to work but unable to secure a job, and if only temporarily out of job. The number of children under sixteen years of age and dependent on the head of the household was separately recorded. OCCUPATION—tabulation in conjunction with industry, major groups recorded. INDUSTRY—classification presented divisions and subgroups (two-digits). OCCUPATIONAL STATUS—categories were employer, employee, self-employed, and helper not on wage or salary.

Special Elements and Features. Orphanhood, infirmities, language, education, war service, and income present in the 1933 census were excluded from this census. Detailed map of capital cities and suburbs; and alphabetical list of metropolitan areas by state with total population by sex, number of dwellings, and occupancy; comparative tables for 1933 and 1947; a brief analysis of previous censuses, and a copy of schedules were all included in the publications.

Quality of the Census. Higher standard of accuracy than the previous censuses was achieved. A postcensal adjustment of population estimates for the years between censuses of 1933 and 1947 was provided. Information regarding race did not furnish a satisfactory indication of ethnic constitution, and information on the number of dependent children could not be accurately obtained. This census presented the highest rate of failure to state age (5.54 per 1,000 inhabitants); however, Whipple's Index classified data on age in category I—highly accurate data.

Publication Plan. Australia. Commonwealth Bureau of Census and Statistics. *Census of the Commonwealth of Australia, 30th June 1947.* Canberra, Government Printer, n.d. Volumes 1-3. Unpublished data are available. Language of publication is English.

1954 (June 30)

The fifth census, conducted by the Commonwealth Bureau of the Census and Statistics, was *de facto*, and self-enumeration was the method used. Householder's schedules and individual slips were the instruments of enumeration. As traditionally done, the census of housing was carried out simultaneously with that of population. Full-blooded aborigines were not counted. Automatic machine tabulation was used. The information gathered here was taken directly from the tables and some explanatory notes accompanying each volume. Apparently the statistician's report was not published. The territorial divisions were the same as 1947.

Definitions and Concepts. AGE—same as 1947 plus tabulated in single years. For the first time unspecified ages were distributed over all ages prior to tabulation. MARITAL STATUS—never married (two groups: under and over age fifteen), married, married but permanently separated, widowed, and divorced. PLACE OF BIRTH—same as 1947. URBAN—metropolitan urban were those areas of the capital cities of the states and the city of Canberra. This normally included the city and the contiguous urban areas. Other urban—all areas outside of the metropolitan urban divisions (included the capital city of the Northern Territory), all separately incorporated cities and towns, and other towns with population of 1,000 and more (except Tasmania, which included towns of 750 and more). NATIONALITY—primarily citizenship. Two main groups were recorded: "British" born in Australia and elsewhere, and "foreign" by name of country. Irish citizens were included in the British group. RELIGION—population was divided into the following groups: Christians (and subgroups), non-Christians (and subgroups), indefinite, no religion, no reply. The answer to the question was optional; therefore, a large number of people chose not to give an explicit statement. RACE—same as 1947. DWELLING—habitation occupied by a household group living together as a domestic unit, whether comprising the whole or only part of a building. ECONOMIC ACTIVITY—classified in two groups: persons in the work force included the ones at work and not at work at the time of the census (unable to secure employment, temporarily laid off from their jobs, not actively seeking work at the time of the census because of sickness or accident, industrial dispute, resting between jobs or for any other reason); and persons not in the work force who were preschool and all children not attending school, full-time students, persons of independent income, the retired, pensioners, annuitants, inmates of institutions, homemakers, or others not engaged in industry, business and so forth. INDUSTRY—groups, subgroups, and individual units according to the Australian Classification of Industries. OCCUPATIONAL STATUS—employer, employee, self-employed, helper not on wage. Persons in the work force but not at work were further classified by cause and time out of work.

Special Elements and Features. Australian life tables, 1953-55; tables with population densities since 1911; analysis of intercensal increases of population 1911-1954; tables with population and occupied dwellings in alphabetical order of localities; cross-classification of characteristics of population; cross-classification of dwelling and householder characteristics. Occupation with the number of dependent children was dropped. Fertility may have been asked, but no tables were published.

Quality of Census. Whipple's Index category not available. Final results published in 1957. Comparison of industry groups with previous census presents difficulties because of changes in the industrial classification.

Publication Plan. Australia. Commonwealth Bureau of Census and Statistics. *Census of the Commonwealth of Australia, 30th June 1954*. Canberra, Government Printer, 1955-1958. Volumes 1-8 and Australian life tables in 40 volumes. Unpublished data are available, and the language of publication is English.

1961 (June 30)

The sixth commonwealth census of population and housing was conducted by the Commonwealth Bureau of Census and Statistics on a *de facto* basis, and self-enumeration was the method used to gather information on household schedules and individual slips. The statistician's report was not published; the information here was taken from table headings and some explanatory notes contained in each individual volume. The territory covered by the census was divided into six states, two internal territories (Northern territory and Australian Capital territory) and six external territories (Papua, New Guinea, Norfolk Island, Nauru, and, for the first time, Christmas Island and Cocos [Keeling] Island).

Definitions and Concepts. AGE, MARITAL STATUS, PLACE OF BIRTH, RELIGION, NATIONALITY, DWELLING—same as 1954. Persons who omitted their marital status were for the first time allocated to a particular group prior to tabulation. FERTILITY—according to 1966 census, fertility analyses for 1954 and 1961 censuses were derived from a 20 percent sample of married women enumerated. However, no tables were presented in the reports. URBAN—same as 1954. RACE—three major groups were presented: European, non-European, and European/other races. This last group refers to persons with European blood to the extent of one-half and blood of non-European race to the extent of one-half. PLACE OF RESIDENCE—only for foreign born persons. Period of residence in Australia was recorded. ECONOMIC ACTIVITY—the concept of inclusion or exclusion from the work force was the same as 1954. INDUSTRY—classification based on Australian Standard Industrial Classification (ASIC), divisions, major groups, and subgroups (three-digits). OCCUPATION—classification based on the Australian Classification of Occupation (ACO) 1961, major groups, groups, and subgroups (three-digits). OCCUPATIONAL STATUS—categories were: employer, employee, self-employed, and helper.

Special Elements and Features. Life tables, tables with population densities since 1911, analysis of intercensal increases of population from 1911 to 1961, table with population and number of occupied dwellings in alphabetical order of localities were present. A list of census publications, including date of issue and price, was included.

Quality of the Census. The boundaries of urban areas, although improved when compared to earlier censuses, were still highly subjective, not providing sufficient comparability from census to census. Whipple's Index classified age data into category I—highly accurate data. Field count statements started being published in September 1961, and final results in the form of census bulletins began in 1962.

Publication Plan. Australia. Commonwealth Bureau of Census and Statistics. *Census of the Commonwealth of Australia, 30th June 1961.* Canberra, 1962-1965. Volumes 1-8 in 38 volumes. Unpublished data are available, and language of publication is English.

1966 (June 30)

The seventh commonwealth census of population and housing was conducted by the same agency, and organization and methods were basically the same as the previous census. Tabulation was computerized. The information gathered here was taken from introductory notes and table headings because the statistician's report was not published. Aborigines were excluded from the majority of tables. The territory covered by the census was divided into six states, two internal territories, and four external territories (Nauru, Norfolk Island, Christmas Island, and Cocos [Keeling] Island). Papua New Guinea took its census separately.

Definitions and Concepts. AGE—as of last birthday in completed years and completed months. Tabulated in single years and standard five-year age groups. URBAN—settlements of 1,000 or more inhabitants. Urban centers and metropolitan centers were as defined in 1961. The boundaries of these areas vary from census to census. For urban centers with a population of 30,000 and over, the criterion of delimitation was the inclusion of all collector's districts of 500 inhabitants or more. For urban centers of less than 30,000 inhabitants, local government area boundaries were adopted. For areas around metropolitan areas (urban centers with a population of at least 75,000 inhabitants and a regional population of at least 100,000) a further boundary was created—statistical divisions, or statistical districts. For areas with a large number of holiday houses, the number of dwellings rather than population was the criterion used. MARITAL STATUS, PLACE OF RESIDENCE, PLACE OF BIRTH, NATIONALITY, and DWELLINGS—same as 1961. HOUSEHOLD—one person or a group of persons living as a domestic unit with common eating arrangements; divided into primary or secondary family units. FAMILY—members of the household related by blood or marriage. The head of the family was also the head of the household. Persons classified as other family members, boarders, and other unrelated persons were excluded from the family tables but included in the household tables. EDUCATION (new)—school attendance, educational attainment (highest degree completed), and educational qualification. RELIGION—the full name of the religious denomination was asked. As in previous censuses, a large number of people failed to answer the question. RACE—schedules were redesigned to obtain more precise data. The term "half-caste" was abolished; instead, the percentage of racial mixture was recorded. FERTILITY—number of children born (both living and dead) to existing marriage. Asked of married women only. ECONOMIC ACTIVITY—reference period was the week before the census. The active were all persons employed (working for pay or profit), owners of businesses, unpaid family helpers, members of the clergy who worked, the temporarily unemployed (laid off), and those looking for work. The inactive were homemakers, children not of school age, students (full-time), the pensioned and retired, persons of independent income, and inmates of institutions. OCCUPATION—major groups, groups and subgroups (three-digits) according to the ACO. INDUSTRY— divisions, subgroups, and units (three-digits) according to the ASIC.

Special Elements and Features. For the first time publications were titled *Census of Population and Housing*, although housing information was always part of the census. Publication format changed from a geographical arrangement to subject volumes. Cross-classification of population and housing characteristics, alphabetical list of localities by state, catalog of census tabulations, and age pyramids for all states and territories were included. Papua New Guinea took a separate census. Education was recorded for the first time.

Quality of the Census. A postenumeration survey was conducted. Age questions were more specific than those of previous censuses. The proportion of persons who failed to state an age was very small. The new criteria adopted for territorial division allowed more reliable comparison of population of different areas; however, comparison with previous censuses was limited. Extensive arrangements were made to obtain as complete coverage of aborigines as possible. As a result a fairly complete enumeration of aborigines in the Northern territory was made. However, data relating to persons of more than half aboriginal mix were insufficiently precise. Whipple's Index rated accuracy of age as category I—highly accurate data. Final results began to appear in 1967.

Publication Plan. Australia. Commonwealth Bureau of Census and Statistics. *Census of Population and Housing, 30th June 1966.* Canberra, 1970-1973. Volumes 1-6 in 38 volumes. Bulletins with final results on the external territories were issued from 1967-1968. Unpublished data are available as are computer tapes with accompanying documentation. Language of publication is English.

1971 (June 30)

The eighth commonwealth census of population and housing was conducted by the Commonwealth Bureau of Census and Statistics on a *de facto* basis, and self-enumeration was the method utilized to record information on household schedules and individual slips. For the first time, the census included aborigines. Tabulation was computerized. The territory covered by the census was divided into six states and two territories, subdivided into local government areas. The Torres Strait Island population was also included.

Definitions and Concepts. URBAN—the term "major urban" was introduced and referred to all urban centers with a population of 100,000 or more, the smaller urban centers were included in the other urban group, and the remainder were classified as rural. The criteria for delimitation of urban boundaries were as follows: urban center—population cluster of 1,000 or more (holiday resorts of less population used the criterion of 250 or more dwellings, of which at least 100 were occupied); major urban centers presented a further boundary—the city— that is, an area that is expected to be socially and economically oriented toward the urban centers; collector's district was a further delimitation presented in all urban centers with 25,000 or more population. AGE—in completed years and months. Tabulated in single years and standard five-year age groups. MARITAL STATUS—categories were: never married, now married, married but permanently separated, divorced, and widowed. PLACE OF RESIDENCE—usual place for persons living in a particular dwelling for the last six months, persons who would live in the dwelling for the following six months, or persons who were found at the date of the census in a particular dwelling and had no usual place of residence. Previous place of residence in 1966 was also asked. Duration of residence in Australia has always been recorded. PLACE OF BIRTH—state or territory of birth for the foreign born. The country of birth of parents was also recorded. NATIONALITY—primarily citizenship. The name of the country was recorded. RACE—was no longer used for the constitutional purposes of reckoning the Australian population and to identify aborigines. The question on race was redesigned stressing that "if of mixed origin, indicate to which he considers himself to belong." The following groups were presented: European origin, aboriginal origin, Torres Strait Islander origin, and others. All "Not Stated" answers were assigned a racial origin in accordance with other information supplied on the schedules. RELIGION—religious denomination recorded. EDUCATION—for persons age five years and over: school attendance (full- or part-time), educational attainment (highest degree completed), educational qualification. Vocational and professional education were specified. Address of school or college was also asked. FERTILITY—asked of all women age fifteen and over: number of children ever born from all marriages, including adoptions but excluding stillbirths; number of children from present marriage, including adoptions but excluding stillbirths; whether presently married and duration. For persons who have been married, the following was asked: Has this person ever been widowed, length of widowhood, or if since remarried, length of last widowhood. Publication with information about fertility was not issued. ECONOMIC ACTIVITY—The term labor force substituted for work force used in previous censuses. Lower age limit was fifteen years. The reference period was the week before the census. Included in the labor force: persons who worked (that is, those who had a job even if they were temporarily absent, or were temporarily laid off without pay for the whole reference week) and those who did not work (that is, did not have a job but were actively looking for work). Persons helping but not receiving salary or wages and who usually worked less than fifteen hours a week were excluded from the labor force. OCCUPATION—classification based on Australian Classification of Occupation and ISCO, revised 1968, major groups, groups, and subgroups (three-digits). INDUSTRY—classification based on Australian Standard Industrial Classification, division, major groups, and subgroups (three-digits). OCCUPATIONAL STATUS—categories were: employer, employee, self-employed, and helper. The number of hours worked per week and place of employment (address, division, and branch or section in which the person works) were also recorded.

Special Elements and Features. The publication format was modified. For the first time aborigines were included in the enumeration. Detailed information on aborigines was printed in a separate volume. New questions: usual place of residence, place of previous residence, place of work, and number of weeks worked. More detailed information on marriage and fertility was asked; tables on fertility were not published, however. Copy of schedule was included.

Quality of the Census. A postenumeration survey was conducted. Whipple's Index rating was not available. Results were published beginning in October 1971 with the field count statements. Fertility data (Bulletin 11), however, were not published.

Publication Plan. Australia. Commonwealth Bureau of Census and Statistics. *Census of Population and Housing, 30 June 1971*. Bulletins (final reports). Canberra, 1972-75. Volumes 1-14 in 67 volumes. Unpublished data and computer tapes are available. Language of publication is English.

1976 (June 30)

The census of population and housing was conducted by the Australian Bureau of Statistics on a *de facto* basis, including persons on vessels in or between Australian ports, but excluding diplomatic personnel. Self-enumeration was the method used to record information on household schedules. Tabulation was computerized. The territory covered by the census was divided into six states and two internal territories (Northern and Australian Capital territories) and subdivided into local government areas. Information is also available at other levels of geographical detail (collection district, statistical division and subdivision, statistical district, and section of state).

Definitions and Concepts. AGE, MARITAL STATUS, PLACE OF BIRTH, NATIONALITY and RELIGION—same as 1971. HOUSEHOLD—same as 1971, that is, a person living alone or group of people living together as a single domestic unit with common eating arrangements. DWELLINGS—like 1971, were divided into two groups, occupied and unoccupied. Occupied dwellings were further subdivided into private and nonprivate (group quarters). PLACE OF RESIDENCE—usual place of residence, place of previous residence one year before the census (1975), and five years before the census (1971). Length of residence in Australia (whether resident or visitor), recorded date of arrival (first arrival and on this visit). URBAN—major urban centers (over 100,000 inhabitants), other urban centers (in between 1,000 and 99,999 inhabitants), bounded rural (200 to 900 inhabitants), and rural (balance). Persons on board vessels or between Australian ports were classified as migratory and shown only as a balancing item in the population of state or territory. RACE—four groups: European, aboriginal, Torres Strait Islander and other origin. At this time, there was no attempt to allocate "not stated" answers among the various race groups. EDUCATION—for persons aged five years and over: school attendance (did not go to school, age left school, still at school), educational attainment, educational qualification according to ISCED, and name and address of educational institution. LANGUAGE—for the first time recorded, for persons five years and over: language spoken at home (aboriginal languages were also recorded). FERTILITY—for women ever married: the number of children from all marriages, including adopted but excluding stillbirths, number of children now living and not now living. For women presently married: the number of children from present marriage and duration of marriage were recorded. ECONOMIC ACTIVITY—the criteria for inclusion in the labor force was basically the same as those in 1971. The following questions were asked: Did this person work last week (the week before the census)? Full- or part-time job? Temporarily laid off without pay? Looked for work? How many hours usually worked per week? For the first time, type of transportation used to get to work. Additional questions: type of pension or benefit received, type of retirement benefit paid, life insurance, place of work, and type of license to drive various kinds of motor vehicle. OCCUPATION—classification based on the Australian Classification of Occupations (twenty-eight additions since 1971), major groups, groups, and subgroups (three-digits); comparable with ISCO. INDUSTRY—classification based on ASIC (three-digits) or (four-digits) for comparison with ISIC. OCCUPATIONAL STATUS—same categories as 1971. INCOME—reinstated (previously asked in 1933). Individual, family, and household income were recorded.

Special Elements and Features. The following questions were added to 1976 census schedules: place of usual residence (one year before the census), serious long term illness, life insurance policies, whether children were minded by someone other than parents for some part of the day, language used at home, age the person left school, license to ride or drive a motor vehicle, type of pension received, retirement benefits, and kind of transportation used to get to work.

Quality of the Census. Postenumeration survey was conducted. Preliminary data became available in October 1976 (state capitals and Darwin) only for selected characteristics. Final results were processed on a sample basis except for the Northern territory for which all the schedules were processed. More detailed information is available in magnetic tapes or microfiche. Whipple's Index category gory I—highly accurate age data.

Publication Plan. Australia. Australian Bureau of Statistics. *1976 Census of Population and Housing.* "Population and dwellings in local government areas and urban centers." (Preliminary). Canberra, 1977-1978. Parts 1-8. "Characteristics of the population: local government areas." (Preliminary). Canberra, 1978. Parts 1-9.

Census of Population and Housing, 30 June 1976. Population and Dwellings: Cross-classified Tables. Canberra, 1979. 9 parts. Unpublished data and computer tapes are available. Language of publication is English.

OTHER STATISTICAL PUBLICATIONS: Issued by Bureau of Statistics, *Internal Migration* (irregularly), *Monthly Summary of Statistics, Pocket Year Book,*

Population and Vital Statistics (quarterly), *Population: Principal Cities and Towns* (annually), *Quarterly Summary of Australian Statistics, Social Indicators* (biennially), *Year Book*. Issued by Department of Immigration and Ethnic Affairs, *Australian Immigration: Consolidated Statistics* (annually).

National Topic Chart

	1947	1954	1961	1966	1971	1976
De facto	X	X	X	X	X	X
Usual residence					X	X
Place of birth	X	X	X	X	X	X
Duration of residence	X	X	X	X	X	X
Place of prev. residence					X	X
Urban/rural	X	X	X	X	X	X
Sex	X	X	X	X	X	X
Age	X	X	X	X	X	X
Relation to household head	X	X	X	X	X	X
Marital status	X	X	X	X	X	X
Children born alive	X			X	X	X
Children living	X				X	X
Citizenship	X	X	X	X	X	X
Literacy						
School enrollment				X	X	X
Ed. attainment				X	X	X
Ed. qualification				X	X	X
National/Ethnic origin	X	X	X	X	X	X
Language						X
Religion	X	X	X	X	X	X
Household composition	X	X	X	X	X	X
Econ. active/inactive	X	X	X	X	X	X
Occupation	X	X	X	X	X	X
Industry	X	X	X	X	X	X
Occupational status	X	X	X	X	X	X
Income						X
Housing	X	X	X	X	X	X

Christmas Island

External Territory of the Commonwealth of Australia

CAPITAL: Flying Fish Cove.
STATISTICAL AGENCY: Central Statistics Office, Flying Fish Cove.
NATIONAL REPOSITORY: Government offices, Flying Fish Cove.
MAIN U.S. REPOSITORY: Population Research Center (Univ. of Texas).

The censuses of Christmas Island were the same as those of Cocos (Keeling) Islands. Occasional variations between them are cited in this entry.

The earliest record of the populations of both Christmas and Cocos dates back to 1891 as part of the Colony of Straits Settlements which also included the Settlement of Singapore, Penang, and Malacca, and the Protective Native States of Malay Peninsula. Since then, the censuses were taken decennially.

1891

The first census was *de facto*, a combination of canvasser and self-enumeration on householder's schedules, and manual tabulation was used. While more detailed information was recorded for the other settlements, for the islands the results presented only total population, age, and nationality.

1901

The second census followed the same organization and scope of the previous one, but this time the schedules were written in English and Malay. The results of Cocos (Keeling) Islands arrived after the report was printed. The tables showed slightly different format with more detailed age groups.

1911

In the third census the islands were presented as part of the Settlement of Singapore, but the results were recorded separately from the rest of the settlement. The census was *de facto*, and the floating population was included. At this time, there was no difference between the number of tables presented for the islands and the rest of the colony. The scope was considerably larger than those of previous enumerations and included the following topics: age, sex, marital status, place of birth, language, race, tribe or nationality, occupation, and religion.

1921

First Pan-Malayan census included the Straits Settlements, the Federated Malay States (Perak, Selangor, Negri Sembilan, and Panang) and the Unfederated Malay States (Johore, Kedah, Perlis, Kelantan, Trengganu, and Brunei). All of them constituted what was called British Malay. Cocos (Keeling) Islands and Christmas Island results were not presented separately in all tables but rather shown as part of the totals for the Settlement of Singapore. House lists, block lists, householder's schedules, seagoing population schedules in English and Malay were the forms used. The scope was about the same as 1911 with more detailed questions about language, such as dialect spoken, and the inclusion of literacy and ability to speak English. The questions about literacy and English proficiency, however, were limited to selected large towns. Tables presented urban and rural subdivisions. Center of census operation was located in Singapore.

1931

Organization and scope of the second British Malay census followed the same format as 1921. Again, most of the tables did not present separate results for Cocos (Keeling) Islands and Christmas Island but rather included them within the totals for the Settlement of Singapore. Questions about literacy and English proficiency, at this time, were rewritten to obtain higher degree of accuracy.

1947 (September 23)

Because of World War II the third Pan-Malayan census, originally planned for 1941, was temporarily abandoned. In addition, the census headquarters was forced to move from Singapore to Ipok, Perak. Conducted by the Pan-Malayan Department of Statistics, the census was *de facto*, but nomadic aborigines, persons in transit, and service personnel were not included in all tables. A combination of self-enumeration and canvasser methods was used on householder's schedules. Card punching and mechanical tabulation were used.

After the Japanese domination the following political changes occurred: the former Federated and Unfederated Malay States and the two Straits Settlements of Penang and Malacca became the Federation of Malaya; Singapore became a separate colony including Singapore Municipality and the remaining area, Christmas Island and Cocos (Keeling) Islands. Labuan was incorporated in the colony of North Borneo, and the Malay State of Brunei was no longer part of the territory covered by the census. Like the previous census the results of the Christmas and Cocos (Keeling) Islands were in most of the tables presented as part of the totals for the colony of Singapore.

The census of housing was taken simultaneously with the population, and the schedules were bilingual in English and Malay.

Definitions and Concepts. URBAN—villages with 1,000 or more inhabitants. (Villages were administered by rural or town boards, contained at least 100 houses and a population of 500 or more.) AGE—last birthday according to the

"English reckoning"; recorded in years or in months for babies. Tables were presented in single years to four then standard five-year age groups. In addition, groups of under five, six to twelve, under fifteen and fifteen to forty-four were tabulated. MARITAL STATUS—categories included single, married (legal or common law), widowed, and divorced. FERTILITY—for the first time the number of children born and the number of children still living was asked of all women fifteen years of age and older. RACE—concept based on the idea of "community"; that is, persons who are bound together by common ties of language, religion, custom, or allegiance were recorded together. In cases of children of mixed marriages or adoption, the name of the community that accepted the individual and to which he claimed to belong was recorded instead of the race or origin. PLACE OF BIRTH—country, state, or settlement of birth was recorded. The year of the first arrival in the Federation of Malaya or colony of Singapore was also asked. The purpose of this question was to come up with an index for internal and external migration as well as to check the results on race. EDUCATION—literacy (ability to read and write in English, Malay, or any other language). OCCUPATION—gainful occupation from which a person receives the greater part of his income and spends most of his time, 31 major groups and 183 subgroups. INDUSTRY—23 divisions and 140 major groups. Occupation and industrial classifications were not based on the United Kingdom scheme but rather developed by the superintendent of the census. OCCUPATIONAL STATUS—wage earner, employer, own-account worker, unpaid family worker.

Special Elements and Features. Model of the schedules, results of enumerations taken during the Japanese occupation, industry and occupation classification, migration statistics, comparative tables for 1931-1947, age pyramids for 1931 and 1947, tables with population counts since 1700s up until early 1800s were all included in the report.

Quality of the Census. The instructions and comments referred to the whole census of Malaya; no separate specifications were given for the islands. Some areas were undercounted mainly because of danger and inaccessibility; others were overcounted due to belief that schedules were to be used for food control program. The census of nomadic population was not synchronous with the general census; it took several months for completion and the results lacked accuracy. Persons in transit were enumerated on special simplified schedules. There was no permanent office for census operation.

Publication Plan. Malaya (Federation). Superintendent of Census. *Malaya Comprising the Federation of Malaya and the Colony of Singapore: A Report on the 1947 Census of Population*, by M.V. del Tufo. London, 1949. (Cited as part of the colony of Singapore.) Language of publication is English.

1957 (June 17)

The seventh census of population of Cocos (Keeling) and Christmas Islands was still taken as part of the colony of Singapore. It was the first time Singapore conducted a census independently from the Federation of Malaya. The census was *de facto*, and canvasser was the method used on householder schedules. Punched card system and mechanical tabulation were adopted. The census of housing was not carried synchronously with the population but was derived from a 10 percent sample taken at the data processing stage.

The results for Christmas Island were presented in separate tables, whereas the results of Cocos (Keeling) Islands were included in the Singapore figures and not separately cited. Reduced number of tables was recorded for Christmas Island.

Definitions and Concepts. HOUSEHOLD—group of persons living together and having common food arrangements. AGE—complete date of birth taken, followed both English and Chinese systems of years. Recorded in standard five-year age groups. MARITAL STATUS and RACE—same as 1947. PLACE OF BIRTH, YEAR OF FIRST ARRIVAL, and OCCUPATIONAL STATUS— results were only for Singapore, not for Christmas Island. EDUCATION—literacy, ability to reåd and write in any language, specifically in English, Malay, Chinese, and Tamil. ECONOMIC ACTIVITY—all persons ten years of age and older, reference period was the week before the census. The active included all persons who were working or looking for work during the reference week. The categories presented were: working more than fifteen hours, fifteen hours or less, and not working but looking for a job. The inactive were homemakers, full-time students, inmates of institutions, pensioners, persons with private income, and the infirm. INDUSTRY—classification based on ISIC but only a few divisions and major groups were recorded. OCCUPATION—only major groups of the Malayan Classification of Occupations 1957 were based on ISCO. OCCUPATIONAL STATUS—not recorded. A note indicated that all persons classified by occupation were employed.

Special Elements and Features. Maps, charts, models of schedules, and abridged life tables are included. Comparison and analysis of the 1947 and 1957 census results are present. Place of birth, year of first arrival, and occupational status left out for Cocos and Christmas. Fertility was dropped.

Quality of the Census. Enumeration was divided into three phases: numbering and listing of houses, preliminary enumeration, and final enumeration; Whipple's Index classified age data of Singapore as whole in category III—approximate data; still no permanent office for census operation; the housing census based on 10 percent sample was found to be inadequate.

Publication Plan. Singapore. Superintendent of Census. *Report on the Census of Population, 1957.* Signapore, 1964. (Cited in separate tables.) Language of publication is English.

1961 (June 30)

Eighth census of the islands but the first under Australian administration. Christmas Island was annexed to Australia in 1958 and Cocos (Keeling) Islands in 1955. The census was *de facto* and self-enumerated. Population and dwelling censuses were taken simultaneously. The information gathered here was taken directly from the tables and some explanatory notes present in each volume, but no special comments on organization or methods were found with respect to enumeration in the islands. Tabulation method is not known.

Definitions and Concepts. AGE—as of last birthday, tabulated in five-year age groups. In addition, two groups (under twenty-one, twenty-one and over) were used. MARITAL STATUS—never married (under and over fifteen years of age), married, married but permanently separated, divorced, and widowed. PLACE OF BIRTH and LENGTH OF RESIDENCE IN THE COUNTRY—name of country of birth and number of years of residence in the country was required from all aliens. NATIONALITY—synonymous with citizenship. Two main groups were recorded: British, which included United Kingdom and colonies, Canada, Australia and New Zealand, Union of South Africa, India, Pakistan, Ceylon, Federation of Rhodesia and Nyasaland, Ghana, Federation of Malaya, the State of Singapore; and foreign—in this case, the name of the country was recorded. RELIGION—religious denominations were divided into two groups: Christians and non-Christians. The answer to the question was optional, and a large number of people chose not to respond. RACE—Europeans, non-Europeans, and Europeans mixed with other races. The last category covered persons of more and less than one-half European blood. ECONOMIC ACTIVITY— classification based on participation in the work force. In the work force—persons at work and persons without a job at the time of the census but who were usually engaged in an industry, occupation, business, trade, or service. Not in the work force—inactive, students, pensioners, inmates of institutions, invalids, persons of independent income, and homemakers. INDUSTRY—Australian Classification of Industry June 1961, major groups, subgroups and categories recorded, but subgroups and categories that had no entry were omitted from the tables. OCCUPATION—Australian Classification of Occupation, 1961, only major groups recorded. OCCUPATIONAL STATUS—employer, self-employed, employee, and helper on wage.

Special Elements and Features. Education (literacy) was not recorded for the islands. Population was not recorded by districts or other smaller geographical unit. Persons who omitted their marital status were allocated a conjugal condition prior to tabulation.

Quality of the Census. The Australian census was classified in Whipple's Index in category I—highly accurate age data, but no special reference was made to Christmas and Cocos (Keeling) Islands. General report for the whole census was not issued; hence, no information concerning methods or organization was published.

Publication Plan. Australia. Commonwealth Bureau of Census and Statistics. *Census of the Commonwealth of Australia.* Volume 7, Territories. Part 5, External territories: population and dwelling. Canberra, 1964. Unpublished data are available, and language of publication is English.

1966 (June 30)

The ninth census of the islands was the second conducted by the Australian Commonwealth Bureau of the Census and Statistics. It was *de facto*, self-enumerated, and the information was compiled from householder's schedules. The results were published in the Census Bulletins 11.1 and 12.1, *Summary of Population*, but were considered preliminary and subject to amendment. However, no other publication was found, and the information gathered here was taken from those bulletins. Tabulation was computerized.

Definitions and Concepts. AGE—as of last birthday, recorded in years and completed months. Tabulated in standard five-year age groups and also under twenty-one, twenty-one to sixty-four and sixty-five and over. MARITAL STATUS, PLACE OF BIRTH, NATIONALITY, LENGTH OF RESIDENCE, and RELIGION—same as 1961. RACE—although part of the Australian census, it was not included in the tables for Christmas Island. ECONOMIC ACTIVITY— to determine inclusion in the work force the following questions were asked: If a person had a job or business during the reference week, although temporarily absent from it? If a person worked at all the week before for profit or payment (persons working as family helper or members of the clergy should answer "yes" to this question, but those doing only unpaid housework should answer "no")? If a person was temporarily laid off without pay? If a person was looking for a job? All persons who answered "yes" to any one of these questions were included in the work force. INDUSTRY—only the major groups of the Australian Standard Industrial Classification were published. OCCUPATION—only the major groups of the ACO. OCCUPATIONAL STATUS—same as 1961.

Special Elements and Features. No data is available for small areas. Education was not included in Christmas Island report. Comparative tables on total population, age, marital status, place of birth, nationality, place of residence, and religion for 1961 and 1966 are present.

Quality of the Census. The Australian census data on age was classified by Whipple's Index as category I—highly accurate data, but there was no specific reference as to whether that of the islands was included in that rating. Only a summary of population was published.

Publication Plan. Australia. Commonwealth Bureau of Census and Statistics. *Census of the Territory of Christmas Island, 30 June 1966. Summary of Population*, by K. M. Archer. Canberra, 1968. (Census bulletin, No. 11-1.) Unpublished data are available, and language of publication is English.

1971 (June 30)

The tenth census of Christmas Island, the third under Australian administration, was *de facto* and self-enumerated on household schedules. Tabulation was computerized. The Australian census did not include the external territories among its publications. The information here was gathered from a facsimile of the schedule and copies of tables sent by the Central Statistics Office of Christmas Island. No information is available for Cocos (Keeling) Islands from this census.

Definitions and Concepts. AGE, MARITAL STATUS, NATIONALITY, and RELIGION—same as 1966. PLACE OF BIRTH—the country of birth and date of first arrival in the territory if born outside of Christmas Island. RACE—the groups recorded were: Caucasian, Ceylonese, Chinese, Cocos Islander, Eurasian, European, Indonesian, Javanaese, Malayan, and Pakistani. If of mixed races, personal choice was used for selection of race. ECONOMIC ACTIVITY—all persons fifteen years of age and older were required to answer the following questions: Did this person have a full- or part-time job or business of any kind the week before the census? Did this person do any work the week before for profit or payment? A negative response to these two questions would exclude a person from the work force. INDUSTRY—classified according to AIC, only major groups. OCCUPATION—classified according to AOC, only major groups. OCCUPATIONAL STATUS—categories were: in the work force and not in the work force. Not in the work force included children not in school, children attending school, pensioners, and those performing home duties. EDUCATION—included in the schedule but no tables were presented.

Special Elements and Features. Tables at this time showed the territory divided into fourteen collector's districts.

Quality of the Census. Extremely reduced amount of information and tables available. No official publication has appeared. Whipple's Index category was I—highly accurate age data.

Publication Plan. (Australian Bureau of Statistics). (*1971 Census of the Territory of Christmas Island*). Canberra, n.d. (a copy of results by collector's districts forwarded by the Department of Home Affairs).

National Topic Chart

	1947	1957	1961	1966	1971
De facto	X	X	X	X	X
Usual residence		(X)			
Place of birth	X	(X)	X	X	X
Duration of residence	X	(X)	X	X	X
Place of prev. residence					
Urban/rural					
Sex	X	X	X	X	X
Age	X	X	X	X	X
Relation to household head	X	X			X
Marital status	X	X	X	X	X
Children born alive	X				
Children living	X				
Citizenship			X	X	X
Literacy	X	X			
School enrollment					
Ed. attainment					
Ed. qualification					
National/Ethnic origin	X	X	X		X
Language		(X)			
Religion			X	X	X
Household composition					
Econ. active/inactive		X	X	X	X
Occupation	X	X	X	X	X
Industry	X	X	X	X	X
Occupational status	X	(X)	X	X	X
Income					
Housing	X		X	X	X

Note: In 1957 (X) means that topics were asked but no tables were presented.

Cocos (Keeling) Islands

External Territory of the Commonwealth of Australia

CAPITAL: West Island.
STATISTICAL AGENCY: not known.
NATIONAL REPOSITORY: Library, Australian Bureau of Statistics.
MAIN U.S. REPOSITORY: Population Research Center (Univ. of Texas).

See Christmas Island entry since censuses were conducted together by the same statistical agencies. Administrative changes that have occurred throughout the years to the Christmas Islands also apply to Cocos (Keeling).

1947

Publication Plan. Same as Christmas Island, 1947.

1957

Publication Plan. Same as Christmas Island, 1957; however, results for Cocos are included in Singapore figures, not separately cited.

1961

Publication Plan. Same as Christmas Island, 1961.

1966

Publication Plan. Australia. Commonwealth Bureau of Census and Statistics. *Census of Territory of Cocos (Keeling) Islands, 30th June 1966. Summary of Population.* [Canberra], 1968. (Census bulletin, No. 12-1). Unpublished data are available, and language of publication is English.

1971

Publication Plan. No publication issued.

National Topic Chart

	1947	1957	1961	1966	1971
De facto	X	X	X	X	X
Usual residence		X			
Place of birth	X	X	X	X	
Duration of residence	X	X	X	X	
Place of prev. residence					
Urban/rural					
Sex	X	X	X	X	
Age	X	X	X	X	
Relation to household head	X	X			
Marital status	X	X	X	X	
Children born alive	X				
Children living	X				
Citizenship			X	X	
Literacy	X	X			
School enrollment					
Ed. attainment					
Ed. qualification					
National/Ethnic origin	X	X	X		
Language		X			
Religion			X	X	
Household composition					
Econ. active/inactive		X	X	X	
Occupation	X	X	X	X	
Industry	X	X	X	X	
Occupational status	X	X	X	X	
Income					
Housing	X		X	X	

Note: In 1957 all results were included into the Singapore figures; no separate tables were
    shown. In 1971, no publication was available.

Cook Islands

New Zealand Dependency

CAPITAL: Avarua, Rarotonga.
STATISTICAL AGENCY: Statistics Office, Central Planning Bureau.
NATIONAL REPOSITORY: Statistics Office, Avarua.
MAIN U.S. REPOSITORY: University of California, Berkeley.

The fifteen component islands of the Cook group are divided into the northern group (Penrhyn, Rakahanga, Minihiki, Pukapuka, Nassau, Suarrow and Palmerston) and the lower group (Mangaia, Rarotonga, Atiu, Mauke, Aitutaki, Mitiaro, Manuae and the inhabited Takutea), which is the principal area of settlement.

During the nineteenth century, several population estimates were made by the missionary groups visiting the islands, but the records were incomplete, and no indication of accuracy was given. The records for Rarotonga's population are more complete than those for the other islands. In 1895 Rarotonga had its first official census, and total population by age for the five districts of the island were recorded. Apparently the sex of each individual was not recorded because six weeks later a supplementary census was requested by the New Zealand government. Despite these two enumerations, accuracy was not achieved. In 1901 another census was taken in Rarotonga, and the results indicated a decreasing population. However, further analysis revealed that the difference of the totals of the two censuses "did not denote a decreasing population so much as an overestimate of people at the 1895 census."

In 1902, after the annexation of the islands to New Zealand, Rarotonga and the other small islands were enumerated, but the detailed results of the census were not found. The first comprehensive census including all the inhabited islands was taken in 1906; and since that time a system of quinquennial censuses was adopted.

These earlier censuses were taken by the Registrar General of the Justice Department on a *de facto* basis, and canvasser was the method used in various forms of schedules. The scope was always very limited as the main interest was to know the total number of inhabitants. The results were published as part of the New Zealand census up until 1966.

Cook Islands

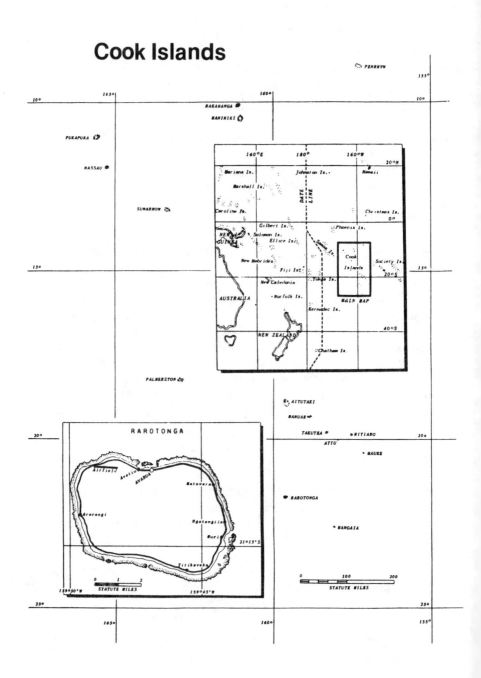

1906

No details of organization were furnished. The scope included: total population divided into natives and half-castes, British born and foreigners, place of birth and residence, approximate age, sex, religion, literacy, and school attendance. The censuses of 1911 and 1916 were the same as 1906.

1921

Household questionnaires, identical to those of the Europeans in New Zealand, were used for the nonnative population in Cook Islands. The scope included: name, relationship to head of household, sex, age, marital status, date of marriage, number of children born alive, number of children still living, industry, occupation, occupational status, period of unemployment, place of birth, allegiance, race, length of residence, country of birth of father, religion, literacy, school attendance, and life insurance. Not all results were published.

The native population, however, was recorded in census books containing the following questions: age, sex, whether full blooded or half-caste, place of birth, usual place of residence, occupation, religion, literacy and school attendance. Like the nonnative population, not all results were published.

1926

Basically the same organization as applied in 1921 was used. Synchronization was still not achieved in all islands. The following tables were published as part of the New Zealand census: native and nonnative total population, sex and place of birth (native and nonnative), occupation (nonnative), religion (native and nonnative), age (native and nonnative), literacy, and school attendance (native). The data, however, are not comparable with previous censuses because the concept of native and nonnative changed; natives and half-castes living with Europeans were no longer considered nonnative population.

1936

The seventh general census of population was also conducted by the Census and Statistics Department in association with the New Zealand census. The organization was similar to the previous census, and the tables published included: total population, age, place of birth, religion and race (native and nonnative population), literacy (native), duration of residence, occupation, nationality, and country of domicile (nonnative).

1945 (September 25)

The eighth general census of population was associated with the census of New Zealand and conducted by the Census and Statistics Department. For the first time, a synchronous census of all islands was achieved. The census was taken on a *de facto* basis, and a combination of canvasser and self-enumeration was adopted. Personal schedules were used by the European part of the population and the natives attached to European dwellings, while book records were used to enumerate the native population. Tabulation was mechanical. Information gathered here was taken from introductory notes and table headings because a general report was not published.

Definitions and Concepts. AGE—recorded in completed years and months and presented in standard five-year age groups. PLACE OF BIRTH—name of the country was recorded from the nonnatives and islands of birth from the natives. RELIGION—natives and nonnatives were classified according to their religious affiliation. A reduced number of denominations was found for natives. The answer to the question was not mandatory, and the verb "object" was used in those cases. RACE—the following categories were recorded for the nonnatives: European, European-Maori, quarter-cast European native, European-Maori-native, European-Chinese-native, European-Chinese-Maori, Chinese-native, Negro-native, and Indian-native. The native population were classified as either full-blood native, three-quarter native or half-native. LITERACY—question asked of native population only, ten years of age and older. Ability to read and write in English as well as in native language. PLACE OF RESIDENCE—duration of residence in number of years was recorded for the nonnatives. ECONOMIC ACTIVITY—questions asked of all persons fifteen years and older. The following groups were classified as persons not actively engaged in gainful occupations: persons performing domestic duties, invalids, "rangatira" (no definition given), and students and youths not working. Occupation was recorded of the nonnative population, and the classification was not presented in separated groups and subgroups but rather in a list of individual occupations in alphabetical order. The native population was presented in a mix of industrial and occupational classification. NATIONALITY—political allegiance and country of domicile were recorded for the nonnative population. WAR SERVICE—number of nonnative persons in service in World War I and World War II and the South African War.

Special Elements and Features. The island of Nassau was not inhabited at the time of the census. The personal schedule used in New Zealand was the same for the European population (nonnatives) in the islands. However, results of marital status, number of dependent children, occupational status, number of working hours, journey to work (traveling time), and unemployment were not available for the islands. A table with native population of village districts was furnished.

Quality of the Census. Whipple's Index made no reference to the accuracy of age data, but introductory notes of the census reported data as fairly accurate and that in some instances estimates rather than actual age were recorded. In addition, "tabulation of occupational distribution of both natives and non-natives has been incorporated for interest, rather than from the point of view of any inherent value contained in the results." No general report was published.

Publication Plan. New Zealand. Census and Statistics Department. *Popula-*

tion census, 1945. Volume 2, Island territories. Auckland, 1947. Language of publication is English.

1951, 1956, 1961

Up until 1945 the results of the censuses were published in conjunction with the New Zealand census. The 1951, 1956, and 1961 censuses were conducted by the Cook Islands Administration, but the only published results were summary tables in the *Annual Reports on the Cook Islands* presented to the New Zealand parliament.

The following mimeographed tables are available for the years 1956 and 1961: (1956) Manuae marital status by age and sex; Manuae racial origin by sex, Manuae religion by sex, Manuae population by age and sex, Manuae occupations, place of birth and fertility.

(1961): Population by districts, sex and island, age of female at birth of the first child, fertility (number of children born to each woman by age of woman and marital status), place of birth by island and sex, racial origin by island and sex, religion by island and sex, marital status by age and sex, and religion by island and sex.

Total number of inhabitants was included in the general report of the New Zealand censuses of the respective years.

1966 (September 1)

Twelfth general census of population and the first taken after independence in 1965. It was the first census to be published in a separate report, and the scope was enlarged to cover aspects of the Cook Islands not previously dealt with. No details related to organization and methods used were furnished by the Justice Department, the agency responsible for the census. The information gathered here was taken from the table headings and introductory notes included in the report. Tabulation was computerized, and the results were published and edited in New Zealand. Population and housing censuses were taken simultaneously.

Thirteen islands were part of Cook Islands—Rarotonga, Aitutaki, Mangaia, Atiu, Mauke, Mitiaro, Manuae, Palmerston, Pukapuka, Nassau, Manihiki, Rakahanga, and Penrhyn. The island of Suwarrow was uninhabited at the time of the census.

Definitions and Concepts. AGE—presented in standard five-year age groups and in single years. MARITAL STATUS—categories were: never married, married, legally separated, widowed, and divorced. The marriageable age was eighteen for males and fifteen for females. Legal separation was based on the New Zealand laws not those of the Cook Islands. FERTILITY—number of children ever born, number of children still living, age of women at birth of the first child. PLACE OF BIRTH—island of birth was asked of natives and country of birth of foreigners. PLACE OF RESIDENCE—present residence and duration were recorded. RACE—the following detailed categories were presented: full-blood

Maori, more than half-caste, half-caste, and less than half-caste. The half-caste were subdivided into C. I. (Cook Island) Maori-European, C. I. Maori-French Polynesian, C. I. Maori-Niuean, and C. I. Maori-other races. The less than half-caste were divided into European-C. I. Maori, European-French Polynesian-C. I. Maori, and other races-C. I. Maori. Full Europeans, full French Polynesians and other Pacific islanders were among other racial groups. RELIGION—religious affiliation recorded, but at this time the category "No religion" and "Object to state" were separately classified. ECONOMIC ACTIVITY—the economically active were all employed persons, unpaid family workers, and the unemployed looking for job. Economically inactive were the retired and persons dependent on public or private support. INDUSTRY—classification based on ISIC, nine divisions and major groups (two-digits). OCCUPATON—based on ISCO, nine major groups, groups, and subgroups (three-digits). OCCUPATIONAL STATUS—categories were: employer, own-account worker, on salary or wages for full time (part time or casually), mainly subsistence, relative assisting, unemployed seeking work (actively engaged), and the retired, and those dependent on public or private support (inactives). INCOME—primary, secondary incomes and income other than salary, wages or own account were recorded. EDUCATION—school attendance, educational attainment, and educational qualification were taken.

Special Elements and Features. Larger scope than the previous censuses that included industrial and occupational classifications, income, education, dwellings, and livestock. Five-year age groups are used in comparative tables for 1956, 1961, and 1966. A table of the economically active female by age and marital status is included.

Quality of the Census. Whipple's Index not available. The introductory notes, however, acknowledged that after the introduction of self-government, there was no time for detailed planning of the census operations and that "a number of technical problems arose, some of which were not fully solved, but valuable experience has been gained . . . for planning future censuses."

Publication Plan. Cook Islands. Census Supervisor. *Population Census, 1966.* Wellington, 1968. Language of publication is English.

1971 (date unknown)

The results were mimeographed in brief by the Statistics Office in Cook Islands and contain the following tables: Rarotonga population by sex (C. I. Maori and other Maori) for each census district. Comparative tables published in the 1976 census indicate that at least the following were also taken: religion, industry, housing amenities, materials of construction. Classified in Whipple's Index category I—highly accurate age data. Unpublished data are available.

1976 (December 1)

The fourteenth general census of population was the second conducted by the Statistics Office of the Central Planning Bureau. The census was *de facto*, and canvassers were used in completing personal and household schedules. Tabulation was semimanual sorting and edge-punch cards. The 1966 and 1971 censuses used computerized tabulation, but for various reasons publication of results was extremely delayed. For this reason the 1976 census returned to the manual system. Population and housing censuses were taken simultaneously. The territory covered by the census included the thirteen islands mentioned in the 1966 census plus Suwarrow (inhabited in 1971 and 1976).

Definitions and Concepts. AGE—date of birth and completed years. Presented in single years standard five-year age groups. PLACE OF BIRTH—same as 1966. PLACE OF RESIDENCE—address at the night of the census, usual place of residence, and previous residence (in 1971) were recorded. EDUCATION—school attendance, educational attainment (class completed and certificate obtained), educational qualification, and specification of vocational education were recorded. RACE—four groups were presented: C. I. Maori, C. I. Maori-European, European, and C. I. Maori-French Polynesian. RELIGION—same as 1966. NATIONALITY—asked only of non-C. I. Maori and recorded according to passport. In addition, residential status (resident, contract worker, or visitor) and length of stay were recorded. FAMILY—nuclear (head, spouse, and unmarried children). However, in the Cook Islands families are extended, including married and unmarried children, grandchildren, parents, parents-in-law, grandparents, uncles, aunts, brothers, sisters, and so forth. MARITAL STATUS—same as 1966. ECONOMIC ACTIVITY—questions asked of all persons fifteen years of age and older. The economically active were: employed for subsistence or cash, unpaid family worker, and unemployed looking for work (experienced or new). Economically inactive included: unpaid domestic workers, students, retired and income recipients, and unemployed not looking for work. All questions were related to work activity two weeks before the census (time reference). OCCUPATION—no indication was given as to whether classification was based on ISCO or not. Only eight major groups were presented. INDUSTRY—no indication was given of whether classification was based on ISIC or not. Only nine divisions were presented. FERTILITY—questions asked of all women fifteen years of age or older: number of children born alive, number of children still living, age at birth of first child, whether last born child was still alive, and date of birth of last child.

Special Elements and Features. Residential status of contract workers was asked for the first time. Ownership and entitlement to land asked in 1971 were dropped. Comparative tables and some unpublished results of earlier censuses were presented. Data on concentration of income distribution, although not collected during the census, were presented based on an employment survey conducted in 1975. Population projections and estimates and an analysis of census results are present in the report. Charts and graphs and copy of the schedules are included. Cross-classification was very limited, and statistical tables on details of occupation and industry are to be published separately.

Quality of the Census. The census planning with mapping and delineation of boundaries of the enumeration areas, preparation of schedules and training of field workers increased the completeness and accuracy of the results. Publication of results was presented in less than a year after enumeration in spite of the fact that data processing was done semimanually. The census office is reestablished for each census. Although with a long history of censuses, synchronization was only achieved in 1945 and publication of results was limited as long as Cook Island results were part of the New Zealand census (up until 1966). Even after that (1971), results were many times reduced to mimeographed pages.

Publication Plan. Cook Islands. Central Planning Bureau. Statistics Office. *1976 Population Census, Preliminary Report.* Rarotonga, [1977]. *Census of Population and Housing, 1976.* Rarotonga, 1977. Language of publication is English.

OTHER STATISTICAL PUBLICATIONS: Issued by Statistics Office, *Quarterly Statistical Bulletin.*

National Topic Chart

	1945	1951	1956	1961	1966	1971	1976
De facto	X		X	X	X		X
Usual residence					X		X
Place of birth	X		X	X	X		X
Duration of residence	X				X		
Place of prev. residence							X
Urban/rural							
Sex	X	X	X	X	X	X	X
Age	X		X	X	X	X	X
Relation to household head	X						X
Marital status			X	X	X		X
Children born alive			X	X	X		X
Children living					X		X
Citizenship	X						
Literacy	X						
School enrollment					X		X
Ed. attainment					X		X
Ed. qualification					X		
National/Ethnic origin	X		X	X	X		X
Language							
Religion	X		X	X	X		X
Household composition							
Econ. active/inactive					X		X
Occupation	X		X	X	X		X
Industry	X				X		X
Occupational status					X		X
Income					X		
Housing							X

Note: The 1951, 1956, 1961 and 1971 census results were extremely reduced and published in mimeographed annual reports.

Fiji

Dominion of Fiji

CAPITAL: Suva.
STATISTICAL AGENCY: Bureau of Statistics.
NATIONAL REPOSITORY: The Government Archives, Suva.
MAIN U.S. REPOSITORY: Population Research Center (Univ. of Texas).

The Fiji Islands are a total of 840 islands of which only 106 are inhabited. The islands were ceded to Britain in 1874 and became an independent parliamentary democracy in 1970. The first census was taken in 1879, but it was a rough count of heads, and it is known to be incomplete. In 1881, a census was "taken upon a somewhat primitive system—the best that could be devised to suit the capacity of the natives at the time, when some approximation to accuracy was all that could be hoped for—but not to be relied upon to produce anything more than a rough estimate of the population." Each successive census sought more comprehensive information, but the records of the censuses prior to 1911 are incomplete as far as details of organization and procedures. A series of decennial censuses started in 1881 and continued until 1921. They began again in 1936 to the present.

1891

A census was conducted by the Registrar's General Office, and the results included the following tables: total population of districts by race and sex; age, place of birth, marital status and occupation of white population; age of half-castes; broad age categories for Indians, Polynesians, Fijians and others by sex; and livestock. A separate table with population by sex and broad age categories was also recorded for the island of Rotuma.

The census of 1901 was the same as that of 1891.

1911

The fifth general census was conducted by the census commissioner on a *de facto* basis. It was mostly self-enumerated, but the Indian population was canvassed. The enumeration of Fijians living in native communities was carried out by the chief of each village. Six different household schedules and one special form for Fijians living in native communities were utilized. The scope included: age, sex, marital status, place of birth and occupation (of Europeans and other

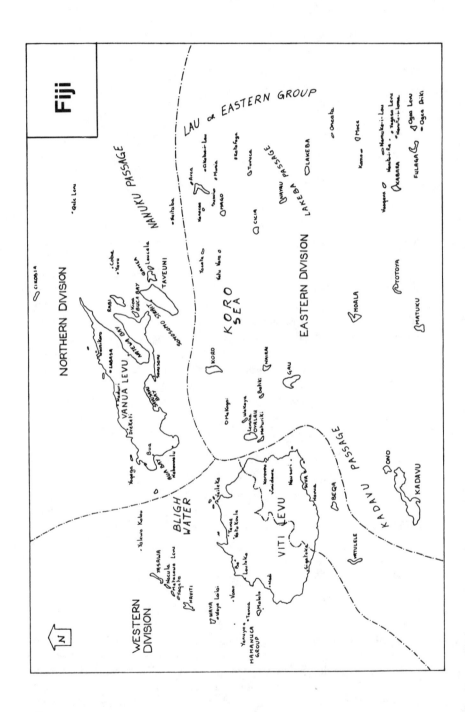

whites, half-castes, and Indians); religion (all races); infirmities (all races); literacy (whites, half-castes, Fijians and Indians); migration (Indians); age, sex, occupation (Fijians); age (Polynesians, Chinese, and others); and livestock (all races). The results of the census of Rotuma were presented in separate tables, including total population, sex, race, age, religion, literacy, and infirmities. For the first time, the Chinese group was presented as a separate component. Before this census, they were included in the general group "others."

The territory covered by the census included seventeen provinces divided into districts, towns, and native Fijian villages. NOTE: The tables of all Fiji censuses are divided by racial groups.

1921

The sixth census was conducted by the census commissioner on a *de facto* basis. A combination of self-enumeration and canvasser was the method used to record information on household schedules. For the first time an attempt was made to publish uniform information on all races. The scope included: age, sex, marital status, occupation, place of birth, religion, infirmities, density (of all races), and literacy (not published for Europeans, half-caste, Chinese, and Japanese). The nineteen provinces were divided into districts and villages. Boundaries and names of provinces changed throughout the history of the censuses; therefore, an index of Fijian villages was furnished in alphabetical order.

1936

The seventh census of population was conducted by the census commissioner on a *de facto* basis. Self-enumeration was the method used to record information on seven different schedules. However, the information recorded was about the same in all schedules. The questionnaires were printed in three languages—English, Fijian, and Hindustani. Scope included: name, relationship to head of household, sex, age, marital status, place of birth, nationality, religion, literacy, school attendance, ability to speak English (new), infirmities, occupation, and industry (new). In addition, types of houses were asked of Fijians living in villages, race of parents was asked of Indians, and race of wives asked of Chinese. Nineteen provinces, Rotuma, and Makongai were covered in the census.

1946 (October 3)

The eighth census of population was conducted by the census commissioner on a *de facto* basis. Unlike 1936, only one type of household schedule was utilized, and it was printed in English, Fijian, and Hindustani. This was the fullest census so far taken in Fiji, including several housing questions and a few more personal ones. Questions on poultry were also asked. Canvasser was the method used and the tabulation was totally manual. For the first time, the census procedures were made uniform for all sections of the population. The distribution of the population was presented by provinces, "tikina," towns, villages, and localities. However, most of the tables were divided by components of population instead of geographical divisions.

Definitions and Concepts. TIKINA—subdivision of a province. AGE—stated in completed years and months. Tabulated in single years and standard five-year age groups. MARITAL STATUS—categories were: never married, married, legally separated, widowed, and divorced. Question was asked of persons thirteen years and older. FERTILITY—For married women only: number of children born alive and number of children now dead. PLACE OF BIRTH—country of birth was recorded and presented in two major groups—British commonwealth and foreign countries. For persons born outside of Fiji, the number of years living in the country was also recorded. Nationality was derived from these questions. RACE—a large list of racial origins was recorded. If the person was of more than two races, particulars were asked, for example, European-Fijian-Samoan. The word "half-caste" was abolished. RELIGION—religious denomination recorded. EDUCATION—school attendance and educational attainment (class reached at school). LANGUAGE—language and literacy were derived from the following questions: In what language can this person read and write? Has this person at least a simple working knowledge of English speech? ECONOMIC ACTIVITY—For persons twelve years of age and older. The gainful occupation concept was used. Economically active were those who earn money, perform a service as unpaid family workers, and those who assist with the production of goods of commercial value. Inactive population included: landlords, the retired, inmates of institutions, children under twelve, students, and homemakers. Those unemployed or performing unpaid domestic duties (other than wives and children) were considered active. The number of weeks worked one year before the census was recorded for the first time. Persons who worked for less than twelve weeks were not included in the active population. OCCUPATION—classification based on New Zealand Classification of Occupations and Industries 1945 (COI) with modifications to suit conditions in Fiji. Twenty-six major groups and subgroups were recorded (two-digits). INDUSTRY—fourteen divisions and major groups (two-digits). OCCUPATIONAL STATUS—categories were: employer, own-account worker, salary or wage earner, unpaid family worker, and not applicable, including not stated. PLACE OF RESIDENCE—usual place of residence (for Fiji residents), and name of the country of usual residence (for nonresidents). INFIRMITIES—blind, dumb, lunatics, and feebleminded were recorded.

Special Elements and Features. Larger number of questions on housing asked. Different racial denominations were adopted. Number of gainfully occupied and number of weeks worked were asked for the first time. Results of Rotuma were tabulated separately as in the previous censuses; however, industry and occupation tables included the results for Rotuma within the total population. An alphabetical list of Fijian villages was provided. Maps and graphs with density, population growth, and division of the colony into census districts were presented.

Quality of the Census. Precautions were taken to ensure accuracy and full count of the population. However, figures for unpaid family workers should be taken carefully because of the misunderstanding of the question by those who follow the Fijian communal system of living. Whipple's Index classified age accuracy into category IV—rough data. No permanent census office.

Publication Plan. Fiji. Census Commissioner's Office. *A Report on the Results of the Census of Population, 1946*, by John W. Gittens. Suva, 1947. Legislative Council Paper, No. 35 of 1947. Language of publication is English.

1956 (September 26)

The ninth census of population was conducted by the census commissioner, who was appointed from outside the territory. The census was *de facto*, and canvasser was the method utilized to record information on household schedules. The schedules were printed only in English, but the instructions were in all three languages. A personal schedule was used in group quarters, and the questions on description of dwellings and relationship to head of the household were omitted. For the first time mechanical tabulation was utilized. The census covered sixteen provinces, including Rotuma. Provinces changed names and boundaries; therefore, comparability becomes difficult from one census to the next.

Definitions and Concepts. HOUSEHOLD—a group of persons of the same family, living in a single dwelling house and sharing food and sleeping arrangements. Servants and visitors who either slept in the house or were fed by the family were considered members of the household. AGE—completed years and birth date; tabulated in single years and standard five-year age groups. FERTILITY—women only, fifteen years of age and older: number of children ever born, number of children still living, number of children now dead, and age of the mother at birth of first child. MARITAL STATUS—categories were: never married, married (legally or common law), widowed, and divorced. PLACE OF BIRTH—for Fiji born, the name of province in which the person was registered as land owner (not of actual birth); for those born outside Fiji, name of the island group or country were recorded. RACE—the following groups were presented: Chinese or part-Chinese, European, Fijian, Indian, part-European, Rotuman, Samoan, and Tongan. RELIGION—exact denomination or sect. The verb "object" was used for those unwilling to answer. ECONOMIC ACTIVITY—economically active were those persons engaged either in subsistence agriculture or in any kind of paid occupation. The economically inactive included persons of independent income, students, pensioners, the retired, inmates of institutions, those performing home duties, and unemployed. The questions were asked of persons fifteen years of age or older. OCCUPATION—only the following groups were recorded: proprietorial, managerial and executives; supervisory and clerical; skilled workers; semiskilled workers; and other workers. The word "status" does not mean occupational status as used traditionally but rather a socioeconomic status related to the ranking of the person's occupation within a particular industry. INDUSTRY—ten divisions and groups (two-digits). The word industry, for census purposes, was used to cover all forms of economic activity from subsistence agriculture to highly specialized professional services.

Special Elements and Features. Usual residence, citizenship, literacy, education, occupational status, and number of weeks worked were dropped from the census. Fertility questions differed and were addressed to all women fifteen years of age and older instead of only married women as in 1946. The question on language was asked only of the Indian population. Housing questions were dropped.

Quality of the Census. Whipple's Index classified age data into category IV—rough data. The census office was still temporary. Completeness of the census was considered satisfactory since only in a few exceptional areas were a few households omitted.

Publication Plan. Fiji. Census Commissioner's Office. *Report on the Census of Population, 1956*, by Norma McArthur. Suva, 1958. Legislative Council Paper, No. 1 of 1958. 1 volume. Language of publication is English.

1966 (September 12)

The tenth census of population, as in 1956, was conducted by a census commissioner from Australia with assistance of local officers. The organization was modeled on the plan of the 1956 census. It was taken on a *de facto* basis; canvasser was the method used to record information on household schedules. A few personal schedules with approximately the same number of questions were supplied to group quarters. The questionnaires were printed in English only, but the instructions for the enumerators were given in three languages (English, Fijian, and Hindustani). Tabulation was mechanical. A precensus was conducted ten days before the general enumeration. The census covered eighteen provinces divided into "tikinas" and enumeration areas, but boundaries of several towns were changed making comparisons difficult between 1956 and 1966.

Definitions and Concepts. URBAN—fourteen specific places based on commercial and administrative functions and presence of public utilities. Only eight had legal status; the others were unincorporated townships. HOUSEHOLD, AGE, MARITAL STATUS, RACE, and LANGUAGE—same as 1956. FERTILITY—all women fifteen years and older: number of children ever born, number of children still living, and age of mother at birth of first child. PLACE OF BIRTH—for Fiji born, the name of the province; for those born outside Fiji, the name of the island group or the name of their country. RELIGION—religious denomination or sect of a religion. It was presented in two major groups—Christians and non-Christians and their respective subgroups. "No religion, not stated, and object" were the three other categories recorded. EDUCATION—asked of all persons fifteen years and older: educational attainment. ECONOMIC ACTIVITY— economically active were: all persons fifteen years of age and older engaged in an industry plus unemployed persons. Reference period was as of the census date. Economically inactive included: dependent persons under fifteen, persons of independent income and the retired, inmates of institutions and the incapacitated, and those engaged in home duties. Economic activity was derived from the following questions: What work does this person do? For whom, and where does he do it? INDUSTRY—as in 1956, the concept extended from subsistence agriculture to highly specialized professional services. Classification included ten divisions and major groups (two-digits). OCCUPATION—same as 1956.

Special Elements and Features. Educational attainment was revived. Differentiation of urban and rural population was only roughly determined. Most tables were still divided by components of population (racial groups) instead of geographical areas.

Quality of the Census. Accuracy of age was improved with comparison between census data and birth registration. Whipple's Index classified accuracy of age data into category III—approximate data. Census maps were prepared, but some were missing; others had poorly defined boundaries, thus bringing errors in coverage and causing difficulties for future comparisons.

Publication Plan. Fiji. Census Commissioner's Office. *Report on the Census of the Population, 1966*, by F. H. A. G. Zwart. Suva, 1968. Legislative Council Paper, No. 9 of 1968. Unpublished data and computer tapes are available. Language of publication is English.

1976 (September 13)

The eleventh census of population was conducted by the census commissioner on a *de facto* basis. Canvasser was the method used to record information on household schedules. More information was obtained in this census than in any other census taken in Fiji. The census office is still temporary; but since 1974 preparatory works and a pilot census were designed to test all phases of the enumeration. Tabulation was for the first time computerized. The census covered the eighteen provinces divided into "tikinas" and localities.

Definitions and Concepts. HOUSEHOLD—a person or group of persons living together and sharing the work and the costs of providing food. Domestic servants and visitors who ate with the other members of the household were included as members. AGE—date of birth. Results presented in single years and standard five-year age groups. RACE—categories: Chinese or part-Chinese, European, Fijian, Indian, part-European, Rotuman, Samoan, Tongan, and so forth. PLACE OF BIRTH—for native born, province, town, village, and locality were recorded. The mother's usual place of residence was also recorded. Foreign born were asked country of birth. PLACE OF RESIDENCE—previous as well as usual place of residence were asked. ORPHANHOOD—whether parents still alive, and whether person's mother present in the household were asked. EDUCATION—school attendance and educational attainment (highest degree completed or still attending). RELIGION—religious denomination recorded. The words "object" and "none" were used if the case applied. ECONOMIC ACTIVITY—time reference was the week before the census. Questions asked only of persons born in 1962 or before. Economically active included persons working plus unemployed (experienced or inexperienced but looking for a job). Inactive population included students, unpaid homemakers, the retired, the disabled, inmates of institutions, those resting, tourists in private households, armed forces, and others. INDUSTRY—classification based on ISIC, divisions and major groups (two-digits). OCCUPATION—Fiji Classification and Dictionary of Occupation, 1975, major groups, groups, and subgroups (three-digits). OCCUPATIONAL STATUS—categories were: employer, self-employed, government wage or salary, private wage and salary, unpaid family worker, villager, and other (inexperienced unemployed and not stated). MARITAL STATUS—categories were: never married, currently married, widowed, and divorced. Marriage order (times married), and whether the first husband or wife was still alive were also recorded. FERTILITY—For all women born in 1962 and before: number of children ever born, number of children still living, and age of mother at birth of the first child.

Special Elements and Features. In addition to the printed results, more detailed information is available on tapes. Previous residence and marriage order were asked for the first time. Occupational status was revived. Language was dropped. Localities within "tikina" are not comparable to 1966 because there is no general agreement about locality names. An alphabetical list of localities was given.

Quality of the Census. The pilot census improved the planning of the enumeration, the layout of the schedules, and the field work. The results of the census were compared with the estimates based on the 1966 census, birth and death registration, and migration statistics; the coverage was considered good. As far as content, the general accuracy was improved, although some questions on economic activity and fertility for persons between fifteen and twenty years of age were sometimes not asked by the enumerators. Whipple's Index category was III—fairly accurate age data. Census office is still reestablished for each census.

Publication Plan. Fiji. Census Commissioner's Office. *Report on the Census of Population, 1976.* Suva, 1977-1979. Volumes 1-3 in 4 volumes. (Parliamentary papers, nos. 13 of 1977, 43 and 44 of 1979). Report on urban boundaries and two analysis volumes were also published. Unpublished data and computer tapes are available. Language of publication is English.

OTHER STATISTICAL PUBLICATIONS: Issued by Bureau of Statistics, *Current Economic Statistics* (quarterly), *Social Indicators for Fiji* (irregularly).

National Topic Chart

	1946	1956	1966	1976
De facto	X	X	X	X
Usual residence	X			X
Place of birth	X	X	X	X
Duration of residence	X			
Place of prev. residence				X
Urban/rural			X	X
Sex	X	X	X	X
Age	X	X	X	X
Relation to household head	X	X	X	X
Marital status	X	X	X	X
Children born alive	X	X	X	X
Children living	X*	X	X	X
Citizenship	X			
Literacy	X**		X†	
School enrollment	X			X
Ed. attainment	X		X	X
Ed. qualification				
National/Ethnic origin	X	X	X	X
Language	X**	X††	X††	
Religion	X	X	X	X
Household composition	X	X	X	X
Econ. active/inactive	X	X	X	X
Occupation	X	X	X	X
Industry	X	X	X	X
Occupational status	X			X
Income				
Housing	X			

*Number of children dead.
**Language and literacy recorded together.
†Derived from school enrollment.
††For Indians only.

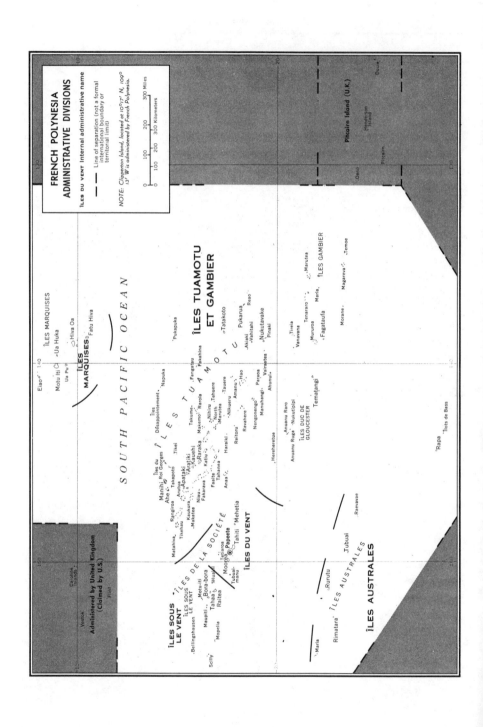

FRENCH POLYNESIA
ADMINISTRATIVE DIVISIONS

ÎLES DU VENT Internal administrative name

— — — Line of separation (not a formal
international boundary or
territorial limit)

0   100   200   300 Miles
0   100   200   300 Kilometers

NOTE: Clipperton Island, located at 10°17' N, 109°
13' W is administered by French Polynesia.

SOUTH PACIFIC OCEAN

ÎLES MARQUISES

Eiao   140
Motu Iti   Ua Huka
Ua Pu   Hiva Oa
ÎLES   Fatu Hiva
MARQUISES

Îles du Georges
Manihi Roi
Ahe   Napuka
Matahiva   Takapoto   Tikei
Tikehau Rangiroa Arutua
Kaukura Apataki
Makatea Niau Kauehi Katiu
Fakarava   Faaite Tahanea
Anaa   Haraiki
Fangatau
Takume   Raroia Fakahina
Makemo   Nihiru Tehuere
North
Marutea
Nukueru
Reitoru
Ravahere   Amanu
Nengonengo   Hao
Manuhangi   Paraoa
Ahunui   Vairaatea
Hereheretue

ÎLES TUA MOTU
ET GAMBIER

ÎLES TUA MOTU

Pukapuka

Tatakoto

Akiaki   Reao
Vahitahi
Nukutavake
Pinaki

Tirela   Marutea
Vanavana
Tenararo
Mururoa   Maria
Fagataufa

Morane   Magareva   Temoe

ÎLES GAMBIER

Anuanu Raro
Anuanu Raga Nukutipipi
ÎLES DUC DE
GLOUCESTER
Tematangi

ÎLES DE LA SOCIÉTÉ

ÎLES SOUS
LE VENT
Mopiti
Tahaa Bora-bora
Raitea   Moorea   Papeete
Tubuai-   Tahiti Mehetia
Bellingshausen   manu
Maupiti   Tetiaroa
ÎLES DU VENT

ÎLES SOUS
LE VENT
Mopelia
Scilly

Raevavae

Rurutu   Tubuai
ÎLES AUSTRALES

Maria   Rapa Îlots de Bass
Rimatara
ÎLES AUSTRALES

Vostok
Caroline
Islands

Administered by United Kingdom
(Claimed by U.S.)

Flint

Pitcairn Island (U.K.)

Oeno   Henderson
Island
Pitcairn   Ducie

French Polynesia

French Overseas Territory (TOM)

CAPITAL: Papeete, Island of Tahiti.
STATISTICAL AGENCY: Institute Territorial de la Statistique (Papeete and INSEE (Paris).
NATIONAL REPOSITORY: Institute Territorial de la Statistique.
MAIN U.S. REPOSITORY: University of California, Berkeley.

Annexed by the French in 1880, it was called French Oceania until 1957. The territory is made up of the Society Islands (Windward and Leeward), the Marquesas, the Australes, and the Tuamotu-Gambiers. Except in secondary sources little has survived from the pre-World War II censuses (1887-1936). Comparative tables have not been present in publications other than those that compare the legal population with previous censuses. Nothing is known of the procedures used nor of the accuracy of the data. In fact, INSEE feels that they were estimates rather than enumerations.

In the post-World War II period the French government has shown more interest in the territorial censuses, but there is still a lack of complete information about the organization and methodology in the publications that offer results for French Polynesia.

As with all French based censuses, the designation of the legal population is somewhat different from the usual. The totaling of two of or all three of the following segments constitutes the legal population for the specific area:

1. "Population municipale"—private households and collective households (inhabited by those who freely choose to reside there, for example, live-in hospital staff, hotel residents).

2. "Population comptée à part"—populations in institutions (inhabited by those who have little or no choice to reside there, for example, military on base, boarding students, prisoners, patients—not staff—in hospitals of all kinds of relatively long term duration, and public works laborers in barracks).

3. "Double compte"—inhabitants of "comptée à part" institutions in one commune who maintain a personal residence in another are counted in both communes.

Generally, the commune legal population is a combination of all three; whereas the legal population of larger administrative units of the whole territory is the total of numbers one and two only.

1946 (June 10)

To satisfy the French decree of a census of the "non-originaire" population (Europeans and assimilated, or nonindigenous), the census of French Oceania was taken of the total population with tables totally separating the "non-originaire" from the "originaire." It was a *de facto* census, using individual schedules, but it is not stated whether it was self-enumerated or canvassed. It could have been both. The major territorial divisions were the island groups with Papeete singled out. The method of tabulation was not mentioned.

Definitions and Concepts. BIRTHPLACE—island or country; those born in France gave "département." Year of arrival for those born outside of the territory was also asked. AGE—year of birth. Tables give real age and generational age in standard five-year age groups. MARITAL STATUS—single, married, widowed, and divorced. No statement if common law included in married or single; traditionally marital status has been legal. FERTILITY— asked of both males and females: number of children ever born alive and the number surviving. RELIGION—general denominations, for example, Catholic or Protestant. NATIONALITY—emphasis on citizenship rather than on ethnic or racial classification. OCCUPATIONS—ten groups only, classified according to industry. OCCUPATIONAL STATUS—employer, employees, own-account worker, and not stated. MIGRATION—only immigration of continental French born and naturalized French citizens.

Special Elements and Features. Separate publications for Oceanians and for nonindigenous populations. It was the first time for data on fertility and citizenship and perhaps for religion, occupation, and occupational status.

Quality of the Census. Uniform individual schedule was used for all French overseas possessions. French Polynesia chose to census the total population rather than just the nonindigenous. Whipple's Index category was not indicated.

Publication Plan. France. INSEE. *Résultats dans les territoires d'outre-mer: Établissements français d'Oceanie.* Paris, 1950. (*Bulletin Mensual de la Statistique d'Outre-Mer [BMSOM]*, série "statistique," nos. 11 and 12.) Language of publication is French.

1951 (September 17)

Many of the other French overseas possessions took only a nonindigenous census this year; French Oceania again enumerated the total population. The census was *de facto*, self-enumerated, and mechanically tabulated. Individual schedules were used. Territorial divisions were the same as 1946.

Definitions and Concepts. MARITAL STATUS, NATIONALITY, and OCCUPATIONAL STATUS are the same as 1946. BIRTHPLACE—same as 1946, plus birthplace of both parents. AGE—date of birth. Tables in real age and generational age in standard five-year age groups. EDUCATION (new) —literacy and educational attainment. OCCUPATION—breakdown by sector (public or private). Classified in INSEE 1947 list. INDUSTRY (new)—"activité collectif"—classification based on INSEE 1949 list. FAMILY COMPOSITION— asked the number of children ever born outside continental France and how many usually reside with the family in the overseas territory. MIGRATION— asked of metropolitan French, other French citizens, and foreigners: age when first arrived in a tropical territory (not necessarily this one) and duration. Usual residence given only by residents who were temporarily absent (less than six months).

Special Elements and Features. First time that education and industry were taken. Religion, while not in the schedule, was included in the tabulations, proba- bly from another source. Continued separation in the tables of the "originaire" and "non-originaire" populations. The "non-originaire" were also included in a sepa- rate publication giving results for the nonindigenous in all the overseas possessions.

Quality of the Census. INSEE, the metropolitan France statistical agency, is becoming more and more involved in the organization, preparation, and publi- cation of the overseas censuses. In the process of tabulation, however, they found many gaps in the data collected. No Whipple's Index rank was cited.

Publication Plan. France. INSEE. *Résultats de recensement de 1951: terri- toires d'outre-mer: 4ᵉ partie, Océanie (ensemble de la population)*. Paris, n.d. (*BMSOM*, serie "statistique," no. 17). *Le Recensement de la population non originaire des territoires d'outre-mer en 1951. Paris, n.d. (BMSOM*, série "étude," no. 33). Language of publication is French.

1956 (September 12)

Taken on a *de facto* and *de jure* basis for the first time, this introduced the rather complicated process of determining the legal (*de jure*) population of a specific geographic division. (See introduction.) It is not known if the census was self-enumerated or canvassed, but the schedule was changed to the house- hold one. The territorial divisions are the same as 1946 and 1951 plus communes.

Definitions and Concepts. HOUSEHOLD—one person living alone or a group of persons who usually live together in the same dwelling and share living arrangements. Residents who were temporarily absent and visitors were so indicated on the schedule. Family members (spouses or unmarried children under twenty-one) who did not reside with the head were also listed (to deter- mine the "famille coupé"). AGE—asked in month and year of birth. Tables of both real age and generational age, in single years and standard five-year age groups. Median age also given. MARITAL STATUS—same as 1946 and 1951 plus an indication of marriages of mixed nationalities. NATIONALITY— more citizenship than ethnic, although the latter can be deduced with some degree of accuracy. Tables indicated French by birth (born in France, in Oceania, and in other French overseas possessions), naturalized French (of Asiatic and other origin), and foreigners (European, Chinese, other Asian, and other nationalities). EDUCATION—educational attainment was asked, but literacy (number of illiterates) was also included in tables. FERTILITY—asked of both males and females age fourteen and over: number of children ever born alive. BIRTHPLACE—department in France or country for foreign born who also indicated the year of arrival in the territory. MIGRATION—immigration, for those born outside the territory only. HOUSEHOLD COMPOSITION— head without spouse or child, married couple without child at home, married couple with children, common-law couple with or without children, single parent. ECONOMIC ACTIVITY—main occupation at the moment of census; unemployed gave last occupation. The inactive were not specified in the tables. The active (employed and unemployed) gave occupation and occupational situation by sector: public (unemployed, civil servant, helper, contracted employee, day-laborer, unknown); semipublic (unemployed, owner, supervisor, employed worker, own-account craftsman, apprentice); private (same as semipublic plus unpaid family worker); military (term of service, career, contracted, extended enlistment, civilian personnel, unknown). From this, the socioeconomic status and socioprofessional category were established. OCCUPATION—classified in INSEE-UN 1954. INDUSTRY—classified by INSEE list.

Special Elements and Features. Presence of tables of socioeconomic status, socioprofessional category, and division by economic sector. Emphasis placed on married couples and household composition. Vital statistics from other sources included to evaluate census results. Median age column located in age tables.

Quality of the Census. Evaluation performed through use of vital statistics. There is progressively greater involvement of INSEE in the conduct of the census. Whipple's Index rating is not cited.

Publication Plan. France. INSEE [and] Ministère de la France d'Outre-Mer. Service des Statistiques. *Recensement général de la population, décembre 1956 (Polynesia Française). Résultats définitifs.* Paris, 1960. Language of publication is French.

In August 1957, the name French Oceania was changed to French Polynesia.

1962 (November 9)

The census was taken on a *de facto* and *de jure* basis, canvassed, and manually and mechanically tabulated. Household schedules were used, one for private households and one for collective households. Territorial division in tables included the communes of Papeete and Uturoa and districts for the remainder of the territory. Island groups are the same as in 1946, 1951, and 1956.

Definitions and Concepts. DWELLING—all or part of any construction used or intended to be used for permanent or temporary housing. HOUSEHOLD— private: one person living alone or a group of persons, related or not, living in the same dwelling and sharing household arrangements; collective and separate count: (see Introduction). Legal population of communes include all three; that of larger administrative areas, numbers one and two. AGE—year of birth only. Tables are in generational age only; tabulated in single years and standard five-year age groups. MARITAL STATUS—same as 1956. BIRTH-PLACE—district and island of birth for native; department for those born in France and overseas territories; country for the foreign born. Tables cross this with district of USUAL RESIDENCE to give internal migration and immigration. NATIONALITY/ETHNIC ORIGIN—type of French citizenship (by birth, marriage, naturalization). French by birth expanded to determine if of Polynesian origin (pure Polynesians and Europolynesians living "a la polynesienne"), "demi" (Europolynesians living "a l'europeenne"), born French of pure or mixed Chinese origin (new), and naturalized French of Chinese origin (new). RELIGION—denominations. EDUCATION—all persons age fifteen and over: literacy in any language and highest degree confirmed. LANGUAGE—derived through literacy question: read or write Tahitian, French, Chinese, or combination of two and three. ECONOMIC ACTIVITY—all persons age fifteen and over; reference period was the preceding twelve months. Active: agricultural workers engaged at least thirty days per year, nonagricultural workers averaging at least one day per week; unpaid family helpers; the underemployed; and the unemployed for less than one year. Inactive: not specified in tables. OCCUPATION and INDUSTRY—classifications were both three-digits and based on ISCO (1958) and ISIC (1958), respectively. OCCUPATIONAL STATUS—according to agricultural or nonagricultural occupations rather than according to economic sector (as in 1956): employer, own-account worker, salaried employee, family worker, tenant farmer, or without status (for example, persons in religious orders). SOCIOPROFESSIONAL CATEGORY [stress on social]—a cross between occupation and occupational status. HOUSEHOLD COMPOSITION—same as 1956.

Special Elements and Features. Economic activity reference period and the number of active per household were new as is determination of naturalized French of Chinese origin. Literacy was taken by question rather than by inference as in 1956. Language is also new.

Quality of the Census. There was no editing of schedules. INSEE actively participated in the census by supplying schedules, instructions, and other printed matter as well as a representative who organized and trained enumerators and served as technical advisor to the local governments. A fixed period of enumeration was adhered to that began with census day. Still no Whipple's Index category was assigned.

Publication Plan. Two publications were issued in French Polynesia that seem preliminary in nature. France. INSEE. *Résultats statistiques du recensement général de la population de la Polynesie Française effectué le 9 novembre 1962.* Paris, n.d. Language of publication is French.

1967

An enumeration ("dénombrement") was taken in the second trimester (April-June) of 1967 by the Service des Affairs Administratives, but the results were rejected by the government, especially for the errors in the urban population. However, the Office de la Recherche Scientifique et Technique Outre-Mer (ORSTOM) issued a publication giving the results for the Leeward Islands part of the Society Islands and stated that the results were worthy of confidence. The scope of the enumeration was smaller than that of the preceding census: sex, age, ethnic groups, religion, birthplace, economically active/inactive, household composition, and socioprofessional category.

1971 (February 8)

"Because of a number of imponderables, it is still not possible to disseminate the final results of the last census (1971)." Two publications were issued with provisional results only. Scope included citizenship, nationality, ethnic origin, birthplace and place of previous residence, sex, age, literacy and educational attainment, urban distinction, and economic activity. No definitions, concepts, organization, or methodological information were given. One segment of the population is designated CEP and is excluded from the tables. The 1977 census indicated the CEP stands for the Centre d'Experimentation du Pacifique (an atomic testing group?).

Quality of the Census. "The hypothesis of overestimation of this census remains most plausible because of the absence throughout the census of tight controls in order to search out and eliminate the frequent double counts, especially of indigenous population censused both in island of origin as well as in island of residence, and of 'faamu,' children who were counted both by natural family and by family of adoption."

Publication Plan. French Polynesia. Service du Plan. Statistique. *Recensement du 8 février 1971. Données individuelles (résultats provisoires).* [Papeete, 1973]. *Recensement du 8 fevrier 1971. Données collectives.* Plus one volume of legal population by commune. Language of publication is French.

1977 (April 29)

Conducted by INSEE, this census also included information on housing. It was *de facto* and *de jure* with tables mainly for the *de jure* population. Individual schedules were used for self-enumeration; however, the enumerators helped in case of need. Tabulation was done by the INSEE team. Territorial division was the same as for preceding censuses.

Definitions and Concepts. For individual islands, groups, and the whole territory, the legal population was the total of all "municipale" plus only the "comptée à part" that was not censused in Polynesia, that is, residents and the temporarily absent outside the territory. For communes it was the "municipale" plus the "comptée à part" censused in another commune as well as those not censused in Polynesia. BIRTHPLACE—same as 1962. MIGRATION—usual residence and duration, year of arrival of foreign born, plus place of previous residence (new). AGE—same as 1962 but tables have only real age (no generational) in standard five-year age groups. MARITAL STATUS—legal status only. EDUCATION—same as 1962. NATIONALITY/ETHNIC ORIGIN—same as 1962. HOUSEHOLD COMPOSITION—size, type of household, and characteristics of head (private households only). ECONOMIC ACTIVITY—asked of all persons age fourteen and over; reference period was as of the moment of the census. The active include all employed and unemployed; the inactive, students, the retired, nonprofessional military, and other without occupation. OCCUPATION—agricultural and nonagricultural; classification by groups: liberal and specialized professions, directors and managers, office workers, business, agriculture, mining and extraction work, transportation and communication, artisans and skilled production workers, semiskilled and other production workers, service workers, and the military. Also tables for seasonal, part-time and unemployed (new). INDUSTRY—according to primary, secondary, and tertiary sectors, subdivided by major industry (one-digit). OCCUPATIONAL STATUS—family worker, agricultural worker, liberal profession, employer and own-account worker, and salaried. SOCIOECONOMIC STATUS—farmers and fishermen, salaried farmers and fishermen, private employers-liberal professions-managers; independent industry and commerce (white-collar) workers, public workers, employed in private sector, laborers in private industry other than agriculture, service personnel, others (artisans and clergy, and so forth). ECONOMIC DEPENDENCY—number of economically active in household.

Special Elements and Features. Duration of present residence, place of previous residence and the unemployed are new. No urban/rural tables are present. Religion, language, and fertility were dropped. Both internal migration and immigration tables were included.

Quality of the Census. "In 1977, all the necessary precautions were taken to avoid the double count of the indigenous (island of origin as well as of residence) and of the 'faamu' (children reported by both natural and adoptive families). It must be recognized that the use of individual schedules and the recruitment of enumerators and supervisors at the commune level greatly facilitated the work of the census." Whipple's Index category was not given.

Publication Plan. France. INSEE. *Résultats du recensement de la population de la Polynésie Française, 29 avril 1977. Études.* Paris, n.d. Computer tapes are available. Language of publication is French.

OTHER STATISTICAL PUBLICATIONS: Issued by Institut Territorial de la Statistique, *Annuaire Statistique, Bulletin de Statistique.*

National Topic Chart

	1946	1951	1956	1962	1967	1971	1977
De facto	X	X	X	X			X
Usual residence			X	X		X	X
Place of birth	X	X	X	X		X	X
Duration of residence	X	X	X				X
Place of prev. residence						X	X
Urban/rural						X	
Sex	X	X	X	X	X	X	X
Age	X	X	X	X	X	X	X
Relation to household head			X	X			X
Marital status	X	X	X	X			X
Children born alive	X		X				
Children living	X						
Citizenship	X	X	X	X		X	
Literacy		X	X	X		X	X
School enrollment							
Ed. attainment		X	X	X		X	X
Ed. qualification							
National/Ethnic origin	X	X	X	X	X	X	X
Language				X			
Religion	X	X		X	X	X	
Household composition			X	X	X		X
Econ. active/inactive		X	X	X	X		X
Occupation	X	X	X	X			X
Industry		X	X	X			X
Occupational status	X	X	X	X	X		X
Income							
Housing						X	X

Gilbert and Ellice Islands

British Colony of Gilbert and Ellice Islands
(See Kiribati and Tuvalu, respectively, for latest censuses.)

CAPITAL: Bairiki, Tarawa.
STATISTICAL AGENCY: Central Government Office, Bairiki.
NATIONAL REPOSITORY: Kiribati National Library.
MAIN U.S. REPOSITORY: Population Research Center (Univ. of Texas).

The original colony consisted of thirty-seven islands and atolls: Gilbert (sixteen islands), Ellice (nine islands), Phoenix (eight islands), Line (three islands), and Ocean Island. Sighted and named by British captains sometime after 1788, they became a British protectorate in 1892. Colony status was assigned in 1915 when Gilberts were united with Ellice groups. In 1978, Ellice Islands gained independence and are now officially called Tuvalu. Gilbert Islands, Ocean Island, Phoenix and Line Islands were combined into a single nation called Kiribati in 1979. A separate entry is given for each of these two nations for their latest censuses.

During the early days of the colonial period the only data on population were estimates made by traders and missionaries who settled in the islands after 1857. Between 1905 and 1916 administrative censuses were taken in several islands of the Gilbert group and all but Niulakita of the Ellice group. The results of these censuses are limited to total population by sex, and their reliability cannot be assessed.

The first uniform census of the colony was taken in 1921; but again only the total numbers of males and females are known.

1931

A second general census of population was taken this year; however, the only published data are contained in the 1947 census. The tables presented each group of islands separately but did not consolidate totals for the colony as a whole. The following are available: number of inhabitants by race, population density, total population by broad age groups, religion, masculinity, and household size.

The decennial census planned for 1941 could not be taken because of World War II.

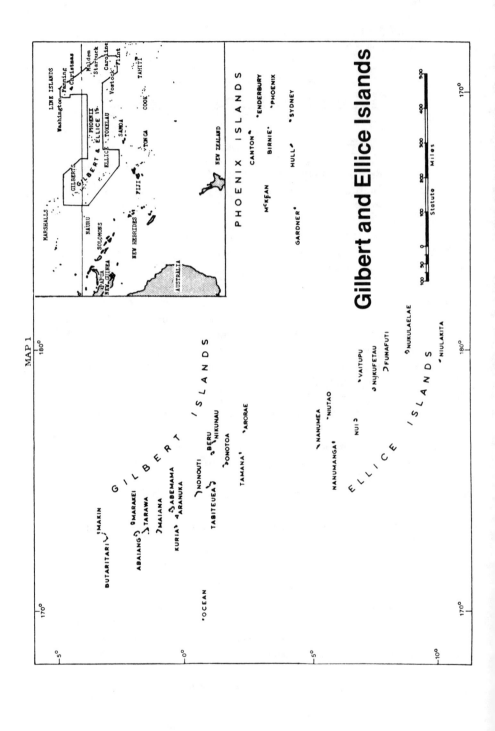

MAP 1

Gilbert and Ellice Islands

1947 (June 9)

The third general census was conducted by the census commissioner on a *de facto* basis with the assistance of the local governments. Household heads recorded information on schedules which were printed in three languages: English, Gilbertese, and Ellice. The islands of Canton and Enderbury were included in the census (without the U.S. subjects present). The islands were divided into village districts.

Definitions and Concepts. AGE—in completed years and months and tabulated in standard five-year age groups. MARITAL STATUS—asked of all persons thirteen years of age and older. Categories were: never married, married, legally separated, widowed, and divorced. DWELLING—every building used permanently or temporarily for human habitation, including group quarters. PLACE OF BIRTH—for native born, the name of the island of birth; for nonnatives, the name of the country and the number of years lived in the colony. British subjects were classified separately. PLACE OF RESIDENCE—for residents, the usual place of residence; for nonresidents (less than a year in the islands), the name of the country. FERTILITY—asked of married women only: number of children born alive and the number of children dead at the time of the census. RACE—the following groups were recorded: Micronesians, Polynesians, Europeans, Mongolians, and most possible combinations among the four. RELIGION—religious denomination recorded. If a child, the religion in which it is to be brought up was named. EDUCATION—for all persons ten years and over: literacy and working knowledge of English were recorded. For persons between the ages of six and sixteen: school attendance. ECONOMIC ACTIVITY—the majority of the Pacific islanders are engaged in subsistence agriculture and the production of copra. Persons are distributed in five groups: recruited workers, government employees, mission employees, other wage earners, and nonwage earners. Question was asked of all sixteen years of age and older. The number of weeks worked full-time was also recorded. OCCUPATION—classification was mixed with industry and varied for each racial group. INDUSTRY—six divisions were recorded: primary industry, secondary industry, transport and communication, trade and commerce, public administration, and professional. OCCUPATIONAL STATUS—categories: employer, own-account worker, and others (including retired persons, wives and children not gainfully occupied, and persons of independent income).

Special Elements and Features. A brief history of the settlement of the islands by successive waves of immigrants was presented. Results of the 1931 census and comparative tables for the censuses of 1905, 1916, 1921, and 1931 were also included. The tables of this census are distributed by racial groups. Copies of the schedule are included in the census report. Students and workers, absent from resident island, were also recorded. Some agriculture and housing questions were included.

Quality of the Census. "Strictly speaking, the census did not meet the criterion of simultaneity." The quality of results for some of the islands was considered not reliable. Whipple's Index ranking was not available.

Publication Plan. Gilbert and Ellice Islands Colony. *A Report on the Results of the Census of Population, 1947,* by F. N. M. Pusinelli. Suva, 1951. 1 volume. Language of publication is English.

1963 (April 30)

The fourth general census of population was conducted by the census commissioner on a *de facto* basis, and the household schedules were completed by trained enumerators (new). The general plan of the enumeration and the questionnaire were based on those used in the 1956 census of Fiji. The schedule was uniform and printed in the three languages common to the islands. Citizens living temporarily in Nauru were included, but their results were tabulated separately. Tabulation was mechanical. Canton and Enderbury were enumerated under the same conditions as in 1947.

Definitions and Concepts. RACE and RELIGION were the same as 1947. FAMILY UNIT—consisted of married couples without children; couples with unmarried children; unaccompanied by relatives and visitors. HOUSEHOLD—a group of persons related or not by blood, living in the same house or part of a house and sharing food arrangements, including live-in servants and visitors. Households were divided into private and collective. AGE—in completed years, and if less than a year, "0" was recorded. Tabulated in single years and standard five-year age groups. MARITAL STATUS—never married, married (legal or common-law marriages), widowed, and divorced were the categories. PLACE OF BIRTH—differed from 1947 in that native born Gilbert and Ellice Islanders reported their home island even if different from island of actual birth. All others gave island or country of birth. FERTILITY—asked of all women fifteen years and older: number of children born alive, number still living, and age of mother at first birth. ECONOMIC ACTIVITY—because the economy of the colony is primarily subsistence agriculture (only phosphate mining provided gainful employment), usual questions on occupation did not result in specific enough responses to classify. All persons age fifteen and over were asked what work they did, for whom, and where at the time of the census. INDUSTRY—was used to describe economic activities, including those not in the work force. Classification presented nine divisions and respective subgroups. Weeks worked full-time was not asked.

Special Elements and Features. Fewer questions were asked in 1963 than in 1947. Literacy, language, infirmities, number of years resident in the colony, number of trees and livestock, and type of housing construction were dropped from the schedule. Economic activity was presented in a different fashion. Life tables and projected population (by age and sex) are available for 1968, 1973, and 1978. Average number of persons in private households and family units were tabulated according to the ethnic origin of the head of household.

Quality of the Census. Enumeration was carried out in two stages, and it is believed that this accounted for particularly full coverage. Preliminary figures for each island and village by sex were tallied during the first visit of the enumerators which provided speedy publication of results. Whipple's Index ranking was not available for this census. The census office is reestablished for each enumeration.

Publication Plan. Gilbert and Ellice Islands Colony. Census Commissioner's Office. *A Report on the Results of the Census of Population, 1963.* Suva, Fiji, 1964. Language of publication is English.

1968 (December 5)

The fifth general census of the colony was conducted by the census commissioner on a *de facto* basis and included citizens living temporarily in the Republic of Nauru. The organization, scope, and household schedules were basically the same as used in 1963. Electronic tabulation was used. The territory covered by the census was divided into island groups, islands, subgroups, and villages.

Definitions and Concepts. URBAN (new)—Tarawa island, with the greatest single concentration of population and accompanying social services and amenities, had the only settlement to be called urban. AGE, FAMILY UNIT, HOUSEHOLD, FERTILITY, MARITAL STATUS, PLACE OF BIRTH, RELIGION were all the same as 1963. ECONOMIC ACTIVITY—essentially the same as 1963 except that unemployed persons were included in the active population. INDUSTRY—the system of classification used was the same, only the subgroups vary to a slight degree from those used in 1963. EDUCATION—data on school attendance were obtained through the question on economic activity. Data are presented for students between the ages of five and nineteen.

Special Elements and Features. Urban/rural distinction was recorded for the first time. Data on school attendance are available. Type of school attended was recorded but no attempt was made to tabulate this data. Maps, graphs, and a copy of the schedules are included in the report.

Quality of the Census. As in 1963, enumeration was carried out in two stages to assure completeness of coverage. The final results were available two years after the census. Whipple's Index category was not assigned.

Publication Plan. Gilbert and Ellice Islands Colony. Census Commissioner's Office. *A Report on the Results of the Census of the Population, 1968,* by F. H. A. G. Zwart and K. Groenewegen. New South Wales, 1970. Language of publication is English.

1973 (December 8/9)

The sixth general census of the colony was conducted by the Census Commission on a *de facto* basis; canvassers recorded information on household and individual schedules. Unlike the previous censuses, persons living temporarily in Nauru were not enumerated. The organization was basically the same as 1968, but the scope was considerably enlarged. The territory covered by the census included: Ocean Island, Gilbert Islands, Ellice Islands and Line Islands. Phoenix

Islands were excluded. The islands were subdivided into villages. Tarawa was also divided into urban and rural areas. Tabulation was computerized.

Definitions and Concepts. URBAN, HOUSEHOLD, MARITAL STATUS, RELIGION and PLACE OF BIRTH were the same as 1968. AGE—date of birth (new) instead of age in completed years. Tabulated in single year and standard five-year age groups. RACE—Gilbertese, Ellice, European, and mixed were the categories. The European group included all persons from Europe, Australia, New Zealand, Canada, the United States, South America, Russia, Israel, and persons whose ancestors principally came from these countries. New Zealand, European, and Maori were distinguished, as well as American, European, Hawaiian, or Negro. FERTILITY—asked of all women born before 1959: number of children ever born alive, number of children still living, date of birth of the first child, and date of birth and sex of the last child. PLACE OF RESIDENCE— usual place and previous place of residence (in 1968). EDUCATION (new) —school attendance for all persons four years of age and older and educational attainment (highest level of education reached) for all persons age twelve and over. Other full-time training was also recorded. ECONOMIC ACTIVITY—for all persons age fifteen and over. Reference period was the week of the census. The population was divided into three groups: inactive in village life, that is, those who were dependent upon others for daily living (students, elderly, the disabled, visitors, homemakers, the retired, inmates of institutions, others) and reason for inactivity; active in village life (subsistence life), or those who win their daily living with work; and active in cash economy, those actually working for pay or profit plus the unemployed looking for a job (new or experienced workers). In addition, part-time jobs (secondary occupation) and other skills not being used were asked. OCCUPATION—recorded only for those active in cash economy. Classification had seven major groups plus subgroups. Some tables excluded new workers. INDUSTRY—classification included eleven divisions and major groups (two-digits). As in occupational classification, some tables excluded new workers. OCCUPATIONAL STATUS—categories were: having own business (employer, own-account worker and unpaid family worker), and wage earner (employee). Employers and own-account workers were also asked the number of employees or unpaid family workers.

Special Elements and Features. School attendance, educational attainment, usual and previous place of residence, occupation, and occupational status were new. Fertility questions differed from previous censuses; date of birth and death of children were recorded for the first time. Age of mother at birth of first child was dropped. Comparative tables of population in islands of usual residence for 1968 and 1973 were included.

Quality of the Census. A postenumeration survey was taken for the first time in the colony. The results indicated that ten households and seventy-two persons were not reported in the census enumeration. The use of birth record cards and the special training given to enumerators improved coverage and accuracy of results (for example, age data). The schedules were pretested in south and rural

Tarawa. Provisional results were available only six months after enumeration; final results, in 1975. Census office is still temporary. Whipple's Index ranking was not given.

Publication Plan. Gilbert and Ellice Islands Colony. Office of Chief Minister. *A Report on the 1973 Census of Population.* Bairiki, 1975. Unpublished data are available. Language of publication is English.

See Kiribati and Tuvalu for censuses taken after independence.

National Topic Chart

	1947	1963	1968	1973
De facto	X	X	X	X
Usual residence	X			X
Place of birth	X	X	X	X
Duration of residence	X			
Place of prev. residence				X
Urban/rural			X	X
Sex	X	X	X	X
Age	X	X	X	X
Relation to household head	X	X	X	X
Marital status	X	X	X	X
Children born alive	X	X	X	X
Children living	X	X	X	X
Citizenship				
Literacy	X			
School enrollment	X		X	X
Ed. attainment				X
Ed. qualification				
National/Ethnic origin	X	X	X	X
Language	X			
Religion	X	X	X	X
Household composition				X
Econ. active/inactive	X	X	X	X
Occupation	X			X
Industry	X	X	X	X
Occupational status	X			X
Income				
Housing	X			

Guam

Guam

United States Territory of Guam

CAPITAL: Agana.
STATISTICAL AGENCY: U.S. Department of Interior.
NATIONAL REPOSITORY: ?
MAIN U.S. REPOSITORY: University of Hawaii Pacific Collection, Honolulu.

The largest and most southern of the group of islands known as the Marianas Islands, Guam was under the dominion of Spain for over 300 years. No population records are known for this period. After the Spanish-American War, the island was ceded to the United States (1898). The first enumeration of the population was made in 1901 when total population by sex was recorded. From then on, local censuses, estimates, and population counts were taken by the naval governors, and the results were published in the form of annual reports with total population divided into native and foreign born and nationality of the foreign born. Subsequent censuses were taken in conjunction with the regular decennial census of population of the United States with exception of 1955 and 1958 censuses, which were conducted by the municipal commissioners.

1920

First census of population was taken in conjunction with the fourteenth decennial census of the United States. The population was enumerated on *de jure* basis, and canvasser was the method used to record information on general schedules. The territory covered by the census was divided into six districts and subdivided into minor civil divisions (barrios, cities, and towns).

The scope included: age, sex, race (color), marital status, place of birth (nativity for foreign born), school attendance, literacy, language, occupation, and number of working children by sex and occupation. Comparative tables with the United States were also given.

1930

Census of population was conducted in conjunction with the fifteenth decennial census of the United States. Population and agriculture censuses were conducted simultaneously. The organization and methods were virtually the same as 1920. The territory was divided into municipalities, barrios, and towns. Urban and rural were distinguished. The scope was the same, but the number of working children were included in the general table of occupation by age.

1940

Census of population and housing was conducted simultaneously with the sixteenth decennial census of the United States. The governor of the island was responsible for the field work. Organization and methods were basically the same as the previous censuses. The following features were added to the questionnaire: family relationship, educational attainment, home tenure, and in addition to the country of birth, persons born in the United States were presented by state of birth. Extensive redistricting took place between 1930 and 1940.

1950 (April 1)

Census of population was taken in conjunction with the seventeenth decennial census of population of the United States and conducted under the supervision of the governor of Guam. The census was *de jure*, and canvassers were used to record information on general schedules. Tabulation was mechanical.

During World War II most of the towns and villages were destroyed, and many communities were dislocated. As a consequence, the division of municipalities into barrios was abandoned, and most of the tables were divided only by municipality, the principal administrative division of the island.

Definitions and Concepts. AGE—as of last birthday in completed years. Presented in standard five-year age groups. Assignment of unknown ages based on related information was used for the first time in 1950. NATIVITY—population was classified according to two basic groups—native and foreign born. CITIZENSHIP—Classification presented three major categories: citizens (natives and naturalized), nationals (natives of Guam and American Samoa were nationals of the United States in 1950 and became citizens when naturalized), and aliens. PLACE OF BIRTH—country of birth based on international boundaries recognized by the United States. HOUSEHOLD—all persons who occupy a house, an apartment, or other group of rooms that constitute a dwelling unit. It included related, as well as unrelated, persons. MARITAL STATUS—categories were: single, married, widowed, and divorced. Separated and common-law marriages were classified as married. RACE (color)—The following groups were recorded: white, Chamorro (full-blood and mixed), other races (Japanese, Koreans, Negroes and other nonwhite not classified as Chamorro). EDUCATION—school enrollment and educational attainment (highest grade completed for the population of twenty-five years and over). ECONOMIC ACTIVITY—lower age limit was fourteen years of age. Period of reference was the year before the census (1949). The population was divided into three groups: worked as civilian for pay or profit or without pay on a family farm or business on full- or part-time basis, in armed forces, and other, including those who did not give information, and those who did not work (homemakers, students, retired, disabled, and inmates of institutions). INDUSTRY—classification based on Standard Industrial

Classification (SIC), reduced form: divisions and major groups (two-digits). OCCUPATION—classification based on Classified Index of Occupations and Industries, 1950, reduced form: seventy-three groups that represent a selection and combination of the 469 adopted in the United States. OCCUPATIONAL STATUS—categories were: private wage and salary worker, government worker, self-employed worker, and unpaid family worker.

Special Elements and Features. Data on economic activity are not comparable with previous census. Occupation data shown in earlier census are not entirely comparable. Industry, occupational status, citizenship, and educational attainment were new. Literacy and language were dropped.

Quality of the Census. See United States entry, 1950, for details on completeness and accuracy of data. Constant misinterpretation by enumerator caused appreciable effect in the statistics of very small communities. Precise allocation of occupation was not possible due to insufficiently specified occupation designations.

Publication Plan. U.S. Bureau of the Census. *Census of Population: 1950. A Report of the Seventeenth Decennial Census of the United States.* Volume 2, Part 51-54. Washington, D.C., 1953. Language of publication is English.

1955 (June 30)

Island-wide census of population was conducted by the municipal commissioners. No details of organization and methods are available, and the total population excluded transients residing in military reservations. The following results were published: total population of municipalities by sex divided into Guamanians, other citizens, and aliens; total number of families; total number of buildings (residential and business); number of eligible voters; number of bona fide farmers; number of employed by sex; number of self-employed; and number of able-bodied males (eighteen to sixty years of age).

Publication Plan. Guam. Office of the Chief Commissioner. *Island-wide Census as of June 30, 1955.* [Agana], n.d. Language of publication is English.

1958 (June 30)

Another island-wide census of population conducted by the municipal commissioners. No details of organization and methods are available, and the total population, like the previous one, excluded transients residing in military reservations. The following results were published: total population of municipalities by sex divided into Guamanians, statesiders, Hawaiians, Filipinos, and others; number of families (Guamanians, others, aliens, and armed forces); number of buildings (residential, business, others, and quonsets); number of eligible voters; bona fide farmers, self-employed, families receiving charity; number of employed by sex; and number of able bodied males (eighteen to sixty years of age).

Publication Plan. Guam. Office of the Chief Commissioner. *Island-wide Census as of June 30, 1958.* [Agana] n.d. Language of publication is English.

1960 (April 1)

Census of population was taken in conjunction with the eighteenth decennial census of population and housing of the United States. Population was enumerated on *de jure* basis, and canvasser was the method utilized to record information on household and individual schedules. All questions were asked on complete count basis. Manual coding and editing with mechanical tabulation was used rather than FOSDIC as in the continental United States. The territory covered by the census was divided into nineteen election districts (new), but comparable figures were not available.

Definitions and Concepts. AGE—same as 1950; however, tabulated in single years up to twenty-one years of age and standard five-year age groups. Median age was also furnished. RACE (color)—the following groups were recorded: white, Chamorro (full-blooded or mixed Chamorro), other races (Negroes, Japanese, Chinese, Korean, Polynesians, and so forth), and mixed parentage (mixed white and nonwhite classified according to nonwhite parent, mixed nonwhite parentage classified according to the race of the father). NATIVITY AND PLACE OF BIRTH—information on country of birth was used to classify the population into two major groups: native (persons born in the United States, territories and possessions), and foreign born. MARITAL STATUS—categories were: never married, married, separated, widowed, divorced. The presence of spouse and relationship with family members and unrelated individuals were also recorded. HOUSEHOLD—the same as 1950 but housing unit instead of dwelling unit was the base for enumeration. FERTILITY (new)—the number of children ever born. Questions were asked of married, widowed, separated, and divorced women, but the data were not limited to legitimate birth because women living with illegitimate child reported themselves as married. However, data on illegitimacy is less complete than that on legitimate births. EDUCATION—school enrollment, educational attainment (highest degree attended and highest degree completed). ECONOMIC ACTIVITY—period of reference was the week before the census. Lower age limit was fourteen years. The labor force included employed (at work, with a job but not at work) and unemployed persons (looking for a job within the past sixty days). Not in the labor force: unpaid family workers doing incidental work (less than fifteen hours per week), homemakers, students, retired, seasonal workers off season and not looking for a job, inmates of institutions, and students were shown separately. The number of weeks worked during the year before the census was recorded. OCCUPATION—classification based on Classified Index of Occupations and Industries, 1960, reduced form: forty-eight occupation groups were recorded (two-digits). INDUSTRY—classification based on CIOI, reduced form: thirty-two groups (two-digits). OCCUPATIONAL STATUS—categories were the same as 1950. INCOME—recorded for the first time: wages or salary income from all jobs; net income from business, professional practice, partnership or farm; and other income (pensions, social security, and so forth).

Special Elements and Features. Fertility, income, and number of weeks worked were new; citizenship was dropped. There is an alphabetical list of cities and villages with the number of inhabitants.

Quality of the Census. See the United States entry, 1960, for general comments on coverage and accuracy of data.

Publication Plan. U.S. Bureau of the Census. *Census of Population: 1960. The Eighteenth Decennial Census of the United States.* Volume 1, Part 54-57. Language of publication is English.

1970 (April 1)

The census of population was conducted in conjunction with the nineteenth decennial census of population and housing of the United States. The census of agriculture was conducted simultaneously.

The population was enumerated on a *de jure* basis, and canvasser was the method used to record information. A single household questionnaire that was machine readable was used for the first time (FOSDIC). Like 1950 and 1960, an individual questionnaire was utilized to enumerate persons living in hotels and group quarters. Sampling was not used in Guam.

Although the census date was April 1, in most of the outlying areas enumeration was delayed from one to three weeks. Tabulation was computerized. The territory covered by the census was divided into nineteen election districts, which for the census were equivalent to counties, and subdivided into cities and villages. Urban and rural population was distinguished. Merizo district included Cocos Island.

Definitions and Concepts. AGE, HOUSEHOLD, FAMILY, FERTILITY, INCOME—same as 1960; however, a different method of computation was used. EDUCATION—same as 1960, but a question on vocational training was added. MARITAL STATUS—categories were: never married, now married, consensually married, widowed, divorced, and separated. The category separated included legally or otherwise absent from spouse. PLACE OF BIRTH—same as 1960. CITIZENSHIP—whether naturalized, permanent alien, temporary alien, or born abroad of American parents. The year of immigration was also recorded. PLACE OF RESIDENCE—usual place, and for the first time, previous place of residence (in 1965). VETERAN STATUS—recorded for the first time: whether the person served in the armed forces and during what war. ECONOMIC ACTIVITY—reference period was the week before the census. Lower age limit was sixteen years. The labor force included all persons classified as employed (at work and with job but not at work) and unemployed (looking for a job during the past four weeks and available to accept job). Unemployed persons who had worked at any time in the past were classified as experienced unemployed. Not in the labor force consisted mainly of students, homemakers, retired, seasonal workers in off season and not looking for a job, inmates of institutions, the disabled, and persons doing only incidental unpaid family work (less than fifteen hours per week). The number of weeks worked was also recorded. OCCUPATION—Main occupation and last occupation if the person were unemployed. Classification based on the Classified Index of Industries and Occupations, 1970, reduced form: thirty-two major groups were presented. INDUSTRY—Classification based on CIIC, 1970, reduced form: forty industry groups (two-digit). OCCUPATIONAL STATUS—same categories as 1960.

Special Elements and Features: Race and nativity were dropped; citizenship returned; year of immigration, veteran status, place of previous residence, and vocational training were recorded for the first time. Economic activity concepts were revised.

Quality of the Census. To improve the usefulness of the 1970 census results, a number of changes were introduced based on evaluation of the previous census, consultation with users of data, and extensive field pretesting. For more detailed information on coverage and accuracy of data, see the United States entry, 1970.

Publication Plan. U.S. Bureau of the Census. *Census of Population: 1970*. Volume 1, Part 54-58. Language of publication is English.

OTHER STATISTICAL PUBLICATIONS: Issued by Economic Research Center, *Annual Economic Report*. Issued by Office of Vital Statistics, *Annual Statistical Report*. Issued by U.S. Department of the Interior, *Annual Report of the Governor of Guam to the Secretary of the Interior*.

National Topic Chart

	1950	1955	1958	1960	1970
De facto					
Usual residence	X			X	X
Place of birth	X			X	X
Duration of residence					X
Place of prev. residence					X
Urban/rural					X
Sex	X	X	X	X	X
Age	X			X	X
Relation to household head	X			X	X
Marital status	X			X	X
Children born alive				X	X
Children living					
Citizenship	X	X	X		X
Literacy					
School enrollment	X			X	X
Ed. attainment	X			X	X
Ed. qualification					
National/Ethnic origin	X			X	
Language					
Religion					
Household composition	X	X	X	X	X
Econ. active/inactive	X	X	X	X	X
Occupation	X			X	X
Industry	X			X	X
Occupational status	X			X	X
Income				X	X
Housing	X			X	X

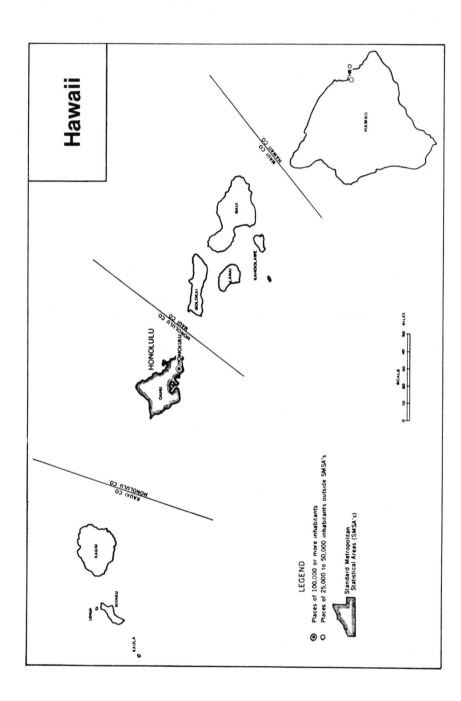

Hawaii

KAUAI CO.
HONOLULU CO.

NIIHAU
LEHUA
KAUAI
KAULA

HONOLULU CO.
MAUI CO.

HONOLULU
OAHU
HONOLULU

MOLOKAI
LANAI
KAHOOLAWE

MAUI

MAUI CO.
HAWAII CO.

HILO

HAWAII

LEGEND

⊙ Places of 100,000 or more inhabitants

○ Places of 25,000 to 50,000 inhabitants outside SMSA's

Standard Metropolitan
Statistical Areas (SMSA's)

SCALE

0   10   20   30   40   50   MILES

Hawaii

State of United States of America

CAPITAL: Honolulu.
STATISTICAL AGENCY: U.S. Bureau of the Census.
NATIONAL REPOSITORY: University of Hawaii, Pacific Collection.
MAIN U.S. REPOSITORY: Population Research Center (Univ. of Texas).

Discovered in 1778, these islands remained a Hawaiian kingdom until 1894, when the native control was abandoned. A republic for a short period, the archipelago was finally annexed to the United States in 1898 and organized as territory in 1900. Hawaii became a state in 1959.

An estimate of the native population was done in 1778. Missionary counts conducted in 1832 and 1836 reported a staggering decline in population, which continued during the following years, as indicated by subsequent censuses. The 1850, 1853, and 1860 enumerations were considered very simple and rudimentary in character. Regularity was not observed and the exact dates of enumeration are not available. Results of these censuses were published in the periodical *The Polynesian* and referred to the total population divided into native (Kanaka), part-native (Hapahaole) and foreign (Haole). According to Andrew W. Lind [*Hawaii's People*. University of Hawaii Press. Honolulu, 1967], the classification of population was based on cultural differences rather than on biological differences. This practice continued until annexation to the United States, when conceptions of race were introduced.

The following censuses were taken regularly at intervals of six years, counting from 1860 (1866, 1872, 1878, 1884, 1890, and 1896).

There is not much difference either in the subjects dealt with or in the manner of presentation of results between 1866 and 1884. The enumerations were conducted by the Board of Education on a *de facto* basis, and the questionnaires were filled by the head of the household or canvassers. No more details on organization were furnished. The territory covered by the censuses was divided into islands (Hawaii, Maui, Molokai, Lanai, Oahu, Kanai, and Niihau) and respective districts. The scope included: total population, age, sex, nationality (natives, half-caste, Hawaiian born of foreign parents, and the country of origin of foreign-born persons), and occupation. The reports were written in English and Hawaiian. In addition, the 1884 census included results for the city of Honolulu by health wards, a map of the city, and religious affiliations data.

1890

Census of population conducted by the general superintendent of the Bureau of Public Instruction. It was considered the most comprehensive census taken to date. The enumeration was carried out on a *de facto* basis, and canvasser was the method used to record information on apparently general schedules (blanks) printed in two languages. The passengers and crews of vessels in transit in the islands were included in the population of Honolulu. Scope included: age, sex, nationality (like the previous ones), marital status, occupation, literacy, school attendance, possession of electoral franchise and ownership of real estate, and the following "statistics of maternity": number of females fifteen years old or over; number of married, divorced, and widowed; number of females with children; number of children born; and number of children still living.

1896

The last census taken under Hawaiian administration, like the previous one, was conducted by the Department of Public Instruction. The organization employed in taking the census was largely modeled on that of New Zealand. The census was *de facto*, and canvassers recorded information on household schedules. Enumerators' books were utilized as a method of checking completeness and accuracy of data. Scope was basically the same as 1890.

1900

First census taken in conjunction with the decennial census of population of the United States. The enumeration was conducted on a *de jure* basis, and canvasser was the method used to record information on general schedules. Tabulation was manual. Scope included: age, sex, race, nativity, place of birth, parentage, marital status, year of immigration (to the United States or other possession and not necessarily to Hawaii), males of voting and militia age, citizenship, school attendance, literacy, language, economic activity, occupation, industry, number of dwellings and persons per dwelling, and number of households and persons per household.

1910

Census of population was conducted in conjunction with the thirteenth decennial census of the United States. The organization and methods were virtually the same as 1900 except that the territory was, for the first time, divided into five counties (Hawaii, Honolulu, Kalawao, Kanai, and Maui), then subdivided into minor civil divisions or districts. Correspondence with previous censuses (1890 and 1900) was provided. The population of Midway and Kahoolawe islands was available for the first time. Separate tables were presented for the cities of Hilo and Honolulu. The scope was the same as 1900.

1920

Census of population was taken in conjunction with the fourteenth decennial census of the United States. The organization, methods, and scope were virtually the same as the previous two censuses. Separate tables were presented for the cities of Hilo and Honolulu, the two urban areas of Hawaii.

1930

Census was conducted under the supervision of the U.S. Bureau of the Census in conjunction with the fifteenth decennial census. No major changes occurred as far as organization and scope of the census.

1940

Census of population was taken, for the first time, simultaneously with a census of housing. In addition to counties, judicial districts, representative districts, and places (cities, towns, and villages), data were also available for census tracts. The scope of the census included the following features: age, race, sex, nativity, parentage, place of birth, year of immigration, citizenship, marital status, school attendance, educational attainment (new), economic activity, occupation, industry, occupational status (new), income (new), and number of months worked in 1939. Labor force replaced gainful workers concept. The number of males of voting age, language ability, and literacy were dropped. The total population also included inhabitants of the following outlying islands: Baker, Canton, Enderbury, Howland, Jarvis, Johnston, and Midway.

1950 (April 1)

The census of population and housing was conducted in conjunction with the seventeenth decennial census of the United States on a *de jure* basis, and canvassers collected information on general schedules. Some of the questions in the schedules were asked on a 20 percent sample basis. The census of agriculture was conducted simultaneously. Tabulation was mechanical. The territory covered by the census included the islands divided into counties and districts. Information was also available for Honolulu standard metropolitan area and minor civil subdivisions such as cities, towns, villages, and places of 1,000 inhabitants or more. Urban/rural populations were distinguished.

Definitions and Concepts. URBAN—places of 2,500 inhabitants or more. SMAs (standard metropolitan areas) consist of a county, or group of contiguous counties, that contains at least one city of 50,000 inhabitants or more. This type of statistical division was new. RACE—concept not based on clear-cut definitions of biological stock and most of the categories referred to nationalities. Categories were: Hawaiians (including part-Hawaiians), Caucasians, Chinese, Filipinos, Japanese, and others (including Koreans, Negroes, other Polynesians, Puerto Ricans, and so forth). Mixtures of Caucasians were classified according to race of nonwhite parent, and mixture of nonwhite races other than Hawaiian was classified according to race of father. AGE—as of last birthday in completed years. For the first time, unknown ages were assigned based on related information. Age was tabulated in single years and standard five-year groups. NATIVITY— two major groups: native (persons born in the United States, its territories and possessions, and persons born in a foreign country of American citizens) and foreign born. CITIZENSHIP—categories: citizen (including native and naturalized) and alien. Data reported only for those twenty-one years old and over. American citizens were also classified according to territorial citizenship. Territorial citizens were persons living in Hawaii for more than a year, except those serving in the armed forces. PLACE OF BIRTH—classification based on the place of birth of parents. Categories were: both parents born in Hawaii; both parents born elsewhere in the United States; one born in Hawaii and the other born in the United States; one born in Hawaii or elsewhere in the United States or territories, and the other in a foreign country; both parents born in foreign country. PLACE OF RESIDENCE—usual place and, for the first time, previous place of residence (August 14, 1945). MARITAL STATUS—categories were: never married, married, widowed, divorced, and separated (new). The category "married" was further divided into "spouse present" and "spouse absent". HOUSEHOLD—persons, related or not by blood, living in the same house, apartment, or other group of rooms or a room that constitutes a dwelling unit. FAMILY—a group of two or more persons, related by blood, marriage, or adoption and living together. EDUCATION—school enrollment (for persons under thirty years of age); educational attainment (for the first time, two questions were asked: years of school enrolled and highest degree completed). FERTILITY—number of children ever born of ever-married women. For the first time recorded after census operations were taken in conjunction with the United States. ECONOMIC ACTIVITY—period of reference was the week before the enumerator's visit. Lower age limit was fourteen years. In the labor force: employed (at work, unpaid family workers, and with a job but not at work) and unemployed looking for work (divided into new workers and experienced workers). Not in the labor force: persons doing only incidental unpaid family work (less than fifteen hours per week), homemakers, unable to work, inmates of institutions, and others (retired, students, too old to work, voluntary idle, and seasonal workers during off season and not looking for job). The number of hours worked during the reference week and the number of weeks worked in 1949 were also recorded. OCCUPATION—classification was based on the Classified Index of Occupations and Industries, 1950, major groups, groups, and subgroups (three-digits). INDUSTRY—Classification based on the Classified Index of Occupations and Industries, 1950, 153 categories were recorded (three-digits). OCCUPATIONAL STATUS—The categories were: private wage and salary worker, government worker, self-employed, and unpaid family worker. INCOME—Gross income from wages and salary, net income from self-employment, and income other than earnings.

Special Elements and Features. The following new features were added: SMAs, place of previous residence, and fertility. The method of assigning unknown ages was introduced, as were two questions to determine educational attainment. Detailed information for Honolulu SMA and for the City of Honolulu were unpublished but are available upon request.

Quality of the Census. For details on completeness of coverage and accuracy of data, see United States entry, 1950. In addition, omission from the labor force of some workers resulted in an understatement in many occupation, industry, and occupational status figures. Precise allocation of occupation was not possible due to insufficiently specified occupation designation.

Publication Plan. U.S. Bureau of the Census. *Census of Population: 1950. A Report of the Seventeenth Decennial Census of the United States.* Volume 2, Part 51-54. Washington, D.C., 1953. Language of publication is English.

1960 (April 1)

Hawaii became the fiftieth state of the United States in 1959; therefore, no special entry is necessary after this date. Refer to the U.S. entry for further details.

National Topic Chart

	1950
De facto	
Usual residence	X
Place of birth	X
Duration of residence	
Place of prev. residence	X
Urban/rural	X
Sex	X
Age	X
Relation to household head	X
Marital status	X
Children born alive	X
Children living	
Citizenship	X
Literacy	
School enrollment	X
Ed. attainment	X
Ed. qualification	
National/Ethnic origin	X
Language	
Religion	
Household composition	X
Econ. active/inactive	X
Occupation	X
Industry	X
Occupational status	X
Income	X
Housing	X

Note: For 1960-1980, see United States.

Kiribati

Republic of Kiribati

CAPITAL: Bairiki, Tarawa.
STATISTICAL AGENCY: Ministry of Home Affairs, Bairiki.
NATIONAL REPOSITORY: Kiribati National Library.
MAIN U.S. REPOSITORY: Population Research Center (Univ. of Texas).

In 1975, the former colony of Gilbert and Ellice Islands was divided. The islands of the Gilbert group, Phoenix group, Line group, and Ocean Island (Banaba) became an independent nation in 1979 under the name of Kiribati. Even though independence was achieved in 1979, their first national census was taken in 1978. Information on censuses previous to this date is located in the Gilbert and Ellice Islands entry.

1978 (December 12-13)

The first census of population and housing was conducted by the census commissioner on a *de facto* basis, including I-Kiribati (the Gilbertese) employed in Nauru. A two-stage enumeration system was utilized, and canvassers recorded information on individual and household schedules. The schedules were printed in English and Kiribati. The territory covered by the census was divided into islands and villages. Tarawa North in this census is the same as Tarawa (rural) in 1973, except that the island of Tanaea is now under the jurisdiction of the urban local government. The island of Ocean changed its name to Banaba in 1973. Phoenix islands and South Line islands were not part of the census as they were uninhabited at the time. Hand-sorting tabulation was performed.

Definitions and Concepts. HOUSEHOLD—person or group of persons, related or not by blood, living in a house, a group of houses, or part of a house, who usually eat food prepared for them in the same kitchen. Households may be private or collective. AGE—date of birth. Tabulated in single years and standard five-year age groups. ORPHANHOOD—for the first time recorded, was derived from the following questions: real mother alive, mother's eldest child, mother living in the household, and real father alive? In addition, the personal number of the mother was recorded. MARITAL STATUS—categories were: never mar-

Kiribati appears on the map of Gilbert and Ellice Islands.

ried, married, widowed, and divorced. RELIGION (voluntary question)—religious affiliation recorded. RACE—the following groups were recorded: I-Kiribati (Gilbertese), Gil-Ellice, Ellice, European, and others. The classification took into consideration the race of the parents. EDUCATION—school attendance (still attending and not attending) and educational attainment (highest class completed). PLACE OF BIRTH—the concept of "home island" was used for persons born in the Gilbert islands. "Home island" meant the island of the person's father, where most land may be expected to be inherited, or the island with which the person has a traditional link; independently of whether it was the actual place of birth or not. For all other persons, the country of birth was recorded. LAND OWNERSHIP—questions asked of persons fifteen years of age and over: land ownership or expectation of inheritance on "home island," and land ownership on any other island. PLACE OF RESIDENCE—questions asked of all persons fifteen years of age and older: usual place of residence, duration of residence, and name of island lived for more than twelve months at any time in their lives. ECONOMIC ACTIVITY—period of reference was the week of enumeration; lower age limit, fifteen years. The population was divided into three groups: active outside cash economy (village life, home duties, or traditional and subsistence sectors); active in cash economy (employed and unemployed looking for work, experienced or new worker); and dependents (visitors, elderly, disabled, inmates of institutions, students, and "resting" or making no significant contribution to the household). The number of years worked and whether received occupational training and for how long were also recorded. OCCUPATION—classification based on ISCO, revised edition, 1968, major groups, groups, and subgroups (three-digits). INDUSTRY—classification based on ISIC, revised edition, 1968, divisions, major, and subgroups (three-digits). OCCUPATIONAL STATUS—categories were: employer, employee, self-employed, and looking for work. FERTILITY—questions asked of all women: number of children born alive, number of children alive on census night, first and last child's date of birth, last child's sex and whether still alive, and age of mother at birth of first child.

Special Elements and Features. Persons employed in Nauru Island were enumerated but tabulated separately. New area measurements for most of the islands were provided and boundaries usually differ from the previous censuses. List of educational levels was provided to avoid confusion over changes in class nomenclature. Orphanhood and land ownership were new features. Questions on place of residence were worded differently. Information on economic activity was more detailed. Detailed information on household composition and characteristics and an approximate *de jure* population were also given.

Quality of the Census. Although one was conducted in the previous census (1973), no postenumeration survey was carried out this time mainly because of lack of qualified personnel. A system of numbering of houses was introduced to improve coverage and facilitate the division of enumeration areas. The accuracy of results was improved with utilization of listing pads on which each person was first listed by name, sex, relationship to head of household, and date of birth. The use of birth registration records since 1898 improved quality of age information. Pilot census was carried out to test applicability of questionnaires and tabulation procedures. Preliminary results were available in 1979 and final results in 1980. Whipple's Index category was not given.

Publication Plan. Kiribati. Ministry of Home Affairs. *Report on the 1978 Census of Population and Housing.* Volume 1. Basic information on tables. Tarawa, 1980. Language of publication is English.

National Topic Chart

	1978
De facto	X
Usual residence	X
Place of birth	X
Duration of residence	X
Place of prev. residence	
Urban/rural	
Sex	X
Age	X
Relation to household head	X
Marital status	X
Children born alive	X
Children living	X
Citizenship	
Literacy	
School enrollment	X
Ed. attainment	X
Ed. qualification	
National/Ethnic origin	X
Language	
Religion	X
Household composition	X
Econ. active/inactive	X
Occupation	X
Industry	X
Occupational status	X
Income	
Housing	X

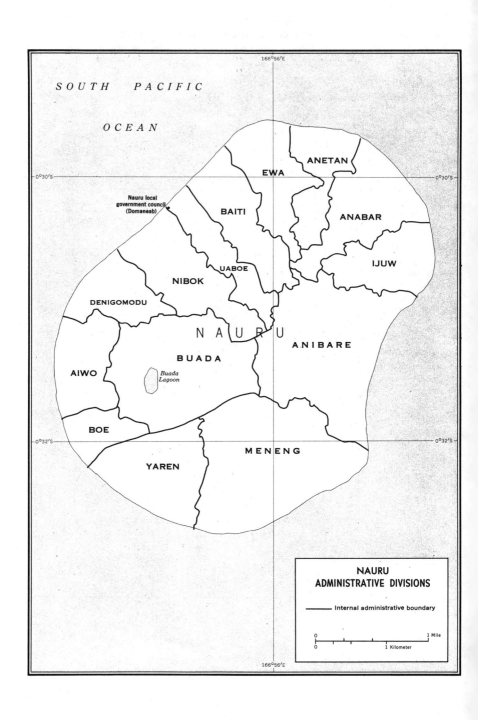

SOUTH PACIFIC

OCEAN

166°56'E

ANETAN

EWA

0°30'S

Nauru local
government council
(Domaneab)

BAITI

ANABAR

NIBOK

UABOE

IJUW

DENIGOMODU

N A U R U

ANIBARE

BUADA

Buada
Lagoon

AIWO

BOE

0°32'S

MENENG

YAREN

NAURU
ADMINISTRATIVE DIVISIONS

——— Internal administrative boundary

0   1 Mile
0   1 Kilometer

166°56'E

Nauru

Republic of Nauru

CAPITAL: Yaren.
STATISTICAL AGENCY: Department of Island Development and Housing.
NATIONAL REPOSITORY: ?
MAIN U.S. REPOSITORY: Population Research Center (Univ. of Texas).

The island of Nauru was discovered in 1798, annexed by Germany in 1888, and occupied by Australia during World War I. Later it was made a mandate territory under the authority of Australia, New Zealand,and Great Britain. All censuses taken in the country were administered by the Australian Commonwealth Bureau of the Census and Statistics. Nauru became independent in 1968. After independence the Department of Island Development and Housing conducted a census in 1977. Only a preliminary report of this census is known to have been issued.

1933

The first census of the mandated territory of Nauru, administered by the Australian CBCS, was *de facto*, and a combination of canvasser and self-enumeration was used. The schedules included the following topics: age, marital status, dependent children, orphanhood, schooling, war service, religion, place of birth, length of residence, language, citizenship, industry, race, occupation, occupational status, causes and duration of unemployment, and income. The tables presented data on the nonindigenous population only, except for the total number of inhabitants.

1947 (June 30)

The second census, conducted by the CBCS, was *de facto* and self-enumerated on household and personal schedules. The census excluded the indigenous population. The nonindigenous population (1,476) included 1,163 Chinese and 51 Gilbert and Ellice Islanders. Tabulation was mechanical. No statistician's report was published; information was gathered directly from tables.

Definitions and Concepts. AGE—as of last birthday, recorded in standard five-year age groups. In addition, two groups, under twenty-one and twenty-one and over, were given separately. Information related to Gilbert and Ellice Islanders was not available. MARITAL STATUS—categories were: never married, married (included permanently separated), widowed, and divorced. The question was asked of persons fifteen years of age and older. Information on the marital status of Chinese and Gilbert and Ellice Islanders was not available. DEPENDENCY—number of persons with dependent children as well as number of dependent children were recorded. Information excluded Chinese and Gilbert and Ellice Islanders. PLACE OF BIRTH—name of country or territory of birth. LENGTH OF RESIDENCE—number of completed years of residence in the country was recorded for Chinese and Gilbert and Ellice Islanders. NATIONAL-ITY—name of the country to which a person owed legal allegiance. No reliable information was available for Chinese persons although they were said to be born in Hong Kong. RACE—three groups were presented: full-blooded European, non-European, and "half-caste" (word used in the census). If half-caste with one parent European, the initials H.C. followed by the race were recorded. If both parents were non-European no initials were used and the race of the father was stated. RELIGION—Two major categories: Christians and non-Christians, followed by the respective denominations. In addition, indefinite, no religion, and no reply were recorded. ECONOMIC ACTIVITY—analyzed in terms of participation or not in the work force. In the work force: included persons at work and not at work (unable to secure employment, temporarily laid off, not actively seeking work because of sickness or accident, industrial dispute, resting between jobs, and so forth). Not in the work force included the inactive, students, pensioners, inmates of institutions, invalids, persons of independent income, and homemakers. INDUSTRY—classification recorded twelve divisions and major groups (Australian Classification). Data excluded Chinese and Gilbert and Ellice Islanders, although the majority were engaged in rehabilitation activities, general services, transportation, and laboring duties. OCCUPATIONAL STATUS—employer, self-employed, employee, and helper (not on wage).

Special Elements and Features. Population was not recorded by districts. Although Chinese and Gilbert and Ellice Islanders constituted the majority of the territory's nonindigenous population, most of the tables excluded information about them.

Quality of the Census. The statistician's report was not published and no details about the results were furnished. Whipple's Index category was not cited.

Publication Plan. Australia. Commonwealth Bureau of Census and Statistics. *Census of the Commonwealth of Australia, 30th June 1947.* Canberra, n.d. One volume on population and one on housing for the external territories. Language of publication is English.

1954 (June 30)

The third census, conducted by the Australian Commonwealth Bureau of Census and Statistics, was *de facto*, and self-enumeration was used on household schedules and individual slips. Tabulation was mechanical. Indigenous population was excluded again from the census. The information gathered here was taken directly from the tables and a few explanatory notes present in each volume. A census of housing was carried out simultaneously.

Definitions and Concepts. AGE—same as 1947, but for the first time unspecified ages were distributed over all ages prior to tabulation. MARITAL STATUS— categories were: never married (those under fifteen and those over fifteen), married, married but permanently separated, divorced, and widowed. PLACE OF BIRTH and LENGTH OF RESIDENCE—same as 1947. NATIONALITY— primarily citizenship. Two main groups were recognized: British (subjects of all territories and commonwealth countries as well as the homeland and Ireland) and foreigners (country of nationality was recorded). RACE—same as 1947. RELIGION—two main groups, Christians and non-Christians as in 1947, but since the question was optional, a large number of people chose not to answer. ECONOMIC ACTIVITY—same as 1947. OCCUPATIONAL STATUS—same as 1947. INDUSTRY—a reduced classification was used (only groups and subgroups of the Australian Classification scheme of June 1954).

Special Elements and Features. Tables refer only to the territory as a whole; there was no distribution of the population by districts or any other territorial division.

Quality of the Census. The indigenous population is included only in the total number of inhabitants. Whipple's Index classified age information within category II—fairly accurate data.

Publication Plan. Australia. Commonwealth Bureau of Census and Statistics. *Census of the Commonwealth of Australia.* Volume 7, Part 5, External territories. Canberra, 1958. Language of publication is English.

1961 (June 30)

The fourth census, conducted by the Australian Commonwealth Bureau of Census and Statistics, was *de facto*, and self-enumeration was used. Population and housing censuses were taken simultaneously. The census, this time, included both indigenous and nonindigenous population. The information gathered here was taken directly from the tables and a few explanatory notes present in each volume. Details on organization and methods are not available.

Definitions and Concepts. AGE, MARITAL STATUS, PLACE OF BIRTH, LENGTH OF RESIDENCE, NATIONALITY, and RELIGION—same as 1954. RACE—European, non-European, and European and other races (persons of mixed races, up to one-half European and up to one-half non-European). ECONOMIC ACTIVITY—concept used was the same as in 1947 and 1954. INDUSTRY—Australian Classification of Industries, June 1961, was used—groups, subgroups, and categories. OCCUPATION—Australian Classification of Occupations was used, major groups only. OCCUPATIONAL STATUS—same as 1954.

Special Elements and Features. Persons who omitted their marital status were allocated a conjugal condition prior to tabulation of results. The total number of indigenous population for 1954 was given to provide intercensal comparisons. Population was not tabulated by districts or other smaller geographic units.

Quality of the Census. There is no statement on the accuracy of the data. Whipple's Index ranking was not given. However, this census did enumerate the total population.

Publication Plan. Australia. Commonwealth Bureau of the Census and Statistics. *Census of the Commonwealth of Australia, 30th June 1961.* Canberra, 1963. Bulletin No. 24 [and] Volume 7, Part 5, External Territories. Canberra, 1965. Language of publication is English.

1966 (June 30)

The fifth census, taken by the Commonwealth Bureau of Census and Statistics, was *de facto*; self-enumeration was the method used to compile the information on household schedules. The results published in Census Bulletin, No. 13-1, *Summary of Population*, were considered preliminary and subject to amendment. However, no other publication was found, and the information gathered here was taken from that bulletin. Tabulation was computerized.

Definitions and Concepts. AGE—as of last birthday, recorded in years and completed months. It was tabulated in standard five-year age groups. There was also a simplified grouping used (under twenty-one, twenty-one to sixty-four, and sixty-five and over). MARITAL STATUS—never married, married, married but permanently separated, divorced, and widowed. PLACE OF BIRTH, NATIONALITY, LENGTH OF RESIDENCE, RELIGION—same as 1961. RACE—was not included although it was taken in Australia. ECONOMIC ACTIVITY—reference period was the week before the census. The active were the employed for pay or profit, and the unemployed whether temporarily or looking for a job. Family helpers and the clergy were considered active. OCCUPATION—classified in major groups only of the Australian system. INDUSTRY—classified in major groups only of the Australian system. OCCUPATIONAL STATUS—same as 1961. EDUCATION—taken in Australia, but not in the external territories.

Special Elements and Features. Very limited amount of information was published on Nauru from this census.

Quality of the Census. Same as 1961.

Publication Plan. Australia. Commonwealth Bureau of Census and Statistics. *Census of Nauru, 30 June 1966.* Census Bulletin No. 13-1. Summary of population. Canberra, 1968. Language of publication is English.

1977 (January 22)

First census of population and housing taken since Nauru's independence in 1968. The preliminary report, the only publication so far available, carried very little about organization and methods utilized in the census and less of definitions. The census was apparently conducted by the Department of Island Development and Industry on a *de facto* basis, but the total population figures included Nauruans known to be absent from the country on census day. Personal and household forms were completed by, or for, every person and household. The scope included: age (standard five-year groups), sex, marital status (single, married, divorced, separated, widowed, consensually married), religion (members of various churches), ethnic groups (Chinese, European, other Pacific Islander, Nauruan), work force (employed persons seventeen years and over), income (monthly income), household size and type, average number of family units, and total number of family units. The figures for total population were also presented by tribes and districts. Number of children ever born was asked, but so far data have not been published.

The data on the preliminary report was manually processed. Large number of forms returned were incorrectly answered, and some enumerators failed to check the completeness of the forms. In addition, some of the questions were not fully comprehended, and it was estimated that about 10 percent of those who stated that they were employed did not list their monthly income. In general, however, the results obtained were considered a true representation of the statistics of the republic, and it was recommended that a census should be taken every five years.

Publication Plan. Nauru. Department of Island Development and Housing. *Preliminary report, Census 1977 in the Republic of Nauru.* Yaren, 1977. Language of publication is English.

National Topic Chart

	1947	1954	1961	1966	1977
De facto	X	X	X	X	X
Usual residence					
Place of birth	X	X	X	X	
Duration of residence	X	X	X	X	
Place of prev. residence					
Urban/rural					
Sex	X	X	X	X	X
Age	X	X	X	X	X
Relation to household head					X
Marital status	X	X	X	X	X
Children born alive					X
Children living					
Citizenship	X	X	X	X	
Literacy					
School enrollment					
Ed. attainment					
Ed. qualification					
National/Ethnic origin	X	X	X	X	X
Language					
Religion	X	X	X	X	X
Household composition					X
Econ. active/inactive	X	X	X	X	X
Occupation	X	X	X	X	
Industry	X	X	X	X	
Occupational status	X	X	X	X	
Income					X
Housing	X	X	X	X	X

New Caledonia

French Overseas Territory (TOM)

CAPITAL: Nouméa.
STATISTICAL AGENCY: Service Statistique de Nouvelle Calédonie.
NATIONAL REPOSITORY: Service de la Statistique, Nouméa.
MAIN U.S. REPOSITORY: Population Research Center (Univ. of Texas).

Discovered by James Cook in 1774, New Caledonia came under French control in 1853, and the first colony was established in 1860. The territory located in Melanesia (Southwest Pacific) consists of the main island (Grande Terre) and its dependencies: Pine Islands, Loyalty Islands, Huon, Belep, Chesterfield, and Walpole Islands.

In 1875 the European population was counted for the first time. The census of 1887 was of both the European and native population. Since 1891 censuses have been taken every five years except when war interfered. In these censuses the population was divided into three categories: the free population (French by birth, born in New Caledonia and elsewhere)—tables of adults and children by sex; the penal population—tables of adults by sex; and the native population (including immigrant labor)—tables of adults by sex and tables of children. The basis of the native population census figures was the tribal register, which was kept up to date by the police and was used up to the 1956 census. The only published results from the censuses through 1936 appear in statistical annuals and the *Journal Officielle*; they consisted mainly of numbers of inhabitants and little else.

1946 (June 20)

The census was *de facto*, of the "non-originaire" population, conducted by the Central Bureau of the Census, self-enumerated on individual schedules, and tabulated in Paris by INSEE, the French statistical agency. The "non-originaires" were those of European stock, Japanese and Algerian Moslims. Those excluded in addition to the native population were Syrian-Lebanese, Chinese, contract labor from Indonesia and Indochina, and those from dependencies of other countries, for example, Arabs from Aden, Indians from British India, and so forth. Territorial division: Grande Terre, subdivided into districts (east and west), communes, and the island dependencies.

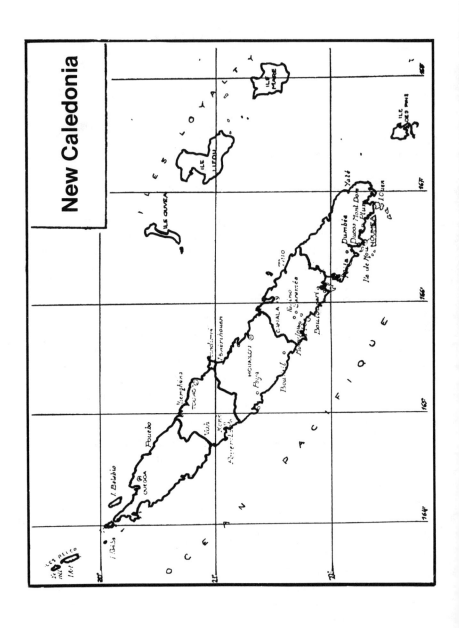

New Caledonia

Definitions and Concepts. AGE—day, month, and year; tables in real age by standard five-year age groups and in generational age by single years. BIRTHPLACE—all persons: department or country and commune. Birthplace(s) of parents used to establish nationality. MARITAL STATUS—single, married, widowed, divorced. FERTILITY—asked of all males and females: number of children born alive (with year of birth) and the number surviving. NATIONALITY—citizenship: French citizens (by birth or naturalization) and foreigners. ECONOMIC ACTIVITY—no reference period stated, assumed to be the moment of the census. Active were those declaring an occupation. OCCUPATION—tabulated in twenty groups, following order of industries. INDUSTRY—tabulated in twenty-one groups, with no systematic classification. OCCUPATIONAL STATUS—employer, employee, own-account worker, not stated, and without activity.

Special Elements and Features. Footnote to Table 2 gives adults and children by sex for 1936.

Quality of the Census. A copy of the schedule that was supposed to have been used contains questions for which there were no tables in the publication of the results, for example, residence in a colony (French possession) or in any tropical country, number of live births occurring in the colony, year of marriage, university or professional degrees earned. "For the first time, some detailed data on the structure of the European and assimilated population have been obtained." No Whipple's Index category cited. The census office is not permanent.

Publication Plan. France. INSEE [and] Service Colonial des Statistiques. *Résultats du recensement de 1946 dans les territoires d'outre-mer. Nouvelle Calédonie*. Paris, n.d. (*Bulletin Mensual de Statistique d'Outre-Mer [BMSOM]*, série "statistique," No. 6) and *Les français d'origine métropolitaine et les étrangers dans les territoires d'outre-mer au recensement de 1946*. Paris, 1950. (*BMSOM*, série "études," no. 18). Language of publication is French.

1951 (October 8)

A census of the "non-originaire" population only. It was *de facto* and conducted by a territorial commission everywhere except Nouméa where the city administration was responsible. It was self-enumerated on individual schedules, and tabulated in Paris by INSEE. Those included were French citizens of European stock and foreign nationals. Excluded were French citizens of non-European stock and other non-Europeans. Territorial division: Grande Terre (in administrative jurisdictions) and the island dependencies.

Definitions and Concepts. BIRTHPLACE, MARITAL STATUS, NATIONALITY, and ECONOMIC ACTIVITY—same as 1946. AGE—same as 1946. Median age was indicated. FERTILITY—for males eighteen and over, females fifteen and over: in addition to number of children born alive, and those surviving, the number of those born outside of France and those who reside with parents in the overseas possessions were asked. EDUCATION—educational attainment (diploma earned), type of education (general or professional). Illiteracy was included in tables, probably by process of elimination.

Special Elements and Features. Sojourn in a tropical country (whether French Union territory or any other tropical country), year of arrival and duration of stay are new in this census. Fertility questions were expanded to emphasize family structure, especially of split families.

Quality of the Census. Most of the data taken on the schedule appears in the results published for New Caledonia.

Publication Plan. France. INSEE. *Premiers résultats du recensement de 1951 dans les territoires d'outre-mer. Population non originaire: 3ème partie, Nouvelle Calédonie.* Paris, n.d. (*BMSOM,* série "statistique," no. 16). And: *Le recensement de la Population non originaire des territoires d'outre-mer en 1951.* Paris n.d. (*BMSOM,* série "études," no. 33). Language of publication is French.

1956 (December 6)

The first of the post-World War II censuses to cover the total population was *de jure* (new); the conduct was the same as 1951. The use of household schedules was new. It was not stated if canvassed or self-enumerated; probably the former. The results were mechanically tabulated in France. Territorial divisions were islands, "arrondissements," communes, localities (and subdivisions) and tribes.

Definitions and Concepts. HOUSEHOLD—one person living alone or a group living in one dwelling with a community of existence, includes live-in servants and boarders. BIRTHPLACE—department in France (or TOM and DOM) or name of country plus year of immigration. AGE—date of birth: tables of real age in standard five-year age groups only. MARITAL STATUS—same as 1951. EDUCATION—literacy (in French, in other languages), type of education (general or professional), and educational attainment (diploma earned). FERTILITY— asked of women fourteen years of age and over: number of children born alive. NATIONALITY and ETHNIC ORIGIN—less emphasis on nationality and citizenship and more on ethnicity. All tables are divided by European and assimilated, Melanesians of New Caledonia, French Polynesians, Hebridians and Wallisians, Indonesians, and Vietnamese. ECONOMIC ACTIVITY—asked of all age fourteen and over; reference period was the moment of the census. Active were divided by sectors (public, semipublic, private, military), which in turn were subdivided by hierarchy. OCCUPATION—tabulated in twenty groups, classed according to industry. INDUSTRY—tabulated in twenty-four groups, classed in major and minor groups. OCCUPATIONAL STATUS—owner, director-manager, employed worker, own-account worker, apprentice, family helper, without work. SOCIOECONOMIC STATUS—cross of occupation and occupational status according to French code adapted for local use. HOUSEHOLD COMPOSITION—private households by size, characteristics of head, and type (spouse and/or children present, relatives or others present); collective households (one table) by type of establishment.

Special Elements and Features. All tables are divided by ethnicity. "Melanesian" means natives, plus tribe; "Caledonians" means European population whose parents were born in New Caledonia.

Quality of the Census. First attempt to have the native population who left tribe of origin censused as residents of an area if they resided there more than six months. No copy of schedule is present. First census of the total population and first *de jure* census of the indigenous population. No Whipple's Index category is cited.

Publication Plan. France. INSEE. *Recensement général de la population de la Nouvelle Calédonie 1956, tableaux statistiques.* Paris, 1962. Language of publication is French.

1963 (May 2)

This was a *de jure* census of the total population, conducted as the previous census, canvassed on household schedules, and tabulated in France by INSEE. Territorial division—same as 1956. First time the French style of determining legal population was used in New Caledonia (see Introduction to Martinique).

The population is divided into "municipale" and "comptée à part." The former is the private household and the collective household (where people freely choose to live). The "comptée à part" population are those who live in institutional establishments with little or no choice in the matter. Unlike larger administrative units, the commune has two legal populations, one based on the commune treated as a separate entity and the other as based on a part of the total territory. Generally, those of the "comptée à part" population who maintain a personal residence in a commune other than that of the institution are double counted if the commune is treated as a separate entity. In 1963 the legal population of a commune (separate) was the total of the "municipale" and the "comptée à part," whether any of the latter had a residence elsewhere or not. As a part of the total territory, the legal population of a commune was the total of the "municipale" and only those of the "comptée à part" who had no residence elsewhere.

Definitions and Concepts. HOUSEHOLD—private: same as 1956. Collective—those living in religious communities, in old age homes, as hotel guests; patients in other than TB, Hansen's and psychiatric treatment facilities, staffs living in all hospitals, schools, and hotels. The "comptée à part" population were the French military living on base; boarding students; public works laborers in barracks; prisoners and reform school inmates; and patients in TB, Hansen's, and psychiatric treatment facilities. USUAL RESIDENCE—commune, tribe, or locality. AGE—date of birth. Tables in generational age, both single years and standard five-year age groups. BIRTHPLACE—same as 1956 plus locality or tribe for the native born. MARITAL STATUS—same as 1956. NATIONALITY and ETHNIC ORIGIN—same as 1956. However, only tables on individual data were divided by ethnicity. EDUCATION—same as 1956. ECONOMIC ACTIVITY—asked of all age fifteen and over; reference period the twelve months preceding census. Active are those employed, family helpers, if those in agriculture worked at least thirty days during reference period, and those in nonagricultural jobs who worked an average of one day per week. Nonactive were not listed by category, only as a total. OCCUPATION—detailed to the three-digit level or more if needed. INDUSTRY—major groups (eight) and minor groups to the second digit level. It was not stated which classification systems were used; probably an adaptation of that used in France. OCCUPATIONAL STATUS—employer, own-account worker (with no employees), salaried, family worker (with or without pay), apprentice, and "culte" (belonging to a religious order). SOCIOECO-NOMIC STATUS—same as 1956. ECONOMIC DEPENDENCY—number of children under fifteen per household and number of economically active in household. HOUSEHOLD COMPOSITION—same as 1956 plus the categories of collective households.

Special Elements and Features. The "legal" population, detailed occupation and industry tables, and twelve month reference period for economic activity were new for New Caledonia. Economic dependency was added and fertility was dropped.

Quality of the Census. No controls were placed on responses given as to occupation and occupational status. Some definitions and a copy of the schedule used are reproduced. No Whipple's Index category is cited.

Publication Plan. France. INSEE. *Analyse des résultats du recensement de la population de Nouvelle-Calédonie (provisoire), 2 mai 1963.* Paris, n.d. And *Résultats statistiques du recensement général de la population de la Nouvelle Calédonie effectué le 2 mai 1963.* Paris, 1965. Language of publication is French.

1969 (March 10)

The conduct of this census was the same as 1963. Territorial division—same as 1963. Legal population for commune (as separate entity)—"municipale" and "comptée à part" minus residents of same commune (because already counted) and commune (as part of whole) "municipale" and "comptée à part" minus those with residence in same or in different commune. Other "comptée à part" are special (prisoners, and patients in TB, Hansen's, and psychiatric facilities), those with residence outside the territory, and those with no residence other than the institution.

Definitions and Concepts: AGE, USUAL RESIDENCE, FERTILITY, EDU-CATION, HOUSEHOLD COMPOSITION, SOCIOECONOMIC STATUS, and ECONOMIC DEPENDENCY—same as 1963. BIRTHPLACE—commune in New Caledonia, department or overseas territory, name of country plus year of arrival in New Caledonia (if born outside), and year of arrival in Nouméa (if born outside). PLACE OF PREVIOUS RESIDENCE (new)—in May 1963. NATION-ALITY—European and assimilated are French (by birth and by naturalization), foreigners (of European stock), all natives of French Overseas Departments (DOM) and Territories (TOM), Indonesians and Vietnamese naturalized French, and Melanesians living "outside of tribe." The autochthon are Melanesians (in tribes) of New Caledonia, French Polynesians, Wallisians and New Hebridians, Vietnamese, and Indonesians. The not stated are grouped as New Hebridians. ETHNIC ORIGIN—in addition to nationality of all persons, the tribal origin and legal status of Melanesians. MARITAL STATUS—same as 1963 plus legally separated included in divorced. ECONOMIC ACTIVITY—asked of all age fifteen and over; reference period was the present. Category—permanent, temporary, seasonal, unemployed, and without occupation (seeking or not seeking work). No statement as to who was considered active or inactive, perhaps assumed as obvious. OCCUPATION—major groups (ten) with minor groups and units (three-digits). INDUSTRY—major groups (eight), minor groups and subdivisions (three-digit). Classifications of both are assumed to be an adaptation of the French systems. OCCUPATIONAL STATUS—employer, own-account worker (without employees), salaried, apprentice, family worker (paid or not).

Special Elements and Features. Fertility was reinstated, and housing was new. Specific definition of European and assimilated and so forth and number of inhabitants in categories of collective and institutionalized population are of interest. A new concept of the legal population of communes is used.

Quality of the Census. More control was exercised over occupation and occupational status responses. No Whipple's Index category was cited, however, and the census office is still not permanent although liaison with INSEE tends to offest this lack.

Publication Plan. France. INSEE. *Résultats statistiques du recensement général de la population de la Nouvelle-Calédonie effectué en mars 1969.* Paris, 1972? No analysis volume has been published as yet. Language of publication is French.

1974 (April 23)

This was not a full census but an enumeration of household heads on ethnicity, migration, and housing. It was canvassed on household schedules for private households and on individual schedules for collective households and the "comptée à part" population. It was *de jure* (with a *de facto* total possible). Territorial division—commune, locality, neighborhood, and tribe. Legal population—same as 1969.

Definitions and Concepts. ETHNIC ORIGIN—all members of private households were classed according to the origin of the household head; the collective and institutionalized populations were classed individually. European and assimilated were all those of European stock, including Australians and New Zealanders. The others were Melanesians of New Caledonia, French Polynesians, Wallisians, Vietnamese, Indonesians, New Hebridians, those born in other DOM and TOM, other non-French Pacific islanders, Japanese, and so forth. USUAL RESIDENCE—included year of arrival in New Caledonia, in Nouméa, or in commune of residence. Results are given for 1960-1974 period.

Special Elements and Features. Housing, including condition and number of inhabitants was given. There is a difference in the definition of European and assimilated.

Quality of the Census. It was of limited scope and not an individual enumeration, but it served its purpose of determining extent of migration and immigration.

Publication Plan. France. INSEE. *Dénombrement de la population de Nouvelle Calédonie.* Paris, 1974. Language of publication is French.

1976 (April 23)

First time the census was conducted under direct responsibility of all local authorities. INSEE helped with preparation of the census, training of enumerators, and control of data collected. Swift publication of results was due to tabulation and analysis performed in New Caledonia. Financial aid was given by FIDES (Fonds d'Investissement et de Développement Economique et Social). This was a *de jure* census canvassed on individual schedules (reinstated), coordinated by household sheets. The territorial divisions are thirty-one communes grouped into administrative zones (Nouméa, West Coast, East Coast, South/Center, Loyalties). Legal population is same as 1969 and 1974.

Definitions and Concepts. ETHNIC ORIGIN—Distribution of population was still more according to ethnic origin (as in 1969 and 1974) than to nationality-citizenship. Definition of European and assimilated was closest to that used in 1974. AGE—date of birth. Age tables are in standard five-year age groups (real age) and single years (generational age). HOUSEHOLD, DWELLING, BIRTHPLACE, MARITAL STATUS, NATIONALITY, HOUSEHOLD COMPOSITION, and ECONOMIC DEPENDENCY—same as 1969. EDUCATION—asked of all age fourteen and over: if attending school, literacy, type of education (general, professional), and education attainment (highest degree confirmed). ECONOMIC ACTIVITY—asked of private household members only, age fourteen and over: permanent, temporary, seasonal. If not working, how long seeking work, experienced worker or new, occupation. If no longer working, what was occupation. OCCUPATION, INDUSTRY, OCCUPATIONAL STATUS, SOCIOECONOMIC STATUS—same as 1969.

Special Elements and Features. Schedules for collective and "comptée à part" populations differed from that of private household in economic activity and usual residence. Questions on unemployment are new.

Quality of the Census. The postenumeration check revealed an undercount of only 0.6 percent. The analyses of the census results are extensive, and the quick publication of results are good factors in this census.

Publication Plan. New Caledonia. INSEE [and] FIDES. *Résultats statistiques du recensement général de la population de la Nouvelle-Calédonie, 23 Avril 1976.* Nouméa, 1977. [and] *Résultats du recensement de la population de la Nouvelle Calédonie, 23 Avril 1976. [Analisis].* [and] *Annexes [tables].* Unpublished data and computer tapes are available with authorization from INSEE (France) only. Language of publication is French.

OTHER STATISTICAL PUBLICATIONS: Issued by Service de la Statistique, *Annuaire Statistique, Informations Statistiques Rapides* (monthly), *Situation Démographique du Territoire* (irregularly).

National Topic Chart

	1946	1951	1956	1963	1969	1974	1976
De facto	X	X				X	
Usual residence		X	X	X	X	X	X
Place of birth	X	X	X	X	X		X
Duration of residence				X	X		
Place of prev. residence					X		X
Urban/rural							
Sex	X	X	X	X	X		X
Age	X	X	X	X	X		X
Relation to household head			X	X	X		
Marital status	X	X	X	X	X		X
Children born alive	X	X	X		X		
Children living	X	X					
Citizenship	X	X	X	X	X		
Literacy			X	X	X		X
School enrollment							X
Ed. attainment		X	X	X	X		X
Ed. qualification							X
National/Ethnic origin	X	X	X	X	X	X	X
Language							
Religion							
Household composition			X				
Econ. active/inactive				X	X		X
Occupation	X	X	X	X	X		X
Industry	X	X	X	X	X		X
Occupational status	X	X	X	X	X		X
Income							
Housing					X	X	

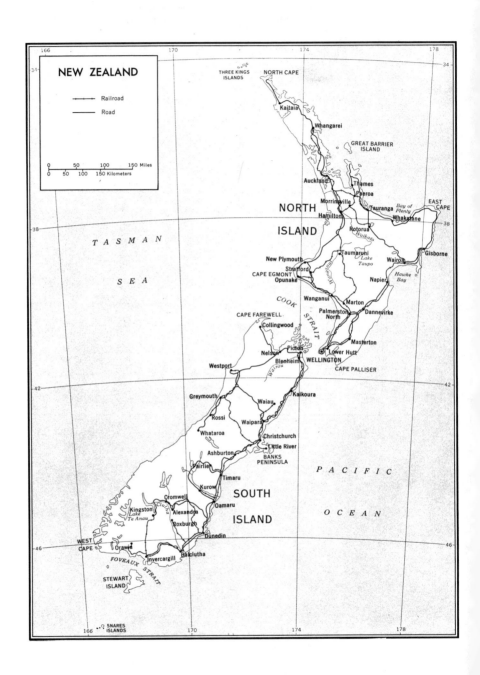

NEW ZEALAND

Railroad
Road

0   50   100   150 Miles
0   50   100   150 Kilometers

THREE KINGS
ISLANDS

NORTH CAPE

Kaitaia

Whangarei

GREAT BARRIER
ISLAND

Auckland
Thames
Paeroa
Morrinsville
Tauranga
Bay of
Plenty
EAST
CAPE

NORTH
Hamilton
Whakatane

ISLAND
Rotorua
Waikato

Taumaruhi
Lake
Taupo
Wairoa
Gisborne

New Plymouth
Stratford
CAPE EGMONT
Opunake
Napier
Hawke
Bay

Wanganui
Marton
Palmerston
North
Dannevirke

TASMAN

SEA

CAPE FAREWELL
Collingwood
Masterton

Nelson
Picton
Lower Hutt
Westport
Blenheim
WELLINGTON
CAPE PALLISER

COOK STRAIT

Wairau

Greymouth
Waiau
Kaikoura

Rossi
Waipara

Whataroa
Christchurch
Ashburton
Little River
BANKS
PENINSULA
Fairlie
Timaru
PACIFIC

Kurow
SOUTH
OCEAN

Cromwell
Kingston
Lake
Te Anau
Alexandra
Oamaru
ISLAND
Roxburgh
Dunedin
WEST
CAPE
Orawia
Clutha
Invercargill
Balclutha
FOVEAUX STRAIT

STEWART
ISLAND

SNARES
ISLANDS

New Zealand

Dominion of New Zealand

CAPITAL: Wellington.
STATISTICAL AGENCY: Department of Statistics, Wellington.
NATIONAL REPOSITORY: Department of Statistics.
MAIN U.S. REPOSITORY: New York Public Library (early years) and Population Research Center (Univ. of Texas).

New Zealand was permanently settled in 1840 and separated from New South Wales, Australia, in 1841. Although some crude form of census operations took place in the early 1840s, what is usually regarded as the first general census of the country was taken in 1851. From then on, censuses were taken with great frequency, but regularity was first achieved with the Census Act of 1858, which instituted triennial general censuses up until 1874. In 1877, a new Census Act provided for the taking of the census in 1878 and 1881 and thereafter in every fifth year.

The nineteen censuses that took place in the country from 1851 to 1936 were *de facto* with supplementary tables prepared on the basis of length of residence, that is, aliens were required to indicate the length of time living in the country. After 1921, duration of residence (domicile) or usual place of residence was part of the schedules, providing information about the *de jure* population.

In 1874 aborigines (Maori) and Chinese started to be enumerated but in a separate census. A number of other censuses were taken simultaneously with the population and housing census, namely those of agriculture, of places of worship and Sunday schools, and of public libraries.

Self-enumeration was used for the Europeans and a combination of canvasser and self-enumeration for the Maoris.

1851

The first general census set the pattern for the subsequent ones. As stipulated by the census ordinance, the country was divided into two provinces. The schedules presented the following features: name, relationship to head of the household (data available but not tabulated until 1926), age, sex, marital status, religion, industry (presented in some dozen groups until 1874, in detailed quasi industrial classification in which personal occupation was more prominent than industry until 1921, and in fully detailed classification thereafter), infirmity, place of birth, literacy, school attendance, and length of residence in the country.

1858

The census act of this year decreed that the census should be taken uniformly throughout the country every three years. Individual and household schedules were used and tabulation was manual. The country was divided into seven provincial districts. The scope was the same as 1851.

1861

The organization and scope were similar to 1858, but length of residence was dropped. Information was obtained for each province and in addition the forty-three electoral districts which were designated census districts.

1864

The same organization and scope as 1861 were used. The number of census districts increased to forty-five, and the military settlers and defense forces were included in the total population.

1867 and 1871

The same as 1861. The number of districts increased to sixty-four.

1874

The first time the Maori census was taken. It was not at the same time as the general census and had a reduced number of questions and a limited amount of tables. Occupation, nationality, and race were added to the 1861 topics used in the general census.

1878

The same scope as 1874, but the results of the Maori census were more accurate. Results by territorial division presented provincial districts, electoral districts, and cities and towns.

1881

It was the first of the quinquennial censuses. The scope was the same as 1874. Household schedules were used. There were tables for the North and South Islands, Chatham Islands, Stewart Islands, and for different tribes of the Maori population.

1886

The general census followed the same pattern as the previous ones since 1874; the Maori census, however, was more elaborate with particulars about sex, age, and principal tribes.

1891

Occupational status was added to the schedules adopted since 1874.

1896

The same as 1891. Mechanical tabulation (punched cards) used for the first time.

1901

Uniformity of schedules and methods of tabulation was achieved in all provinces. A question about naturalization was introduced, and length of residence was revived. The rest of the schedule followed the same pattern adopted in 1891.

1906

The schedules adopted the same format and number of questions as 1901 census. The separate enumeration of Maoris was made at this time by the native agents. A third count was taken to include the population of Cook Islands, Niue, and other South Pacific islands now part of New Zealand.

1911

Questions about duration of marriage and number of children born were added to the schedules previously adopted. The word "object" was used to indicate refusal to state religious affiliation. The census of Maoris, Niueans, Cook Islanders, and other Pacific islanders was still taken separately.

1916

The schedules adopted the same format as 1911 but a question about number of children living was added to it. The territorial division included provincial districts, counties (more rural), and boroughs (more urban). For statistical purposes metropolitan areas and suburban areas were created and were made up of cities and boroughs.

1921

Major changes were made in the schedules adopted previously, and the following features were added: orphanhood, father's birthplace, number of dependent children, insurance (life) and place of domicile (usual place of residence). On the other hand, infirmity was dropped. The territorial division also presented changes. Provincial districts and counties remained unchanged but what were previously called metropolitan and suburban areas were now called urban areas. The urban areas included cities, boroughs, and town districts of 1,000 or more inhabitants.

1926

Another major change took place as far as scope of the census. A new policy was adopted in which certain questions that were unlikely to experience major changes in a short period of time were dropped. Therefore, compared with its predecessor the 1926 census was considerably reduced. The following features were dropped: duration of marriage, number of children born, number of children living, place of birth, father's place of birth, nationality, literacy, school attendance, and insurance. On the other hand, income was added. For the first time, the Maori population was enumerated in one day; previously it had been impossible to relegate the census to a single day. The schedules were written in both English and Maori, thus permitting a larger number of self-enumerations.

1931

Financial conditions caused by worldwide economic depression resulted in the abandonment of this census.

1936

The scope of the census was basically the same as the 1926 with the reinstatement of the question about place of birth. The number of supplementary censuses taken along with population was reduced to a census of poultry. A special volume was dedicated to unemployment with specifications about duration of unemployment and cause. Special schedules were still used for the Maori population.

See Table 4 for quick referral to the topics added and dropped in the early censuses. Name, relationship to head of household, age, sex, marital status, religion and industry were present in all censuses.

The quinquennial sequence was interrupted for the second time in 1941 because of World War II. The Finance Act of 1940 provided for the taking of the census no earlier than 1941 and no later than 1945. The next census was taken in September of 1945, and the 1946 census was abandoned. The scope of the censuses varied considerably in the following years. Some features related to armed forces included in the 1945 census were later abandoned. In substitution the increasing interest in the living standards of the people led to a considerable number of questions on living conditions and social and economic characteristics. Extensive comments about increase and location of population were part of every census after 1945. In addition, after 1951 life tables became part of the general report. Data about education and literacy had been abolished from the census schedules after 1921 but were reinstated in 1966.

Censuses of poultry and war service have been taken simultaneously with the census of population and housing since 1945.

Table 4
Changes in Early New Zealand Censuses 1851-1936

Years	Added	Dropped
1851, 1858	Infirmity Place of birth Literacy School attendance Length of residence	—
1861, 1864, 1867, 1871	—	Length of residence
1874, 1878, 1881, 1886	Occupation Nationality Race	—
1891, 1896	Occupational status	—
1901, 1906	Naturalization Length of residence	—
1911	Duration of marriage Number of children born	—
1916	Number of children living	—
1921	Orphanhood Father's place of birth Dependent children Life insurance Domicile (usual residence)	Infirmity
1926	Income	Duration of marriage Number of children born Number of children living Place of birth Father's place of birth Nationality Literacy School attendance Life insurance
1931	No census was taken	
1936	Place of birth	—

1945 (September 25)

The twentieth census, conducted by the Census and Statistics Department, was *de facto*, but it included supplementary tables prepared on the basis of resident population (*de jure*). The territory of New Zealand proper consisted of both the North and South Islands, and Stewart, Chatham, and adjacent islands. Cook and Niue Islands, although within the extended boundaries of the country, were treated separately. From 1945 on only two kinds of schedules were used by Europeans—dwelling and personal. A special Maori schedule was used, with simplified scope and headings and questions printed in both English and Maori. Self-enumeration was mostly used. Territorial divisions were provincial districts, urban areas, and counties. Tabulation was mechanical. A housing census was taken simultaneously.

Definitions and Concepts. AGE—stated in years and completed months. Recorded in single and five-year age groups. MARITAL STATUS—asked of persons sixteen years of age and over. The categories recorded were: never married, married, legally separated, widowed, and divorced. URBAN—urban areas (1,000 and more inhabitants). Within the urban areas were included boroughs, cities, and town districts. DEPENDENT CHILDREN—understood as all living children under sixteen years of age, including stepchildren and the adopted. The question was asked of all men and women. Although not explicit, it was safely assumed that the great bulk of the children under that age were financially dependent upon their parents. RELIGION—detailed list of religious denominations was provided, and the word "object" used to indicate those who declined to state. PLACE OF BIRTH—the name of the country of birth was asked, and if born overseas the place and length of residence in New Zealand was also required. If born in British Isles, specification of which country was necessary. RACE—if European (that is, white), respondent classified as such; if non-European, specified race; and if more than one race, stated closely as possible the degree of each. ECONOMIC ACTIVITY—the population was divided into active and inactive. See Occupational Status for groups. INDUSTRY—classification was similar to ISIC, divisions, major, and subgroups (three-digits). OCCUPATION—detailed classification was used (three-digit). OCCUPATIONAL STATUS—classification included the economically active (employer, own-account worker, working for wages, unemployed, and family worker) and inactive (invalids, children under fifteen, housewives, unpaid domestic workers, full-time students, the retired, and those of independent income). Armed forces were presented within the group of working for wages. UNEMPLOYMENT—in addition to causes and time of unemployment, whether or not looking for a job was asked. A classification of unemployed by occupation was also given. INCOME—gross income for the twelve months before the census was asked of all but the Maori who did not record income until 1951. WAR SERVICE—whether the respondent had served overseas or not and in what country.

Special Elements and Features. There was an extensive discussion about movement of population from rural to urban areas and a summary of the population census of Tokelau and Western Samoa was included. The general report was not published. The following were added to the schedule: number of working hours, traveling time from and to work, intended changes of industry and occupation, postponed retirement, and number of working days lost. The results of the Maori census were published separately. An alphabetical list of townships and localities by county with total population was included.

Quality of the Census. The enumeration of Maoris followed the same organization applied previously; that is, special schedules with simple and reduced number of questions were used. Comparison between Maori and European data presented difficulties. Since no general report was published, the information gathered here had to be taken from introductory notes on each one of the topics. No postenumeration survey was conducted. Whipple's Index was category II—fairly accurate age data for the total population and category III—approximate data for the Maori population.

Publication Plan. New Zealand. Census and Statistics Department. *Population Census, 1945.* Wellington, 1947-1952. In addition to the eleven subject volumes, there were interim returns published. Language of publication is English.

1951 (April 17)

The twenty-first census, conducted by the Census and Statistics Department, was *de facto* with additional tables presented on the basis of usual place of residence. Dwelling and individual schedules were used by both Europeans and Maoris for the first time. Also, results of the Maori population were included in the general tabulations. Self-enumeration was mainly used, but since the schedules were written in English interpreters were needed at times. The territorial division was the same as 1945. The enumeration in Cook Island, Niue Island, Tokelau, and Western Samoa was carried out at a different date. Tabulation was mechanical. The total population now included Kermadec and Campbell islands.

Definitions and Concepts. MARITAL STATUS, DEPENDENCY, RELIGION, RACE, INCOME and WAR SERVICE—same as 1945. AGE—same as 1945 but was tabulated in single years and five-year age groups. PLACE OF BIRTH and DURATION OF RESIDENCE were put together in one question in the schedule—name of country where born, and if born overseas, number of years living in New Zealand. In addition, usual place of residence was also recorded. ECONOMIC ACTIVITY—comparison with previous censuses is limited to total number of people actively and not actively engaged in industry. Comparison on an industrial basis is not possible because in 1945 the Maori population was tabulated by occupation alone. Tables presented data for those under sixteen and sixteen and over in several age groups. INDUSTRY—codes were modified to agree with international standards (division, major group, and unit) (three-digits). OCCUPATION—Previously a detailed classification had been adopted, but the information acquired from the answers was not sufficient for a correct classification. In order to conform with ISCO a condensed version was used, twelve major groups only (one-digit). OCCUPATIONAL STATUS—categories included: employer, own-account worker not employing labor, working for wages, unemployed or seeking work, family worker not receiving wages. The choice of categories excluded the economically inactive from the classification. For the first time the name of the employer was asked. The question about number of hours worked was sustained, but the questions about traveling time, intended change of industry and occupation, and postponed retirement were dropped.

Special Elements and Features. The number of questions was intentionally reduced as compared to 1945. That is, certain questions concerning employment and facilities and location of dwelling were considered subject to periodic inquiry only, and "questions about postponed retirement and proposed peacetime industry and occupation were omitted since they related only to immediate post-war conditions." The general report was issued this time. There were also copies of the schedules used, life tables, and a list of population by domicile (county, city, borough, town).

Quality of the Census. The shortage of staff for mechanical tabulation and verification of census data may have affected the results, but Whipple's Index classified age of the total population in category I—highly accurate age data and for the Maoris, category II—fairly accurate data.

Publication Plan. New Zealand. Census and Statistics Department. *Population Census, 1951.* Wellington, 1953-1956. Seven subject volumes, a general report, results of the poultry census, maps, and life tables were published. Language of publication is English.

1956 (April 17)

The twenty-second census, conducted by the Department of Statistics under the authority of Census Act 1955, was *de facto* with supplementary tables prepared on the basis of the usual place of residence. Dwelling and individual schedules were used by both Europeans and Maoris. The scope was similar to the 1951 census, increasing only the number of questions regarding dwellings. The censuses of Tokelau Islands, Cook and Niue Islands, and the trust territory of Western Samoa were taken separately (September 25 of the same year). Poultry and war service censuses were still conducted along with the census of population and housing. Total population and territorial divisions were the same as 1951.

Definitions and Concepts. AGE, MARITAL STATUS, DEPENDENT CHILDREN, PLACE OF BIRTH, DURATION OF RESIDENCE, RELIGION, and INCOME were the same as 1951. RACE—the question was stated in the same way as 1951, but this time persons with half or more Maori blood were classified with the Maori population and those with under half, with other races. ECONOMIC ACTIVITY—lower age apparently was sixteen; however, industrial and occupational classification tables presented data on the under sixteen years of age as well. Those engaged in industry (the active) were employers, own-account workers, wage or salary earners, the unemployed, and relative assisting. The not actively engaged were the retired, persons of independent income, and those dependent on public or private support. INDUSTRY—changes were introduced and the classification was identical to that of ISIC, division, major group, and unit (three-digits). OCCUPATION—in 1951 occupational classification was condensed but the demand for a more detailed tabulation was so strong that a full occupational classification based on ISCO was introduced (four-digits). OCCUPATIONAL STATUS—the categories used were those employed to indicate economic activity (see above). If retired, the former industry and occupation were requested. Number of hours worked per week and name of employer were also recorded.

Special Elements and Features. A copy of the schedules was included. There are diagrams and commentaries accompanying each volume. Housing questions were expanded.

Quality of the Census. Whipple's Index classified age data as category I—highly accurate. Fundamental changes in industrial and occupational classification schemes were made because of growing complexity of economic organizations, which prevented comparative analysis with previous results.

Publicaton Plan. New Zealand. Department of Statistics. *Population Census, 1956.* Wellington, 1957-1961. Nine subject volumes, general report, census of poultry, and life tables were published. Language of publication is English.

1961 (April 18)

The twenty-third census was organized and conducted in basically the same way as 1956 by the Department of Statistics. The population of Cook, Niue, and Tokelau Islands were excluded, as was the Ross dependency, which is usually uninhabited except for navy personnel. Tabulation was mechanical. There were some changes in territorial division. Provincial districts were replaced by statistical areas. The new unit is larger than urban areas and counties but smaller than provincial districts. This made it possible to divide large areas such as Auckland province into four statistical areas with different economic conditions.

Definitions and Concepts. AGE—same as 1956. MARITAL STATUS, DEPENDENT CHILDREN, PLACE OF BIRTH, RACE, RELIGION, DURATION and USUAL PLACE OF RESIDENCE, and INCOME were also the same as 1956. HOUSEHOLD—the term was used in the sense of total occupants, related or not, of a permanent private dwelling. DWELLING—building, construction, or tenement that is wholly or partly used as habitation. ECONOMIC ACTIVITY— for statistical purposes the labor force included all persons who worked twenty or more hours per week for wages, salary, or financial reward; persons who assisted relatives in gainful occupation without financial reward; and persons unemployed but seeking work. The inactive population included the retired, persons of independent income, those dependent on public or private support, homemakers, children, and so forth. INDUSTRY—detailed classification based on ISIC adapted to suit New Zealand needs, divisions, major groups, and individual groups (three-digits). OCCUPATION—major changes from the classificaton adopted in

1956 were introduced and comparison with the previous census is difficult. Detailed classification based on ISCO, major groups, group, subgroups, and unit (four-digits). Number of hours worked per week, name of employer, and time occupied in traveling from and to work were additional inquiries. OCCUPATIONAL STATUS—same as 1956. Retired persons were requested to state former industry and occupation and the unemployed, their usual industry and occupation.

Special Elements and Features. The general report presented tables and comments about school enrollment and education in general. It was proposed that a question about educational attendance and qualifications be included in the 1966 census. Rate of urban increase was indicated. A list of the population by townships and localities in each county in alphabetical order, copies of the census schedules, and a table with life expectancy at birth were included.

Quality of the Census. Whipple's Index classified age data in category I—highly accurate. Regularity of census taking has been achieved. Industry and occupation classifications have been constantly updated in accordance with the international standards. Final results began to be published one year after the census.

Publication Plan. New Zealand. Department of Statistics. *Population Census, 1961*. Wellington, 1962-1965. Same pattern of volumes as in 1956. Unpublished data are available and language of publication is English.

1966 (March 22)

The twenty-fourth census was also organized and conducted in the same manner as 1956 and 1961. It was *de facto* and included some tables based on usual place of residence. Self-enumeration was used for all persons. Territorial division was the same as 1961. This was the first census to be processed on computers, which allowed many additional cross-classifications and the inclusion of new tables. Total population still included Kermadec and Campbell Islands. The island territories of Tokelau and Niue had their censuses taken in September 1966. Cook Islands became a self-governing nation in August 1965 and consequently took a census separately. Ross dependency had been inhabited for some years by persons maintaining scientific bases and was also enumerated separately.

Definitions and Concepts. The inquiries related to AGE, MARITAL STATUS, RACE, PLACE OF BIRTH, DURATION OF RESIDENCE, USUAL PLACE OF RESIDENCE, RELIGION, INCOME, and DEPENDENT CHILDREN were the same as the 1961 census. HOUSEHOLD—included all persons residing in a single dwelling whether related or not. EDUCATION—The topic was revived and included for the first time since 1921. Educational attainment, educational classification, and school enrollment for all persons fifteen years of age and older were asked. ECONOMIC ACTIVITY, INDUSTRY, OCCUPATION, and OCCUPATIONAL STATUS followed the same pattern used in 1961. The question about traveling to and from work, however, was dropped.

Special Elements and Features. There is an index to statistical areas, urban areas, counties, cities and boroughs, town districts, and county towns. An alphabetical listing of the population of townships and localities and the population, area and density of all territorial divisions are also included. The use of the computer expanded detail and cross-classifications in the results. The question on education was reinstated.

Quality of the Census. The issuance of final results began in 1967. The format of printed reports adopted areal volumes to cope with the statistical areas and city subdivisions. Whipple's Index classified age data in category I—highly accurate data.

Publication Plan. New Zealand. Department of Statistics. *New Zealand Census of Population and Dwellings, 1966.* Wellington, 1967-1971. Nine statistical area supplements, four city subdivisions, one summary result, and ten subject reports (including a general report) were published. Unpublished data are available. Language of publication is English.

1971 (March 23)

The twenty-fifth census, conducted by the Department of Statistics, was *de facto* with additional tables presented on the basis of usual place of residence. Dwelling and individual schedules continued to be used, and the results were processed by computer. The schedules underwent extensive change and more questions were included. Self-enumeration was used but interpreters were employed when language difficulties required assistance. The total population of New Zealand in addition to North and South Islands, Chatham Islands and Stewart Islands, included Kermadec and Campbell Islands. Cook Islands, Niue, and Tokelau Islands were excluded. The statistical division was introduced. It referred to nonadministrative regions with basic requirements of population of at least 75,000 with a community of social and economic interests centered on a large city. New boundaries were created for urban areas, counties, and the remaining subdivisions.

Definitions and Concepts. AGE, MARITAL STATUS, RACE, INCOME, RELIGION, HOUSEHOLD, PLACE OF BIRTH, USUAL RESIDENCE are the same as 1966. FERTILITY (new)—asked of all ever-married women: the number of children born alive. PLACE OF RESIDENCE—the question referred both to residence one year before in 1970, and five years before the census, in 1966. EDUCATION—school enrollment, educational attainment (number of years completed at each level and the highest level completed), and educational qualification (specific subject or field). ECONOMIC ACTIVITY—same as 1966. The question about time spent traveling to and from work was reinstated, and location of place of work and means of transportation were added for the first time. INDUSTRY, INCOME, OCCUPATION, and OCCUPATIONAL STATUS were the same as 1966. WAR SERVICE—asked for the war in which served (World Wars I and II were the only ones separately specified in the tables). There were separate figures for the Maori population in this topic.

Special Elements and Features. There is an index of statistical divisions, statistical areas, urban areas, counties, cities and boroughs, town districts, and county towns as well as an alphabetical listing of population of townships and localities. Maps of the location of total population as well as Maori population are included. Fertility, education, and labor force characteristics were reinstated and expanded.

Quality of the Census. No postenumeration survey was conducted. The Department of Statistics, a permanent office of different censuses, has assured regularity, accuracy, and updating of such topics as occupational classification. The final results began to appear in 1972. Whipple's Index category was I—highly accurate age data.

Publication Plan. New Zealand. Department of Statistics. *New Zealand Census of Population and Dwellings, 1971.* Wellington, 1972-1977. Nine volumes for territorial areas, one summary, twelve subject volumes (including a general report) were published. Unpublished data are available. Language of publication is English.

1976 (March 23)

The twenty-sixth general census of population and housing was conducted by the Department of Statistics on a *de facto* basis, with additional tables for the *de jure* population. Self-enumeration was the method mostly used to record information on individual and household schedules. The tabulation was computerized, and the territory was divided into statistical areas, statistical divisions, main urban areas, and local authority subdivisions (cities, towns, Thames-Coromandel district, counties, communities, district communities, and town districts). The total population included the same islands as 1971.

Definitions and Concepts. AGE—in years and completed months. Tabulated in single years and standard five-year age groups. URBAN—cities, boroughs, town districts, and communities with 1,000 or more inhabitants. Main urban areas are cities and their adjacent urbanized areas or suburbs. HOUSEHOLD—the total occupants of one permanent private dwelling. Households may consist of one family only, other family household (family with another person or two families), nonfamily (multiperson household), and one person. MARITAL STATUS—categories were: never married, married, legally separated, widowed, and divorced. FAMILY—nuclear family and persons related by blood, marriage, or adoption. FERTILITY—asked of all females sixteen years and over who were ever married: number of children born alive. PLACE OF BIRTH—two groups were distinguished: born in New Zealand and born overseas (country of birth recorded and duration of residence in the country). PLACE OF RESIDENCE—usual place, and duration of residence for foreign born. ETHNIC ORIGIN—derived from the following questions: whether of full European descent, whether full New Zealand Maori, Cook Islands Maori, Indian, and so forth. If more than one origin, full details were asked, for example, three-fourths European one-fourth New Zealand Maori, or one-half New Zealand Maori one-half Samoan. The definition of Maori changed in 1974 to include descendants of Maoris who were less than half in origin. RELIGION—religious profession in which the person was brought up. Like the previous censuses, the word "object" was used in case of no answer offered. EDUCATION—asked of persons fifteen years and over: school attendance (level attended and attendance during the twelve months before the census). ECONOMIC ACTIVITY—lower age limit was fifteen years. Economically active population included persons working for financial reward for a minimum of twenty hours per week, persons temporarily unemployed and looking for work at census date, and unpaid family workers. Inactive population were those who did not work at all, persons who worked less than twenty hours per week, inmates of institutions, the retired, students, homemakers, and invalids. OCCUPATION—classification was based on ISCO (four-digits). INDUSTRY—classification based on ISIC, major divisions, divisions, and major groups (three-digits). OCCUPATIONAL STATUS—categories were: employer of labor, own-account worker, wage and salary earner, unemployed, and relative assisting. INCOME—estimated gross income from all sources other than social security benefits. Those owning their own business or persons of independent income recorded their net income before tax. SOCIAL SECURITY—asked were types of social security type benefits, including war pensions and allowances, received during the year before the census.

Special Elements and Features. The volume with the general report is not yet available, but the scope of the census was reduced in comparison with the 1971 census. Publication format was changed slightly. The designations of territorial divisions were also changed. An alphabetical list of counties, townships, and localities and their respective populations and boundaries of urban areas changed since 1971 are also supplied.

Quality of the Census. Preliminary counts were issued soon after the census date; the provisional results, in September 1976; and the final results began to appear in March 1977. Whipple's Index is not yet available. Further details on organization and conduct will be available when the general report is issued.

Publication Plan. New Zealand. Department of Statistics. *1976 Census of Population and Dwelling.* Wellington, 1977— . Ten subject volumes, thirteen areal and eleven subject publications (provisional in nature) were published. Unpublished data and computer tapes are available. Language of publication is English.

1981

Only provisional figures for local authority areas have been published from the 1981 census.

OTHER STATISTICAL PUBLICATIONS: Issued by Department of Statistics, *Information Service* (irregularly), *Monthly Abstract of Statistics, Official Yearbook, Pocket Digest of Statistics* (annually), *Population and Migration* (annually), *Quarterly Demographic Bulletin, Social Trends in New Zealand, Statistics Bulletin* (miscellaneous series).

National Topic Chart

	1945	1951	1956	1961	1966	1971	1976
De facto	X	X	X	X	X	X	X
Usual residence	X	X	X	X	X	X	X
Place of birth	X	X	X	X	X	X	X
Duration of residence	X	X	X	X	X	X	X
Place of prev. residence						X	
Urban/rural	X	X	X	X	X	X	X
Sex	X	X	X	X	X	X	X
Age	X	X	X	X	X	X	X
Relation to household head	X	X	X	X	X	X	X
Marital status	X	X	X	X	X	X	X
Children born alive						X	X
Children living							
Citizenship							
Literacy							
School enrollment					X	X	X
Ed. attainment					X	X	X
Ed. qualification					X	X	
National/Ethnic origin	X	X	X	X	X	X	X
Language							
Religion	X	X	X	X	X	X	X
Household composition	X	X	X	X	X	X	X
Econ. active/inactive	X	X	X	X	X	X	X
Occupation	X	X	X	X	X	X	X
Industry	X	X	X	X	X	X	X
Occupational status	X	X	X	X	X	X	X
Income	X	X	X	X	X	X	X
Housing	X	X	X	X	X	X	X

Niue

New Zealand Associate State

CAPITAL: Alofi.
STATISTICAL AGENCY: Secretary of the Government; Government of Niue, Alofi.
NATIONAL REPOSITORY: Central Office of the Niue Government.
MAIN U.S. REPOSITORY: University of California at Berkeley and Population Research Center (Univ. of Texas).

The island of Niue was annexed to New Zealand in 1901 and was initially administered as part of the Cook Islands. Since 1903 Niue has had its own administration.

Starting in 1827, the missionaries kept the records of births and deaths of the inhabitants of the island, which was divided into three settlements—Avarua, Arorangi, and Takitumu. The first mission "census" of Avarua and Arorangi was taken in 1840, and in 1854 all three settlements were part of the missionary count, which included number of inhabitants, sex, and broad age groups. After this date information on population of the island became very scarce. Two sets of missionary "censuses" taken in 1859 and 1875 were later published in annual reports, but they were considered not accurate and incomplete.

The first official census was taken in 1902 as part of the New Zealand census but no details are known as far as organization and methods used. The results were limited to number of inhabitants by sex.

The earlier censuses were taken by the registrar general of the Justice Department. They were *de facto*, and canvasser was the method used in various schedules. The scope was always very limited as the main interest was to know the total number of inhabitants. The results were published in conjunction with the New Zealand census up until 1966.

1906

The system of quinquennial census was adopted. The scope included: total population of natives classified by sex and broad age groups. The twenty-one inhabitants (sixteen males and five females) of the white and half-caste population were excluded from the census.

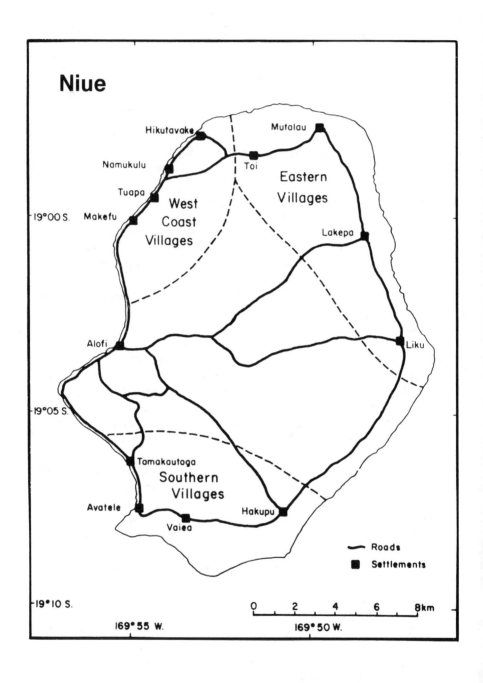

Niue

Hikutavake
Mutalau
Namukulu
Toi
Tuapa
West
Coast
Villages
Eastern
Villages
Makefu
19°00 S.
Lakepa
Alofi
Liku
19°05 S.
Tamakautoga
Southern
Villages
Avatele
Hakupu
Vaiea

— Roads
■ Settlements

0   2   4   6   8km

19°10 S.

169°55 W.
169°50 W.

1911

The third general census, besides total population, recorded literacy in English, school attendance, and number of livestock and coconut palms. At this time the white and half-caste populations were included. In addition, an extract from the report by the resident commissioner was published with comments about occupations and religious denominations.

1916

The same as 1911.

1921

Household questionnaires, identical to those of the Europeans in New Zealand, were used for the nonnative population. The scope included: name, relationship to head of household, sex, age, marital status, date of marriage, number of children born alive, number of children still living, industry, occupation, occupational status, period of unemployment, place of birth, citizenship, race, length of residence, country of birth of father, religion, literacy, school attendance, and life insurance. However, not all results were published (only age, literacy, school attendance, number of livestock, and coconut palms).

The native population, however, was recorded in census books containing the following questions: age, sex, whether full blood or "half-caste," place of birth, usual place of residence, occupation, religion, literacy, and school attendance. Like the nonnative population, not all the results were published.

1926

Basically the same organization as was used in 1921. The following tables were published as part of the New Zealand census: native and nonnative total population, sex and place of birth (native and nonnative), literacy, and school attendance (native). The data, however, is not comparable with the previous censuses since the concept of native and nonnative changed; that is, natives and "half-caste" living with Europeans were no longer considered part of the nonnative population.

1936

The seventh general census of population also was conducted by the Census and Statistics Department in association with the New Zealand census. The organization was similar to the previous census, and the tables published included total population, age, place of birth, religion, and race for native and nonnative population. Literacy was asked only of natives whereas duration of residence, occupation, nationality, and country of domicile were asked only of nonnatives.

1945 (September 25)

The eighth general census of population was associated with the census of New Zealand and conducted by the Census and Statistics Department. The census was taken on a *de facto* basis and a combination of canvasser and self-enumeration was adopted. Personal schedules were used by the European part of the population as well as the natives attached to European dwellings, while book records were utilized to enumerate the other natives. Tabulation was mechanical. Information gathered here was taken from introductory notes and table headings because a general report was not published. Niue was divided into twelve districts.

Definitions and Concepts. AGE—recorded in completed years and months and presented in five-year age groups. PLACE OF BIRTH—name of the country was recorded for the nonnatives and the island of birth for the natives. RELIGION—natives and nonnatives were classified according to their religious affiliation. Reduced number of denominations was found for natives. The answer to this question was not mandatory and the verb "object" was used in those cases. RACE—the nonnatives were classed as European or Chinese. The native population was classified as either full-blood native, three-quarter native or half native. EDUCATION—the question was asked of native population only, ten years of age and older: ability to read and write English as well as the native language. PLACE OF RESIDENCE was asked and DURATION OF RESIDENCE—in number of years was recorded for the nonnatives. ECONOMIC ACTIVITY—asked of all persons fifteen years and older. The following groups were classified as persons not actively engaged in gainful occupations: persons performing domestic duties, invalids, "rangatira" (no definition given), students, and youth not working. Occupation was recorded for the nonnative population, and the classification was not presented in separated groups and subgroups but rather in a list of individual occupations in alphabetical order. The native population was presented in a mix of industrial and occupational classifications. Almost all the natives were under one occupation, planter. NATIONALITY—political allegiance and country of domicile were recorded for the nonnative population.

Special Elements and Features. The personal schedule used in New Zealand was the same for the European population in Niue; however, the results of marital status, number of dependent children, occupational status, number of working hours, journey to work (traveling time), and unemployment were not available for the island. A table with native population of village districts was furnished. Niue was divided into twelve districts.

Quality of the Census. Whipple's Index made no reference to the accuracy of age data, but introductory notes of the census reported data as fairly accurate and added that in some instances an estimate rather than actual age was recorded. In addition, "tabulation of occupational distribution of both natives and non-natives has been incorporated for interest, rather than from the point of view of any inherent value contained in the results." The general report was not published.

NOTE: Unpublished data for 1902, 1906, 1911, 1916, 1921, and 1926 through 1945 are available from the central office of the Niue Government.

The 1951, 1956, 1961, and 1966 censuses were conducted by the Niue Island administration, but the only published results were summary tables in the *Annual Reports* presented to the New Zealand parliament. Tables with the number of inhabitants by sex for each of the above censuses are found in the New Zealand census reports for the respective year.

1971 (September 27)

The thirteenth general census of population was considerably larger than the four previous ones and served as the basis for the planning of future enumerations. The census was conducted by the Department of Justice on a *de facto* basis, and canvasser was the method used on personal and dwelling schedules. Housing and population censuses were taken simultaneously, and the results were published in separate reports. No additional details were furnished as far as organization and methods; therefore, the information contained here was based on the introductory part and table headings.

Definitions and Concepts. AGE—presented in single year and standard five-year age groups. MARITAL STATUS—asked of all persons fifteen years and older. The categories were: never married, married, legally separated, divorced, and widowed (results were published for the first time). FERTILITY—for the first time the number of living children per female was recorded. Age at birth of the first child was also asked. RELIGION—The following religious denominations were present: Ekalesia Niue, Latter Day Saints, Roman Catholic, Jehovah's Witness, and Seventh Day Adventist. PLACE OF BIRTH—Niuean descent was distinguished from non-Niuean descent. The name of the island or country of birth as well as duration of residence in the island were recorded. EDUCATION—school enrollment, educational attainment (complete years of attendance), educational qualification (degree, certificate, and diploma), professional trade and vocational qualifications. ECONOMIC ACTIVITY—asked of all persons fifteen years and older. The economically active were wage and salary earners, those assisting the family, and the unemployed looking for job. Inactive were the retired, students, and housewives. Number of hours worked per week, location of work place, and means of transportation were recorded. OCCUPATION—classification limited to ten major groups. Tables were presented that distinguished those of Niuean descent from non-Niuean. OCCUPATIONAL STATUS—categories were: employer, self-employed, wage and salary earner, unemployed, relative assisting, the retired, full-time student, and housewife. INDUSTRY—classification included only the following groups: public service, retail trading, building services, transport services, and planting. INCOME—annual estimated income of persons by village.

Special Elements and Features. Also present in the census report were migration to and from New Zealand (1966-1970); villages by fruit, crops, and livestock; household occupants, total hours worked per household; households by aggregate total income; and vehicles and boats by village. There is also a table on the resident population by sex for 1966 and the intercensal increase/decrease for each village since then.

Quality of the Census. Whipple's Index classified age data into category III—approximate data. This census was the most comprehensive as yet published. It was pointed out that one of the major failings of the census was the absence of comparable data and summary results of unpublished enumerations.

Publication Plan. Niue Island. Census Officer. *Census of Population and Dwellings, Niue Island, 1971.* Wellington, 1974. Language of publication is English.

1976 (September 28)

The fourteenth general census of population was taken simultaneously with the housing census and conducted by the Department of Justice. It was *de facto* and canvassed on personal and household/dwelling schedules. Tabulation was computerized. A pilot survey was conducted in 25 percent of the households.

Definitions and Concepts. HOUSEHOLD—consisted of one or more persons, related or not, sleeping in the same house and sharing food arrangements. Visitors, boarders, or occupants of any type of out-building on the land of the head of the household were included. An additional question—whether parents were alive or deceased— was also recorded. AGE—date of birth (and if unknown, estimated year). Data presented in single years and standard five-year age groups. PLACE OF BIRTH—natives and foreigners distinguished. If foreigner, country of birth, whether visitor or resident, and number of years resided in Niue. The natives were asked the number of years resided outside the island. RACE—The racial origin or descent was asked. Correct description such as full-blooded was taken, and if of more than one origin, percentage of blood of each race was recorded. HOME VILLAGE—asked only of persons who were of Niuean descent— to measure internal migration. RELIGION—not a compulsory question, specific denominations were recorded. EDUCATION—school attendance (full-time), educational attainment (highest degree completed), and educational qualification (including professional, vocational, and business degrees or certificates). MARITAL STATUS—asked of all persons fifteen years of age and older. Categories were the same as 1971. ECONOMIC ACTIVITY—asked of all persons fifteen years and older. Niueans often have more than one activity, but for the census only the main activity performed the week before the enumeration was taken. Economically active included persons working to earn money, growing or catching food for own use, temporarily not working because of sickness or holiday, not working but actively looking for paid work (for the first time or not). Economically inactive were those who did unpaid domestic duties, full-time students, and others living on pensions or social benefit or who were dependent on any other kind of public or private support. The number of hours worked, name of employer (company or firm), place of work, and means of transportation were also recorded. OCCUPATIONAL STATUS—employer, working on own account and not employing labor, working for salary or wages, unpaid family worker, and unemployed. INDUSTRY—classification presented eight divisions with major groups (two-digits). OCCUPATION—classification presented seven major groups with subgroups (two-digits). INCOME—estimated annual gross income during the year ending March 1976. Included wages, salaries, war pensions, remittances from overseas, and so forth. FERTILITY—asked of all females fifteen years of age and older: number of children ever born, number of children still living (in the household or elsewhere), number of children dead, and age of mother at first birth.

Special Elements and Features. There is an analysis of demographic data of the 1976 census (population distribution, migration, population projections, fertility, and mortality). It also discusses the results of the mini-census conducted in 1979. (An analysis volume was published in 1980 or 1981.) Other items included were a history with comparative tables for the censuses 1901-1976, methods and organization of the 1976 census, maps, graphs, and a copy of the schedules used. The results of several tables have been rounded. A reference was made about the similarities of the 1971 and 1976 censuses, which may help in further research on comparability between the two.

Quality of the Census. A pilot survey conducted in 25 percent of the households improved completeness of enumeration and served as a check on the questionnaires. An extensive training program was developed to improve the quality of work of the enumerators. Age reporting was considered accurate and almost complete. Only five were "not stated." These were compared to the birth registration records. The size of the country and the easy access to its small population contributed to the accuracy and completeness of the data. The rounding process created some small inconsistencies in the tables. Whipple's Index rating was category I—highly accurate age data.

Publication Plan. Niue Island. Department of Justice. *1976 Census of Population and Housing. Report.* Noumea, New Caledonia, 1978-1981? One volume of basic information and one volume of analysis. Computer tapes are available. Language of publication is English.

1981

"The establishment of the Planning Division of the Central Office in 1980 made it possible to centralize all activities relating to census taking in the future. It follows that the processing of the 1981 census data is now the responsibility of the Assistant Secretary to Government (Planning)."

National Topic Chart

	1945	1951	1956	1961	1966	1971	1976
De facto	X	X	X	X	X	X	X
Usual residence							X
Place of birth	X					X	X
Duration of residence	X					X	X
Place of prev. residence							
Urban/rural							
Sex	X	X	X	X	X	X	X
Age	X					X	X
Relation to household head	X					X	X
Marital status						X	X
Children born alive							X
Children living						X	X
Citizenship	X						
Literacy	X						
School enrollment						X	X
Ed. attainment						X	X
Ed. qualification						X	X
National/Ethnic origin	X			X	X	X	X
Language							
Religion	X					X	X
Household composition						X	X
Econ. active/inactive	X					X	X
Occupation	X					X	X
Industry	X					X	X
Occupational status						X	X
Income						X	X
Housing						X	X

Norfolk Island

Australian External Territory

CAPITAL: Kingston.
STATISTICAL AGENCY: Australian Bureau of Statistics.
NATIONAL REPOSITORY: ?
MAIN U.S. REPOSITORY: Population Research Center (Univ. of Texas).

Norfolk, a small volcanic island in the South Pacific Ocean, was discovered by Captain James Cook in 1774. For a short time the island was a penal colony under the jurisdiction of New South Wales. Since then it has been one of the Australian external territories, governed by an administrator and a local council.

Unlike the other external territories (Papua New Guinea and Nauru), Norfolk Island did not have aboriginal or native populations. Pitcairn Islanders, southern European in appearance, were transferred to settle in Norfolk in 1855.

Since 1921 the population censuses of the territory have been carried out as an adjunct to the Australian census.

1921

The first census administered by the Commonwealth Bureau of Census and Statistics was *de facto* and self-enumerated with assistance by collectors.

The scope was quite large, covering age, place of birth, nationality, length of residence in the territory, race, religion, industry, grades of occupation (occupational status), causes and duration of unemployment, marital status, literacy, and school attendance.

1933

Second census, conducted by the Australian Commonwealth Bureau of Census and Statistics, was *de facto* and mostly self-enumerated. The scope included the following topics: age, marital status, number of dependent children, orphanhood, schooling, war service, religion, place of birth, length of residence in the territory, language, nationality (citizenship), race, industry, occupation, occupational status, unemployment causes and duration, and income.

1947 (June 30)

The third census, conducted by the Australian Commonwealth Bureau of Census and Statistics, was *de facto* and self-enumerated on household and personal schedules. Tabulation was mechanical. The information gathered here was taken directly from the tables; the statistician's report was not published.

Definitions and Concepts. AGE—as of last birthday in completed years. Tabulated in standard five-year age groups. In addition, two groups—under twenty-one and twenty-one and over—were given separately. MARITAL STATUS—the categories were: never married, married (included permanently separated), widowed, and divorced. DEPENDENCY—number of persons with dependent children and number of dependent children (no older than sixteen years of age). PLACE OF BIRTH—name of country or territory of birth. LENGTH OF RESIDENCE—required of all aliens and recorded in completed years of residence. NATIONALITY—that is, citizenship. Name of the country to which a person owes legal allegiance. RACE—population was divided into three groups: full-blooded European, non-European, and half-caste (expression used in the census). If half-caste with one parent European, the initials H. C. followed by the race were recorded; if both parents were non-European, only the race of the father was stated. RELIGION—two major categories: Christians and non-Christians, followed by respective denominations. In addition, indefinite, no religion, and no reply were recorded. ECONOMIC ACTIVITY—analyzed in terms of participation or not in the work force. In the work force included persons at work and not at work (unable to secure employment, temporarily laid off, not actively seeking work because of sickness or accident, industrial dispute, resting between jobs, and so forth). Not in the work force included inactive, students, pensioners, inmates of institutions, invalids, persons of independent income, and homemakers. INDUSTRY—recorded twelve divisions with major groups (Australian Classification). OCCUPATIONAL STATUS—employer, self-employed, employee, and helper (not on wage).

Special Elements and Features. Population was not recorded by districts as it was done in Papua New Guinea. No separate reference was made to indigenous population. Occupation was not taken.

Quality of the Census. Statistician's report to this census was not published, hence there is no specific information as to organization, conduct, methods, or definitions used. No Whipple's Index category was assigned.

Publication Plan. Australia. Commonwealth Bureau of Census and Statistics. *Census of the Commonwealth of Australia, 30th June, 1947.* Volume 1, Part 7, External territories. There is also a comparable volume on housing (Volume 3, Part 26). Language of publication is English.

1954 (June 30)

The fourth census, conducted by the Australian Commonwealth Bureau of Census and Statistics, was *de facto*, and self-enumeration the method used.

Householder's schedules and individual slips were the instruments of enumeration. Tabulation was mechanical. The information gathered here was taken directly from the tables, and some explanatory notes that are present in each volume. A census of housing was realized simultaneously with population.

Definitions and Concepts. AGE—the same as 1947, but for the first time unspecified ages were distributed over all ages prior to tabulation. MARITAL STATUS—categories were: never married (under and over fifteen years of age), married, married but permanently separated, divorced, and widowed. PLACE OF BIRTH and LENGTH OF RESIDENCE—the same as 1947. NATIONALITY—primarily citizenship. Two main groups were recognized. British (subjects of all territories and commonwealth countries as well as the homeland and Ireland) and foreign, the name of the country of nationality was recorded. RACE—the same as 1947. Pacific island race included Polynesians and other South Sea islanders. RELIGION—two main groups, Christians and non-Christians as in 1947; but the answer to the question was optional, therefore a large number of people chose not to respond. ECONOMIC ACTIVITY—the same as 1947. OCCUPATIONAL STATUS—the same as 1947. INDUSTRY—reduced classification; major groups and subgroups of the Australian Classification of Industry of June 1954.

Special Elements and Features. Tables referred only to the territory as a whole; there was no distribution of the population by districts or any other territorial division.

Quality of the Census. Whipple's Index classified age information within category III—approximate data. No information as to organization, methods, definitions, and so forth is available, since statistician's report was not published.

Publication Plan. Australia. Commonwealth Bureau of Census and Statistics. *Census of the Commonwealth of Australia.* Volume 7, Part 5, External territories. Canberra, 1958. Language of publication is English.

1961 (June 30)

The fifth census, conducted by the Australian Commonwealth Bureau of Census and Statistics, was *de facto*, and self-enumeration was the method used on household schedules. Population and dwelling censuses were taken simultaneously. The information gathered here was taken directly from the tables and some explanatory notes present in each volume. Tabulation was mechanical.

Definitions and Concepts. AGE, MARITAL STATUS, PLACE OF BIRTH, LENGTH OF RESIDENCE, NATIONALITY and RELIGION—same as 1954. RACE—European, non-European, and European and other races (persons of mixed races, up to one-half European and up to one-half non-European). ECONOMIC ACTIVITY—concept of inclusion or exclusion in the work force was the same adopted in 1947 and 1954. INDUSTRY—Australian Classification of Industries, 1961, was used; major groups only.

Special Elements and Features. Persons who omitted their marital status were, for the first time, allocated a conjugal condition prior to tabulation. Population was not recorded by districts or other smaller geographical unit.

Quality of the Census. Little or no information on methods and definitions is available. Analysis of the data is also lacking. There was no Whipple's Index category assigned to Norfolk, but the Australian census was rated Category I—highly accurate age data.

Publication Plan. Australia. Commonwealth Bureau of Census and Statistics. *Census of the Commonwealth of Australia.* Volume 7, Part 5, External territories. Canberra, 1965. Language of publication is English.

1966 (June 30)

The sixth census taken by the Commonwealth Bureau of Census and Statistics was *de facto* and self-enumeration was the method used on household schedules. The results were published in Census Bulletin number 10.1, *Summary of Population*, but it was considered preliminary and subject to amendment. However, no other publication was found, and the information gathered here was taken from that bulletin. Tabulation was computerized.

Definitions and Concepts. AGE—as of last birthday, recorded in years and completed months. It was tabulated in standard five-year age groups and also under twenty-one, twenty-one to sixty-four and sixty-five and over. MARITAL STATUS—categories were: never married, married, married but permanently separated, divorced, and widowed. PLACE OF BIRTH, NATIONALITY, LENGTH OF RESIDENCE, RELIGION—same as 1961. RACE was not included although it was taken in the Australian census. ECONOMIC ACTIVITY— lower age limit was not stated. Reference period was the week before the census. The active were the employed, the temporarily unemployed, and those looking for work. Family helpers and working clergy were included in active. INDUSTRY— classification was according to ASIC, only major groups. OCCUPATION— classification was ACO, only major groups. OCCUPATIONAL STATUS—same as 1961. EDUCATION—not taken in Norfolk, although it was included in the Australian census.

Special Elements and Features. Results were given only for the island as a whole, no districts. There are some comparative tables, 1961-1966. Race was dropped.

Quality of the Census. Although the question of age was more specific than in the previous census, Whipple's Index classified the information in category III—approximate age data.

Publication Plan. Australia. Commonwealth Bureau of Census and Statistics. *Census of Population and Housing, 30 June 1966.* Bulletin No. 10-1. *Census of the Territory of Norfolk Island. Summary of Population.* Canberra, 1968. Language of publication is English.

1971 (June 30)

It is not known if the Norfolk Island Administration took the census in this year; the publication available is a copy of tables comparing 1966 and 1971 results. The tables covered the following topics: AGE, LINEAL DESCENDANTS OF ORIGINAL SETTLERS, NUMBER OF VISITORS, MARITAL STATUS,

PLACE OF BIRTH, NATIONALITY, RELIGION, OCCUPATION (major groups), INDUSTRY (major groups), LENGTH OF VISIT. Details of census of dwellings were also recorded. Whipple's Index is category I—highly accurate age data.

National Topic Chart

	1947	1954	1961	1966	1971
De facto	X	X	X	X	X
Usual residence					
Place of birth	X	X	X	X	X
Duration of residence	X	X	X	X	X
Place of prev. residence					
Urban/rural					
Sex	X	X	X	X	X
Age	X	X	X	X	X
Relation to household head					
Marital status	X	X	X	X	X
Children born alive					
Children living					
Citizenship	X	X	X	X	X
Literacy					
School enrollment					
Ed. attainment					
Ed. qualification					
National/Ethnic origin	X	X	X		X
Language					
Religion	X	X	X	X	X
Household composition					
Econ. active/inactive	X	X	X	X	X
Occupation			X	X	X
Industry	X	X	X	X	X
Occupational status	X	X	X	X	X
Income					
Housing	X	X	X	X	X

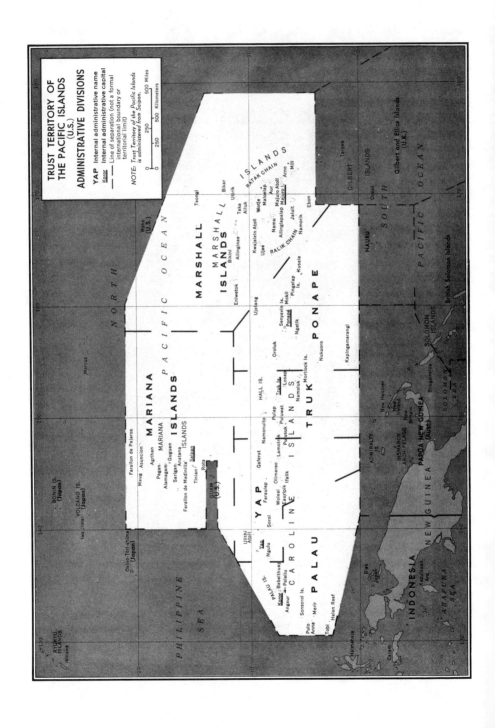

TRUST TERRITORY OF
THE PACIFIC ISLANDS
(U.S.)
ADMINISTRATIVE DIVISIONS

YAP Internal administrative name
Koror Internal administrative capital
— Line of separation (not a formal
international boundary or
territorial limit)

NOTE: Trust Territory of the Pacific Islands
is administered from Saipan.

Pacific Islands, Trust Territory

**Former United States trust territory;
see recently created countries below**

CAPITAL: Saipan.
STATISTICAL AGENCY: Office of Planning and Statistics, High Commissioner's Office, Saipan.
NATIONAL REPOSITORY: ?
MAIN U.S. REPOSITORY: New York Public Library and Population Research Center (Univ. of Texas).

Three groups of islands (Carolines, Marshalls, and Marianas except Guam) cover an expanse of about 3,000,000 square miles. There are more than 3,000 islands of which only 100 are inhabited. Under an agreement by the Security Council of the United Nations, they came under the administration of the United States on April 2, 1947. Previously, the islands had been under the administration of the Japanese government.

In 1981, the trust territory agreement terminated and the Caroline Islands became the federated States of Micronesia (FSM); Palau Islands became the Republic of Belau; Marshall islands, a separate state; and the Marianas, the U.S. Commonwealth of Northern Mariana Islands.

Censuses of population taken quinquennially between 1920 and 1940 were conducted by the South Seas Bureau of Japan. Figures from those earlier censuses were published by the Foreign Affair Association of Japan, *Japan Yearbook, 1943-44 and 1938-39*, Kenkyusha Press, Tokyo, Japan.

In 1950, the U.S. Department of the Navy published a report on the administration of the islands with total population results.

In 1955, the total number of inhabitants was published by the U.S. Department of the Interior in its annual report on the territory.

1958 (first half of the year)

The census was conducted by the Office of the High Commissioner from December 1957 to June 1958. It was the first complete enumeration since the area became a trusteeship of the United Nations administered by the United States. Apparently the census was taken on a *du jure* basis; canvasser was the method utilized to record information on the schedules. Tabulation was mechanical. The report carries very little about organization and methods, and no definitions or concepts were supplied. Information gathered here was taken from introductory notes and table headings. The territory covered by the census was divided into seven districts (Marshalls, Palau, Ponape, Rota, Saipan, Truk, and Yap), subdivided into municipalities or islands.

Definitions and Concepts. AGE—tabulated in standard five-year age groups and median age. PLACE OF BIRTH—two major groups: born in the territory and born outside or not reported. ETHNIC GROUPS—most tables were tabulated by ethnic groups. The following groups were recorded: Chamorro, Kapingamarangi-Nukuoran, Kusaiean, Marshallese, Palauan, Ponapean, Trukese, Ulithi-Woleaian, and Yapese; and among the outside groups, American, other, and not reported. Persons of mixed ethnicity were classified according to ethnic group of mother. MARITAL STATUS—asked of persons fourteen years of age and over. Categories: single, married, widowed or divorced, separated, and not reported. FERTILITY—for ever-married women fifteen years and older: number of children ever born. HOUSEHOLD—distinguished private (related or not) from the quasi household (institutional and others). EDUCATION—educational attainment (years of school completed). The school system changed from what it had been in previous years. LANGUAGE—ability to speak and read in English and Japanese. OCCUPATION—questions asked of all persons fourteen years of age and older. Eleven occupation groups were recorded.

Special Elements and Features. Maps and comparative table with total population from 1925 to 1958 are in the report.

Quality of the Census. Apparently simultaneity was not observed, since the enumeration took six months. Although censuses have been taken since 1920, results available are limited to total population. The present census was the first one published in a regular census report and contained considerable detailed data. The results from the 1958 census were also included in the 1960 census of the United States.

Publication Plan. Pacific Islands (Trust Territory). High Commissioner's Office. *Census Report 1958, Trust Territory of the Pacific Islands.* Agana, Guam, 1959. Language of publication is English.

1970 (April 1)

Census of population taken under the supervision of the U.S. Bureau of the Census, in conjunction with the nineteenth decennial census of population of the United States. The enumeration was carried out on a *de jure* basis, and canvassers recorded information on machine readable (FOSDIC: Film Optical Sensing Device) household questionnaire (new). An individual schedule was utilized to enumerate persons living in hotels and group quarters. There was no sampling used. Tabulation was computerized. The territory covered by the census was divided into six districts (Mariana, Marshall, Palau, Ponape, Truk, and Yap), subdivided into municipalities, islands, atolls, and places. A census of housing (new) was taken simultaneously.

Definitions and Concepts. AGE—in completed years and, for the first time, the date of birth was recorded. Tabulated in single years and standard five-year age groups. Median age was also presented. HOUSEHOLD—all persons, related or not by blood, living in the same housing unit. FAMILY—two or more persons, living in the same household, related by blood, marriage, or adoption. Families living in group quarters were not recorded. FERTILITY—number of children ever born. Question asked of all married, divorced, widowed, and separated women. EDUCATION—school enrollment and educational attainment. A question on vocational training was asked for the first time. MARITAL STATUS—categories were: never married, now married, consensually married, widowed, divorced, and separated. The presence of spouse was also recorded, and the category "separated" included legally or otherwise absent from spouse. PLACE OF BIRTH—country of birth according to international boundaries as recognized by the United States and if native, whether born in the United States or other territory or possession. CITIZENSHIP—whether naturalized, permanent alien, temporary alien, or born abroad of American parents. PLACE OF RESIDENCE—usual and previous place of residence (in 1965). VETERAN STATUS—recorded for the first time whether the person served in the armed forces and during what war. ECONOMIC ACTIVITY—reference period was the week before the census. Lower age limit was sixteen years of age. The labor force included all persons classified as employed (at work and with a job but not at work) and unemployed (looking for a job during the past four weeks, and available to accept a job). Unemployed persons who had worked at any time in the past were classified as experienced workers as opposed to new workers. Not in the labor force consisted mainly of students, homemakers, retired, seasonal workers in off season and not looking for a job, inmates of institutions, the disabled, and persons doing only incidental unpaid family work (less than fifteen hours during the reference week). The number of weeks worked was also asked. OCCUPATION—main occupation or last occupation, if unemployed. Classification based on Classified Index of Industries and Occupations, but presented in a condensed form—thirty-two occupational groups (two-digits). INDUSTRY—Classification based on CIIO but a reduced format of only forty industry groups (two-digits). OCCUPATIONAL STATUS—categories were: private wage and salary worker, government worker, self-employed, and unpaid family worker. INCOME—from earnings (wage, salary, commissions, own nonfarm business, professional practice or partnership, and own farm income), from other than earnings (social security, retirement, welfare), and from other sources.

Special Elements and Features. Previous place of residence, citizenship, school attendance, family composition, economic activity, industry, occupational status, and income were all recorded for the first time. This was the first housing census taken. Race and language were dropped from the schedules. Changes in territorial divisions have occurred in between 1958 and 1970. Copy of schedule was available.

Quality of the Census. To improve the usefulness of the 1970 census results, a number of changes were introduced based on the evaluation of previous censuses, consultation with users of data, and extensive field pretesting. However, according to the census report, "Doubts were felt concerning the reliability of the census, particularly because certain municipalities and islands within the Territory with known populations were reported either as uninhabited or having populations much smaller than had been previously reported." Whipple's Index category does not specify trust territory age data.

Publication Plan. U.S. Bureau of the Census. *Census of Population: 1970.* Volume 1, Part 54-58. Language of publication is English.

1973 (September 18)

The census of population was carried out by the High Commissioner, based on a plan developed by Ko Groenewegen, demographer of the South Pacific Commission. The census was basically *de facto*, but information about *de jure* population was also collected. Results excluded military and civil population at the Kwajalein Missile Range facilities (2,619 expatriate employees and 1,848 expatriate dependents). Canvasser was the method used to record information (two-stage system) on household questionnaires. Each questionnaire distinguished three types of persons: resident present (RP), nonresident temporarily present (NRTP), and resident temporarily absent (RTA). Tabulation was computerized. The territory was divided into municipalities, districts, district centers, and subdistrict center.

Definitions and Concepts. URBAN—population living in district centers that have direct access to any utilization of the cash economy and certain modern conveniences and public services. AGE—date of birth (month, day, and year). Persons born during the Japanese period of administration were assisted with a Japanese calendar of conversion dates. Tabulated in single year and standard five-year age groups. MARITAL STATUS—categories were never married, married (legal and common law), widowed, and divorced (separated included). PLACES OF BIRTH—country of birth for foreign born and district and municipality of birth for native born. PLACE OF RESIDENCE—usual place and home area (place or district where the person is originally from or place where the person has land rights). CITIZENSHIP—two groups were distinguished: citizens and noncitizens. For census purposes, in cases where one parent was a trust territory citizen, parents decided the citizenship of their children. EDUCATION— school attendance and educational attainment (highest school level attended). Persons without education were also recorded. RELIGION—response not compulsory. Religious denominations recorded. FERTILITY—asked of all women born in 1959 and before: number of children ever born alive, number of children still living, date of birth of the last child, whether the last child was still alive, and sex of the last child. FAMILY UNIT—based on the concept of conjugal family nucleus. However, person living alone in the household was also considered as a family unit. HOUSEHOLD—group of people who live together and share food arrangements. Two types of households were presented: private and group household. ECONOMIC ACTIVITY—reference period was the week before the census. Lower age limit was fourteen years. The population was divided into two major groups: persons at work and persons not working. The first group was subdivided into those who worked in village economy (persons producing goods for their own use and needs or selling some products for cash as supplementary income); and those who worked in money economy (persons working for wages or salaries, working in their own business or profession, or working without pay for a relative). The not working population was subdivided into unemployed looking for a job and economically inactive persons (housewives, students, retired, persons of independent income, the disabled, inmates of institutions, and so forth). Number of hours worked during the reference week was also recorded. OCCUPATION—asked only of persons engaged in the money economy. If unemployed, the last occupation was recorded. If employed in two or more money earning jobs, the occupation in which the most time was spent was asked. The classification was based on the International Labor Organization classification (ISCO) and the trust territory government's list of occupations (three-digits). Persons engaged in village economy were asked the main activity and six options were presented—growing food, fishing, copra, livestock, handcrafts, and others. OCCUPATIONAL STATUS—questions asked only of those engaged in money economy. Categories were: employer, self-employed, wage/salary earner (government), wage/salary earner (private), unpaid family worker, and other (miscellaneous work).

Special Elements and Features. Census conducted by the local authorities on a *de facto* basis. Income and place of previous residence were dropped. Urban population was distinguished. Fertility questions were expanded. Religion was recorded. Economic activity concepts were different from the ones adopted in the 1970 census. Copy of the schedule, maps, and list of unpublished tables are included.

Quality of the Census. A postenumeration survey (PES) was conducted, but it was stated that the results of the survey were not necessarily better than those of the census. "They [the PES results] provide a good 'second opinion,' not a fully objective yardstick." More details of the PES can be found in the same report. Pilot surveys were conducted in each district to test the questionnaire as well as the personnel involved in the census operations. The final results were published in 1975. Whipple's Index category was not available. The census office is reestablished for each census.

Publication Plan. Pacific Islands (Trust Territory). High Commissioner's Office. *1973 Population of the Trust Territory of the Pacific Islands*. Saipan, Mariana Islands, 1975. Unpublished data are available. Computer tapes are available from East-West Population Institute, Honolulu. Language of publication is English.

1980 (April 1)

This census was taken by the U.S. Bureau of the Census. No information is available as yet.

OTHER STATISTICAL PUBLICATIONS: Issued by Office of Planning and Statistics, *Bulletin of Statistics* (quarterly). Issued by U.S. Department of State, *Trust Territory of the Pacific Islands* (annually).

National Topic Chart

	1958	1970	1973
De facto			X
Usual residence	X	X	X
Place of birth	X	X	X
Duration of residence			
Place of prev. residence		X	
Urban/rural			X
Sex	X	X	X
Age	X	X	X
Relation to household head	X	X	X
Marital status	X	X	X
Children born alive	X	X	X
Children living			X
Citizenship		X	X
Literacy			
School enrollment		X	X
Ed. attainment	X	X	X
Ed. qualification			
National/Ethnic origin	X		
Language	X		
Religion			X
Household composition		X	X
Econ. active/inactive		X	X
Occupation	X	X	X
Industry		X	X
Occupational status		X	X
Income		X	
Housing		X	

Papua New Guinea

Papua New Guinea

CAPITAL: Port Moresby.
STATISTICAL AGENCY: National Statistical Office.
NATIONAL REPOSITORY: National Statistical Office, Library.
MAIN U.S. REPOSITORY: Population Research Center (Univ. of Texas).

The island of New Guinea consisted of three separate entities: on the western half, Netherland New Guinea, now Irian Jaya (part of Indonesia); and on the eastern half, both the trust territory of New Guinea and the territory of Papua, administered by Australia. In 1949 the two territories and the islands of the Bismark archipelago were combined administratively. Papua New Guinea was first granted autonomy (1973) and then in 1975 became independent.

Before 1966 the population censuses of the territories were carried out as an adjunct to the Australian census and were restricted to enumeration of nonindigenous persons only.

1921

First census, administered by the Australian Commonwealth Bureau of Census and Statistics, was *de facto*, and a combination of canvasser and self-enumeration methods was used. The scope was quite large covering age, place of birth, nationality, length of residence in the country, race, religion, industry, grades of occupation (occupational status), causes and duration of unemployment, marital status, literacy, and school attendance. The mandated territory of New Guinea had the census taken separately but followed the same organization. The schedules presented the same number of questions, except for the question related to unemployed.

1933

Second census, conducted by the Australian Commonwealth Bureau of Census and Statistics, was *de facto* and mostly self-enumerated. The scope for both territories was the same: age, marital status, number of dependent children, orphanhood, schooling, war service, religion, place of birth, length of residence in the country, language, nationality (citizenship), race, industry, occupation, occupational status, unemployment causes and duration, and income.

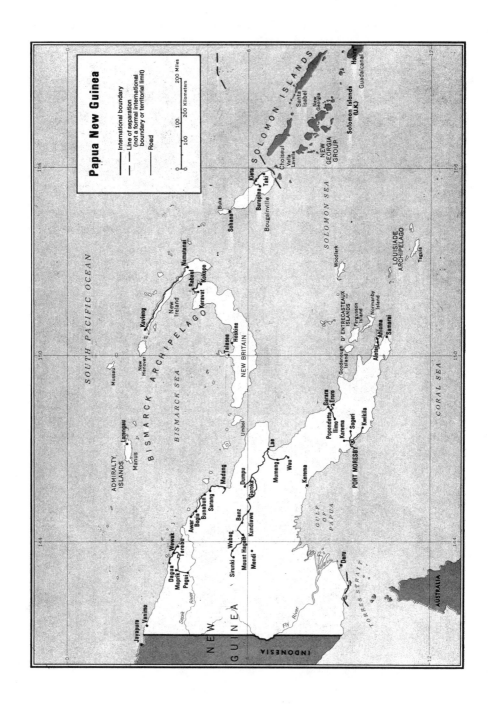

Papua New Guinea

International boundary

Line of separation
(not a formal international
boundary or territorial limit)

Road

0   100   200 Miles
0   100   200 Kilometers

1947 (June 30)

The third census, conducted by the Australian Commonwealth Bureau of Census and Statistics, was *de facto*. It was self-enumerated on household schedules and individual slips. As previously, indigenous population was excluded. The region started to be called the territory of Papua-New Guinea, but still the tables presented the results separately. Mechanical tabulation was used. Information gathered here was taken from the tables; apparently the statistician's report was not published.

Definitions and Concepts. AGE—as of last birthday in completed years. Standard five-year age groups were tabulated. In addition, two groups, under twenty-one and twenty-one and over, were given separately. MARITAL STATUS—the categories were: never married, married (included permanently separated), widowed, and divorced. DEPENDENCY—number of persons with dependent children and number of dependent children (no older than sixteen years of age). PLACE OF BIRTH—name of the country or territory of birth. LENGTH OF RESIDENCE—required of all aliens and recorded in completed years of residence. NATIONALITY—that is, citizenship: name of the country to which a person owes legal allegiance. RACE—population was divided into three groups: full-blooded European, non-European, and "half-caste" (expression used in the census). If half-caste with one parent European the initials H. C. followed by the race were recorded; if both parents were non-Europeans no initial was used and the race of the father was stated. RELIGION—two major categories: Christians and non-Christians. In addition, indefinite, no religion, and no reply were also recorded. ECONOMIC ACTIVITY—analyzed in terms of participation or not in the work force. In the work force included persons at work and not at work (unable to secure employment, temporarily laid off, not actively seeking work because of sickness or accident, industrial dispute, resting between jobs, and so forth). Not in the work force included the inactive, students, pensioners, inmates of institutions, invalids, persons of independent income, and homemakers. INDUSTRY—classification included twelve divisions and major groups of Australian Industrial Classification (two-digits). OCCUPATIONAL STATUS— employer, self-employed, employee, and helper (not on wage).

Special Elements and Features. Unlike the other external territories (Nauru and Norfolk Island) Papua New Guinea recorded population distribution for each district.

Quality of the Census. No Whipple's Index category was available, nor was there information on the completeness and accuracy of results.

Publication Plan. Australia. Commonwealth Bureau of Census and Statistics. *Census of the Commonwealth of Australia, 30th June 1947.* Volume 1, Part 7, External territories. Canberra, n.d. Language of publication is English.

1954 (June 30)

The fourth census, conducted by the Australian Commonwealth Bureau of Census and Statistics, was *de facto*, and self-enumeration the method used on household schedules and individual slips. The indigenous were excluded from the census. Automatic machine tabulation was used. The information gathered here was taken directly from the tables and some explanatory notes present in each volume. A census of housing was realized simultaneously. Distribution of population and dwellings by districts was also shown.

Definitions and Concepts. AGE—same as 1947 but for the first time unspecified ages were distributed over all ages prior to tabulation. MARITAL STATUS—categories were: never married (two groups—under and over fifteen years of age), married, married but permanently separated, divorced, and widowed. PLACE OF BIRTH—same as 1947. LENGTH OF RESIDENCE—same as 1947. NATIONALITY—synonymous with citizenship. Two main groups were recorded. British, which included British subjects by birth or naturalization of all commonwealth countries, territories, and possessions, as well as the homeland and Ireland; and foreign (name of country recorded). RACE—same as 1947 plus the classification was extended to show separately those persons whose parents were both non-European either of whom was wholly or partly descended from the aborigines of Papua New Guinea. RELIGION—two main groups—Christians and non-Christians as in 1947. The answer to the question was optional; therefore, a large number of people chose not to give explicit statements. ECONOMIC ACTIVITY—same as 1947. OCCUPATIONAL STATUS—same as 1947. INDUSTRY—reduced classification, only groups and subgroups of the Australian Classification of Industries of June 1954 were included.

Special Elements and Features. Unlike the other territories, Papua New Guinea presented population and dwellings results by districts.

Quality of the Census. Whipple's Index classified age information of Europeans in Papua within category I—highly accurate data—but information of nonindigenous in New Guinea was classified as category II—fairly accurate data. Still the major part of the population (indigenous) was not enumerated.

Publication Plan. Australia. Commonwealth Bureau of Census and Statistics. *Census of the Commonwealth of Australia.* Volume 7, Part 5, External territories. Canberra, 1958. Language of publication is English.

1961 (June 30)

The fifth census, conducted by the Australian Commonwealth Bureau of Census and Statistics, was *de facto* and self-enumerated. Population and dwelling censuses were taken simultaneously. The census still excluded indigenous population but included migratory population; that is, persons on ships in Papuan and New Guinean waters at the time of the census. The information gathered here was taken directly from the tables and some explanatory notes present in each volume.

Definitions and Concepts. AGE, MARITAL STATUS, PLACE OF BIRTH, LENGTH OF RESIDENCE, NATIONALITY, and RELIGION—same as 1954. RACE—four groups: European, non-European, half European and half other races, and other non-European races (both parents non-European, one of whom is wholly or partly aboriginal native of the territory). ECONOMIC ACTIVITY—the concept of inclusion and exclusion in the work force was the same adopted in 1947 and 1954. INDUSTRY—Australian Classification of Industries, June 1961, groups and subgroups only (with exception of an adaptation of the individual industry category within the subgroup, rural industries). OCCUPATION— major and subgroups of the ACO (new). OCCUPATIONAL STATUS—the same as 1954.

Special Elements and Features. Persons who omitted their marital status were allocated a conjugal condition prior to tabulation. The migratory population was enumerated.

Quality of the Census. Census still limited to nonindigenous population. No Whipple's Index was available, nor was information on completeness and accuracy of results included.

Publication Plan. Australia. Commonwealth Bureau of Census and Statistics. *Census of the Commonwealth, 30th June 1961.* Census Bulletin No. 16. Summary of non-indigenous population and dwellings for the territory of Papua and New Guinea. [and] Volume 7, Part 5, External territories. Canberra, 1965. Language of publication is English.

1966 (June 30)

First census conducted by the Bureau of Statistics of Papua New Guinea. Unlike the previous censuses, it included indigenous as well as nonindigenous population. The nonindigenous population was enumerated on a *de facto* basis at a single point in time (June 30). The indigenous, however, due to difficulties of illiteracy and accessibility to remote areas, were enumerated between June 20 and July 9 on both a *de facto* and *de jure* basis. A combination of canvasser and self-enumeration was the method. Two types of schedules were necessary—the household one was used in areas where most of the population was literate, and the interview questionnaire, which had the same number of questions and was designed to accommodate canvassing where needed. The nonindigenous population was completely enumerated as well as the indigenous living everywhere except inside rural villages. The rural village population, however, was estimated based on sample of approximately 10 percent of the total number of rural villages. Tabulation was computerized.

Definitions and Concepts. URBAN—places with 500 or more inhabitants (excluding separately located schools, hospitals, missions, plantations, rural settlements, and rural villages, regardless of population size). RURAL VILLAGES—villages recorded by the Department of District Administration (except for those included in urban areas) including persons living in small schools, missions, trade stores, and aid posts located close to a village. RURAL NONVILLAGE—separately located schools, missions, plantations, rural settlements, defense establishments, and centers with less than 500 inhabitants. AGE—date of birth stated as accurately as possible in day, month, and year. If not known, careful estimate was made. Tabulated in single years and standard five-year age groups, also under twenty-one, twenty-one to sixty-four, and sixty-five and over. MARITAL STATUS—the household schedules presented the following categories: never married (under twelve and twelve years of age and older), married (whether to more than one wife), married but permanently separated, divorced and not re-married, and widowed. The interview questionnaire stressed that any kind of marriage between indigenous persons should be classed as married. PLACE OF BIRTH—if born in the territory, the subdistrict; if born outside, name of the country was required. In addition, length of residence was asked of persons born outside of the territory. NATIONALITY—nationality or citizenship of the per-son. A person born in the territory was considered Australian or Australian Protected. Australian citizens had British nationality (Irish was also included). For all the other aliens the name of country of citizenship was required. RACE— the person's race, regardless of where born. If of mixed races, particulars were asked (parents' race). RELIGION—Christian, non-Christian, indefinite, and no reply. LANGUAGE—ability to speak simple English, Pidgin (lingua franca of the territory of New Guinea), or Police Motu (lingua franca of Papua). This question was asked of all persons ten years of age and over. EDUCATION— questions were asked of all persons ten years of age and older. Literacy (ability to read and write in English, Pidgin, Police Motu, or any other language), school attendance, educational attainment (highest grade completed), and educational qualification. Very detailed classification differentiating university degrees and professional levels for all fields of study. ECONOMIC ACTIVITY—all persons ten years of age and older. The work force included four major categories: wholly money-raising, mainly money-raising with some subsistence, mainly subsistence with some money-raising, and wholly subsistence. Money-raising work force referred to the first three categories above mentioned. INDUSTRY— took into consideration only the persons included in the mainly money-raising work force; that is, the first two categories of the work force (groups, subgroups, and categories of the Australian 1966 Classified List of Industries). OCCUPA-TION—considered only persons included in the money-raising work force; clas-sification presented groups, minor groups, and categories of the Australian Clas-sified List of Occupations. OCCUPATIONAL STATUS—employer, self-employed, employee, and unpaid helper. In addition, subsistence status and subsistence occupation based on wholly and mainly subsistence work force were recorded as well as number of hours worked, name of employer, and address of the place of work.

Special Elements and Features. The economy of the territory was divided into monetary, subsistence, and transitional sectors. This is the first time the indige-nous population was counted. Urban, education, and language were new.

Quality of the Census. "The preliminary bulletins numbers 1-38 may be taken as the final figures." A complete enumeration of all rural villages was not possible. Age data for the indigenous was imprecise and inaccurate; neverthe-less, it provided for the first time a broad picture of the age structure of the whole territory. No Whipple's Index category was available.

Publication Plan. Papua New Guinea. Bureau of Statistics. *Census of Papua and New Guinea, 1966. Preliminary bulletins.* Konedobu, 1966-1970. Nos. 1-38. Unpublished data are available. Language of publication is English.

1971 (July 5 to 16)

Second census was also conducted by the Bureau of Statistics of Papua New Guinea. The census covered indigenous as well as nonindigenous population, but the coverage rules applied to the urban and rural nonvillage sections differed from those applied to the rural village sectors. The enumeration for the first group was *de facto*, and for the rural villages a partial *de jure* and *de facto* approach was used. A combination of canvasser and self-enumeration methods was used, and the forms were written in English, Pidgin, and Motu languages.

Following the same pattern of 1966, not all rural villages were enumerated, only a sample of 10 percent of the population living in those areas. The census date also differed. For the part of the population that was self-enumerated, the census moment was July 7. For those who were interviewed, the period from July 5 to July 16 was used.

A postenumeration survey was carried out in 110 rural villages out of the 1,280 that were included in the 10 percent sample. The tabulation was computerized.

Definitions and Concepts. AGE—same as 1966. In addition, the following groups were recorded: twelve years of age and over, sixteen years and over (minimum legal age for entry into the money-raising work force), and eighteen years and over (minimum voting age). URBAN AREAS—places with at least 500 inhabitants and a minimum population density of 500 persons per square mile. PLACE OF BIRTH, LENGTH OF RESIDENCE, MARITAL STATUS, and EDUCATION—same as 1966. RACE—unlike 1966, no specific criterium was used to define a person's race. Instead, it was the race the respondent considered he or she belonged to. LANGUAGE—same as 1966, plus the language spoken at home. ECONOMIC ACTIVITY—persons were classified according to the activity in which they spent most of their time. The following were the five categories of activities: mainly money-raising, mainly subsistence, mainly unpaid home duties, mainly students attending school, and mainly other activities. Classification by industry, occupational status, and occupation considered only persons within the money-raising work force. Money-raising work force included all persons who worked for money the week before the census, persons temporarily absent from work for money, and the unemployed. INDUSTRY— Australian Industrial Classification, major and minor groups; also sectors (government, nongovernment). OCCUPATION—major and minor groups; classified according to Australian Occupational Classification. OCCUPATIONAL STATUS— employee, unpaid helper, self-employed with paid help, and self-employed without paid help. FERTILITY—number of children still living (only for indigenous).

Special Elements and Features. Number of surviving children by age of mother was reported (limited to indigenous women, ten years of age and over). A question about radio listening habits was added.

Quality of the Census. The census office is reestablished for each census. Whipple's Index classified age data into category IV—rough data. A postenumeration survey was taken. Comparisons between 1966 and 1971 censuses are not always possible due to some differences in definitions and classifications used, particularly in economic activity. Serious underenumeration occurred in certain areas.

Publication Plan. Papua New Guinea. Bureau of Statistics. *1971 Census. Characteristics of the Population.* Konedobu, 1974. In addition to the twenty-seven bulletins of this set, there were preliminary releases and a census monograph. Computer tapes are available. Language of publication is English.

1980 (September/October)

Papua New Guinea became independent in 1975. The third national census of population (including indigenous as well as nonindigenous) was conducted by the National Statistical Office, formerly the Bureau of Statistics.

In the two previous censuses, only a sample of the population of rural villages was enumerated. The total population of these areas was estimated based on these samples. In 1980 an attempt was made to enumerate every person in the country. In order to accomplish this, it was necessary to spread the rural enumeration over several months. People in urban and some other accessible areas were enumerated in two weeks (September and October).

The population in urban and rural nonvillage establishments were enumerated on a *de facto* basis, and population living in rural villages were enumerated on a *de jure* basis, except for those who spent the night before the census in an urban or rural nonvillage area. Canvasser was the method used to record information, but further details on organization are still not available. The territory covered by the census was divided into provinces and districts and subdivided into urban areas, rural villages, and rural nonvillages.

Definitions and Concepts. URBAN AREAS—places with 500 persons or more and a population density of a minimum of 500 persons. This definition was similar to the one adopted in 1971, but in 1980 density criterion was applied more loosely; therefore, the boundaries of these areas are larger. RURAL VILLAGE—consists of all traditional villages, hamlets, and so forth in rural areas. RURAL NONVILLAGES—all persons living in rural areas in places like plantations, mission stations, government out-stations, sawmills, agricultural research stations, boarding schools, settlements schemes, migrant settlements, and so forth.

The bulletins available, in addition to the information already given, carried the following tables: population by province, 1971 and 1980; population in urban and rural areas by province, 1980; population by districts, 1980; population of provinces by census divisions, 1980. The final census figures were expected to be available after mid-1981; however, they have not yet been published.

OTHER STATISTICAL PUBLICATIONS: Issued by National Statistical Office, *Abstract of Statistics* (quarterly), *Summary of Statistics* (annually).

National Topic Chart

	1947	1954	1961	1966	1971	1980
De facto	X	X	X	X	X	X
Usual residence				X	X	X
Place of birth	X	X	X	X	X	
Duration of residence	X	X	X	X	X	
Place of prev. residence						
Urban/rural				X	X	X
Sex	X	X	X	X	X	
Age	X	X	X	X	X	
Relation to household head						
Marital status	X	X	X	X	X	
Children born alive						
Children living					X	
Citizenship	X	X	X	X	X	
Literacy				X	X	
School enrollment				X	X	
Ed. attainment				X	X	
Ed. qualification				X	X	
National/Ethnic origin	X	X	X	X	X	
Language				X	X	
Religion	X	X	X	X	X	
Household composition						
Econ. active/inactive	X	X	X	X	X	
Occupation		X	X	X		
Industry	X	X	X	X	X	
Occupational status	X	X	X	X	X	
Income						
Housing	X	X	X	X	X	

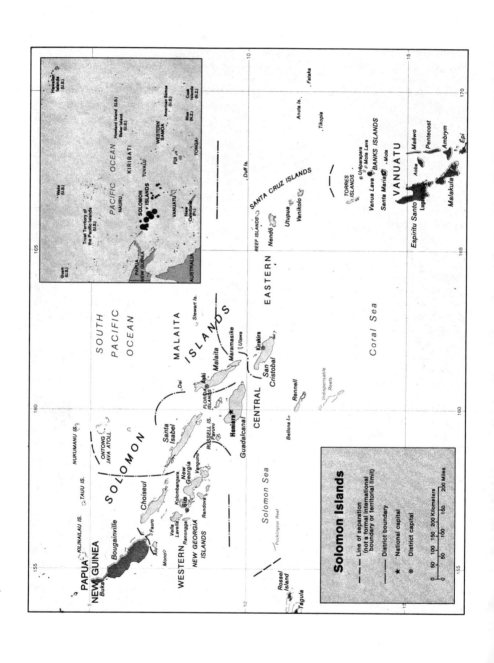

Solomon Islands

Line of separation
(not a formal international
boundary or territorial limit)

District boundary

★ National capital

◉ District capital

0 50 100 150 200 Kilometers

0   50   100   150   200 Miles

Solomon Islands

Solomon Islands

CAPITAL: Honiara.
STATISTICAL AGENCY: Statistics Office, Ministry of Finance.
NATIONAL REPOSITORY: Solomon Islands National Library.
MAIN U.S. REPOSITORY: Population Research Center (Univ. of Texas).

The group of volcanic islands was discovered by European navigators in 1568 and became a British protectorate in 1890s. Although self-governed since 1976, final independence was obtained in 1978.

The population statistics available for the period preceding 1920 were rough estimates which tended to either exaggerate population numbers or underestimate them. The depopulation process widely believed to have occurred in the nineteenth century was discussed in recent research which found periods of decline alternated with periods of growth. Furthermore, according to the census report, "population losses in one part of the territory may have been wholly or partly offset by gains in another."

The first "census" ever taken in the islands was carried out in 1931. It was conducted by district officers over a period of several months. The method of enumeration was not uniform for all islands. In some areas, a "device of four-cornered tallysticks, each corner being painted a different colour" was utilized to classify the population by sex and age groups. The almost total illiteracy of the population and the impossibility of enumeration in several areas made this attempt of a headcount seriously inaccurate. In other areas not even a population count was attempted, and the results were based on missionary records and on the judgment of government officials. The scope of the census included: total population classified by sex, age, occupation (males only), religion, and race.

In 1948, the system of administrative districts was reorganized. The former eight-district system was reduced to four (Eastern, Western, Malaita, and Central). Except for Ysabel Island which was transferred from Western to Central District in 1956, this territorial division has been maintained up to now.

The census planned for 1949 was abandoned because of the opposition by leaders and supporters of the "Marching Rule" movement. For several years after 1950 little attention was paid to the collection of population data.

1959 (November 5-30)

This was a sample census of population conducted under the supervision of Norma McArthur. The lack of enough personnel with educational qualifications to work in census operations and the difficulty of communication among the islands made the taking of a full census impossible. Melanesians were only sampled while the other components of the population were completely enumerated. The census was *de jure* for all areas, except Honiara, which was enumerated on a *de facto* basis. Honiara and the Melanesian sample were enumerated simultaneously (November 6); the other districts were enumerated on November 16. Canvassers recorded information on household schedules. The schedules were a condensed version of the questionnaire used in other Polynesian territories and in Fiji in 1956.

The territory was divided into four districts and then into subdistricts. Tabulation was mechanical, and the scope included name, relationship to head of household, present and absent population during enumeration, sex, age, number of children born alive, number of children still living, age of the mother at birth of first child, marital status, race, place of birth, and religion.

Comparative tables for 1949, 1952, 1953, 1954, and 1959, maps, graphs, copy of schedules, and a complete census report with methodology and analysis of results were also furnished.

Publication Plan. Solomon Islands (British). Western Pacific High Commission. *Report on the Population Census of 1959*, by Norma McArthur. Honiara, 1961. Language of publication is English.

1970 (February 1)

This was the first general census of population. It was conducted by the census commissioner on a *de facto* basis, and canvasser was the method used to record information on household schedules. Due to little temporary international migration in 1959, the total *de jure* population can be considered virtually equal to the *de facto* population on that date; therefore, the results may be compared to 1970 census data. The tabulation was computerized, and the territory was divided into four districts (Western, Malaita, Central, and Eastern) and subdivided into council areas, wards, and villages. However, all census tables are based on a breakdown of the data by council areas.

Definitions and Concepts. URBAN—the government statistician considered Honiara city the only urban settlement. AGE—in completed years as of last birthday, and if a person was under one year of age "0" was recorded. Tabulated in single years and standard five-year age groups. HOUSEHOLD—a group of persons who normally eat together the food prepared for them in the same kitchen. Therefore, it also included persons who slept in different dwellings as long as they ate together. Households were divided into private and collective. FAMILY UNIT—the basic family unit consisted of couples with or without children. One person household and one parent with children were also considered a family unit. MARITAL STATUS—categories were never married, married (church, civil law or custom), widowed, and divorced. PLACE OF BIRTH—for persons born in Solomon Islands, the name of the council area was recorded. If foreign born, the name of the country of birth was recorded. Migration was calculated by comparing place of birth and area of enumeration. FERTILITY—questions asked of females fifteen years of age and over: number of children ever born, number of children still living, age of mother at birth of first child, and number of years since the last child was born. RACE—components of population recorded: Melanesian, Polynesian, Chinese, Gilbertese, European, Ellice, Fijian, part-European, part-Chinese, and all others. RELIGION—the question was not compulsory. Religious groups recorded: Christian Fellowship Church, United Church, Diocese of Melanesia, Roman Catholic, South Sea Evangelical Church, Seventh Day Adventist, pagan, and others. EDUCATION—question asked of Melanesians and Polynesians fifteen years of age and over: school attendance to "standard 7." (Standard 7 is the highest grade of the senior primary schools.) This level was considered a satisfactory base for literacy measurement.

Special Elements and Features. Included in the report were a brief demographic history of the protectorate, maps, graphs, age pyramids, an historical calendar (a list of important events for each district), and a copy of the schedule. The following tables were also included: population by districts from 1917 to 1945, vital statistics (births and deaths) from 1926 to 1941, population of subdistricts of Malaita from 1931 to 1940, labor recruiting from 1915 to 1940, and comparative tables for 1931, 1959, and 1970. A list of each locality and its population in each council area was also present.

Quality of the Census. Whipple's Index classified age accuracy into category III—approximate data. Intensive training was given to enumerators and detailed mapping of the protectorate into council areas and wards was made. Census report with final results was published in 1970. The census office is reestablished for each census but is a part of the permanently established Statistics Office.

Publication Plan. Solomon Islands (British). Western Pacific High Commission. *Report on the Census of the Population, 1970,* by K. Groenewegen. Southampton, England, n.d. Language of publication is English.

1976 (February 7-8)

The second full census of population was conducted by the Statistics Division, Ministry of Finance, on a *de facto* basis, and canvassers recorded information on household schedules. A two-stage system was utilized, and the tabulation was computerized. The territory covered by the census was divided into districts, council areas, islands, wards, and localities. Most of the tables, however, contain a breakdown of the data by council areas.

Definitions and Concepts. URBAN—the towns of Honiara, Gizo, Auki, and Kira-Kira. AGE—date of birth (month and year), tabulated in single years and standard five-year age groups. RACE—ethnic origin. The following groups were recorded: Polynesian, Melanesian, European, Gilbertese, Ellice, Fijian, part-European, part-Chinese, and others. Data on Gilbertese and Ellice were tabulated together. PARENTHOOD—vital status of parents was determined by the question: Is natural father alive? Is natural mother alive? PLACE OF BIRTH—island or town (only Honiara, Gizo, Auki, and Kira-Kira were specified) of birth was recorded for the native born, and island or country of birth if foreign born. In addition, it was asked whether the person was born in a clinic or hospital. MARITAL STATUS—categories were not married or single, married (civil, religious, or common-law marriage), widowed, divorced, and separated. RELIGION—the only question for which the answer was not compulsory. Religious affiliations recorded. LANGUAGE—the first local language spoken as a child (new). A large number of languages was included. EDUCATION—school attendance and for the first time educational attainment (highest degree completed). School attendance was recorded for all levels and not just through seventh grade as in 1970. If foreign born, the grade and the country where educated were asked. PLACE OF RESIDENCE—duration of residence in the area of enumeration in months and years. HOUSEHOLD—a group of people, related or not, who live together in one or more closely connected houses and share common eating arrangements. FERTILITY—questions were asked of all women fifteen and over: number of children ever born alive, number of children still alive and living at home with the mother, number of children who are living elsewhere, number of children now dead, whether the last child is still alive, and date of birth of this child. ECONOMIC ACTIVITY—lower age limit was fifteen years of age. Period of reference was the week before the census. Questions were asked only of those who had worked to earn money for three or more days during the reference period. The intention was to provide usable information on participation in the cash economy at a particular point in time. A table with the number of persons not attending school and not working for money was also provided. OCCUPATION—classification compatible with ISCO, major groups and groups (two-digits). INDUSTRY—classification comparable with ISIC, divisions and major groups (two-digits). OCCUPATIONAL STATUS—only self-employed and wage/salary earner were listed.

Special Elements and Features. Economic activity, language, educational attainment, and duration of residence were recorded for the first time. School attendance was expanded. Fertility questions differed from the ones in 1970. Included in the report were maps of the islands with council areas, wards, and enumeration areas indicated plus a copy of the schedule.

Quality of the Census. Provisional results were released in 1976 (manual count), the preliminary data in 1977 (computer analysis), and the final results started to be released in 1980. Detailed demographic analysis of results is to be published. The classification of racial components is not directly comparable among the four censuses. Whipple's Index rating was not available. Pilot censuses were taken to test questionnaires and the effectiveness of the enumerators' instructions for the final census.

Publication Plan. Solomon Islands. Statistics Office. *Report on the Census of Population, 1976.* Honiara, 1980. Volume 1, Basic information. Provisional and preliminary results were also published. Unpublished data and computer tapes (from South Pacific Commission) are available. Language of publication is English.

Honiara had population and housing census in 1979 and 1981 as well.

OTHER STATISTICAL PUBLICATIONS: Issued by Statistics Office, *Quarterly Digest of Statistics, Statistical Year Book.*

National Topic Chart

	1959	1970	1976
De facto		X	X
Usual residence	X		
Place of birth	X	X	X
Duration of residence			X
Place of prev. residence			
Urban/rural		X	X
Sex	X	X	X
Age	X	X	X
Relation to household head	X	X	X
Marital status	X	X	X
Children born alive	X	X	X
Children living	X	X	X
Citizenship			
Literacy		X	
School enrollment		X	X
Ed. attainment			X
Ed. qualification			
National/Ethnic origin	X	X	X
Language			X
Religion	X	X	X
Household composition		X	X
Econ. active/inactive			X
Occupation			X
Industry			X
Occupational status			X
Income			
Housing			

Tokelau Islands

Tokelau Islands Dependency (New Zealand)

CAPITAL: Administered from Apia, Western Samoa.
STATISTICAL AGENCY: Department of Statistics, Wellington.
NATIONAL REPOSITORY: ?
MAIN U.S. REPOSITORY: Population Research Center (Univ. of Texas).

Very little is known about the population and less on the censuses taken in the three islands (Fukaofo, Atafu, and Nukunono) that form the Tokelau group. From 1916 to 1925, the islands, evidently lacking European residents, were part of the Gilbert and Ellice Islands. The first uniform census of Tokelau was taken in 1921 under British administration, but a published report is not available, and only total population is on record.

In 1926, Tokelau Islands separated from the British colony and the New Zealand government took over the administration of the islands. A system of quinquennial censuses was adopted and the enumerations were conducted by Western Samoa. The results were published as part of the New Zealand census report for that year. No details of organization and methods used are known, and the information here was taken from table headings and introductory notes published in the New Zealand report.

1926

The census was conducted by Western Samoa, and the results sent to New Zealand included total population, religion, literacy, school attendance, sex, age, and race.

1936

The same conduct and scope were used that appeared in the 1926 census.

1945-1971

The censuses of 1945, 1951, 1956, 1966, and 1971 were all taken as of September 25 of the respective year. They were conducted by the Western Samoan administration and perhaps were *de facto*. The 1945 census results for Tokelau gave more information than the later censuses: total population for 1936 and 1945 by sex (twenty-six members of the U.S. armed forces stationed there were excluded), race (Tokelau Islanders and Samoans), and religion (London Missionary Society and Roman Catholic).

Publication Plan. New Zealand. Census and Statistics Department. *Population Census, 1945*. Volume 2, Island territories. Auckland, 1947.

The results of the remaining censuses consist of only one table published in the New Zealand reports that gave total number of inhabitants by sex and religion. Annual reports presented to the New Zealand House of Representatives also reported the total populations of each island.

There was mention of a "census" taken September 26, 1972, but only total population by sex and a brief paragraph on religious affiliation were published in the annual report for that year. The same amount of information for 1976 was published in the 1980 annual report.

National Topic Chart

	1945	1951	1956	1961	1966	1971
De facto	X	X	X	X	X	X
Usual residence						
Place of birth						
Duration of residence						
Place of prev. residence						
Urban/rural						
Sex	X	X	X	X	X	X
Age						
Relation to household head						
Marital status						
Children born alive						
Children living						
Citizenship						
Literacy						
School enrollment						
Ed. attainment						
Ed. qualification						
National/Ethnic origin	X					
Language						
Religion	X	X	X	X	X	X
Household composition						
Econ. active/inactive						
Occupation						
Industry						
Occupational status						
Income						

Tonga

Kingdom of Tonga

CAPITAL: Nuku'alofa.
STATISTICAL AGENCY: Statistics Department.
NATIONAL REPOSITORY: No library in the country, Statistics Department.
MAIN U.S. REPOSITORY: Population Research Center (Univ. of Texas) and East-West Population Institute.

The Kingdom of Tonga consists of 150 small islands that were first visited by Dutch navigators at the beginning of the seventeenth century. Regular contact, however, was established in 1826 with the arrival of European missionaries. The islands became a British protectorate in 1900. In 1903, regulations for taking a census were established, but the first published census results appeared in 1921. After a gap of twelve years, biennial censuses were taken between 1933 and 1939. However, "these censuses were no more than a count of heads, and they left no records whatsoever as to how the fieldwork was carried out. Only the bare results were published." The tables available show the total number of inhabitants distributed into broad age groups, sex, and nationality. After 1939, estimates of population were made at the end of each year.

1956 (September 26)

This was the first population census to be based on modern census concepts and methodologies. The Census Act provided that a census should be taken "from time to time." The census officer was responsible for the census, which was carried out on a *de facto* basis. Canvassers recorded information on household schedules that were printed in two languages, English and Tongan. Mechanical tabulation was utilized. The territory covered by the census was divided into five districts and then divided into subdistricts and villages.

Definitions and Concepts. AGE—in completed years and months, and the date of birth. Tabulated in single years and standard five-year age groups. MARITAL STATUS—categories were: married, single, widowed, and divorced. PLACE OF BIRTH—if born in the kingdom, the name of village and district of birth; if born elsewhere, the name of the country. The countries were divided into two groups: United Kingdom and countries of the Commonwealth of Nations, and other European countries (United States included). FERTILITY (new)—asked of

Tonga

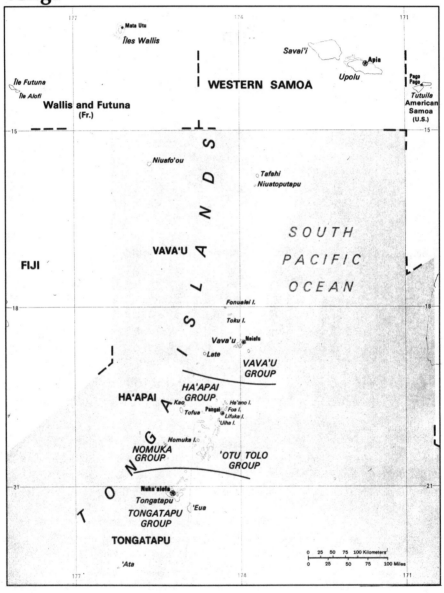

women fifteen years of age and older: number of children born alive; number of children still living, and those who are now dead; and age of mother at birth of first child. HOUSEHOLD—person or group of persons, related or not, living in the same housekeeping community and sharing food arrangements. DWELLING—any building used permanently for human habitation. RACE—population was distributed into four categories: Tongan, European, part-European, and all others. RELIGION—religious denominations were recorded, not based on active membership. ECONOMIC ACTIVITY—lower age limit was fifteen years. Period of reference was not cited, apparently the date of the census. Economic activity was derived from three questions: What work does this person do, for whom and where? The difficulty of classification was due to the fact that the number of persons with no specific or regular occupation far outnumbered those regularly employed. INDUSTRY—defined as a collection or group of related types of work, occupation, or employment. Classification for male population was presented in thirty-three groups (six divisions and subgroups), including dependents, prisoners, and students as well. Classifications of female population presented twenty-three groups (six divisions and subgroups) including domestic duties as well.

Special Elements and Features. For the first time, organization and methods were published in a regular census report. Uniform schedules and mechanical methods of tabulation were utilized. It was the most extensive census taken up to date; therefore, most of the features were recorded for the first time. Type of dwelling and number of persons per household were also recorded.

Quality of the Census. Schedules were pretested in each village six weeks before the census, and enumeration was carried out in two stages to assure completeness and accuracy of data. Although the Census Act provided that a census should be taken "from time to time," no reference as to regularity was made. The census office was temporary. It was stated that "every possible precaution was taken to insure accuracy and complete count of the population. The census office staff and enumerators, however, were no more familiar with census procedure than the population at large and any omission or apparent neglect of standard practice should be taken in this light." Whipple's Index category was not available.

Publication Plan. Tonga. Census Office. *Report on the Results of the 1956 Census*, by M. U. Tupouniua. Nuku'alofa, 1958. Language of publication is English.

1966 (November 29)

The seventh census of population (second modern census) was conducted by the census officer on a *de facto* basis, and canvasser was the method used to record information on household questionnaires. The schedules were printed in English and Tongan. The organization and content of schedules were basically the same as 1956 except that an additional question on land ownership was asked. Tabulation was computerized for the first time. The territory covered by the census was divided into six districts (Niuafo'ou was uninhabited in 1956) and subdivided into subdistricts and villages. The enumeration spread over a period of two weeks.

Definitions and Concepts. AGE, RACE, MARITAL STATUS, FERTILITY, HOUSEHOLD, and RELIGION—same as 1956. PLACE OF BIRTH—for persons born in the kingdom, the name of the village and district of birth; if born elsewhere, the name of the island group, territory, or country of birth were recorded. ECONOMIC ACTIVITY—lower age limit was fifteen years. No reference period was mentioned, apparently the day of the census. The same questions asked in 1956 were repeated in this schedule. The population was divided into: those not engaged in industry (persons less than fifteen years, students fifteen years and over, all women and older daughters who were engaged in home duties, persons of independent means who had retired, and inmates of hospitals and prisons), and those engaged in industry. The word "industry" is used to indicate all forms of economic activities from subsistence agriculture to the specialized professional services. INDUSTRY—all types of work were grouped according to the following headings: agriculture, commerce, government and administration, transport and communication, services, parts manufacturing and processing, domestic, and unclassified. Occupation and industry were presented together. It is important to notice that that part of the population classified as not actively engaged in industry were included within the industrial classification. Occupations were examined only in broad outline to show the general interest of the population. LAND—question asked of all Tongan males sixteen years and over: land ownership (new).

Special Elements and Features. The island of Niuafo'ou, uninhabited in 1956, was resettled in 1958 and included in the enumeration. Computerized tabulation was utilized for the first time. The type of dwelling, number of persons per household, and livestock belonging to the household were also recorded. The question on land ownership was the only new feature.

Quality of the Census. As in 1956, enumeration was carried out in two stages to assure completeness and accuracy of data. Final results were available in 1968. Whipple's Index was not available, but it was stated that "ages in this census were probably as accurate as one could hope until the population of the Kingdom became more conscious of chronological time."

Publication Plan. Tonga. Census Office. *Report on the Results of the 1966 Census*, by Sione N. Fiefia. Nuku'alofa, 1968. Language of publication is English.

1976 (November 30)

The census of population and housing was conducted by the census officer on a *de jure* basis (new). Canvasser was the method used to gather information on household schedules. This census, in addition to the information on individuals and households, provided the first comprehensive statement on education and employment characteristics. Questions on fertility and land ownership were also expanded. Tabulation was computerized and the territory was divided into five divisions (Niuatoputapu and Niuafo'ou were unified) and subdivided into districts and villages.

Definitions and Concepts. HOUSEHOLD—person or persons, related or not by blood, who live in the same house and take their meals together. The household may include boarders and lodgers unless they have separate cooking facilities and a different entrance. In addition, households were divided into private and collective (institutions). FAMILY—members of the household who are related by blood, adoption, or marriage. AGE—as of last birthday in completed years and date of birth. Tabulated in single years and standard five-year age groups. Age at first marriage was also recorded. MARITAL STATUS—categories were: never married, married (legal and common-law marriages), widowed, divorced, or separated. PLACE OF BIRTH—for persons born in the kingdom, village and district of birth. For persons born overseas, the country only was recorded. PLACE OF RESIDENCE—usual place and duration of residence (number of years residing continuously). The mother's usual place of residence was also recorded. RACE—Tongan, European, part-European, other Pacific islanders and others (Asian, African) were the groups recorded. RELIGION—same as 1966. The following groups were recorded: Free Wesleyan, Roman Catholic, Free Church of Tonga, Church of Tonga, Latter Day Saints, Seventh Day Adventists, Anglican Church, Assemblies of God, and all others. EDUCATION—recorded for the first time. Questions asked of all persons five years and over: literacy (ability to read and write in Tongan and English), school attendance, educational attainment (highest degree completed), and educational qualification. FERTILITY—For all women fifteen years and over reported as ever married: number of children born alive and those born in 1975, number of children still living, age of mother at birth of first child. ECONOMIC ACTIVITY—period of reference was the week before the census. Lower age limit was fifteen years of age. Economically active population included: employed (at work or on leave), unemployed looking for a job (new and experienced workers), and unpaid family workers. Inactive population: homemakers, students, physically disabled, income recipients, and others. The number of days worked during the reference week and reasons for not working were also recorded. OCCUPATION—main and secondary occupations. Classification presented major groups, groups, and subgroups (three-digits). INDUSTRY—divisions, major groups, and subgroups (three-digits) were recorded. OCCUPATIONAL STATUS—categories were: own-account worker, employer, government worker (salary and wage earner), semigovernment worker (salary and wage earner), private (salary and wage earner), and unpaid worker. LAND—land ownership and size of land (for males sixteen and over and widowed females).

Special Elements and Features. There were new questions related to each household: number of children ever born during the last year (1975), number of persons who died during the last year (1975). In addition to all regular housing questions, number of boats owned, number of livestock, land ownership, land cultivation, and tenure were asked. New questions relating to individuals were:

duration of residence, usual place of residence, mother's usual place of residence, age at marriage, literacy, school attendance, educational attainment, educational qualification, occupation, occupational status, number of days worked during the reference week, and reasons for not working.

Quality of the Census. Remapping of the country with description of blocks was made, and prelisting of buildings and houses was also prepared prior to actual enumeration. The change from *de facto* to *de jure* basis of enumeration meant that the results of this census are not directly comparable to those of earlier censuses. Because of the amount of information recorded, it was felt necessary to introduce checks at different stages of the recording and data processing. The span of time required for enumeration (three days) was shorter than that of the previous census. Final results were available in 1978. Whipple's Index was category I—highly accurate age data.

Publication Plan. Tonga. Census Office. *Census of Population and Housing. Volume I Administrative Report and Tables.* Nuku'alofa, 1979(?). There is no mention nor citation of a Volume 2 as yet. Unpublished data are available. Language of publication is English.

OTHER STATISTICAL PUBLICATIONS: Issued by Statistics Department, *Statistical Abstract.*

National Topic Chart

	1956	1966	1976
De facto	X	X	
Usual residence			X
Place of birth	X	X	X
Duration of residence			X
Place of prev. residence			
Urban/rural			
Sex	X	X	X
Age	X	X	X
Relation to household head	X	X	X
Marital status	X	X	X
Children born alive	X	X	X
Children living	X	X	X
Citizenship			
Literacy			X
School enrollment			X
Ed. attainment			X
Ed. qualification			X
National/Ethnic origin	X	X	X
Language			
Religion	X	X	X
Household composition			X
Econ. active/inactive	X	X	X
Occupation			X
Industry	X	X	X
Occupational status			X
Income			
Housing	X	X	X

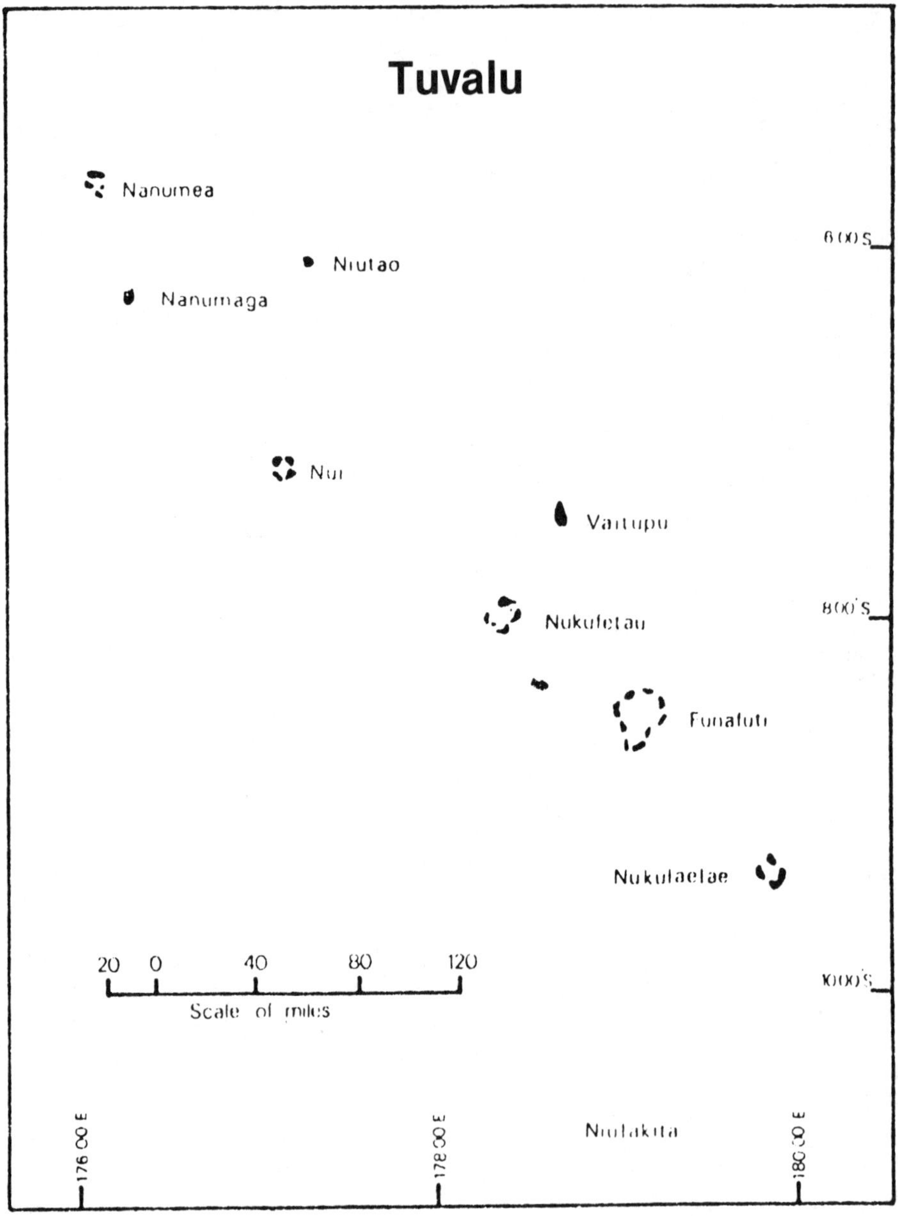

Tuvalu

Nanumea

6 00 S

Niutao

Nanumaga

Nui

Vaitupu

8 00 S

Nukufetau

Funafuti

Nukulaelae

```
20    0       40      80      120
 └─┴───┴───────┴───────┴───────┘
      Scale  of  miles
```

10 00 S

176 00 E

178 00 E

Niulakita

180 30 E

Tuvalu

Tuvalu

CAPITAL: Funafuti.
STATISTICAL AGENCY: Statistical Officer, Ministry of France.
NATIONAL REPOSITORY: Tuvalu Government Library and Archives, Ministry of Social Services.
MAIN U.S. REPOSITORY: Population Research Center (Univ. of Texas).

In 1975 the former colony of Gilbert and Ellice Islands was divided. The nine islands that constituted the Ellice group (Nanumea, Nanumanga, Niutao, Nui, Vaitupu, Nukufetau, Funafuti, Nukulaelae, and Niulakita) became an independent nation in 1978 under the name of Tuvalu.

The first census of population and housing of the country was carried out in 1979, and information of censuses previous to this date is located in the Gilbert and Ellice Islands entry.

1979 (May 27-28)

The census of population and housing was conducted by the census commissioner on a *de facto* basis. It included Tuvaluans who were resident in Nauru. A two-stage enumeration system was utilized, and canvassers recorded information on individual and household schedules. For the first time, a housing census was taken simultaneously with the census of population. The territory covered by the census was divided into islands and villages. Hand-sorting tabulation was performed.

Definitions and Concepts. HOUSEHOLD—group of persons, related or not by blood, living in a house, a group of houses, or part of a house who usually eat food prepared for them in the same kitchen. Households may be private or collective. AGE—date of birth; tabulated in single years and standard five-year age groups. ORPHANHOOD—for the first time recorded, was determined through the following questions: real mother alive, mother's eldest child, mother living in the household, real father alive? In addition, the personal number of the mother was recorded. MARITAL STATUS—categories were: never married, married, widowed, and divorced. RELIGION (voluntary question)—religious groups recorded. RACE—the following groups were recorded: Tuvaluan, Tuvalu/Kiribati, Tuvalu/other, other Pacific, and European. Classification took into consideration the race of the parents. EDUCATION—school attendance (still attending and not attending) and educational attainment (highest class completed). PLACE OF BIRTH—the concept "home island" was used for persons born in Tuvalu. "Home island" meant the island of the person's father, where most land might be expected to be inherited, or the island with which the person had a traditional link, independently of whether it was the actual place of birth or not. For all other persons, the country of birth was recorded. LAND OWNERSHIP—questions asked of persons fifteen years of age and over: land ownership or expectation of inheritance on "home island," and land ownership on any other island. PLACE OF RESIDENCE—questions asked of all persons fifteen years of age and older: usual place of residence, duration of residence, and name of island lived for more than twelve months at any time in their lives. ECONOMIC ACTIVITY—Period of reference was the week of enumeration; lower age limit, fifteen years. The population was divided into three groups: active outside cash economy (village life, home duties or traditional and subsistence sectors); active in cash economy (employed and unemployed looking for work, experienced or new worker); and dependents (visitors, elderly, disabled, inmates of institutions, students, and "resting" or making no significant contribution to the household). The number of years worked, whether received occupational training and for how long, were also recorded. OCCUPATION—classification based on ISCO, revised edition, 1968, major groups, groups, and subgroups (three-digits). INDUSTRY— classification based on ISIC, revised edition, 1968, divisions, major groups, and subgroups (three-digits). OCCUPATIONAL STATUS—categories were: employer, employee, self-employed, and looking for work. FERTILITY—questions asked of all women: number of children born alive, number of children alive on census night, first and last child's date of birth, last child's sex and whether still alive, and age of mother at birth of first child.

Special Elements and Features. Brief census history and analytical methodology of the data are included. Orphanhood and land ownership were new features. Questions on places of residence were worded differently. Information on economic activity was more detailed as was information on household composition and characteristics. For the first time, extensive data on characteristics of dwellings were collected in Tuvalu. Birth rates, death rates, and abridged model life tables for indigenous population were furnished. Population projections are included.

Quality of the Census. Pilot census was carried out to test applicability of questionnaires. Postenumeration survey was taken in thirteen enumeration areas selected randomly, 52 percent of all households. "Because of the very small scale of the census operation nearly all of the missed persons could be enumerated at a later stage. A very low proportion of not reported persons in the census, combined with the fact that there were actually more people missed by the PES itself than by the census, may have made the survey a rather superfluous exercise."

The use of birth registration records for comparability improved the quality of age information. A system of numbering of houses was introduced to provide better coverage and also to facilitate the creation of enumeration areas. The accuracy of results was improved with the utilization of listing pads on which each person was listed first by name, sex, relationship to head of household, and date of birth. Whipple's Index category is not available.

Publication Plan. Tuvalu. Census Commissioner's Office. *A Report on the Results of the Census of the Population of Tuvalu, 1979*. Funafuti, 1980. 1 volume. Unpublished data are available. Language of publication is English.

National Topic Chart

	1979
De facto	X
Usual residence	X
Place of birth	X
Duration of residence	X
Place of prev. residence	
Urban/rural	
Sex	X
Age	X
Relation to household head	X
Marital status	X
Children born alive	X
Children living	X
Citizenship	
Literacy	
School enrollment	X
Ed. attainment	X
Ed. qualification	
National/Ethnic origin	X
Language	
Religion	X
Household composition	X
Econ. active/inactive	X
Occupation	X
Industry	X
Occupational status	X
Income	
Housing	X

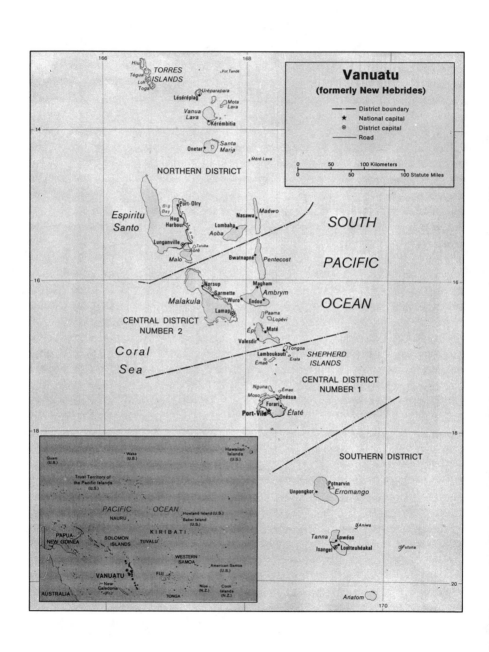

Vanuatu

Republic of Vanuatu

CAPITAL: Port-Vila.
STATISTICAL AGENCY: Bureau of Statistics.
NATIONAL REPOSITORY: Bureau of Statistics.
MAIN U.S. REPOSITORY: Population Research Center (Univ. of Texas).

Vanuatu consists of a 400 mile chain of volcanic islands (fourteen large ones and numerous small ones). Discovered in 1606 by Portuguese navigators, it was first called Australia del Espíritu Santo. In 1774 most of the islands were renamed the New Hebrides by Captain James Cook, but no records with specific population have survived. Settlement of the islands started after the discovery of sandalwood at the beginning of the nineteenth century. French and British settlers disputed the control of the islands until 1906 when the Anglo-French Condominium of New Hebrides was established. Population counts and estimates were made by various sources, but data available are limited only to a few of the inhabited islands. The first official estimate of population related to 1910, but results show discrepancies between the numbers reported by French and British sources.

Administrative censuses were taken up to 1946. The 1946 census was taken on a *de jure* basis, and the results included total population divided into autochthonous and nonautochthonous and were published in the French census for the "territoires Français d'outre-mer et des pays étrangers." Accuracy of data, however, was comparable to the mission counts.

In 1957, a census of the nonnative population was taken, apparently on a *de facto* basis, but no details on organization and methods were furnished. The territory was divided into four administrative divisions (Northern, Central I, Central II, and Southern). The results published by INSEE, however, presented total population only by administrative divisions; all the other tables related to the country as a whole. The scope included: age, sex, nationality, marital status, year of arrival, fertility, education, economic activity, occupation, industry, occupational status, and relationship to head of the household.

In 1965, a survey of Greater Vila was made, but no details on organization, methods or scope were furnished.

1967 (May 28)

This was the first general census of population of the Condominium of New Hebrides. It was directed by Norma McArthur and J. F. Yaxley, and the enumeration was conducted on a *de facto* basis. A combination of canvasser and self-enumeration was the method utilized to record information on household schedules. The schedules were printed in English and French. Enumeration was taken in two stages, tabulation was mechanical, and data were presented mainly by ethnic groups and by legal status. The territory covered by the census was divided into administrative districts, islands and villages.

Definitions and Concepts. URBAN—places with 100 and more households. AGE—age at last birthday and if under one year, "0" was recorded. Tabulated in single years and standard five-year age groups. MARITAL STATUS—categories were: never married, married (in church or by custom), widowed, and divorced. RACE—the following groups were recorded: New Hebridean, European, Chinese, Vietnamese, other Melanesian, Polynesian and Micronesian, part-European, all other mixed and all others. FERTILITY—asked of all women fifteen years and over: number of children ever born, number of children still living, and age of the mother at birth of first child. PLACE OF BIRTH—island of birth for New Hebrideans and country of birth for foreign born. RELIGION—religious affiliation, groups: Presbyterian, Anglican, Melanesian Mission, Roman Catholic, Seventh Day Adventist, French Protestant, Church of Christ, Apostolic, other Christian, other religions, custom, no religion and objection. HOUSEHOLD—a group of persons who ate together the food prepared for them in the same kitchen. Most of the persons also lived together in the same building. However, there were many cases (mainly of single males and widowers) who were dispersed throughout various houses for sleeping but came together to eat: these were included in the household. Households were divided into private and nonprivate. FAMILY UNIT—a married couple with or without children. NATIONALITY—called legal status and divided into: New Hebridean, British, of British jurisdiction, French, and of French jurisdiction. EDUCATION—school attendance only. ECONOMIC ACTIVITY—Lower age limit was fourteen years of age; no period of reference was mentioned (apparently the day of the census). All persons who declared themselves as working were considered active. Two groups were distinguished: subsistence activity and production activity. The word industry was used to cover all forms of economic activity from pure subsistence to cash economy. The economically inactive population included school children and students, persons of independent income or retired and not dependent, inmates of institutions and the incapacitated, those involved in home duties, and all others. INDUSTRY—classification presented thirty-four groups. The group, subsistence and village agriculture, was the only group with subdivisions. OCCUPATIONAL STATUS—the term used in the census was "status within industry," and the following categories were recorded: professional, managerial and executive, supervisory and clerical, skilled and semiskilled workers.

Special Elements and Features. Table on population in urban and peri-urban areas of Vila and Santos islands, age pyramid, maps, and copy of the schedule are also included. A list of settlements for each island was provided. Number of households, family units, and household size were also recorded.

Quality of the Census. Because the Condominium of New Hebrides had no census tradition, enumeration encountered opposition in some of the islands and many schedules were only partially completed. Although the census date was May 28, in some of the areas of Tanna and Santo Bush, enumeration only started in July. Preenumeration work included: detailed list of settlements with approximate population of inhabited islands, delimitation of urban and rural areas, training of enumerators, and enumerators' maps. Without birth registration and only a few missionary records of births, the age of many people had to be estimated. There was no permanent census office. Whipple's Index classified age accuracy within category IV—rough data.

Publication Plan. France. INSEE. *Le recensement du Condominium des Nouvelles-Hébrides, 1967. Principaux résultats*. Paris, n.d. And New Hebrides. Director of Census. *Condominium of New Hebrides. A Report on the First Census of Population, 1967*. Sidney, 1968. Languages of publication are French and English, respectively.

1972 (October 29)

A census of population and housing was taken of the urban areas of Vila and Luganville (Santo). It was *de facto*, and a combination of canvassed and self-enumerated was the method used to record information on household questionnaires. The Condominium Bureau of Statistics conducted the census, and the tabulation was computerized. Vila was divided into town, municipal council area, and Greater Vila; Santo was divided into town and municipal council area. The scope included: age, sex, marital status, nationality, race, duration of residence, electoral status, school attendance, educational attainment, postschool qualifications, economic activity, occupation, occupational status, number of hours worked, and place of birth. Housing questions were also included.

Publication Plan. New Hebrides. Condominium Bureau of Statistics. *Recensement de la population et de l'habitat, Port-Vila et Luganville, 29 octobre 1972/Census of Population and Housing. . . .* Port-Vila, 1973. 2 volumes. Language of publication is bilingual, French and English.

1979 (January 15/16)

The second general census of population was conducted under the supervision of J. J. Wagner, statistician of the National Statistics and Economic Studies Institute. The Bureau of Statistics was involved in the preparation and the collection of information. It was the first census conducted simultaneously on a *de facto* and *de jure* basis. Canvasser was the method used to record information on three kinds of questionnaires: household, collective household, and individual.

Final results are not yet available; the information gathered here was taken from preliminary and provisional results published in 1980.

The territory was divided into four districts (Northern, Central I, Central II, and Southern), islands, villages, and places. Only total population by age and sex is available, and the reports carried very little on organization and methods followed and less on definitions of concepts. Comparative tables of *de facto* population of 1967 and 1979 by administrative districts, islands, enumerator's areas, and urban areas are also available.

This census was originally planned for 1977, but it was postponed and coordinated simultaneously with preparation of electoral rolls for general election. This was one of the reasons for the population in some areas having refused to be counted. Alternative procedures were taken which involved enumeration by indirect methods (data recorded based on information available in the area), simple estimate of population household by household with no questionnaires filled, census forms completed in men's meeting-house, questionnaires filled with omission of some questions, or the same answer recorded for all persons on nationality, religion and occupation.

The total number of persons who refused to be counted or were not indirectly enumerated was 2,675 or 2.4 percent of the resident population. Based on these results, it was assumed that the overall results would not be changed. All publications are available in French and English.

Publication Plan. New Hebrides. Ministry of Public Administration, District Affairs and Local Authorities. *General Population Census, 15-16 January 1979.* Port-Vila, 1980. Three preliminary volumes. Unpublished data are available. Language of publication is French and/or English.

National Topic Chart

	1957	1967	1972	1979
De facto	X	X	X	X
Usual residence				X
Place of birth		X	X	
Duration of residence			X	
Place of prev. residence				
Urban/rural		X	X	X
Sex	X	X	X	X
Age	X	X	X	X
Relation to household head	X	X	X	
Marital status	X	X	X	
Children born alive	X	X		
Children living		X		
Citizenship	X	X	X	
Literacy	X			
School enrollment		X	X	
Ed. attainment	X		X	
Ed. qualification	X		X	
National/Ethnic origin		X	X	
Language				
Religion		X		
Household composition	X			
Econ. active/inactive	X	X	X	
Occupation	X		X	
Industry	X	X		
Occupational status	X	X	X	
Income				
Housing				

Wallis
and
Futuna

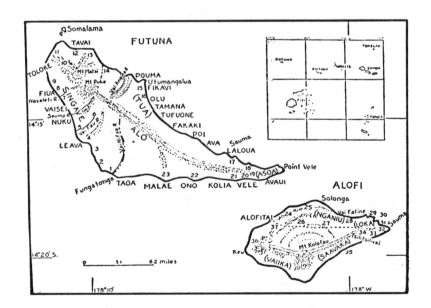

Wallis and Futuna

French Overseas Territory (TOM)

CAPITAL: Mata Utu, Wallis Island.
STATISTICAL AGENCY: INSEE (Paris).
NATIONAL REPOSITORY: ?
MAIN U.S. REPOSITORY: Population Research Center (Univ. of Texas).

Formerly dependencies of New Caledonia, these islands became a French Overseas Territory in 1961. Wallis has three districts subdivided into nineteen villages, and Futuna has two districts with ten villages. Alofi Island was not enumerated as it is used for farming and not usually inhabited.

There was mention of figures by sex for the years 1921, 1953, and 1961, but no source was cited. The first census of Wallis and Futuna was that administered in 1969 by INSEE, the statistical agency of France. The second was taken in 1976.

1969 (March 10)

The census was *de jure*, canvassed on household schedules, and tabulated in France. The territorial division was as listed above. The legal population was simplified—the total of private and collective households and the institutionalized (in this case, military housed on base and boarding students).

Definitions and Concepts. HOUSEHOLD—one person living alone or a group of persons, related or not, living in the same dwelling and sharing meals, budget, and so forth (private). The collective households were religious communities, retirement and old age homes, patients in hospitals (not TB, Hansen's, or psychiatric), hotel and pension residents, and hospital, boarding school, and hotel staffs living on the premises. "Comptée à part" were military living on base, boarding students, prisoners, patients in TB, Hansen's, and psychiatric hospitals, and public works laborers housed in barracks. PLACE OF PREVIOUS RESIDENCE—taken but there is no table in the existing publication for residence in 1963. May be available from INSEE (Paris). BIRTHPLACE—commune for native born, name of department or territory for French citizens, or name of country for foreigners. AGE—month and year of birth. Tables have single years by generational age, and real age by standard ten-year age groups. MARITAL STATUS—single, married, widowed, and divorced (including legally separated).

FERTILITY—women age fifteen and over: number of children born alive. NATIONALITY—citizenship: French or foreigner, with ethnic origin for the French (Melanesian, Wallisian, and so forth). Tribe given for French Melanesians. EDUCATION—literacy and educational attainment (highest diploma received). HOUSEHOLD COMPOSITION—by size, type (based on spouse and/or children present), and characteristics of head. ECONOMIC ACTIVITY—all age fifteen and over. No specified reference period stated, assumed to be at moment of census. Categories: permanent, temporary, seasonal, unemployed, without employment (homemakers, students, and so forth). OCCUPATION—twenty groups to suit local conditions. Classification is more or less in the order of the list used in France. INDUSTRY—six major groups, selected as most pertinent to the territory. OCCUPATIONAL STATUS—employer, own-account worker (no employees), salaried worker, family worker (with or without pay). SOCIOECONOMIC STATUS—crossing of occupation with status. Code is adapted to the conditions of the territory. ECONOMIC DEPENDENCY—number of children under fifteen in household and number of economically active per household.

Special Elements and Features. Only main results were published; more data are available from INSEE (Paris). Ages of children lumped "under 10." Housing may have been taken, but there are no tables in the publication.

Quality of the Census. "Responses of the censused with regard to occupation and status were not controlled." Lack of detail in published tables was not deemed of importance to INSEE. Emphasis was mainly on the Wallisians, little on Futunians.

Publication Plan. France. INSEE. *Recensement de la population de Wallis et Futuna, mars 1969. Principaux résultats.* Paris, 1970? Unpublished data are available from INSEE (Paris). Language of publication is French.

1976 (March 26)

Taken simultaneously in both islands, the census was *de jure* and was canvassed on individual schedules that were combined with a household sheet for both private and collective households. It was computer tabulated in Noumea, New Caledonia. Housing data was also taken. The legal population is the total of private and collective households plus the absent residents (boarding students and compulsory military service members). No double count was used for villages. Territorial division is the same (as noted in the introduction of this entry).

Definitions and Concepts. HOUSEHOLD—same as 1969. PLACE OF PREVIOUS RESIDENCE—taken only if it was in New Caledonia. USUAL RESIDENCE—of all persons including visitors. AGE—day, month, and year of birth. Tables in generational age by single years and by standard five-year age groups in real age. BIRTHPLACE—same as 1969 plus year of arrival in territory for all born elsewhere. MARITAL STATUS—same as 1969. NATIONALITY—citizenship: French by birth, naturalized (plus former nationality), and foreigners. ETHNIC ORIGIN—European/assimilated, Futunian, Wallisian, other. EDUCATION—school attendance for age fourteen and over, literacy (in Futunian, in

Wallisian, in French), educational attainment (highest degree confirmed, vocational training completed). ECONOMIC ACTIVITY—all age fourteen and over. Reference period was the moment of census. The active are the employed (permanent, seasonal), and unemployed seeking work. The inactive are students, the retired, members of compulsory military service, those without profession, and those temporarily employed. OCCUPATION—included former profession for the retired. Classification was an adaptation of the list used in France (thirty-six groups). INDUSTRY—name, type, and activity of establishment. Six broad groups, subdivided into twenty-eight subgroups. Classification was an adaptation of the list used in France. OCCUPATIONAL STATUS—employer, own account, salaried, family worker. SOCIOECONOMIC STATUS—crossing of occupation and status (French code).

Special Elements and Features. Languages spoken can be determined to some degree by the literacy question. Information is available about the unemployed (how long, with experience, and profession). Return migration from New Caledonia (commune in New Caledonia, arrival and departure dates, reason for stay) was presented. Fertility was dropped. Housing tables were published this time. The temporarily employed were switched from active (1969) to inactive in this census.

Quality of the Census. Both main and final result volumes were published. There is more detail for villages and in occupation and industry. The direction of INSEE and publication financed by FIDES (Fonds d'Investissement Économique et Social) helped in bringing out a good census. "The operations posed no difficulties and the undercount should be close to zero percent." A Whipple's Index category was not available.

Publication Plan. France. INSEE [and] FIDES. *Résultats statistiques du recensement général de la population des îles Wallis et Futuna, 26 mars 1976.* Paris, 1977? (Main). *Résultats du recensement de la population des Wallis et Futuna, 26 mars 1976.* Noumea, n.d. (Final). Unpublished data are available. Language of publication is French.

National Topic Chart

	1969	1976
De facto		
Usual residence	X	X
Place of birth	X	X
Duration of residence		X
Place of prev. residence	X	X
Urban/rural		
Sex	X	X
Age	X	X
Relation to household head	X	X
Marital status	X	X
Children born alive	X	
Children living		
Citizenship	X	X
Literacy	X	X
School enrollment		X
Ed. attainment	X	X
Ed. qualification		
National/Ethnic origin	X	X
Language		X
Religion		
Household composition	X	X
Econ. active/inactive	X	X
Occupation	X	X
Industry	X	X
Occupational status	X	X
Income		
Housing		X

Western Samoa

Now officially known as Samoa

CAPITAL: Apia.
STATISTICAL AGENCY: Department of Statistics, Apia.
NATIONAL REPOSITORY: Nelson Memorial Library, Apia.
MAIN U.S. REPOSITORY: Population Research Center (Univ. of Texas).

Samoa (name changed in 1977) consists of two large islands (Upolu and Savai'i) and two small islands (Manono and Apolina), which later were incorporated into Upolu. It is believed that European explorers had visited the islands from 1722 on, but the earliest recorded estimate of the population was made by an exploring expedition from the United States in 1839 (47,000 inhabitants). Subsequent estimates were made up to 1882 that showed a rapid decline of population. The main causes were epidemics and intertribal warfare. Under German administration, the population censuses, taken in 1900, 1902, 1906, and 1911, also recorded births, deaths, and migration.

The New Zealand administration started in 1917, and censuses have been taken regularly since then. In 1918, an influenza epidemic caused the loss of one-fifth of the population; but since that year health conditions have improved, and the population has increased steadily. The early censuses of 1921, 1926, 1936, and 1945 were extremely limited, presenting very few tables, which were believed to be inaccurate. Also, ages were not observed chronologically; instead, the population was classified in sociological groups to which approximate ages were assigned. The following censuses of 1951, 1956, and 1961 were also taken under New Zealand administration.

On January 1, 1962, Samoa became the first independent Polynesian state to be established in modern times. Since the establishment of the new government, three other censuses have been conducted (1966, 1971, and 1976).

A brief account of the extended family ("matai") system in Samoa (both American and former Western) is of fundamental importance for the understanding of its society and its economic activities. A "matai" is the head of the "aiga" (extended family), which is the basic unit of the social system in Samoa. The family supports the "matai" in all social and economic matters concerning the "aiga." In return, the "matai" is responsible for providing leadership and direction to his people as well as the distribution of the "aiga" revenue necessary for

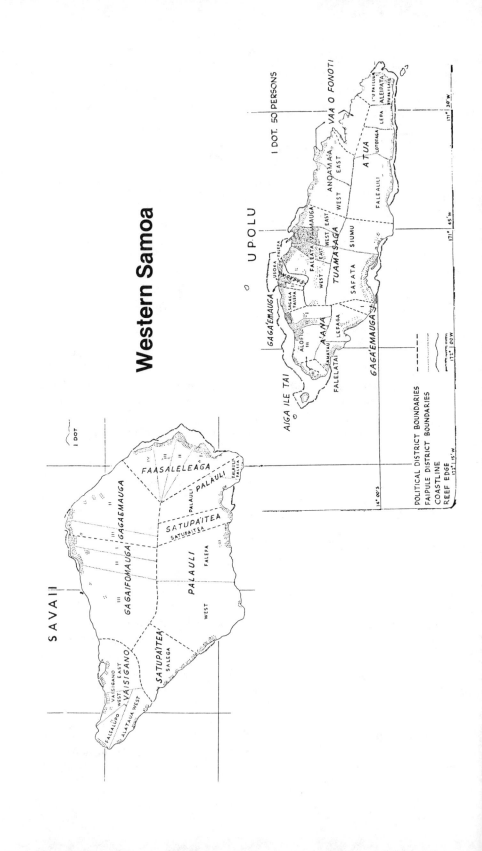

the members' subsistence. The "matai" has the rights to certain land (customary land). The electoral system of the country is closely tied to the "matai" system. For census purposes, persons who are under a "matai" were asked the district where their "matai's" title is registered, and if the head of the family has more than one "matai" title, the village of the title he intends to use in the election was recorded.

1945 (September 25)

The census of population was conducted under New Zealand administration on a *de facto* basis, and canvasser was the method used for enumeration. The two islands of Manono and Apolina were not included as they were uninhabited. The census was synchronized with that of the other island territories administered by New Zealand, but the preparation, organization and actual conduct of the census were severely handicapped due to staff illness and various unexpected circumstances. Therefore, the results were limited to a few tables. The total population excluded U.S. armed forces and persons on board overseas vessels.

Definitions and Concepts: AGE—the population was not recorded chronologically but rather classified in sociological groups (under six, six to sixteen, sixteen to twenty-one, and twenty-one and over) for Europeans and part-Europeans; and groups of two, two to fifteen, and fifteen and over for native born. MARITAL STATUS—categories were: never married, married, separated, widowed, and divorced (recorded only for Europeans). RELIGION—Unlike the New Zealand Maoris, the Samoans have no purely native variant of religious belief; nearly all adhere to one or the other missions maintained in the islands. Religious groups were recorded for all three groups (European, part-European, and natives). COUNTRY OF BIRTH—the majority of Europeans and part-Europeans recorded their country of birth as being Western Samoa. RACE—based on the concept of descent. Samoans were pure or mixed descendents of Polynesians or other Pacific islanders. The Europeans and part-Europeans included Chinese and other Pacific islanders who had not adopted Samoan status.

Special Elements and Features. The major problem encountered in the censuses up to 1966 was the unsatisfactory racial classification of the population. Most of the statistics available were defined in terms of legal status, and the laws governing the status of individuals such as Europeans or Samoans have changed from time to time creating difficulties as far as consistency of answers and comparability among censuses. Comparative tables for 1921, 1926, 1936, and 1945 results were presented.

Quality of the Census. Because of staff illness substitute officers were used without previous training. They could not overcome the difficulties, and consequently the enumeration lacked coherent planning. The final results were not as accurate as desired. The utilization of traditional age grouping provides insufficient data for comparisons with future censuses.

Publication Plan. New Zealand. Department of Island Territories. *Population Census, 1945*. Volume 2, Island Territories: Cook Islands and Niue, Tokelau Island, Western Samoa. Auckland, 1947. Language of publication is English.

1951 (September 25)

The fifth census of population conducted under New Zealand administration was taken on a *de facto* basis, and canvasser was the method utilized to record information. No further details as far as organization and methods adopted in the census were furnished. The territory covered by the census was divided into traditional political districts, "fipule" districts, villages and subvillages, and Apia urban district. This census was the first detailed set of statistics and became the basis for future analysis of demographic changes.

Definitions and Concepts. AGE—in completed years. Tabulated in standard five-year age groups for the first time. Single years up to five years of age were also presented. MARITAL STATUS—for the first time marital status was recorded for Samoans. Categories were: never married, married, widowed and not remarried, divorced, legally separated, and married by custom. The last category was not applied to the European population. FERTILITY (new)—asked of women fifteen years and older: number of children ever born. Although not explicitly mentioned, fertility was asked only of women ever married (tables do not present data for single women). RACE—groups recorded: Samoan (persons of Polynesian or other Pacific island blood, whether of pure or mixed descent, but not including persons of mixed blood who are Europeans) and European or part-European (including Chinese and their children and excluding any persons with Samoan status). Data were considered too unsatisfactory to be tabulated due to the large amount of unstated and inaccurate answers. EDUCATION—literacy (ability to read and write in vernacular or English) and school attendance (government or mission schools). PLACE OF BIRTH—two groups recorded: born in Samoa and foreign born (country of birth and duration of residence were asked). CITIZENSHIP—country of allegiance and method of acquiring Samoan nationality (by birth, marriage, or naturalization). RELIGION—for the first time the declaration of religious denomination was optional. It is curious to note that no Samoan exercised the privilege. Samoans have been converted to Christianity, and the church of mission plays the most important part in the social life of the people. ECONOMIC ACTIVITY—the population was divided into the following groups: children under five years of age and not attending school, children attending school, those employed in village economy ("nofo-aiga"), those employed for remuneration, and not stated (including retired and dependents). OCCUPATION—broad occupation groups, including housewife, the retired, or dependent, but excluding children attending or not attending school. WAR SERVICE—questions asked only of the European population (full- or part-Europeans): country with whose force the person served and whether receiving war pension.

Special Elements and Features. Tables of racial classification alone were not presented; however, other tables had the basic division European and Samoan. In the results on total population, occupation, school attendance, and war service, the European group was subdivided into part-European and full-European. Fertility was recorded for the first time. Age was tabulated in standard five-year age groups (new). Also included were maps, housing occupancy (size and type), and a separate table for urban population of Apia. Education, citizenship, and economic activity were new.

Quality of the Census. Although 1951 was the first comprehensive census in the country, there was a general uncertainty on the accuracy of results. Marital status and fertility data were not reliable and should be considered only an accurate estimate. Results of economic activity presented a large number of unstated answers, revealing more accurately the minimal number of occupied persons rather than expressing occupational classification. The number of Samoans for each district serves only as a reference for later censuses. Whipple's Index category was not available.

Publication Plan. New Zealand. Department of Island Territories. *Population Census, 25 September 1951.* Wellington, 1954. One general volume was published. Language of publication is English.

1956 (September 25)

The sixth census of population taken under New Zealand administration was conducted by a census commissioner. The census was *de facto*, and canvasser was the method utilized to record information on household and individual schedules. The schedules were printed in Samoan for outer districts and in Samoan or English for the Apia urban area. A two-stage enumeration system was applied and record books were used for obtaining preliminary figures. Tabulation was manual. Territorial divisions were basically the same as 1951.

Definitions and Concepts. AGE—in completed years and date of birth. Tabulated in single years and standard five-year age groups. MARITAL STATUS—categories were: never married, married (legally or common law), widowed, and divorced. HOUSEHOLD—all those who shared the place of sleeping, including servants, visitors, or boarders. Institutions and vessels in port on the night of the census were regarded as households. If in an institution there were separate quarters for any of the staff, such quarters were considered separate households. FAMILY—relationship to the "matai" or head of the household was recorded. FERTILITY—asked of all women fifteen years and over: number of children born who are still living, number of children born who are now dead, and age of the mother at birth of the first child. PLACE OF BIRTH—if born in Samoa, name of island; if born outside, the island group or the name of the country was recorded. RACE (descent)—the following groups were recorded: Samoan, part-Samoan, European, other Pacific islanders, and others. RELIGION—churches and missions recorded, and the verb "object" used to indicate persons who did not wish to answer the question. EDUCATION—school attendance recorded and tabulated as part of the economically inactive population. ECONOMIC ACTIVITY—because of the structure of the village agricultural system in which the majority of people are engaged, each person was asked whether he was a "matai" (head of the family) or a "nofo-aiga" (person at home engaged in village agriculture). A "matai" may be classified as having paid employment but not a "nofo-aiga." The population was divided into two groups: gainfully occupied, including males engaged in village agriculture ("nofo-aiga"), males and females in full-time paid employment, and government employees (full and part-time). The nongainfully occupied population included: children under fifteen years of age (attending school or not), homemakers, the retired, pensioners, persons of independent income, and inmates of institutions. No question was asked about unemployment. INDUSTRY—classification presented eight broad industrial groups. OCCUPATION—broad major groups within each industry, with the main purpose of separating the group of owners and managers as an occupational class. The other occupations were ranked on the basis of skill required.

Special Elements and Features. The census report included organization and methods adopted, analysis of population change, density, and distribution. Copy of schedules, administrative report, and maps were also included. Citizenship, literacy, and war service were dropped.

Quality of the Census. Although date of birth was recorded, the number of corrections made by enumerators to ensure consistency with stated age reduced the value of the figures. The two-stage enumeration system improved accuracy of results. The difficulties of racial classification remained, however. Whipple's Index category was not available. Final results were published in 1958.

Publication Plan. Western Samoa. Census Commissioner's Office. *Report on the Population Census, 1956,* by Kathleen M. Jupp. Wellington, N. Z., 1958. Language of publication is English.

1961 (September 25)

The last census taken under New Zealand administration was *de facto*, and canvasser was the method used to record information on household and individual schedules. The organization of the census was based on that of 1956. The tables presented were almost identical except for some modifications on summary tables and the addition of information on dwellings and family units. The schedules were printed in English only, and the tabulation was mechanical. The islands of Manono and Apolina were included in the total for Upolu.

Definitions and Concepts. AGE, MARITAL STATUS, RELIGION, HOUSEHOLD, FERTILITY, EDUCATION, PLACE OF BIRTH, and RACE—same as 1956. ECONOMIC ACTIVITY—the principal occupation; the population was divided into the following groups: those working in paid employment, working in "aiga" (village agriculture), not working (dependent on wage or money earner, dependent on "aiga," retired and unemployed); and those working in other business or on own account. The economically active were persons who furnished the supply of labor available for the production of economic goods and services. Inactives were those dependent on wage or money earners (children, students, and homemakers), those dependent on "aiga" (including the same groups), and others not economically active (persons of independent income and inmates of institutions). OCCUPATION—like 1956 it was presented within industry. INDUSTRY—classification presented nine broad groups including the unemployed.

Special Elements and Features. For the first time housing questions were recorded (type of construction and number of persons living in each dwelling). Pyramids of the distribution of the population by age, sex, and ethnic groups were presented comparing results for 1956 and 1961.

Quality of the Census. As in the previous census, two-stage enumeration system was used to assure accuracy. Whipple's Index classified age accuracy into category II—fairly accurate data.

Publication Plan. New Zealand. Department of Island Territories. *Population Census, 1961.* Apia, 1962. Language of publication is English.

1966 (November 21)

The first census of population taken after the independence of Samoa (January 1962) was conducted by a census commissioner, and largely based on the previous two censuses to maintain comparability. The census was *de facto*, and canvasser the method used to record information on household and individual schedules. Mechanical tabulation was utilized. For census purposes, the two major islands (Upolu and Savai'i) were divided into political districts, "faipule" districts, villages, subvillages, and plantation or other areas. The results for Manono and Apolina islands were included in Upolu.

Definitions and Concepts. AGE, MARITAL STATUS, RELIGION, HOUSE-HOLD—same as 1956 and 1961. RACE—basically the same as 1961, but this time Chinese were not included in the European group. PLACE OF BIRTH—if native born, name of the island and village of birth; if foreign born, the island group or country of birth was recorded. In addition, foreign-born persons were asked the year of immigration to the country. LANGUAGE (new)—ability to speak Samoan and ability to speak English. EDUCATION—literacy was revived (not recorded since 1951), school attendance, and educational attainment (highest class attended). FERTILITY—for females fifteen years and over: number of children ever born, number of children still living, and age of mother at birth of first child. ECONOMIC ACTIVITY—Economically active population included those working for paid employment, those unemployed at the time of the census, those working in "aiga" (subsistence agriculture), and own-account workers. Unemployed persons were asked reasons for unemployment and number of weeks since last worked. It is important to notice that those classified as unemployed were previously working as wage earners. Persons employed at the time of the census were also asked the number of weeks worked during the last twelve months, and number of hours worked per week. Persons working in village agriculture were asked whether they were full- or part-time workers, and if part-time workers, the percentage of time spent on the job and secondary occupation. The economically inactive population included: persons dependent on wage or money earner (homemakers, children attending school or not, invalids, the elderly, and so forth), persons dependent on village agriculture (same groups), and retired persons. OCCUPATION—as in 1956 and 1961, occupations were presented as subgroups of industrial divisions, separating proprietors, managers, and overseers in each group from the others. INDUSTRY—broad classification; the following divisions were presented: village agriculture; other agriculture, forestry, fishing and mining; manufacturing and construction; commerce; transport and communications; total service; personal service and entertainment; government administrative and protective services; and professions.

Special Elements and Features. New features were language, educational attainment, and literacy (reinstated). Analysis of results and comparative tables for 1961 and 1966 censuses, a table with total population since 1839, maps of the country and Apia urban area, and charts of religious distribution were all included. The number of dwellings, size of household, and types of construction were also recorded.

Quality of the Census. The lack of a permanent census office and qualified personnel created difficulties for the organization of census operations. The use of mechanical tabulation improved accuracy of results, but the identification of persons of mixed races remained a problem. Whipple's Index classified age data into category II—fairly accurate data. Preliminary results were available a month after enumeration.

Publication Plan. Western Samoa. Bureau of Statistics. *Population Census, 1966.* Apia, 1968. *Apia Urban Area Population Census, 1966.* Apia, 1968. Language of publication is English.

1971 (November 3)

The second census of population taken after independence was conducted by the Department of Statistics and with assistance of the U.N. Development Programme. For the first time, the census of population and housing were taken simultaneously. The census was *de facto*, and canvasser was the method utilized to record information on two kinds of schedules: population interview schedule (house and personal questionnaires), and housing interview schedule. A two-stage enumeration system was used and tabulation was computerized. The territory covered by the census was divided into four major regions (Apia urban area, northwest Upolu, rest of Upolu, and Savai'i) and subdivided into "faipule" districts.

Definitions and Concepts. HOUSEHOLD—all occupants of a housing unit who share common housekeeping arrangements and provision of food. Visitors and boarders who occupied a separate room and provide their own food are not included. If the boarders, however, paid money to the head of the household to provide them with food, they were part of the household. AGE—as of last birthday in completed years, plus date of birth. Tabulated in single years and standard five-year age groups. MARITAL STATUS—asked of all persons fourteen and over. Categories were: never married, married (legally or common law), separated, divorced, and widowed. RELIGION—groups recorded: Congregational Christian, Roman Catholic, Methodist, Latter Day Saints, Seventh

Day Adventist, Church of England, no religion, and objection to the question. PLACE OF BIRTH—if native born, the name of the village and "faipule" district; if foreign born, country of birth. PLACE OF RESIDENCE (new)—usual place and previous place of residence in 1970. CITIZENSHIP—legal nationality replaced the concept of race. Groups recorded: citizen of Samoa (by birth, by descent, or by naturalization) and alien (country of citizenship recorded). LANGUAGE—ability to speak English, Samoan, or any other language. EDUCATION—literacy was recorded for persons ten years and older (ability to read and write in English, Samoan, or any other language), educational attainment recorded of persons six years and older (highest degree completed, or highest professional, technical qualifications, and field training), and school attendance recorded of persons five years and older (full- or part-time students). FERTILITY—asked of females fourteen years and over: number of children ever born alive, number of children still alive and living with the mother, number of children still alive but not living with the mother, age of the mother at birth of the first child, number of children born alive during the twelve months preceding the census, and of those how many were still living. ECONOMIC ACTIVITY— asked of all persons ten years of age and older. Period of reference was the week before the census. Economically active population included those employed (working primarily to earn money; working to grow, gather, or catch food; and persons having a job but not at work) and unemployed looking for job (both new and experienced workers). Economically inactive population: attending school, homemakers, independent income recipient, unable to work, and others. The number of hours worked and the means of livelihood (source of income) during the year before the census were also recorded. The source of income was that from which the person derived his living (economic activity, pension, benefits, property or other investments, and support by other person). OCCUPATION— main and secondary occupations were recorded. Classification based on ISCO, major and minor groups (two-digits). INDUSTRY—classification based on ISIC, divisions and major groups (two-digits). OCCUPATIONAL STATUS—recorded for the first time. Categories were: employer, employee, own-account worker, unpaid family worker (in agriculture and outside agriculture), and person not classified by status. TENURE OF AGRICULTURAL HOLDING—the type of holding operated (crop, livestock and poultry, mixed holdings) and type of land operated (Samoan land, freehold land owned, and freehold land leased).

Special Elements and Features. For the first time, housing and population censuses were taken simultaneously. Usual and residence in 1970, occupational classification separate from industry, and occupational status were new. Citizenship was reinstated, and race was dropped. The questions on fertility were expanded. List of the main occupations in the country; code list of political and "faipule" districts and villages per island; table with increased and decreased village population between 1966 and 1971 due to changes in village and district boundaries; and maps, charts, copy of schedules and codes used for occupational and industrial classifications were also furnished.

Quality of the Census. A complete list of villages by "faipule" districts, and a list of buildings in villages with identifying numbers were part of the preparations for the census, reducing over- and underenumerations. For the first time in the country, every housing unit was identified, and its location established without duplication. A postcensus check to determine the accuracy of the census indicated that it was quite satisfactory, and very few persons were missed in the final census count. Comparability of the 1971 census with the last three censuses was not always possible because of changes of boundaries and the addition of new tables. The date of publication of final results is not known, but judging from previous censuses, results were probably issued within two years after enumeration. Whipple's Index category was I—highly accurate age data.

Publication Plan. Western Samoa. Department of Statistics. *Census of Population and Housing, 1971.* Apia [1972?]. Computer tapes are available. Language of publication is English.

1976 (November 3)

The third census of population after independence was also taken simultaneously with a census of housing. The Department of Statistics conducted the census on a *de facto* basis, and enumeration, like the previous ones, was carried out according to the "two-stage enumeration system." Canvasser was the method utilized to record information on household schedules and individual questionnaires. Tabulation was computerized and the territorial division was the same adopted in 1971.

Definitions and Concepts. AGE—date of birth (day, month, year). If the date was not known, the estimated age in completed years was recorded. Tabulated in single years and standard five-year age groups. MARITAL STATUS—question asked of persons fifteen years and over instead of fourteen and over. Categories were the same as the ones in 1971. RELIGION and PLACE OF RESIDENCE— the same as 1971. EDUCATION—basically the same as 1971, except that literacy was dropped. FERTILITY—questions asked of women fifteen years and over: number of adopted children still living, number of children born alive, number of children still living, and number of children born alive during the twelve months before the census. CITIZENSHIP—two groups distinguished: Samoan citizen and alien or foreign citizen. The country of citizenship of aliens was recorded. ECONOMIC ACTIVITY—the concepts were the same as those of 1971. OCCUPATION—only major groups were tabulated (one-digit); classification was based on ISCO. INDUSTRY—classification was based on ISIC, but only major divisions were tabulated. OCCUPATIONAL STATUS—the categories were the same as 1971. The category "unpaid family worker" was not subdivided.

Special Elements and Features. The number of questions on the schedules was reduced as compared to 1971. Place of birth, literacy and language, number of hours worked, and means of livelihood were dropped. Fertility questions were reduced and worded differently. Occupations and industries were tabulated only at the level of major groups and major divisions. A list of unpublished data was provided. Maps, charts, and copy of the schedules were included.

Quality of the Census. The lack of mapping was dealt with as in the previous censuses, that is, the enumerators themselves provided the mapping of census enumeration blocks. The data process operations did not take place in the country but at the Electronic Data Processing Service in Suva, Fiji. Final results were published in 1978 and 1979. Whipple's Index rating was not available. The census office is permanent.

Publication Plan. Western Samoa. Department of Statistics. *Census of Population and Housing, 1976.* Apia, 1978-1979. Volume 1, administrative report and tables. Volume 2, analytical report. Unpublished data and computer tapes are available. Language of publication is English.

OTHER STATISTICAL PUBLICATIONS: Issued by Department of Statistics, *Annual Statistical Abstract, Quarterly Statistical Bulletin.*

National Topic Chart

	1945	1951	1956	1961	1966	1971	1976
De facto	X	X	X	X	X	X	X
Usual residence						X	X
Place of birth	X	X	X	X	X	X	
Duration of residence							
Place of prev. residence						X	X
Urban/rural		X	X	X	X	X	X
Sex	X	X	X	X	X	X	X
Age	X	X	X	X	X	X	X
Relation to household head		X	X	X	X	X	X
Marital status	X	X	X	X	X	X	X
Children born alive		X	X	X	X	X	X
Children living			X	X	X	X	X
Citizenship		X				X	X
Literacy		X			X	X	
School enrollment		X	X	X	X	X	X
Ed. attainment					X	X	X
Ed. qualification							
National/Ethnic origin	X	X	X	X	X		
Language					X	X	
Religion	X	X	X	X	X	X	X
Household composition					X	X	X
Econ. active/inactive		X	X	X	X	X	X
Occupation		X	X	X	X	X	X
Industry			X	X	X	X	X
Occupational status						X	X
Income							
Housing						X	X

APPENDIXES

International Population Charts

COUNTRIES (areas in square miles), CAPITALS, AND MAJOR CITIES

```
            — = No census in that five-year group
          (p) = Provisional results
           na = Not available
  [blank cell] = Not known if taken or will take,
                 1980-84 column only
```

	1945-1949	1950-1954	1955-1959	1960-1964	1965-1969	1970-1974	1975-1979	1980-1984
LATIN AMERICA and CARIBBEAN								
Antigua-Barbuda (171)	41,757	—	—	54,299	—	65,525	—	na
St. Johns (Cap.)	10,965	—	—	21,396	—	21,814	—	na
Argentina (1,072,067)	15,893,827	—	—	20,013,793	—	23,364,431	—	27,947,446
Buenos Aires (Cap.)	2,982,580	—	—	2,966,634	—	2,972,453	—	2,922,829
Cordoba	369,866	—	—	586,015	—	798,663	—	(p) 998,007
Rosario	467,937	—	—	646,293	—	798,292	—	(p) 935,471
Bahamas (5,382)	—	84,841	—	130,220	—	169,534	—	(p) 209,505
Nassau (Cap.)	—	na	—	na	—	4,655	—	na
Freeport	—	na	—	na	—	15,546	—	22,301
Barbados (166)	192,800	—	—	232,333	—	235,229	—	(p) 248,983
Bridgetown (Cap.)	13,486	—	—	11,452	—	8,868	—	(p) 7,552
Belize (8,867)	59,220	—	—	90,121	—	119,934	—	(p) 144,857
Belize city (Cap.)	21,886	—	—	32,824	—	39,050	—	(p) 39,887

International Population Charts (Continued)

COUNTRIES (areas in square miles), CAPITALS, AND MAJOR CITIES

— = No census in that five-year group
(p) = Provisional results
na = Not available
[blank cell] = Not known if taken or will take, 1980-84 column only

	1945-1949	1950-1954	1955-1959	1960-1964	1965-1969	1970-1974	1975-1979	1980-1984
Bermuda (21)								
Hamilton (Cap.)	—	38,530	—	56,056	—	52,330	—	67,761
	—	2,816	—	2,763	—	3,314	—	1,624
Bolivia (424,162)								
La Paz (Cap.)	—	3,019,031	—	—	—	—	4,647,816	
Santa Cruz	—	321,073	—	—	—	—	654,713	
Cochabamba	—	42,746	—	—	—	—	237,128	
	—	80,795	—	—	—	—	194,156	
Brazil (3,286,470)								
Brasilia (Cap.)	—	51,944,397	—	70,992,343	—	94,508,554	—	(p)119,961,470
São Paulo	—	na	—	141,742	—	537,492	—	(p) 1,176,748
Rio de Janeiro	—	2,198,096	—	3,164,804	—	5,924,615	—	(p) 8,490,763
Belo Horizonte	—	2,377,451	—	3,307,163	—	4,251,918	—	(p) 5,093,496
Salvador	—	352,724	—	642,912	—	1,235,030	—	(p) 1,774,712
	—	417,235	—	649,453	—	1,005,216	—	(p) 1,501,219
British Virgin Isl. (133)								
Road Town (Cap.)	6,505	—	—	7,921	—	9,672	—	12,034
	na	—	—	na	—	na	—	2,479
Cayman Islands (9,281)								
Georgetown (Cap.)	—	—	—	8,511	—	10,068	16,677	
	—	—	—	2,705	—	3,812	7,617	

Chile (286,396)	—	5,932,995	—	7,374,115	—	8,884,768	—	(p) 11,275,440
Santiago (Cap.)	—	1,350,409	—	1,907,378	—	2,730,895	—	(p) 3,672,374
Valparaíso	—	218,829	—	252,865	—	255,360	—	na
Colombia (455,355)	—	11,548,172	—	17,484,508	—	20,666,920	—	—
Bogotá (Cap.)	—	648,324	—	1,697,311	—	2,557,461	—	—
Cali	—	284,186	—	637,929	—	901,714	—	—
Medellín	—	358,189	—	772,887	—	1,053,964	—	—
Costa Rica (19,653)	—	800,875	—	1,336,274	—	1,871,780	—	na
San José (Cap.)	—	111,820	—	168,938	—	215,441	—	na
Cuba (44,218)	—	5,829,029	—	—	—	8,569,121	—	9,706,369
Havana (Cap.)	—	1,210,920	—	—	—	1,751,216	—	1,924,886
Santiago de Cuba	—	163,237	—	—	—	277,600	—	345,289
Dominica (305)	47,624	—	—	59,916	—	69,549	—	na
Roseau (Cap.)	9,752	—	—	10,417	—	9,949	—	na
Dominican Republic (18,704)	—	2,135,872	—	3,047,070	—	4,009,458	—	(p) 5,647,977
Santo Domingo (Cap.)	—	181,553	—	369,980	—	668,507	—	na
Santiago	—	67,701	—	85,640	—	155,506	—	na
Ecuador (105,685)	—	3,202,757	—	4,476,007	—	6,521,710	—	na
Quito (Cap.)	—	319,221	—	510,286	—	782,671	—	na
Guayaquil	—	331,942	—	567,895	—	907,013	—	na
El Salvador (8,260)	—	1,855,917	—	2,510,984	—	3,554,648	—	
San Salvador (Cap.)	—	161,951	—	255,744	—	337,171	—	
Falkland Islands (4,618)	2,239	2,230	—	2,172	—	1,957	—	
Stanley (Cap.)	1,252	1,135	—	1,074	—	1,079	—	

International Population Charts (Continued)

COUNTRIES (areas in square miles), CAPITALS, AND MAJOR CITIES

— = No census in that five-year group
(p) = Provisional results
na = Not available
[blank cell] = Not known if taken or will take, 1980-84 column only

	1945-1949	1950-1954	1955-1959	1960-1964	1965-1969	1970-1974	1975-1979	1980-1984
French Guiana (37,740)	29,260	27,863	—	33,505	44,392	55,125	—	na
Cayenne (Cap.)	na	13,362	—	18,615	24,518	30,461	—	na
Grenada (133)	72,387	—	—	88,677	—	92,775	—	
St. George's (Cap.)	5,772	—	—	7,303	—	6,313	—	
Guadeloupe (687)	278,464	229,120	—	283,223	312,724	324,530	—	na
Basse-Terre (Cap.)	na	11,837	—	13,978	15,690	15,457	—	na
Guatemala (42,042)	—	2,790,868	—	4,287,997	—	5,160,221	—	(p) 6,043,559
Guatemala city (Cap.)	—	294,344	—	572,671	—	700,504	—	(p) 749,784
Guyana (83,000)	369,678	—	—	560,330	—	699,848	—	na
Georgetown (Cap.)	73,509	—	—	72,964	—	63,184	—	na
Haiti (10,714)	—	3,097,220	—	—	—	4,329,991	—	na
Port-au-Prince (Cap.)	—	185,606	—	—	—	543,012	—	na
Honduras (43,277)	1,200,542	1,368,605	—	1,884,765	—	2,656,948	—	na
Tegucigalpa (Cap.)	86,462	99,948	—	134,075	—	273,894	—	na
San Pedro Sula	46,282	54,268	—	58,632	—	150,991	—	na

Location									
Jamaica (4,244)	—	—	—	1,609,814	—	—	1,797,400	—	—
Kingston (Cap.)	—	—	—	109,800	—	—	106,791	—	—
Martinique (426)	—	261,595	—	290,030	320,030	—	324,832	—	na
Fort-de-France (Cap.)	—	66,006	—	84,811	96,943	—	100,576	—	na
Mexico (761,601)	—	25,791,017	—	34,923,129	—	—	48,225,238	—	(p) 67,382,581
Mexico D.F. (Cap.)[1]	—	3,050,442	—	4,870,876	—	—	6,874,165	—	(p) 9,373,353
Mexico city	—	2,233,914	—	2,832,133	—	—	2,902,969	—	na
Guadalajara	—	377,016	—	736,800	—	—	1,193,601	—	na
Monterrey	—	333,422	—	596,939	—	—	858,107	—	na
Montserrat (33)	—	14,333	—	12,168	—	—	11,458	—	12,073
Plymouth (Cap.)	—	2,103	—	1,950	—	—	1,267	—	1,623
Netherlands Antilles (395)	—	—	—	188,914	—	—	218,390	—	
Willemstad (Cap.)	—	—	—	45,546	—	—	na	—	
Nicaragua (57,143)	—	1,057,023	—	1,535,588	—	—	1,877,952	—	na
Managua (Cap.)	—	109,352	—	234,580	—	—	396,279	—	na
Panama[2] (28,753)	—	805,285	—	1,075,541	—	—	1,428,082	—	(p) 1,830,175
Panama (Cap.)	—	127,874	—	273,440	—	—	348,704	—	(p) 388,638
Panama Canal Zone (362)	—	52,822	—	42,122	—	—	44,198	—	
Paraguay[3] (157,048)	—	1,328,452	—	1,816,890	—	—	2,357,955	—	na
Asunción (Cap.)	—	206,634	—	305,160	—	—	388,958	—	na
Perú[4] (496,222)	—	—	—	10,420,357	—	—	13,538,208	—	na
Lima (Cap.)	—	—	—	1,752,277	—	—	3,241,051	—	na
Callao	—	—	—	204,990	—	—	313,316	—	na
Arequipa	—	—	—	250,746	—	—	420,801	—	na

COUNTRIES (areas in square miles), CAPITALS, AND MAJOR CITIES

— = No census in that five-year group
(p) = Provisional results
na = Not available
[blank cell] = Not known if taken or will take, 1980-84 column only

	1945-1949	1950-1954	1955-1959	1960-1964	1965-1969	1970-1974	1975-1979	1980-1984
Puerto Rico[5] (3,435)	—	2,210,703	—	2,349,544	—	2,712,033	—	na
San Juan (Cap.)		227,767		432,377		452,377		na
Río Piedras		132,438		143,989				na
Ponce		99,492		114,286		128,233		na
St. Kitts-Nevis[6] (138)	46,243			56,693		44,884		(p) 44,404
Basse-Terre (Cap.)	na			15,579		12,771		na
St. Lucia (233)	70,113			86,108		99,806		115,783
Castries (Cap.)	7,146			4,353		3,615		
St. Vincent (150)	61,647			79,948		86,314		na
Kingstown (Cap.)	4,833			4,308		17,117		na
Suriname (63,251)		184,700		329,400		384,900		na
Paramaribo (Cap.)		74,300		110,867		102,297		na
Trinidad and Tobago (1,979)	557,970			827,957		931,071		(p) 1,059,825
Port-of-Spain (Cap.)	92,793			93,954		62,680		(p) 54,919

	C1	C2	C3	C4	C5	C6	C7
Turks and Caicos (202)	—	—	5,668	—	5,558	—	(p) 7,436
Grand Turk (Cap.)	—	—	2,180	—	2,287	—	(p) 3,146
Uruguay (68,548)	—	—	2,595,510	—	2,788,429	—	
Montevideo (Cap.)	—	—	1,159,085	—	1,179,986	—	
Salto	—	—	57,958	—	80,088	—	
Venezuela (352,143)	5,034,838	—	7,523,999	—	10,721,522	—	na
Caracas D.F. (Cap.)	709,602	—	1,257,515	—	1,860,637	—	na
Caracas city	495,064	—	786,863	—	1,035,499	—	na
Maracaibo	238,882	—	412,872	—	651,574	—	na
Virgin Islands (*U.S.*) (132)	26,665	—	32,099	—	62,468	—	(p) 95,591
Charlotte Amalie (Cap.)	11,469	—	12,880	—	12,220	—	(p) 11,756
NORTH AMERICA							
Canada (3,851,809)	14,009,429	16,080,791	18,238,247	20,014,880	21,568,311	22,992,604	(p) 24,105,163
Ottawa (Cap.)	202,045	222,129	268,206	290,741	302,241	304,462	na
Montreal	1,021,520	1,109,439	1,191,062	1,222,255	1,214,352	1,080,546	na
Toronto	675,754	667,706	672,407	664,584	712,786	633,318	na
Quebec	164,016	170,703	171,979	166,984	186,088	177,082	na
Greenland (840,000)	21,412	26,933	33,140	39,600	46,531	49,630	—
Godthaab (Cap.)	1,962	3,357	4,305	5,781	8,209	8,912	—
St. Pierre-Miquelon (93)	4,354	4,822	5,025	5,235	5,840	—	na
United States (3,615,122)	151,325,798	—	179,323,175	—	203,211,926	—	226,504,825
Washington, D.C. (Cap.)	802,178	—	763,956	—	756,510	—	637,651
New York	7,891,957	—	7,781,984	—	7,894,862	—	7,071,030
Chicago	3,620,962	—	3,550,404	—	3,366,957	—	3,005,072
Los Angeles	1,970,358	—	2,479,015	—	2,816,061	—	2,966,763

International Population Charts (Continued)

COUNTRIES (areas in square miles), CAPITALS, AND MAJOR CITIES

— = No census in that five-year group
(p) = Provisional results
na = Not available
[blank cell] = Not known if taken or will take, 1980-84 column only

	1945-1949	1950-1954	1955-1959	1960-1964	1965-1969	1970-1974	1975-1979	1980-1984
United States (Continued)								
Philadelphia	—	2,071,605	—	2,002,512	—	1,948,609	—	1,688,210
Houston	—	596,163	—	938,219	—	1,232,802	—	1,594,086
Detroit	—	1,849,568	—	1,670,144	—	1,511,482	—	1,203,339
OCEANIA								
American Samoa[7] (76)	—	18,937	20,157	20,051	—	27,159	—	32,395 (p)
Pago Pago (Cap.)	—	1,586	—	1,251	—	2,451	—	3,058 (p)
Australia (2,974,581)	7,579,358	8,986,530	—	10,508,186	11,550,462	12,755,638	13,548,472	na
Canberra (Cap.)	15,156	28,277	—	56,449	92,308	158,880	196,538	na
Sydney	1,484,434	1,863,161	—	2,183,388	2,446,345	2,807,828	3,021,982	na
Melbourne	1,226,923	1,524,111	—	1,911,895	2,110,168	2,503,450	2,604,035	na
Christmas Isl. (62)	866	—	2,619	3,099	3,391	2,691	—	2,871
Cocos (Keeling) Isl. (1.5)	1,814	—	na	606	684	na	—	
Cook Islands (93)	14,088	15,079	16,680	18,378	19,247	21,323	18,128	
Rarotonga (Cap.)	5,574	6,048	7,212	8,676	9,971	11,748	9,802	

606

Region (Capital)							
Fiji (7,083) / Suva (Cap.)	259,638 / 11,398	— / —	345,737 / 37,371	— / —	476,727 / 54,157	— / —	588,068 / 63,628	na / na
French Polynesia (1,544) / Papeete (Cap.)	55,424 / 12,417	62,678 / 15,214	76,327 / 17,288	84,551 / 19,903	98,400 / na	119,168 / 25,342	137,382 / na	na / na
Gilbert-Ellice Isl.[8] See Kiribati and Tuvalu respectively								
Guam[9] (209) / Agana city (Cap.) / Agana Heights	— / —	59,498 / 1,330 / 858	38,578 / 1,343 / 2,548	67,044 / 1,642 / 3,210	— / —	84,996 / 2,116 / 3,156	— / —	(p) 105,821 / na / na
Hawaii (6,425) / Honolulu (Cap.)	— / —	499,794 / 248,034	— / —	632,772 / 294,194	— / —	769,913 / 324,871	— / —	(p) 964,680 / 365,114
Kiribati (Gilbert) (264) / Tarawa (Cap.)	29,884	— / —	— / —	40,679	46,398	50,025	56,213 / 20,148	
Nauru (8)	2,855	3,473	—	4,613	6,057	—	7,254	
New Caledonia (7,335) / Nouméa (Cap.)	62,700 / —	65,500 / —	68,480 / 22,235	86,519 / 32,586	100,579 / 41,853	131,665 / 59,052	133,233 / 56,078	
New Zealand[10] (103,736) / Wellington (Cap.) / Aukland	1,720,671 / 123,771 / 123,457	1,939,472 / 120,072 / 127,406	2,174,062 / 122,070 / 136,540	2,414,984 / 123,969 / 143,583	2,676,919 / 131,655 / 149,989	2,862,631 / 136,782 / 151,580	3,129,383 / 138,938 / 150,708	3,175,737 / 135,094 / 144,963
Niue[11] (100) / Alofi (Cap.)	4,253 / 844	4,553 / —	4,707 / 989	4,864 / 1,107	5,194 / 1,117	4,990 / 1,045	3,578 / 960	
Norfolk Isl. (13)	938	942	—	844	1,147	1,683	—	
Pacific Isl., T.T.[12] (707)	—	54,843	70,724	—	—	115,251		na

International Population Charts (Continued)

COUNTRIES (areas in square miles), CAPITALS, AND MAJOR CITIES

— = No census in that five-year group
(p) = Provisional results
na = Not available
[blank cell] = Not known if taken or will take, 1980-84 column only

	1945-1949	1950-1954	1955-1959	1960-1964	1965-1969	1970-1974	1975-1979	1980-1984
Papua New Guinea[13] (178,260)	9,439	17,755	—	25,330	2,184,986	2,489,935	—	2,978,057
Port Moresby (Cap.)	—	—	—	—	41,848	76,507	—	123,624
Solomon Islands[14] (11,500)	—	—	124,076	—	—	160,998	196,823	
Honiara (Cap.)	—	—	3,548	—	—	11,191	14,942	
Tokelau Islands (4)	1,388	1,580	1,619	1,870	1,900	1,655	na	
Tonga (289)	—	—	56,838	—	77,429	—	90,085	
Nuku'alofa (Cap.)	—	—	9,202	—	15,685	—	18,312	
Tuvalu (Ellice) (10)	4,487	—	—	5,444	5,782	5,887	8,730	
Funafuti (Cap.)	—	—	—	—	—	—	2,120	
Vanuatu[15] (5,700)	—	—	4,026	—	77,988	—	112,596	
Vila (Cap.)	—	—	—	—	7,738	12,541	14,797	

Wallis-Futuna (106)	68,197	—	—	—	8,362	—	9,192	na
Mata Utu (Cap.)	—	—	—	—	566	—	558	na
Western Samoa (1,093)	—	84,909	97,327	114,427	131,377	146,627	151,983	na
Apia (Cap.)	—	11,840	18,153	21,153	25,480	30,261	32,099	na

NOTE: For exact date of the census, see entry for each country.

[1] Mexico. Since December 29, 1970, the boundaries of the Distrito Federal coincide with those of Mexico City. Data for the Mexico City Metropolitan Area were not available in the 1970 census but were estimated by the Centro de Estudios Económicos y Demográficos at 8,589,630. The 1980 census data for the same area are not yet available.

[2] Panama. The 1980 census included the Panama Canal Zone.

[3] Paraguay. The 1950 census excluded 12,881 persons not tabulated. The Indian jungle population was estimated at 17,000 persons, and underenumeration was calculated at 50,067. The 1970 total population excluded adjustments for underenumeration, and an allowance of 35,000 was estimated for jungle population. The population of Asunción in 1950 and 1962 included the region of Lambaré.

[4] Peru. The 1961 total population figure included estimated indigenous population.

[5] Puerto Rico. The city of Rio Piedras was annexed to San Juan in time for the 1970 census.

[6] St. Kitts-Nevis-Anguilla. The 1970 and 1980 total population figures excluded Anguilla.

[7] American Samoa. Tutuila was divided into three districts in 1974, and Swain Island was annexed to Manua.

[8] Gilbert and Ellice Islands. Ellice became independent in 1978 as Tuvalu and Gilbert in 1979 as Kiribati. The 1973 census of Gilbert and Ellice Islands did not include Phoenix and Southern Line Islands.

[9] Guam. The censuses of 1955 and 1958 were conducted by the municipal commissioners, and the figures for total population excluded personnel living on the military reservations.

[10] New Zealand. Figures for total population include the islands of Kermadec and Campbell and exclude New Zealand armed forces living overseas.

[11] Niue. A minicensus was taken in 1979.

[12] Pacific Islands, trust territory. The 1970 population figures exclude Kwajalein Island (3,960 persons).

[13] Papua New Guinea. Census figures up to 1961 included nonindigenous population only. From 1966 on, both segments of the population were enumerated.

[14] Solomon Islands. The Melanesian population in the 1959 census was only sampled and estimated at 117,620 persons.

[15] Vanuatu (New Hebrides). The 1957 census enumerated the nonnative population only. The urban census of 1972 covered only Port Vila and Luganville.

METROPOLITAN AREAS (pop. one million or more)
LATEST CENSUS FIGURES AVAILABLE

(C) = City limit because no metropolitan area
(MA) = Metropolitan area
(SMSA) = Standard Metropolitan Statistical Area

Country, Metropolitan Area	Population
ARGENTINA (1980)[1]	
Buenos Aires (Cap.)	2,908,001 (p)
Buenos Aires (Greater)	6,802,222 (p)
AUSTRALIA (1976)	
Sydney (MA)	3,021,982
Melbourne (MA)	2,604,035
BRAZIL (1980)	
São Paulo (MA)	12,578,045 (p)
Rio de Janeiro (MA)	9,018,961 (p)
Belo Horizonte (MA)	2,543,576 (p)
Recife (MA)	2,346,196 (p)
Pôrto Alegre (MA)	2,232,370 (p)
Salvador (MA)	1,766,075 (p)
Fortaleza (MA)	1,581,457 (p)
Curitiba (MA)	1,441,743 (p)
Brasília, DF (MA)	1,176,748 (p)
Belém (MA)	1,000,357 (p)
CANADA (1976)	
Toronto (MA)	2,803,101
Montreal (MA)	2,802,485
CHILE (1970)	
Santiago (Greater)	2,819,547
COLOMBIA (1973)	
Bogotá (Special District)	2,861,913
Medelín (C)	1,163,868
CUBA (1970)	
Havana (C)	2,152,570
MEXICO (1980)	
Mexico City (Cap.)[2]	9,373,353 (p)
Guadalajara (1970, C)	1,193,601
PERU (1972)	
Lima (MA)	3,302,523

Country, Metropolitan Area	Population
UNITED STATES (1980, SMSA's)	
New York	9,119,737
Los Angeles	7,477,657
Chicago	7,102,328
Philadelphia	4,716,818
Detroit	4,352,762
San Francisco	3,252,721
Washington, D.C.	3,060,240
Dallas-Fort Worth	2,974,878
Houston	2,905,350
Boston	2,763,357
Nassau-Suffolk	2,605,813
St. Louis	2,355,276
Pittsburgh	2,263,894
Baltimore	2,174,023
Minneapolis-St.Paul	2,114,256
Atlanta	2,029,618
Newark	1,965,304
Anaheim-Santa Ana-Garden Grove	1,931,570
Cleveland	1,898,720
San Diego	1,861,846
Miami	1,625,979
Denver-Boulder	1,619,921
Seattle-Everett	1,606,765
Tampa-St.Petersburg	1,569,492
Riverside-San Bernardino-Ontario	1,557,080
Phoenix	1,508,030
Cincinnati	1,401,403
Milwaukee	1,397,143
Kansas City	1,327,020
San Jose	1,295,071
Buffalo	1,242,573
Portland	1,242,187
New Orleans	1,186,725
Indianapolis	1,166,929
Columbus	1,093,293
San Antonio	1,071,954
Ft. Lauderdale-Hollywood	1,014,043
Sacramento	1,014,002
URUGUAY (1975)	
Montevideo (C)	1,173,254
VENEZUELA (1970)	
Caracas (MA)	2,183,935

1. The metropolitan area of Buenos Aires is generally considered as Gran Buenos Aires plus Capital Federal.
2. The metropolitan area of Mexico City according to the Centro de Estudios Económicos y Demográficos includes the Distrito Federal plus eleven municipalities of the State of Mexico. This figure, however, is not yet available.

International Topic Charts

AGE

S = single years
G = groups

LATIN AMERICA AND CARIBBEAN

	1945-1949	1950-1954	1955-1959	1960-1964	1965-1969	1970-1974	1975-1979	1980-1984
Antigua-Barbuda	SG			SG		G		
Argentina	SG			SG		SG		
Bahamas		SG		SG		SG		
Barbados	SG			SG		SG		
Belize	SG			SG		SG		
Bermuda		SG		SG		SG		
Bolivia		SG					SG	
Brazil		SG		SG		SG		
British Virgin Isl.	SG			SG		SG		

	C1	C2	C3	C4	C5
Cayman Isl.	SG		SG		
Chile	SG		SG	SG	
Colombia	SG		SG	G	
Costa Rica	SG		SG	SG	
Cuba	SG			SG	
Dominica	SG		SG		SG
Dominican Republic	SG		SG	SG	
Ecuador	SG		SG	G	
El Salvador	SG		S	SG	
Falkland Isl.	G		G	G	G
French Guiana	SG	SG	SG	SG	SG
Grenada	SG		SG	SG	SG
Guadeloupe	SG	SG	SG	G	
Guatemala	SG		SG	SG	
Guyana	SG		SG		SG

International Topic Charts (Continued)

AGE

	1945-1949	1950-1954	1955-1959	1960-1964	1965-1969	1970-1974	1975-1979	1980-1984
Haiti		G					SG	
Honduras	G	G		SG			SG	
Jamaica				SG			SG	
Martinique	SG	G		SG	SG		SG	
Mexico		SG		SG			SG	
Montserrat	SG			SG			SG	
Netherlands Antilles				S/SG	G		SG	
Nicaragua		SG		SG			SG	
Panama		G		SG			G	
Panama C.Z.		G		SG			SG	
Paraguay		G		SG			SG	

Peru				G		SG	
Puerto Rico			SG	SG		SG	SG
St. Kitts-Nevis		SG		SG		SG	SG
St. Lucia		SG		SG		SG	SG
St. Vincent		SG	SG	SG		SG	SG
Suriname			SG	SG		G	
Trinidad-Tobago		SG		SG		SG	SG
Turks-Caicos				SG		SG	
Uruguay				SG		SG	SG
Venezuela			SG	SG	SG	SG	
Virgin Isl. (U.S.)			G	SG	SG	SG	
NORTH AMERICA							
Canada		SG	SG	SG	SG	SG	SG
Greenland	SG		G	SG	SG	SG	SG
St. Pierre-Miquelon			SG	SG	SG	SG	
United States			SG	SG		SG	SG

International Topic Charts (Continued)

AGE

S = single years
G = groups

	1945-1949	1950-1954	1955-1959	1960-1964	1965-1969	1970-1974	1975-1979	1980-1984
OCEANIA								
American Samoa		G	SG	SG		SG/SG		
Australia	G	SG	SG	SG	SG	SG	SG	
Christmas Isl.	SG	G	G	G	G	G		
Cocos (Keeling) Isl.	SG	G	G	G	G			
Cook Isl.	G	G	G	G	SG		SG	
Fiji	SG	SG	SG	SG	SG	SG	SG	
French Polynesia	G	G	SG	SG	G	G	G	
Gilbert-Ellice Isl.	G			SG	SG	SG		
Guam		G		SG	SG	SG		
Hawaii		SG		SG	SG			

Country						
Kiribati (Gilbert)						SG
Nauru	G		G	G		G
New Caledonia	SG		SG	SG	SG	SG
New Zealand	SG		SG	SG	SG	SG
Niue	G				SG	SG
Norfolk	G		G	G	G	
Pacific Isl., T.T.	G	G	G	G	SG/SG	
Papua New Guinea			SG	SG	SG	SG
Solomon Isl.		G			SG	SG
Tokelau						
Tonga		SG		SG		SG
Tuvalu (Ellice)				SG		SG
Vanuatu (New Hebrides)		G		G	G	G
Wallis-Futuna				SG	SG	SG
Western Samoa	G	SG	SG	SG	SG	SG

CITIZENSHIP

X = tables present
/ = two censuses within the same group of years

LATIN AMERICA AND CARIBBEAN

	1945-1949	1950-1954	1955-1959	1960-1964	1965-1969	1970-1974	1975-1979	1980-1984
Antigua-Barbuda								
Argentina	X			X		X		
Bahamas						X		
Barbados								
Belize								
Bermuda		X		X		X		
Bolivia		X						
Brazil		X		X		X		
British Virgin Isl.								

Cayman Isl.					
Chile				X	
Colombia				X	
Costa Rica	X			X	
Cuba	X			X	
Dominica					
Dominican Republic			X	X	
Ecuador			X	X	
El Salvador	X		X	X	
Falkland Isl.	X		X		X
French Guiana		X	X		
Grenada					
Guadeloupe		X	X	X	
Guatemala			X		
Guyana					
Haiti	X			X	

International Topic Charts (Continued)

CITIZENSHIP

X = tables present
/ = two censuses within the same group of years

	1945-1949	1950-1954	1955-1959	1960-1964	1965-1969	1970-1974	1975-1979	1980-1984
Honduras	X		X	X			X	
Jamaica								
Martinique				X	X			
Mexico			X	X				
Montserrat								
Netherlands Antilles				X/X				
Nicaragua			X	X				
Panama			X	X				
Panama C.Z.			X			X		
Paraguay			X	X				
Peru			X			X		

Puerto Rico			X			
St. Kitts-Nevis						
St. Lucia						
St. Vincent						
Suriname			X			
Trinidad-Tobago						
Turks-Caicos						
Uruguay			X			
Venezuela	X		X		X	
Virgin Isl. (U.S.)	X		X		X	
NORTH AMERICA						
Canada	X		X		X	
Greenland	X	X	X			X
St. Pierre-Miquelon	X	X	X	X	X	
United States	X	X	X		X	

International Topic Charts (Continued)

CITIZENSHIP

X = tables present
/ = two censuses within the same group of years

	1945-1949	1950-1954	1955-1959	1960-1964	1965-1969	1970-1974	1975-1979	1980-1984
OCEANIA								
American Samoa						X		
Australia	X			X	X	X	X	
Christmas Isl.				X	X	X		
Cocos (Keeling) Isl.				X	X			
Cook Isl.	X							
Fiji	X							
French Polynesia	X		X	X		X		
Gilbert-Ellice Isl.								
Guam		X	X			X		
Hawaii		X				X		

	(1)	(2)	(3)	(4)	(5)	(6)
Kiribati (Gilbert)						
Nauru	X		X	X		
New Caledonia	X		X	X		
New Zealand		X				
Niue	X					
Norfolk	X		X	X	X	
Pacific Isl., T.T.					X/X	
Papua New Guinea	X		X	X	X	
Solomon Isl.						
Tokelau						
Tonga						
Tuvalu (Ellice)						
Vanuatu (New Hebrides)		X	X	X	X	
Wallis-Futuna			X	X	X	X
Western Samoa	X					X

International Topic Charts (Continued)

DE FACTO, DE JURE

DF = *De facto*
DJ = *De jure*
/ = Two censuses within the same group of years

	1945-1949	1950-1954	1955-1959	1960-1964	1965-1969	1970-1974	1975-1979	1980-1984
LATIN AMERICA AND CARIBBEAN								
Antigua-Barbuda	DF			DF + DJ		DF + DJ		
Argentina	DF			DF		DF		
Bahamas			DF	DJ		DJ		
Barbados	DF			DF		DF		
Belize	DF			DF + DJ		DF		
Bermuda		DF + DJ		DF		DF		
Bolivia		DF					DF	
Brazil		DF + DJ		DF + DJ		DF + DJ		DF + DJ
British Virgin Isl.	DF			DF + DJ		DF		

Country				
Cayman Isl.		DF + DJ		DF
Chile	DF	DF		DF
Colombia	DF	DF		DF
Costa Rica	DJ	DJ		DJ
Cuba	DJ			DJ
Dominica	DF	DF		DF
Dominican Republic	DF + DJ	DF		DF
Ecuador	DJ	DF		DF
El Salvador	DF	DF		DF
Falkland Isl.	DF	DF		DF
French Guiana	DF + DJ	DJ	DJ	DF
Grenada	DF	DF		DF
Guadeloupe	DF + DJ	DF + DJ	DJ	DF
Guatemala	DF	DF		DJ
Guyana	DF	DF		DF

International Topic Charts (Continued)

DE FACTO, DE JURE

DF = *De facto*
DJ = *De jure*
/ = Two censuses within the same group of years

	1945-1949	1950-1954	1955-1959	1960-1964	1965-1969	1970-1974	1975-1979	1980-1984
Haiti		DJ				DJ		
Honduras		DF		DF		DJ		
Jamaica				DF + DJ		DJ		
Martinique	DF	DF + DJ		DF + DJ	DJ			
Mexico		DJ		DJ		DJ		
Montserrat	DF			DF + DJ		DF		DF
Netherlands Antilles				DJ/DJ	DJ	DJ		
Nicaragua		DF		DF		DF		
Panama		DF		DF		DF		
Panama C.Z.		DJ		DJ		DJ		
Paraguay		DF		DF		DF		

626

Peru			DF		DF		
Puerto Rico	DJ		DJ		DJ		
St. Kitts-Nevis	DF		DF + DJ		DF + DJ		
St. Lucia	DF		DF		DF		
St. Vincent	DF		DF		DF		
Suriname		DJ	DF		DJ		
Trinidad-Tobago	DF		DF		DF		
Turks-Caicos			DF + DJ		DF + DJ		
Uruguay			DF			DF	
Venezuela		DF	DF		DJ		
Virgin Isl. (U.S.)		DJ	DJ		DJ		DJ
NORTH AMERICA							
Canada		DJ	DJ	DJ	DJ	DJ	
Greenland	DJ	DJ	DF	DJ	DJ	DJ	
St. Pierre-Miquelon		DF	DF	DF	DF		
United States		DJ	DJ		DJ		DJ

627

DE FACTO, DE JURE

DF = De facto
DJ = De jure
/ = Two censuses within the same group of years

	1945-1949	1950-1954	1955-1959	1960-1964	1965-1969	1970-1974	1975-1979	1980-1984
OCEANIA								
American Samoa		DJ	DF	DJ		DJ/DF		
Australia	DF	DF		DF	DF	DF	DF	
Christmas Isl.	DF		DF	DF	DF	DF		
Cocos (Keeling) Isl.	DF		DF	DF	DF			
Cook Isl.	DF		DF	DF	DF		DF	
Fiji	DF		DF	DF	DF		DF	
French Polynesia	DF		DF + DJ	DF + DJ			DF + DJ	
Gilbert-Ellice Isl.	DF			DF	DF	DF		
Guam		DJ		DJ		DJ		DJ
Hawaii		DJ		DJ		DJ		DJ

	1	2	3	4	5	6	7
Kiribati (Gilbert)							DF
Nauru	DF	DF		DF	DF	DF	DF + DJ
New Caledonia	DF	DF	DJ	DJ	DJ	DJ	DJ
New Zealand	DF	DF	DF	DF	DF	DF	DF
Niue	DF	DF	DF	DF	DF	DF	DF
Norfolk	DF	DF		DF	DF	DF	
Pacific Isl., T.T.	DF		DJ		DJ	DJ/DF	
Papua New Guinea	DF	DF		DF	DF + DJ	DF + DJ	DF + DJ
Solomon Isl.	DF		DJ	DF	DF	DF	DF
Tokelau	DF	DF	DF	DF	DF	DF	
Tonga			DF	DF	DF	DF	DJ
Tuvalu (Ellice)						DF	DF
Vanuatu (New Hebrides)			DF	DF	DF	DF	DF + DJ
Wallis-Futuna					DJ	DJ	DJ
Western Samoa	DF		DF	DF	DF	DF	DF

International Topic Charts (Continued)

EDUCATION

L = literacy
S = school enrollment
A = educational attainment
/ = two censuses within this group of years

LATIN AMERICA AND CARIBBEAN

	1945-1949	1950-1954	1955-1959	1960-1964	1965-1969	1970-1974	1975-1979	1980-1984
Antigua-Barbuda	LS				SA	A		
Argentina	L				LSA	LSA		
Bahamas			L		LSA	A		
Barbados	LS				LSA	SA		
Belize	LS				SA	SA		
Bermuda			L		LA	SA		
Bolivia		LSA						LSA
Brazil		LA			LSA	LSA		

Country				
British Virgin Isl.	LS		LS	SA
Cayman Isl.			LSA	SA
Chile		LSA	LSA	LSA
Colombia		LA	LA	LSA
Costa Rica		LSA	LSA	LSA
Cuba		LSA		LSA
Dominica	L		SA	SA
Dominican Republic		LSA	LSA	LSA
Ecuador		LA	LSA	LSA
El Salvador		LSA	LSA	LSA
Falkland Isl.	S	S	S	S
French Guiana		LA	LA	LA
Grenada	LS		SA	SA
Guadeloupe		LA	LA	LA
Guatemala		LSA	LSA	LSA
Guyana	LS		SA	SA

International Topic Charts (Continued)

EDUCATION

L = literacy
S = school enrollment
A = educational attainment
/ = two censuses within this group of years

	1945-1949	1950-1954	1955-1959	1960-1964	1965-1969	1970-1974	1975-1979	1980-1984
Haiti		LA						LSA
Honduras	LSA	LA		LSA				LSA
Jamaica				LSA				SA
Martinique	LSA	LA		LA	LA			S
Mexico		LSA		LSA				LSA
Montserrat	LS			LSA				SA
Netherlands Antilles				SA/LSA				SA
Nicaragua		LSA		LSA				LSA
Panama		LSA		LSA				LSA
Panama C.Z.		SA		SA				SA
Paraguay		LSA		LSA				LSA

Country					
Peru			LSA	LSA	
Puerto Rico		LSA	LSA	LSA	
St. Kitts-Nevis	LS		LSA	SA	
St. Lucia	L		SA	SA	
St. Vincent	L		SA	SA	
Suriname			A		
Trinidad-Tobago	L		SA	SA	
Turks-Caicos			LSA	SA	
Uruguay			LSA		LSA
Venezuela		LSA	LSA	LSA	
Virgin Isl. (U.S.)		SA	SA	SA	
NORTH AMERICA					
Canada		SA	SA		SA
Greenland		SA	SA	SA	
St. Pierre-Miquelon	LA	LA	LA	A	
United States		SA	SA	SA	SA

International Topic Charts (Continued)

EDUCATION

L = literacy
S = school enrollment
A = educational attainment
/ = two censuses within this group of years

	1945-1949	1950-1954	1955-1959	1960-1964	1965-1969	1970-1974	1975-1979	1980-1984
OCEANIA								
American Samoa		SA		SA		SA/SA	SA	SA
Australia					SA	SA	SA	
Christmas Isl.			L					
Cocos (Keeling) Isl.			L					
Cook Isl.			L		SA		SA	SA
Fiji		LSA			LA		SA	SA
French Polynesia		LA	LA	LA		LA	LA	
Gilbert-Ellice Isl.		LS			S	SA		
Guam		SA		SA		SA		

Kiribati (Gilbert)						SA
Nauru						
New Caledonia	A	LA	LA	LA		LSA
New Zealand				SA	SA	SA
Niue	L			SA	SA	
Norfolk						
Pacific Isl., T.T.		A	A		SA/SA	
Papua New Guinea				LSA	LSA	
Solomon Isl.					LS	SA
Tokelau						
Tonga						LSA
Tuvalu (Ellice)						SA
Vanuatu (New Hebrides)		LA	LA	S		
Wallis-Futuna				LA		
Western Samoa	LS	S	S	LSA	LSA	SA

635

International Topic Charts (Continued)

ETHNIC AND RACIAL ORIGIN AND LANGUAGE

R = Ethnic and racial origin
L = Language
/ = two censuses within the same group of years

LATIN AMERICA AND CARIBBEAN

	1945-1949	1950-1954	1955-1959	1960-1964	1965-1969	1970-1974	1975-1979	1980-1984
Antigua-Barbuda	R				R		R	
Argentina								
Bahamas			R					
Barbados	R				R		R	
Belize	RL				RL		R	
Bermuda			R		RL		R	
Bolivia			RL	RL				L
Brazil				RL	R		R	
British Virgin Isl.	R				R		R	

Cayman Isl.			R		R
Chile					
Colombia					
Costa Rica		RL	R		
Cuba		R	R		R
Dominica	RL		RL		R
Dominican Republic		RL	RL		
Ecuador			L		
El Salvador	R	R	R		R
Falkland Isl.	R	R	R		R
French Guiana	R	R	R	R	
Grenada	R	R	R	R	R
Guadeloupe		R			R
Guatemala		RL	RL		R
Guyana	R	R			R
Haiti		R			R

International Topic Charts (Continued)

ETHNIC AND RACIAL ORIGIN AND LANGUAGE

R = Ethnic and racial origin
L = Language
/ = two censuses within the same group of years

	1945-1949	1950-1954	1955-1959	1960-1964	1965-1969	1970-1974	1975-1979	1980-1984
Honduras	R							
Jamaica				R		R		
Martinique		R		R	R			
Mexico		L		L		L		
Montserrat		R		R		R		
Netherlands Antilles				R/RL	R	R		
Nicaragua		L		L				
Panama		L						
Panama C.Z.		R		R				
Paraguay		L		L				
Peru		L						L

Puerto Rico		RL	L	L
St. Kitts-Nevis	R		R	R
St. Lucia	RL		R	RL
St. Vincent	R		R	R
Suriname		R	RL	R
Trinidad-Tobago	R		R	R
Turks-Caicos			R	R
Uruguay				
Venezuela			R	R
Virgin Isl. (U.S.)		R	R	R
NORTH AMERICA				
Canada		RL	RL	RL
Greenland				
St. Pierre-Miquelon		R	R	R
United States		R	RL	RL

639

International Topic Charts (Continued)

ETHNIC AND RACIAL ORIGIN AND LANGUAGE

R = Ethnic and racial origin
L = Language
/ = two censuses within the same group of years

	1945-1949	1950-1954	1955-1959	1960-1964	1965-1969	1970-1974	1975-1979	1980-1984
OCEANIA								
American Samoa		RL		R		R		
Australia	R	R		R	R	R		RL
Christmas Isl.			R	R	R	R		
Cocos (Keeling) Isl.	R		R	R				
Cook Isl.	R		R	R	R			R
Fiji	RL		RL		RL			R
French Polynesia	R		R	RL	R	R		R
Gilbert-Ellice Isl.	RL			R	R	R		
Guam		R		R				
Hawaii		R		RL		RL		

Country							
Kiribati (Gilbert)	R						R
Nauru	R	R	R		R		R
New Caledonia	R	R	R	R	R	R	R
New Zealand	R	R	R	R	R		R
Niue	R				R		R
Norfolk	R	R	R		R	R	
Pacific Isl., T.T.			RL				
Papua New Guinea	R	R	R	RL	R	R	R
Solomon Isl.		R		R			R
Tokelau	R						
Tonga		R		R	R		R
Tuvalu (Ellice)						RL	R
Vanuatu (New Hebrides)				R		R	
Wallis-Futuna		R		R	R	R	
Western Samoa	R	R	R	RL	RL	L	RL

641

International Topic Charts (Continued)

FERTILITY

B = Children ever born
S = Still living
/ = two censuses within the same group of years

	1945-1949	1950-1954	1955-1959	1960-1964	1965-1969	1970-1974	1975-1979	1980-1984
LATIN AMERICA AND CARIBBEAN								
Antigua-Barbuda	BS			B				
Argentina				B		BS		
Bahamas				B				
Barbados	BS			B		B		
Belize	BS			B		B		
Bermuda		BS		BS		BS		
Bolivia								BS
Brazil		BS		BS		BS		
British Virgin Isl.	S			B		B		

	1	2	3	4
Cayman Isl.			B	B
Chile			B	BS
Colombia				BS
Costa Rica				BS
Cuba		B		BS
Dominica	BS		B	B
Dominican Republic		B		BS
Ecuador				BS
El Salvador				BS
Falkland Isl.				
French Guiana	BS			
Grenada	BS	B	B	
Guadeloupe			B	
Guatemala	BS		B	BS
Guyana			B	B

643

International Topic Charts (Continued)

FERTILITY

B = Children ever born
S = Still living
/ = two censuses within the same group of years

	1945-1949	1950-1954	1955-1959	1960-1964	1965-1969	1970-1974	1975-1979	1980-1984
Haiti						B		
Honduras								
Jamaica				B		B		
Martinique	BS	B			B			
Mexico		B		B		B		
Montserrat	BS			B		BS		
Netherlands Antilles				B/B		BS		
Nicaragua				B		BS		
Panama		B				B		
Panama C.Z.				B		B		
Paraguay				B		BS		

Peru				B	BS
Puerto Rico		B		B	B
St. Kitts-Nevis	B			B	B
St. Lucia	BS			B	B
St. Vincent	BS			B	B
Suriname				BS	
Trinidad-Tobago	BS			B	B
Turks-Caicos				B	B
Uruguay						BS
Venezuela	B			B	B
Virgin Isl. (U.S.)				B	B

NORTH AMERICA

Canada				B	B
Greenland				B	
St. Pierre-Miquelon		BS	B	B	
United States		B		B	B

International Topic Charts (Continued)

FERTILITY

B = Children ever born
S = Still living
/ = two censuses within the same group of years

OCEANIA

	1945-1949	1950-1954	1955-1959	1960-1964	1965-1969	1970-1974	1975-1979	1980-1984
American Samoa			S	B		B/BS	BS	BS
Australia		BS			B	BS	BS	
Christmas Isl.		BS						
Cocos (Keeling) Isl.		BS						
Cook Isl.			B	B	BS		BS	
Fiji		BS	BS		BS		BS	
French Polynesia		BS	B					
Gilbert-Ellice Isl.		BS		BS	BS	BS		
Guam				B	B	B		
Hawaii	B			B	B			

646

Country						
Kiribati (Gilbert)						BS
Nauru						B
New Caledonia	BS	BS		B	B	B
New Zealand					B	BS
Niue					S	S
Norfolk						
Pacific Isl., T.T.			B	B	B/BS	B/BS
Papua New Guinea					B	B
Solomon Isl.			BS	BS	BS	BS
Tokelau						
Tonga			BS	BS	BS	BS
Tuvalu (Ellice)			BS			BS
Vanuatu (New Hebrides)			B	B		B
Wallis-Futuna				B		
Western Samoa		B	BS	BS	BS	BS

International Topic Charts (Continued)

HOUSEHOLD COMPOSITION

X = Tables present
/ = two censuses within the same group of years

	1945-1949	1950-1954	1955-1959	1960-1964	1965-1969	1970-1974	1975-1979	1980-1984
LATIN AMERICA AND CARIBBEAN								
Antigua-Barbuda	X			X				
Argentina				X		X		
Bahamas						X		
Barbados	X			X		X		
Belize	X			X		X		
Bermuda								
Bolivia			X				X	
Brazil			X	X		X		
British Virgin Isl.	X			X				

	1	2	3	4	5
Cayman Isl.	X				
Chile	X		X	X	
Colombia	X		X	X	
Costa Rica	X		X	X	
Cuba	X			X	
Dominica	X		X		
Dominican Republic	X		X	X	
Ecuador	X		X	X	
El Salvador	X		X	X	
Falkland Isl.					
French Guiana		X	X	X	
Grenada					X
Guadeloupe		X	X	X	
Guatemala	X		X		
Guyana	X		X		X
Haiti	X			X	

International Topic Charts (Continued)

HOUSEHOLD COMPOSITION

X = Tables present
/ = two censuses within the same group of years

	1945-1949	1950-1954	1955-1959	1960-1964	1965-1969	1970-1974	1975-1979	1980-1984
Honduras				X		X		
Jamaica				X				
Martinique	X			X	X			
Mexico		X		X		X		
Montserrat				X		X		X
Netherlands Antilles					X			
Nicaragua		X		X				
Panama		X		X		X		
Panama C.Z.						X		
Paraguay								
Peru								

Puerto Rico		X		X		X	
St. Kitts-Nevis		X		X			X
St. Lucia		X		X			X
St. Vincent		X		X			
Suriname				X		X	
Trinidad-Tobago		X		X			X
Turks-Caicos		X		X			
Uruguay	X	X		X			
Venezuela		X		X		X	
Virgin Isl. (U.S.)		X		X	X		
NORTH AMERICA							
Canada	X	X	X	X		X	
Greenland	X	X	X	X		X	
St. Pierre-Miquelon		X	X	X			
United States		X		X		X	

651

International Topic Charts (Continued)

HOUSEHOLD COMPOSITION

X = Tables present
/ = two censuses within the same group of years

	1945-1949	1950-1954	1955-1959	1960-1964	1965-1969	1970-1974	1975-1979	1980-1984
OCEANIA								
American Samoa		X				X/X		
Australia	X			X	X	X	X	
Christmas Isl.								
Cocos (Keeling) Isl.								
Cook Isl.								
Fiji	X		X		X		X	
French Polynesia			X	X	X		X	
Gilbert-Ellice Isl.						X		
Guam		X		X		X		
Hawaii	X			X		X		

Kiribati (Gilbert)	X					
Nauru	X		X	X		X
New Caledonia					X	
New Zealand	X	X	X	X	X	X
Niue	X	X				
Norfolk						
Pacific Isl., T.T.		X/X				
Papua New Guinea		X	X	X		X
Solomon Isl.	X	X				
Tokelau						
Tonga	X					
Tuvalu (Ellice)	X	X				
Vanuatu (New Hebrides)					X	
Wallis-Futuna	X		X	X		
Western Samoa	X	X	X	X		

International Topic Charts (Continued)

INCOME

X = Tables present

/ = two censuses within the same group of years

LATIN AMERICA AND CARIBBEAN

	1945-1949	1950-1954	1955-1959	1960-1964	1965-1969	1970-1974	1975-1979	1980-1984
Antigua-Barbuda								
Argentina								
Bahamas							X	
Barbados		X		X		X		
Belize						X		
Bermuda								
Bolivia								
Brazil				X		X		
British Virgin Isl.						X		

Cayman Isl.	X		
Chile			
Colombia			
Costa Rica	X	X	
Cuba			
Dominica			
Dominican Republic		X	X
Ecuador			
El Salvador			
Falkland Isl.			
French Guiana			
Grenada	X	X	
Guadeloupe			
Guatemala			
Guyana	X		
Haiti			

International Topic Charts (Continued)

INCOME

X = Tables present
/ = two censuses within the same group of years

	1945-1949	1950-1954	1955-1959	1960-1964	1965-1969	1970-1974	1975-1979	1980-1984
Honduras								
Jamaica				X		X		
Martinique								
Mexico		X		X		X		
Montserrat						X		
Netherlands Antilles				X/X		X		
Nicaragua								
Panama		X		X		X		
Panama C.Z.				X		X		
Paraguay								
Peru				X		X		

	Col 1	Col 2	Col 3
Puerto Rico	X	X	X
St. Kitts-Nevis	X		
St. Lucia	X		
St. Vincent	X		
Suriname			
Trinidad-Tobago	X		
Turks-Caicos	X		
Uruguay			
Venezuela	X	X	X
Virgin Isl. (U.S.)	X	X	X
NORTH AMERICA			
Canada	X	X	X
Greenland			
St. Pierre-Miquelon			
United States	X	X	X

International Topic Charts (Continued)

INCOME

X = Tables present
/ = two censuses within the same group of years

	1945-1949	1950-1954	1955-1959	1960-1964	1965-1969	1970-1974	1975-1979	1980-1984
OCEANIA								
American Samoa				X		X		
Australia								X
Christmas Isl.								
Cocos (Keeling) Isl.								
Cook Isl.					X			
Fiji								
French Polynesia								
Gilbert-Ellice Isl.								
Guam				X		X		
Hawaii		X		X		X		

Country						
Kiribati (Gilbert)						
Nauru	X					
New Caledonia		X				
New Zealand		X	X	X	X	X
Niue			X	X		X
Norfolk				X		
Pacific Isl., T.T.			X			
Papua New Guinea						
Solomon Isl.						
Tokelau						
Tonga						
Tuvalu (Ellice)						
Vanuatu (New Hebrides)						
Wallis-Futuna						
Western Samoa						

International Topic Charts (Continued)

INDUSTRY

X = Tables present
/ = two censuses within the same group of years

	1945-1949	1950-1954	1955-1959	1960-1964	1965-1969	1970-1974	1975-1979	1980-1984
LATIN AMERICA AND CARIBBEAN								
Antigua-Barbuda				X		X		
Argentina				X		X		
Bahamas				X		X		
Barbados				X		X		
Belize				X		X		
Bermuda				X		X		
Bolivia		X						X
Brazil		X		X		X		
British Virgin Isl.				X		X		

Country					
Cayman Isl.	X		X		
Chile	X		X	X	
Colombia	X		X	X	
Costa Rica	X		X	X	
Cuba	X			X	
Dominica			X		X
Dominican Republic	X		X	X	
Ecuador	X		X	X	
El Salvador	X		X	X	
Falkland Isl.	X				
French Guiana		X	X		X
Grenada	X		X		X
Guadeloupe	X		X	X	
Guatemala	X	X	X		X
Guyana	X		X	X	
Haiti	X		X		

International Topic Charts (Continued)

INDUSTRY

X = Tables present
/ = two censuses within the same group of years

	1945-1949	1950-1954	1955-1959	1960-1964	1965-1969	1970-1974	1975-1979	1980-1984
Honduras		X		X		X		
Jamaica				X		X		
Martinique	X			X	X	X		
Mexico		X		X		X		
Montserrat	X			X		X		
Netherlands Antilles				X/X		X		
Nicaragua		X		X		X		
Panama		X		X		X		
Panama C.Z.		X		X		X		
Paraguay		X		X		X		
Peru				X		X		

	1	2	3	4	5	6	7
Puerto Rico		X		X		X	
St. Kitts-Nevis		X		X			X
St. Lucia		X		X			X
St. Vincent		X		X			X
Suriname				X			
Trinidad-Tobago		X		X			X
Turks-Caicos		X		X			
Uruguay	X			X			
Venezuela		X		X		X	
Virgin Isl. (U.S.)		X		X		X	
NORTH AMERICA							
Canada		X		X		X	
Greenland	X	X	X	X	X	X	
St. Pierre-Miquelon		X	X	X	X	X	
United States		X		X		X	

International Topic Charts (Continued)

INDUSTRY

X = Tables present
/ = two censuses within the same group of years

OCEANIA

	1945-1949	1950-1954	1955-1959	1960-1964	1965-1969	1970-1974	1975-1979	1980-1984
American Samoa				X		X		
Australia	X	X		X	X	X	X	
Christmas Isl.	X		X	X	X	X		
Cocos (Keeling) Isl.	X		X	X	X			
Cook Isl.	X				X		X	
Fiji	X		X	X	X		X	
French Polynesia		X	X	X		X		
Gilbert-Ellice Isl.	X			X	X	X		
Guam		X		X	X	X		
Hawaii		X		X	X	X		

664

	1	2	3	4	5	6	7
Kiribati (Gilbert)							X
Nauru	X	X		X	X		
New Caledonia	X	X	X	X	X		X
New Zealand	X	X	X	X	X	X	X
Niue	X					X	X
Norfolk	X	X		X	X	X	
Pacific Isl., T.T.						X/X	
Papua New Guinea	X	X		X	X	X	
Solomon Isl.							X
Tokelau							
Tonga			X		X		X
Tuvalu (Ellice)							X
Vanuatu (New Hebrides)			X		X		
Wallis-Futuna					X	X	X
Western Samoa			X	X	X		X

International Topic Charts (Continued)

MARITAL STATUS

X = Tables present
/ = two censuses within the same group of years

LATIN AMERICA AND CARIBBEAN

	1945-1949	1950-1954	1955-1959	1960-1964	1965-1969	1970-1974	1975-1979	1980-1984
Antigua-Barbuda	X			X		X		
Argentina	X			X		X		
Bahamas		X		X		X		
Barbados	X			X		X		
Belize	X			X		X		
Bermuda		X		X		X		
Bolivia		X						X
Brazil		X		X		X		
British Virgin Isl.	X			X		X		

Cayman Isl.	X				
Chile	X		X	X	
Colombia	X		X	X	
Costa Rica	X		X	X	
Cuba	X		X	X	
Dominica	X				X
Dominican Republic	X		X	X	
Ecuador	X		X	X	
El Salvador	X		X	X	
Falkland Isl.	X		X	X	X
French Guiana		X	X	X	X
Grenada	X			X	X
Guadeloupe		X	X	X	
Guatemala	X		X	X	X
Guyana	X				X
Haiti	X		X		

International Topic Charts (Continued)

X = Tables present
/ = two censuses within the same group of years

MARITAL STATUS

	1945-1949	1950-1954	1955-1959	1960-1964	1965-1969	1970-1974	1975-1979	1980-1984
Honduras	X	X		X		X		
Jamaica				X		X		
Martinique	X	X		X	X	X		
Mexico		X		X		X		
Montserrat	X			X		X		
Netherlands Antilles				X/X	X	X		
Nicaragua		X		X		X		
Panama		X		X		X		
Panama C.Z.		X		X		X		
Paraguay		X		X		X		
Peru				X		X		

	1	2	3	4	5	6	7
Puerto Rico		X		X		X	
St. Kitts-Nevis		X		X			X
St. Lucia		X		X			X
St. Vincent		X		X			X
Suriname				X		X	
Trinidad-Tobago		X		X			X
Turks-Caicos		X		X			
Uruguay	X			X			
Venezuela		X		X		X	
Virgin Isl. (U.S.)		X				X	
NORTH AMERICA							
Canada	X	X	X	X	X	X	
Greenland	X	X	X	X	X	X	X
St. Pierre-Miquelon		X	X	X	X	X	
United States		X		X		X	

International Topic Charts (Continued)

MARITAL STATUS

X = Tables present
/ = two censuses within the same group of years

OCEANIA

	1945-1949	1950-1954	1955-1959	1960-1964	1965-1969	1970-1974	1975-1979	1980-1984
American Samoa			X		X	X/X		
Australia	X		X		X	X	X	
Christmas Isl.	X			X	X	X		
Cocos (Keeling) Isl.	X			X	X			
Cook Isl.			X		X	X	X	
Fiji	X		X		X		X	
French Polynesia	X		X	X	X		X	
Gilbert-Ellice Isl.	X			X	X	X		
Guam			X	X	X	X		
Hawaii			X	X	X	X		

Kiribati (Gilbert)	X						
Nauru	X		X	X		X	X
New Caledonia	X	X	X	X	X	X	X
New Zealand	X	X	X	X		X	X
Niue	X	X					
Norfolk		X	X	X		X	X
Pacific Isl., T.T.		X/X			X		
Papua New Guinea		X	X	X		X	X
Solomon Isl.	X	X	X		X		
Tokelau							
Tonga	X	X	X	X	X		
Tuvalu (Ellice)							
Vanuatu (New Hebrides)		X	X	X	X	X	
Wallis-Futuna	X		X				X
Western Samoa	X	X	X	X		X	X

International Topic Charts (Continued)

MIGRATION

U = Usual place
P = Previous place
D = Duration of residence
/ = two censuses within the same group of years

	1945-1949	1950-1954	1955-1959	1960-1964	1965-1969	1970-1974	1975-1979	1980-1984
LATIN AMERICA AND CARIBBEAN								
Antigua-Barbuda	UD			UD		U		
Argentina				UDP		UDP		
Bahamas				UD				
Barbados	D			UDP		UDP		
Belize				UD		UD		
Bermuda			UD	UD		U		
Bolivia							UP	
Brazil			U	UDP		UDP		

British Virgin Isl.	U	UD		UD
Cayman Isl.	U	UD		
Chile	UDP	UDP		
Colombia	DP	DP		
Costa Rica	UD	UDP	U	
Cuba	UD		UD	
Dominica	U	UD		UD
Dominican Republic				
Ecuador	UDP	DP	U	
El Salvador	UP		U	
Falkland Isl.				
French Guiana	U	U		
Grenada	U	UD		D
Guadeloupe	U	U		U
Guatemala	UP	DP	UP	UP
Guyana	UDP	UD		

International Topic Charts (Continued)

MIGRATION

U = Usual place
P = Previous place
D = Duration of residence
/ = two censuses within the same group of years

	1945-1949	1950-1954	1955-1959	1960-1964	1965-1969	1970-1974	1975-1979	1980-1984
Haiti		U				UDP		
Honduras						UDP		
Jamaica				UD		UDP		
Martinique	UD	U		U	U			
Mexico		U		UDP		UDP		
Montserrat		U		UDP		UD		
Netherlands Antilles				UD/UD		UD		
Nicaragua						UP		
Panama				DP		UP		
Panama C.Z.		U		U		UDP		

Paraguay		UP	D	
Peru		UDP	D	
Puerto Rico		UDP	UP	U
St. Kitts-Nevis		U	UD	D
St. Lucia		U	UD	D
St. Vincent		U	UD	D
Suriname			UDP	U
Trinidad-Tobago		UDP	UD	D
Turks-Caicos		UD	U	
Uruguay	UDP		DP	
Venezuela		UDP	UD	D
Virgin Isl. (U.S.)		UP	U	U
NORTH AMERICA				
Canada		UP	UP	UD
Greenland		U	U	U
St. Pierre-Miquelon		U	U	
United States		UDP	UDP	UDP

675

International Topic Charts (Continued)

MIGRATION

U = Usual place
P = Previous place
D = Duration of residence
/ = two censuses within the same group of years

	1945-1949	1950-1954	1955-1959	1960-1964	1965-1969	1970-1974	1975-1979	1980-1984
OCEANIA								
American Samoa		U		U		UP/U		
Australia	D	D		D	D	UDP	UDP	
Christmas Isl.	D			D	D	D		
Cocos (Keeling) Isl.	D		D	D	D			
Cook Isl.	D				UD		UP	
Fiji	UD						UP	
French Polynesia	D	UD	UD	U		UP	UDP	
Gilbert-Ellice Isl.	UD					UP		
Guam		U		U		UDP		

676

Hawaii		UP		UDP		UDP	UD	
Kiribati (Gilbert)							UD	
Nauru	D	D		D	D			
New Caledonia	U	U	U	UD	D	U	UP	
New Zealand	UD	UD	UD	UD	UDP	UDP	UD	
Niue	D	D		D	UD	D	UD	
Norfolk	D	D		D	D	D		
Pacific Isl., T.T.		D	U	D		UP/U		
Papua New Guinea	D			UD	UD	UD		U
Solomon Isl.			U		D			
Tokelau							UD	
Tonga							UD	
Tuvalu (Ellice)							UD	
Vanuatu (New Hebrides)						D	U	
Wallis-Futuna							UDP	
Western Samoa					UP	UP	UP	

International Topic Charts (Continued)

OCCUPATION

X = Tables present
/ = two censuses within the same group of years

	1945-1949	1950-1954	1955-1959	1960-1964	1965-1969	1970-1974	1975-1979	1980-1984
LATIN AMERICA AND CARIBBEAN								
Antigua-Barbuda	X				X	X		
Argentina	X				X	X		
Bahamas		X			X	X		
Barbados	X				X	X		
Belize	X				X	X		
Bermuda		X			X	X		
Bolivia		X					X	
Brazil		X			X	X		
British Virgin Isl.	X				X	X		

Country					
Cayman Isl.	X		X		
Chile	X		X	X	
Colombia	X		X	X	
Costa Rica	X		X	X	
Cuba	X			X	
Dominica	X		X		X
Dominican Republic	X		X	X	
Ecuador	X		X	X	
El Salvador	X		X	X	
Falkland Isl.	X		X	X	X
French Guiana		X	X		X
Grenada	X		X	X	X
Guadeloupe	X	X	X	X	
Guatemala	X		X	X	
Guyana	X		X	X	X
Haiti	X			X	

International Topic Charts (Continued)

X = Tables present
/ = two censuses within the same group of years

OCCUPATION

	1945-1949	1950-1954	1955-1959	1960-1964	1965-1969	1970-1974	1975-1979	1980-1984
Honduras	X	X		X		X		
Jamaica		X		X		X		
Martinique	X	X		X	X	X		
Mexico		X		X		X		
Montserrat	X			X		X		
Netherlands Antilles				X/X		X		
Nicaragua		X		X		X		
Panama		X		X		X		
Panama C.Z.		X		X		X		
Paraguay		X		X		X		
Peru				X		X		

Puerto Rico		X		X		X
St. Kitts-Nevis	X			X		X
St. Lucia	X			X		X
St. Vincent	X			X		X
Suriname				X		
Trinidad-Tobago	X			X		X
Turks-Caicos				X		X
Uruguay				X		
Venezuela		X		X		X
Virgin Isl. (U.S.)		X		X		X
NORTH AMERICA						
Canada	X	X		X		X
Greenland	X		X	X	X	X
St. Pierre-Miquelon		X	X	X	X	X
United States		X		X		X

International Topic Charts (Continued)

OCCUPATION

X = Tables present
/ = two censuses within the same group of years

OCEANIA

	1945-1949	1950-1954	1955-1959	1960-1964	1965-1969	1970-1974	1975-1979	1980-1984
American Samoa		X		X		X/X		
Australia	X			X	X	X	X	
Christmas Isl.	X		X	X	X	X		
Cocos (Keeling) Isl.	X		X	X	X			
Cook Isl.	X		X	X	X		X	
Fiji	X		X	X	X		X	
French Polynesia	X	X	X	X			X	
Gilbert-Ellice Isl.	X					X		
Guam		X		X		X		
Hawaii		X		X		X		

682

Kiribati (Gilbert)	X						
Nauru				X		X	X
New Caledonia	X		X	X	X	X	X
New Zealand	X	X	X	X	X	X	X
Niue	X	X	X				X
Norfolk		X	X	X			
Pacific Isl., T.T.		X/X			X		
Papua New Guinea		X	X	X			
Solomon Isl.	X						
Tokelau							
Tonga	X				X		
Tuvalu (Ellice)	X						
Vanuatu (New Hebrides)		X			X		
Wallis-Futuna	X		X				
Western Samoa	X	X	X	X	X	X	

International Topic Charts (Continued)

OCCUPATIONAL STATUS

X = Tables present
/ = two censuses within the same group of years

LATIN AMERICA AND CARIBBEAN

	1945-1949	1950-1954	1955-1959	1960-1964	1965-1969	1970-1974	1975-1979	1980-1984
Antigua-Barbuda	X			X		X		
Argentina	X			X		X		
Bahamas				X		X		
Barbados	X			X		X		
Belize	X			X		X		
Bermuda		X		X		X		
Bolivia		X					X	
Brazil		X		X		X		
British Virgin Isl.	X			X		X		

Country	1	2	3	4	5
Cayman Isl.	X		X		
Chile	X		X	X	
Colombia	X		X	X	
Costa Rica	X		X	X	
Cuba	X			X	
Dominica	X		X		X
Dominican Republic	X		X	X	
Ecuador	X		X	X	
El Salvador	X		X	X	
Falkland Isl.					
French Guiana		X	X		X
Grenada	X		X	X	X
Guadeloupe	X	X	X	X	
Guatemala	X		X		X
Guyana	X		X	X	
Haiti	X				

International Topic Charts (Continued)

OCCUPATIONAL STATUS

X = Tables present
/ = two censuses within the same group of years

	1945-1949	1950-1954	1955-1959	1960-1964	1965-1969	1970-1974	1975-1979	1980-1984
Honduras		X		X		X		
Jamaica				X		X		
Martinique		X		X	X	X		
Mexico		X		X		X		
Montserrat	X			X		X		
Netherlands Antilles				X/X		X		
Nicaragua		X		X		X		
Panama		X		X		X		
Panama C.Z.		X		X		X		
Paraguay		X		X		X		
Peru				X		X		

	1	2	3	4	5	6	7
Puerto Rico		X		X		X	
St. Kitts-Nevis		X		X			X
St. Lucia		X		X			X
St. Vincent		X		X			X
Suriname				X			
Trinidad-Tobago		X		X			X
Turks-Caicos		X		X			
Uruguay	X			X			
Venezuela		X		X		X	
Virgin Isl. (U.S.)		X		X		X	
NORTH AMERICA							
Canada		X		X		X	X
Greenland	X	X	X	X		X	
St. Pierre-Miquelon		X	X	X	X	X	
United States		X		X		X	

International Topic Charts (Continued)

OCCUPATIONAL STATUS

X = Tables present
/ = two censuses within the same group of years

	1945-1949	1950-1954	1955-1959	1960-1964	1965-1969	1970-1974	1975-1979	1980-1984
OCEANIA								
American Samoa				X		X		
Australia	X	X		X	X	X	X	
Christmas Isl.	X			X	X	X		
Cocos (Keeling) Isl.	X		X	X	X			
Cook Isl.					X		X	
Fiji	X						X	
French Polynesia	X	X	X	X	X		X	
Gilbert-Ellice Isl.	X					X		
Guam		X		X		X		
Hawaii		X		X		X		

	1	2	3	4	5	6
Kiribati (Gilbert)	X					
Nauru			X		X	X
New Caledonia	X		X	X	X	X
New Zealand	X	X	X	X	X	X
Niue	X	X				
Norfolk		X	X		X	X
Pacific Isl., T.T.		X/X				
Papua New Guinea		X			X	X
Solomon Isl.	X					X
Tokelau						
Tonga	X					
Tuvalu (Ellice)	X				X	X
Vanuatu (New Hebrides)		X	X	X		
Wallis-Futuna	X				X	X
Western Samoa	X	X				

International Topic Charts (Continued)

PLACE OF BIRTH

X = Tables present
/ = two censuses within the same group of years

LATIN AMERICA AND CARIBBEAN

	1945-1949	1950-1954	1955-1959	1960-1964	1965-1969	1970-1974	1975-1979	1980-1984
Antigua-Barbuda		X				X		
Argentina		X				X		
Bahamas				X		X		
Barbados		X				X		
Belize		X				X		
Bermuda				X		X		
Bolivia				X			X	
Brazil				X		X		
British Virgin Isl.		X		X		X		

Country	1	2	3	4	5
Cayman Isl.	X		X		
Chile	X		X	X	
Colombia	X		X	X	
Costa Rica	X		X	X	
Cuba	X			X	
Dominica	X		X		X
Dominican Republic	X		X	X	
Ecuador	X		X	X	
El Salvador	X		X	X	
Falkland Isl.	X		X	X	X
French Guiana		X	X	X	X
Grenada	X		X		X
Guadeloupe		X	X	X	
Guatemala	X		X	X	X
Guyana	X				X
Haiti	X		X	X	

International Topic Charts (Continued)

PLACE OF BIRTH

X = Tables present
/ = two censuses within the same group of years

	1945-1949	1950-1954	1955-1959	1960-1964	1965-1969	1970-1974	1975-1979	1980-1984
Honduras		X		X		X		
Jamaica				X		X		
Martinique	X	X		X	X			
Mexico		X		X		X		
Montserrat	X			X		X		
Netherlands Antilles				X/X	X	X		
Nicaragua		X		X		X		
Panama		X		X		X		
Panama C.Z.		X		X		X		
Paraguay		X		X		X		
Peru				X		X		

	1	2	3	4	5	6	7
Puerto Rico		X		X		X	
St. Kitts-Nevis		X		X			X
St. Lucia		X		X			X
St. Vincent		X		X			X
Suriname				X		X	
Trinidad-Tobago		X		X			X
Turks-Caicos		X		X			
Uruguay	X			X			
Venezuela		X		X		X	
Virgin Isl. (U.S.)		X		X		X	
NORTH AMERICA							
Canada	X	X		X		X	X
Greenland	X	X	X	X	X	X	
St. Pierre-Miquelon		X	X	X	X	X	
United States		X		X		X	

International Topic Charts (Continued)

PLACE OF BIRTH

X = Tables present
/ = two censuses within the same group of years

OCEANIA

	1945-1949	1950-1954	1955-1959	1960-1964	1965-1969	1970-1974	1975-1979	1980-1984
American Samoa			X	X		X/X		
Australia	X	X		X	X	X	X	
Christmas Isl.	X			X	X	X		
Cocos (Keeling) Isl.	X		X	X	X			
Cook Isl.	X		X	X	X		X	
Fiji	X		X		X		X	
French Polynesia	X		X	X	X	X	X	
Gilbert-Ellice Isl.	X			X	X	X		
Guam		X		X		X		
Hawaii		X		X		X		

	1	2	3	4	5	6	7
Kiribati (Gilbert)	X						
Nauru			X	X		X	X
New Caledonia	X		X	X	X	X	X
New Zealand	X	X	X	X	X	X	X
Niue	X	X					X
Norfolk		X	X	X		X	X
Pacific Isl., T.T.		X/X			X		
Papua New Guinea		X					X
Solomon Isl.	X	X	X	X	X	X	
Tokelau							
Tonga	X		X		X		
Tuvalu (Ellice)	X						
Vanuatu (New Hebrides)		X	X				
Wallis-Futuna	X		X				
Western Samoa		X	X	X	X	X	X

International Topic Charts (Continued)

RELIGION

X = Tables present
/ = two censuses within the same group of years

	1945-1949	1950-1954	1955-1959	1960-1964	1965-1969	1970-1974	1975-1979	1980-1984
LATIN AMERICA AND CARIBBEAN								
Antigua-Barbuda	X			X		X		
Argentina	X			X		X		
Bahamas		X		X		X		
Barbados	X			X		X		
Belize	X			X		X		
Bermuda		X		X		X		
Bolivia								
Brazil			X	X		X		
British Virgin Isl.	X			X		X		

Country				
Cayman Isl.	X	X		
Chile	X	X	X	
Colombia				
Costa Rica				
Cuba				
Dominica	X	X		X
Dominican Republic		X	X	
Ecuador				
El Salvador				
Falkland Isl.	X	X	X	X
French Guiana				
Grenada	X	X		X
Guadeloupe		X		
Guatemala		X	X	
Guyana	X	X		X
Haiti	X			

International Topic Charts (Continued)

RELIGION

X = Tables present
/ = two censuses within the same group of years

	1945-1949	1950-1954	1955-1959	1960-1964	1965-1969	1970-1974	1975-1979	1980-1984
Honduras	X							
Jamaica				X		X		
Martinique						X		
Mexico		X		X		X		
Montserrat	X			X		X		
Netherlands Antilles				X/X		X		
Nicaragua		X		X				
Panama								
Panama C.Z.				X				
Paraguay		X						
Peru		X		X		X		

Puerto Rico				
St. Kitts-Nevis	X	X		X
St. Lucia	X	X		X
St. Vincent	X	X		X
Suriname		X		
Trinidad-Tobago	X	X		X
Turks-Caicos	X	X		
Uruguay				
Venezuela				
Virgin Isl. (U.S.)				
NORTH AMERICA				
Canada	X	X	X	
Greenland				
St. Pierre-Miquelon				
United States				

International Topic Charts (Continued)

RELIGION

X = Tables present
/ = two censuses within the same group of years

OCEANIA

	1945-1949	1950-1954	1955-1959	1960-1964	1965-1969	1970-1974	1975-1979	1980-1984
American Samoa						X		
Australia	X	X			X	X		X
Christmas Isl.				X	X	X		
Cocos (Keeling) Isl.				X	X			
Cook Isl.	X		X	X	X	X		X
Fiji	X		X	X	X	X		X
French Polynesia	X	X		X	X	X		
Gilbert-Ellice Isl.	X			X	X	X		
Guam								
Hawaii								

Kiribati (Gilbert)	X						X
Nauru	X					X	X
New Caledonia	X	X	X	X	X	X	X
New Zealand	X	X	X	X	X	X	X
Niue		X	X	X			
Norfolk		X	X	X	X		
Pacific Isl., T.T.		X	X				
Papua New Guinea				X		X	X
Solomon Isl.	X	X			X		
Tokelau							X
Tonga	X	X	X		X	X	
Tuvalu (Ellice)	X						
Vanuatu (New Hebrides)			X				
Wallis-Futuna		X	X	X	X		
Western Samoa	X	X	X	X	X	X	X

International Topic Charts (Continued)

URBAN/RURAL

X = Tables present
/ = two censuses within the same group of years

	1945-1949	1950-1954	1955-1959	1960-1964	1965-1969	1970-1974	1975-1979	1980-1984
LATIN AMERICA AND CARIBBEAN								
Antigua-Barbuda								
Argentina	X			X		X		
Bahamas			X					
Barbados	X			X		X		
Belize	X			X				
Bermuda								
Bolivia			X				X	
Brazil	X		X			X		
British Virgin Isl.								

	1	2	3	4
Cayman Isl.	X		X	
Chile	X	X	X	
Colombia	X	X	X	
Costa Rica	X	X	X	
Cuba	X		X	
Dominica	X	X		
Dominican Republic	X	X	X	
Ecuador	X	X	X	
El Salvador	X	X	X	
Falkland Isl.		X	X	X
French Guiana				X
Grenada		X	X	
Guadeloupe	X	X	X	
Guatemala	X	X	X	
Guyana	X			X
Haiti	X		X	

International Topic Charts (Continued)

URBAN/RURAL

X = Tables present
/ = two censuses within the same group of years

	1945-1949	1950-1954	1955-1959	1960-1964	1965-1969	1970-1974	1975-1979	1980-1984
Honduras	X	X		X		X		
Jamaica				X		X		
Martinique	X	X		X		X		
Mexico		X		X		X		
Montserrat				X		X		X
Netherlands Antilles								
Nicaragua		X		X		X		
Panama		X		X		X		
Panama C.Z.				X		X		
Paraguay		X		X		X		
Peru				X		X		

Region/Country	1	2	3	4	5	6	7	8
Puerto Rico			X		X		X	
St. Kitts-Nevis			X		X			X
St. Lucia			X		X			X
St. Vincent			X					X
Suriname							X	
Trinidad-Tobago			X		X			X
Turks-Caicos								
Uruguay		X			X		X	
Venezuela			X		X		X	
Virgin Isl. (U.S.)			X		X			
NORTH AMERICA								
Canada		X	X	X	X	X	X	
Greenland								
St. Pierre-Miquelon								
United States	X		X		X		X	

International Topic Charts (Continued)

URBAN/RURAL

X = Tables present
/ = two censuses within the same group of years

	1945-1949	1950-1954	1955-1959	1960-1964	1965-1969	1970-1974	1975-1979	1980-1984
OCEANIA								
American Samoa								
Australia		X		X	X	X	X	
Christmas Isl.								
Cocos (Keeling) Isl.								
Cook Isl.							X	
Fiji					X			
French Polynesia						X		
Gilbert-Ellice Isl.					X	X		
Guam						X		
Hawaii				X	X	X		X

706

Kiribati (Gilbert)								
Nauru								
New Caledonia								
New Zealand	X	X	X	X	X	X	X	
Niue								
Norfolk								
Pacific Isl., T.T.					X	X	X	
Papua New Guinea					X	X		X
Solomon Isl.						X	X	
Tokelau								
Tonga								
Tuvalu (Ellice)								
Vanuatu (New Hebrides)					X	X	X	
Wallis-Futuna								
Western Samoa	X		X	X	X	X	X	

Variant Country Names and Capital Cities Cross-Reference

Agana, *see* Guam

Alofi, *see* Niue

Anguilla, *see* St. Kitts-Nevis-Anguilla

Apia, *see* Western Samoa

Asunción, *see* Paraguay

Australasia: formerly British Colonies in Australia, Tasmania, New Zealand, and Melanesia; presently refers to British Commonwealth nations of the Southwest Pacific (Australia, New Zealand, Fiji, and Western Samoa)

Bairiki, *see* Kiribati; *see also* Gilbert and Ellice Islands

Balboa Heights, *see* Panama Canal Zone

Banda Oriental (up to 1825), *see* Uruguay

Basse-Terre, *see* Guadeloupe

Basseterre, *see* St. Kitts-Nevis-Anguilla

Belau, Republic of, *see* Pacific Islands Trust Territory

Belmopan, *see* Belize

Bismarck Archipelago, *see* Papua New Guinea

Bogotá, *see* Colombia

Brasília, *see* Brazil

Bridgetown, *see* Barbados

British Guiana, *see* Guyana

British Honduras, *see* Belize

British Solomon Islands, *see* Solomon Islands

British West Indies: consists of most of the West Indies (Bahamas, Lesser Antilles, Leeward and Windward Islands) plus Bermuda

Buenos Aires, *see* Argentina

Canberra, *see* Australia

Canton and Enderbury, *see* Kiribati; *see also* Gilbert and Ellice Islands

Caracas, *see* Venezuela

Castries, *see* St. Lucia

Cayenne, *see* French Guiana

Central American Federation (1823-1838), *see* Costa Rica, El Salvador, Guatemala, Honduras, and Nicaragua

Charlotte Amalie, *see* Virgin Islands (U.S.)

Cockburn Town, *see* Turks and Caicos

Curaçao, *see* Netherlands Antilles

Curaçao Territory (pre-1949): refers to Netherlands Antilles

Danish West Indies, *see* Virgin Islands (U.S.)

DOM: Départements d'Outre-Mer (French Overseas Departments), *see* Guadeloupe, French Guiana, Martinique, St. Pierre and Miquelon, and Réunion (Africa).

Dutch Antilles, *see* Netherlands Antilles

Dutch Guiana, *see* Suriname

Dutch West Indies, *see* Netherlands Antilles

Easter Island (Isla de Pascuas, Rapa Nui), *see* Chile

Eastern Samoa, *see* American Samoa

Ellice Islands, *see* Tuvalu; *see also* Gilbert and Ellice Islands

Federated States of Micronesia, *see* Pacific Islands Trust Territory

Fidji, *see* Fiji

Flying Fish Cove, *see* Christmas Island

Fort-de-France, *see* Martinique

French Establishments in Oceania, *see* French Polynesia

French Oceania, *see* French Polynesia

Friendly Islands, *see* Tonga

Funafuti, *see* Tuvalu

Galapagos Islands, *see* Ecuador

Georgetown, *see* Cayman Islands

Georgetown, *see* Guyana

Gilbert and Ellice Islands, *see also* Kiribati and Tuvalu respectively

Godthaab, *see* Greenland

Greater Antilles, *see* Cuba, Jamaica, Hispaniola (Haiti and Dominican Republic), and Puerto Rico

Greater Colombia, *see* Colombia and Ecuador

Grønland, *see* Greenland

Guiana, *see* either Suriname (Dutch), Guyana (formerly British), or French Guiana

Guyane Française, *see* French Guiana

Hamilton, *see* Bermuda

Harvey Islands, *see* Cook Islands

Havana, *see* Cuba

Hayti, *see* Haiti

Hispaniola (Island), *see* Dominican Republic and Haiti

Honiara, *see* Solomon Islands

Hoorn Island, *see* Futuna of Wallis and Futuna

Inini, *see* French Guiana

Islas Malvinas, *see* Falkland Islands

Keeling Islands, *see* Cocos (Keeling) Islands

Kingston, *see* Jamaica

Kingston, *see* Norfolk

Kingstown, *see* St. Vincent and the Grenadines

La Paz, *see* Bolivia

Leeward Islands: as part of West Indies, refers to British Virgin Islands, Antigua, St. Kitts-Nevis-Anguilla, Montserrat, Guadeloupe, St. Martin, St. Barts, and St. Eustatius. As part of British West Indies, refers to the first four only

Lesser Antilles: consists of Leeward Islands (British Virgin Islands, Antigua, St. Kitts-Nevis-Anguilla, Montserrat), Windward Islands (Dominica, St. Lucia, St. Vincent and the Grenadines, and Grenada), Trinidad and Tobago, and Barbados

Lima, *see* Peru

Managua, *see* Nicaragua

Mariana Islands, *see* Pacific Islands Trust Territory

Marshall Islands, *see* Pacific Islands Trust Territory

Mata Utu, *see* Wallis and Futuna

Melanesia: consists of Bismarck Archipelago, Fiji, New Caledonia, Solomon Islands, and Vanuatu

Micronesia: consists of Pacific Islands Trust Territory, Guam, Nauru, and Kiribati

Micronesia, Federated States of, *see* Pacific Islands Trust Territory

Montevideo, *see* Uruguay

Naoero, *see* Nauru

Nassau, *see* Bahamas

Navigators Islands, *see* Western Samoa

Nederlandse Antillen, *see* Netherlands Antilles

Netherlands Guiana, *see* Suriname

Nevis, *see* St. Kitts-Nevis-Anguilla

Newfoundland and Labrador, *see* Canada

New Grenada, *see* Colombia, Ecuador, Panama, Venezuela

New Guinea, *see* Papua New Guinea

New Hebrides, *see* Vanuatu

New Spain, *see* Mexico, Cuba

Northern Mariana Commonwealth, *see* Pacific Islands Trust Territory

Noumea, *see* New Caledonia

Nouvelles-Hébrides, *see* Vanuatu

Nuku'Alofa, *see* Tonga

Oceania: consists of Melanesia, Micronesia, and Polynesia

Ottawa, *see* Canada

Pago Pago, *see* American Samoa

Papeete, *see* French Polynesia

Paramaribo, *see* Suriname

Pelau, *see* Pacific Islands Trust Territory

Pleasant Island, *see* Nauru

Plymouth, *see* Montserrat

Polynesia: consists of French Polynesia, Cook, Niue, Hawaii, Tonga, Tokelau, and Tuvalu

Port-au-Prince, *see* Haiti

Porto Rico: name changed to Puerto Rico in 1932

Port Moresby, *see* Papua New Guinea
Port of Spain, *see* Trinidad and Tobago
Port-Vila, *see* Vanuatu

Quito, *see* Ecuador; also referred to whole
country while a Spanish territory

Rarotonga, *see* Cook Islands
Rio de Janeiro, *see* Brazil
Road Town, *see* British Virgin Islands
Roseau, *see* Dominica

Saba, *see* Netherlands Antilles
Saint Christopher, *see* St. Kitts-Nevis-
Anguilla
Saint-Domingue, *see* Haiti
St. Georges, *see* Grenada
St. John's, *see* Antigua
Saipan, *see* Pacific Islands Trust Territory
Salvador, *see* El Salvador
Samoa i Sisifo, *see* Western Samoa
Sandwich Islands, *see* Hawaii
San José, *see* Costa Rica
San Juan, *see* Puerto Rico
San Salvador, *see* El Salvador
Santiago, *see* Chile
Santo Domingo, *see* Dominican Republic
Savage Island, *see* Niue
Snake Island (Anguilla), *see* St. Kitts-Nevis-
Anguilla
Somers Island, *see* Bermuda
Stanley, *see* Falkland Islands
Statia, *see* St. Eustatius in Netherland Antilles
Suva, *see* Fiji

Tahiti, *see* French Polynesia
Tegucigalpa, *see* Honduras
Tobago, *see* Trinidad and Tobago
TOM: Territoires d'Outre-Mer (French Over-
seas Territories), *see* French Polynesia,

New Caledonia, Wallis and Futuna,
Mayotte (Africa), and French Southern
and Antarctic territories
Trust Territory of Pacific Islands, *see* Pa-
cific Islands Trust Territory
Tuvalu (Ellice), *see also* Gilbert and Ellice
Islands

Union Isles, *see* Tokelau Islands

Vielles Colonies (French Old Colonies), *see*
Guadeloupe and Martinique
Virgin Islands, *see* British Virgin Islands,
or Virgin Islands (U.S.)

Washington, D.C., *see* United States
Wellington, *see* New Zealand
West Island, *see* Cocos (Keeling) Islands
West Indies: consists of Bahamas, Greater
Antilles, Lesser Antilles, Barbados, Lee-
ward and Windward Islands
West Indies Associated States: now only
two out of six remain, *see* St. Kitts-Nevis-
Anguilla and Antigua
West Indies Federation, *see* Jamaica, Dom-
inica, St. Lucia, Grenada, British Virgin
Islands, Antigua, Montserrat, St. Kitts-
Nevis-Anguilla, St. Vincent, and Trini-
dad and Tobago
Willemstad, *see* Netherlands Antilles
Windward Islands: as part of the West In-
dies, *see* Martinique, Dominica, St. Lucia,
Grenada, St. Vincent and Grenadines
Windward Islands (British), *see* Dominica,
St. Lucia, Grenada, St. Vincent
Windward Islands (Dutch): located in West
Indies Leeward Group, *see* Netherlands
Antilles

Yaren, *see* Nauru

About the Authors

DOREEN GOYER is a Librarian-Social Science/Humanities Research Associate IV at the Population Research Center of the University of Texas, Austin. She is the author of *National Population Censuses, 1945-1976: Some Holding Libraries* and the *International Population Census Bibliography Revision and Update, 1945-1977*, as well as several reports for the APLIC-International.

ELIANE DOMSCHKE is a Social Science/Humanities Research Associate I at the Population Research Center of the University of Texas, Austin. She holds a Master's Degree from the University of Texas, previously taught history of Philosophy for university candidates, and served in the Secretariat of Finance for the state of Guanabara, Brazil.

DATE DUE